"David VanDrunen here continues his sterling work of recovering and re-presenting the Reformed doctrine of the two kingdoms. That there is a biblical-theological account of natural law may be a surprise to those who have habitually thought of natural law in secularized terms. But such law is a divine gift, playing its part in every era. VanDrunen shows that it is a revealed truth, confirmed in experience, and that it undergirds 'the kingdoms of this world.'"

— PAUL HELM
Regent College

"VanDrunen speaks clearly, carefully, and incisively into contemporary debates about natural law. He fills an important interdisciplinary niche that warrants the attention of political theorists and philosophers in addition to theologians and biblical scholars. . . . For anyone who wants to think more biblically about natural law, this book is essential reading."

— JESSE COVINGTON
Westmont College

EMORY UNIVERSITY STUDIES IN LAW AND RELIGION

John Witte Jr., General Editor

BOOKS IN THE SERIES

Faith and Order: The Reconciliation of Law and Religion
Harold J. Berman

Rediscovering the Natural Law in Reformed Theological Ethics
Stephen J. Grabill

*Lex Charitatis: A Juristic Disquisition on Law
in the Theology of Martin Luther*
Johannes Heckel

*The Best Love of the Child:
Being Loved and Being Taught to Love as the First Human Right*
Timothy P. Jackson, ed.

*The Ten Commandments in History:
Mosaic Paradigms for a Well-Ordered Society*
Paul Grimley Kuntz

Religious Liberty, Volume 1: Overviews and History
Douglas Laycock

Religious Liberty, Volume 2: The Free Exercise Clause
Douglas Laycock

Building Cultures of Trust
Martin E. Marty

*Suing for America's Soul: John Whitehead, The Rutherford Institute,
and Conservative Christians in the Courts*
R. Jonathan Moore

Theology of Law and Authority in the English Reformation
Joan Lockwood O'Donovan

*Power over the Body, Equality in the Family:
Rights and Domestic Relations in Medieval Canon Law*
Charles J. Reid Jr.

Religious Liberty in Western Thought
Noel B. Reynolds and W. Cole Durham Jr., eds.

*Hopes for Better Spouses: Protestant Marriage and Church Renewal
in Early Modern Europe, India, and North America*
A. G. Roeber

Political Order and the Plural Structure of Society
James W. Skillen and Rockne M. McCarthy, eds.

*The Idea of Natural Rights:
Studies on Natural Rights, Natural Law, and Church Law, 1150-1625*
Brian Tierney

The Fabric of Hope: An Essay
Glenn Tinder

Liberty: Rethinking an Imperiled Ideal
Glenn Tinder

Religious Human Rights in Global Perspective: Legal Perspectives
Johan D. van der Vyver and John Witte Jr., eds.

Divine Covenants and Moral Order: A Biblical Theology of Natural Law
David VanDrunen

*Natural Law and the Two Kingdoms:
A Study in the Development of Reformed Social Thought*
David VanDrunen

Early New England: A Covenanted Society
David A. Weir

God's Joust, God's Justice: Law and Religion in the Western Tradition
John Witte Jr.

Religious Human Rights in Global Perspective: Religious Perspectives
John Witte Jr. and Johan D. van der Vyver, eds.

Justice in Love
Nicholas Wolterstorff

Divine Covenants and Moral Order

A Biblical Theology of Natural Law

David VanDrunen

WILLIAM B. EERDMANS PUBLISHING COMPANY

GRAND RAPIDS, MICHIGAN / CAMBRIDGE, U.K.

Published 2014 by
Wm. B. Eerdmans Publishing Co.
2140 Oak Industrial Drive N.E., Grand Rapids, Michigan 49505 /
P.O. Box 163, Cambridge CB3 9PU U.K.

Printed in the United States of America

20 19 18 17 16 15 14   7 6 5 4 3 2 1

Library of Congress Cataloging-in-Publication Data

ISBN 978-0-8028-7094-0

www.eerdmans.com

Contents

CONTENTS

Preface

This book represents the continuation of a larger project, the first major part of which was also published in the Emory University Studies in Law and Religion.[1] In that volume I explored the place of natural law in Reformed theology from the sixteenth century to the present, especially in its relation to the doctrine of the two kingdoms. I concluded that the ideas of natural law and the two kingdoms played an important role in Reformed social thought through the nineteenth century, and I reflected on why much of twentieth-century Reformed theology largely ignored these ideas, or even came to regard them as foreign to the spirit of Reformed Christianity.

Though this prior volume was historical in focus, I did suggest that contemporary Reformed Christians ought to reconsider the doctrines of natural law and the two kingdoms. Reformed theologians of yesteryear utilized these categories in theological and social contexts very different from our own, but I expressed my conviction that they are rooted in Scripture and remain exceedingly relevant for helping Christians think clearly about living godly lives in early-twenty-first-century Western society. I also noted my own hope "to offer a detailed biblical, theological, and ethical defense of the Reformed natural law and two kingdoms doctrines, revised in certain respects and applied to important concrete social issues" (14). The present volume seeks to fulfill part of that goal by presenting a thorough (though of course not comprehensive) study of natural law in Scripture while addressing many crucial questions of theology and ethics along the way.[2] I now hope to extend this project to a third volume,

---

1. David VanDrunen, *Natural Law and the Two Kingdoms: A Study in the Development of Reformed Social Thought* (Grand Rapids: Eerdmans, 2010).

2. I have also fulfilled part of that goal in a separate work, intended primarily for a

in which I plan to build on the conclusions developed here and to explore their relevance for some perennial issues of legal and political theory, including justice, authority, religious freedom, and economic organization. Many of the paths that book is likely to take are anticipated in the present work.

If my goal in writing this had been to win as much agreement and as few critics as possible, I undoubtedly should have written a different — and shorter — book. It would have been relatively easy and uncontroversial to argue that *some* concept of natural law is at work in Scripture and deserves recognition in Christian theology and ethics. But I judged that writing a thin study of natural law in Scripture would not be nearly as helpful or fun as constructing a thick account that probes the theological foundations undergirding the many biblical texts that reflect the reality of a natural moral order. Accordingly, in the chapters that follow I engage in an ambitious, cross-disciplinary endeavor that stretches the bounds of my own scholarly expertise, to be sure. But natural law is hardly the tame kind of subject likely to remain content within the narrow confines of most modern scholarship. Any theory of natural law likely to do any semblance of justice to the topic will have to cross several disciplines, so I can only hope that a place remains for such an inquiry in contemporary academia.

In producing this book I owe a considerable debt of gratitude to the Center for the Study of Law and Religion at Emory University, and especially to John Witte and Amy Wheeler. I am so thankful for the hospitable, stimulating, and peaceful environment that the Center provided for me while I enjoyed a study leave several years ago, during which time I officially began the research and writing that turned into this book. Prof. Witte also had the brilliant idea of putting together a "virtual symposium" on a draft of the book and then ensured that it came to pass. Submitting my work to a group of distinguished scholars from a variety of academic fields was intimidating, but I know without a doubt that the final product is considerably better than it would have been without this experience. Thus I offer many thanks to John, Amy, and their colleagues at the Center for such generous encouragement along the way and for giving me the honor of contributing again to their admirable Studies in Law and Religion. Thank you also to Eerdmans for their fruitful collaboration with the folks at Emory in promoting this series, and for bringing this volume to the light of day.

Gratitude is thus also due to those willing to participate in the virtual

---

popular audience, in which I presented a biblical and theological case for a version of the two kingdoms doctrine; see *Living in God's Two Kingdoms: A Biblical Vision for Christianity and Culture* (Wheaton, IL: Crossway, 2010).

symposium from far and near: William Brown, Jonathan Burnside, Andrew Das, Paul Helm, Russell Hittinger, David Novak, and Nicholas Wolterstorff. The challenges, prodding, suggestions, and encouragement were much appreciated and spurred many fruitful revisions to my work, from tiny details to systemic considerations. Thanks to you all for taking the time to read and comment on a long manuscript still far from being a finished product.

My home institution, Westminster Seminary California, remains a wonderfully supportive community for theological reflection and ministerial training. I am grateful to the board, faculty, students, and staff for their various contributions to the collegiality on such regular display around campus. I thank the board and faculty for granting me two study leaves — one coinciding with the very beginning of this project and one with its very end — that provided extended times of intensive research and writing so conducive for bringing a project like this together. Sincere thanks to faculty colleagues who provided comments on various parts of this manuscript at various stages of development: Steve Baugh, Dennis Johnson, Charles Telfer, Josh Van Ee, and especially Bryan Estelle, John Fesko, and Mike Horton. But I hate to name only a few in the seminary community. On countless occasions over the years — in the classroom, at the Warfield Seminar, or on other informal occasions — this community has provided spiritual nourishment and intellectual stimulation for which I should be even more grateful than I am.

And before I move on from the seminary, a special word of thanks to Anna Speckhard Smith for cheerful, timely, and insightful research assistance, and for her unenviable labor of putting together the bibliography by the date I requested. May your hard-won expertise in goring oxen bring you wealth and renown.

Many other people provided me with helpful insights on a variety of occasions, either on drafts of chapters, on basic research questions, or on particular intellectual issues perplexing to me. I fear I am forgetting some of them, but let me at least mention Eric Enlow, Greg Forster, D. J. Goodwiler, Brian Hecker, Tom Johnson, Shane Lems, Robert Lotzer, David Noe, Scott Pryor, Manfred Svensson, Matt Tuininga, and Jens Zimmerman. I'm grateful to you all for your time and wisdom. Thank you too to my family's pastor, Zach Keele — for many things, but here especially for all those keen exegetical insights delivered from the pulpit on the Lord's Day that found their way into my research notes first thing on Monday morning, some of which you may recognize in the pages that follow, even when unacknowledged.

Abundant thanks, as always, to Katherine and Jack, wife and son *par excellence* and the best imaginable companions in a happy home.

Some material scattered through the book has been published previously and appears here in modified form. I thank the respective editors and publishers for their kind permission to adapt the following essays for use in this volume: "Wisdom and the Natural Moral Order: The Contribution of Proverbs to a Christian Theology of Natural Law," *Journal of the Society of Christian Ethics* 33 (Spring/Summer 2013): 153-68; "A Natural Law Right to Religious Freedom: A Reformed Perspective," *International Journal for Religious Freedom* 5.2 (2012): 135-46; "Natural Law and Mosaic Law in the Theology of Paul: Their Relationship and Its Social-Political Implications," in *Natural Law and Evangelical Political Thought,* ed. Jesse Covington, Bryan McGraw, and Micah Watson (Lanham, MD: Lexington, 2012), 85-108; "The Two Kingdoms and the Social Order: Legal and Political Theory in Light of the Covenant with Noah," *Journal of Markets and Morality* 14 (Fall 2011): 445-62; "Israel's Recapitulation of Adam's Probation under the Law of Moses," *Westminster Theological Journal* 73 (Fall 2011): 303-24; a review of *Eccentric Existence: A Theological Anthropology,* by David Kelsey, in *Themelios* 35 (November 2010): 523-25; "Natural Law in Noahic Accent: A Covenantal Conception of Natural Law Drawn from Genesis 9," *Journal of the Society of Christian Ethics* 30 (Fall/Winter 2010): 131-49; and "Bearing Sword in the State, Turning Cheek in the Church: A Reformed Two Kingdoms Interpretation of Matthew 5:38-42," *Themelios* 34 (November 2009): 322-34.

Introduction

Alister McGrath has observed: "The idea that human morality might ultimately be grounded in something built into the fabric of the universe itself has obstinately refused to die out. It possesses a certain intuitive plausibility, even if its conceptual clarification has proved to be immensely difficult."[1] McGrath is surely correct on each count. In the present day, when the world is so morally fragmented, the idea of a natural and universally binding moral law perhaps seems more implausible than it ever has. Yet in such a world, which also speaks so earnestly of human rights and seeks some way to ensure social peace in the midst of moral fragmentation, the search for a natural law that transcends particular cultural boundaries is as relevant as ever.

Even so, another new book on natural law demands a defense. The present volume draws from the reservoirs of Western Christian reflection on natural law, yet offers a constructive theory of natural law that is distinctive in certain respects, in terms of its approach to the subject and its substantive conclusions. I develop this theory seeking to recover four centuries of Reformed theological conviction about natural law that has been curiously neglected for much of the past century. This attempted recovery of Reformed natural law thought, furthermore, taps into important streams of natural law theory before the Reformation, especially in the realist tradition. Yet I pursue this task in a historically unusual way, through a biblical-theological approach that draws upon important Reformed theological themes, especially the doctrine of the biblical covenants. I exegete numerous texts from all over Scripture in close interaction with contemporary biblical scholarship, and I seek to integrate my

---

1. Alister McGrath, *The Open Secret: A New Vision for Natural Theology* (Malden, MA: Blackwell, 2008), p. 295.

1

conclusions from these texts into a larger theological framework that explains the character and role of natural law in the unfolding drama of God's dealings with this world from creation to consummation.

I defend the writing of this book not only on the basis of its uniqueness in the annals of Christian natural law theory but also on account of its timing. Much of the recent literature on natural law has moved in directions that anticipate and even invite a book such as this. Three developments in particular come to mind. First, many writers have repudiated the kind of natural law theory, often associated (imprecisely) with the Enlightenment, that masquerades as the product of autonomous human reason, unconstrained by any authority outside itself. Second, many authors have called for a reintegration of natural law theory with biblical ethics and its traditional theological moorings. Third, a number of Protestant scholars have argued that natural law has played an important role historically in the theological and moral traditions stemming from the Reformation. Some of them have even attempted to construct and defend theories of natural law, despite skepticism about natural law in many Protestant circles during the past century and continuing to the present.

These developments are encouraging. Christians indeed ought to reject natural law theories rooted in illusions of autonomous human reason freed from the restraints of external authority. Furthermore, integrating theories of natural law more thoroughly with the biblical narrative and with broader theological doctrine should only help to strengthen such theories and make them more plausible to thoughtful Christians. At the same time, these encouraging developments have not as yet fulfilled their promise. Recent authors have done relatively little actual exegesis of Scripture in the service of natural law theory, and most recent Protestant attempts to forge constructive theories of natural law give scant attention to what Reformation theology might contribute to this endeavor.

In the context of this recent literature, which is encouraging but has not yet delivered on its promise, this book offers a Reformed biblical theology of natural law. It is genuinely an account of *natural law*, in organic continuity with broader Christian natural law traditions, including the famous medieval formulation of Thomas Aquinas. Yet it is also a *Reformed biblical theology*[2]

2. I would like the term "biblical theology," as used here and in the book's title, to remain somewhat vague. In one sense I use the term simply to highlight that I engage in the study of theology through the exegesis of biblical texts. I do not mean to use the term in a technical sense to indicate that I pursue the discipline of "biblical theology" as distinguished from, say, exegetical theology, systematic theology, or moral theology. To some degree, however, I do pursue the discipline of biblical theology in the more technical sense, since I let the

of natural law, since I believe, in the spirit of the Reformation, that Christian doctrine and ethics must be reformed according to the word of God. Thus I develop this account primarily through the exegesis of Scripture, as hermeneutically guided by classic Reformed covenant theology. By grounding natural law in God's covenants with all creation, this theology of natural law rejects the idea of human autonomy but instead interprets natural law in terms of humanity's relationship to God and accountability before him. By presenting natural law in connection with the series of covenants (plural) revealed through biblical history, rather than as an ahistorical reality, this account seeks to place natural law in the context of the whole story of Scripture, identifying both its universal relevance for the human race and its relation to God's particular work of redemption as it culminates in the first and second comings of Jesus Christ. By presenting natural law in connection with these biblical covenants, furthermore, this account utilizes a theological theme distinctively important in the Reformed tradition, and thus this account constitutes not simply a defense of natural law by a Protestant, but a Protestant exposition of natural law.[3] Through this biblical theology of natural law I hope both to provide all readers with a stimulating case that will advance broader discussions of this topic and to convince my fellow Reformed Christians of the importance of natural law for Christian faith and life.

Why should Christians, even Protestant Christians, deem natural law an important issue? Perhaps chiefly, they should do so because Scripture itself teaches that *all* human beings, made in God's image and situated within a broader created order, know their basic moral obligations before God and their accountability to him as their ruler and judge. And because these obligations are universal, Scripture also presents them as foundational for *Christians'* understanding of their moral responsibilities, both as citizens of broader civil societies and as members of the church of Jesus Christ. Some readers will

---

redemptive-historical unfolding of the divine covenants in Scripture determine the structure of much of the book. In the end I engage in elements of exegetical, biblical, systematic, and moral theology, and despite the tendency of the modern academy to keep these disciplines separate, I cannot really imagine doing good theology — at least in the present volume — without engaging them all.

3. J. Budziszewski (speaking as a Roman Catholic) has recently remarked that what is needed is an evangelical explanation of natural law theory, not an evangelical theory of natural law. See his closing essay in *Natural Law and Evangelical Political Theory,* ed. Jesse Covington, Bryan McGraw, and Micah Watson (Lanham, MD: Lexington, 2012). If one substitutes "Reformed" for "evangelical" for greater precision, I believe I am attempting the latter and not simply the former.

likely agree with these claims and yet, wearied by the interminable debates about natural law and skeptical of many versions of natural law theory, prefer to examine such issues under some rubric other than "natural law." These readers may still find much to appreciate in this book, even while objecting to the natural law terminology, but I deal with these issues in terms of "natural law" both because I do not find the term objectionable per se (our universal human moral obligations are both "natural" and "law") and because Western Christian theology (including Reformed theology) has for so long used this term as it has wrestled with these issues.

In the remainder of this introduction I first place my project in contemporary context through interaction with a number of recent natural law theorists and then summarize my argument and how I develop it in subsequent chapters. Finally, I set my project in historical context, with particular attention to the Thomistic tradition.

Natural Law in Recent Constructive Proposals

In recent years a number of scholars have produced major works on natural law, and their labors form an important part of the context of my present project. Among notable examples are books by Roman Catholics Robert George, Russell Hittinger, Jean Porter, and Matthew Levering, and by Protestants Craig Boyd, J. Daryl Charles, and Alister McGrath.[4] Jewish scholar David Novak also wrestles with many of the same issues in his work, and I interact with his claims at several points in subsequent chapters.[5] With the exception of George — who attempts to ground his natural law theory in practical reason alone, without recourse to a philosophy of nature, and defends his theory's legitimacy independent of God's existence — the writers mentioned above generally seek to distinguish natural law theory from the pretensions of autonomous human

---

4. Robert P. George, *In Defense of Natural Law* (Oxford: Clarendon, 1999); Russell Hittinger, *The First Grace: Rediscovering the Natural Law in a Post-Christian World* (Wilmington, DE: ISI Books, 2003); Jean Porter, *Nature as Reason: A Thomistic Theory of the Natural Law* (Grand Rapids: Eerdmans, 2005); Matthew Levering, *Biblical Natural Law: A Theocentric and Teleological Approach* (Oxford: Oxford University Press, 2008); Craig A. Boyd, *A Shared Morality: A Narrative Defense of Natural Law Ethics* (Grand Rapids: Brazos, 2007); J. Daryl Charles, *Retrieving the Natural Law: A Return to Moral First Things* (Grand Rapids: Eerdmans, 2008); and McGrath, *The Open Secret*.

5. David Novak, *Natural Law in Judaism* (Cambridge: Cambridge University Press, 1998).

reason and support the reintegration of natural law theory with biblical studies and broader theological doctrine. Appendix 1 provides a summary of the work of each of these eight authors.

As expressed at the outset, I find many positive and encouraging aspects in most of these contemporary natural law proposals. I heartily resonate with their rejection of conceptions of autonomous human reason, their interest in grounding natural law in a rich theology and anthropology, and their support of reintegrating natural law theory with biblical ethics. Nevertheless, in my judgment the recent literature only scratches the surface of Scripture's teaching on natural law and has not connected natural law with the full range of Christian doctrine as it might.

First, the recent literature often acknowledges the need to connect natural law to Scriptural teaching, but provides little detailed biblical exegesis or attention to the broader biblical story of God's dealings with creation generally and the human race specifically. Though relatively few in number, several insightful biblical scholars have recently presented studies on natural law–related themes in Scripture.[6] Yet such studies have played a minimal role in shaping the natural law theories of the writers mentioned at the opening of this section. These writers identify Scripture as an important source for understanding natural law, but engage biblical scholarship sparsely, if at all. Levering is an exception to these observations. He interacts with biblical scholars such as John Barton and Markus Bockmuehl, who have wrestled with natural law as a Scriptural theme, and he attends to several relevant passages in Scripture itself. Nevertheless, even Levering presents little rigorous biblical exegesis and considers only a small part of the biblical corpus.[7] Another exception is Novak, who has insightfully identified natural law at work in many places in the Hebrew Bible. But for a Christian natural law theorist, who also recognizes the New Testament as Scripture and who reads the Hebrew Bible as the Old Testament that anticipates the New, Novak's work has inevitable limitations.

Second, in addition to its paucity of rigorous biblical exegesis, the recent

---

6. See e.g. Markus Bockmuehl, *Jewish Law in Gentile Churches: Halakhah and the Beginning of Christian Public Ethics* (Grand Rapids: Baker Academic, 2000); John Barton, *Understanding Old Testament Ethics: Approaches and Explorations* (Louisville: Westminster John Knox, 2003); and James Barr, *Biblical Faith and Natural Theology* (Oxford: Clarendon, 1993). For a couple of opinions among scholars working in the field of biblical theology, see Charles H. H. Scobie, *The Ways of Our God: An Approach to Biblical Theology* (Grand Rapids: Eerdmans, 2003), pp. 174-75, 184; and Francis Watson, *Text and Truth: Redefining Biblical Theology* (Grand Rapids: Eerdmans, 1997), pp. 242-67.

7. Levering interacts with Barton and Bockmuehl in *Biblical Natural Law,* chap. 1.

natural law literature also lacks a well-defined sense of how exactly natural law relates to the larger biblical narrative. This narrative begins with creation, proceeds through a fall into sin, continues through a series of divine dealings with humanity in salvation and judgment, climaxes with the life, death, resurrection, and ascension of Jesus Christ, and will be consummated by Christ's second coming and the establishment of a new heavens and new earth. Even when the contemporary literature properly identifies biblical texts that pertain to natural law, it too often exhibits what Francis Watson calls the "tendency to interpret scriptural texts relating to creation in isolation from their canonical contexts."[8] Though Christianity is a historical religion, grounded in temporal divine acts of judgment and salvation, many Christian writers have conceived of natural law as an ahistorical ontological reality that communicates timeless moral truth. It is not obvious how one might weave natural law into the fabric of the historical biblical narrative.

A few examples illustrate these observations. Boyd, through his quest to develop a "narrative" defense of natural law, admirably seeks to get away from the tendency to treat natural law as an abstract and ahistorical ontological reality. Yet the narratives he tells are the story of the evolutionary development of human nature and the history of interpretation of natural law. Whatever the relevance of such narratives, a crucial narrative missing is the biblical narrative of creation, fall, redemption, and consummation. A similar observation applies to Porter's theory, given its focus on evolutionary biology and the medieval scholastic natural law tradition but lack of attention to the biblical narrative. In the theories of both Boyd and Porter the supernatural perfecting of the natural is an important theme, but they do not explain how this theme is to be understood in the context of the objective divine acts of redemptive history. Levering, who also emphasizes the supernatural perfecting of the natural, does have interest in the progress of biblical history from old covenant to new covenant, especially as described by the Apostle Paul.[9] In light of my argument in this volume, Levering addresses many of the right issues, but does not adequately capture the profound implications of Pauline soteriology and eschatology for a Christian theology of natural law.

Charles and McGrath also do not situate natural law within the larger biblical story. A recurring tension in Charles's work is illustrative. In a number of places Charles promotes natural law as a means to facilitate Christians'

---

8. Watson, *Text and Truth*, p. 266. "Canonical context" refers to the meaning of a particular biblical text in relation to the broader canon of Scripture.

9. See Levering, *Biblical Natural Law,* chap. 4.

coexistence in this world with unbelievers. Natural law, he explains, provides a way to engage in genuinely moral conversations in a pluralistic world and thus to avoid the contemporary tendency toward relativism. Yet in many of the very contexts in which he makes such claims he speaks of natural law as a tool for the *redemptive transformation* of society.[10] One could raise a conceptual objection that the quest to coexist peacefully and the quest to transform redemptively seem to be distinct endeavors. But the deeper issue is that the story of God's providential preservation of the present world and the redemptive story of incarnation, crucifixion, resurrection, and consummation are interrelated but should not be conflated. Where precisely does natural law fit in the development and interconnection of these two biblical stories? The fact that Charles does not wrestle with this question bears fruit in the one instance in which he engages in an extended analysis of a particular passage of Scripture, Paul's address on Mars Hill in Acts 17. Charles never clarifies how and why the strategies of this sermon, which is clearly evangelistic and aimed at the religious conversion of Paul's audience, are applicable in the context of civil coexistence in a religiously pluralistic society, as Charles suggests.[11]

Though McGrath's project has a very different tenor from Charles's, it raises questions that are not entirely different. McGrath deals with natural law as an aspect of a broader natural theology that, when seen properly, discloses the kingdom of God and the redemption of the present creation by virtue of Christ's incarnation. McGrath's interest in the relationship among natural theology, natural law, and the Christian doctrine of salvation is in some ways a welcome development, since many historic theories of nature hardly bothered to address the issue at all. But can nature's disclosure of God and his law be understood *entirely* within a soteriological framework, as either the disclosure of God's kingdom through the incarnation (for those who see properly) or the veiling of the same (for those who see poorly)? As I argue below, Scripture also speaks of a natural disclosure of God and his law in the work of creation and providence, distinct from the work of redemption, a disclosure that serves as the presupposition and foundation of the divine revelation of salvation in Christ. With respect at least to these concerns, McGrath does not situate natural law in the context of the entire story of the biblical narrative.

A third issue is that contemporary natural law theorists do not place

---

10. For the coexistence theme, see e.g. Charles, *Retrieving the Natural Law,* pp. 23-24, 154; for the redemptive transformation theme, see e.g. *Retrieving the Natural Law,* pp. 23, 24-25 n. 57, 315.

11. See Charles, *Retrieving the Natural Law,* pp. 45-54.

natural law in the context of the broad system of Christian doctrine as fully as they might. This is connected to the previous point, for exploring the relation of natural law to the biblical narrative of creation, fall, redemption, and consummation entails exploring the relation of natural law to fundamental *loci* of systematic theology such as anthropology, hamartiology, Christology, soteriology, ecclesiology, and eschatology. This is a crucial issue, in my judgment. Many Christians — particularly Protestants — will continue to be suspicious of natural law if it cannot be set compellingly in the context of a broader biblical and systematic theology. As James Barr has noted, in his wide-ranging study of natural theology in Scripture, "What is required is not just a few words, or the exegesis of a few words, but a wide vision and perspective within which the status of the question might be seen. Exegesis alone will not alter people's minds, until they perceive an alternative total perspective through which they can see not only the biblical material but also an explanation of how it affects a wide range of personal stands and theological problems."[12]

Of particular interest here is the absence of a distinctly and historically *Protestant* theology of natural law in the contemporary literature. Neither Boyd nor Charles develops a systematic theological foundation for natural law. Instead, the theology of Aquinas is their touchstone. Whether in Boyd's evaluation of divine-command ethics or in Charles's appeals to fellow evangelicals, the burden of both writers vis-à-vis Protestant theology seems to be negative rather than positive. That is, they do not show how a rich (and distinctive) theology of natural law can be built on a Protestant theological foundation, but simply try to demonstrate that Protestant theology is not opposed to a doctrine of natural law.[13]

There are many good reasons for Protestants to regard Thomas Aquinas as an illustrious theologian of the Western Christian church and to identify many aspects of continuity between his theology of natural law and that of the Protestant Reformers, an issue I revisit at length below. Nevertheless, the Reformation engaged Western Christianity on a number of doctrines crucial to a theological understanding of natural law, including but not limited to the image of God, the effects of the fall on human reason and volition, the relationship of nature and grace, and the relationship of law and faith. For those who embrace the Reformation generally — and, as in my own case, the Reformed

---

12. Barr, *Biblical Faith and Natural Theology*, p. 50.

13. For a helpful, though brief, study that does seek to move in the positive direction, see Thomas K. Johnson, *Natural Law Ethics: An Evangelical Proposal* (Bonn: Verlag für Kultur und Wissenschaft, 2005), especially pp. 131-34.

theological tradition particularly — appeal to Thomas cannot be sufficient. Natural law is intimately connected to conceptions of the image of God, the powers of human reason, and a person's standing before the law of God, among many other things, and thus the reformation of these latter doctrines demands the reformation of the theology of natural law as well. Protestants and Roman Catholics after the Reformation continued to share many convictions about basic moral problems, but Charles's assertion that the Reformers had theological disputes with the Roman church but "maintained *full continuity* with their Catholic counterparts" with regard to ethics is not accurate.[14] As with many other aspects of Christian doctrine, the very idea of a *reformed* Christianity indicates that a Protestant understanding of natural law should exhibit both continuity and discontinuity with the pre-Reformation theological traditions.

McGrath's claim that the testimony of nature reveals the redemptive work of the kingdom of God may appear rigorously and distinctively Protestant in its sharp rebuke of human reason's ability to read God in nature by its own autonomous power. But his claim that nature speaks about the last things rather than the first things — that it speaks about the things of the age to come rather than the things of this age — makes the eschatological swallow the protological. This marks a significant break from the whole Western tradition — Roman Catholic and Protestant — of thinking about natural law and matters germane. Conflating the natural and the supernatural falls short of providing a historically Protestant theological foundation for natural law, just as remaining content with a Thomistic view of nature and grace also does.

In my judgment what is still lacking, then, is a theological-ethical exploration of natural law that is grounded in the thorough exegesis of Scripture, set in the context of the larger biblical story of creation, fall, preservation, redemption, and consummation, and developed upon a distinctively Protestant theological foundation. I present this study as an attempt to provide just this, noting that my theological foundation is not simply "distinctively Protestant" but more specifically Reformed. As Novak has constructed a theological account of natural law "constituted from within the sources of the Jewish tradition,"[15] so I aim to construct a theological account of natural law from the resources already present within the Reformed tradition.

---

14. See Charles, *Retrieving the Natural Law,* p. 125. I think for example of the way that the Reformation's doctrine of justification triggered a rethinking of the important moral issue of Christian liberty, as expressed for example in Martin Luther's essay "The Freedom of the Christian"; John Calvin, *Institutes of the Christian Religion,* 3:19; and the Westminster Confession of Faith, chap. 20.

15. Novak, *Natural Law in Judaism,* p. 11.

The Argument, Assumptions, and Structure of This Book

Two resources in the Reformed tradition especially important for this volume are its longstanding affirmation of the reality of natural law and its utilization of the biblical covenants as an organizing principle of theology. In this section I reflect briefly first upon the place of natural law in the Reformed tradition and then upon the character of Reformed covenant theology. The early Reformed tradition offers some important and suggestive hints as to the relationship of natural law and the biblical covenants, but this relationship was, I believe, an underdeveloped theme.[16]

As I have argued at length in a recent work, natural law was a standard feature of Reformed theology from the Reformation to the early twentieth century, though in the past century it largely fell out of favor among Reformed theologians, either by neglect or outright opposition.[17] Although John Calvin and many other leading figures of the early tradition spoke about natural law in certain ways distinct from their medieval predecessors and understood it in vital connection to other aspects of Reformed doctrine, on the whole they seemed to affirm natural law as a catholic Christian idea that was not especially controversial and not in particular need of theological reform. They presented relatively little explicit reflection on how their distinctive Reformed under-standing of a range of Christian doctrines ought to reconfigure a theology of natural law.

In the development of Reformed orthodoxy in the two centuries follow-ing the Reformation, natural law continued to be a ubiquitous presence tied intimately to multiple points in the fabric of its system of doctrine. Reformed

---

16. Many early Reformed theologians, for example, believed that natural law was part of the original endowment of human nature as created in the image of God and as such con-stituted an aspect of Adam's obligation under the covenant of works. In some ways this has been a persistent theme in Reformed theology, though not without significant ambiguity. For sources and analysis of the ambiguity, see David VanDrunen, "Natural Law and the Works Principle Under Adam and Moses," in *The Law Is Not of Faith: Essays on Works and Grace in the Mosaic Covenant,* ed. Bryan D. Estelle, J. V. Fesko, and David VanDrunen (Phillipsburg, NJ: Presbyterian and Reformed, 2009), pp. 286-91. For a recent Reformed work suggesting, though not developing in detail, the intimate connection between natural law and the cove-nant of works, see Michael S. Horton, *Lord and Servant: A Covenant Christology* (Louisville: Westminster John Knox, 2005), p. 94.

17. David VanDrunen, *Natural Law and the Two Kingdoms: A Study in the Development of Reformed Social Thought* (Grand Rapids: Eerdmans, 2010); along similar lines, cf. Stephen Grabill, *Rediscovering the Natural Law in Reformed Theological Ethics* (Grand Rapids: Eerd-mans, 2006).

orthodox theologians connected natural law to such significant matters as the divine attributes, the image of God, the New Testament Sabbath, the Mosaic law, civil authority, Christian liberty, and the final judgment.[18] Though many of these doctrines had a distinctive Reformed flavor in comparison to how other Christian traditions understood them, however, the early Reformed theologians generally did not develop *natural law itself* in a distinctively Reformed way. The existence of a law of nature and its general association with the moral law summarized in the Decalogue could be assumed from the earlier medieval natural law traditions and contemporary Roman Catholic and Lutheran theologies. Like so many Christian theologians before them, the early Reformed theologians appealed to Romans 2:14-15 as a biblical proof-text and defined a relationship between natural and Mosaic law similar to that of their predecessors.

In the present, when the general validity of natural law can no longer be readily assumed, either in Reformed theological circles or in the broader cultural ethos, a more detailed and robust exposition of natural law seems in order. I attempt to provide such an exposition through the integration of natural law with Reformed covenant theology.[19] This approach builds a detailed theology of natural law from the Reformed tradition's own resources rather than staking out a place for natural law within Reformed Christianity by imposing foreign theological constructs upon it. Yet by working with covenantal themes that are explicitly biblical I also hope to commend my conclusions to those working in other Christian traditions and hence to contribute to broader discussions about the place of natural law in Christian theology and ethics.

From the early days of Reformed Christianity its theologians identified the divine covenants recorded in Scripture as a major theme in the development of the biblical story and thus made it a key organizing principle of their

18. Many of these connections are evident in the numerous references to natural law in the Westminster Confession and Catechisms, the confessional standards of traditional Presbyterian churches worldwide since the mid-seventeenth century. See Westminster Confession of Faith 1.1; 1.6; 4.2; 10.4; 20.4; 21.1; 21.7; and Westminster Larger Catechism 2, 17, 60, 121, 151.

19. In *Natural Law and the Two Kingdoms* I explored the intimate connection of historic Reformed views of natural law with historic Reformed views of the two kingdoms doctrine. I stand in that tradition of framing natural law within the context of the two kingdoms. I believe that seeking to understand natural law through Reformed covenant theology is essentially the same endeavor, since a theology of the kingdom(s) and a theology of the covenants are so organically interrelated (as I have argued in David VanDrunen, *Living in God's Two Kingdoms: A Biblical Vision for Christianity and Culture* [Wheaton: Crossway, 2010]). Nevertheless, in this present volume it has seemed better to me to use the latter rather than the former as the chief theological motif for grounding natural law.

theological systems.[20] The most basic and important idea that came to characterize mature Reformed covenant theology is the distinction between the *covenant of works* (also referred to as the covenant of life, covenant of nature, or covenant of creation — I employ the latter term here) and the *covenant of grace*. God made the former with Adam, as the federal representative of the human race, before the fall into sin, promising eternal life in confirmed blessedness if he proved obedient and threatening condemnation and death if not. Following the primeval sin, God instituted the covenant of grace. In this covenant God also held out the prospect of eternal life in confirmed blessedness, but offered it not as a reward for personal obedience (now impossible for fallen human beings) but as a gracious gift to be received by faith in the Lord Jesus Christ, who perfectly obeyed God's will as the first Adam should have done and took upon himself the penalty for human sin. Thus the covenant of grace provides a way of salvation that both displays God's rich mercy and satisfies the claims of divine justice.[21] Reformed theologians understood this covenant of grace to be administered in different ways through biblical history, by a series of distinct but organically connected covenantal arrangements, especially with Abraham, Israel at Sinai, and the New Testament church. (A terminological note: I agree with this traditional Reformed notion that there is a single, organically unified covenant of grace throughout biblical history, with distinct administrations. As explained again in Chapter 6, however, I will generally refer to the "covenants of grace" rather than the "covenant of grace" when I have the Abrahamic, Mosaic, and new covenants in view. I do not mean

20. See R. Scott Clark, "Christ and Covenant: Federal Theology in Orthodoxy," in *Companion to Reformed Orthodoxy*, ed. Herman Selderhuis (Leiden: Brill, 2013), pp. 403-28; Richard A. Muller, "Divine Covenants, Absolute and Conditional: John Cameron and the Early Orthodox Development of Reformed Covenant Theology," *Mid-America Journal of Theology* 17 (2006): 11-56; and Geerhardus Vos, "The Doctrine of the Covenant in Reformed Theology," in *Redemptive History and Biblical Interpretation: The Shorter Writings of Geerhardus Vos*, ed. Richard B. Gaffin Jr. (Phillipsburg, NJ: Presbyterian and Reformed, 1980), pp. 234-67.

21. For confessional summary of these points, see especially the Westminster Confession of Faith, chaps. 7 and 11. In order to capture the relationship between the work of Christ and the covenant of grace made with sinners in the midst of history, many Reformed theologians also identified a third biblical covenant, often called the *covenant of redemption* (or referred to by its common Latin title, the *pactum salutis*). The covenant of redemption described an eternal, intra-Trinitarian covenant by which the divine persons counseled together to ordain the plan of salvation to be accomplished in the coming of the Son and the sending of the Spirit. For description and defense of this idea of the covenant of redemption, see David VanDrunen and R. Scott Clark, "The Covenant before the Covenants," in *Covenant, Justification, and Pastoral Ministry: Essays by the Faculty of Westminster Seminary California*, ed. R. Scott Clark (Phillipsburg, NJ: Presbyterian and Reformed, 2007), pp. 167-96.

to detract from their organic unity but simply to avoid confusion for readers unfamiliar with parochial Reformed language.)[22]

The covenant with Noah after the great flood was not a major point of focus for classic Reformed covenant theology, but it is very important for the present volume. Many Reformed theologians have taken this covenant to be one of the covenants of grace. Other Reformed theologians, impressed by the fact that God made this covenant with every living creature and offered no promise of salvation in it, treated this as a covenant distinct from the covenants of grace, though not wholly unrelated to them. According to the latter theologians, this is a universal covenant by which God preserves the natural order and human society.[23] I hold this view and will defend it at length. Grounding postlapsarian natural law in the Noahic covenant, so understood, permits one to affirm both the universal relevance of the natural law for all human beings and the origin of natural law in the character and will of God. The "natural" need not be simplistically contrasted with the "covenantal," as if one is rational and the other a revelation of the divine will.[24] The natural *is* a covenantal reality. Thus this view of the Noahic covenant provides a *theological* understanding

22. Thus Reformed readers should not think that my use of "covenants of grace" terminology reflects any disagreement with the closing sentence of the Westminster Confession of Faith, 7.6: "There are not therefore two covenants of grace, differing in substance, but one and the same, under various dispensations."

23. Among Reformed theologians who have held views akin to this, see Herman Witsius, *The Economy of the Covenants between God and Man: Comprehending a Complete Body of Divinity*, 2 vols., trans. William Crookshank (1822; reprint, Phillipsburg, NJ: Presbyterian and Reformed, 1990), 2:239 (originally published in 1677); Wilhelmus à Brakel, *The Christian's Reasonable Service*, 4 vols., trans. Bartel Elshout (Ligonier, PA: Soli Deo Gloria, 1992-95), 4:384 (originally published in 1700); A. Kuyper, *De Gemeene Gratie* (Kampen: J. H. Kok, 1945), pp. 11-100 (originally published in 1902-4); Herman Bavinck, *Reformed Dogmatics*, vol. 3, *Sin and Salvation in Christ*, ed. John Bolt, trans. John Vriend (Grand Rapids: Baker, 2006), pp. 218-19 (originally published in 1895-1901); Geerhardus Vos, *Biblical Theology: Old and New Testaments* (Grand Rapids: Eerdmans, 1949), pp. 56, 62-63; Meredith G. Kline, *Kingdom Prologue: Genesis Foundations for a Covenantal Worldview* (Overland Park, KS: Two Age Press, 2000), pp. 164, 244-62; Michael Horton, *God of Promise: Introducing Covenant Theology* (Grand Rapids: Baker, 2006), chap. 6; and VanDrunen, *Living in God's Two Kingdoms*, pp. 78-81.

24. Something of this contrast lingers even in Jewish scholars intrigued by connections between natural law and the so-called Noachide commands binding upon Gentiles. A good example appears in Nahum Sarna, *Genesis* (Philadelphia: Jewish Publication Society, 1989), p. 377. As I read David Novak, some of his analysis of these questions also reflects this contrast (e.g., see *Natural Law in Judaism*, pp. 13, 145), though in more recent works the contrast seems muted and perhaps in part overcome; e.g., see *The Jewish Social Contract: An Essay in Political Theology* (Princeton: Princeton University Press, 2005), chap. 2.

of natural law without identifying natural law ethics with a *uniquely Christian* ethics. The natural law remains critically important for Christians as they continue to live in this world preserved through the Noahic covenant, but the ethics of this natural law cannot be collapsed into the ethics of the kingdom of God as announced by Jesus, whose uniqueness, anchored in the redemptive work of Christ and faith in him, must be accounted for.[25]

My basic argument in this book is that God promulgates the natural law in covenant relationships with human beings, who are rulers of the created world under him. He did so originally in a covenant of creation, with Adam as divine image-bearer and representative of the human race, in which natural law made known both humanity's basic moral obligations and humanity's eschatological destiny of new creation upon performance of the obligations. After the fall into sin, God continues to promulgate natural law, though in refracted form through the covenant with Noah, by which he preserves the first creation while postponing its final judgment. In the midst of this human history governed by God's preservative grace under the covenant with Noah, God also has enacted a plan of salvation by which human beings will attain the original goal, the new creation, through the work of the Lord Jesus Christ. As God gathers a redeemed people through a series of gracious covenants through history, he calls them to continue acknowledging and honoring the norms of the natural law in common with all humanity, even while he reveals with increasing clarity their citizenship in the new creation, in which the natural law, as it now exists, no longer binds.

Before describing my case in more detail through a summary of the arguments developed in each chapter, I first provide some points of clarification on a few key issues for this volume: its working definition of natural law, its understanding of covenant, its approach to Scripture, and its purpose and audience.

In regard to the first of these points, I am hesitant to present a short definition of natural law, due to all the nuances and clarifications that any brief

---

25. Porter notes that Protestant scholars writing about natural law generally focus upon the theological significance of the natural, which leads to seeing natural law as a basis for a distinctively Christian theological ethic. She seems to equate the "theological" reflection on natural law with what is distinctively "Christian" and herself wants to make natural law and Scripture a unified source for Christian ethics. See *Nature as Reason*, pp. 325-26, 332. While my exploration of the theological significance of the natural does fit her basic description of Protestant tendencies, I believe that interpreting the Noahic covenant as a universal covenant of common grace permits theological analysis of natural law even while distinguishing it from what is *uniquely* Christian.

definition would demand. Nevertheless, I offer the following, which I believe accurately, though incompletely, captures the ideas I develop in the following chapters: natural law consists in *the obligations and consequences incumbent upon and known by human beings as image-bearers of God and participants in the protological moral order.*[26] As this definition hints, I affirm that natural law is *law,* since it communicates binding obligations and consequences from an authority (God) outside of human persons themselves. But this is not law in the contemporary positivistic sense of a collection of discrete rules. Rather, I treat natural law as law in the sense of being a normative moral order communicated through nature, though this moral order can be helpfully summarized through general rules (such as "have dominion" and "be fruitful and multiply," or the principles of the Decalogue). This does not mean that the natural moral order is itself a complete ethical system, for it requires individuals and societies to put it into concrete application through their divinely bestowed creative freedom, and this can happen potentially in many different cultural forms. But *the natural moral order itself is divine revelation,* and precedes special revelation insofar as God always delivers the latter to human beings whom he created as participants in the natural order and designed by nature to respond to God in certain ways.[27] As I argue especially in Chapter 8, perhaps the key human attribute necessary for understanding the natural law (as moral order) and putting it into practice is *wisdom.*[28]

Second, a few comments on my use of "covenant" may be helpful. As with "natural law," I am also hesitant to offer a neat and concise definition of "covenant." One reason is that the various covenants in Scripture do not all take the same form. Historically, Reformed theologians have identified basic

---

26. When seeing this reference to "moral order" (here or in the book's title), some readers may think of Oliver O'Donovan's influential volume *Resurrection and Moral Order: An Outline for Evangelical Ethics,* 2nd ed. (Grand Rapids: Eerdmans, 1994). Though O'Donovan does not approach his subject in terms of "natural law" (for reasons he explains), many of the questions he wrestles with there are the same as those I address here. Many of O'Donovan's conclusions are attractive, particularly his defense of the created moral order as an objective reality. Yet I do not find sufficient (or even entirely clear) how he explains the relationship between the original created order and the eschatological new creation, a question central for his book, as well as for mine.

27. This distinction between natural revelation (of which natural law is an aspect) and special revelation (the spoken or written word of God, ordinarily delivered through prophets) is standard in Reformed theology; e.g., Herman Bavinck, *Reformed Dogmatics,* vol. 1, *Prolegomena,* ed. John Bolt, trans. John Vriend (Grand Rapids: Baker, 2003), chaps. 10-11.

28. I find quite congenial and useful the way O'Donovan concisely defines "created order," "wisdom," and "moral law," among other terms, in *Resurrection and Moral Order,* p. 191.

criteria that characterize biblical covenants (for example, they involve contracting parties, conditions, promises, and penalties),[29] but they recognized certain distinctions between different kinds of covenants, most notably the difference between the requirement of perfect personal obedience for blessing in the covenant of works at creation and the free bestowal of blessing upon sinners, received by faith alone, in the covenants of grace. The biblical covenants have been a topic of considerable interest to recent generations of biblical scholars. Some of them, like earlier Reformed theologians, have recognized the importance of covenant as a unifying theme in the Scriptures.[30] Though biblical scholars have developed competing proposals, they recognize the presence of different kinds of covenants, differentiated by the type of relationship between the covenanting parties and the kind of obligations one or both parties assume.[31] In the chapters that follow I understand the biblical covenants to be solemn and ordinarily oath-bound agreements that establish God and human beings in formal relationships that entail obligations for both parties and consequences for fidelity or lack thereof.[32] As we will see in subsequent chapters, however, the nature of these relationships, the types of obligations, and the conditions for reception of blessing and curse vary significantly from covenant to covenant.

Third, stating a few words about my approach to Scripture is important

29. E.g., see Louis Berkhof, *Systematic Theology*, 4th ed. (1949; reprinted Grand Rapids: Eerdmans, 1993), p. 213.

30. E.g., see Richard E. Friedman, "The Hiding of the Face: An Essay on the Literary Unity of Biblical Narrative," in *Judaic Perspectives on Ancient Israel*, ed. Jacob Neusner et al. (Philadelphia: Fortress, 1987), p. 215, as quoted in Scott W. Hahn, *Kinship by Covenant: A Canonical Approach to the Fulfillment of God's Saving Promises* (New Haven: Yale University Press, 2009), p. 25: "If we could delete all references to covenant [in the Old Testament] — which we cannot do, precisely because it is regularly integral to its contexts — we would have an anthology of stories. As it is we have a structure that can house a plot." Cf. Paul R. Williamson, *Sealed with an Oath: Covenant in God's Unfolding Purpose* (Downers Grove, IL: InterVarsity, 2007), pp. 29-30: "Covenant is without a doubt one of the most important motifs in biblical theology, attested to not only by the traditional labels applied to the respective parts of the Christian Bible, but also by the fact that the concept looms large at important junctures throughout the Bible. It underpins God's relationship with Noah, Abraham, Israel, the Levitical priesthood and the Davidic dynasty. It is also used with respect to God's relationship with the reconstituted 'Israel' of the future. Therefore, while 'biblical' and 'covenant theology' must certainly not be confused as synonymous, covenant is indisputably one of the Bible's core theological themes."

31. For a concise description of how various scholars have identified the different types of biblical covenants, see Hahn, *Kinship by Covenant*, pp. 28-31.

32. I recognize that some biblical covenants are made between two human parties. Though I will mention a couple of these, my chief concern for purposes of this theology of natural law is the series of divine-human covenants.

in light of the space I devote to biblical exegesis. All of the biblical books have human authors, who display their own particular gifts and utilize a range of literary genres, and these different authors present distinct perspectives even when treating similar subjects. Yet I affirm with historic Christianity that all of Scripture is God's word; that is, God is also the author of the biblical books — indeed, the ultimate author — and the prophets and apostles who served as their human authors wrote under divine inspiration and with divine authority. This means, most significantly for this volume, that I believe all the teaching of Scripture is coherent and internally harmonious, despite the multiple human authors with the various genres they employ and perspectives they present. Furthermore, I adhere to the traditional Reformation axiom, dating back to the early church, that Scripture is its own best interpreter. This implies that biblical interpreters today should use clearer parts of Scripture to understand less clear parts. It also implies that later parts of Scripture that interpret earlier parts provide normative guidance for our own interpretation of the latter (though it is also true, in the other direction, that earlier parts of Scripture are crucial background for understanding later parts).[33] In light of these convictions, I not only seek to do careful exegesis of particular texts in their original context but also to interpret them in light of the entire canon of Scripture.[34]

---

33. I recognize that with these comments I wade into an area of significant scholarly debate (outside of my own fields of specialty) and, certainly with respect to using the New Testament (NT) to interpret the Old Testament (OT), I am taking a position different from what is typically found among scholars engaged in grammatical-historical exegesis. An influential book on the question of how the NT interprets the OT has been Richard Longenecker, *Biblical Exegesis in the Apostolic Period* (Grand Rapids: Eerdmans, 1975). Without wishing to oversimplify challenging questions about the apostolic hermeneutic and Christians' use of it today, I would disagree with Longenecker's essential conclusion that contemporary Christian exegetes should follow the apostolic hermeneutic insofar as it follows grammatical-historical norms; see *Biblical Exegesis in the Apostolic Period,* p. 219. As a general matter, it seems to me that the direction should be reversed: rather than the apostles' interpretation of the OT being normed by the standards of the contemporary grammatical-historical exegesis, contemporary grammatical-historical exegesis should be subservient to the apostles' interpretation of the OT. On these matters I appreciate the approach in Dan McCartney and Charles Clayton, *Let the Reader Understand: A Guide to Interpreting and Applying the Bible,* 2nd ed. (Phillipsburg, NJ: Presbyterian and Reformed, 2002), pp. 63-69. For a recent book exploring related issues, see Christopher R. Seitz, *The Character of Christian Scripture: The Significance of a Two-Testament Bible* (Grand Rapids: Baker Academic, 2011).

34. What will also be evident to readers is that I deal with Scripture in terms of the completed canon. If, as Scobie puts it, "a canonical biblical theology is not based on historical reconstructions, but on the Bible in its completed form," then my book is a kind of canonical biblical theology. See Scobie, *The Ways of Our God,* p. 183.

The fourth and final point of clarification concerns the purpose and audience of this book. This book offers a *theological* account of natural law, organically related to broader Christian traditions of natural law thought, but developed here specifically through the exegesis of relevant parts of Scripture in the context of the biblical story as a whole. I do not engage natural law through nontheological disciplines such as philosophy, biology, sociology, or cultural anthropology. This is not meant to prohibit or discourage others from doing so (quite the contrary), but does seek to provide important theological foundation, justification, and boundaries for Christians who pursue such work. I also do not offer a detailed strategy for bringing the claims of natural law to bear in the pluralistic public square or extensively develop how natural law should serve as a foundation for or check upon civil law, though these too are important matters for which a biblical theology of natural law should provide much material for further reflection.

Is knowledge of the natural law itself unavailable apart from knowledge of such a biblical theology of natural law? No. The very point of the concept of natural law is that objective moral obligations are known, in some way and to some degree, by all human beings. What this study seeks to provide is a biblical explanation of what this natural law is, why it exists, and what relation it has to the divine plan of salvation in Jesus Christ. Thus the audience for this book is primarily Christians, who, though thankful for the knowledge of God's law that exists even among those who know nothing of this biblical background, wish to understand the biblical-theological foundations of natural law, at least in order to clarify their own natural knowledge of God's law and to be better able to integrate this knowledge with their broader Christian faith and life. Accordingly, this volume also serves as a general study in Christian ethics and moral theology, rather than as simply a narrow study in natural law. Non-Christians may also benefit from this book if they wish to understand better what Christians believe and what their Scriptures teach about natural law, as well as about the gospel of Jesus Christ, in whom the natural order of the present world will be brought to consummation.

In light of these points of clarification, I now provide an overview of how my argument develops in the following chapters. Part 1 (Chapters 1-5) deals with the covenantal foundations of the natural moral order and how Scripture describes the role of natural law with respect to the human race in general. I begin with the covenant of creation that governed the original world and then consider the covenant with Noah that governs creation as fallen yet divinely sustained. These covenants are *protological,* in that they are God's means for ruling the *first creation,* that is, this present world in which we live.

Chapter 1 addresses the covenant of creation and focuses particularly on Genesis 1–2. In this covenant God revealed himself in the natural order and especially in human persons as created in the divine image. God made human beings, as image-bearers, to know by nature their basic moral obligations before God and to understand their eschatological destiny of life in a new creation. Designed to image the Creator God as he revealed himself in Genesis 1–2, human beings were to be culturally creative, lovingly generous, and perfectly just.

In Chapter 2 I explore the Noahic covenant of Genesis 8:20–9:17, a covenant of preservation or "common grace" (a term I introduce in the next section). The fall into sin brought devastating consequences upon the natural order and human nature, and thus the natural law did not pass unchanged into the postlapsarian world. In Genesis 9 God entered into a covenant with both the natural order and the human race, promising to uphold and preserve his creation, albeit in fallen form. God promised to uphold the regularity of the cosmic order and reaffirmed the nature of humanity as his own image, and thereby continues to reveal his law by nature. Genesis 9 indicates that this natural law provides at least a basic, minimal ethic designed for the preservation of the social order. It also hints at a broader cultural responsibility for the human race that resembles humanity's cultural responsibility under the covenant of creation, but only as refracted for a fallen context. Yet rather than orient human beings by nature to life in a new creation, as in the original covenant with Adam, the image of God preserved in the Noahic covenant reminds them of their condemnation because of sin before a just God. The covenant with Noah itself provides no eschatological hope, only temporal preservation.

Chapters 3-4 continue Part 1 by examining a number of subsequent Old Testament texts and considering God's government of the nations of the world through the natural law, as they live under the auspices of the Noahic covenant. In distinction from God's special covenant people — the Abrahamic, Israelite, and church communities — God holds the nations of the world accountable to him primarily through the natural law rather than through his revealed word. Consistent with what Genesis 9 suggests, Chapter 3 argues that there are both a negative and a positive side to God's postlapsarian government of the world through natural law. Negatively, the story of Sodom in Genesis 18–19 manifests how the natural law maintains a witness to God's righteous judgment against sin, through a great anticipation of the final judicial reckoning, which was postponed, but not canceled, by the Noahic covenant. Positively, the story of Abraham's conflict with Abimelech in Genesis 20 shows the natural law as God's instrument for maintaining a sense of justice and civil order among a pagan people who were foreigners to Abraham's covenant household. Chapter 4 extends this analysis through a study of the Old Testament prophetic oracles against foreign nations and the court scenes in Daniel. I argue that these texts also display God holding the nations of the world accountable to his judgment through the natural law, in ways consistent with what the Noahic covenant indicates.

Chapter 5 concludes Part 1 through a detailed study of that *locus classicus* of Christian natural law theory, Romans 1:18–2:16. I argue that this text does indeed speak of natural law, and in fact provides the most focused biblical description of the revelation of divine law in nature, especially in its universal relevance in God's just government of the world. Romans 1:18–2:16 both confirms the conclusions of previous chapters regarding natural law under the Noahic covenant and enriches the picture as to what this natural law requires.

In Part 2 I explore the covenants of grace, as they are progressively revealed through redemptive history, and the significance of natural law for God's redeemed people at each stage in this history. While the covenant of creation and covenant with Noah are *protological,* in that they govern the natural moral order of this present creation, the covenants of grace reveal the *eschatological* realities of the new creation, incipiently in the Old Testament and more fully in the New Testament, until the new creation is fully manifest at the second coming of Christ. These redemptive covenants do not themselves govern the protological natural order, but point beyond it to an eschatological natural order to be revealed on the last day. Yet until that day these covenants show great interest in how God's people should conduct themselves while still living in this present world, and for this task natural law continues to play a crucial role.

Chapter 6 introduces the covenants of grace and examines the Abrahamic covenant in particular. Though God's promises of redemption began long before, his covenant with Abraham marks the first formalized covenant relationship that promises the grace of salvation. Though this covenant pointed to a coming Messianic seed and the blessing of redemption for all peoples, it distinguished but did not separate the covenant people from the pagan nations around them, calling them to live in their midst as sojourners and active participants in their cultural life. In this context, God desired his covenant people to learn his ways of righteousness and justice, revealed in part through the natural law. Natural law also served as the common objective moral standard enabling them to enjoy a measure of peaceful coexistence with some foreign cities around them.

Chapter 7 considers the next great biblical covenant, the covenant with

Israel, through Moses, at Mount Sinai. This chapter confronts a weighty but difficult issue, the relationship of Mosaic law and natural law. The New Testament interprets the Mosaic covenant as a temporary arrangement designed to prepare God's people of old in various ways for the coming Messiah. Chapter 7 focuses on one of the ways it accomplished this task, namely, by bringing Israel through a recapitulation of Adam's experience in the covenant of creation. The Mosaic law played a key role in this dynamic, detailing the people's obligations to God and promising them blessing upon obedience and threatening curse upon disobedience. In doing so, the Mosaic law reflected both the substance and the sanctions of the natural law. I argue that God intended the Mosaic law (in part) to be a republication of the natural law designed for the unique circumstances of Old Testament Israel. The Mosaic law thereby served to make Israel a microcosm of the whole human family, showcasing the plight of all sinful humanity living under the protological natural law.

Chapter 8 turns to the Old Testament wisdom literature, particularly Proverbs. Proverbs significantly enriches this volume's portrayal of natural law by highlighting the presence of a moral order pervading this world. Though Proverbs originated during Israel's life under the Mosaic covenant, it provides moral instruction not through written law but by training readers how to observe and reflect upon the natural moral order and then to draw appropriate practical conclusions that lead to success and flourishing. Wisdom — understood as perception of the natural moral order and effective structuring of one's life within its bounds — was absolutely necessary for Israel if she was to put the Mosaic law into faithful practice. But Proverbs also portrays wisdom as an international phenomenon, attainable to a certain degree even by those outside the special covenant people. Thus Proverbs further testifies both to the significance of natural law for the covenant community and to the presence and power of natural law in the broader world.

Part 2 concludes with a study of natural law and the new covenant. In this crucial Chapter 9 I argue that through the life, death, resurrection, and ascension of the Lord Jesus Christ, as the Last Adam, believers in him have passed through the judgment coming upon the human race under the protological natural law and have become citizens of the new creation even now. Their identity is chiefly defined by this new creation, which is the eschatological consummation of the first creation and its natural order. Yet until Christ's second coming Christians live in the overlap of two ages, for though citizens of the age-to-come, God calls them for a time to continue living peaceful and productive lives in this present age. To put my point concisely, under the new covenant Christians have been released from the protological natural law at an ultimate level, since they no longer stand under its judgment and are citizens of a new creation with its own consummated, eschatological moral order. Yet at a penultimate level they must continue to live within the structures of this present world and thus under the authority of the protological natural law. Thus the natural law still plays a crucial normative role for the moral lives of New Testament believers, even while their distinctive moral identity in Christ simultaneously gives testimony to the imminent passing away of the natural law in its present form, at the consummation of all things in the new creation.

The book concludes with Chapter 10, which first summarizes and integrates the arguments of previous chapters. I then explain why I believe developing a sound theology of natural law is useful and even necessary for Christians seeking to live faithful, productive, peaceful, and vigilant lives in this "present evil age" (Gal. 1:4). Finally, the chapter closes with reflections on the implications of natural law for some key issues in political and legal theory, including the nature of justice and the good of religious liberty.

This Present Project and the Broader
Christian Natural Law Traditions

As already mentioned, this biblical theology of natural law is organically connected to historic Christian natural law traditions. In the remainder of the chapter I explain this claim in more detail. To summarize, I believe that my project, in many significant ways, stands in continuity with the perennially important natural law theory of Thomas Aquinas, but also is biblically *reformed* in other important respects. I present this project in the spirit of the Reformation, which was not a total break with the medieval heritage but a reform movement. In addition, though my proposal is basically premodern, insofar as it roots natural law in an objectively real and meaningful created order and ultimately in the authority of God himself,[35] it is also modern, insofar

---

35. As a broad generalization, people in classical and premodern times, as Steven D. Smith puts it, understood the world they inhabited to be "intrinsically normative or purposeful"; see *The Disenchantment of Secular Discourse* (Cambridge, MA: Harvard University Press, 2010), p. 21. In contrast, the modern world seeks to stamp its own meaning upon the world, rather than discover its meaning. The now-famous words of Justice Kennedy in the *Casey* decision of the United States Supreme Court perhaps emblematize the modern attitude as well as anything: "At the heart of liberty is the right to define one's own concept of existence, of meaning, of the universe, and of the mystery of human life." As Alasdair MacIntyre describes it, the modern perspective on ethics is characterized by "emotivism," "the doctrine that all

as it understands natural law in a way (critically) supportive of the modern Western experiment in religious liberty, in the face of the perceived crisis of secular liberalism in the West.

Thomas Aquinas was not the first natural law theorist and was obviously not the last. But however one evaluates the soundness of his understanding of natural law, it has proven to be the most enduring and perennially relevant in the history of Christian thought. In light of its eminent status, I focus this section on reflecting where my biblical theology of natural law stands in relation to Thomas's understanding. Without seeking to be exhaustive, I first identify six points at which I see significant continuity between Thomas's understanding and my own project and then two areas where I believe important biblical and theological considerations suggest the need for reform in Thomistic theory.

A first point at which I see my project's continuity with Thomas is his metaphysical and epistemological realism. Thomas believed that things in this world (including human beings) have objectively meaningful natures, and that human nature entails certain obligations and rights, knowledge of which is accessible to the human mind.[36] I too affirm these ideas. An important theme in Thomas's metaphysics and epistemology, and, correspondingly, in his understanding of natural law, was his notion of *participation*. Thomas's most basic definition of natural law, in fact, makes use of this theme: natural law is the "participation of the eternal law in the rational creature" *(participatio legis aeternae in rationali creatura).*[37] Since, for Thomas, eternal law represents the government of the universe by the divine reason,[38] such words may suggest some point of intersection between the human and divine minds, some mea-

---

evaluative judgments and more specifically all moral judgments are *nothing but* expressions of preference, expressions of attitude or feeling, insofar as they are moral or evaluative in character." See *After Virtue: A Study in Moral Theory,* 2nd ed. (Notre Dame: University of Notre Dame Press, 1984), pp. 11-12.

36. I recognize that how exactly to characterize Thomas's epistemology is a disputed question. Without wishing to delve into more technical debates, I take Eleanore Stump's general summary as accurate: "Like Aristotle, Aquinas is a metaphysical realist. That is, he assumes that there is an external world around us and that it has certain features independently of the operation of any created intellect, so that it is up to our minds to discover truths about the world, rather than simply inventing or creating them. On Aquinas's account, the human intellect was created by God for the purpose of discovering such truths about the world." See *Aquinas* (New York: Routledge, 2003), p. 231.

37. *Summa Theologiae,* 1a2ae 91.2. English translations are taken from *Summa Theologica,* trans. Fathers of the English Dominican Province (New York: Benzinger, 1948).

38. *Summa Theologiae,* 1a2ae 91.1.

sure of univocity between God and humanity, and therefore a compromise of the fundamental Christian doctrine of the absolute distinction between the infinite creator and his finite creation. But Thomas did not intend his words to convey this meaning. He rejected a univocal understanding of the God-human relationship and argued instead for an *analogical* relationship. In other words, there is an absolute difference between the being and mind of God and the being and mind of human beings, but within this absolute difference is also a likeness or similarity. Thus rational and moral human attributes reflect those of God, such that human beings can bear his image and be true causes of effects in this world, without thereby compromising God's identity as the first cause of all things.[39] In Thomas's definition of natural law mentioned above, therefore, human beings (as rational creatures) are enabled to play a genuine role in the government of the world while always standing under God's supreme government, doing works that are truly their own while existing under God's ultimate causality.[40] Though I do not utilize the terminology of "participation" in the technical metaphysical way that Thomas does, my treatment of the image of God, in the context of the covenant of creation and the Noahic covenant (especially in Chapters 1-2), communicates many of the same ideas: though there is an absolute distinction between God and human beings, God has made them in his image, to exercise rule in this world under his ultimate authority, as they know by nature a moral standard that reflects God's own character and his own actions in his government of the world.

A second point at which I see my project's continuity with Thomas's thought is his conception of human nature being ordered to something beyond itself. Below I critically engage some important aspects of Thomas's famous paradigm — grace perfects nature — but here I wish to express appreciation for his affirmation, following many prominent theologians before him, that humanity's ultimate end, established before the fall into sin and renewed

---

39. For helpful discussion of related points, see Reinhard Hütter, "Attending to the Wisdom of God — from Effect to Cause, from Creation to God: A *relecture* of the Analogy of Being according to Thomas Aquinas," in *The Analogy of Being: Invention of the Antichrist or the Wisdom of God?* ed. Thomas Joseph White, O.P. (Grand Rapids: Eerdmans, 2011), pp. 209-45.

40. Thomas's definition of natural law, in its immediate context, reads: "The rational creature is subject to Divine providence in the most excellent way, in so far as it partakes of a share of providence, by being provident both for itself and for others. Wherefore it has a share of the Eternal Reason, whereby it has natural inclination to its proper act and end: and this participation of the eternal law in the rational creature is called the natural law." See *Summa Theologiae*, 1a2ae 91.2. I am grateful to Russell Hittinger and Manfred Svensson for helpful counsel to me on this issue.

through salvation in Christ, was something unattainable within the confines of the original creation. For Thomas, humanity's highest end is the beatific vision of God, attained through supernatural grace.[41] Despite some significant differences with Thomas's scheme, my account also understands God to have created human beings for an eschatological end transcending the present world and to have renewed their hope of attaining it through the work of Christ.

A third point of continuity with Thomas's thought is his sensitivity to the movement of human beings through a state of original integrity to a fallen condition and then to a state of grace. For Thomas, the human nature with which God endowed his image-bearers at creation survived, but was wounded by, the fall; and grace, through Christ, both heals the wounds of nature and elevates it to its supernatural end.[42] I critically evaluate some aspects of this scheme as well, but the historical movement from a covenant of creation (concerning human nature's original integrity) to a covenant of common grace (concerning human nature's preservation, though in a corrupted state), which in turn is foundational for the covenants of grace (concerning human nature's redemption through Christ), is a central dynamic for my present project.

Fourth, Thomas understood the natural law more in terms of a moral order than a series of discrete rules. Natural law, for Thomas, is encapsulated in one rule — pursue good and shun evil — but this is so general that it is of little concrete usefulness. More specific rules (such as those of the Decalogue) can also be understood through practical reason, but even these do not capture the natural law comprehensively, for natural law pertains to all things to which human beings are inclined by nature.[43] Though again I develop these matters differently, the idea of natural law in terms of moral order rather than discrete rules is also important to the theology of natural law for which I argue in subsequent chapters.

A fifth point of continuity lies in the relation Thomas perceived between natural law and human civil law. For Thomas, human law ought to be grounded in the natural law, and any "law" not grounded in natural law is a

---

41. *Summa Theologiae,* 1a2ae 3.8; 109.5. Among earlier theologians, Augustine, for example, saw humanity as destined for eschatological life even before the fall, upon condition of faithful obedience: God created man "in such sort, that if he remained in subjection to His Creator as his rightful Lord, and piously kept His commandments, he should pass into the company of the angels, and obtain, without the intervention of death, a blessed and endless immortality." See *The City of God,* trans. Marcus Dods (New York: Random House, 1950), p. 406 (Book 12, Section 21).

42. *Summa Theologiae,* 1a2ae 109.

43. *Summa Theologiae,* 1a2ae 94.2-3; 100.1.

perversion of law.[44] Yet there is no single civil code that is necessarily derived from natural law, for human beings must exercise prudence and be attentive to social circumstances in order to apply the moral foundation of the natural law in suitable and effective ways for particular times and places.[45] Though my present study does not focus on civil law per se, I do portray the natural moral order as the soil from which civil law ought to grow. Yet, with Thomas, I do not view natural law itself as teaching a detailed political system or policy agenda, but as providing basic moral boundaries within which responsible human agents can develop concrete legal systems.

Sixth and finally, I see continuity with Thomas's work in his interest in integrating natural law into a broader biblical moral theology. For Thomas, human beings know natural law by reason, but Thomas was not content to examine natural law independently of Scripture. Not only did he believe that Scripture teaches about natural law,[46] but he also interpreted the content and effects of natural law in conjunction with the content and effects of biblical commands, or what he called "divine law." For example, he believed that natural law lay at the heart of the moral core of the Mosaic law and also undergirded its judicial aspect.[47] Though my conclusions do not always match Thomas's, interest in such integration of natural law and biblical moral teaching pervades this volume, whose longest chapter, in fact, concerns the relation of natural law and Mosaic law.

These aspects of continuity between Thomas's theory of natural law and my proposal in the present volume are, I believe, substantive and significant. My project stands in organic continuity with this most enduring of medieval accounts of natural law. But as a Reformed theologian I also believe that the reformation of medieval church and theology was necessary for the health of Christianity. Accordingly, as I approach a Thomistic perspective on natural law critically, in the light of my reading of Scripture with the church and especially with the Reformed tradition, I also see matters of discontinuity between Thomas's theory and what I develop here. I mention two in particular, one that I discuss briefly and the other at greater length.

The first matter of discontinuity relates to the larger metaphysics in which Thomas's understanding of natural law is embedded. The embedding in a metaphysics is not a problem; presumably every coherent view of natural

---

44. *Summa Theologiae*, 1a2ae 95.2.
45. *Summa Theologiae*, 1a2ae 95.2; 96.2.
46. E.g., in Romans 2:14; see *Summa Theologiae*, 1a2ae 91.2.
47. *Summa Theologiae*, 1a2ae 100.1; 104.1, 3.

law involves some metaphysical ideas, whether explicitly or implicitly, whether developed theologically or philosophically. Rather, I wish briefly to engage Thomistic metaphysics in regard to God's existence and the implications for natural law. In Thomistic metaphysics one begins with a philosophical study of this world and the being that one experiences in this world, and thereby comes to identify the essence of human nature and a more detailed metaphysics generally. The philosopher cannot gain knowledge of God's being itself through this study, but can draw conclusions about the existence of a God who is the first cause. The existence of God, therefore, is metaphysically demonstrated *a posteriori,* not something presumed from the outset of investigation.[48]

Many Reformed theologians working within so-called Kuyperian or neo-Calvinist circles have been critical of this metaphysical approach.[49] Though I have reservations about some aspects of these circles' interpretation of Thomas (about which more below), I believe they identify a genuine difficulty at this point. My chief concern about this Thomistic approach to metaphysics is twofold: it presumes that human beings can investigate nature while holding accountability to God in abeyance (at least for a time), and it seems to make natural knowledge of God and one's place before him (at best) a privilege of the learned. A number of biblical texts call such ideas into question. Scripture indeed teaches a knowledge of God in nature, but not one that comes at the end of a philosophical investigation. It is not so much that human beings find God in nature as that through nature God proclaims and reveals himself to them: "The heavens declare the glory of God, and the sky above proclaims his handiwork. Day to day pours out speech, and night to night reveals knowledge" (Ps. 19:1-2); "The wrath of God is revealed from heaven against all ungodliness and unrighteousness of men, who by their unrighteousness suppress the truth. For what can be known about God is

48. For a recent explanation of these themes and a robust defense of Thomistic metaphysics, see Thomas Joseph White, O.P., *Wisdom in the Face of Modernity: A Study in Thomistic Natural Theology* (Ave Maria, FL: Sapientia Press of Ave Maria University, 2009).

49. Perhaps none more critical than Cornelius Van Til; see e.g. *Christian Apologetics* (Phillipsburg, NJ: Presbyterian and Reformed, 1976), pp. 8-9. He writes: "While claiming to hold to the Christian theory of reality Thomas Aquinas and his modern followers in effect follow Aristotle in speaking first of being in general and in introducing the distinction between divine being and created being afterwards. The consequences are fatal both for systematic theology and for apologetics. For systematic theology it means that God is not unequivocally taken to be the source of man's being and the controlling power over his actions. Every doctrine is bound to be false if the first and basic doctrine of God is false." It is worth noting that Thomas, despite his metaphysical method, does in fact affirm God as the source of man's being and the controlling power over his actions.

plain to them, because God has shown it to them. For his invisible attributes, namely, his eternal power and divine nature, have been clearly perceived, ever since the creation of the world, in the things that have been made. So they are without excuse" (Rom. 1:18-20). The created world relentlessly impresses upon human beings not only the existence but also something of the character of God. And it does this clearly, such that all humans know their basic moral obligations before him (though they suppress this knowledge) and are held duly accountable. I do not claim that Scripture treats serious intellectual reflection as worthless for understanding the natural law (a point refuted at least by Proverbs). But biblical teaching makes suspect any metaphysical method that permits investigation of nature by philosophers who function as uncommitted even to the very existence of God during the course of their investigation, and Scripture calls into question any model that makes only those with sophisticated philosophical training capable of understanding the existence of God through nature. Nature confronts every person at every moment with God and his claims, and at every moment demands a response, to which God holds each accountable. If this is the case, then a decision about God cannot be postponed until the end of a long process of investigating nature. I take it that the Thomistic approach falls short on this point,[50] and I will attempt to defend the point in subsequent chapters (though I make only modest epistemological claims concerning natural law, because I do not believe a *biblical* theology of natural law permits more than this).

A second point at which I see discontinuity between Thomas's account of natural law and my own demands a more lengthy discussion: the famous Thomistic formula that grace does not destroy nature, but perfects it *(gratia non tollat naturam sed perficiat).*[51] In many respects, the way one resolves the so-called nature and grace issue is fundamental for any Christian theory of natural law, and this is true for the present book. Here I wish to bring into the discussion a certain Reformed school of thought mentioned above, sometimes referred to as Kuyperian or neo-Calvinist. Though this has not been a unified movement, those associated with it display important affinities in thought and characteristically build upon the work of late-nineteenth- and

---

50. Perhaps illustrated well by White's defense and description of Thomistic metaphysics in the following words: "The primary being, for Aquinas, has an ontological priority with regard to all others, but *for us* this is discovered last." See *Wisdom in the Face of Modernity*, p. 160. At the same time, I recognize that Thomas does not necessarily delay consideration of God in his writings; he approaches similar subjects in different ways depending upon what he is writing and why.

51. E.g., *Summa Theologiae*, 1a 1.8, ad.2.

early-twentieth-century Dutch figures Abraham Kuyper and Herman Bavinck. I reflect on neo-Calvinist views of natural law more specifically in Appendix 2. Here I wish to interact with its views on nature and grace and its critique of Thomas on this score, as a way to probe Thomas's position. In short, while I think neo-Calvinist critiques raise good issues, they do not always deal with Thomas himself entirely fairly and do not provide an adequate theological response to the problems that are in fact present in Thomas's understanding of nature and grace.

The precise shape of Thomas's view of nature and grace is a debated matter, even within Thomistic Roman Catholic circles. Many of the most penetrating Roman Catholic theologians of the twentieth century wrestled with questions of nature and grace. Some suggested that neo-scholastic thinkers such as Cajetan and Suarez had corrupted Thomas's view by positing a realm of "pure nature" and obscuring the allegedly more intimate connection of nature and grace in Thomas's thought.[52] Without wishing to delve deeply into these intra-Catholic debates, I summarize Thomas's view of nature and grace in the following way: God created human beings with a certain kind of nature, which had its own natural and proximate ends. At their creation, however, God also bestowed supernatural gifts of grace upon them, which served to elevate human nature to enable them to do works meritorious of a supernatural end, namely, the beatific vision of God. Thus unfallen humanity was able to attain this supernatural end by grace. Through their fall into sin, however, human beings lost their supernatural gifts. Their human nature remained, though in a damaged and weakened state. In the economy of redemption, God restores to human beings the supernatural gifts of grace, which not only heal the powers of nature that they retained in damaged form, but also enable them again to do meritorious works by which they can attain the supernatural beatific vision. Thus, both before and after the fall, grace does not destroy but perfects nature.[53]

Many prominent figures within neo-Calvinist circles are quite critical of Thomas and the so-called medieval synthesis of Greek philosophy and

---

52. See especially the work of Henri de Lubac, S.J.; e.g., *The Mystery of the Supernatural,* trans. Rosemary Sheed (New York: Herder & Herder, 1967); cf. Hans Urs von Balthasar, *The Theology of Karl Barth,* trans. John Drury (New York: Holt, Rinehart & Winston, 1971), pp. 217-47; and Karl Rahner, "Concerning the Relationship between Nature and Grace," in *Theological Investigations,* vol. 1 (Baltimore: Helicon, 1969), pp. 297-317. For a strong critique of de Lubac's interpretation of Thomas by a contemporary Roman Catholic scholar, see Steven A. Long, *Natura Pura: On the Recovery of Nature in the Doctrine of Grace* (New York: Fordham University Press, 2010).

53. See *Summa Theologiae,* 1a 95; 1a2ae 109.

Christian theology.[54] The nature/grace motif is one of their prime targets for critique. As mentioned above, I do not always believe their critiques deal accurately with Thomas himself or offer the most helpful solutions to issues that I believe are indeed problematic in Thomas's theology. I now describe three aspects of their critique and offer some reflection on them.

One common aspect of neo-Calvinist critique is that Thomas's view implies that nature is inherently defective, because even before the fall nature required a superadded gift of grace in order to keep its internal tensions in check and to transcend its inherent limitations, and this compromises biblical affirmation of the goodness of the original creation.[55] This critique raises a legitimate point of concern with respect to the presence of concupiscence in the prelapsarian natural human condition. Though all Christian theologians must struggle to explain how Adam was created very good yet was also able to sin, positing an inherent tension between his higher and lower natural faculties is, I agree, an unsatisfactory move. But in other respects it is not clear how a neo-Calvinist critique of supernatural gifts added on to Adam's natural endowments, as a general idea, can gain serious traction. For one thing, early Reformed theologians continued to speak of Adam's original condition in terms of natural and supernatural gifts, and thus the Reformation may not have represented a sharp break with medieval theology on this issue, as sometimes suggested.[56] Furthermore, even when describing Adam's pre-fall state in distinctively Reformed terms, neo-Calvinists continue to suggest that God gave him some kind of additional endowment beyond what is reckoned as natural. Bavinck, for example, argues that Adam did not have natural knowledge of or ability to attain eschatological beatitude, but attained such only through God's establishment of the covenant of works (which thus effectively functions as a *donum superadditum* of a different sort).[57]

A second common aspect of neo-Calvinist critique of Thomas and the medieval synthesis regards the effects of the fall. According to this critique, the

---

54. E.g., see Herman Bavinck, *Reformed Dogmatics*, vol. 2, *God and Creation*, ed. John Bolt, trans. John Vriend (Grand Rapids: Baker Academic, 2004), pp. 539-48; Herman Dooyeweerd, *Roots of Western Culture: Pagan, Secular, and Christian Options*, trans. John Kraay (Toronto: Wedge, 1979), chap. 5; and Cornelius Van Til, *The Defense of the Faith* (Philadelphia: Presbyterian and Reformed, 1955), pp. 86-95, 149-56.

55. E.g., see Bavinck, *Reformed Dogmatics*, 2:546-47 (though Bavinck critiques "Rome" generally here, Thomas is often within his purview in this larger section).

56. See the helpful discussion of this point in Paul Helm, *Calvin at the Centre* (Oxford: Oxford University Press, 2010), pp. 313-22.

57. Bavinck, *Reformed Dogmatics*, 2:571.

medieval synthesis held that human beings at the fall lost their supernatural gifts but not their natural gifts, and this idea does not properly account for the damage to human nature stemming from Adam's first transgression.[58] One difficulty here is that Thomas himself clearly did not believe that human nature remained intact after the fall (though some later Roman Catholic thinkers may have spoken in this way), for he taught that natural human powers were weakened and damaged by sin.[59] It is true that Reformed theologians have ordinarily spoken of the effects of the fall on human nature as more grave than did Thomas, but Thomas did wrestle seriously with sin and its effects. Also interesting to consider here is the neo-Calvinist claim that its categories of "common grace"/"saving grace" provide a better paradigm than does Thomas's "nature"/"grace" categories for working through the issues at stake.[60] As with the first point of critique, it is not evident here that neo-Calvinists offer an alternative that is really so different from Thomas's understanding. Neo-Calvinists agree with Thomists that nature was not destroyed by the fall, and affirm that human beings retain their human nature, however damaged, even apart from God's work of redemption. What the category of common grace seems to do is explain *how* God preserves something of humanity's original condition despite the devastation of the fall, while the category of nature identifies what it is that remains (which in turn is the material on which saving grace works). The categories of common grace/special grace and nature/grace seem to be complementary, rather than in competition.[61]

A third important point of neo-Calvinist critique is that, insofar as the nature/grace terminology is retained, their "grace-restores-nature" paradigm is better than the Thomistic "grace-perfects-nature." Some writers suggest that the former paradigm is crucial to understanding certain neo-Calvinist thinkers or even neo-Calvinism generally.[62] What does it mean, then, to assert that grace restores nature? Read literally, it suggests that what grace does is *recover*

58. E.g., see Bavinck, *Reformed Dogmatics,* 3:43. Though not mentioning Thomas in particular, he says that, for the "Roman Catholic dualism . . . cast aside by the Reformation," "fallen nature is actually totally identical with uncorrupted nature" and "the natural gifts continue intact."

59. E.g., see *Summa Theologiae,* 1a2ae 109.2.

60. E.g., see Herman Bavinck, "Calvin and Common Grace," in *Calvin and the Reformation,* ed. William Park Armstrong (New York: Fleming H. Revell, 1909), 99-130.

61. As was the case for Calvin, as Helm has argued in *Calvin at the Centre,* pp. 325, 333.

62. According to John Bolt, for example, "The fundamental theme that shapes Bavinck's entire theology is the Trinitarian idea that grace restores nature." See "Editor's Introduction," in Bavinck, *Reformed Dogmatics,* 1:18.

nature as it was before the fall, for "restoration" seems to presume an initial state of integrity to which something returns. Were this really what the paradigm means, it would be very problematic theologically, for Scripture never portrays redemption as returning human beings to their condition before the fall, but rather as granting eschatological gifts that Adam himself did not enjoy in Eden. But neo-Calvinist writers do not in fact intend the language of restoration to teach a return to a protological Paradise. Bavinck, perhaps the figure most associated with the grace-restores-nature paradigm, sometimes uses such language in the same breath as he asserts that grace brings nature to its highest state of existence, that is, to something much greater than its condition before the fall.[63] Once put this way, however, one wonders why "grace does not destroy nature but perfects it" is really such a bad way to put it.

This raises the question again whether there is as large a difference between the Thomistic and neo-Calvinist models as sometimes suggested (interestingly, both "restoration" and "perfection" are terms Scripture uses to describe redemption[64]). The suggestion that there is not such a large difference gains plausibility from recent neo-Calvinist popular literature. This literature does not portray redemption in terms of a return to Eden, but does speak of it as putting human beings back on the track originally set before Adam and enabling them to carry out his cultural mandate once again, which in turn promotes and contributes to the coming of the kingdom and its full realization in the new creation.[65] This contemporary neo-Calvinist vision bears notable similarities to Thomas's: both paradigms envision redemptive grace as enabling human beings to do the sorts of things that Adam was originally supposed to do and to attain an eschatological state of beatitude at the end of the process. Of course, to the extent that contemporary neo-Calvinists maintain a traditional Reformed soteriology, their views must differ from Thomas's position on nature and grace in significant ways, especially on whether the work

---

63. E.g., see *Reformed Dogmatics*, 3:577: "It is the same treasure that was promised in the covenant of works and is granted in the covenant of grace. Grace restores nature and takes it to its highest pinnacle, though it does not add to it any new and heterogeneous constituents." Cf. 2:573: "Christ does not [merely] restore his own to the state of Adam before the fall. He acquired and bestows much more, namely, that which Adam would have received had he not fallen. He positions us not at the beginning but at the end of the journey that Adam had to complete. He accomplished not only the passive but also the active obedience required; he not only delivers us from guilt and punishment, but out of grace immediately grants us the right to eternal life."

64. Among other examples, see Acts 3:21 and Hebrews 12:23.

65. E.g., see Albert M. Wolters, *Creation Regained: Biblical Basics for a Reformational Worldview* (Grand Rapids: Eerdmans, 1985), pp. 11, 57-60, 63-64.

performed as part of this restored Adamic task is in some sense meritorious of the future beatitude. But in my judgment it is difficult to see how speaking of "grace-restores-nature" provides any great advantage over speaking of "grace-perfects-nature."[66]

I would like to suggest, therefore, a different sort of Reformed response to Thomas's nature/grace paradigm, one that sets the ideas of nature and natural law in the context of Reformed covenant theology. What follows is a basic sketch, the substance of which I unpack in the subsequent chapters of this book.

First, what about the situation before the fall into sin? For now I will refer not to "nature" and "grace" but to "first creation" and "new creation." This is not to deny that things have natures or to get hung up on semantics, but there are certain advantages to these terms I will explain below. At the beginning, God made the first creation destined for consummation in the new creation. At the center of this about-to-unfold historical dynamic were human beings, created to live in the first creation but also, through faithful service to God in it, to attain consummation in the new creation where they would rest and reign with God (who himself labored righteously in his work of creation and then entered his state of rest). God made human beings with a nature upright and righteous, though protological and fallible, and in this natural condition and by their natural powers they were fully able to fulfill the task God gave to them and thus to attain the promised reward of the consummated new creation. I avoid speaking here of "supernatural" gifts or gifts of "grace" that God gave to human beings in addition to their natural endowments, because I wish to affirm that the ability to fulfill their divinely established commission in the world was a constitutive gift of the original creation, not a proleptic gift of the eschatological new creation. This is not to say that human beings were on some kind of ontologically level ground with God so as to enable them to earn something from him, but that God as a free gift created human beings in his image, in a covenant relationship (the covenant of creation). As an image-bearer in covenant with God, Adam was naturally enabled to follow God's archetypal pattern of ruling well in this world and then attaining rest in an eschatological new creation as a just reward.[67] In this context, the (original)

---

66. Perhaps supporting this observation is the fact that neo-Calvinist writers at times use the traditional Thomistic language and the fact that Thomists sometimes use the preferred neo-Calvinist language. Bavinck, for example, can write: "Grace repairs *and perfects* nature"; see *Reformed Dogmatics,* 3:226 (italics added). Long, on the other hand, says that Thomas held nature to be *"restored"* in grace; see *Natura Pura,* p. 82.

67. In Bavinck's words, "there was a merit *ex pacto* (arising from a covenant), not *ex*

natural law was a law directing human beings in this image-bearing task of ruling the first creation toward the goal of attaining the new creation.

Putting this in terms of first creation/new creation (instead of nature/ grace) helps to make clear that the chief dynamic here is *historical* (or horizontal), not vertical (which the very language of *super*natural perfection suggests, and which Thomas's use of neo-Platonic metaphysics does not discourage). The first creation/new creation terminology should also make clear that the ultimate eschatological goal is not something wholly other than the original state (some kind of second creation *ex nihilo*), but its consummation. Thomas, I am confident, would appreciate both of these points. But my decision not to use the terminology of "grace" does get to substantive differences with Thomas, for while Thomas uses "grace" as a way to express the *similarities* between the way to heavenly beatitude before the fall and the way after the fall, I refrain from using "grace" precisely in order to capture the *differences* between them. In short, for Thomas human beings could merit the beatific vision through a gift of supernatural grace both before and after the fall; for the project I develop here, human beings before the fall could merit the new creation through the proper use of their natural endowments, while human beings after the fall need a gift of grace to attain the new creation because they cannot merit it in any respect. I return to this last point again shortly.

After the fall, the human history initiated at creation continued, but was diverted from its original straight path toward consummation in the new creation. The dynamic of the revised historical process is twofold: God preserves the original creation (and with it a general human history) and God enacts a plan of salvation that achieves human attainment of the new creation, which was humanity's original goal. Both aspects of this dynamic may again be understood covenantally: the preservation of the original creation through the covenant with Noah and the attainment of the new creation by a plan of salvation through the covenants of grace. In the postlapsarian context the traditional nature/grace language becomes much more amenable to my project. Grace, indeed, does not destroy nature; *(common) grace preserves nature* and *(saving) grace consummates nature.*

First, then, (common) grace preserves nature. One of God's great works

---

condigno." See *Reformed Dogmatics*, 2:544. As I explain further in Chapter 1, my claims here may help point to a way through traditional debates between the intellectualist and voluntarist traditions about the relationship of natural law to God's reason and will. I argue in this book that natural law does indeed reflect the very holiness and righteousness of God, but only insofar as God reveals himself through nature in a particular covenant relationship with humanity, into which he freely and willingly enters.

after the fall is preservation of the original creation, including human nature, though in fallen and corrupted form. Though this work obviously began immediately upon the fall, God later made a covenant with Noah by which he formally established the terms of his preservative work. By this covenant God bestows common grace upon creation — "common" in that God gives it promiscuously. Human nature still exists, since human beings continue to be image-bearers of God, having reason and will and retaining a continuing responsibility to rule in this world under God's ultimate authority. But sinful human beings have damaged reason and wounded wills, using their authority in this world for many wicked ends. Their eschatological horizon now points not to a new creation attainable through faithful service to God but to condemnation at the final judgment, which the Noahic covenant has postponed but not canceled. God continues to impart natural law, which is organically continuous with the natural law imparted in the covenant of creation but is now refracted through the Noahic covenant of common grace, in a way fit for a fallen-but-preserved world. It lays upon human beings natural obligations for things that serve to preserve their existence and to promote a limited and penultimate flourishing within this present creation. This natural law also reminds human beings of their accountability before God and preserves a sense of their eschatological orientation, though now it offers no hope of a good outcome.

The second aspect of the post-fall dynamic is that (saving) grace consummates nature. Through the covenants of grace God provides a way of salvation such that human beings attain the original goal, the consummated new creation. This happens, however, not by putting human beings back somewhere on the track upon which Adam originally set out to get there, either in terms of a Thomistic gift of supernatural grace enabling them to do acts meritorious of the beatific vision or in terms of a neo-Calvinist renewed pursuit of the original creation mandate. Rather, by the covenants of grace God forms a new community from among fallen humanity. Its members rest by faith on the Lord Jesus Christ, who personally fulfilled Adam's original commission by being a perfect image-bearer of God in the present creation and thereby achieved the goal of the new creation in his ascension. Those who believe in him are already justified (as if they themselves had faithfully completed the original human commission) and already adopted as heirs of the new creation, of which they are now citizens. But God also calls believers to pilgrimage for a time in this present world — fallen but preserved under the Noahic covenant of common grace — until the day of Christ's return, at the consummation, when the new creation will be fully revealed.

During this interim time, these justified participants in the covenants of grace are to live moral lives that are in many respects unique, in the way they anticipate the glorified life of the new creation. But God also calls them in Christ to continue to respect and obey the natural order preserved by the Noahic covenant, and sanctifies them for more faithful obedience to the natural law.

PART 1

CHAPTER 1

Natural Law under the Covenant of Creation

A biblical theology of natural law appropriately begins at the outset of the biblical story. Accordingly, this chapter undertakes a detailed exegetical consideration of several important matters in Genesis 1 and 2, in their own context and in the broader context of the canon of Scripture and Christian doctrine. I argue that these two chapters lay a foundation for a full-orbed theology of natural law, and this foundation is crucial background for the ideas developed in the rest of the book.

Of particular importance is the image of God, a concept relevant to biblical studies, Christian theology, and natural law. In biblical studies, the terse statements of Genesis 1:26-27 concerning human creation in the divine image and likeness have generated a large body of literature. In Christian theology, the image of God has served as the key organizing theme of theological anthropology, with reverberations in other areas of theology such as the doctrine of the Trinity, Christology, and soteriology. In regard to natural law, the idea that the image of God somehow defines human nature could hardly be more relevant. Yet, for the most part, the topic of the image of God has not facilitated fruitful interdisciplinary conversation among exegetes, theologians, and natural law theorists. Scholars have observed a frequent disconnect between doctrinal studies of the image of God and exegetical studies of Genesis 1:26-27,[1] and re-

---

1. E.g., see J. Richard Middleton, *The Liberating Image: The* Imago Dei *in Genesis 1* (Grand Rapids: Brazos, 2005), p. 17. For an earlier example, see Phyllis A. Bird, "'Male and Female He Created Them': Gen 1:27b in the Context of the Priestly Account of Creation, *HTR* 74, no. 2 (1981): 130-32. Bird notes that Karl Barth stated a desire to develop his doctrine of the image from the biblical text and that he was conversant with Old Testament literature, but that his doctrine, like those of many other theologians, ultimately manipulated the biblical text rather than explained it. Many writers have noted the effect of Barth's theological constructions

cent constructive theories of natural law do not engage the relevant exegetical literature.[2]

In contrast, I develop the initial aspects of a theology of natural law in this chapter through interaction with contemporary exegetical studies of Genesis 1:26-27 and attention to many historic doctrinal issues associated with the image of God. Though the presence of a covenant in Genesis 1–2 is a controversial issue, the traditional Reformed doctrine of the covenant of creation (or covenant of works) will serve as an integrating feature of my conclusions and will serve to connect these conclusions with the argument of subsequent chapters.

The argument of this chapter unfolds as follows. First I define what the image of God (and human nature) was in the original creation: the image consisted in being God's physical/visible representative on earth, entrusted with an official, royal-judicial commission to exercise dominion on earth in knowledge, righteousness, and holiness, toward the goal of eschatological enthronement in the age-to-come. The image, understood in these terms, is not a static ontological reality but a dynamic, historically/teleologically/eschatologically oriented office that entails being equipped for a task, performing the task, and attaining a goal.[3] This defined human nature as originally created. What human beings were made to be and what they were made to do cannot be separated, and hence human nature was inherently ethical. Second, I place this conception of the image in the context of the Reformed doctrine of the covenant of creation. I explain and defend the idea of a covenant at creation and argue that the creation of human beings in the divine image toward the goal of their eschatological enthronement was itself a covenantal act of God. Finally, drawing upon my conclusions about the image of God and the covenant of creation, I describe the character of natural law in the world as originally created. This natural law cannot be understood as static deontological

---

upon several decades of exegetical study of Genesis 1, but see especially Gunnlaugur A. Jónsson, *The Image of God: Genesis 1:26-28 in a Century of Old Testament Research* (Lund: Almqvist & Wiksell, 1988), pp. 61-131. Since Bird's article, some doctrinal studies of the image have drawn constructively from exegetical studies; e.g., Stanley J. Grenz, *The Social God and the Relational Self: A Trinitarian Theology of the* Imago Dei (Louisville: Westminster John Knox, 2001).

2. This is true at least of the significant studies by Robert George, Jean Porter, Russell Hittinger, Matthew Levering, J. Daryl Charles, Craig Boyd, and Alister McGrath mentioned in the Introduction.

3. If the image of God is understood in this way, I believe its central place in Christian anthropology is justified, despite the learned and fascinating case to the contrary by David H. Kelsey in *Eccentric Existence: A Theological Anthropology*, 2 vols. (Louisville: Westminster John Knox, 2009). For a brief engagement with Kelsey's work, both sympathetic and critical, in relation to my proposals on natural law and the image of God, see Appendix 3.

principles but as a moral order by which human beings were normatively directed toward a creatively fruitful life in exercising righteous royal dominion in this world toward the eschatological goal. The original natural law required the exercise of both love and justice. It required love in terms of abundant generosity toward fellow creatures and required justice in terms of giving to all their due and exercising retribution for wrongdoing. Such love and justice reflected the likeness of the God who revealed himself in creation both as abundantly generous toward the world and as the just enforcer of his law.

The Image of God at Creation

The biblical theology of natural law developed in this book depends upon a proper understanding of the image of God. Fundamental in what follows is the idea that the image of God bestowed in the first creation (what I will call the "protological image") is not identical to the image of God as preserved after the fall into sin (what I will call the "fallen image") and that neither of these is identical to the image of God bestowed upon believers in Christ as a gift of the new creation (what I will call the "eschatological image"). There is organic continuity, but not identity, among them. The image of God should be understood in the context of humanity's original orientation toward an eschatological destiny, its deflection from that destiny, and the attainment of that destiny in the work of Christ.[4] God made human beings to progress

---

4. My approach to the image differs somewhat from that of Francis Watson, *Text and Truth: Redefining Biblical Theology* (Grand Rapids: Eerdmans, 1997), chap. 7. I have great appreciation for his attempt to read all of Scripture in the light of Christ and thus, in light of Jesus' being the image of God, to see in Jesus what it means to be truly human. According to Watson, the Christ event reorients our reading of texts like Genesis 1:26-28 so that through Jesus we see the true nature of the rule entrusted to human beings, that is, the overcoming of death. As my argument in this and subsequent chapters should make clear, I claim that Jesus did indeed attain the original destiny of the human race, as defined in Genesis 1–2, which was rule not only over this world but also over the world to come (to borrow words from Heb. 2:5). But the attainment of this destiny through Christ's conquest of death was not exactly what the image originally meant. Death was a phenomenon that entered the human world after the fall into sin; thus the original meaning of being human was the attainment of rule, without any need to overcome death. Jesus became a human image-bearer because of the fall and now there is no way to know what it means to be truly human without him, but this was not so from the beginning. The protological image, therefore, was in an important sense not Christological, and Genesis 1:26-28 must be read as setting forth a somewhat different anthropology from (though organically related to) that found in the New Testament emerging from redemption in Christ.

historically from one state of existence to another, and thus human nature as expressed in the image of God must be conceived dynamically rather than statically (unlike what has often been the case in Christian theology).[5] Such an understanding of human nature promises to have significant implications for a theology of natural law, if indeed human beings know a moral law *by nature.*

In the first section of this chapter I develop a definition of the proto-logical image of God and thereby identify the character of human nature as originally created. In subsequent sections I connect my conclusions explicitly to matters of covenant and natural law.

The Royal Exercise of Dominion as God's Representative

During the last several decades a remarkable consensus has emerged among biblical scholars seeking the meaning of the image and likeness of God in Genesis 1:26-27. Gunnlaugur Jónsson already recognized this emerging consensus in 1988 in his exhaustive study of the history of interpretation of Genesis 1:26-28,[6] and with the exception of a few dissenters biblical exegetes have maintained this consensus to the present.[7] An increasing number of theologians,

---

5. Some contemporary biblical scholars and theologians have explored the idea of the image as historically dynamic and eschatologically oriented. Among biblical scholars, David J. A. Clines makes helpful observations in his influential article, "Humanity as the Image of God," in *On the Way to the Postmodern: Old Testament Essays, 1967-1998,* vol. 2 (Sheffield: Sheffield Academic Press, 1998) [originally published as "The Image of God in Man," *Tyndale Bulletin* 19 (1968): 53-103], pp. 496-97. Among theologians, this idea has also shaped the conclusions of Wolfhart Pannenberg, *Systematic Theology,* vol. 2, trans. Geoffrey W. Bromiley (Grand Rapids: Eerdmans, 1994), chap. 8; and Grenz, *The Social God,* especially chaps. 4-6.

6. Jónsson, *The Image of God,* pp. 219-23.

7. The relevant literature includes Clines, "Humanity as the Image of God," pp. 482-95; Bird, "'Male and Female He Created Them,'" pp. 139-44; Bruce R. Reichenbach, "Genesis 1 as a Theological-Political Narrative of Kingdom Establishment," *Bulletin for Biblical Research* 13, no. 1 (2003): 60-63; Middleton, *The Liberating Image,* chap. 2; W. Randall Garr, *In His Own Image and Likeness: Humanity, Divinity, and Monotheism* (Leiden: Brill, 2003), chap. 7; Jon D. Levenson, *Creation and the Persistence of Evil: The Jewish Drama of Divine Omnipotence* (San Francisco: Harper & Row, 1988), pp. 112-17; W. J. Dumbrell, *Covenant & Creation: A Theology of the Old Testament Covenants* (Carlisle: Paternoster, 1984), pp. 33-34; Meredith G. Kline, *Images of the Spirit* (Grand Rapids: Baker, 1980), chap. 1; Gordon J. Wenham, *Word Biblical Commentary,* vol. 1, *Genesis 1–15* (Waco, TX: Word, 1987), pp. 31-32; Victor P. Hamilton, *The Book of Genesis Chapters 1–17* (Grand Rapids: Eerdmans, 1990), pp. 135, 138; Nahum M. Sarna, *Genesis* (Philadelphia: Jewish Publication Society, 1989), p. 12; Charles H. H. Scobie, *The Ways of Our God: An Approach to Biblical Theology* (Grand Rapids: Eerdmans, 2003), pp. 158-59;

attentive to developments in the exegetical literature, have begun incorporating its insights into their broader dogmatic treatment of anthropology.[8] The core idea of the consensus is that the image and likeness refer to the exercise of royal dominion as God's representative on earth. Advocates of this idea frequently relate the biblical statements to Egyptian and/or Mesopotamian views circulating in the ancient Near East and often speak of the image as holistic (as opposed to residing in some particular ontological feature of the human person).[9]

As Jónsson and others have noted, this consensus emerged in the wake of James Barr's seminal work, which called for a more modest use of word studies and emphasized the importance of context for determining the meaning of biblical words and sentences.[10] Trying to determine the meaning of צלם ("image") and דמות ("likeness") in Genesis 1:26-27 solely by use of word studies is fraught with difficulties. Perhaps most importantly, both terms refer to a variety of things in the Old Testament (OT) and thus neither can be given a single, airtight definition that determines its use in Genesis 1. Furthermore, word studies cannot determine whether the terms "image" and "likeness" are meant to convey two distinct aspects of the human person or are overlapping and even interchangeable terms describing the same reality in slightly different ways. Additional philological complications surround the translation and significance of the two prepositions, ב and כ, which precede "image" and "likeness" respectively. They too bear different shades of meaning in the OT. If these prepositions bear their usual meaning in 1:26, yielding a translation such as "in the image and according to the likeness," then understanding image

---

and Stephen G. Dempster, *Dominion and Dynasty: A Theology of the Hebrew Bible* (Downers Grove, IL: InterVarsity, 2003), pp. 57-62.

8. Among other examples, see Pannenberg, *Systematic Theology*, 2:203-4; Grenz, *The Social God*, pp. 197-200; Michael S. Horton, *Lord and Servant: A Covenant Christology* (Louisville: Westminster John Knox, 2005), pp. 105-8; J. Wentzel van Huyssteen, *Alone in the World? Human Uniqueness in Science and Theology* (Grand Rapids: Eerdmans, 2006), chap. 3; and J. V. Fesko, *Last Things First: Unlocking Genesis 1-3 with the Christ of Eschatology* (Fearn: Mentor, 2007), pp. 47-48.

9. Among a long list of recent scholars who have highlighted the holistic character of the image are Hamilton, *Genesis Chapters 1-17*, p. 137; Andreas Schüle, "Made in the 'Image of God': The Concepts of Divine Images in Genesis 1-3," *Zeitschrift für die Alttestamentliche Wissenschaft* 117, no. 1 (2005): 7, 11; Clines, "Humanity as the Image of God," pp. 480-82; and Fesko, *Last Things First*, pp. 47-48. More than a century ago this was emphasized in Herman Bavinck, *Reformed Dogmatics*, vol. 2, *God and Creation*, trans. John Vriend, ed. John Bolt (Grand Rapids: Baker Academic, 2004), pp. 533, 554-55.

10. James Barr, *The Semantics of Biblical Language* (Oxford: Clarendon, 1961).

and likeness as distinct concepts becomes more probable. But Genesis 5:3 tantalizingly reverses the prepositions ("in his likeness, according to his image"), suggesting the interchangeability of image and likeness. Thus some exegetes have argued that ב in Genesis 1:26 and 5:3 does not bear its usual meaning but should be translated as "according to" or "as" (the so-called *beth essentiae*), which makes its meaning similar or virtually equivalent to כ in these verses.[11]

At best, a word-study approach suggests a number of possible readings of "image" and "likeness" in Genesis 1:26-27 but provides nothing definitive. This indeterminacy creates the temptation to choose a reading that fits a certain predetermined theological conception of human nature, thus making the text proof for what one already believes for extra-textual reasons. A number of significant theological issues are implicated by the interpretive difficulties presented by Genesis 1:26-27. For example, much classic Christian theology has associated the image with the soul rather than the body, but word studies of "image" show that the term very often refers to something visible and physical.[12] Another example is that classic Christian theology has often understood the image to refer to certain ontological human attributes that resemble divine attributes, but while word studies of "likeness" indicate that the term connotes similarity, they do not specify the nature of that similarity in Genesis 1.[13] Furthermore, the Eastern Orthodox and Roman Catholic traditions have historically made a clear distinction between the image and the likeness, while Protestant theology has tended to equate them, adding a potentially complex theological layer to attempts to define the terms.[14] Finally, the suggestion by

11. That ב could be translated in these alternative ways is demonstrated by Exodus 6:3 (where it clearly means "as") and Exodus 25:40 (where it clearly means "according to"). Among writers who defend the virtual equivalence of the two prepositions in Genesis 1:26 are Clines, "Humanity as the Image of God," pp. 470-75; Sarna, *Genesis*, p. 12; Wenham, *Genesis*, pp. 28-29; Henri Blocher, *In the Beginning: The Opening Chapters of Genesis* (Downers Grove, IL: InterVarsity, 1984), p. 85; and Bavinck, *Reformed Dogmatics*, 2:432. Garr mounts a rigorous counterargument in favor of the distinction between the two prepositions in *In His Own Image and Likeness*, chap. 6.

12. For a recent example of a largely word-study approach that emphasizes the visible character of "image," and proceeds to argue for an appropriately modified theological understanding of the image of God, see R. Larry Overstreet, "Man in the Image of God: A Reappraisal," *Criswell Theological Review* 3 (Fall 2005): 43-70.

13. However, a study of this term in Ezekiel, for example, indicates its potential richness in Genesis 1:26; see the brief but suggestive comments in Garr, *In His Own Image and Likeness*, pp. 123-24.

14. From an Eastern Orthodox perspective, see Vladimir Lossky, *Orthodox Theology* (Crestwood, NY: St. Vladimir's Seminary Press, 2001), pp. 71-73; for an example of the dis-

Wolfhart Pannenberg that human creation "*in* the image and *according* to the likeness" means that an image and likeness of God already existed prior to the appearance of human beings (namely, the Son of God) means that a possible weighty organic connection between God's Trinitarian nature and human image-bearing is directly affected by the translation of the little prepositions ב and כ.[15]

In my judgment, the contemporary shift toward interpreting the creation of human beings in the "image" and "likeness" of God *in the context of Genesis 1:1–2:3* has offered a salutary way forward. If for no other reason, this shift respects Barr's compelling claim that individual words have meaning only as they function within sentences as parts of larger texts. If the words צלם and דמות generally indicate visible representation and resemblance, as so many biblical scholars believe, then the context of the original creation story provides great insights into the character of this representation and resemblance.

The contemporary exegetical consensus also provides notable confirmation of important insights in Reformed thinking about the image. While much of the broader Christian tradition has located the image in certain ontological features of the human person (such as rationality or volitionality) and in the soul over against the body, Reformed theologians have tended to take a more holistic view of the image (involving both body and soul) and sometimes have highlighted the exercise of dominion.[16] Holistic

---

tinction in the medieval West, see Thomas Aquinas, *Summa Theologiae*, 1a 93.9; compare a representative Reformed treatment in Bavinck, *Reformed Dogmatics*, 2:532-33.

15. See Pannenberg, *Systematic Theology*, 2:216.

16. John Calvin writes: "Though the primary seat of the divine image was in the mind and the heart, or in the soul and its powers, there was no part even of the body in which some rays of glory did not shine"; see *Institutes of the Christian Religion,* trans. Henry Beveridge (Grand Rapids: Eerdmans, 1953), 1.15.3; cf. John Calvin, *Commentaries on the First Book of Moses Called Genesis*, vol. 1, trans. John King (Grand Rapids: Eerdmans, 1963), pp. 94-95. According to Wolfgang Musculus: "Therefore it remains that we were created as the image and likeness either of his *quality* or of his *power* to rule all things. And here the views of Christians are divided. Some understand it of the rational soul, in which there is memory, intellect and volition, so that humans were created as God's image according to [the soul]; and thus they situate the image of God in the inner person as understanding, wisdom, thoughtfulness and upright living. . . . Others expound [it] of the power and dignity to rule all things, according to which man was created according to the image of God and constituted lord over the earth and all the things that are in it. . . . I prefer to follow this view rather than the one which breathes philosophical subtlety and is, moreover, of such a kind that with equal reason the angels, too, could be seen as created according to God's image. Indeed, if it is fitting to consider reason, wisdom, volition, intellect, and other things of this kind in this matter and to lodge the image of God in those things, nothing prevents angels, who are in any case much more righteous than we,

views of the image also appear elsewhere at times among non-Reformed theologians.[17]

In what follows I offer a series of brief arguments that the image and likeness of God, in the context of Genesis 1:26-27, refers to human beings as commissioned with the royal exercise of dominion as God's representatives in this world. These arguments therefore constitute a defense of the general consensus among contemporary biblical scholars about the image in Genesis 1. After presenting these arguments I address another important aspect of the protological image which, though not unrecognized, is underappreciated in the contemporary literature: the eschatological destiny inherent in the image. Upon completing these arguments I will be prepared to offer a general definition of human nature as originally created.

The Dominion Mandate

The obvious and central consideration that commends interpreting the image as representative kingship is the creation mandate, in which God sets before the newly created human beings the command to be fruitful and multiply

---

from also being named as created according to God's image. For they draw considerably nearer to God's wisdom and understanding than we do. Yet Scripture does not attribute to them as it does to us, that they were made according to God's image and likeness. Why? Namely, because they were not constituted lords of earth and beasts, a dignity God expressly conferred on humankind." See *Genesis 1-11*, Reformation Commentary on Scripture, Old Testament I, ed. John L. Thompson (Downers Grove, IL: IVP Academic, 2012), p. 47. Herman Witsius distinguishes between the image "antecedently" (the soul's spiritual and immortal nature and capacities), "formally" (righteousness and holiness), and "consequentially" (immortality and dominion). See *The Economy of the Covenants between God and Man*, 2 vols., trans. William Crookshank (1822; reprinted, Phillipsburg, NJ: Presbyterian and Reformed, 1990), 1:57. The Westminster Shorter Catechism (answer 10) states: "God created man male and female, after his own image, in knowledge, righteousness, and holiness, with dominion over the creatures." Perhaps most helpfully, see Bavinck, *Reformed Dogmatics*, 2:554-62.

17. Among patristic writers, Gregory of Nyssa writes: "The language of Scripture . . . expresses it concisely by a comprehensive phrase, in saying that man was made 'in the image of God,' for this is the same as to say that he made human nature participant in all good; for if the deity is the fullness of good, and this is his image, then the image finds its resemblance to the archetype in being filled with all good." See *Genesis 1-11*, Ancient Christian Commentary on Scripture, Old Testament I, ed. Andrew Louth (Downers Grove, IL: InterVarsity, 2001), p. 34. The Lutheran theologian Johannes Brenz states: "In the beginning, not just one part but the whole person was created to be an image of facsimile similar to God"; see *Genesis 1-11*, Reformation Commentary, p. 46.

and to exercise dominion over the other creatures. Genesis 1:26 states God's intention in this matter and then 1:28 records the divine command itself: "Then God said, 'Let us make man[18] in our image, after our likeness. And let them have dominion over the fish of the sea and over the birds of the heavens and over the livestock and over all the earth and over every creeping thing that creeps on the earth.' . . . And God blessed them. And God said to them, 'Be fruitful and multiply and fill the earth and subdue it and have dominion over the fish of the sea and over the birds of the heavens and over every living thing that moves on the earth.'" The placement of this mandate in immediate conjunction with the account of human creation in the image and likeness of God raises questions about what this dominion was meant to be and what relationship this dominion bears to the image itself.

Though the details of what this dominion entailed only become clear through consideration of the nature of God's own exercise of dominion in Genesis 1, as explored below, an initial and very important point is drawn from the language of 1:26-28 itself. This exercise of dominion involves an exertion of *power* that is particularly associated with *royal* activity. It is not a general call to manage the affairs of this world but a specific commission for powerful, kingly rule.

A number of scholars have commented on the connotations of mastery and subjugation in the relevant Hebrew words used in 1:26 and 28, רדה ("have dominion" or "rule") and כבש ("subdue"). In response to accusations that the Judeo-Christian doctrine of creation presented in Genesis 1 is a root cause of contemporary environmental crises, many theologians and exegetes have helpfully emphasized the themes of stewardship, justice, and generosity latent in the text. Such counterarguments are warranted and salutary, and as Richard Bauckham puts it, "Their 'dominion' is within the created order, not, like God's, transcendent above it."[19] Yet forgetting that God really put human beings in charge of this world would miss a key aspect of the biblical story. Ruling and subduing are not terms to describe middle-management. כבש is a strong term in the OT.[20] רדה can convey rulership imposed upon conquered enemies, such as the rule of Israel's enemies over the covenant people as a consequence of their disobedience (Lev. 26:17) or that of the messianic son over his enemies

---

18. The English translation of Scripture I use in this book reads "man" in Genesis 1:26, but it refers to both male and female, as Genesis 1:27 itself makes clear.

19. Richard Bauckham, *Living with Other Creatures: Green Exegesis and Theology* (Waco, TX: Baylor University Press, 2011), p. 14.

20. Garr, *In His Own Image and Likeness*, p. 171, describes it as a "harsh" term, though it is not only used in that way in the OT.

(Ps. 110:2). Though the word is not used in the OT exclusively of kings, it frequently conveys a sense of royal function or prerogative, whether of a righteous Israelite king (e.g., 1 Kgs. 5:4 [4:24 in English]; Ps. 72:8-9) or a foreign monarch (e.g., Isa. 14:6). The one wielding such rule invariably holds a position of superior power.[21] It is interesting that God sometimes warns his people against the exercise of such "rule" in a ruthless manner (e.g., Lev. 25:43, 46, 53; Ezek. 34:4), which suggests that רדה is not inherently a negative term but that the power it constitutes is readily abused. The context of Genesis 1 provides plenty of reason to conceive of human dominion as intended to be just and benevolent, but this initial mandate that God gives to human beings clearly commissions them to rule creation with a sense of superior royal authority.

What then is the relationship of this dominion mandate to human identity as the image of God? However one understands the grammatical connection between "Let us make man" and "let them have dominion" in 1:26, positing a total lack of relationship between bearing the image and exercising dominion is highly implausible. A more difficult question is whether the exercise of dominion is merely the *consequence* of the image, as suggested by some modern and ancient interpreters,[22] or actually constitutes the image. A few considerations shed light on this issue.

Initially, the grammar of 1:26 likely, though not definitively, indicates that "let them have dominion" is the beginning of a purpose clause. If this is the case, the proper translation might be: "Let us make man in our image, after our likeness *so that he might have dominion* over the fish of the sea. . . ." This reading depends upon taking וירדו ("let them have dominion") as an indirect volative indicating purpose, which is grammatically possible.[23] Another grammatical possibility is taking the initial ו in וירדו as a conjunctive *waw* that joins two clauses "not otherwise logically related,"[24] yielding a translation such as "Let us make man . . . and let him have dominion. . . ." Context, therefore, must

21. E.g., see Bird, " 'Male and Female He Created Them,' " pp. 154-55; and Garr, *In His Own Image and Likeness*, p. 156.

22. Among modern interpreters who take this position, in various forms, are Gerhard von Rad, *Genesis: A Commentary*, rev. ed. (Philadelphia: Westminster, 1972), p. 59; Wenham, *Genesis 1–15*, pp. 31-32; Blocher, *In the Beginning*, p. 90; Watson, *Text and Truth*, p. 293; and Grenz, *The Social God*, p. 197. Grenz describes this view as the "near consensus in recent years." This coheres with a position held by many seventeenth-century Reformed scholastic theologians; e.g., see Witsius, *Economy of the Covenants*, 1:57, as explained above.

23. Paul Joüon, S.J., e.g., cites Genesis 1:26 as an example of this grammatical construction: see *A Grammar of Biblical Hebrew*, trans. and rev. T. Muraoka (Rome: Editrice Pontificio Instituto Biblico, 1991), 2:381.

24. This is the understanding of Genesis 1:26 adopted in Bruce K. Waltke and M. O'Con-

determine which construction to prefer. Two contextual considerations make the purpose clause in 1:26 the compelling choice and indicate that exercising dominion is *at least* the direct consequence of image-bearing and, more likely, constitutive of the image itself.

First, the fact that human beings are created in the image and likeness of *God* militates against disconnecting the image and dominion. Genesis 1 presents God, whose image and likeness humanity bears, as none other than a king who exercises supreme dominion over all creation. I examine below some details of the text in order to identify characteristics of divine (and thus also human) dominion, but for now it suffices to note that the God of Genesis 1 is a God who acts. The only things the text says about God are what he does. Since it is *this* God whom the first human beings were made to image, the image cannot be defined independently of human action. The image and likeness of a God who acts must be human beings who act. The move from naming humans as the image and likeness to specifying human action in 1:26 is entirely expected in the light of Genesis 1:1-25. In context, bearing the image and exercising dominion must be organically connected. As Genesis 1 presents the being and action of God the Creator as inseparable, so also it presents the being and action of his image-bearer.[25]

Second, the inseparability of being and action in several nonhuman creatures in Genesis 1 confirms this conclusion. These examples unveil a general divine purpose to make creatures designed for performance. Genesis 1 has no interest in a thing's ontology apart from its function, but presents its function as inherent to what it is. A first example is 1:6-7. In 1:6 God says: "Let there be an expanse in the midst of the waters, and let it separate the waters from the waters." The general pattern of this verse — God's word creating something followed immediately by a statement of what its function is — is exactly the same as 1:26, and the use of ויהי ("and let it be" [separating the waters from the waters]) anticipates the language of וירדו ("let them have dominion") in 1:26. Is there, narrowly, a purpose clause in 1:6 and is there, more broadly, an inherent identity between what the expanse is and what it does? An affirmative answer to both questions is compelling. The expanse, which God calls "heaven"

---

nor, *An Introduction to Biblical Hebrew Syntax* (Winona Lake, IN: Eisenbrauns, 1990), pp. 653-54.

25. I wish to acknowledge a potentially difficult ethical question that arises when the image of God is connected with the exercise of dominion, namely, whether human beings who are incapable of such action (such as embryos or the comatose) are therefore not image-bearers. I believe there are good reasons to think they are, though I will not burden this already long chapter by engaging the argument.

in 1:8, by its very nature stands in between the waters above and the waters below. The expanse performs its work of separation simply by being what it is. Genesis 1:7 describes two actions of God — making the expanse and separating the waters — but they are manifestly two sides of a single action. For God to make the expanse was to separate the waters; for the expanse to exist was to maintain and regulate the separation. A similar dynamic animates creation of the lights in 1:14-18. These verses also exhibit a general pattern and grammatical features similar to 1:26. God speaks a word of creation and ordains the function of what he has created — in this case, multiple functions: separating the day from the night (and the light from darkness), serving as signs, seasons, days, and years, giving light upon the earth, and ruling day and night. Again it is impossible to understand the nature of the luminaries apart from their function. Simply *being* the sun in the place where God put it is *to perform* the tasks that God ordained for it. As David J. A. Clines remarks, "The act of creation of the sun and moon includes within itself the purpose that they are to serve. Their giving of light is not the same thing as their being set in the firmament, yet their being set there cannot be fully defined without reference to their function as luminaries."[26]

The conclusion for interpreting 1:26 that Clines (among others) draws from this evidence is that "dominion is so immediate and necessary a consequence of the image, it loses the character of a mere derivative of the image and virtually becomes a constitutive part of the image itself."[27] In agreement with this verdict, I conclude that 1:26 should indeed be read as containing a purpose clause and that the exercise of dominion is not simply a happy consequence of image-bearing but an inherent aspect of image-bearing. As with the expanse of the heavens, the lights in the expanse, and even God himself, so it is with human beings as the image and likeness of God: what a thing is cannot be defined apart from what it does.

God's Royal Dominion in Genesis 1

Having taken this initial but important step in describing the image and likeness of God presented in Genesis 1:26-27, we face another question: What

---

26. Clines, "Humanity as the Image of God," p. 491.

27. Clines, "Humanity as the Image of God," pp. 490-92. For similar conclusions drawn from this evidence, see also Bird, " 'Male and Female He Created Them,' " p. 138; and Middleton, *The Liberating Image*, pp. 53-54.

exactly is the nature of this dominion that defines the image? As observed above, the terms used in 1:26 and 28 indicate that human beings possess an office of authority over the other creatures, but what is to be done with this high position? To answer these questions I return to an issue raised briefly above: God's own exercise of dominion in Genesis 1. If exercising dominion is a constitutive aspect of being like God, then exploring how God himself exercises dominion promises to be fruitful for understanding the image. Several aspects of the divine dominion in Genesis 1 stand out: his efficacious speaking and naming, his righteous decrees and judgments, and his beautiful and bountiful ordering of all things.

God's Royal Dominion through Speaking and Naming

One of the striking things about Genesis 1 is that the Creator is a *speaking* God. Unlike the mute gods of the nations, whom the OT prophets mocked (e.g., Ps. 115:5; Isa. 44:6-23), the God of Genesis 1 keeps speaking — and what he says always comes to pass. Nothing demonstrates God's sovereign control of creation as clearly as this. As Graeme Auld observes, 40 percent of the verbs indicating divine action in Genesis 1 are verbs of speech, and the other things that God does, such as making, separating, granting, and sanctifying, were accomplished by his word.[28] Elsewhere the OT reflects upon the efficacious divine speech of creation: "By the word of the Lord the heavens were made, and by the breath of his mouth all their host" (Ps. 33:6). The very form of the language God uses throughout Genesis 1 — "Let the . . ." — suggests that God's powerful speech is more than simply a raw display of sovereign control but is specifically the work of a king. The language communicates an authority inherent in the speaker. Many earthly monarchs, both Israelite and pagan, use such language to issue their own decrees (e.g., 2 Kgs. 12:4-5; Ezra 1:2-4).[29] One of God's speaking acts in Genesis 1 is *naming* the things that he has made (1:5, 8, 10). Giving something a name constituted an act of authority in the ancient Near East and in the OT Scriptures. When pagan kings conquered Israel they demonstrated their superior position by changing the names of the Israelite rulers (see 2 Kgs.

---

28. Graeme Auld, "*Imago Dei* in Genesis: Speaking in the Image of God," *Expository Times* 116 (May 2005): 261.

29. See also Middleton, *The Liberating Image,* pp. 65-66. For discussion of the priestly aspect of God's speaking in Genesis 1, see Mark S. Smith, *The Priestly Vision of Genesis 1* (Minneapolis: Fortress, 2010), p. 67.

23:34; 24:17; Dan. 1:7). By naming the day and night, heaven, land, and sea in the first three days, God asserts his royal authority over time itself and over the three great regions of creation.[30]

In larger biblical context, this royal divine speech is evidence of God's *wisdom*. This is the first of several wisdom-related themes to note in this chapter, themes that anticipate the fuller discussion in Chapter 8. One of the striking things in the opening section of Proverbs is how God created the world by wisdom (3:19-20; 8:22-31) — by which wisdom human kings also reign (8:15-16). Through the entirety of the book, Proverbs praises the skill and effectiveness of a wise tongue. All the words of wisdom are true and righteous (see 8:7-8). Wise people speak adeptly and bring about flourishing for themselves and those around them. As William Brown puts it, "the sapiential word is a world-producing word."[31]

The idea that Genesis 1 presents God as a king is strengthened, and also further defined, by the covenantal character of this text. If indeed Genesis 1 presents God as entering into a covenant with creation (a claim I argue below), then it thereby highlights his royal identity, for in the OT God enters covenants as a great king. In his covenant with Abraham, Isaac, and Jacob, for example, God exercises his royal prerogative by changing the names of his human counterparts (Gen. 17:5; 32:28). In his covenant with Israel, enacted at Mount Sinai, God manifests himself as a king in numerous ways (see e.g. Exod. 19:5-6). The widely recognized parallels between various OT covenants and the forms of various ancient Near Eastern treaties add further evidence. Insofar as Genesis 1 evokes the aura of covenant, it presents God as the supreme and transcendent suzerain king entering into covenant with his vassal world. Kings are covenant-makers. These considerations bring God's royal authority in Genesis 1 into sharper focus. God may be a sovereign monarch, but he will not be an indifferent or arbitrary one. As a king in relationship with his world he has an interest in its affairs and takes on commitments for his future conduct toward it.[32]

What sorts of things does Genesis 1 reveal about this royal God who

---

30. See Reichenbach, "Genesis 1 as a Theological-Political Narrative," p. 59.

31. William P. Brown, *The Ethos of the Cosmos: The Genesis of Moral Imagination in the Bible* (Grand Rapids: Eerdmans, 1999), p. 303.

32. The relationship of the biblical covenants to ancient Near Eastern treaties is a complicated issue that has generated a great deal of literature. Further discussion of this issue and citation of some of the relevant literature appear later in the chapter. Among recent writers that specifically connect the ancient Near Eastern treaties with the identity of God as a king in Genesis 1, see Reichenbach, "Genesis 1 as a Theological-Political Narrative," p. 49; and Mid-

enters into covenant with creation, and thus what does it indicate about the terms for their future relationship? On the one hand, it reveals God as a just king who decrees equitable judgments and, on the other hand, it reveals God as a fruitful, loving, and generous king who instills beauty and bounty in his world. Both of these aspects — and not one to the exclusion of the other — are crucial for understanding the character of God the Creator and, I believe, crucial for understanding the image of God and natural law in the original creation.

The Justice of God's Dominion

First, Genesis 1 reveals God as a just king who decrees equitable judgments. Though many contemporary Western readers think instinctively of kings, legislators, and judges as holding different offices with clearly defined spheres of authority (executive, legislative, and judicial respectively), the opening chapter of Scripture teaches no doctrine of the separation of powers. To say that Genesis 1 presents God as king is to ascribe legislative, judicial, and executive power to him simultaneously. God exercises his legislative authority in following up many creative fiats with instructions for his creatures' conduct. For example, after creating the expanse in the midst of the waters he says "let it separate the waters from the waters" (1:6) and after creating the dry land he says "let the earth sprout vegetation, plants yielding seed, and fruit trees bearing fruit in which is their seed" (1:11). Most notably and climactically, God immediately follows his decree to create human beings in his image with the decree that they should exercise dominion (1:26; cf. 1:28). More legislative action follows in the next chapter, both the implicit command to work and to guard the Garden of Eden (2:15) and the explicit prohibition of eating from the tree of the knowledge of good and evil (2:16-17).

God's judicial authority is also on display. Six times Genesis 1 describes God looking at what he has made and issuing a verdict upon it, and hence upon the quality of his own work: "And God saw that it was good" (1:4, 10, 12, 18, 21, 25). At the conclusion of the six days God takes in the entire panorama of creation and proclaims his assessment of the whole: "And God saw everything that he had made, and behold, it was very good" (1:31). The next verses declare God's work of creation "finished" and describe him entering his rest

---

dleton, *The Liberating Image*, pp. 66-70. On the connection between naming in Genesis 1 and the ancient Near Eastern treaties, also see Horton, *Lord and Servant*, p. 110.

(2:1-3). God submits himself to his own judgment and attains vindication (2:1-3).[33] With the close of Genesis 1 God has completed his creative labors and left each creature with its appropriate task.

With God already manifest as a legislator and judge the text invites us to wonder how well the man and woman will perform their responsibilities and what verdict God will render upon them. Adam first succeeds in naming the animals, but then they disobey the command not to eat from the tree of the knowledge of good and evil (3:6), and they provoke a threefold judgment of God — against the serpent, the woman, and the man (3:14-19). That God comes to Eden in judgment can hardly be doubted given 3:14-19, but the full effect of his judicial power may be obscured by the common English translation that he arrives on the scene to walk in the Garden "in the cool of the day" (3:8). Pleasant as this sounds, the description of God's entrance is probably meant to elicit fear rather than delight. The "sound of the Lord" (קול יהוה) is likely not the patter of footsteps but the very "voice of the Lord" (קול יהוה) that thunders and terrifies creation seven times in Psalm 29. God's "walking" (מתהלך) in the Garden is likely not an evening stroll but the "walking and storming" (הולך וסער) of the sea before Jonah was thrown overboard (Jonah 1:11) or the "walking" (מתהלכת) of the torches among the living creatures in Ezekiel's terrifying vision of the wheels (Ezek. 1:13). "The cool of the day" is likely not the chill that arrives at sunset but, quite literally, the "spirit of the day" (לרוח היום), which might be glossed as "the [S]pirit of the [D]ay [of Judgment]," an anticipation of what later biblical writers would call "the Day of the Lord." The man and woman hide, then, likely not to keep a secret from God while he gets his exercise but with the same motivation as the sinners who, at the opening of the sixth seal, "hid themselves in the caves and among the rocks of the mountains, calling to the mountains and rocks, 'Fall on us and hide us from the face of him who is seated on the throne, and from the wrath of the Lamb, for the great day of their wrath has come, and who can stand?'" (Rev. 6:15-17).[34] Propitious as were the seven favorable verdicts of Genesis 1, the verdict of condemnation in Genesis 3 is devastating. And God's executive authority follows swiftly on the heels of his judicial decision (3:23-24).

What is the character of the Creator's justice displayed at the outset of

33. For discussion of God's "judicial pronouncement" upon his own work, culminating in his enthronement on the seventh day, see Kline, *Images of the Spirit,* pp. 109-12.

34. For an argument in support of a similar interpretation of Genesis 3:8, see Jeffrey Niehaus, "In the Wind of the Storm: Another Look at Genesis 3:8," *VT* 44, no. 2 (1994): 263-67. See also Kline, *Images of the Spirit,* chap. 4. For a contrary view, see Christopher L. K. Grundke, "A Tempest in a Teapot? Genesis III 8 Again," *VT* 51, no. 4 (2001): 548-51.

Genesis? The idea of justice is often considered under a twofold heading; I use Nicholas Wolterstorff's terms, *primary* and *rectifying* justice.[35] Primary justice (e.g., commutative and distributive) refers to the positive obligations and corresponding rights that people have with respect to one another. Rectifying justice (e.g., retributive and restorative) refers to the equitable response to wrongdoing that inflicts a proportionate harm upon offenders and seeks to put victims back into their original position.

When I refer to God's justice in the original creation I am not thinking chiefly of primary justice, though there are some important things to say about this. It is difficult to conceive of what obligations God had to creatures — or what rights they could claim from him — prior to their creation. Of course, the general biblical description of God indicates that he created in accord with his goodness and other attributes, and thus he would not have made evil things or an evil social order. Yet there were a myriad of good things that God could have created, and nothing could conceivably claim a right to be created at all or to be created as some particular good thing. In creating as he did, however, God took upon himself certain obligations toward his creatures. God could not, consistent with his own character, treat human beings in the same way he treats rocks. The requirements he imposed upon various creatures were just because they corresponded to their respective natures. God could not justly have required human beings to create *ex nihilo,* given the way he made them; nor could he justly have required them to be fruitful and multiply had he not made them with reproductive capacities. Furthermore, given the nature and moral requirements God gave them, God was presumably obligated to provide means for their sustenance. Human beings could not have existed or acted as divine image-bearers if there was no food supply. In light of these considerations, I believe we can refer to God as just in his original creation in terms of primary justice. Yet in thinking about God's positive bestowal of good things upon his creation it seems more helpful to me to consider them under the theme of God's love — a fruitful, abundant, and generous love that overflowed bountifully to his creation. God was certainly just in creating, obligating, and providing for his creatures as he did, but his lavish goodness far surpasses anything we might say was his creatures' due. I return to this subject below.

When I refer to God's justice with respect to the original creation I affirm chiefly that God is just in his judgments. On the positive side, he rendered favorable verdicts upon his own work, and would have rendered a favorable

---

35. Nicholas Wolterstorff, *Justice: Rights and Wrongs* (Princeton: Princeton University Press, 2008). Wolterstorff focuses upon primary justice in this book.

verdict upon human beings had they successfully completed theirs. On the negative side, God issued a just threat of punishment for disobedience. Here is where rectifying justice — specifically, retributive justice — comes technically into view.[36] God's retributive justice, as portrayed in Genesis 1-2, is proportionate and strict. His own work was *perfect* and thus received a *seven*fold declaration of goodness. Conversely, if the man and the woman would commit but one sin they would be condemned to death. God sets no middle ground and no gray area before them. As it turns out, in Genesis 3 and beyond, God is not yet done with the human race, but their subsequent relationship will be on different terms and he will give them no second chance to fulfill their mission in its original form.[37] In God's protological relationship with humanity, as described in Genesis 1-2, his retributive justice is strict and he promises no mercy or forgiveness. The threatened punishment is also proportionate: those who rejected *life* were condemned to *death*.[38]

This primordial revelation of God's justice seems to anticipate the principle underlying the *lex talionis,* the law of retaliation. Both Scripture and many ancient legal codes articulated the *lex talionis* in simple formulas, such as "eye for an eye and tooth for a tooth." Behind such simple formulas lurks

36. There seems to be no divine restorative justice in view in the early chapters of Genesis. God is the ultimate "victim" of human sin, and human beings themselves cannot repair the damage they caused. As the representative of the whole human race (see Rom. 5:12-19; 1 Cor. 15:21-22, 47-49; and my discussion in Chapter 9), other human beings are not so much the victim of Adam's first sin as vicarious participants in it who share his guilt. The rest of the created order, in its nonrational way, does indeed seem to be a victim of the human fall, as exemplified in God's curse of the ground because of Adam (Gen. 3:17-18). I am open to the idea that — not in the abstract but in light of who God is and the way in which he freely made the world in the first place — God had some intrinsic obligation to bring the world to its original destiny of being consummated in a new creation ruled by human beings (see Heb. 2:5-9). In this sense some notion of restorative justice may come into play with respect to the original creation, but it would be wrapped up in a display of grace, redemption, and forgiveness that far transcends considerations of justice.

37. For discussion of relevant themes in the early chapters of Genesis, with some different conclusions from my own, see J. Krašovec, "Punishment and Mercy in the Primeval History (Gen 1-11)," *Ephemerides Theologicae Lovanienses* 70 (April 1994): 5-33.

38. Though he does not develop the idea at length, I believe J. Budziszewski is correct to say: "without a direct revelation from the Author of the law, it is impossible to know whether the possibility of forgiveness is real. . . . Apart from an assurance that the debt can be forgiven — an assurance which transcends what human reason can find out on its own — no human being dares to face the law straight on." See *The Line Through the Heart: Natural Law as Fact, Theory, and Sign of Contradiction* (Wilmington, DE: ISI, 2009), p. 35. In the covenant of creation there was indeed no divine revelation promising forgiveness, as discussed further below.

a basic judicial principle that remains an ideal for any just legal system, even when the *lex talionis* is rarely or never applied literally. This basic principle is proportionality. Punishment should not be too lax or too harsh, but should match the wrong.[39] (Though not immediately obvious, the *lex talionis* idea, I believe, can account for just concerns about restoring the victim as well as punishing the offender; Chapter 10 will explain why.) I suggest that this principle of proportionality underlies the presentation of divine justice toward humanity in Genesis 1–3. The penalty of death may initially seem too harsh for the sin of eating a piece of fruit. But if God's command regarding the tree of the knowledge of good and evil was ultimately a call to render holistic obedience to his Creator (see below for more on this point), then the penalty of death appears in a new light. God demanded complete devotion from Adam — his whole self — and thus exacting Adam's whole self from him in death maintains the talionic principle of proportionality. Furthermore, Scripture elsewhere describes the final judgment of the wicked in terms of the *lex talionis*.[40] Therefore, if my subsequent argument is correct that the judgment threatened in Genesis 2 ultimately refers to the final judgment, which God did not fully bring in Genesis 3 but postponed until Christ's second coming, this is further evidence that God's protological justice portrayed in Genesis 1–2 is talionic. In subsequent chapters I explore how the *lex talionis* theme is developed in Scripture and serves an important role in a biblical theology of natural law.

The presentation of God in these royal-judicial terms is strengthened and magnified if the mysterious "let *us* make man in *our* image, after *our* likeness" (1:26) is interpreted as a reference to God's speech in the midst of the angelic council, his royal court. According to this view, Genesis 1:26 anthropomorphically reveals God as a king seated in splendor on his royal throne, attended by a majestic host, and issuing judicial decrees. Scholars have suggested a number of interpretations of this first person plural. Some take it as a

---

39. These ideas are thoroughly discussed in William Ian Miller, *Eye for an Eye* (Cambridge: Cambridge University Press, 2006).

40. E.g., see 2 Pet. 2:13 ("suffering wrong as the wage for their wrongdoing [ἀδικούμενοι μισθὸν ἀδικίας]"); Rev. 11:18 ("Your wrath came, and the time for the dead to be judged . . . , and for destroying the destroyers of the earth"); Rev. 16:6 ("For they have shed the blood of saints and prophets, and you have given them blood to drink. It is what they deserve!"); and Rev. 18:6-7a ("Pay her back as she herself has paid back others, and repay her double for her deeds; mix a double portion for her in the cup she mixed. As she glorified herself and lived in luxury, so give her a like measure of torment and mourning"). The talionic theme in the last of these is more evident if "double" is better translated "equivalent," as argued in Meredith G. Kline, "Double Trouble," *JETS* 32 (June 1989): 177.

plural of self-exhortation,[41] others as indicating duality within the Godhead (specifically with regard to the Spirit referred to in 1:2),[42] and others as intra-Trinitarian speech.[43] In recent years most scholars, from a variety of theological perspectives, have adopted versions of the heavenly court view.[44] Though I believe other considerations in Genesis 1 inchoately manifest God's Trinitarian nature,[45] in my judgment the evidence clearly favors the heavenly court interpretation of 1:26. For interested readers I have provided a defense of this view in Appendix 4. If this view is correct, 1:26 itself reveals God, who makes humans in his image, as a glorious royal figure establishing justice on earth.

To summarize the argument of this section: God's royal dominion is exercised in Genesis 1 as a king seated upon his heavenly throne and surrounded by his angelic council, issuing righteous decrees and making equitable judgments upon earth. His justice is upright and unassailable. His laws are just and the punishment threatened for violating them is severe.

The Generous Bounty of God's Dominion

Understanding the nature of God's royal dominion in Genesis 1 also requires recognizing the fruitfulness, generosity, and love that he exhibits toward creation. He is a God of beauty and bounty as well as justice. Only in recognizing both aspects of divine action is the nature of the original image of God properly apprehended.

41. E.g., U. Cassuto, *A Commentary on the Book of Genesis,* Part 1, *From Adam to Noah,* trans. Israel Abrahams (Jerusalem: Magnes, 1972).

42. E.g., Clines, "Humanity as the Image of God," pp. 463-64; Blocher, *In the Beginning,* p. 84; and Hamilton, *The Book of Genesis Chapters 1–17,* p. 135.

43. This view, often associated with Augustine, has been historically popular among Christian interpreters as a primordial revelation of God's triune nature. For a recent defense, see Fesko, *Last Things First,* p. 43.

44. Most thoroughly, see Garr, *In His Own Image and Likeness.* Other proponents include Bruce K. Waltke, *Genesis: A Commentary* (Grand Rapids: Zondervan, 2001), p. 65; Sarna, *Genesis,* p. 12; Wenham, *Genesis 1–15,* pp. 27-28; von Rad, *Genesis,* pp. 58-59; Middleton, *The Liberating Image,* pp. 55-60; and Kline, *Images of the Spirit,* pp. 22-23.

45. I concur with the sentiment expressed by Thomas A. Smail concerning the Trinitarian reading of Genesis 1:26: "Exegetically the point has no basis in the text, but theologically the instinct that the whole passage requires a trinitarian context to make full sense of it was right on target." See "The Image of the Triune God," *IJST* 5 (March 2003): 4. Looking simply at Genesis 1:1-3 discloses God the Father who initiates the work of creation (1:1), God the Spirit who hovers over the waters (1:2), and God the Son who is the Word of God (1:3).

First, several features of Genesis 1 reveal God's creating work as one of beauty and order. The very literary comeliness of Genesis 1 provides an initial hint that the creation it describes is beautiful. Biblical interpretation hangs not only upon a bare analysis of the propositions stated in the text but also upon an appreciation for the way in which the words are communicated. Form, in other words, shapes the substance. Many scholars have explored the artful literary structure of Genesis 1:1–2:3. The pattern of fiat and fulfillment, the formation of creation kingdoms in days 1-3 and the filling of these kingdoms in days 4-6, the sevenfold repetition of various themes, and the modification of language to signal the climax of God's work in the creation of humanity are among the many features that display the author's literary skill.[46] But ultimately the literary artistry magnifies the divine author rather than the human author of Scripture, for the beauty of the text is a faint reflection of the beauty of the creator's handiwork. The orderliness of the emerging creation is displayed in both covert and overt ways. Covertly, the pattern of creating kingdoms in days 1-3 and filling these kingdoms in days 4-6 subtly reveals the balance and proportion of creation. Overtly, the repetition of the phrase "according to its/their kind(s)" announces that God has put everything in this world in its proper place. Even the revelation of divine justice in Genesis 1:1–2:3 (as further unfolded through Genesis 2–3) adds to the specter of beauty pervading the narrative. Philosophers classically have recognized the inherent relationship between justice and beauty (through their mutual dependence on ideas such as order and proportionality),[47] and biblical writers also exalt the beauty of God's visible revelation in connection with the revelation of his justice.[48]

Second, a fruitfulness and bounty permeate this beautiful order established in creation. Genesis 1 gives the impression not of scarcity but abundance, a world bursting at the seams. The earth sprouts vegetation, the plants yield seed, and the trees bear fruit (1:11-12). The waters "swarm with swarms of

---

46. Many writers have explored the literary features of Genesis 1. Middleton, *The Liberating Image*, pp. 74-77, has a brief but helpful discussion of the relation of the literary structure and the revelation of God himself, in the context of questions about the image of God.

47. Elaine Scarry has revived and explored the classic connection between justice and beauty in her idiosyncratic but stimulating book, *On Beauty and Being Just* (Princeton: Princeton University Press, 1999).

48. The Psalms are replete with examples. Psalm 97:2, for instance, states that "Clouds and thick darkness are all around him; righteousness and justice are the foundation of his throne," and the two parts of Psalm 19 juxtapose themes of beauty and justice: "The heavens declare the glory of God. . . . The law of the Lord is perfect . . ." (19:1, 7). Another relevant theme may be the prophets' confrontation with the visible majesty of God and their simultaneous sense of their own guilt, exemplified most clearly in Isaiah 6:1-5.

living creations" in order to "fill the waters in the seas" and the birds "multiply on the earth" (1:20-22). The earth brings forth living creatures (1:24-25). The birds, fish, and human beings are commanded to "be fruitful and multiply" (1:22, 28). The creator is a God of bounty.

Third, Genesis 1 also reveals him as a God of generosity and empowerment.[49] Though the cry of Psalm 115:1 — "not to us, O Lord, not to us, but to your name give glory" — would be entirely fitting for all the creatures fashioned in Genesis 1, the text portrays God as sharing his authority, fruitfulness, and enjoyment of creation. He does not keep things for himself, as it were, but draws his handiwork into the dynamic of production and enjoyment. On day 1 God "separated the light from the darkness" (1:4) while on day 4 the lights in the heavens were made "to separate the day from the night" (1:14). This apparently refers to the same event, since in both verses the Hebrew word refers to *making* a separation, which the heavenly lights could hardly do if the light and darkness were already separated before the heavenly lights' creation. Hence, in this apparent example of the concurrence of primary and secondary causation, God enlists creatures in the accomplishing of his work and even in some sense shares credit for it.[50] God also grants authority to his creatures in anticipation of the ongoing administration of the world. He calls the sun and moon, for example, "to rule" the day and the night (1:16) and gives to human beings the commission to "have dominion" over the other creatures and to "subdue" the earth (1:26, 28). As God's work has been fruitful so he calls upon creatures to share in his fruitfulness (1:22, 28). The swarming and filling of the creation kingdoms observed above, though primarily evidence of God's abundance, are actually attributed to created things themselves as he calls them to abound. To anticipate a point emphasized below, God made his image-bearers not only to work as he worked but also to rest as he rested. Human beings were created to look back upon their own finished work one day and to be enthroned in sabbatical rest. The creator is a sharing and lavishing God.

49. See Middleton, *The Liberating Image,* chap. 7, for some stimulating material on these issues. Some of Middleton's conclusions in this chapter are different from mine, however. Most notable is his desire to take these themes in a direction sympathetic to the "openness of God" theology (see p. 294 n. 70). I also differ from his concluding reflections in which he asserts the convergence of God's love in creation with his love in redemption, and hence of Genesis 1:1–2:3 with John 3:16 (see p. 297). My difficulty with this latter move is more nuanced than my difficulty with his sympathy to openness theology; see Chapter 9 of the present volume for detailed discussion of this and related issues.

50. See also William P. Brown, *The Seven Pillars of Creation: The Bible, Science, and the Ecology of Wonder* (Oxford: Oxford University Press, 2010), pp. 44-46.

This evidence of God's fruitfulness and bounty provides another example of the theme of *wisdom* in Genesis 1. After reflecting on God creating the world through wisdom (Prov. 8:22-31), the preface of Proverbs concludes with imagery of wisdom having built a house (9:1). Wisdom's work is well ordered and constructive, but also bountiful and generous. The house of wisdom is filled with meat and wine for those within (9:2), and wisdom calls to others to share in her abundance (9:3-6) and to engage in their own work of building homes bountifully furnished (see 24:3-4).[51] Read in larger biblical context, then, the opening of Genesis presents God as a wise creator.

These considerations compel the conclusion that the creation narratives reveal both the divine justice and the divine love. Defining the relationship of love and justice is a perennial challenge for theology and ethics, and it will be a recurring theme in following chapters. At this point, however, I suggest a way of understanding the relationship of divine love and (rectifying) justice *in the original creation, as revealed in Genesis 1-2*. In short, Genesis 1-2 reveals a divine love for creation — and particularly human beings — that is abundantly generous and bestows participation in all sorts of good. But the love revealed in Genesis 1-2 is not a merciful or forgiving love, for the text also threatens strict retributive justice upon humanity's disobedience, without giving any hope of mitigation in case of rebellion. God bestows high honors and blessings upon the man and woman and holds out the prospect of greater honors and blessings to come, but even one violation of their responsibilities as image-bearers will bring judgment. Thus Scripture reveals God *in his work of creation* as a God of abundant generosity but not of mercy.

The Reflection of Divine Dominion in Human Dominion

I now turn back specifically to the image and likeness of God. Earlier in this chapter I argued that the exercise of royal dominion is a constitutive aspect of bearing God's image and not simply a consequence of it. In the preceding pages I have explored the nature of God's own royal dominion as presented in Genesis 1-2, toward the goal of understanding how human beings were to exercise dominion. Since God called human beings to bear forth his likeness in the exercise of dominion, the nature of divine dominion must inform the nature of human dominion.[52] What can we conclude about the nature of

---

51. See Brown, *Ethos of the Cosmos*, pp. 297-98.
52. This is a significant theme throughout Jonathan Burnside, *God, Justice, and Society:*

human dominion based upon the preceding conclusions about the dominion of God?

First, the fact that God exercised dominion through speaking, and specifically naming, creates expectation that his image-bearers would follow a similar practice. This is precisely what occurs in Genesis 2. God brings the beasts and birds to Adam, and as he himself had "called" [וַיִּקְרָא] things by name (1:5, 8, 10), so he sees what Adam would "call" [יִקְרָא] them (2:19). There is even an echo of the fiat-fulfillment pattern in this episode, for "whatever the man called every living creature, that was its name." The very first recorded human action was a successful imitation of divine action: Adam acted and it came to pass. The same pattern of God's bringing and Adam's calling recurs in 2:22-23 after the formation of the woman.[53] I noted above that in larger biblical context effective and creative speech is a function of wisdom. As God exercised wise dominion through speaking and naming, so did Adam.

Second, protological humanity also reflected God's identity as a king enthroned in the heavenly court in judicial capacity. Like God, human beings were to render right judgments. Adam's work of naming is a good example of this. When giving things their names, Adam properly recognized that no animal was a suitable partner for him, but that the woman was. Adam delivered right judgments because in wisdom he discerned the proper nature and function of things.

We also see this likeness to divine judicial authority, I suggest, in God's probationary test of Adam through the tree of the knowledge of good and evil. The meaning of "knowing good and evil" is a disputed question, but it probably indicates Adam's responsibility to render righteous judgment.[54] The whole

---

Aspects of Law and Legality in the Bible (Oxford: Oxford University Press, 2011); see e.g. pp. 70-73, 104-5, 152-62.

53. For reflection on Adam's speaking and naming as a function of the image of God, see Auld, "*Imago Dei* in Genesis," p. 261.

54. Among those advocating versions of this position are William N. Wilder, "Illumination and Investiture: The Royal Significance of the Tree of Wisdom in Genesis 3," *WTJ* 68 (Spring 2006): 51-69; Meredith G. Kline, *Kingdom Prologue: Genesis Foundations for a Covenantal Worldview* (Overland Park, KS: Two Age, 2000), pp. 105-7; Blocher, *In the Beginning*, pp. 132-33; E. W. Heaton, *Solomon's New Men: The Emergence of Ancient Israel as a National State* (New York: Pica, 1974), pp. 160-61; and W. Malcolm Clark, "A Legal Background to the Yahwist's Use of Good and Evil in Genesis 2–3," *JBL* 88 (Sept. 1969): 266-78. Some commentators take "good and evil" to mean "everything"; e.g., see Krašovec, "Punishment and Mercy," pp. 7-8; Sarna, *Genesis*, p. 19; von Rad, *Genesis*, pp. 81-82; and Cassuto, *A Commentary on the Book of Genesis*, 1:112-13. Another writer speaks of knowing good and evil as a reference to experiential knowledge gained through response to the command of 2:16-17; see Chris A.

question is complicated by the need to interpret "knowing good and evil" in the light of three considerations: its use elsewhere in the OT, the fact that the tree of the knowledge of good and evil was off limits and hence that eating of it was a wicked act, and God's declaration in 3:22 that, after they ate of it, "the man has become like one of us in knowing good and evil." To put the question concisely: why was eating from the tree of the knowledge of good and evil considered a wicked act when Adam, the image-bearer, actually became like God in knowing good and evil as a result of eating? This question is answered and the relevant evidence best taken into account if one interprets the tree of the knowledge of good and evil as a test of Adam's fidelity to his commission to be a just royal judge under the authority of God as supreme king.

The use of the phrase "knowing good and evil" and related expressions elsewhere in the OT provides strong evidence for interpreting this idea in a royal-judicial sense in Genesis 2–3. The attribution of knowledge of good and evil to the two great Israelite kings, David and Solomon, provides the clearest evidence that such knowledge is the particular province of monarchs as they render judgment. 2 Samuel 14 describes a ruse by Joab to restore Absalom to the presence of his father David. Joab sends a wise woman from Tekoa to present a concocted judicial appeal to the king. In the course of her conversation with David the woman states, "your servant thought, 'The word of my lord the king will set me at rest,' for my lord the king is like the angel of God to discern [know] good and evil" (14:17). Here the phrase refers to a king's judicial decision that grants relief to a person bereft of justice. The same is true in 1 Kings 3. Solomon initially asks for wisdom in order to *judge* [לשפט] God's people, "that I may discern between good and evil" (3:9). After his wise judicial ruling involving the two women claiming the same living child, the people "perceived that the wisdom of God was in him to do justice" (3:28). Thus the recognition that he *does justice* is evidence that God has answered Solomon's request for wisdom to *discern good and evil*. A number of similar expressions occur throughout the OT that have clear judicial connotations and often take place in a royal or quasi-royal context.[55] Even in texts in which the knowing of good and evil does not have an immediately obvious reference to juridical decision-making, a judicial overtone often lies in the background.[56]

Vlachos, *The Law and the Knowledge of Good & Evil: The Edenic Background of the Catalytic Operation of the Law in Paul* (Eugene, OR: Pickwick, 2009), pp. 139-42.

55. E.g., see Gen. 24:50; 31:24, 29; 2 Sam. 13:22; and Isa. 7:16.

56. In Deuteronomy 1:39, for example, Moses states that the children "who today have no knowledge of good or evil" would not be condemned with their rebellious parents but would one day enter the promised land. In light of Israel's commission to be a "kingdom of

In light of the immediate context — particularly God's exercise of judicial authority as a king seated in the midst of his heavenly court and the human commission to exercise dominion — it is compelling to understand the references to "knowing good and evil" in Genesis 2–3 in line with this common OT meaning of the phrase. This still leaves some difficult interpretive questions. If Adam was to image God through the exercise of dominion, then the knowing of good and evil (that is, making just judicial decisions) would seem to be a good thing for him to do. Yet eating from the tree of the knowledge of good and evil was prohibited (2:17), knowing good and evil was promoted by the serpent (3:5), and Adam's becoming "like one of us in knowing good and evil" is the cause of his expulsion from Eden (3:22-24) — all of which suggests that knowing good and evil was a bad thing for Adam.

The solution to this apparent difficulty, I suggest, is that the drama of Genesis 2–3 concerns *how well* Adam would know good and evil rather than *whether* Adam would know good and evil. In either obeying *or* disobeying the command not to eat of the tree (the serpent's temptation made some sort of decision necessary) Adam would know good and evil — the question was whether he would exercise judicial authority in the proper way. This is obscured if the command about the tree is taken as an arbitrary test imposed by God. The Garden of Eden was a holy sanctuary, and God called Adam to be not only a king (as discussed at length in this chapter) but also a priest.[57] As a priest, Adam was responsible for *guarding* [שמר] the Garden (and not simply for being a primordial landscaper or farmer).[58] The command in 2:16-17 is indeed a test, but not an arbitrary one. God was testing Adam's general commission to exercise dominion over the other creatures and to subdue the earth (1:26, 28), the whole of which was also a

---

priests" (Exod. 19:6), the children's inability to exercise the requisite judicial authority meant that they were not guilty of failing in their commission as were those who had come of age. Another example is 2 Samuel 19:35 [19:36 in Hebrew], where Barzillai declines David's invitation to move to Jerusalem in part because, at his advanced age, he could no longer understand good and evil. Whatever Barzillai exactly meant by this statement, it is worth noting that he is effectively declining an invitation to be connected to David's royal court.

57. For discussion of many issues related to Adam's priestly identity, see generally Smith, *The Priestly Vision*.

58. Guarding a holy place is the work of priests later in the OT (Num. 3:6-7, 32, 38; 18:1-7). See e.g. Gordon J. Wenham, "Sanctuary Symbolism in the Garden of Eden Story," in *I Studied Inscriptions from before the Flood*, ed. Richard S. Hess and David Toshio Tsumura (Winona Lake, IN: Eisenbrauns, 1994), p. 401; and G. K. Beale, *The Temple and the Church's Mission: A Biblical Theology of the Dwelling Place of God* (Downers Grove, IL: InterVarsity, 2004), pp. 66-70.

holy sanctuary.[59] By guarding Eden from anyone or anything that would defile it, Adam would, in microcosmic fashion, fulfill his original mandate. The tree of the knowledge of good and evil was to be the means for testing. In Genesis 3 the reader learns precisely how the tree came to serve this role. The serpent entered the Edenic sanctuary as an intruder and Adam, alongside the woman during her conversation with the serpent (3:6), presumably should have exerted his authority over the creature, rejected his overtures, and driven out this defiler from the holy Garden, thereby fulfilling simultaneously his various duties in 1:26, 28, and 2:15-17. In whichever choice he made, therefore, Adam would necessarily be exercising a judicial role, for good or ill.

What was the precise character of his unrighteous exercise of judicial authority? Whatever else might be said, Adam completely reversed the authority structure of the original creation. God was to be the supreme king, human beings under him, and the other creatures under human authority. By his actions in Genesis 3, Adam elevated himself over God (by rejecting his commandment in favor of his own desire) and elevated the serpent over himself, thereby making the serpent the supreme king, humanity under him, and God beneath them all. Ezekiel 28 provides interesting commentary. God condemns the king of Tyre, whom he set in "Eden, the garden of God" as a "blameless" and "anointed guardian cherub" (28:13-15). But God drove him out, not because he acted as a king (which was his proper position), but "because your heart is proud, and you have said, 'I am a god. I sit in the seat of the gods, in the heart of the seas . . .'" (28:2). These obvious allusions to Genesis 1–3 and the overt comparison of the king of Tyre to Adam add further evidence that Adam was indeed a king and a judge, but failed to exercise his authority in the righteous way. Instead of being *like* God and remaining "for a little while lower than the angels" (Heb. 2:7), Adam instead sought to force himself into the heavenly court and even above it, forcing his will upon God and his servants.

This in turn explains why God speaks of Adam becoming "like one of us in knowing good and evil" and promptly expels him from Eden because of it. God was evidently stating an ironic truth. Adam had indeed become like God and his angels by rendering judicial judgment in the Garden — this was inevitable and was meant to happen in any case. But in seeking to be like God not in the subordinate sense proper to an image-bearer but in a usurping sense

---

59. E.g., see S. Dean McBride Jr., "Divine Protocol: Genesis 1:1–2:3 as Prologue to the Pentateuch," in *God Who Creates: Essays in Honor of W. Sibley Towner,* ed. William P. Brown and S. Dean McBride Jr. (Grand Rapids: Eerdmans, 2000), pp. 11-15.

that confused likeness with identity, Adam failed his test and incurred divine judgment. God, with the assistance of his obedient angelic servants, restores the proper authority structure (3:24).

If this interpretation of the tree of the knowledge of good and evil is accurate, then it is further evidence that God created human beings to exercise dominion in his likeness by rendering just judicial decisions, with respect to the proper channels of authority in the original created order. This work of knowing good and evil, done well, would have been another expression of wisdom, as the example of Solomon illustrates (1 Kgs. 3:9, 28).[60]

A third characteristic of God's dominion in Genesis 1–3, as examined above, was its beauty and bounty in ordering the world and bestowing generous gifts upon it. The creator did not keep his wealth and goodness to himself but called creatures to participate in the enjoyment of them. According to Genesis 1–2, human image-bearers were also to reflect this characteristic of the divine dominion. For example: "So God created man in his own image, in the image of God he created him; male and female he created them" (1:27). God made "man" in the plural. Human beings were not meant to bear God's image as solitary individuals or to live without mutual interaction. Although some writers have unduly emphasized the last phrase in 1:27 as definitive for what constitutes the image of God,[61] the clear statement that human beings are social creatures meant to live in community is surely significant. Rather than being turned inward, human beings were to be turned outward and to be other-regarding. God freely entered relationship with his image-bearers, and they in turn necessarily entered relationship with one another, most intimately in marriage (2:20-24).

The reflection of God's generosity and bounty is more explicitly evident in the command following the blessing in 1:28: "be fruitful and multiply and fill the earth." As God filled the world with an abundance of creatures, even causing the waters to "swarm" with living creatures, so human beings were

60. For discussion of the biblical relationship between Solomon and Adam, see John A. Davies, "'Discerning between Good and Evil': Solomon as a New Adam in 1 Kings," *WTJ* 73 (Spring 2011): 39-57. In regard to Genesis 3:5-6, Eve seems to have recognized properly that knowing good and evil through the tree of testing, and hence becoming like God, was intimately connected with wisdom.

61. I think here especially of Karl Barth's famous claims, in light of his understanding of Genesis 1:27, that the image of God is about entering and being in relationship; see e.g. *Church Dogmatics* III/1 (London: T. & T. Clark, 2004), pp. 181-91. For detailed discussion of Barth's views on the image and its influence on subsequent scholarship, see Jónsson, *The Image of God,* Part 3.

to fill the earth through their own reproductive fruitfulness. They were not to keep their share in God's dominion and enjoyment of his world to themselves, but to share it in turn with many descendants. The call to generosity also seems present in God's placing Adam in the Garden "to work it and keep [i.e., guard — ולשמרה] it" (2:15). Though the mandate to "subdue" the earth communicates a strong sense of human superiority, their authority was to be exercised for the good of the earth and not at its expense. In providing priestly protection for the holy Garden, Adam was to preserve its purity and thereby maintain, in this part of the earth, the order God imparted to it.

Once again the text draws us into the orbit of biblical wisdom. As discussed above, the work of wisdom displayed in God's creative labor is constructive and bountiful, like the erection of a house filled with sumptuous food and drink meant for sharing (Prov. 8:22–9:6). Correspondingly, people who acquire wisdom build their own well-provisioned houses (Prov. 24:3-4) and are generous to those around them (e.g., Prov. 28:27).

The idea that the character of God's dominion sheds light upon the proper character of human dominion, and thus upon the meaning of the image and likeness of God, has thus proven to be helpful. Like God the supreme king, human beings were made to exercise authority by speaking and naming, by rendering righteous judgments, and by displaying their creator's fruitful generosity for the well-being of all creation. Human beings, as image-bearers, were quite literally called to do God's work on earth under his supreme authority. This conclusion, drawn from Genesis 1–2 itself, is corroborated by the claim of many scholars that "image and likeness" in Genesis 1:26-27 reflects the use of similar terms in Mesopotamian and/or Egyptian sources, indicating *representation*.[62] Human beings, created to rule the world under God, are his royal representatives here on earth.

---

62. There is a great deal of literature on this subject. The relevant Egyptian and Mesopotamian background includes evidence of "image" and "likeness" terminology to describe either a statue erected to represent an absent king or to describe a king (or perhaps a priest) who functions as the god's representative on earth. An early pioneer on this topic was Hans Wildberger, "Das Abbild Gottes: Gen. 1,26-30," *Theologische Zeitschrift* 21 (1965): 245-59, 481-501. Among the many subsequent writers with whom I have interacted in this chapter who have explored the implications of this ancient Near Eastern background for understanding the biblical image of God, see Fesko, *Last Things First*, pp. 47-48; Middleton, *The Liberating Image*, chap. 3; Horton, *Lord and Servant*, pp. 105-8; Garr, *In His Own Image and Likeness*, chap. 7; Grenz, *The Social God*, pp. 197-200; Levenson, *Creation and the Persistence of Evil*, pp. 112-17; Pannenberg, *Systematic Theology*, 2:216; Dumbrell, *Covenant & Creation*, pp. 33-34; Sarna, *Genesis*, p. 12; Hamilton, *Genesis Chapters 1–17*, pp. 135, 138; Wenham, *Genesis*, pp. 31-32; Reichenbach, "Genesis 1 as a Theological-Political Narrative," pp. 60-63; Bird, "'Male and Female,'" pp. 139-44; and Clines, "Humanity as the Image of God," pp. 482-95.

Preliminary Conclusion

To this point in the chapter I have defended a preliminary definition of the protological image of God, in line with a broad consensus among contemporary biblical scholars about the general ideas underlying Genesis 1:26-27. I have presented the protological image as a commission or office to exercise royal dominion as God's representative on earth. The revelation of God's own exercise of dominion in Genesis 1–3, furthermore, indicates that image-bearing human dominion was to take place through speaking and naming, through rendering right judgments, and through a bounteous generosity that seeks the good of all creation. Yet these tasks required human beings to have certain attributes, and Genesis 5:3 indicates that to bear one's image involves a certain natural resemblance between the parties.[63] The protological image of God, therefore, involved both what human beings *are* and what they are *to do*. It is neither exclusively ontological nor exclusively functional, and cannot be attributed to the soul to the exclusion of the body.[64]

Paul's statements in Ephesians 4:24 and Colossians 3:10 seem to confirm this preliminary conclusion. When he speaks in these verses of Christians being "created after the likeness of God in true righteousness and holiness" and "being renewed in knowledge after the image of its creator" he alludes back to Genesis 1:26[65] and suggests that the image borne in redemption is in organic continuity with the image as originally displayed. As evident both in these verses themselves and in their immediate contexts, Paul describes the image not merely as the *capacity* for rational or moral behavior but especially as the exercise of moral and rational *excellence*.

This holistic understanding of the protological image of God, focused upon the proper execution of a royal office, is substantively rich. But there is still one more aspect of the image to identify in order to capture the biblical teaching.

63. See the helpful comments on this point in Brown, *The Seven Pillars*, p. 42.

64. This conclusion resembles that of my colleague Michael Horton in *Lord and Servant*, chap. 4. In refusing to identify the image with any particular human attribute or quality, yet seeking to avoid reductionism in the other direction by making the image nothing but relation, Horton distinguishes between "prerequisite attributes" that make human beings suitable candidates for image-bearing and the image "itself." As he puts it, "While my proposal rejects any identification of the image of God with any faculty or substance, mental or physical, can there be any doubt that human beings are uniquely suited among the creation to be covenant partners with God? And can we not point out fairly obvious prerequisites such as certain natural capacities for deliberative reason, intentional relationality, moral agency, and linguisticality?" (p. 104).

65. See comments in Watson, *Text and Truth*, p. 281.

Toward the Goal of Eschatological Enthronement

The final aspect of the protological image of God involves a crucial, though underappreciated, part of the dynamic of Genesis 1–2.[66] The protological image of God was not about the indefinite exercise of dominion as God's representative on this earth, but about its exercise *toward an eschatological goal.* In other words, the commission as image-bearer did not require the exercise of dominion as an endless task but as a task to be completed. The original human state was not "a state of indefinite probation."[67] The protological image was oriented toward a goal, the original human destiny. Human beings were meant to complete their task as protological image-bearers so that they might become eschatological image-bearers. This idea reflects the views of many Christian theologians from a number of traditions, who have recognized an eschatological goal for the human race even before the fall (though they have not necessarily understood it in terms of the image of God).[68]

One idea with ancient roots in Christian theology is that God made human beings in a state of immaturity, as little children (though perhaps with adult bodies), with the expectation that they would grow in maturity over time through their experience in this world and thereby attain to adulthood.[69]

66. Among theologians who have given sustained attention to this matter in their treatment of the image of God are Horton, *Lord and Servant,* chaps. 4-5; Grenz, *The Social God,* chaps. 5-6; and Pannenberg, *Systematic Theology,* vol. 2, chap. 8.

67. See Geerhardus Vos, *Biblical Theology: Old and New Testaments* (Grand Rapids: Eerdmans, 1948), pp. 31-32. Vos was a Reformed exegete and theologian whose overall interpretation of the progress of biblical revelation in this work is very congenial to my claims in this book. Here he asserts, without exploring the implications of the image of God in much detail, that the first human beings had no *natural* knowledge of their calling to attain to an eschatological goal beyond the confines of the originally created world. I will discuss related issues in other Reformed theologians below when dealing with the covenant of creation as a natural covenant.

68. E.g., see Augustine, *The City of God,* 12.21; Augustine, *Genesis 1-11,* Ancient Christian Commentary, p. 39; John of Damascus, *The Orthodox Faith,* 2.11; Thomas Aquinas, *Summa Theologiae,* 1a2ae 3.8; 109.5; and Francis Turretin, *Institutes of Elenctic Theology,* 3 vols., trans. George Musgrave Giger, ed. James T. Dennison Jr. (Phillipsburg, NJ: Presbyterian and Reformed, 1992-1997), 1:583-86.

69. The general idea seems to derive back at least to Irenaeus in the third century. Cassuto's treatment of the text in *A Commentary on the Book of Genesis,* 1:113 provides an interesting example from a prominent twentieth-century biblical scholar. Subsequently, Wilder, in "Illumination and Investiture," expresses certain sentiments in this direction, though within the framework of the Reformed doctrine of the covenant of works, within which I too am working. I am attracted to much of Wilder's interpretation of Genesis 1-3, though I find his

While it seems plausible to speculate that Adam and Eve were to grow in wisdom through the pursuit of their commission, what I have in mind is somewhat different from this ancient view. Genesis 1–2 itself suggests that God made the primordial humans capable of performing their commission and accountable for doing so from the outset. In Genesis 1:26-28 God immediately gives the newly created human beings a comprehensive task and in Genesis 2:7-20 God puts Adam right to work after granting him life. Adam, in fact, successfully and wisely completes his initial work of naming the animals (2:19-20). In short, and building upon my interpretation of the tree of the knowledge of good and evil above, I suggest that the first human beings were created ready to do their task, that through obedience to this task they would have attained their destiny, and that attaining it would have happened by a decisive act of God (analogous to his decisive act of judgment in Genesis 3 whereby they were disqualified from their original goal).[70]

But why see the destiny of eschatological enthronement as a constitutive aspect of the image in Genesis 1–2? Earlier I described how human dominion was to reflect God's dominion. This route promises to be fruitful again, for Genesis 1:1–2:3 presents God as working toward and attaining an eschatological goal. The text is permeated with a sense of historical movement that is capped by a scene of arrival. This sense is produced most prominently by the sabbatical pattern that frames the narrative. Far from this being an incidental or ornamental characteristic of the text, Jon Levenson notes that the "formal feature that most strikingly sets Genesis 1:1–2:3 off from its Egyptian, Mesopotamian, and Israelite antecedents and parallels is its heptadic structure. In

---

thesis that Adam was eventually supposed to eat from the tree of the knowledge of good and evil unconvincing.

70. Though I generally wish to avoid extra-biblical speculation, it seems necessary to assume that had Adam sustained his probation he would not have been brought immediately to eschatological enthronement with God, though his right to it would have been guaranteed. Without continuing to live for some extended period of time in the original creation, Adam would not have been able to be fruitful and multiply and thus to fill and subdue the earth as a whole, as envisioned in the original mandate (Gen. 1:28). For discussion of relevant issues, see e.g. Beale, *The Temple and the Church's Mission,* chap. 3. Had he sustained his probation, however, Adam would, by necessity, have been freed from the threat of sanctions inherent in the natural law, since he would have already successfully passed through its judgment, though much of the moral substance of the natural law would presumably still be binding upon him during this period (enforcing retributive justice would seem to be unnecessary). Anticipating the argument of Chapter 9, I suggest that there is an analogy (though not identity) between this provisional state of Adam between successful probation and eschatological enthronement and New Testament Christians' present provisional state between justification and glorification.

none of the other literature that we have examined so far do we find anything reminiscent of the schema of seven days of creation that dominates the overture to the Bible."[71] Building upon the work of Umberto Cassuto, Levenson observes how patterns of sevens or multiples of sevens absolutely pervade Genesis 1:1–2:3.[72]

The text begs us, therefore, to take the seven-day pattern seriously and to explore its significance. One remarkable characteristic of the creation week is the absence on the seventh day of many features shared by the first six days. The first six days, for example, are marked by the recurrence of the divine fiats and their fulfillment, of God's viewing his handiwork and pronouncing it good, and the refrain of "evening and morning." All of these are absent on the seventh day. Most significant, perhaps, is that the seventh day witnesses no earthly labor on God's part. For six days God is very busy with the world, calling things into being, making separations, giving things names, and evaluating his work. God performs none of these actions on the seventh day. In contrast to the many acts of creation and organization of this world in 1:1-31, 2:1-2 simply pronounces this work "finished." Following these statements, the text says that God "rested . . . from all his work" (2:2). Here, unlike anything seen in Genesis 1, God acts not with reference to his creation but with reference to himself only. The third and fourth divine actions of the seventh day are also self-referential.

Another unique feature of the seventh day is how it brings closure. While the narrative proceeds through Genesis 1 constantly leaving the impression that there is more for God to do, the account of the seventh day imposes the impression of finality. The king's work is "finished" and he now rests enthroned. Of course this does not mean the end of history altogether. In hindsight, the second part of the work of the sixth day, concerning human creation (1:26-31), sets up readers for a dramatic story to follow.[73] But this subsequent story will be the story of this world as determined by *human* action — how would the man and woman do in the commission God granted them? From now on responsibility for ruling and filling the earth shifts from God to his human representatives. God will indeed have more dealings with his world, but as far as his work of *creation* is concerned he has done all there is to do.

71. Levenson, *Creation and the Persistence of Evil,* p. 66.

72. Levenson, *Creation and the Persistence of Evil,* pp. 66-68. See also Smith, *The Priestly Vision,* p. 87; and Brown, *The Seven Pillars,* p. 37.

73. Garr closes his work on the image of God with suggestive comments about the open-endedness of the account of human creation at the end of Genesis 1. A continuing story remains to be told. See *In His Own Image and Likeness,* pp. 239-40.

There is no "evening and morning" on the seventh day because the seventh day is removed from the passage of time and the flow of history which characterizes the first six days. God has accomplished all that he set out to do, has arrived at the goal, and now has nowhere else to go. The description in 2:2-3 even suggests that the seventh day, in its transcendence of time, never draws to a close. This is how the New Testament interprets the seventh day. According to Hebrews 4:1-11, God has invited human beings throughout history to share in his (apparently ongoing) seventh-day rest.

One other aspect of God's arrival at the seventh day deserves attention: he enters his rest only after receiving judicial approbation. As considered above, God's royal dominion bears a judicial character in Genesis 1–3 which culminates in his judgment against the serpent, the woman, and the man. But before judging others God renders judgment upon himself. Six times in Genesis 1 he looks upon the mounting evidence and pronounces his own work "good." These are preliminary verdicts, however, for after his last act of creation he views it all and declares it "very good" (1:31). God has put himself through a test, passed his own trial, and attained his much-deserved rest.

All of this is richly suggestive for a theology of the image of God. God's dominion includes not only working within this world but also passing a judicial test and entering into a rest that transcends this world. If human dominion was meant to resemble the divine dominion, then it seems that human dominion must also include working in this world, passing a judicial test, and entering into an eschatological rest.[74] Since the heptadic structure of Genesis 1:1–2:3 is so prominent and pervasive, and thus so definitive for this initial biblical revelation of God, the sabbatical pattern should apply to human beings as well if they were truly to bear God's likeness. God's *work itself* cannot be understood apart from his rest, for work performed toward a historically defined goal is essentially different from work performed aimlessly and indefinitely. To be the image and likeness of God Adam must have performed his work with a historically defined goal in view. Thus the very unfolding of events in Genesis 1–3, in which human beings explicitly resemble God in being commissioned to do royal work in this world and in being brought to judicial trial, invites the conclusion that, had they been obedient, God would

74. This is the conclusion in Horton, *Lord and Servant*, p. 129. Despite the similarity of many of my claims to Middleton's, this is a point where our conclusions diverge. While Middleton properly ascribes significance to God's seventh-day rest in 2:2-3 as the signal that God has delegated authority over this world to his human representatives, he does not see the entrance into rest as itself constitutive of the image and likeness of God. See Middleton, *The Liberating Image*, p. 212.

have proclaimed their work "very good" and welcomed them into a state of rest, their work also "finished."

This conclusion, not explicitly stated in Genesis 1–3 but, in my judgment, inescapable from what is said there, is confirmed by later biblical interpretation of the creation story. Two clear examples are the explanation of the fourth commandment in Exodus 20 and the understanding of the seventh day of creation expressed in Hebrews 4. In the Exodus version of the Decalogue, God grounds Israel's keeping of the Sabbath day in his own work of creation: "For in six days the Lord made heaven and earth, the sea, and all that is in them, and rested the seventh day. Therefore the Lord blessed the Sabbath day and made it holy" (20:11). The fourth commandment therefore interprets God's sabbatical pattern in Genesis 1:1–2:3 as normative for understanding the active human reflection of God's image and likeness.[75] Hebrews 4:1-11 speaks of God inviting human beings to join him in his seventh-day rest of Genesis 2:2-3. The author of Hebrews identifies the reference to "my rest" in Psalm 95:11 as the very rest of God at the conclusion of creation (4:3-5). Though the unbelieving people of Israel were excluded from that rest in the days of Moses and Joshua (4:2, 8), there "remains for some to enter it" (4:6). That is, "there remains a Sabbath rest for the people of God" (4:9) and present-day believers should "strive to enter that rest" (4:11). Hebrews 4:1-11, therefore, interprets God's rest of Genesis 2:2-3 as intended for human participation. Reading these verses in context solidifies the case for applying this to Adam's original condition. A previous section in Hebrews begins: "Now it was not to angels that God subjected the world to come, of which we are speaking" (2:5). The author then quotes Psalm 8:4-6 to explain that God subjected it not to angels but to human beings: "What is man, that you are mindful of him, or the son of man, that you care for him? You made him a little while lower than the angels; you have crowned him with glory and honor, putting everything in subjection under his feet" (2:6-8). Thus, long before he offers his interpretation of God's seventh-day "rest" (4:1-11), the author has already looked back to God's original work of creation to find proof that human beings are destined for a royal life in "the world to come."

75. In this context the "seventh day" recurs every week, of course. But this commandment also comes in a larger context that points toward a final rest. God leads his people through the wilderness with the goal of arriving at the Promised Land of rest — setting out from Sinai and arriving at Zion. This theme is explored at length in Jon Levenson, *Sinai and Zion: An Entry into the Jewish Bible* (San Francisco: HarperSanFrancisco, 1985). Michael S. Horton has built upon Levenson's work in a theological context similar to mine in this present book; see especially *People and Place: A Covenant Ecclesiology* (Louisville: Westminster John Knox, 2008), pp. 290-93.

Read together, Hebrews 2 and 4 portray human beings as created not to work indefinitely in this world but to image God by working and then joining him in his kingly rest.

Following the lead of Genesis 1:1–2:3 itself as well as later biblical interpretation of its seven-day structure, I conclude that a sufficient definition of the protological image includes an eschatological dimension. The image and likeness of God in Genesis 1:26-27 is thus a commission or office for human beings to establish their royal dominion as God's representative on earth in order that they might join him in a triumphant rest that transcends the earth they have subdued. The protological image oriented human beings in a historically dynamic direction, toward completing their work of dominion and then entering a state in which they could look back at their work of dominion as complete.

The Image of God and Protological Human Nature

From my interpretation of the image of God in Genesis 1:26-27, I now draw some conclusions about human nature as originally created. A conception of human nature is crucial for a doctrine of natural law. Whether defined in a thin or a thick sense, some understanding of human nature must underlie claims about a law that is naturally known by and obligatory upon human beings. As observed in the Introduction and Appendix 1, this need to identify human nature has driven advocates of natural law such as Jean Porter and Craig Boyd to explore the insights of contemporary biology and other advocates such as Russell Hittinger and Matthew Levering (and Porter) to recover and develop the anthropology of their Roman Catholic (and particularly Thomistic) heritage.[76] Even a Roman Catholic proponent of natural law such as Robert George, who generally shuns the need to establish a metaphysical basis for natural law, acknowledges that his theory must identify what the true "human goods" are and what constitutes "integral human fulfillment."[77] In one way or

---

76. See Jean Porter, *Nature as Reason: A Thomistic Theory of the Natural Law* (Grand Rapids: Eerdmans, 2005); Russell Hittinger, *The First Grace: Rediscovering the Natural Law in a Post-Christian World* (Wilmington, DE: ISI, 2003); Craig A. Boyd, *A Shared Morality: A Narrative Defense of Natural Law Ethics* (Grand Rapids: Brazos, 2007); and Matthew Levering, *Biblical Natural Law: A Theocentric and Teleological Approach* (Oxford: Oxford University Press, 2008).

77. E.g., see Robert P. George, *In Defense of Natural Law* (Oxford: Clarendon, 1999), pp. 49-53.

another, what human beings know by nature about their basic moral obligations depends upon what sort of creatures they are.

Philosophy, evolutionary biology, cultural anthropology, and other academic disciplines may suggest many things about what a human being "is," but when we address this question theologically we come face to face with one fundamental answer: a human being *is* the image of God. Whether in terms of the image as originally created, the image as fallen but preserved, or the image as re-created, Scripture gives no other basic definition of what makes a human being a human being. It may be true that if we begin with certain preconceptions about what sorts of things human "nature" could or could not entail, then the biblical concept of the image of God may not yield perfectly satisfactory results. But if we seek to develop a theological conception of human nature, with Scripture as our guide, then defining the image of God is precisely the route to be pursued. Scripture provides no precedent or justification for abstracting a notion of humanness that could exist independently of bearing the divine image.[78]

How should protological human nature be defined in light of my conclusions about the image of God? Since the image of God was holistic, human nature at creation should be understood holistically. The original human beings were body and soul. They had constitutive attributes ordained to their proper exercise. They were creatures designed to complete a task in this world and to attain to a royal "rest" in a "world to come." In other words, protological human nature was constituted by three things: human beings' attributes, commission, and destiny. The idea of human "nature" as a static concept is foreign to Scripture and is thus insufficient theologically. Human nature is a historically dynamic concept that is inherently ethical and eschatologically oriented. Human beings were thus not simply creatures with certain rational, volitional, or moral attributes. They were also kings with a commission to fulfill.[79] This

78. Contra Kline, *Images of the Spirit,* pp. 13, 37. See the discussion in Horton, *Lord and Servant,* chap. 4, which builds on Kline's work but takes a position like that advocated here, identifying the image of God with humanness. See also the cordial critique of Kline on this point in Paul Helm, "Image of the Spirit and Image of God," in *Creator, Redeemer, Consummator: A Festschrift for Meredith G. Kline,* ed. Howard Griffith and John R. Muether (Greenville, SC: Reformed Academic Press, 2000), pp. 211-14.

79. As Michael Horton puts it, for the biblical writers humanness is "ultimately a narrative-ethical rather than a metaphysical-ontological" matter; see *Lord and Servant,* p. 94. Horton immediately adds: "This is not to assume that my account avoids its own ontological/metaphysical scheme (the impossibility of which is insufficiently appreciated . . .). Yet it means that these presuppositions at least strive to be grounded in the concrete revelation of God and humanness as we pick out the characters in the biblical drama and its didactic notations rather

already suggests a point to which I will return toward the end of this chapter. If protological human nature was inherently ethical and eschatological, then a conception of natural law built upon this notion of human nature is not vulnerable to objection from the naturalistic fallacy.[80] Objecting that "ought" cannot be derived from what "is" presumes a conception of nature (what "is") that is by definition non-ethical and non-eschatological. If protological human nature itself cannot be defined apart from the commission to complete a task, however, then any question about human nature is simultaneously and inescapably also a question about natural law.[81]

This biblical-theological conception of human nature may bear resemblance to a conception of human nature derived from evolutionary biology, insofar as both refuse to see human nature as static but rather as historically dynamic. But in contrast to the standard perspective of evolutionary biology, which takes human nature as (primarily) passively caught up in an ongoing and goal-less process of evolutionary flux,[82] the biblical-theological conception identifies a particular historic origin of human nature and the historic attainment of an eschatological goal, and understands this goal to be attained as a consequence of proper human action.[83] This biblical-theological conception

---

than starting with ostensibly universal givens of anthropological science. Neither the Creator nor creation can be named apart from the drama of creation, fall, redemption, and consummation."

80. Critics of natural law from David Hume to the present have complained about the move from "is" to "ought," often thought to be inherent to natural law reasoning. Even a strong proponent of natural law such as Robert George sees the complaint as basically legitimate, and this concession clearly drives his attempt to ground a natural law theory in practical reason without recourse to metaphysics; see *In Defense of Natural Law*, pp. 17, 75, 84-85, 89. A critical reviewer of a couple of my earlier writings on natural law accused me of falling prey to this fallacy, though the accusation was based upon an obvious misreading of one of my arguments. See Nelson D. Kloosterman, "Review Article: *A Biblical Case for Natural Law*," *Ordained Servant* 16 (2007): 101-7; for my response, see David VanDrunen, "VanDrunen in the Hands of an Anxious Kloosterman: A Response to a Review of *A Biblical Case for Natural Law*," *Ordained Servant* 16 (2007): 107-13.

81. For a similar response to charges against natural law, in the context of their own constructive projects, see Burnside, *God, Justice, and Society*, 70-73; Porter, *Nature as Reason*, p. 123; and Boyd, *A Shared Morality*, chap. 6.

82. See e.g. Ernst Mayr, *What Evolution Is* (New York: Basic Books, 2001), chap. 4.

83. This is not to say that we learn nothing about being human from modern biology or even that serious attempts to engage evolutionary biology in the quest to develop a contemporary theory of natural law (such as those of Porter or Boyd) have no value. I do believe, however, that Christian engagement with other disciplines, meant to enrich understanding of human nature or natural law, ought to take place within the general framework of a biblical-theological conception of human nature.

also bears certain resemblances to a classic Thomistic understanding of human nature as teleologically oriented and of human beings as having an ultimately supernatural end. But subtle, though significant, differences exist here too. Whereas the Thomistic understanding posits a human nature that must be perfected by an additional supernatural gift of grace in order to attain its supernatural end, the biblical-theological conception advocated here posits that protological human nature *itself* was oriented toward its eschatological end and that *natural* human abilities were precisely what had to be exercised in order to attain that end.[84] To be sure, this is not because of any ontological parity between God and humanity, but because of the way in which God freely chose to make human beings and because of the nature of his relationship with them which he sovereignly established. I now turn to consider this relationship.

The Covenant of Creation

This book seeks to develop a Christian theology of natural law in the context of the biblical covenants. Thus far, the present chapter has focused upon neither natural law nor the idea of covenant. Following the lengthy discussion of the protological image of God and human nature in the preceding pages, I now consider these two matters, beginning with covenant, as they relate to the story of the original creation told in Genesis 1–2. Though the Hebrew term for covenant, ברית, does not appear in Scripture until Genesis 6:18, classic Reformed theology has understood God's prelapsarian relationship with Adam to be covenantal in nature. In this section, I first briefly outline the historic Reformed understanding of the covenant of creation and show its similarities to my interpretation of the image of God in the preceding pages. Then I defend the decision to characterize God's prelapsarian relationship with Adam as a covenant and argue that this covenant of creation ought to be understood as a covenant of nature and not simply as an arrangement superimposed upon nature. This has significant implications for a doctrine of natural law, which I address specifically in the final section of this chapter.

---

84. Furthermore, whereas the traditional Thomistic conception tends to downplay (though not deny) the bodily and social nature of the supernatural end, I believe a biblical-theological conception must see eschatological human nature as bodily and social at its core. In regard to the Thomistic conception, I think for example of the treatment of the beatific vision in Thomas Aquinas, *Summa Theologiae,* Suppl., 92.1-2. The bodily aspect of eschatological human nature is evident from the many biblical texts that teach a bodily resurrection; its social aspect is also evident in many texts (e.g., Rom. 8:29; Rev. 19:9).

The Features of the Covenant of Creation in Classic Reformed Theology

The Westminster Confession of Faith, one of the traditional secondary standards of Presbyterian churches worldwide since its composition in the mid-seventeenth century, defines the covenant of creation (often referred to as the "covenant of works" or "covenant of life") in the following way: "The first covenant made with man was a covenant of works, wherein life was promised to Adam, and in him to his posterity, upon condition of perfect and personal obedience" (VII.2). This brief statement represents the broad consensus (if not unanimous opinion) among the orthodox Reformed theologians of this era and later centuries, and it bears resemblance to important aspects of my interpretation of the image of God in the preceding pages. To present the basic elements of this classic Reformed doctrine in a little more detail, I use the presentation offered by Herman Witsius (1636-1708) in his *The Economy of the Covenants between God and Man,* one of the most important Reformed works on the biblical covenants. Witsius discussed this covenant under four general headings: its contracting parties, its law or condition, its promises, and its sanctions.

First, Witsius identifies the contracting parties of the covenant as God and Adam, with Adam as "the head and root, or representative of mankind."[85] In this discussion he emphasizes Adam's identity as the image of God. Witsius distinguishes three aspects of the image: "antecedently" it consists in attributes such as the faculties of understanding and will, "formally" it consists in the soul's endowment with righteousness and holiness, and "consequentially" it consists in the immortality of the whole person and dominion over creation.[86] Witsius understands Adam as being in relationship with God as an image-bearer and interprets the image in terms of both what human beings are and what they are to do (and even in terms of their destiny). Thus far the similarity of Witsius's presentation to my interpretation of the image of God in Genesis 1:26-27 is clear.[87]

Second, Witsius considers the law (or condition) of this covenant. He

---

85. Witsius, *Economy of the Covenants,* 1:51.

86. Witsius, *Economy of the Covenants,* 1:57.

87. I did not give great attention above to Adam's role as the representative of the human race, due to limitations of space and the desire to focus upon the most immediately relevant issues. In light of the question of humanity's eschatological destiny this is obviously not an irrelevant issue to the present study, however. Witsius defends Adam's representative office in *Economy of the Covenants,* 1:58-60. For a more recent Reformed defense of this position, see e.g. John Murray, *The Imputation of Adam's Sin* (Grand Rapids: Eerdmans, 1959), chap. 2.

identifies its law or condition as basically twofold, the natural law and what he calls the "symbolical law," that is, the command concerning the tree of the knowledge of good and evil in Genesis 2:16-17. The natural law, he explains, is the rule of good and evil inscribed on the human conscience and binding upon human beings by divine authority, even from creation. Its substance is expressed in the Decalogue and is not arbitrary but grounded in "the very nature of God and man."[88] The "symbolical law" was a probationary test, examining Adam's devotion to God.[89] Adam's obligation before these laws, Witsius continues, was perfect obedience.[90] This emphasis upon human beings having a *natural* moral obligation before God to render *perfect* obedience at creation again resembles my earlier conclusions about the protological image of God. In further discussion below I will draw conclusions similar to Witsius's concerning the legal nature of this obligation, its substantive connection to the Decalogue, and its foundation in God's nature.

Third, Witsius considers the "promises" of this covenant. He states that "God promised Adam life eternal, that is, the most perfect fruition of himself, and that for ever, after finishing his course of obedience."[91] Though he says that the issue "remains doubtful," he concludes that it is "more probable" that this eternal life would have been enjoyed in "heaven" rather than in "paradise."[92] Fourth and finally, he identifies the "penal sanction" of the covenant. The sanction is death, as threatened in Genesis 2:17, and this death includes the death of the body, the miseries of this life, spiritual death (the separation of the soul from God), and eternal death. Witsius is particularly concerned to show how this penalty is consistent with God's justice.[93] His views on the promises and sanction of the covenant are again similar to my treatment of the protological image of God. As image-bearers of God, human beings were to express the likeness of God not only in his earthly working but also in his eschatological resting, and they were also to resemble God in his revelation as a royal judge who renders just verdicts.

In short, my conclusions about the image of God in Genesis 1:26-27 closely resemble the principal features of the classic Reformed doctrine of the covenant of creation, as represented by Witsius. This suggests it is appropriate to consider my treatment of the protological image of God a contempo-

88. Witsius, *Economy of the Covenants*, 1:63-68.
89. Witsius, *Economy of the Covenants*, 1:68.
90. Witsius, *Economy of the Covenants*, 1:69-70.
91. Witsius, *Economy of the Covenants*, 1:73.
92. Witsius, *Economy of the Covenants*, 1:76.
93. Witsius, *Economy of the Covenants*, 1:82-104.

rary expression of the classic Reformed covenant of creation doctrine. Before making this claim conclusively, however, I offer a brief defense of calling the relationship between God and Adam at creation a "covenant," in spite of the absence of the word ברית in Genesis 1–2.

The Original Divine-Human Relationship as a Covenant

The question whether God and humanity were in *covenant* before the fall into sin may seem remote and irrelevant to a theology of natural law. It is true, I believe, that one might agree with all my other substantive claims in this chapter without being convinced of a prelapsarian covenant. Nevertheless, there are good reasons for recognizing such a covenant, and doing so helps to clarify certain important aspects of the account of natural law I am developing in this book. (As a reminder: in the Introduction I described biblical covenants as "solemn and ordinarily oath-bound agreements that establish God and human beings in formal relationships that entail certain obligations for both parties and certain consequences for fidelity or lack thereof.")

The most obvious objection to seeing a covenant in Genesis 1–2 is the absence of the term "covenant" in this text. This has little weight, however, for the OT elsewhere records events not originally described by the word "covenant" but explicitly interpreted as covenants later in biblical history, as even critics of the idea of a prelapsarian covenant recognize.[94]

I mention four reasons for recognizing a covenant in Genesis 1–2. First, and most tenuously, Hosea 6:7 arguably looks back at God's original relationship with Adam and uses the term "covenant" to describe it: "But like Adam they transgressed the covenant; there they dealt faithlessly with me" (Hos. 6:7). Admittedly, this is a contested translation. Scholars have offered different proposals for how to translate כאדם, "like Adam" or "as [at] Adam" being the most likely (Adam was the name of a city on the Jordan River). But writers have provided good arguments for seeing a reference to the man Adam here,[95]

94. E.g., 2 Samuel 7 never refers to God's dealings with David as the establishment of a covenant, but 2 Samuel 23:5 and Psalm 89:19-37 both interpret it as a covenant explicitly. Among critics of the idea of a prelapsarian covenant, this point is recognized, e.g., in Paul R. Williamson, *Sealed with an Oath: Covenant in God's Unfolding Purpose* (Downers Grove, IL: InterVarsity, 2007), p. 58.

95. For a good argument in this direction, and a thorough review of literature on this question, see Byron G. Curtis, "Hosea 6:7 and Covenant-Breaking like/at Adam," in *The Law Is Not of Faith: Essays on Works and Grace in the Mosaic Covenant,* ed. Bryan D. Estelle,

and if this conclusion is sound there is explicit biblical precedent for calling God's original relationship with Adam a "covenant."

Second, the presentation of God as king in Genesis 1:1–2:3 suggests a covenantal reading of this creation account. The relation of the biblical covenants to the ancient Near Eastern suzerainty-vassal treaties has been a vibrant area of OT research over the past several decades. Though many questions in this field of study remain disputed, the significant formal parallels between these treaties and many aspects of the Mosaic covenant (particularly as presented in Deuteronomy) seem undeniable. In the ancient Near East, great kings (suzerains) made treaties with subject peoples (vassals) and these treaties regulated their relationship. In a similar way, God as the great king entered into covenant with his people Israel and governed them by means of documents (the biblical books) that set forth their corresponding expectations and obligations.[96] In context, therefore, God's presenting himself at the beginning of Genesis as the supreme king of creation was not an appeal to an abstract concept. Reading Genesis 1:1–2:3 not as an isolated piece of literature but as the opening of the Pentateuch as a whole thus signals that we are meeting the great *covenant-making* God. He speaks and he puts his creation under obligation to him. Other places in the OT even use covenantal terminology, such as the word "decree" (חק), to describe how God puts the world under his authority at creation. Psalm 148:5-6, for example, addresses the sun, moon, stars, and heavens and says: "Let them praise the name of the Lord! For he commanded and they were created. And he established them forever and ever; he gave a *decree,* and it shall not pass away." Jeremiah 31:35-36, in an allusion to Genesis 1, also uses this language: "Thus says the Lord, who gives the sun for light by day and the fixed order [חקת] of the moon and the stars for light by night. . . . If this fixed order [החקים] departs from before me, declares the Lord, then shall the offspring of Israel cease from being a nation before me forever." In a similar statement two chapters later, Jeremiah actually uses the word "covenant" (ברית) to refer to God's relationship with the day and night, apparently as established at creation (Jer. 33:20-21).[97]

J. V. Fesko, and David VanDrunen (Phillipsburg, NJ: Presbyterian and Reformed, 2009), pp. 170-209.

96. Among early pioneers of research on this topic, see e.g. George E. Mendenhall, *Law and Covenant in Israel and the Ancient Near East* (Pittsburgh: Biblical Colloquium, 1955); Dennis J. McCarthy, *Treaty and Covenant: A Study in Form in the Ancient Oriental Documents and in the Old Testament* (Analecta Biblica 21; Rome: Pontifical Biblical Institute Press, 1963); and Meredith G. Kline, *Treaty of the Great King* (Grand Rapids: Eerdmans, 1963).

97. Many similar claims are made in Middleton, *The Liberating Image,* pp. 65-70.

Third, the remarkable parallels between Genesis 1–2 and God's later dealings with Noah and Israel also suggest reading the creation account in a covenantal light. Scripture explicitly uses the language of covenant to describe God's relationship with both Noah and Israel. Again, given that Genesis 1–2 should not be read as an isolated text but as the beginning of the larger story of the Pentateuch, the fact that the creation account is echoed in later stories of covenant establishment casts a covenantal pall on Genesis 1–2. After Genesis 6–7 recounts the destruction of the original creation by the flood, Genesis 8 depicts the formation of a renewed creation that calls the mind back to the description of the original creation. In addition to a great deal of common vocabulary, Genesis 8 describes a wind/Spirit that blows over the waters, the emergence of dry land, the sprouting of vegetation, a seven-day pattern marking Noah's sending of the dove, and God's attainment of a "rest" (— הניחה 8:21; compare Exod. 20:11). This culminates in the covenant that God makes with all of this restored creation — including human beings, the earth, and all living creatures — in 8:20–9:17, as I explore in Chapter 2.[98] God's entering into a covenant with Israel through Moses also manifests strong parallels with Genesis 1–2. God brings Israel out of Egypt through the waters, he gives them his commands, he places them in a good and prosperous land, he puts them under probation by threatening curses of death and expulsion from the land if they are disobedient (and corresponding blessings if they are obedient), and in the end casts them into exile. The tabernacle and temple are microcosmic representations of the world as a whole and Mount Zion is portrayed as a new Eden.[99] Since these ectypal events later in the biblical story take place in an explicitly covenantal context, it is compelling to interpret the archetypal event as a covenantal event.

Fourth and finally, the kinds of things that characterize covenants elsewhere in Scripture are present in Genesis 1–2. In these chapters God brings human beings into a formal relationship with him, imposes obligations on them,

---

98. Many scholars note this pattern; for helpful summaries of the evidence see e.g. Sarna, *Genesis*, pp. 49-50; and Waltke, *Genesis*, pp. 127-29. Among those exploring the pattern from a Reformed perspective similar to mine, see Kline, *Kingdom Prologue*, pp. 220-24; and Warren Austin Gage, *The Gospel of Genesis: Studies in Protology and Eschatology* (Winona Lake, IN: Carpenter, 1984), chap. 2.

99. Many scholars have also noted these patterns; see e.g. Levenson, *Sinai and Zion*, pp. 111-35. Among Reformed writers see Kline, *Images of the Spirit*, chap. 2; Meredith G. Kline, *God, Heaven and Har Magedon: A Covenantal Tale of Cosmos and Telos* (Eugene, OR: Wipf & Stock, 2006), chap. 5; Beale, *The Temple and the Church's Mission*, chaps. 2-3; and Gage, *The Gospel of Genesis*, pp. 49-58. Also see Chapter 7 of this present volume.

takes obligations upon himself, and identifies consequences for his human partners' response. One might object that this requires seeing "covenant" in such broad terms that it excludes aspects of covenant-making that seem intrinsic to it, such as sealing the relationship with an oath.[100] But biblical covenants in fact take a number of different forms,[101] and so understanding "covenant" in broad terms seems inevitable. And while oath-swearing may indeed be an essential aspect of biblical covenants, many of them do not use the words "oath" or "swear" but simply record solemn words of commitment, command, promise, and/or threat — exactly what we find from God in Genesis 1–2.

As noted at the beginning of this section, one might agree with my other substantive claims in this chapter without recognizing a specifically *covenantal* relationship between God and humanity in Genesis 1–2. But there is considerable evidence for seeing a covenant here, and this clarifies some important aspects of my account of natural law. For one thing, it highlights the organic continuities (alongside the many discontinuities) between God's relationship with humanity before the fall and his explicitly covenantal relationships with human beings after the fall. This is especially true for the Noahic and Mosaic covenants, which echo the covenant of creation in important respects. Recognizing a covenant before the fall, furthermore, helps to demonstrate that the natural law was a personal and historical reality, not an abstract and ahistorical reality, obligating human beings in their historical movement toward an eschatological goal and within a vital *relationship* with God. I also discuss below how the idea of covenant can helpfully modify the Thomistic idea of natural law as participation in God's eternal law.

The Covenant of Creation as a Covenant of Nature

Since my interpretation of the image of God in Genesis 1:26-27 mirrors the chief features of the classic Reformed doctrine of the covenant of creation, it seems accurate to describe my theology of the protological image of God as a contemporary expression of this doctrine. This provokes one final question for this section: Since the image of God constitutes human nature, was the covenant of creation *natural* and, if so, in what sense? Reformed theologians

---

100. E.g., see Williamson, *Sealed with an Oath,* p. 58.

101. For a taxonomy of how various scholars have identified the different types of biblical covenants, see Scott W. Hahn, *Kinship by Covenant: A Canonical Approach to the Fulfillment of God's Saving Promises* (New Haven: Yale University Press, 2009), pp. 28-31.

sometimes referred to this covenant as a "covenant of nature,"[102] and I believe this conclusion is sound and helpful.

I have argued elsewhere that an unresolved ambiguity concerning this issue has lurked within Reformed covenant theology. Many eminent Reformed theologians have argued that human beings by nature knew their moral obligations before God and knew that consequences awaited the outcome of their actions. Some of them explained this by appealing to the image of God.[103] The difficulty arises in their attempt to identify the reason for God's entering into a *covenant* with the human race when there was already this rather full-orbed *natural* relationship between God and human beings. What exactly did the covenant add to their natural relationship, assuming that it was not simply superfluous? Was there some aspect of their obedience to God or some element of the promise or threat that was unknown by nature and needed supernatural specification?[104]

The answer I have proposed is that distinguishing the natural and the covenantal in the opening chapters of Genesis is itself a false move that creates this needless dilemma.[105] It would be better to see the creation of human be-

102. E.g., Witsius writes that this terminology is justified because the covenant is "founded upon and coeval with nature." See *Economy of the Covenants*, 1:64.

103. See David VanDrunen, "Natural Law and the Works Principle under Adam and Moses," in *The Law Is Not of Faith*, pp. 286-89. Among the Reformed sources cited there are the Larger Catechism of Zacharias Ursinus, in Lyle D. Bierma, with Charles D. Gunnoe Jr., Karin Y. Maag, and Paul W. Fields, *An Introduction to the Heidelberg Catechism: Sources, History, and Theology* (Grand Rapids: Baker Academic, 2005), pp. 164-65, 168-69; John Owen, "A Dissertation on Divine Justice," in *The Works of John Owen*, vol. 10, ed. William H. Goold (reprint, Edinburgh: Banner of Truth, 1967), pp. 517-19; John Owen, *The Works of John Owen*, vol. 11, *An Exposition of the Epistle to the Hebrews*, ed. William H. Goold (London/Edinburgh, 1850; Philadelphia: Leighton, 1869), pp. 336-37, 347, 388, 405; Turretin, *Institutes of Elenctic Theology*, 1:575-77; 2:2; Wilhelmus à Brakel, *The Christian's Reasonable Service*, 4 vols., trans. Bartel Elshout (Ligonier, PA: Soli Deo Gloria, 1992-95), 1:357-60; Witsius, *Economy of the Covenants*, 1:71-72; Herman Bavinck, *Reformed Dogmatics*, vol. 2, *God and Creation*, trans. John Vriend, ed. John Bolt (Grand Rapids: Baker, 2004), pp. 564-67; Westminster Confession of Faith, 4.2; Westminster Larger Catechism, 17; and the Irish Articles, 21.

104. See VanDrunen, "Natural Law and the Works Principle," pp. 289-91. Among the Reformed sources cited there are Witsius, *Economy of the Covenants*, 1:76-82; à Brakel, *The Christian's Reasonable Service*, 1:384; Turretin, *Institutes*, 1:574-77; and Bavinck, *Reformed Dogmatics*, 2:564-65, 567, 571-74. See also footnote 67 regarding Geerhardus Vos's claim that the *natural* human state was one of indefinite probation.

105. See VanDrunen, "Natural Law and the Works Principle," p. 291; I am here following the suggestion of Kline, *Kingdom Prologue*, p. 92. See also Michael Horton, *The Christian Faith: A Systematic Theology for Pilgrims on the Way* (Grand Rapids: Zondervan, 2010), p. 332. A different view, though from a generally sympathetic theological perspective, is presented in

ings in God's image *as itself* an act of covenant establishment. As the redemptive act of Christ's crucifixion itself established the new covenant (Matt. 26:28; Mark 14:24; Luke 22:20; Heb. 9:11-28), reflecting the OT precedent of establishing or confirming covenants by a sacrificial act (Gen. 15:7-21; Exod. 24:3-8), so the creative act of making human beings in the divine image, through God's solemn word, established the original covenantal relationship. If my interpretation of the image and likeness of God in the context of Genesis 1–2 is accurate, then there is no element of the covenant of creation, as traditionally understood in Reformed theology, that is not already a constitutive aspect of the human race's natural relationship to God.[106] By their image-bearing nature human beings were morally obligated before God, and by their image-bearing nature they were destined for eschatological life. The absence of any covenant-making ceremony and of the word ברית in Genesis 1–2 may be explained by the fact that humanity's very creation established a covenantal relationship requiring no further establishment or confirmation.

In my judgment there is one aspect of the divine-human relationship described in Genesis 1–2 that possibly calls this conclusion into question. In Genesis 2:15-17 God places Adam in the Garden of Eden with a special command "to work it and keep [guard] it" and to refrain from eating of the tree of the knowledge of good and evil upon the pain of death. The text does not indicate that there is something about this particular geographical location or about the fruit of this particular tree that would have indicated to Adam, simply as a divine image-bearer, that he had special responsibilities toward them. It seems that God provides information and obligation here that Adam could only know by supernatural revelation. This conclusion appears sound, but it does not require rejecting the idea that the covenant of creation was a covenant of nature established in the act of creation itself. The commands of 2:15-17 are best understood, in my judgment, not as *supplementing* Adam's natural moral obligation but as *focusing* it. As I argued earlier in this chapter, the command to work and to guard the Garden served as a concrete test of Adam's general

---

Guy Prentiss Waters, *The Federal Vision and Covenant Theology: A Comparative Analysis* (Phillipsburg, NJ: Presbyterian and Reformed, 2006), pp. 25-26, 42. The Westminster Confession of Faith 7.1 speaks of the divine-human relationship conceived apart from covenant. This could be read in a way consistent with the view that covenant was something added on to creation. I read it to be stating truths somewhat abstractly and theoretically; in any case, it does not affirm that such a noncovenantal state of affairs ever obtained historically.

106. A possible exception is that Adam was representative of the entire human race, though in any case this idea is also not expressed in any of the supernatural words spoken by God to Adam in Genesis 1–2.

and natural obligation to subdue the earth. Likewise, the command to refrain from eating of the tree of the knowledge of good and evil would become a concrete test of his general and natural obligation to exercise dominion over the creatures. The commands of 2:15-17 did reveal something that Adam could not have known simply by his image-bearing nature, although this additional knowledge was not substantive but, we might say, procedural.

In light of these conclusions about the presence of covenant in the opening chapters of Genesis, I believe that the following conclusion is in order: God's creation of human beings in his image and likeness was itself an act establishing a covenant, whose terms would be focused (though not substantively changed or supplemented) in the supernaturally revealed commands of Genesis 2:15-17. This covenant of creation is what Reformed theology has classically understood as the covenant of works.

Natural Law in the Covenant of Creation

We now arrive directly at the main point of the chapter: the identity of natural law in the covenant of creation. In light of the character of the image and likeness of God in Genesis 1:26-27 and of the covenantal context in which God entered into relationship with the human race, I conclude that God, through nature itself, imposed moral obligations upon human beings that are rightly characterized as *natural law,* and that this natural law directed them toward a creative and loving fruitfulness and the exercise of justice, holding out the penalty of death upon disobedience and the promise of life upon obedience.

Natural Moral Obligation, Natural Law

The extended discussion of the protological image of God earlier in this chapter was not a tangential exploration of an important Christian doctrine. If we wish to know what human nature is from a Christian theological perspective then we must know what the image of God is, for Scripture directs us to think of humanness in terms of the image and likeness of God. My conclusions steered away from defining the image of God (and hence human nature) in terms of biological features or rational or moral attributes. Bearing the image of God includes such things, but is hardly exhausted by them. Instead, Genesis 1–3, read on its own terms as well as in light of later biblical interpretation of these chapters, provides a conception of protological human nature that is

86

holistic. It encompasses soul and body and entails both attributes and a commission to exercise dominion toward the attainment of an eschatological goal.

This means that moral obligation is *inherent* to human nature. The common accusation that natural law ethics violates the naturalistic fallacy — deriving "ought" from "is" — raises pressing questions only if nature (what "is") is conceived as basically and essentially *nonmoral*. In such a conception nature simply *is*, and whether nature has anything to do with morality depends upon whether human reason can derive certain obligations from it. A very different conception of human nature emerges from the biblical-theological understanding of the image of God defended in this chapter. Whatever other objections might be leveled against it, this conception cannot be accused of committing the naturalistic fallacy. To know human nature, as situated in the broader natural world, was to know human moral obligation. To bear the image of God was to be commissioned to exercise dominion in this world under God toward the goal of a royal rest. By nature, human beings were called to be kings in knowledge, righteousness, and holiness. Moral obligation, therefore, was not something that human beings could know only from the outside, by positive divine command. Moral obligation was something that human beings could know by knowing themselves, in relation to the world around them. And yet this natural moral knowledge was in no sense autonomous, for God was the covenantal creator of human nature and he oriented his image-bearers toward communion with himself. Natural moral obligation derived from God and directed to God.

Admittedly, Genesis 1–2 does not explain *how* human beings naturally know these things, and I do not wish to force an epistemological theory upon the text. We will have to keep this issue in mind and return to it in subsequent chapters.

Are the protological natural moral obligations rightly termed *law?* If we are not captive to modern positivistic conceptions, in which only explicit commands of the legislator, enshrined in statutes, are rightly regarded as "law," then describing natural human moral obligation as natural law is entirely appropriate. In classic Christian theology "law" could refer to an ordering principle (whether written or not), deriving from one in authority, directing a person or thing toward a fitting end. Thomas's theology of law provides a prominent example.[107] In the Anglo-American legal tradition, the common law was a body of unwritten

---

107. See e.g. Aquinas, *Summa Theologiae*, 1a2ae 90. Rémi Brague offers helpful comments on Thomas's view of law as order in *The Law of God: The Philosophical History of an Idea*, trans. Lydia G. Cochrane (Chicago: University of Chicago Press, 2007), p. 224. See also relevant discussion in Budziszewski, *The Line Through the Heart*, pp. 10-17.

rules of conduct embodied in, but not reducible to, relevant judicial precedents.[108] In neither classic Christian theology nor the common law tradition could law be identified with a series of written statutes. The idea of law as an ordering principle, by which someone in authority directs a person toward a fitting end, seems highly fitting to describe the natural moral obligation ingrained in the protological image of God. This natural moral obligation derives from God, the supreme king of creation, it orders human conduct in this world, and it directs human beings toward the attainment of an eschatological goal.

This idea of seeing natural law in Genesis 1–2 in terms of an ordering principle gains further plausibility from the many things I have noted that link these chapters to the biblical wisdom literature.[109] The idea of wisdom, in Proverbs particularly, involves the perception of a natural moral order and the skill to structure one's life effectively and fruitfully within its bounds.[110] As I explore in some detail in Chapter 7 and especially Chapter 8, law (an objective reality) and wisdom (its subjective apprehension) are not the same thing, yet each should be understood in relation to the other. Biblical law is given in part to build wisdom in its recipients, while wisdom is necessary to interpret and apply (the always noncomprehensive) biblical law. In short, the subtle yet pervasive wisdom theme in Genesis 1–2 points to the presence of a natural moral order, to be understood and honored through the judicial task of discerning "good and evil." This natural moral order is what I have in mind by referring to natural law in the covenant of creation.

Two other brief points provide some linguistic rationale for seeing natu-

---

108. Among classic studies of the common law, see Arthur R. Hogue, *The Origins of the Common Law* (Bloomington: Indiana University Press, 1966); and Theodore F. T. Plunckett, *A Concise History of the Common Law,* 5th ed. (Boston: Little, Brown & Co., 1956).

109. In addition to the positive links between wisdom in Proverbs and the divine and human work in Genesis 1–2, there are many negative links between the conception of folly in Proverbs and the conduct of Adam, Eve, and the serpent in Genesis 3. For several examples, see Walter Brueggemann, *In Man We Trust: The Neglected Side of Biblical Faith* (Atlanta: John Knox, 1972), pp. 56-57. These negative links, by implication, strengthen the evidence for the positive links.

110. Understood in this way, the natural law leaves a broad scope for human freedom to shape societies and cultures in a variety of wholesome ways. There is not a single proper cultural expression of natural law morality. This raises further important questions about how wide this discretionary scope is and where the boundaries of the natural moral order precisely lie, questions explored, e.g., by Jean Porter in "Does the Natural Law Provide a Universally Valid Morality?" in *Intractable Disputes about the Natural Law: Alasdair MacIntyre and Critics,* ed. Lawrence S. Cunningham (Notre Dame: University of Notre Dame Press, 2009), pp. 53-95. See Chapter 10 of the present volume for further comment.

ral *law* in the covenant of creation. First, Scripture uses the Greek term "law," νόμος, in Romans 2:14-15 to refer to natural human moral obligation in the postlapsarian condition (see Chapter 5 for detailed discussion of this text). Thus, for Christian readers there seems little reason to refuse to use the term for natural human moral obligation before the fall. Second, the command in Genesis 2:17 uses common Hebrew legal language.[111] If, as argued above, 2:17 is not simply an arbitrary divine command but a focusing of the general dominion mandate (1:26, 28) given to human beings as image-bearers, then the fact that the command in 2:17 is overtly legal in nature indicates that their natural obligation and relationship toward God bore a legal character.

In light of these considerations — which reflect understandings of "law" in the Christian natural law tradition, the Anglo-American common law tradition, and the biblical literature — the general human moral obligations inherent to those bearing the protological image of God are appropriately termed natural law. "The law does not simply stand over against the creature as a heteronomous authority, but belongs to the creature's own identity. The law of God and the image of God are therefore two sides of the same coin."[112] Or as the Westminster Larger Catechism (17) puts it, "After God had made all other creatures, he created man male and female . . . , made them after his own image, in knowledge, righteousness, and holiness; having the law of God written in their hearts, and power to fulfill it, and dominion over the creatures. . . ."[113] This conclusion is not meant to deny that God gave commands to the first human beings by special revelation as well, as indicated in Genesis 1:28 and 2:16-17, but it does imply that what God specially revealed must have

---

111. For one thing, the grammatical form of the command — לֹא תֹאכַל — is a common way for the OT to state particular laws. It is the same form used to express most of the commands of the Decalogue in Exodus 20:4-17, for example. Furthermore, adding a sanction through a motive clause after the command — "for in the day that you eat of it you shall surely die" — is also common in biblical legal literature. For further discussion of the legal tenor of the command in Genesis 2:17, see Vlachos, *The Catalytic Operation*, pp. 134-35; and Bryan D. Estelle, "The Covenant of Works in Moses and Paul," in *Covenant, Justification, and Pastoral Ministry: Essays by the Faculty of Westminster Seminary California*, ed. R. Scott Clark (Phillipsburg, NJ: Presbyterian and Reformed, 2007), pp. 110-12.

112. Horton, *Lord and Servant*, pp. 101-2. This quotation comes from a description of earlier Reformed understanding of the image of God, though it also expresses Horton's own view.

113. Or as the Lutheran theologian Johannes Brenz wrote, commenting on Genesis 2:16-17, God "did not recite the Decalogue because it had already been engraved on creation for Adam: he understood it well and intelligently, and he took pleasure especially in observing it. This is natural law. . . ." See *Genesis 1–11*, Reformation Commentary, p. 90.

resonated with what they knew by nature. The voice of God in the ear echoed and clarified the voice of God in the heart and mind.

Natural Law and the Divine Nature

Did this natural law actually reflect God's own moral nature?[114] In the Christian tradition some writers (in the intellectualist trajectory) have argued that the natural law does indeed reflect God's moral nature and hence necessarily takes the form it does. Other writers (in the voluntarist trajectory) have argued that natural law is the product of God's will and not necessarily of his nature, and thus that God could have made the world differently and could have made at least some of the precepts of the natural law the opposite of what they in fact are (for example, God might have *required* stealing or lying in the natural law).[115]

The approach to natural law pursued in this chapter suggests an answer to this question (especially in light of my treating natural law as divine revelation — that is, *natural* revelation in distinction from God's *special* revelation through the spoken or written prophetic word). Since protological human nature was defined by the image and likeness of God, natural human moral obligation must have reflected God's nature, but reflected it *as revealed in the covenant of creation.* There is no direct knowledge of God as he is in himself. What humans know about God they know through his revelation of himself, and this revelation comes in covenantal relationship.[116] In the covenant of creation God revealed himself in a certain way. Christians trust that this revelation was true, but it was certainly not exhaustive; the covenant of creation does not

114. By God's "nature" I refer to those characteristics or attributes Scripture ascribes to him, and particularly here his *moral* attributes. God's nature, unlike human nature, is not derived from outside himself. Yet Scripture portrays God as unable to act against his own character; for example, he cannot lie (Titus 1:2; Heb. 6:18).

115. Reformed writers have taken various positions, and they resemble the range of views in medieval theology. From his mid-seventeenth-century vantage point Francis Turretin identified three principal views among the Reformed, and adopted a view leaning in the intellectualist direction; see *Institutes of Elenctic Theology,* 2:9-12.

116. Thus, while Wolterstorff addresses a legitimate concern in broader context, his speaking of God having moral obligations toward us prior to making covenants with us is something of an abstraction. What knowledge of God do we have apart from what he has revealed in covenantal relationship? See *Justice,* pp. 283-84. For further discussion of this point, along lines similar to my own, see C. Scott Pryor, "Looking for Bedrock: Accounting for Human Rights in Classical Liberalism, Modern Secularism, and the Christian Tradition," *Campbell Law Review* 33, no. 3 (2011): 632-38.

reveal everything there is to know about God. These considerations put old medieval and Reformation-era debates in perspective. Protological natural law reflected God's nature, but it reflected God's nature not absolutely — i.e., God's nature as it is in itself — but as revealed in a particular covenant relationship, the covenant of creation. This means that though protological natural law reflected God's nature (because God's covenantal revelation of himself is true) there is not necessarily only one form that natural law can take. If God would establish a different covenant relationship with the natural order and reveal himself in a different way in this covenant, then natural law would presumably take a different form, reflecting this new revelation of God. (Presumably this new covenantal revelation about God and natural law would not *contradict* the revelation about God and natural law under the covenant of creation, even if they would not be identical to each other.) In the next chapter, I argue that this is precisely what transpires in the covenant with Noah in Genesis 8:20–9:17.

Thus, on the one hand, the Thomistic tradition is correct to assert, over against voluntaristic conceptions, that the natural law is rooted in the divine nature. Yet, on the other hand, I suggest it would be better to express this not through the idea of the rational mind's participation in the eternal law of the divine mind, but through God's natural revelation of himself in a concrete covenant relationship. Human "participation" in God's government of the world is mediated by covenant.

Creative and Loving Fruitfulness

The moral substance of the protological natural law, reflecting the revelation of God's own moral nature, may be summarized in a twofold manner. First, the protological natural law required creative and loving fruitfulness. The original image-bearers had an obligation by nature to express creativity and love in imitation of God's fruitfulness in fashioning the world. Here I recap my previous discussion of the issue and suggest how we might define this fruitfulness in a recognizably legal form.

When he created this world God exercised supreme creativity and fruitfulness, calling all things into being and putting them in their proper order. In doing so he did not selfishly hoard the goods of creation for his own solitary enjoyment, but displayed an abundance, bounty, and generosity in enriching his handiwork and entrusting it with responsibilities. Human dominion, if it was to reflect the divine dominion, would reflect this loving and generous rule of God. Many Christian theological traditions have looked to the Decalogue as a written expression of the natural law.[117] While its particular historical context determines the particular form in which the Decalogue is communicated in Exodus 20 and Deuteronomy 5, the substantive principles underlying the Decalogue do, I believe, provide a helpful summary of the fruitfulness that the first human beings were obligated to display under the protological natural law.

In the first three commandments (on the traditional Reformed numbering), for example, God instructs people to render him proper worship and honor, and this was inherent in the nature of the protological image. Human beings were bound first and foremost to show proper love and generosity toward God himself. The very identity of human nature as not self-defining but an image and likeness of God implies proper subordination under him. Human beings were not made lords of creation, but vice-lords under the Creator to whom all homage is due. Human beings were to name many things in creation as an expression of their rightful authority, but as vice-lords they had no authority to name God, who alone can name himself and prescribe how his name is used. In the fourth commandment the pattern of work and rest is explicitly grounded in the image of God in creation, and highlights the purposeful productivity that was to characterize protological human existence. This fruitfulness toward the Creator, summarized in the first through fourth commandments, was also to overflow to the creation, summarized in the fifth through tenth commandments. As God exercised benevolent authority over creation, so also human beings were to exercise benevolent authority over creation as God entrusted it to them (Gen. 1:26, 28). As God created and sustained life in this world, so human beings were to be fruitful as procreators, sharing and extending the gift of life to new generations (1:28). As God entered into covenant relationship with his human creation in bonds of fidelity, so human beings were to live in harmonious social relationship with one another, as exemplified most profoundly in the mutually beneficial and intimate union of marriage (1:27; 2:20-24). As God expressed his ownership over this world by fashioning, naming, and commanding it, so human beings became able to claim ownership of the creatures of the world (though under God's ultimate ownership) (1:26, 28-29) and to claim possession of the land of Eden in particular as a place upon which to pour their labors (2:15).[118] As God spoke true

117. One might observe that Thomas Aquinas, Martin Luther, and John Calvin all made this basic assertion. E.g., see Aquinas, *Summa Theologiae* 1a2ae 100.1; 100.3; Martin Luther, "How Christians Should Regard Moses," in *Luther's Works*, vol. 35, ed. E. Theodore Bachmann (Philadelphia: Fortress, 1960), pp. 172-73; and John Calvin, *Institutes of the Christian Religion*, 2.8.1.

118. Many Christian theologians have been skeptical of the idea of *private* property

and productive words in calling things into being and assigning them names, so human beings were to promote truth and enrich the rest of creation by their speech (2:19-20). And as God himself freely showered his bounty upon creation, so human beings called to do likewise could not simultaneously covet the goods of others.

The protological natural law, therefore, can be expressed and summarized in the substantive principles underlying the Decalogue. Natural law in the covenant of creation directed human beings to abound in creative and loving generosity toward God and toward their fellow creatures. Loving God and neighbor was part of human moral obligation from the very beginning. But this love prescribed in the protological natural law (like the love prescribed in the Decalogue) did not include the obligation to show mercy or to forgive. Considering the second aspect of the moral content of protological natural law explains why.

The Pursuit of Justice

The second substantive aspect of protological natural law is the obligation to pursue proportionate retributive justice. (As discussed above, I do not mean to ignore or deny the obligation to *primary* justice, without which the obligation to retributive justice would make no sense, but this former obligation seems encompassed in my description of creative and loving fruitfulness in the previous section.) Earlier in the chapter I discussed this issue in terms of divine dominion and how it was to be reflected in human dominion. Genesis 1–2 reveals God as a royal legislator and judge and announces that God will enforce his law, mentioning no provision for atonement or forgiveness. One sin was all it took to provoke God's judgment. Human beings were ordained to live with God in the royal rest of the seventh day, but God consigned them to death upon commission of their crime. Genesis 1–2 itself reveals God's justice not as indulgent and lenient but as strict and proportionate.[119] If the first hu-

---

before the Fall. I see no compelling reason for such skepticism, but am content to leave that question open here.

119. The fact that mercy did enter the picture in Genesis 3 after the fall may seem to belie my claim. I would affirm that the full manifestation of God's retributive justice was delayed, but the subsequent biblical story teaches that it will be made manifest at the final judgment (as proleptically portrayed at various times in biblical history, such as in the great flood and the destruction of Sodom). Scripture also teaches subsequently that God provides a way of salvation from this judgment, but this way of salvation was not itself revealed in Genesis 1–2. These issues will arise again in later chapters, beginning in Chapter 2.

man beings were to reflect God's image and likeness in matters of justice, then presumably they also should have exercised such retributive justice in matters under their jurisdiction. The one specific judicial controversy explicitly under their jurisdiction in Genesis 1–3 — regarding the tree of the knowledge of good and evil and the serpent's temptation — seems to confirm this conclusion. Adam and Eve showed the serpent plenty of lenience and indulgence, but sinned in failing to bring retribution against the serpent, who had compromised the holiness of the Garden God commanded them to guard.

The relationship between love and justice — particularly as concepts of mercy and forgiveness threaten to drive a wedge between them — is a perennial controversy in ethics and will be a recurring topic in this book. For now my claim is that *in the covenant of creation,* according to the moral obligation inherent in the *protological image of God,* natural law prescribed a love that was bountiful and generous but not merciful and forgiving, precisely because this natural law also prescribed an exacting retributive justice. Justice, in all its aspects, is a good that must be upheld (which ultimately remains true even when mercy and forgiveness enter the picture later in the biblical story).[120] The eschatological orientation of the covenant of creation and the protological natural law may be helpful to keep in mind. Under the covenant of creation, natural law was designed to lead to finality and to bring closure. It was meant to govern this world decisively: Would human beings fulfill their commission and enter into God's seventh-day rest, or not? Protological natural law was not designed to maintain a provisional or precarious justice but to provide a clear answer to this question. As we will see in the next chapter, however, a different analysis of natural law and the justice it upholds is required after the fall into sin and the establishment of the covenant with Noah.

---

120. In subsequent chapters I will explain how I believe the relationship of love and justice under the covenant of common grace and the covenants of grace differs from their relationship as I have just articulated it under the covenant of creation. Some of the most learned and helpful books on the relationship of love and justice written by Christian ethicists in recent years do not, in my judgment, satisfactorily identify the uniqueness of God's *redemptive* love but conflate it with God's general love exhibited in creation. Among works I have in mind are Eric Gregory, *Politics & the Order of Love: An Augustinian Ethic of Democratic Citizenship* (Chicago: University of Chicago Press, 2008); and Timothy P. Jackson, *The Priority of Love: Christian Charity and Social Justice* (Princeton: Princeton University Press, 2003). The very end of a book I have cited often in this chapter also conflates God's creative and redemptive love without identifying distinctions between them; see Middleton, *The Liberating Image,* p. 297. I will also interact subsequently with Nicholas Wolterstorff's *Justice in Love* (Grand Rapids: Eerdmans, 2011), especially in Chapter 9, and particularly with respect to his claims about retributive justice and Christian love.

CHAPTER 2

Natural Law under the Noahic Covenant

The previous chapter developed a theology of natural law in the original creation, during the state of human integrity before the fall into sin. Building primarily upon exegesis of Genesis 1–2, I argued that the original creation, including human nature, was eschatologically oriented. As God himself labored in this world and then entered his triumphant rest on the seventh day, so he made human beings to image him by exercising faithful dominion under his ultimate authority in the original creation and then to join him in triumphant rest in a consummated new creation. Against this background I concluded that natural law did not consist of static deontological principles but was a moral order by which God normatively oriented human beings for a creatively fruitful life in exercising righteous royal dominion in this world toward the eschatological goal. This implies that the protological natural law of the original creation was never intended to endure in unchanging form forever. A natural law meant to direct human beings toward a goal could not continue to obligate them in identical ways if they attained the goal. Presumably, God designed natural law to be consummated along with the consummation of human nature and creation as a whole.

As it turned out, the divine image-bearers did not faithfully complete their commission and thus God did not bless them with eschatological consummation. But neither did he destroy his creation. Instead, God preserved this world in fallen condition and ordained a different kind of human history to unfold.

In this chapter I begin to describe the character and purpose of natural law in this fallen but preserved creation. Though this chapter does not attempt to define exhaustively what this natural law is, it lays crucial foundation for all the chapters that follow. Here I continue to reject the bifurcation of the "natural" and the "covenantal," arguing instead that God now maintains and governs nature precisely through a covenant relationship, specifically the covenant with Noah enacted after the great flood (Gen. 8:20–9:17). The present chapter examines this covenant and how it serves as the means by which God promulgates the natural law and thereby governs the entire human race in its fallen condition. The remaining chapters in Part 1 (Chapters 3-5) fill in and round out the basic conclusions of this chapter by examining many texts through the rest of Scripture that describe God's dealings with the nations of the world under the natural law. Then in Part 2 I consider the significance of this natural law for the chosen people with whom God has entered redemptive covenant relationships.

My basic argument in this chapter is that God established the post-diluvian Noahic covenant with all of creation and thus with the entire human race. By this covenant God preserves (but does not redeem) the world and maintains human beings in his image, and thereby continues to promulgate natural law. This natural law is in organic continuity with the natural law of the original creation, but as refracted through the covenant with Noah. It too is a *protological* natural law, in that it regulates human life in this present (nonconsummated) created order. Genesis 8:20–9:17 indicates that this natural law communicates at least a bare minimalist ethic designed to promote the maintenance of human society, though the text also implicitly suggests that natural law is a broader moral order that directs fallen human beings toward a constructive cultural task and reveals their ultimate accountability to God himself, a suggestion confirmed in later chapters. Grounding natural law in the covenant with Noah furthers my goal (also the goal of many other contemporary Christian natural law theorists) of providing a theologically based and biblically rich account of natural law that is in no sense associated with illusions of *autonomous* human reason. Yet by portraying natural law as a divinely ordained moral standard that obligates all human beings, whatever their religious profession, this account also suggests that natural law should be *theologically* interpreted though it does not provide a *uniquely Christian* ethic grounded in Christ's work of redemption.

This chapter first discusses some preliminary issues setting my discussion of the Noahic covenant in its biblical and theological context. Second, I describe the principal features of the Noahic covenant through a detailed exegetical study. Third, I identify the human responsibilities established in the Noahic covenant. Finally, I defend the specific conclusion that the Noahic covenant is a covenant of nature and that, as such, it establishes and regulates a natural law that continues to be morally obligatory for the entire human race until the end of the world at Christ's second coming. Interested readers may see Appendix 5 for reflection on how my understanding of the Noahic covenant and natural law compares to the idea of the Noahide laws in traditional Jewish ethics.

Biblical and Theological Background to the Noahic Covenant

Genesis 3 records the story of humanity's fall into sin and God's judgment in response. Though the first couple's disobedience to their commission prohibited attainment of the new creation, God did not destroy the original creation or his human image-bearers. Instead, he preserved them, in fallen form. Human beings would enjoy many good things in the world (such as procreation and harvesting crops from the earth), but also experience God's curse in these very things (through painful childbirth and agricultural toil) (Gen. 3:16-19). Bodily death would mark the end of each person's journey in this world (3:19), but the promise of a coming "offspring" of "the woman" provided initial hope that God's original purpose for creation — the attainment of a consummated new creation — might somehow be achieved after all. Genesis 4:1–6:4 describes the early history of this world that God preserves in fallen form, a history marked by both great injustice and the advance of civilization — the latter, apparently, largely achieved by the line of unbelieving Cain rather than by the godly line of Seth (4:20-22). God brought this initial stage of history to a drastic end through the judgment of the great flood (Gen. 6:5–7:24), but then took away the flood waters (8:1-19) and resumed human history in its fallen but preserved form, this time through a formal covenant (8:20–9:17).

What has become of the image of God and human nature in this preserved but fallen condition? Scripture indicates that human beings retain their reason and will. Scripture (in the Noahic covenant, for example) also continues to call human beings the image of God and to regard them as responsible for exercising benevolent rule in this world under God's ultimate authority. Yet Scripture simultaneously describes them as corrupt in all their attributes and activities. "Every intention of the thoughts of [their] heart was only evil continually" (Gen. 6:5); "although they knew God, they did not honor him as God or give thanks to him, but they became futile in their thinking, and their foolish hearts were darkened" (Rom. 1:21). Therefore it seems best, I suggest, to speak not of human beings having *lost* the image (as if God took away some constitutive faculty or moral responsibility from them) but of human beings as *corrupted* image-bearers. Instead of properly exercising their constitutive faculties in the service of royal dominion, they reason poorly, will badly, and therefore rule destructively. They are unable to fulfill Adam's original commission and thus to attain the new creation through faithful obedience to God. Yet, as considered at length below, by God's restraining providence they are able to achieve much that is genuinely, though penultimately, good through the exercise of their fallen reason and will. In short, fallen human beings retain the image of God and hence their nature, but no longer use their gifts or exercise their responsibilities well.

In the Introduction I suggested that it is best not to say that grace-perfects-nature (as do Thomists) or grace-restores-nature (as do neo-Calvinists). Instead, a better short formula is twofold: (common)-grace-preserves-nature and (saving)-grace-consummates-nature. The remainder of Part 1 focuses upon the former, while Part 2 addresses the latter. My argument here in Chapter 2 is that the Noahic covenant with all creation after the flood was a covenant of *common grace* — common in the sense that God bestows this grace indiscriminately, among the godly and the ungodly. This covenant is God's means for preserving the original creation; or, to put it another way, this covenant is God's means for preserving nature — human nature as well as of other created things — but not for bringing the original creation to its consummation through a work of salvation.

Despite their considerable attention to the important Old Testament (OT) theme of covenant generally, biblical scholars have devoted relatively little work to the covenant with Noah. L. Dequeker noted this dearth of scholarship in an article on the Noahic covenant back in 1972, and apparently little has changed, for James Barr and Katharine Dell made similar observations in 2003 and Aaron Chalmers in 2009.[1] Perhaps, as some of them speculate, the main covenantal action-line in the OT concerns the relationship of God and Israel, and that is seemingly not the concern of Genesis 9.[2] Yet even a major

---

1. See L. Dequeker, "Noah and Israel: The Everlasting Divine Covenant with Mankind," in *Questions disputées d'Ancien Testament: Méthode et théologie*, ed. C. Brekelmans (Leuven: Leuven University Press, 1972), p. 115; James Barr, "Reflections on the Covenant with Noah," in *Covenant as Context: Essays in Honour of E. W. Nicholson*, ed. A. D. H. Mayes and R. B. Salters (Oxford: Oxford University Press, 2003), p. 11; Katharine J. Dell, "Covenant and Creation in Relationship," in *Covenant as Context,* p. 111; and Aaron Chalmers, "The Importance of the Noahic Covenant to Biblical Theology," *Tyndale Bulletin* 60, no. 2 (2009): 207-8.

2. One scholar explicitly recognizing the fundamental importance of this covenant for the larger biblical story is Daniel J. Elazar, *Covenant & Polity in Biblical Israel: Biblical Foundations & Jewish Expressions* (New Brunswick, NJ: Transaction, 1995), p. 111: "Genesis 9 is one of the key chapters of the whole Bible, describing as it does the first covenant between God and man and the foundation for the moral obligations of all humans. It is also the chapter in which,

study such as Robert Murray's *The Cosmic Covenant,* which looks far beyond the borders of ancient Israel and seeks to find a theology of creation in the OT covenants relevant for contemporary problems such as ecology, gives little explicit attention to the postdiluvian covenant.[3] Given that the Noahic covenant has been of minor concern to biblical scholars, it is little surprise that recent natural law theorists — even those with particular interest in the relation of natural law to biblical revelation — have not explored it. Yet Genesis 8:20–9:17 raises many matters potentially relevant for an understanding of natural law, including the stability of the natural order, the continuation of human society through procreation and pursuit of justice, and the image of God.

Though I do not follow any one particular exegete or theologian in my reading of Genesis 8:20–9:17, I am indebted to an interpretive tradition within Reformed covenant theology. This tradition takes the Noahic covenant not as one of the covenants of redemptive grace (such as the Abrahamic, Mosaic, and new covenants), but as a distinct covenant of preservation (or common grace).[4] In this chapter I seek to apply this understanding of the Noahic covenant to the question of natural law. I agree with the claim of a recent Reformed

according to the Talmud, the principle of formal government was introduced as one of God's seven commandments and part of His covenant with Noah. In essence, it is the chapter that describes the new foundation of the postdiluvian earth on a more formal and structured basis."

3. See Robert Murray, *The Cosmic Covenant: Biblical Themes of Justice, Peace and the Integrity of Creation* (London: Sheed & Ward, 1992). Pages 32-38 and 101-2 contain brief discussion of the covenant with Noah.

4. E.g., see Herman Witsius, *The Economy of the Covenants between God and Man: Comprehending a Complete Body of Divinity,* 2 vols., trans. William Crookshank (1822; reprint, Phillipsburg, NJ: Presbyterian and Reformed, 1990), 2:239 (originally published in 1677); Wilhelmus à Brakel, *The Christian's Reasonable Service,* 4 vols., trans. Bartel Elshout (Ligonier, PA: Soli Deo Gloria, 1992-95), 4:384 (originally published in 1700); A. Kuyper, *De Gemeene Gratie* (Kampen: J. H. Kok, 1945), pp. 11-100 (originally published in 1902-04); Herman Bavinck, *Reformed Dogmatics,* vol. 3, *Sin and Salvation in Christ,* trans. John Vriend (Grand Rapids: Baker, 2006), pp. 218-19 (originally published in 1895-1901); Geerhardus Vos, *Biblical Theology: Old and New Testaments* (Grand Rapids: Eerdmans, 1949), pp. 56, 62-63; Meredith G. Kline, *Kingdom Prologue: Genesis Foundations for a Covenantal Worldview* (Overland Park, KS: Two Age Press, 2000), pp. 164, 244-62; and Michael Horton, *God of Promise* (Grand Rapids: Baker, 2006), chap. 6. Among recent Reformed writers who interpret the Noahic covenant as redemptive as well as preservative, see O. Palmer Robertson, *The Christ of the Covenants* (Phillipsburg, NJ: Presbyterian and Reformed, 1980), chap. 7; and Mark D. Vander Hart, "Creation and Covenant: Part One," *Mid-America Journal of Theology* 6, no. 1 (1990): 10-13. John Murray does not treat the Noahic covenant as specifically redemptive, but in emphasizing its noncontractual and gracious character he suggests that it could be seen as providing "the essential features of a divine covenant with men"; see *The Covenant of Grace: A Biblico-Theological Study* (1953; Phillipsburg, NJ: Presbyterian and Reformed, 1988), pp. 12-16.

theologian who, though never developing a natural law theory, saw "universal natural revelation" as grounded in God's "common grace covenanting" in Genesis 8:20–9:17.[5]

This approach to natural law in the present world, I believe, makes several helpful contributions to a biblical theology of natural law. First, by grounding natural law in God's covenantal action, it refutes the idea that natural law implies human moral autonomy. Second, it provides an explicitly biblical description of the divine origins of natural law. Third, rooting the natural law of the present world in the Noahic covenant, rather than in the covenant of creation, provides a conception of natural law that accounts for the fall, the reality of human sin, and the curse on nature.[6] The Noahic covenant, unlike the covenant of creation, was designed for a fallen world rather than a sinless world. Fourth, by grounding natural law in the Noahic covenant, rather than in the covenants of redemptive grace, my conception ensures that natural law is both universal and nonredemptive. This covenant communicates a law that fosters preservation of this world, not a gospel or a way of life fit for the new heavens and new earth.

The Characteristics of the Noahic Covenant

Specifying several characteristics of the Noahic covenant provides important background for subsequent examination of its moral obligations for human beings and its relationship to natural law. Thus in this section I identify the parameters, duration, scope, and purpose of this covenant.

The Parameters of the Noahic Covenant

Many scholars believe that the postdiluvian Noahic covenant consists only of the material found in Genesis 9:8-17. Standard critical scholarship assigns

---

5. Kline, *Kingdom Prologue*, p. 261.

6. Thus, while I would agree with Michael S. Horton's statement that unbelievers continue to "stand in a personal covenantal relation to God," I believe it would be better to identify the primary ground for their image-bearing as the Noahic covenant rather than "the original covenant of creation." See *Lord and Servant: A Covenant Christology* (Louisville: Westminster John Knox, 2005), p. 118. Given what Horton says elsewhere about the Noahic covenant in *God of Promise*, chap. 6, however, there seems to be little substantive difference between us on these matters.

8:20-22 to J (the Yahwist author) and then 9:1-17 to P (the Priestly author), but many writers think the latter consists of two distinct sections, 9:1-7 and 9:8-17. Regardless of one's views on the sources underlying the text, the text itself presents plausible reasons for dividing 8:20–9:17 into three distinct sections and identifying only the last with the covenant itself. Genesis 9:1-7 is marked by an *inclusio*, beginning and ending with the command to "be fruitful and multiply" and fill the earth, and it appears to have an internal coherence and integrity as it regulates human and animal conduct in the postdiluvian world. Furthermore, there is also an *inclusio* of sorts in 9:8-17, whose opening and closing verses begin with the statement "God said to Noah." Most strikingly, the word "covenant" appears numerous times in 9:8-17 but is absent in the previous verses.[7] In addition, 8:20-22 describes events distinct from what transpires in both 9:1-7 and 9:8-17. For example, 8:21-22 records what God says "in his heart" — in other words, he talks to himself. In contrast, both 9:1 and 9:8 announce that God speaks "to Noah and [to] his sons."[8]

Despite the plausibility of these arguments for associating the post-diluvian Noahic covenant with Genesis 9:8-17 only, weighty counter-considerations commend taking the entirety of 8:20–9:17 as delineating the covenant. First is the substantive similarity across the sections. For example, though some different Hebrew vocabulary is used in 8:20-22 and 9:8-17, the substance of what God says to himself in the former closely resembles what he says to Noah in the latter. In 8:21-22 God states his intention neither to curse the *ground* nor to *strike down every living creature* while the *earth* endures. In 9:9-11, in comparison, God tells Noah that, by the terms of the covenant between him and *every living creature,* he will never again send a flood to *destroy the earth* or to *cut off all flesh.* What God publicly commits himself to in 9:8-17 is substantively the same as what God internally committed himself to in 8:21-22. If 9:8-17 is explicitly covenantal, then 8:20-22 is at least a prologue to the covenant. Genesis 8:20-22 is therefore an important aid in interpreting the covenantal words spoken to Noah, disclosing the intention behind the

---

7. James Barr, a proponent of limiting the postdiluvian covenant to 9:8-17, emphasizes this lack of "covenant" language in 9:1-7, especially since it is assigned to P, who uses the term so profusely in the immediately following verses; see "Reflections on the Covenant with Noah," pp. 19-22.

8. The arguments for this case and citations of scholarly proponents have been summarized in Steven D. Mason, "Another Flood? Genesis 9 and Isaiah's Broken Eternal Covenant," *JSOT* 32, no. 2 (2007): 180-83. The arguments of this article were subsumed within the author's subsequent monograph: Steven D. Mason, *"Eternal Covenant" in the Pentateuch: The Contours of an Elusive Phrase* (New York: T. & T. Clark, 2008), pp. 66-87.

proclamation.[9] Second, significant features of the text unite 9:8-17 with 9:1-7. Stephen Mason has argued, for example, that the language of ואתם ("and you" or "as for you") . . . ואני ("and I" or "as for me") (9:7, 9) is a common OT construction for linking the responsibilities of two parties in a single discourse, often in a covenantal context. Mason points especially to God's covenant with Abraham in Genesis 17, where the language אני . . . ואתם (17:4, 9) sets forth first God's commitments and then Abraham's responsibilities. In Genesis 9, the two supposedly separate sections, 9:1-7 and 9:8-17, are united by this linguistic construction. Thus, though "covenant" is not explicitly mentioned until 9:9, the preceding verses seem to enunciate the terms of the covenant.[10]

Since these thematic and linguistic features link the three sections of 8:20–9:17, I read this as a unified text presenting the postdiluvian Noahic covenant. Genesis 8:21-22 records God's subjectively expressed commitments, 9:1-7 records his blessing upon humanity and its obligations, and 9:8-17 records God's public commitments in explicitly covenantal terms. Identifying the features of this covenant, therefore, requires consideration of evidence drawn from 8:20–9:17 in its entirety.

The Duration of the Noahic Covenant

Genesis 8:22 identifies the duration of the postdiluvian Noahic covenant: "*While the earth remains,* seedtime and harvest, cold and heat, summer and winter, day and night, shall not cease." The terse statement in 8:22 indicates that this covenant will last as long as the earth, which in turn suggests that the earth

---

9. If correct, Dequeker's observation about Isaiah 54:9, borrowed from E. Kutsch, bolsters this conclusion. According to him, Isaiah's reference to "the days of Noah," when God "swore that the waters of Noah should no more go over the earth," is a reference to Genesis 8:21-22, for God's speaking to his heart in the latter seems a more obvious candidate for what Isaiah had in mind when he states that God swore an oath. See Dequeker, "Noah and Israel," p. 128. This claim seems debatable to me, since only 9:15 (not 8:21-22) mentions the waters upon the earth and Isaiah could very reasonably interpret God's making a covenant in 9:8-17 as the swearing of an oath, given the tight connection between covenant-making and oath-taking throughout Scripture. Nevertheless, a case might be made that Isaiah could have interpreted God's speaking to his heart in Genesis 8:21 as a specifically oath-swearing action, given his own earlier description of God's oath in Isaiah 45:23: "By myself I have sworn. . . ."

10. See Mason, "Another Flood?" pp. 184-86. Mason also mentions several conceptual features of 9:1-7 that add further evidence for taking these verses as covenantal in nature, such as the themes of "enemies overtaking God's people" and "indiscriminate bloodshed" that are rich covenant motifs elsewhere in the Old Testament. See Mason, "Another Flood?" pp. 186-94.

(at least in its present form) will not endure forever.[11] This will be important for the interpretation of the Noahic covenant presented below. Genesis 9:11 and 9:15 also bear on this issue. God's intentions in 8:21-22 do not mean that he will never again bring great judgment upon the earth, only that he will never again destroy it with "the waters of the flood." Second Peter 3:1-13 picks up this point and teaches that at Christ's second coming the present heavens and earth will undergo radical dissolution (though not annihilation), not by water but by fire.

Might this covenant be terminated earlier? Mason argues for reading Genesis 9:1-17 as a unified covenantal text in order to show that the Noahic covenant is *bilateral* and hence breakable, and that Isaiah 24 announces God's judgment for its violation.[12] While human beings do have responsibilities in this covenant, however, that fact does not necessarily make it bilateral. Genesis 8:20–9:17 contains no conditional statements threatening punishment for disobedience (as found repeatedly in the bilateral covenant in Deuteronomy, for example). Furthermore, whether or not the "everlasting covenant" of Isaiah 24:5 refers to the Noahic covenant, the imagery throughout Isaiah 24–27 suggests that these chapters describe the end of the present age and the appearance of the new heavens and new earth.[13] Though earth's inhabitants will presumably be judged on that day for violating the terms of the Noahic covenant, this does not mean the Noahic covenant might end earlier if human beings behave especially badly. Genesis 8:21 already factors human wickedness into the equation: "I will never again curse the ground because of man, for the intention of man's heart is evil from his youth." God makes the covenant *precisely because of human rebellion*. From the outset God sets the termination of this covenant at the end of this world (8:22), and nothing in the text indicates that something might change this.[14]

The Scope of the Noahic Covenant

The next issue concerns the scope of the Noahic covenant, which is *universal.* As Jonathan Burnside puts it, "It is impossible to imagine a more inclusive

---

11. Genesis 9:16 refers to this covenant as "everlasting," but it is important to note that the Hebrew word עוֹלָם does not carry the technical meaning of never having an end but only implies lasting a very long time.

12. See generally Mason, *"Eternal Covenant" in the Pentateuch.*

13. See Chapter 4 for discussion of Isaiah 24–27.

14. See similar conclusion in Chalmers, "The Importance of the Noahic Covenant," pp. 209-10.

covenant than this."[15] First, the Noahic covenant encompasses all human beings from that time forward. God speaks to "Noah and [to] his sons" (9:1, 8) and establishes his covenant "with you and with your offspring after you" (9:9), even "for all generations to come" (9:12). Second, the Noahic covenant also includes "every living creature" (9:9-13, 15-17). The sweep of 9:10 is all-inclusive: "the birds, the livestock, and every beast of the earth with you, as many as came out of the ark; it is for every beast of the earth." Third, God states that this covenant is with "the earth" itself (9:13). Finally, the Noahic covenant envelops the forces and functions of the natural order. Never again will a flood of extraordinary proportions destroy the earth and all life on it (8:21; 9:11), but regularity will prevail: "seedtime and harvest, cold and heat, summer and winter, day and night, shall not cease" (8:22). Unlike the later OT covenants, such as the Abrahamic, Mosaic, or Davidic, God does not set apart a particular people in distinction from the rest of the world. The Noahic covenant embraces all human beings without exception and even includes the rest of creation, animate and inanimate, within its scope.

The Purpose of the Noahic Covenant

The purpose of the Noahic covenant is perhaps the most difficult characteristic to identify. A full study of the issue requires investigation of the explicit purposes mentioned in Genesis 8:20–9:17, linguistic issues, and questions about the place of the postdiluvian Noahic covenant in canonical context. I argue that the purpose of the postdiluvian Noahic covenant is *preservation*. It holds out no provision for attaining a state of eschatological consummation, either by human obedience or by way of a gracious salvation. While this covenant is related to later biblical covenants in God's larger purposes for accomplishing his plans in history, it is not organically united with them but is of fundamentally different nature.

That the preservation of the natural and social order is at least one important purpose of this covenant is hardly disputable. With respect to the broader created order, the covenant promises the withholding of destruction (8:21; 9:11, 15) and the uninterrupted alternation of seasons and cycles of nature (8:22). The covenant also promises the maintenance of a delicate harmony in animal-human relations (9:2-4). God's explicit commands, furthermore, aim

---

15. Jonathan Burnside, *God, Justice, and Society: Aspects of Law and Legality in the Bible* (Oxford: Oxford University Press, 2011), p. 35.

to maintain the human social order, through reproduction (9:1, 7), proper eating (9:3-4), and the administration of justice (9:5-6). In broader context what is preserved is the original creation, as re-formed after the flood. A number of textual features make Genesis 8 a reenactment of God's creating work in Genesis 1:1–2:3. As noted in Chapter 1, these two texts contain many parallels, including similar vocabulary, the presence of the wind/Spirit over the waters, the emergence of dry land, the sprouting of vegetation, a seven-day pattern marking Noah's sending of the dove, and God's attainment of "rest." There are also parallels with respect to human work. The command to "be fruitful and multiply" in 9:1, 7 reiterates the creation mandate in 1:28 and, though Genesis 9 does not use the language of having dominion and subduing the earth found in 1:26, 28, the statements about human superiority over animals and the enforcement of justice in 9:2-6 evoke the dominion idea. Genesis 8–9, therefore, presents God's actions after sending the flood as a re-forming of the world he originally made and a reestablishment of the creatures' roles within it. This is the world God promises to preserve.

But comparing Genesis 8–9 to the original creation account also reveals some significant differences between them, and they indicate that the Noahic covenant promises to preserve this re-formed creation but does *not* promise to bring it to eschatological consummation. Four differences seem especially relevant. First, in Genesis 8–9 God does not look upon his work as he completes it and declare it (very) good. Second, the description of God's rest in 8:21 (smelling an "aroma of rest") is muted, without the feel of a grand coronation scene as in 2:1-3. Third, 9:1-7 intentionally omits the language of dominion and subduing. Finally, 8:20–9:17 contains no conditional statements and gives no probationary command to Noah. These differentiating features are linked by a common theme that reveals a great difference between God's creating the world and his re-forming it. The original creation account directs readers toward consummation, both of God's work and of human work in God's likeness. As explored in Chapter 1, God put his own work through a judicial test and it came through approved ("very good"), and therefore he entered his seventh-day rest enthroned above the world he made, his creating work "finished." God made human beings in his own image, to work and to rest as he did. He put them under probation through the tree of the knowledge of good and evil in order to focus their responsibilities and to elicit a judicial verdict. In Genesis 8–9, in contrast, God does not put his own work to the test and receive judicial approbation, or enjoy a grand coronation scene thereafter. It portrays human dominion in less glorious ways (hinting that postdiluvian human dominion will look different from that commissioned in Genesis 1), and sets forth no condition or probation that will bring about a particular response from Noah and thereby evoke a judicial decree and the attainment of a consummated new creation. The Noahic covenant will simply continue until the end of the present earth, no matter how well human beings fulfill their responsibilities within it. God did not design it to bring human work and the whole world to a glorious consummation, but to sustain human work and the present world for an extended period of time.

Genesis 8–9 also describes a covenant without salvation from sin and evil. The Noahic covenant presumes the presence of sin and evil but promises only to manage sin and mitigate its effects, not to eliminate it or to forgive its perpetrators. Sin is backdrop for this covenant from the outset: "I will never again curse the ground because of man, for the intention of man's heart is evil from his youth" (8:21). These words hearken back to a similar statement in Genesis 6:5, which in that setting *provoked* God to send the flood. Genesis 8, however, presents human wickedness as the reason why God stays his hand. This is curious, but seems to indicate that God must establish a covenantal relationship with creation to restrain his wrath, lest sin incite him to bring another devastating act of judgment upon the world. Human sin requires proactive preventative measures.

Yet God never promises salvation from sin or elimination of sin. God commits himself to withhold another judgment by flood and to uphold the regularity of the cycles of nature. God addresses the potential conflict between human beings and animals by instilling in animals the fear and dread of humans (9:2). Human beings are to resolve their own conflicts through judicial action (9:6). All of these remedies manage and mitigate evil without eliminating it. The covenant presumes tension within the human community and within animal-human relationships, and though it sets boundaries upon the scope of natural disasters it does not rule them out altogether. The nature of the covenant sign is instructive. At least one fundamental difference sets apart the rainbow from typical covenant signs later in Scripture, such as circumcision, the Passover, baptism, and the Lord's Supper. The rainbow does not signify the shedding of blood, a common symbol throughout Scripture of the forgiveness of sins (see Heb. 9:22).[16] This covenant also says nothing of eschatological life

16. Expressing this point well is Vos in *Biblical Theology*, pp. 62-63, where he writes: "that **the berith is a berith of nature** appears from the berith-sign; the rainbow is a phenomenon of nature, and absolutely universal in its reference. All the signs connected with redemption are bloody, sacramentally dividing signs." A potential objection to my nonredemptive argument here, especially concerning the lack of a promise to forgive sins, is the description of Noah's sacrifice in Genesis 8:20, which God smells and finds pleasing, and which seems to prompt

or a consummated new creation. God speaks of how things will operate in this world "while the earth remains," but is silent about what happens next. The Noahic covenant, therefore, preserves the world through keeping sin and evil within boundaries but gives no final relief from them.

Answering an Objection

Before continuing the main storyline of this chapter, I should address a potentially serious objection to the conclusion just drawn. Some writers argue that the Noahic covenant of 8:20–9:17 is organically related to God's prediluvian covenant with Noah in Genesis 6:18 and to the later biblical covenants, and hence conclude that the Noahic covenant of 8:20–9:17 has a redemptive aspect.[17] I respond to such claims in this subsection to defend the idea that the Noahic covenant is simply preservative. Readers who find this discussion overly technical or tedious may skip this subsection without losing the thread of my larger argument.

My basic response is that the postdiluvian Noahic covenant is connected to these other biblical covenants insofar as God has a unified plan for history and all of his covenants serve that plan, and that without the Noahic covenant

---

the subsequent promises of the Noahic covenant beginning in 8:21. Whatever the full explanation for the role of this sacrifice in the larger Noah narrative, it does not play any apparent redemptive role. The sacrifice comes *after* God's saving actions toward Noah in rescuing him from the flood, and hence it seems to be an act of consecration rather than of expiation. God's words that follow his smelling the sacrifice, furthermore, promise only temporary preservation and not forgiveness of sin or eschatological life. God's grace in this covenant is common and preservative, not saving.

17. For example, William Dumbrell sees the postdiluvian covenant in Genesis 9 as organically connected to the covenant that God established with Noah in Genesis 6:18 before the flood, and as ultimately rooted in a covenant at creation. He therefore concludes that God, after the flood, is refusing "to permit the divine purposes to be frustrated" and that this has "redemptive consequences." Whatever the ambiguity in this statement, Dumbrell later states clearly that the postdiluvian covenant cannot be "limited to a pledge of stable order" as "merely providing an example of God's general providential care." He appeals to the way the rest of Scripture interprets the story of Noah, seeing the postdiluvian Noahic covenant as organically connected to the earlier and later biblical covenants that promise redemption and interpreting it in this light. See W. J. Dumbrell, *Covenant & Creation: A Theology of the Old Testament Covenants* (Carlisle: Paternoster, 1984), pp. 33, 39. A Reformed writer who follows Dumbrell's analysis closely is Vander Hart, "Creation and Covenant," pp. 10-13. Another Reformed author, Robertson, writing before Dumbrell, takes a similar position; see *The Christ of the Covenants*, pp. 109-11.

there would be no world in which God could exercise his redemptive work, and no world to be brought to consummation. Nevertheless, the covenant in Genesis 8:20–9:17 is unique and cannot be situated in an organic line of continuity with these other biblical covenants. To explain and defend this response I first examine the covenant in 8:20–9:17 in relation to the prediluvian covenant with Noah mentioned in Genesis 6:18.

The first explicit reference to a "covenant" in Scripture, and the only one prior to Genesis 9, is in Genesis 6:18. Are these distinct covenants or actually one covenant with Noah mentioned both before and after the flood?[18] If this is only a single covenant, it adds weight to the claim that Genesis 8:20–9:17 has a redemptive flavor as well as a divine pledge of preservation, since in 6:18 God promises salvation for Noah from his judgment in the flood. A popular argument in favor of the one-covenant view relies upon a disputed understanding of the Hebrew verb קוּם, which describes God's "establishing" or "making" a covenant with Noah in Genesis 9:9-17. Some scholars have asserted that in a covenantal context this verb refers to maintaining or confirming an *already existing* covenant rather than making a new covenant.[19] If Genesis 9:9-17 refers only to the confirming or maintaining of a covenant already in effect, then most likely it confirms the covenant previously mentioned in Genesis 6:18.[20] This conclusion extends the inquiry, however, because קוּם describes God's covenant-making in 6:18 as well. This leads some to conclude that the

18. Among those arguing for one covenant are U. Cassuto, *A Commentary on the Book of Genesis*, Part II, *From Noah to Abraham* (Jerusalem: Magnes, 1964), pp. 68, 130; Dumbrell, *Covenant & Creation*, pp. 28, 33, 42-46; Robertson, *The Christ of the Covenants*, pp. 109-10 n. 2; and J. V. Fesko, *Last Things First: Unlocking Genesis 1–3 with the Christ of Eschatology* (Fearn: Mentor, 2007), pp. 87-88, 112-13. Among those arguing for two distinct covenants are Mason, *"Eternal Covenant" in the Pentateuch*, pp. 48-66; Stephen G. Dempster, *Dominion and Dynasty: A Theology of the Hebrew Bible* (Downers Grove, IL: InterVarsity, 2003), p. 73 n. 33; and Kline, *Kingdom Prologue*, pp. 230-62.

19. Among proponents of this view are Jacob Milgrom, *Leviticus 23–27* (New York: Doubleday, 2001), pp. 2343-45; Kline, *Kingdom Prologue*, p. 232; Dumbrell, *Covenant & Creation*, pp. 25-26; Gordon J. Wenham, *Word Biblical Commentary*, vol. 1, *Genesis 1–15* (Waco, TX: Word, 1987), p. 175; Bruce K. Waltke, *Genesis: A Commentary* (Grand Rapids: Zondervan, 2001), pp. 136, 146; and Cassuto, *Genesis*, Part II, p. 68.

20. Kline, however, claims that the covenant "confirmed" in Genesis 9:8-17 was made in 8:21–9:7, and thus he holds that the covenants in 6:18 and 8:20–9:17 are distinct. In other words, God does not make a covenant in 9:8-17 but confirms a covenant that has been made in the immediately previous words (8:21–9:7). See Kline, *Kingdom Prologue*, pp. 232, 246. I am inclined to agree with Mason when he acknowledges appreciation for Kline's two-covenant view but concludes that he is forced into making "some tenuous judgments" because of his insistence on translating קוּם as "confirm." See Mason, *"Eternal Covenant,"* p. 65 n. 48.

postdiluvian Noahic covenant is organically linked not only to the covenant in 6:18 but also to a covenant with Adam at creation. Another possible argument in favor of a one-covenant view is the relative lack of content specified in the covenant of 6:18, which invites the conclusion that a further unpacking of its content awaits — precisely what Genesis 9 provides. According to this view, therefore, the covenant of 6:18 continues in effect after the flood.

In my judgment, the argument based upon the meaning of קום in a covenantal context is not decisive and the argument based upon content fails completely. I do not have the technical expertise in the Hebrew language to offer a definitive conclusion about the use of the word קום, but it is worth noting that though the קום-as-confirm view garnered the support of some scholars for a time (often with little argument), two recent writers, from notably different perspectives, have made rigorous arguments to the contrary. John Day argues that קום is simply the way in which P (the author of both 6:18 and 9:9-17 according to common source-critical views) refers to the making of a new covenant.[21] Mason notes that the range of meaning of קום is "vast and diverse" and that it is used in various ways in covenantal contexts. Thus he initially concludes that קום at least *could* mean something other than ratifying a preexisting covenant in Genesis 6:18 and 9:8-17.[22] Given the range of meaning of קום generally, and even its diverse use in the hiphil in covenantal contexts, it seems sound to side with Mason and not to presuppose what it *must* mean in Genesis 6 or 9 but to examine the context for insight into how it is used in these places.[23]

As Mason mentions, one of the chief arguments against the two-covenant view is that we must look to Genesis 9 to discover what the 6:18 covenant was referring to, since there is so little content to the covenant specified in 6:18. The content of Genesis 8:20–9:17, however, is precisely what shows the profound distinction between God's prediluvian and postdiluvian dealings with Noah. Both the parties and the purposes are different. First, the covenant in 6:18 is thoroughly particularistic while the covenant of 8:20–9:17 is emphatically universalistic. In 6:18 God simply states that his covenant is with "you," that is, Noah. Perhaps God's partners in this covenant also include Noah's sons, wife, and daughters-in-law and the animals brought upon the ark (which the text proceeds to mention in 6:18-19), but even in this case the whole point is

---

21. John Day, "Why Does God 'Establish' rather than 'Cut' Covenants in the Priestly Source?" in *Covenant as Context*, pp. 91-109.

22. Mason, *"Eternal Covenant,"* pp. 48-55.

23. See also *Theological Dictionary of the Old Testament*, vol. 2, ed. G. Johannes Botterweck and Helmer Ringgren (Grand Rapids: Eerdmans, 1975), p. 260.

to *separate* and *distinguish* a tiny part of humanity and the animal kingdom from the rest, given the immediate background of 6:17: "I will bring a flood of waters upon the earth to destroy all flesh in which is the breath of life under heaven. Everything that is on the earth shall die." In sharp contrast, God's words in 8:20–9:17 repeatedly highlight that there is nothing in creation excluded from the postdiluvian covenant. Its universal embrace includes all human beings, every living creature, the cycles of nature, and the earth itself. These observations also suggest important differences between the 6:18 covenant and the original covenant of creation. The covenant of creation at least makes no point to exclude any part of the created order from its purview, and its universal outlook, communicated through the broad scope of the dominion entrusted to humanity and the commission to be fruitful and multiply (1:26, 28), bears considerable resemblance to 9:1-7. All told, identifying the parties of the covenants provides one strong reason not to see the covenant of 6:18 as a confirmation of the covenant of creation and not to see the covenant of 8:20–9:17 as a confirmation of the covenant of 6:18.

Second, the purposes of the covenants in 6:18 and 8:20–9:17 are significantly different, again suggesting two distinct covenants rather than one organically unified covenant. To put it simply, while 8:20–9:17 promises preservation of the world while judgment is kept at bay, 6:18 provides for salvation for a small remnant in the midst of a devastating and universal judgment. The salvific character of 6:18 is especially evident in the literary structure of the first section of the flood narrative (6:13-22). Genesis 6:13-16 unfolds in three stages, an announcement of judgment (6:13), a command to build the ark (6:14), and specific instructions about the ark (6:15-16). In parallel fashion, 6:17-21 unfolds in three stages, an announcement of judgment (6:17), the establishment of the covenant with a view toward Noah's entering the ark (6:18), and instructions about the ark (6:19-21). The parallel between 6:18 and 6:14 highlights that this covenant has special reference to the ark as a refuge from the judgment that will envelop the world.[24] This means that the purposes of the 6:18 covenant have been fulfilled by the time the narrative introduces the postdiluvian covenant. In 8:1 "God remembered Noah" (a statement with strong covenantal overtones) and completed his saving action toward him by making the waters recede and dry land appear once again (8:1-19).[25] The purpose of the 6:18 covenant is therefore starkly different from the purpose of

---

24. A similar argument in more detail appears in Kline, *Kingdom Prologue*, pp. 230-31.

25. On the covenantal implications of God's remembering, see Kline, *Kingdom Prologue*, p. 231.

the covenant in 8:20–9:17, which simply preserves the entire world and keeps judgment out of the picture altogether.[26] This evidence also means that the purpose of the 6:18 covenant is distinct from the purpose of the covenant of creation, which was revealed in a context without sin or evil and provided a means for human beings, by obedience to their royal commission, to attain an eschatological rest.

In short, the postdiluvian Noahic covenant must be clearly distinguished from the prediluvian Noahic covenant, in that the prediluvian covenant promised salvation for a remnant through an otherwise universal judgment while the postdiluvian covenant promised preservation for the whole of creation by holding off such a judgment. But does subsequent biblical material suggest that the postdiluvian Noahic covenant has redemptive purposes? Several scholars have identified thematic similarity between the Noahic covenant and God's later promises to Israel.[27] A number of writers also argue that OT prophetic visions of a renewed or glorified earth, marked by peace and harmony in the universe, are rooted in the promises of the Noahic covenant. Though some scholars may only wish to claim that the Noahic covenant is the platform upon which God performs his salvific, eschatological work, many suggest that the Noahic covenant is organically united to these later covenant promises, an anticipation of coming blessings.[28]

---

26. For another clear statement on the salvific purposes of the covenant in 6:18 (though without a clear commitment on the relationship of the prediluvian and postdiluvian covenants), see Claus Westermann, *Genesis 1–11: A Commentary*, trans. John J. Scullion, S.J. (Minneapolis: Augsburg, 1984), p. 422. For additional arguments in support of a two-covenant view, in interaction with several counterarguments, see Mason, *"Eternal Covenant,"* pp. 55-66.

27. Most recent and comprehensive is Mason's extended argument in *"Eternal Covenant,"* pp. 227-29. See also Dell, "Covenant and Creation in Relationship," pp. 111-33; and Dequeker, "Noah and Israel," pp. 115-29.

28. Robertson, *The Christ of the Covenants*, pp. 121-23, calls the Noahic covenant "redemptive" in line with later biblical covenants and connects it to Romans 8:18-25 and the deliverance of the entire universe from the curse. Mason, *"Eternal Covenant,"* as summarized on pp. 229-30, treats the Noahic covenant as an eternal covenant that is at least organically linked to the other "eternal" covenants later in Scripture and perhaps simply one facet of a single overarching eternal covenant running through Scripture. This eternal Noahic covenant "is to restore the kingdom on earth to its intended state." Dell, "Covenant and Creation," p. 131, writes: "God's final will is for peace and harmony in an ideal creation. The Noahic covenant is the pivot around which this promise of a bright future revolves, and it is a magnet for these passages that I have gathered together under the creation/covenant synthesis." Though Dequeker is generally favorable to uniting the covenants with Noah and with Israel, he writes some things that, in my judgment, suggest that the Noahic covenant could be merely a stage upon which God's covenants with Israel are played out rather than part of a single overarching covenant

In my judgment, thematic similarities between the Noahic covenant and the later OT covenant promises do *not* suggest an underlying organic unity among them. God's covenant with all creation through Noah creates a stage for the unfolding drama of the later eschatological promises of salvation, and thus a broad harmonious relationship exists among them in this sense. But examination of the thematic similarities reveals a very big difference in the way these themes develop. The Noahic covenant promises only the preservation of the earth from a flood and the maintenance of the ordinary cycles of nature. It presumes the presence of sin and evil in the human, animal, and cosmic orders and pledges to manage and constrain this evil but not to expunge it. The later biblical covenant promises look forward to a time in which sin and evil are entirely banished from all orders of creation. The promise of preservation *in the midst of* evil is not the same as the promise of salvation *from* evil. Preventing undue violence between humans and animals through a fear instilled in the latter (Gen. 9:2) is categorically different from the imagery of a perfect peace and harmony among lion and lamb and cobra and child characteristic of the Messianic age (Isa. 11:1-9).

Hosea 2:18, which some writers cite to highlight the continuities between the Noahic covenant and later covenant promises to Israel (and ultimately to the new covenant church), actually illustrates the clear distinctions between them. Hosea 2:18 states: "And I will make for them a covenant on that day with the beasts of the field, the birds of the heavens, and the creeping things of the ground. And I will abolish the bow, the sword, and war from the land, and I will make you lie down in safety." It is true that "in anticipation of future redemptive activity for Israel, Hosea employs the distinctive categories of the universe found in God's covenant with Noah."[29] But what Hosea anticipates is the *abolition* of conflict from the human social order. Whereas the covenant with Noah ordained a legal system to mitigate violence on the earth, Hosea speaks of a covenant that will usher in an age in which bow, sword, and war are eliminated altogether. A society that possesses no weapons can hardly be faithful to the Noahic order of Genesis 9:6: "whoever sheds the blood of man, by man shall his blood be shed." Where there are no weapons there is no bloodshed, whether in unjust violence or in just retribution. Hosea looks forward to the end of the Noahic order, when "the earth remains" (Gen. 8:22)

---

relationship with unified purposes. For example, he writes: "The 'covenantal' promises given to the forefathers of Israel are relevant, theologically speaking, only in the context of the preservation — solemnly confirmed by God — of human life on earth." See "Noah and Israel," p. 127.

29. Robertson, *The Christ of the Covenants*, p. 111.

no longer. He speaks not about the future of this present creation, but about its consummation in an eschatological new creation.

To look at this from a slightly different angle, there *is* an organic continuity among the later major biblical covenants — the Abrahamic, Mosaic, Davidic, and new covenants — that finally blossoms to eschatological fulfillment in the new heavens and new earth. The Abrahamic covenant looked forward to the day when Abraham's descendants, as a great multitude, would inherit the land of Canaan (Gen. 15:7-21; 17:8). Thus God initiated the events leading up to the covenant at Sinai and Israel's entrance into Canaan by remembering his covenant with Abraham (e.g., Exod. 3:6-8). When Israel was unfaithful to the law of Sinai God repeatedly withheld final judgment and bestowed mercy precisely because of his fidelity to that previous covenant (e.g., Exod. 32:11-14). God entered into covenant with David and established his royal line in order to bless Israel and to fulfill the provisions of the law of Moses (Deut. 17:14-20; 2 Sam. 7:4-16). When Christ came and established the new covenant, he did so as the Son of David, to rule upon his throne (e.g., Luke 1:32). Christ and the new covenant were the fulfillment of the Abrahamic promises and the very things to which the Mosaic law pointed (Gal. 3:15-29). Finally, in the new heavens and new earth God will climactically announce the great summary of these covenants: "they will be his people, and God himself will be with them as their God" (Rev. 21:1-3).

But Scripture does not place the Noahic covenant within this organic unity linking the rest of these covenants in the grand biblical story of redemption. Never does a subsequent biblical covenant look back to Noah and announce that it fulfills or consummates that covenant. Scripture at times cites the days of Noah as an *analogy* for what happens later, but this is different from looking back to the Noahic covenant and announcing organic fulfillment.[30] Several New Testament texts speak of the flood as an anticipation of the final judgment and speak of God's rescue of Noah in the ark as an anticipation of

---

30. A good example is Isaiah 54:9-10: "'This is like the days of Noah to me: as I swore that the waters of Noah should no more go over the earth, so I have sworn that I will not be angry with you, and will not rebuke you. For the mountains may depart and the hills be removed, but my steadfast love shall not depart from you, and my covenant of peace shall not be removed,' says the Lord, who has compassion on you." Here the promises of the later covenant of peace are not identified with the promises to Noah, but likened to them. In fact, reference to the removability of the mountains and hills might reflect the temporality of the Noahic covenant intended from its inception (Gen. 8:21). In contrast to the Noahic covenant, which cannot prevent the eventual dissolution of the natural order, the coming covenant of peace will establish a truly indestructible steadfast love of God for his people.

Christian salvation (e.g., Matt. 24:36-44; 1 Pet. 3:18-22; 2 Pet. 3:5-7). This high-lights a claim argued above: the prediluvian covenant with Noah in Genesis 6:18 is a fundamentally different covenant from the postdiluvian covenant in 8:20–9:17, and the former, as a covenant of salvation, provides a foretaste of God's later salvific work that the latter does not.[31]

To summarize, in the postdiluvian Noahic covenant (Gen. 8:20–9:17) God promised the temporary *preservation* of this world, with its cosmic and social orders, not the redemption or eschatological consummation of this world. In Chapter 1, I argued that the original goal of creation was to attain a new creation as the consummation of the first creation and that the covenant of creation was designed to achieve that goal. The Noahic covenant of Genesis 8:20–9:17, in contrast, provides no means to attain a new creation but simply maintains the present, fallen creation by postponing the final judgment. The later biblical covenants — the Abrahamic, Mosaic, Davidic, and new — will prove to be God's means for bestowing salvation upon the world and bring-ing about the new heavens and new earth. We will revisit the story of these subsequent covenants in Chapters 6-9 and explore their importance for a full-fledged biblical theology of natural law.

---

31. For a discussion of the relation of the preservative postdiluvian Noahic covenant to redemptive covenants elsewhere in Scripture, which comes to similar conclusions as I offer here, see Kline, *Kingdom Prologue*, pp. 245-50. With regard to several themes considered in the previous paragraphs, Kline writes in his characteristically blunt manner: "From this radical difference in their prospects concerning the order of nature it is obvious that the covenant of Genesis 8:20ff. is not to be identified with the Covenant of Grace (specifically, as adminis-tered in the Gen 6:18 covenant). Identification of the two has been mistakenly argued on the ground that the postdiluvian covenant, like the redemptive covenant, has a creational aspect: it concerns the realm of nature and wildlife and has ordinances appertaining thereto. But such a vague, oversimplified appeal to a shared world-of-nature aspect will not do. It blurs vital distinctions and ignores pronounced differences. The fact is that the specific character of the nature provision of the covenant of Genesis 8:20ff., a provision merely for the postponement of the final creational curse not for the consummation of the blessing of nature, contradicts any identification of this covenant with the covenant of Genesis 6:18 or with redemptive covenant in general and demands that it rather be distinguished from all such administrations of saving grace and separately classified as a covenant of common grace. To do otherwise is to introduce hopeless confusion into one's biblical-theological analysis and the resultant world-and-life view." See *Kingdom Prologue*, p. 249.

Human Moral Obligation in the Noahic Covenant

We now examine the moral obligations the Noahic covenant places upon human beings. This section takes us a step closer to specifying some initial conclusions about natural law in the fallen world of the present day. Though Genesis 9:1-7 sets forth the human obligations within the Noahic covenant, this covenant is not, strictly speaking, bilateral in nature. From the outset, God establishes the duration of the covenant — as long as the earth "remains" (8:22) — and gives no provisions for triggering an earlier termination point. The best way to describe this covenant, then, is as a unilateral covenant with regulations.[32]

The Noahic covenant gives essentially three explicit obligations to human beings. The first is to "be fruitful and multiply," a command appearing in both 9:1 and 9:7. The second obligation is negative: though God gives them animals to eat (9:3), he forbids them from eating meat with blood still in it (9:4). This command sets constraints upon humanity's exercise of authority over animals; God delivers them into human hands (9:2), but not for reckless abuse.[33] I take it that the covenant intends not to require cooking steaks well done but to prohibit human beings from pouncing on an animal and eating it alive, as animals do to other animals. Humans should act like humans; they are to treat animals *humanely*.[34] The third obligation of the Noahic covenant is

32. This is the position of Kline, *Kingdom Prologue*, p. 246. Over against this is Mason, who argues very helpfully for including 9:1-7 within the Noahic covenant but concludes that this covenant is bilateral and thus breakable by human misconduct; see *"Eternal Covenant,"* pp. 66-87; and Mason, "Another Flood," pp. 177-98. Other scholars arguing for a unilateral interpretation include Dumbrell, *Covenant & Creation*, pp. 28-31; Westermann, *Genesis 1–11*, p. 473; and Waltke, *Genesis*, pp. 146, 154.

33. Here I disagree with Kline's interpretation, curious in context, that the prohibition of blood is a cultic matter pertaining to sacrifice. Hence, though Kline takes the postdiluvian covenant broadly as a covenant of common grace applicable to all people regardless of their cultic standing before God, he interprets Genesis 9:3-4 as an island of particular instruction to those who are true worshipers of him. See *Kingdom Prologue*, pp. 253-62. Though Kline's general theological concerns are understandable, there is no internal warrant in the text for such an interpretation and it seems to undermine his broader case for seeing the Noahic covenant as a universal covenant of preservation or common grace (a compelling view, as I argue above). Historic Judaism, it may be noted, includes the eating of a torn limb as one of the seven Noachide laws binding upon Gentiles.

34. I am grateful to my colleague Joshua Van Ee for several discussions we have had on this issue. Some of his views were defended in "Adam and Other Carnivores: Questions Regarding Primitive Vegetarianism in Genesis 1:28-30" (paper presented at the International Society of Biblical Literature annual conference, London, 2011).

that human beings are to exercise proportionate retributive justice against the murderer: "Whoever sheds the blood of man, by man shall his blood be shed, for God made man in his own image" (9:6).[35] Since the text itself does not put this in imperative form, and what exactly God ordains here is not immediately clear, a few additional comments on this verse are in order.

A popular interpretation of Genesis 9:6 is that the text appeals to the image of God in order to explain why murder is such a terrible crime: the murderer has extinguished the life of one bearing God's image.[36] This is a natural reading of the text and rightly recognizes that the image of God imparts an inviolable human dignity. But there are good reasons to think that Genesis 9:6 speaks more about human duties than human rights. The text appeals to the image of God not (at least primarily) to explain why murder deserves a severe penalty but to explain why the penalty will be administered "by man."[37]

As discussed in Chapter 1, the main point of the image of God in Genesis 1:26-27 is the royal-judicial commission to exercise dominion and subdue the earth. Without any intervening biblical material suggesting a change in focus, reference to the image in Genesis 9:6 should be read as an appeal to this royal-judicial commission. Thus when someone sheds the blood of man, "*by man* shall his blood be shed." Human beings are creatures with authority.

35. In defense of putting the comma after the first "man," rather than after the second (producing a reading such as "whoever sheds the blood of man by man, his blood shall be shed"), see Markus Zehnder, "Cause or Value? Problems in the Understanding of Gen 9,6a," *Zeitschrift für Die Alttestamentliche Wissenschaft* 122, no. 1 (2010): 82. Some scholars have preferred the reading "for man" or "in exchange for man" to "by man," seeing a *beth pretii* here; e.g., see Johan Lust, "'For Man Shall His Blood Be Shed' Gen 9:6 in Hebrew and in Greek," in *Tradition of the Text: Studies Offered to Dominique Barthelemy in Celebration of His 70th Birthday,* ed. Gerard J. Norton and Stephen Pisano (Fribourg: Biblical Institute of the University, 1991), pp. 91-102; and Jacob Milgrom, *Leviticus 1–16* (New York: Doubleday, 1991), p. 705. Zehnder shows the strong evidence for the reading "by man" (though he thinks there is something of a double meaning to the phrase marking both causation and value); see "Cause or Value?" pp. 83-89; see also Victor P. Hamilton, *The Book of Genesis Chapters 1–17* (Grand Rapids: Eerdmans, 1990), p. 315.

36. Among writers taking this view, often with little or no argument in support, are Charles H. H. Scobie, *The Ways of Our God: An Approach to Biblical Theology* (Grand Rapids: Eerdmans, 2003), p. 159; Francis Watson, *Text and Truth: Redefining Biblical Theology* (Grand Rapids: Eerdmans, 1997), pp. 280, 291-92, 299; Dempster, *Dominion and Dynasty,* pp. 59, 73; Cassuto, *Genesis,* Part II, p. 127; Wenham, *Genesis 1–15,* pp. 193-94; and Nahum M. Sarna, *Genesis* (Philadelphia: Jewish Publication Society, 1989), p. 62.

37. Writers defending this position include Mason, "Another Flood?" pp. 192-93; W. Randall Garr, *In His Own Image and Likeness: Humanity, Divinity, and Monotheism* (Leiden: Brill, 2003), p. 163; and Kline, *Kingdom Prologue,* pp. 252-53.

When justice is violated they should exercise their judicial office to rectify the disorder.[38] As in Genesis 1, God is the ultimate judge and enforcer of justice (9:5), but he has delegated this task in part to his human under-lords (9:6).[39]

This interpretation of Genesis 9:6 means that the statement "Whoever sheds the blood of man, by man shall his blood be shed" is prescriptive rather than simply descriptive. The image of God is an inherently ethical concept. To appeal to the image of God is to appeal to an understanding of how human beings are supposed to conduct themselves. Genesis 9:6 is a normative statement of human justice: the so-called *lex talionis*. What the Mosaic law (and many other human legal systems) would later express as "eye for eye, tooth for tooth" (Exod. 21:23-25; Lev. 24:18-21; Deut. 19:21) is here expressed as, we might say, "blood for blood." I discuss natural law and the *lex talionis* in more detail below. Here I simply note that the *lex talionis* expresses the idea of proportionate justice: the punishment must fit the crime.[40] (I also note that the *lex talionis* can account for the restoration of victims as well as the punishment of wrongdoers.)[41] Already in the prediluvian history God ordained that proportionate justice be administered in response to criminal wrongdoing: "If anyone kills Cain, vengeance shall be taken on him *sevenfold*" (Gen. 4:15). The distortion of this principle of perfect sevenfold justice, captured by Lamech's boast, "If

38. Some writers have claimed that taking 9:6 as an appeal to human rights creates an odd tension in the text: the very thing that makes killing so wrong (human dignity as the image of God) demands that another killing take place. See e.g. Lust, " 'For Man Shall His Blood Be Shed,' " pp. 91-102. While capital punishment may be a troubling issue to many in any case, taking the view I defend should mitigate some of this alleged tension.

39. James Barr puzzlingly seems to have missed this whole line of thought in *Biblical Faith and Natural Theology* (Oxford: Clarendon, 1993), pp. 158-59, where he states that viewing the image of God as exercising dominion over the world, the most common contemporary interpretation, "fits less well, or not at all" in Genesis 9:6. For reflections on how a comparison of this larger text with the stories of Adam and Eve and Cain and Abel further highlights the significance of God's delegation of judicial authority to human beings in Genesis 9:6, see Devora Steinmetz, "Vineyard, Farm, and Garden: The Drunkenness of Noah in the Context of Primeval History," *JBL* 113, no. 2 (1994): 193-207.

40. The best exploration of this theme of which I am aware is that of William Ian Miller, *Eye for an Eye* (Cambridge: Cambridge University Press, 2006). As Wenham puts it, regarding Genesis 9:6, "The tight chiastic formulation (shed, blood, man, man, blood, shed) repeating each word of the first clause in reverse order in the second emphasizes the strict correspondence of punishment to offence." See *Genesis 1–15*, p. 193.

41. I discuss this issue in Chapter 10. At least two ways in which the *lex talionis* shows concern for victims are through providing an appropriate expression of the just desire for vengeance and through its ability to indicate a just value for material compensation (even often in cases of physical harm, in lieu of literal mutilation of the perpetrator).

Cain's revenge is *sevenfold,* then Lamech's is *seventy-sevenfold"* (Gen. 4:24), illustrates the perversity of human society before the flood. Thus now, in the re-formed postdiluvian world, God reestablishes the practice of proportionate retributive justice in the covenant with Noah.[42]

In the bigger picture, what are we to make of these three explicit moral obligations of the Noahic covenant: procreation, eating (within limits), and administering proportionate retributive justice? My initial conclusion is that these obligations constitute a republication of the original creation mandate (Gen. 1:26-28) in modified form.

A number of similarities between 9:1-7 and 1:26-28 are evident. Generally, while the mandate of 1:26-28 falls after the account of God's original creation of the world, the mandate of 9:1-7 follows the account of God's re-formation of the world after the flood. Furthermore, in 9:1, 7 God twice repeats the command in 1:28: "be fruitful and multiply." Other considerations arise from the thematic similarities between 9:2-6 and 1:26-29. One similar theme is the relationship between humanity and the animal kingdom. In 1:26 God commands his human creation to have dominion "over the fish of the sea and over the birds of the heavens and over the livestock and over all the earth and over every creeping thing that creeps on the earth," and repeats a somewhat shorter list in 1:28. In comparison, in 9:2 God instills the fear and dread of humanity upon "every beast of the earth and upon every bird of the heavens, upon everything that creeps on the ground and all the fish of the sea." Into Noah's hand "they are delivered." A second common theme is food. At creation God gives "every plant yielding seed" and "every tree with seed in its fruit" for eating (1:29). After the flood the list includes "every moving thing that lives" and "the green plants" — in other words, "everything" (9:3). The image of God is another common theme. God creates humanity in his image and likeness in 1:26-27 and then after the flood reaffirms that "God made man in his own image" (9:6).

---

42. This description of humanity's royal commission in terms of rendering judgment, or adjudication, not only reflects the work of both God and human beings in the covenant of creation but also anticipates a common theme that I will identify in subsequent chapters. Where Scripture speaks of natural law, the work of human judgment is often in the picture. Oliver O'Donovan argues that the act of judgment is *the* authority possessed by civil government; see *The Ways of Judgment* (Grand Rapids: Eerdmans, 2005). See also O'Donovan's argument in *The Desire of the Nations: Rediscovering the Roots of Political Theology* (Cambridge: Cambridge University Press, 1996). However, he also claims that civil government has been stripped of all authority but judgment by the resurrection of Christ; see *The Ways of Judgment,* pp. 4-5. This claim is undermined by the fact that judgment is precisely the authority mentioned in Genesis 9:6. Romans 13:1-7 reads more like an affirmation of the Noahic covenant than an ascription of a new kind of authority.

Alongside these similarities are also significant differences, which support my conclusion that 9:1-7 republishes the original creation mandate in *modified* form.[43] One difference is that the human royal rule commissioned in 9:1-7 is considerably muted compared to 1:26, 28. Rather than a grand summons to rule and subdue all other creatures, 9:2 informs Noah that God himself has put the fear of humanity in animals and 9:6 simply tells the human community to punish murderers. Second, this muted dominion mandate is to be pursued in the context of ongoing conflict within the world. A remarkable feature of the original creation account is the lack of conflict. Unlike the gods of the ancient Near Eastern creation myths, God faces no opposition as he creates and the first human beings receive work to do but not in the context of scarcity, disease, or natural disaster.[44] One particular source of opposition will arise as a probationary test of their obedience (the serpent of Genesis 3), but he appears not as a constitutive aspect of the fabric of creation but as an intruder. Under the Noahic covenant, in contrast, conflict and hostility form an integral part of the natural and social orders. Animals and humans live in an uneasy tension (9:2) and human beings will be killed, both by animals and each other (9:5-6). Third, unlike the covenant of creation, the Noahic covenant envisions no completion of the dominion task and attainment of an eschatological state. It deals simply with the ongoing performance of the task in order to sustain human existence and to maintain an uneasy and partial peace in society. God instills fear in animals to keep animal-human tension in check, but does not eliminate the tension itself. Human-human conflict is mitigated through judicial procedures that enforce penalties, which are neither too severe nor too lax, but again the conflict itself is not expunged. The Noahic covenant holds out no hope of attaining a perfect and lasting peace, only of avoiding a war of all against all. The dominion Noah's descendants can achieve is but a shadow of the dominion Adam was supposed to achieve.

These considerations indicate that Adam's original creation mandate, per se, does not continue to obligate human beings after the fall. Instead, what binds postlapsarian humanity is the original mandate *as refracted through the Noahic covenant,* in ways fit for a fallen but preserved world.

On the face of it, this refracted Noahic mandate appears to be a minimalist ethic, not a comprehensive program for the advance of human civili-

---

43. Kline makes the same basic point in saying: "there is both continuity and discontinuity between the creational kingdom program and the common grace cultural order." See *Kingdom Prologue,* p. 251.

44. To be sure, that human beings were to "subdue" the earth suggests that the nonhuman world had a certain wild and untamed character.

zation. By requiring procreation, eating (with constraints), and proportionate retributive justice the Noahic covenant highlights some basic necessities for the survival of the human race rather than holistic human flourishing.[45] Procreation, eating, and justice, furthermore, all concern intrahuman affairs and do not explicitly or directly concern the worship of God or other matters of religious devotion. Given the preservative purpose of the Noahic covenant discussed above, finding such a minimalist ethic here seems to make a good deal of sense. And if the wicked behavior that provoked the dissolution of human society in the flood — the "sons of God" taking as many of the "daughters of men" as they chose (Gen. 6:2) — was in fact "politically sanctioned rape,"[46] it is no wonder that concerns about procreation and justice stand out in the postdiluvian covenant. At the very least, we may tentatively conclude that the *focus* of the Noahic covenant is upon some basic intrahuman affairs concerning the survival of the race, not upon comprehensive human flourishing in a right relationship with God.

Upon a little reflection, however, many features of Genesis 9:1-7 suggest that a thicker ethic may in fact undergird this apparently thin ethic lying on the surface of the text. If the human race is not only to be fruitful but also to *multiply* (9:1, 7), then procreation must be accompanied by social structures that ensure the raising and training of children and not simply their birth. This suggests that the Noahic covenant has marriage and family relationships in view, as well as broader social structures that can regulate relationships among different families and provide a forum for the formation of new families from one generation to another. The provisions and regulations about eating (9:3-4) also seem to presume some deeper realities about the human condition. Eating plants and animals requires *work* on the part of human beings, and growing crops and tending livestock depends upon some conception of property rights.

---

45. Though I do not mean to allude to his work by referring to a "minimalist" natural law ethic in Genesis 9:1-7, nor to embrace the legal positivism of which he was a notable proponent, some readers may note a certain terminological and even substantive similarity here with H. L. A. Hart's notion of "the minimum content of natural law." Given that the concern of law "is with social arrangements for continued existence," according to Hart, "reflection on some very obvious generalizations . . . concerning human nature and the world in which men live, show that as long as these hold good, there are certain rules of conduct which any social organization must contain if it is to be viable. . . . Such universally recognized principles of conduct which have a basis in elementary truths concerning human beings, their natural environment, and aims, may be considered the *minimum content* of Natural Law." See *The Concept of Law*, 2nd ed. (Oxford: Oxford University Press, 1997), pp. 192-93.

46. David Novak, *Natural Law in Judaism* (Cambridge: Cambridge University Press, 1997), pp. 36-37. See also Burnside, *God, Justice, and Society*, p. 78.

The exercise of retributive justice (9:6), furthermore, becomes necessary only when there is a broader society in which people meet and exercise claims toward and against one another, and it also requires some sort of legal system in which claims can be heard, evaluated, and enforced.

The appeal to the image of God in Genesis 9:6 also suggests that a thicker ethical task underlies the minimalist ethic explicit in the text, given my argument that the image is a holistic reality involving humanity's natural attributes put to use in the royal rule of this world in the likeness of God. Three things stand out in particular.

First, God displays a rich creative fruitfulness after the flood that looks much like his creative fruitfulness at creation. As discussed above, the story of the re-forming and re-inhabiting of the earth in Genesis 8:1-20 echoes the original creation account in striking ways. The waters abate so that dry ground appears, vegetation springs forth from the ground, and the various creatures are again to "swarm" and fill the earth. Also similar to the creation account is God's generosity after the flood. God does not make the earth abound in order to hoard its riches for himself, but calls the creation to share in his work and to participate in his fruitfulness. The ground plays its role in bringing forth vegetation (8:11) and the animals are both to "swarm" and to "be fruitful and multiply" (8:17). Human beings are to be fruitful and multiply and to appropriate and enjoy the bounty of creation for their own well-being through eating both plants and animals (9:1-7). The fact that human beings continue to bear the image of this God suggests that they are called to a creative fruitfulness and generosity toward others. God still summons human beings to love. Their image-bearing commission to be like God, therefore, suggests a thicker ethic than the minimalist ethic explicit in 9:1-7.

Second, the revelation of God's justice in the Noahic covenant comes with an interesting and significant twist. I argued in Chapter 1 that God threatened strict retributive justice for disobedience in Genesis 2, without offering any prospect for forgiveness. As it turned out, after the fall God withheld the full manifestation of his judgment and permitted human history to unfold in a fallen state. But by the beginning of the Noah story human sin has exhausted God's forbearance. "The Lord saw that the wickedness of man was great in the earth, and that every intention of the thoughts of his heart was only evil continually. And the Lord was sorry that he had made man on the earth and it grieved him to his heart. So the Lord said, 'I will blot out man whom I have created from the face of the land . . .'" (Gen. 6:5-7). The massive destruction of the ensuing flood looks like the severe retributive justice readers of Genesis 1–2 may have expected to come after the rebellion of Adam and Eve. (Matthew

24:36-44 and 2 Pet. 3:5-7 confirm this suggestion by portraying the flood as a foretaste of the final judgment of the last day, which God postponed in Genesis 3 but did not abrogate; we return to this issue in Chapters 3 and 4). But following the flood God restores life on earth, and though he continues to see the same wickedness in humanity that he saw before the flood — "the intention of man's heart is evil from his youth" (Gen. 8:21) — this time it triggers not a catastrophic flood but the promise of preservation in the Noahic covenant. In this covenant God neither enforces retributive justice in its full severity (such as he will enforce at the final judgment upon those unreconciled to him)[47] nor promises the forgiveness of sins or an eschatological salvation (such as he bestows in the redemptive covenants of grace, ultimately through Jesus Christ), but resumes the loving *forbearance* (or perhaps *longsuffering*) he had shown prior to the flood, and this time he guarantees it will endure "while the earth remains" (Gen. 8:22). The Noahic covenant, therefore, reveals him as a God of *justice, tempered by forbearance.*

This suggests that human beings, still called to bear God's image in this world, also ought to show loving forbearance in their pursuit of justice (though this covenant provides no basis for them to *forgive* wrongs). Human beings can only image the God they know, and the God they know is the one who reveals himself in concrete covenantal relationships. Thus, though Genesis 9:6 promulgates the *lex talionis* straightforwardly, the context indicates that human society should temper its administration of proportionate retributive justice with a dose of forbearance.[48] The impossibility of the alternative con-

47. See 2 Pet. 2:13; Rev. 11:18; 16:6; 18:6-7, which, as noted in Chapter 1, describe the final judgment in terms reminiscent of the *lex talionis*. Though his analysis of these issues is not identical to mine, J. Budziszewski makes a similar comparison of the partial manifestation of retribution in the judgment of magistrates now and its full manifestation on the last day; see *The Line Through the Heart: Natural Law as Fact, Theory, and Sign of Contradiction* (Wilmington, DE: ISI Books, 2009), pp. 116-17.

48. Relevant here is Nicholas Wolterstorff's discussion of clemency and forgiveness in the ancient pagan writers; see *Justice in Love* (Grand Rapids: Eerdmans, 2011), pp. 178-87. Wolterstorff argues that these writers had strong conceptions of clemency or equity, but these did not entail *forgiveness*. In Seneca's clemency, for example, the wrong is still held against the wrongdoer. According to Wolterstorff, they did not hold to a conception of forgiveness in part because they held to the negative side (at least) of the reciprocity code (i.e., the *lex talionis*). To me, this makes a great deal of sense. Retributive justice is known through the natural law, and thus its claims were impressed upon the consciences of the ancient pagans. But as discussed below, especially in Chapter 9, true forgiveness is understandable, and consistent with the claims of retributive justice, only through Christ's atonement as revealed in Scripture, of which the pagan writers were ignorant.

firms this conclusion. Seeking to impose a proportionate penalty for every wrong against a fellow human being would surely overwhelm a legal system, erode goodwill among persons, and grind all productive activity to a halt. The exigencies of life in a fallen society, in other words, demand a considerable measure of forbearance toward one's fellow human beings. When and how much is not clear. Genesis 9:6 states the talionic principle only with regard to the most heinous intrahuman crime, murder, which subtly indicates the propriety of pursuing retributive justice only for more serious matters, such as the violence that triggered the flood (see Gen. 6:11-13). Evidently a measure of wisdom is necessary in order to administer justice in ways that contribute to the preservation of society's peace and order, rather than detract from it. These considerations suggest, therefore, that the Noahic covenant indeed requires a thicker ethic than the thin and minimalist ethic on the surface of 9:1-7.

Third and finally, if human beings still exist in the image of God, then human identity remains intimately dependent upon their creator, indicating that they retain some sort of relationship and accountability to God. The minimalist ethic on the face of Genesis 9:1-7 never explicitly mentions worship or religious devotion. But the inherently God-oriented character of human nature suggests that God continues to solicit due honor from all human beings, which in turn adds more evidence for a richer ethic in the Noahic covenant than may at first appear.

My tentative conclusion at this point is that the Noahic covenant focuses upon a bare minimalist ethic concerning intrahuman affairs, designed to preserve the existence of human society, in accord with God's purposes in this covenant. But even to carry out this minimalist ethic, human beings need to form a broad range of social structures and engage in a range of other activities, through the exercise of wisdom. Furthermore, the reality of the divine image indicates that they are to render proper honor to their creator, before whom they lie accountable. While the Noahic covenant is thus not unconcerned about holistic (though imperfect) human flourishing and people's relationship with God, its chief interest is human sustenance and a modicum of social order. To solidify and clarify this tentative conclusion we will keep an eye on this thin ethic/thick ethic dynamic in the chapters that follow.

Natural Law in the Noahic Covenant

Against this background material on the characteristics and moral obligations of the Noahic covenant, I now specifically address the question of natural law. In Chapter 1, I argued for a covenant of creation that was "natural." It was natural first of all because God entered into covenant with his human image-bearers in the very act of creating them. This covenant was also natural in a second sense. The obligations this covenant imposed upon human beings were not arbitrary divine decrees foreign to human nature but were consonant with human nature, fit for life within the natural order, and naturally known to them. Even the command prohibiting them to eat from the tree of the knowledge of good and evil, though arbitrary in its bare outward form, served to bring their natural, image-bearing obligations into focus. Because the human obligations in this covenant were legal in character and naturally perceived, I identified these obligations as a protological natural law.

In this section I argue for something analogous in the Noahic covenant. This covenant deals with the natural order generally and deals specifically with human beings according to their nature. The obligations of the covenant are not arbitrary but in accord with the nature of human beings as (fallen) image-bearers of God. There is a protological natural law after the fall, therefore, and since the flood God issues natural law through the covenant with Noah. Natural law is God's law for all human beings in the context of this universal covenantal relationship.[49]

Genesis 8:20–9:17 is a natural covenant, first, with respect to the created order broadly. God promises to restrain his wrath against the ground and against every living creature (Gen. 8:21) and reestablishes regular cycles of days and seasons (8:22). He also speaks of the animal kingdom (9:2-4) and restates his commitment to sustain the regular cycles of nature (9:11-17). God promulgates human obligation in the very same covenantal economy by which he ordains the existence, continuation, and functions of the natural order. This feature of both the covenant of creation and the Noahic covenant distinguishes them from the redemptive covenants of grace with Abraham, Israel, David, and the New Testament church, to be considered in Part 2, which have no immediate effect upon the order of nature and do not promulgate natural law.

The Noahic covenant is also natural with respect to its obligations, which are not arbitrary but fully consonant with human nature and known by nature. This is evident, first, from the fact that the obligations in Genesis 9:1-7 are similar to the basic obligations in Genesis 1:26-28 (alongside the dissimilarities

---

49. Burnside also interprets these obligations in terms of natural law: "Because Genesis 9:1-7 is addressed to all humanity, it is another example of a text which makes explicit universal knowledge of certain norms. In this sense, the Noahide laws are an example of natural law in the Bible." See *God, Justice, and Society,* p. 79.

discussed above). As argued in Chapter 1, these obligations were necessary implications of being created in God's image. The republishing of these commands in the Noahic covenant (in modified form) suggests that this covenant too deals with human beings in full accord with their nature.

More decisive, and confirming this conclusion, is the motive clause in Genesis 9:6: "Whoever sheds the blood of man, by man shall his blood be shed, *for God made man in his own image.*" Motive clauses "are the grammatically subordinate sentences in which the motivation for the commandment is given," the most common of which in the OT begins with the conjunction כִּי, as is the case in Genesis 9:6.[50] *Why* should bloodshed be punished with bloodshed? Because God made human beings in his own image. The reason is not God's arbitrary good pleasure or a pragmatic desire to deter crime, but the character of human nature. The fall into sin and God's curse upon the world have not altered the basic connection between human nature and the fundamental human tasks restated here. The Noahic covenant deals with human beings according to the kind of creatures they are.

The form of Genesis 9:6 may provide interesting confirmation. This verse has both legal and proverbial overtones, such that "whether its origin is legal or proverbial is indeterminable."[51] Given the interrelated origins of law and social custom, it is entirely plausible that we find here a legal principle expressing proverbial wisdom. As discussed in Chapter 1, modern positivistic conceptions should not shackle a theology of natural law. Historically both Christian theology and Western jurisprudence have considered law an ordering principle, not simply the explicit commands of the sovereign. As such, law may be written or unwritten. Law ordinarily reflects the customs of the people it governs, and law that does not do so tends to create social discord.[52] Chapter 7 will consider how Israel's divinely inspired law, for all its distinctive features, bore a close relationship to ancient Near Eastern social custom. If human law tends to originate in custom, then the simultaneously legal and proverbial flavor of Genesis 9:6 should not be surprising. Law and wisdom are

---

50. See B. Gemser, "The Importance of the Motive Clause in Old Testament Law," in *Supplements to Vetus Testamentum,* vol. 1 *Congress Volume* (Leiden: Brill, 1953), pp. 50, 53. For broader discussion of כִּי, in purpose clauses and elsewhere, see A. Schoors, "The Particle כִּי," in *Remembering All the Way . . . : A Collection of Old Testament Studies Published on the Occasion of the Fortieth Anniversary of the Oudtestamentisch Werkgezelschap in Nederland* (Leiden: Brill, 1981), pp. 240-76.

51. Wenham, *Genesis 1-15,* p. 193.

52. I discuss these issues in David VanDrunen, *Law & Custom: The Thought of Thomas Aquinas and the Future of the Common Law* (New York: Peter Lang, 2003).

intimately related elsewhere in the OT.[53] Thus it is plausible that Genesis 9:6 expresses a legal principle grounded in social custom so familiar that it had donned a proverbial cast. If so, we have further reason to speak of *natural law* in the Noahic covenant — that is, something both *natural* and *legal.*

First, the wording of Genesis 9:6 suggests the presence of *law.* Motive clauses are a strikingly distinctive feature — a "peculiarity" — of OT law in comparison to other ancient Near Eastern legal codes. While rare in these other codes, motive clauses are appended to well over half of the laws in Leviticus and Deuteronomy.[54] To Hebrew readers, Genesis 9:6 must have sounded like the statement of a law. In addition, the principle asserted — the *lex talionis* — is overtly legal. The *lex talionis* appears three times explicitly in the Mosaic law (Exod. 21:23-25; Lev. 24:18-21; Deut. 19:21) and is arguably one of the fundamental principles of its jurisprudence. Other ancient Near Eastern legal codes, older than the Pentateuch even on an early dating of the latter, also state the *lex talionis.*[55] Thus it is compelling to read Genesis 9:6 as a statement of law.

But it is also compelling to see a proverbial element of Genesis 9:6 and, behind this, something genuinely *natural.* Though meant to be read prescriptively, Genesis 9:6 is stated descriptively: "Whoever sheds the blood of man, by man shall his blood be shed." Like so many biblical proverbs, Genesis 9:6 describes the way things work in the course of human affairs, with strong moral force underlying the descriptive statement. The *lex talionis* in 9:6, expressing the principle of proportionate justice, seems to reflect the "sevenfold" justice God prescribed in response to murder in Genesis 4:15. Perhaps the *lex talionis* pre-dated the flood and the postdiluvian Noahic covenant simply alludes back to a conventional principle for handling legal disputes in primeval history. In any case, the talionic principle (whether enforced literally or not) was known in the ancient Near East after the flood, such that a statement expressing the principle as a statement of fact (such as Genesis 9:6) would have seemed true to life.

---

53. For example, Gemser notes the intriguing parallels between Leviticus 19:35ff. and Proverbs 11:1; 20:10, 23 and between Exodus 23:7 and Proverbs 17:15. See "The Importance of the Motive Clause," pp. 65-66. See also the extended discussion in Chapters 7-8 of the present book.

54. See Gemser, "The Importance of the Motive Clause," pp. 51-52. See also R. Sonsino, *Motive Clauses in Hebrew Law* (Chico, CA: Scholars, 1980).

55. E.g., see several of the laws of Hammurabi, in G. R. Driver and John C. Miles, *The Babylonian Laws,* 2 vols. (Oxford: Clarendon, 1952), §§196, 197, 200, which read that "if a man has put out the eye of a free man, they shall put out his eye," that "if he breaks the bone of a (free) man, they shall break his bone," and that "if a man knocks out the tooth of a (free) man equal (in rank) to him(self), they shall knock out his tooth."

Does this proverbial character of the principle imply that it is natural, in the sense of an objective, universally known (if not universally acknowledged) moral *obligation?* Being proverbial does not necessarily mean a principle is naturally obligatory, even when it is as widespread and transcultural as the *lex talionis.*[56] I suggest, however, that the *lex talionis* reflects insight about a just (though easily abused) human instinct toward restoring the balance after one has wronged another[57] and about how human beings need to conduct themselves if they are to maintain orderly societies that redress wrongdoing without spiraling into chaos, through constraining feuds and de-escalating cycles of violence. The *lex talionis,* in other words, arguably encapsulates part of humanity's natural moral obligation within the confines of a fallen and evil world. And this conclusion, suggested by the semi-proverbial form of the opening of Genesis 9:6, is confirmed by the motive clause at the end of the verse. By administering justice through the *lex talionis* the human race acts according to nature in the best sense: according to its identity as those who bear the image and likeness of God.

The preceding discussion raises important epistemological questions: How exactly do human beings know these natural moral obligations? How to discern between good and evil social customs? Like Genesis 1–2, Genesis 9 provides little explicit insight into these epistemological issues. Yet the discussion above suggests that insight from human custom may be at least part of the answer to the question of how one knows the natural law. The fact is, it does not seem too difficult for most people, across cultures, to understand the

56. For examination of how the *lex talionis* has been expressed and applied in a variety of cultures, see especially Miller, *Eye for an Eye.*

57. Many scholars not writing from a Christian perspective recognize this idea embedded in Genesis 9:6. See e.g. Peter French, *The Virtues of Vengeance* (Lawrence: University Press of Kansas, 2001), p. 97: "Personal and vicarious moral anger can be and ought to be placated by hostile responsive action taken against its cause. Wrongful actions require hostile responses. That is the basic form of the rule of retaliation, the principle of positive retribution. That, despite its seeming lack of fit with the body of moral principles upheld in our culture, is actually one of the primary foundations of morality. It is a foundation that is settled in passions, attitudes, emotions, and sentiments, not in reason. It embodies our concept of moral wrongness, provides the muscular element without which moral wrongness, wickedness, evil and like concepts would be without impact in our lives. It links our cares, the noncognitive aspects of our moral lives, our expectations and beliefs, and our ideals to action. And because of it vengeance may be a virtue and is sometimes necessary to maintain the moral order." See also Susan Jacoby, *Wild Justice: The Evolution of Revenge* (New York: Harper & Row, 1983), p. 9: "On a practical level, the human desire for retribution requires no elaborate philosophical rationalization. A victim wants to see an assailant punished not only for reasons of pragmatic deterrence but also as a means of repairing a damaged sense of civic order and personal identity."

necessity of pursuing the chief matters of concern for the Noahic natural law — procreation, eating plants and animals, and proportionate retributive justice — and this precisely because of their fundamental importance for survival of human society and of the species itself. Human practices that run against the grain of securing such goods are inherently self-destructive. Conversely, those that promote such goods tend to commend themselves for their usefulness to human well-being and to endure over time. Thus longstanding social custom can offer *evidence* of the demands of the natural law (though in a sinful world this is never definitive).

My conclusion in this section is that the obligations placed upon the human race in Genesis 9:1-7 are natural moral obligations, grounded in the original creation of human beings in the image of God and continuing in the present fallen world. As in Genesis 1–2, these obligations are legal in character and naturally known. People across cultural divides customarily practice these obligations (however imperfectly) — procreation, eating of plants and animals humanely, and pursuit of proportionate retributive justice with forbearance — providing evidence of an enduring human instinct toward these society-preserving activities. Hence we may accurately describe the human obligations within the Noahic covenant as *natural law* and we have good reason to assert that the Noahic covenant — as the formal reestablishment of the postlapsarian natural order — is the foundation for the ongoing presence and force of natural law in the world today.

Conclusion

In this chapter I have argued that the postdiluvian Noahic covenant is foundational for a theological understanding of natural law in the fallen world. Since the end of the flood and as long as "the earth remains" (Gen. 8:22), God governs the natural and social orders and sustains human beings as his image-bearers by means of this covenant. Through it God communicates a natural knowledge of his law to all human beings, imparting obligations that are not arbitrary, but consonant with human nature and necessary for its survival. This natural law exists in organic continuity with natural law as it existed under the covenant of creation, but is also different in important respects, reflecting the effects upon human nature and the broader natural order brought about by the fall into sin and God's curse upon creation (tempered by his common grace). Human nature and human identity as divine image-bearer did not essentially change, but were marred and corrupted. Before the fall God destined the original creation to reach a state of consummation. Accordingly, natural law commissioned human beings, as image-bearers of a God who created and then rested, to exercise royal rule in this world and thereby to attain the eschatological new creation. After the fall God preserves the original creation in a fallen condition, and since the flood does so through his covenant with Noah. In terms I used in the Introduction, *common grace preserves nature.*

In accord with this situation, natural law continues to commission human image-bearers to exercise a species of rule in this world, in likeness to God's preservative rule under the Noahic covenant. The text of Genesis 9:1-7 presents the natural moral obligations of the covenant in thin and minimalist fashion: procreating, eating plants and animals (within bounds), and pursuing proportionate retributive justice. This indicates that the chief focus of the Noahic order and its natural law is the sustenance of the species and maintenance of basic social peace. Thus humanity's postlapsarian natural obligations bear organic continuity with their prelapsarian natural obligations, but take a somewhat truncated form. God himself seems to do most of humanity's original work of subduing the other creatures (Gen. 9:2; cf. 1:28) and the original dominion mandate shrinks into the responsibility to remedy intrahuman wrongs through the *lex talionis* (Gen. 9:6; cf. 1:26). This is because God designed human beings in their state of integrity to fulfill their natural obligations and thereby to attain eschatological consummation, while fallen human beings preserved under the Noahic covenant are unable to complete such a task. Thus natural law now primarily aims to maintain the present world, not to point the way toward consummation. Yet several considerations in 9:1-7 and surrounding context suggest that this Noahic natural law also communicates a richer and thicker ethic that requires social institutions such as family and state, human industry, generosity toward fellow human beings, and homage toward God. Thus, though its focus is upon preservation of human society, the natural law of the Noahic covenant also hints at a broader moral order and at a limited and penultimate human flourishing that God allows his image-bearers to attain, to some degree, through the blessing of common grace.

A comparison of natural law under the covenant of creation and natural law under the Noahic covenant with respect to retributive justice also displays their simultaneous difference and organic continuity. The natural law is *natural* in important part because it is an implication of the image-bearing nature of humanity: to bear God's image entails being called to a moral task in his likeness. But human persons can only bear the image of the God they know, and the God they know is the one who has entered into concrete covenant relationship with them and revealed himself to them in this relationship.

While God originally revealed himself in the covenant of creation as a God who would administer retributive justice strictly, in the Noahic covenant he revealed his retributive justice tempered by forbearance and longsuffering. Under this latter covenant, therefore, bearing God's image entails pursuing proportionate retributive justice, but in ways tempered by forbearance, according to a wisdom that seeks the common good of human society rather than its harm.

These initial conclusions about natural law in the postlapsarian world already suggest some significant implications for thinking about natural law's relationship to civil law and social life generally. Christian theologians classically have considered natural law foundational for civil law (without this meaning that natural law imposes one ideal model for civil law or that every natural law issue is necessarily subject to civil law regulation).[58] This chapter's conclusions provide biblical-theological foundation for this idea. Since God maintains the world and the human social order through the Noahic covenant, it must be this covenant's natural law that provides the moral substance from which human beings should give shape to their civil law. Since proportionate retributive justice is one of the moral issues upon which the Noahic covenant specifically focuses, presumably civil law's chief concern should be identifying natural human responsibilities toward one another and rectifying wrongs committed in intrahuman conflicts. Since the Noahic covenant requires proportionate retributive justice as tempered by forbearance, but without specifying exactly how that should work out, there is no single ideal "natural law" civil code or public policy. Each society must develop its own legal systems and rules, consistent with the natural law but according to its own wisdom in particular circumstances.[59] Finally, since retributive justice must be tempered by forbearance, social life in a fallen world must be decidedly nonutopian:[60] fallen human societies can never remedy every wrong and attain the ideal so-

---

58. E.g., see Thomas Aquinas, *Summa Theologiae*, 1a2ae 91.3; 95.2; Martin Luther, "Temporal Authority: To What Extent It Should be Obeyed," in *Luther's Works*, vol. 45, ed. Walther I. Brandt (Philadelphia: Muhlenberg, 1962), pp. 127-28; John Calvin, *Institutes of the Christian Religion*, 4.20.16; and Francis Turretin, *Institutes of Elenctic Theology*, vol. 2, trans. George Musgrave Giger, ed. James T. Dennison Jr. (Phillipsburg, NJ: Presbyterian and Reformed, 1992-97), p. 2.

59. This is another conviction common in broader Christian natural law thought. E.g., see Aquinas, *Summa Theologiae* 1a2ae 95-97; Calvin, *Institutes of the Christian Religion*, 4.20.16; and Turretin, *Institutes*, 2:167.

60. This suggests that my theology of natural law stands somewhere in the tradition of Augustinian realism with respect to social and political life.

cial order. The quest to right wrongs is an admirable good, yet must serve the common good and the preservation of society, not destroy what is left of it.[61]

The analysis of natural law and the image of God in this chapter raises other possible implications for understanding human social life. God preserves a culturally productive human society and ordains the practice of human justice by means of the Noahic *covenant*. God is a covenant-making God. This may suggest that his image-bearers are to be covenant-making people, particularly in regard to establishing social arrangements among themselves that promote at least the preservation of human society, and perhaps even its partial flourishing, in accord with the purposes of the Noahic covenant. It is an intriguing suggestion since many communities have formed social laws and institutions through covenants and treaties of various sorts, and Scripture presents Abraham doing exactly this shortly after the account of Noah (see Gen. 21:22-34).[62]

This chapter's conclusions also have implications for disputed social questions about religious pluralism and religious liberty. In the Introduction, I stated that the theology of natural law developed in this book is basically a premodern version of natural law, but that its embrace of religious liberty also gives it a modern flavor. This chapter has provided some crucial foundation for my positive view of religious liberty. For one thing, God established the Noahic covenant with the entire human race and gave no religious qualification for participation in its blessings and activities. If God called all human beings generally to the pursuit of procreation, eating, and justice (and whatever other obligations this covenant entails), without excluding people for reason of religious profession, then excluding people for this reason is inherently problematic. Also significant is how Genesis 9:6 commands the pursuit of justice and authorizes the use of coercion through the *lex talionis,* which concerns *intrahuman* disputes and the injuries one person inflicts upon another. It does not speak of human beings prosecuting each other for wrongs inflicted upon God. Therefore to prohibit a person from engaging in a particular kind of religious practice, which does not injure another person but allegedly injures God, seems to transgress the boundaries of rightful human authority under

61. Perhaps the South African Truth and Reconciliation Commission represents a good example of this principle at work. The Commission did not seek to punish every wrong committed during the apartheid era, recognizing the destructiveness and even impossibility of such a task, but to bring truth to light for the purpose of reconciling estranged parties and promoting the future well-being of South African society.

62. See also David Novak, *The Jewish Social Contract: An Essay in Political Theology* (Princeton: Princeton University Press, 2005), pp. 45-46.

the Noahic covenant. For these basic reasons, I suggest, the Noahic covenant provides crucial biblical-theological foundation for the right to religious freedom. This initial conclusion does not suggest that religious observance is unimportant, but simply that now is not the time at which God wills to bring the human race into judgment for lack of proper devotion to him. These questions concerning natural law, civil law, and social life will reemerge in subsequent chapters, and I will revisit them in most detail in Chapter 10.

This chapter's analysis of natural law in the present world — fallen but preserved through God's covenant with Noah — is foundational for the arguments that unfold in all subsequent chapters. In Chapters 3-5 I seek to confirm and enrich this chapter's conclusions by examining God's government of the nations of the world and how he holds them accountable to himself not through special prophetic revelation but through his natural law. Not until Chapters 6-9 do I examine the significance of natural law for the moral life of Abraham's household, the people of Israel, and the New Testament church, that is, those with whom God has also entered *redemptive* covenant relationship.

CHAPTER 3

Judgment on Sodom, Justice in Gerar: Natural Law in Genesis 19–20

The previous chapter argued that God's postdiluvian covenant with Noah is foundational for a theological understanding of natural law after the fall into sin. After the fall God did not bring the world to final judgment, but preserved the order of nature, in a fallen condition, through his common grace. Since the great flood he does so through a formal covenant relationship with the entire human race and all of creation (Gen. 8:20–9:17). As part of this general preservation of nature God maintains the natural law, which exists in organic continuity with the prelapsarian natural law but has now been refracted for a fallen world through the Noahic covenant.

In the book of Genesis the storyline soon turns to Abraham and God's special covenant relationship with his household and descendants. These biblical stories also implicitly provide a kind of report on how things are going among the nations of the world as God governs them under the Noahic covenant and thus through the natural law. This chapter looks specifically at Genesis 19 and 20, which provide poignant — and contrasting — aspects of this report. In the cities of Sodom and Gomorrah, life under the Noahic covenant is going very badly, and God brings radical judgment upon them; in the city of Gerar, life under the Noahic covenant seems to be going relatively well, and its king treats Abraham with decency and civility when he sojourns within its territory.

This examination of Genesis 19–20 confirms the observation in Chapter 2 that the text of Genesis 9:1-7 sets forth a bare, minimalist ethic that is the focus of God's government of the world through the natural law under the Noahic covenant, an ethic concerned with the basic sustenance of human society. In Genesis 19 God brings radical judgment within history upon cities that egregiously violate even this minimal moral standard and Genesis 20 provides evidence of the continuing testimony of the natural law in a city that generally observes its basic norms. But Genesis 19–20 also confirms my claim that even Genesis 9:1-7, read in context, suggests that a richer and thicker natural moral order underlies this minimalist ethic explicit on the surface of the text. This natural moral order points toward a limited and penultimate human flourishing in this fallen world. For example, the norms of procreation (Gen. 9:1, 7) require proper sexual and familial relations, and proportionate retributive justice (9:6) requires proper judicial procedures. And undergirding all of this should be humility and recognition of one's place in the world, especially before God.

This chapter, therefore, serves to confirm and enrich many of the conclusions of the previous chapter concerning God's government of the nations of the world through the natural law by means of the Noahic covenant of common grace. We first consider the dark side of the story in the account of Sodom in Genesis 19 and then examine the brighter side in the narrative of Abraham's sojourn in Gerar in Genesis 20. In Chapter 6 we will revisit some details of these texts in order to reflect upon Abraham's relation to these foreign nations and what this indicates about the significance of natural law for the moral life of those in redemptive covenant with God.

Natural Law and God's Judgment against Sodom

At the beginning of human history God held out the hope of eschatological life but also threatened the judgment of death for disobedience (Gen. 2:16-17), as considered in Chapter 1. Upon the fall into sin, God postponed the final judgment, but the rest of Scripture indicates that he did not cancel it. The postponement of final judgment enabled the continuation of human history and its activities, with their joys and sorrows (3:16-19), and opened the prospect for the coming of a messianic deliverer (3:15). Yet the specter of judgment looms large as the biblical story proceeds. After a concise account of the generations following Adam (Genesis 4–5), Scripture speaks of the profound wickedness of humanity and records God's judgment upon it through the flood of Noah's day (Genesis 6–7). The great flood, in its universal extent and devastation, seems like the judgment we might have expected after the rebellion in Eden. But though the Scriptures would later look back to the flood as a preeminent harbinger of the final judgment (e.g., Isa. 24:18; 26:20; Luke 17:26-27; 2 Pet. 3:5-7),[1] it was not the final judgment itself. God made the waters recede, caused the earth to take shape

---

1. See e.g. the discussion in Daniel R. Streett, "As It Was in the Days of Noah: The Prophets' Typological Interpretation of Noah's Flood," *Criswell Theological Review* 5 (Fall 2007): 33-51.

again in a new creation scene, and entered into a covenant of preservation with every living creature to enable the resumption of human history (Gen. 8:1–9:17).

Insofar as God promised never again to destroy the earth with a flood (9:11, 15), this covenant not only further postponed the final judgment but also announced that the final judgment would never again be so thoroughly anticipated. Until the last day God would not bring another worldwide reckoning as a foretaste of the great assize. But God did not foreclose his right to impose judgment upon particular people and places, in ways that would also provide a glimpse of the final judgment, albeit on a smaller scale. As the Genesis story progresses this is exactly what God does.

The first example comes already in Genesis 11:1-9. The people of the earth, proudly wishing to make a name for themselves, unite at Babel to build a tower to the top of heaven. God responds in judgment by confusing their language and dispersing them over the earth. This judgment itself sounds relatively minor, and Scripture never again explicitly mentions the name of Babel. But the Old Testament (OT) prophets make clear that the proud spirit of Babel revives in the subsequent city that blossoms on the plain of Shinar and seeks to seize the heights of heaven, Babylon (e.g., see Isa. 14:13-14; Dan. 4:22). In the New Testament (NT) Babylon becomes the symbol of the great world-city to be overthrown on the day of final judgment (Revelation 18). God's judgment upon the hubris of Babel is thus a type of the universal judgment to come upon all the world. Several chapters later comes another type of the last judgment: the fiery destruction of Sodom and Gomorrah (Gen. 18:22–19:29). I examine some later biblical examples in Chapter 4, but this judgment upon Sodom and Gomorrah provides the focus for the first section of the present chapter.

The parallels between the destruction of the flood and the judgment upon Sodom, and the corresponding rescue of Noah and Lot (Abraham's nephew who lived in Sodom), are numerous. Both Noah and Lot were reckoned among the "righteous" (Gen. 6:9; 18:23, 25; 19:29; 2 Pet. 2:7). Both were the only ones whom God distinguished from their wicked neighbors, and both of their immediate families were also spared. In both cases God's judgment was absolutely devastating for every living thing (Gen. 7:21-23; 19:24-25). As God opened the "heavens" and made "rain" fall in the days of Noah (7:11-12), so in the days of Lot the Lord "rained" fire and brimstone "out of heaven" upon Sodom and Gomorrah (19:24).[2] In bigger context, Scripture presents both

---

2. For further comments on this parallel, see Robert Alter, *Genesis: Translation and Commentary* (New York: W. W. Norton, 1996), p. 88; and Robert Alter, "Sodom as Nexus: The Web of Design in Biblical Narrative," *Tikkun* 1 (1986): 34.

judgments as proportionate and fitting, expressing God's standard of judgment as reflected in the *lex talionis*.[3] After their deliverance, both Noah and Lot fell victim to drunkenness and were sexually exploited by their children (9:20-22; 19:30-38).[4] They were "righteous," yet sinners whose rescue depended upon grace. The NT confirms these unmistakable parallels within the Genesis text. Second Peter associates the judgment of the flood and the corresponding salvation of Noah with the judgment upon Sodom and the corresponding salvation of Lot. They are both proof that "the Lord knows how to rescue the godly from trials, and to keep the unrighteous under punishment until the day of judgment" (2:5-9). Second Peter 3 further develops this day-of-judgment theme. As "the world that then existed" was destroyed by the flood, so "the heavens and earth that now exist" are kept for a judgment of fire (3:5-7). Likewise, Jude 6-7 looks back to the destruction of Sodom and Gomorrah as an "example" of "the judgment of the great day" by "undergoing a punishment of eternal fire." Jesus comments that "the day when the Son of Man is revealed" will be like "the day when Noah entered the ark, and the flood came and destroyed them all" and when "Lot went out from Sodom" and "fire and sulfur rained from heaven and destroyed them all" (Luke 17:26-30).

The OT also links Sodom and its neighboring cities to a coming day of judgment in a variety of ways (e.g., Deut. 29:23; Isa. 1:9-10; 13:19; Jer. 49:18; 50:40; Lam. 4:6; Hos. 11:8; Amos 4:11; Zeph. 2:9).[5] God had promised to Noah that he would never again cut off all flesh "by the waters of the flood" (Gen. 9:11) and would sustain the natural order "while the earth remains" (8:22). In

---

3. As human wickedness before the flood (Gen. 6:1-2, 5, 11-12) reversed God's original blessing and commission of human beings at creation (1:28-29), so in the flood God reversed the effects of his speech at creation that made life on earth possible at all, wiping out the distinction between the dry land and the seas (1:9-10) and between the waters below and the waters above (1:6-7). Likewise in Genesis 19:1-29, as the men of Sodom made their land terribly inhospitable for their fellow human beings through their wickedness, so God made the land radically inhospitable for them through the fire and brimstone. My thanks to Jonathan Burnside for his suggestions on this matter.

4. On Noah being sexually exploited, see footnote 23 below.

5. Some scholars note that Genesis 19 is the Genesis passage most frequently cited in the rest of Scripture; see Terence E. Fretheim, *The Book of Genesis*, in *The New Interpreter's Bible*, vol. 1 (Nashville: Abingdon, 1994), p. 473; and Robert Ignatius Letellier, *Day in Mamre, Night in Sodom: Abraham and Lot in Genesis 18 and 19* (Leiden: Brill, 1995), pp. 241-42. Weston W. Fields, *Sodom and Gomorrah: History and Motif in Biblical Narrative* (Sheffield: Sheffield Academic Press, 1997), p. 158, comments that later biblical use of the Sodom theme to describe divine judgment emphasizes the judgment's sudden and spectacular nature, its totality, and its perpetuity.

accord with these promises, the biblical writers expect a coming day of universal desolation, by fire rather than water, when the earth in its present form will remain no more. In the meantime, God destroyed Sodom with fire, reminiscent of the judgment of the flood and foreshadowing the final judgment.

The question arises as to why God singles out *Sodom,* or any of the other locales I consider in the next chapter, as the place to bring a great local judgment in anticipation of the final judgment, even while he continues to preserve the rest of the world all around. Scripture provides no exact calculus for determining a tipping point that triggers these great local judgments, but in the case of Sodom and the locales discussed in the next chapter, the recipients of such judgments are guilty of extreme wrongs — of atrocities. Genesis 19:1-11 presents life in Sodom as shockingly perverse, and the rest of Scripture treats it as such.[6] Though all of the major figures in Genesis, whether patriarch or pagan, are portrayed as mixed characters, with a variety of good and bad traits, Genesis 19 depicts the men of Sodom as unambiguously evil.

What exactly are the atrocities of the Sodomites? As far as the biblical text indicates, God had given no prophetic revelation to Sodom. Accordingly Genesis 19 does not expose their wickedness in terms of disobedience to a special divine command or lack of faith in a divine promise of salvation. My analysis in Chapter 2 suggests that God and Sodom were in relationship through the covenant with Noah, and thus we might expect God to hold Sodom accountable for violation of their obligations under the Noahic natural law. The biblical account is consistent with this hunch. In the events of Genesis 19, Sodom's sexual perversity and flagrant disregard for justice confirm the rumors that had reached God's ears (Gen. 18:21).[7] They are not guilty simply of transgressing some of the remote moral implications of the Noahic covenant, but of egregiously violating the bare minimalist ethic explicit in Genesis 9:1-7, meant to ensure the basic sustenance of human society. Specifically, they fail to pursue procreatively fruitful sexuality and proportionate justice. The judgment against Sodom, a preview of the final judgment, is a poignant reminder that

---

6. In subsequent biblical texts Sodom and Gomorrah "symbolize the worst that can be imagined" (Fretheim, *Genesis,* p. 473), and Sodom "is the biblical version of anti-civilization" (Alter, "Sodom as Nexus," p. 32). According to Fields (*Sodom and Gomorrah,* pp. 171-72), Sodom is *archetypically* wicked.

7. Among writers identifying these two things as the particular sins of Sodom, see also Claus Westermann, *Genesis 12–36: A Commentary,* trans. John J. Scullion, S.J. (Minneapolis: Augsburg, 1985), p. 301; and Bruce K. Waltke (Cathi J. Fredricks), *Genesis: A Commentary* (Grand Rapids: Zondervan, 2001), p. 276.

all people know these fundamentals of the natural law and that God holds all people accountable for their violation.[8]

God's remarkable encounter with Abraham in Genesis 18, and their conversation about judgment and mercy, is an intimate part of the larger story concerning Sodom, but I will return to this account in Chapter 6 when discussing natural law and the Abrahamic covenant. In this section I focus upon Genesis 19:1-11 and the events that transpire within the walls of Sodom, after God's two angelic delegates, in human guise, take their leave from Abraham and journey to the city (18:22). We see here Sodom's violation of the fundamentals of the natural law through their sexual perversity and their mockery of justice.

Sexual Immorality in Sodom

Even before the people of Sodom perform a single action (in Gen. 19:4), this text communicates in clear but subtle ways that something is amiss in the city. When the angels come to Sodom it is already evening (19:1). This seemingly mundane comment creates an ominous feeling, since in this text, as elsewhere in Scripture, darkness and night are affiliated with evil.[9] As the day wanes, Lot is sitting in the city gate (19:1), often a place bustling with commercial and judicial activity in an ancient town.[10] When Lot alone approaches the angels and offers them hospitality, therefore, the reader is left wondering why none of the natives of Sodom, but only a sojourner, bothers to greet these visitors.[11] Lot's initial invitation compounds these negative vibes about Sodom. Even

---

8. Some commentators offer similar observations. E.g., Fretheim, *Genesis*, p. 476, writes: "Sodom is condemned, not because they have no faith in God, but because of the way in which they treat their brothers and sisters. God holds the nonchosen accountable for such behaviors. This assumes an understanding of natural law, wherein God's intentions for all people are clear in the creational order (cf. the oracles of the prophets against the nations, e.g., Amos 1–2)." Nahum Sarna, *Genesis*, in *The JPS Torah Commentary* (Philadelphia: The Jewish Publication Society, 1989), p. 132, writes: "The indictment of Sodom lies entirely in the moral realm; there is no hint of cultic offense, no whisper of idolatry. As with the Flood story, the Sodom and Gomorrah narrative assumes the existence of a universal moral law that God expects all humankind to follow."

9. See discussions in Fields, *Sodom and Gomorrah*, pp. 103-08; and Letellier, *Day in Mamre*, pp. 59-60.

10. See Alter, *Genesis*, p. 84; Victor P. Hamilton, *The Book of Genesis: Chapters 18–50* (Grand Rapids: Eerdmans, 1995), p. 32; Waltke, *Genesis*, 275; and Sarna, *Genesis*, pp. 133-34.

11. See William John Lyons, *Canon and Exegesis: Canonical Praxis and the Sodom Narrative* (Sheffield: Sheffield Academic Press, 2002), p. 216.

before hearing their plans he invites them to spend the night at his house and then to "rise up early and go on your way" (19:2). Lot's intention, it seems, is to get them out of town as quickly as possible, hinting that Sodom is not a nice place to stay or be seen.[12] Finally, Lot's anxious insistence that the visitors not sleep in the town square confirms readers' bad first impression of Sodom: "he pressed them strongly" (19:3).[13] Would something bad happen to them if they sleep there?

The provenance of Lot's anxiety becomes quickly evident in the following verses. After dinner, the entire male population of Sodom gathers outside Lot's house demanding that he bring out his guests so that they might "know them." Lot begs them to refrain and even offers to bring out his daughters in their place. They ridicule him and move to break down the door. The angels then pull Lot back into the house and strike the men with blindness, though the men continue to grope for the door unsuccessfully (19:4-11).

Readers have traditionally understood this story as describing the Sodomites' quest to gang-rape the angelic visitors. The straightforward reading of the text itself, combined with the narrative's obvious parallels to Judges 19 and the NT's references to the "sensual conduct" and "unnatural desire" (2 Pet. 2:7; Jude 7) of the men of Sodom, have made this the obvious and accepted interpretation. Sodom has thus come to be associated with homosexuality and its name borrowed to describe homosexual behavior ("sodomy" and "sodomize"). The change of perspective on homosexuality in much of Western society in recent years, however, has prompted numerous rereadings of Genesis 19:1-11 that seek either to downplay the significance of the homosexual element in the story or even to assert that homosexual rape was not the intention of the Sodomites at all. Identifying the "sin of Sodom" has become a disputed issue.

I conclude, based upon Genesis 19:1-11 itself and later biblical interpretation of this text and related themes, that any myopic focus upon homosexual conduct as *the* sin of Sodom is indeed problematic,[14] but that the homosexual element of the Sodomites' attempted action is part of the equation. The citizens of Sodom exemplify an extreme breach of humane social relations and the radical overturning of the Noahic moral order. This is particularly manifest in two ways, their derisive corruption of both sexual propriety and justice. What binds together these two manifestations of their radical violation of natural

---

12. See Waltke, *Genesis*, p. 275.

13. See Letellier, *Day in Mamre*, p. 147.

14. As John Calvin puts it, "they were not contaminated with one vice only, but were given up to all audacity in crime, so that no sense of shame was left them." See John Calvin, *Commentaries on Genesis*, vol. 1, trans. John King (Grand Rapids: Baker, 2003), pp. 496-97.

law is how they strike at the heart of what it means to be an image-bearer of God and express a self-centered pride and hatred of the other.

I consider first their sin of egregious sexual immorality as described in Genesis 19:4-5. Before we can evaluate the moral character of their conduct we must establish what exactly the men of Sodom intended to do when they surrounded Lot's house and shouted, "Where are the men who came to you tonight? Bring them out to us, that we may know them." A number of inter-connected arguments support the traditional understanding that their purpose was gang rape. First, the term "to know" makes a sexual interpretation of their demand at least possible. The Hebrew word, ידע, has a variety of meanings in the OT. In the vast majority of occurrences it does not carry sexual connota-tions, but more than a dozen times it does, including a couple with reference to male homosexual acts. Second, Lot's counter-offer of his daughters in 19:8 strongly supports a gang-rape interpretation of 19:5. When a common word, such as ידע, has a variety of possible meanings, the context in which a particu-lar use appears is crucial. Lot says: "Behold, I have two daughters who have not *known* any man. Let me bring them out to you, and do to them as you please. Only do nothing to these men. . . ." Lot, therefore, answers the Sodomites by using the same term they used, and his use has an explicit sexual meaning. The larger purpose of Lot's response is also telling. Lot offers his daughters as a reciprocal exchange: he seeks to assuage the men by letting them do to his daughters something similar to what they planned against his guests. By identifying his daughters in terms of their sexual status — as virgins — he demonstrates his understanding that the Sodomites have sexual exploits in mind. Unless Lot, who has lived among the men of Sodom for many years, has radically misunderstood their purposes, his response indicates that they have come to rape.[15]

Third, the numerous parallels between Genesis 19:1-11 and the story of the Levite's concubine in Judges 19 further confirm that the Sodomites in-tended to perform gang rape.[16] In this latter account the men of Gibeah de-mand to "know" a male guest in the city. The master of the house where he is staying counter-offers his virgin daughter and his guest's concubine, and

15. For supporting arguments, see e.g. Hamilton, *Genesis*, pp. 34-35; Robert A. J. Gag-non, *The Bible and Homosexual Practice: Texts and Hermeneutics* (Nashville: Abingdon, 2001), pp. 73-74; Donald J. Wold, *Out of Order: Homosexuality in the Bible and the Ancient Near East* (Grand Rapids: Baker, 1998), chap. 5; Letellier, *Day in Mamre*, pp. 156-57; and Lyons, *Canon and Exegesis,* pp. 227-28.

16. On the similar motifs in Genesis 19 and Judges 19, see especially Fields, *Sodom and Gomorrah.*

the Gibeonites, though never formally agreeing to the counter-offer, proceed to "know" and "abuse" the concubine all night. The same basic storyline and terminology refer to gang rape that is actually carried out. Finally, some of the later OT and NT references to Sodom characterize the city as sexually corrupt. Ezekiel 16 is an intriguing example. Though other, nonsexual, sins are associated with "Sodom," particularly in 16:49, this reference to Sodom falls within a broader indictment of Judah that is pervaded with sexual overtones. Two NT statements are more explicit. Second Peter 2:7 speaks of Sodom's ἀσέλγεια, which refers to licentiousness or sensuality that often includes a sexual dimension. Jude 7 speaks of how Sodom "indulged in sexual immorality" (ἐκπορνεύσασαι) and "pursued unnatural desire," or, more literally, went after "other flesh" (σαρκὸς ἑτέρας).

A couple of recent counter-proposals on Genesis 19:4 are worth considering briefly. Brian Doyle, for example, noting that ידע most often carries no sexual connotation, argues that the "people of Sodom were not out on a frenzied search for sexual gratification, their ultimate plan was 'to know' the divine presence and thereby rise above the divine in an act of hubris."[17] Though Doyle offers interesting exegetical suggestions concerning the terms "door" and "opening" in Genesis 18–19, his interpretation of the Sodomites' intentions rests upon a few conclusions I judge to be unwarranted. One conclusion is that Lot completely misunderstood what the Sodomites wanted when they came to his door. Given the story later in Genesis 19 concerning Lot and his daughters, the idea that Lot might play the buffoon with the city's citizens is not far-fetched. But Lot had lived in Sodom or its environs for a long time, and was a prominent enough sojourner to be accorded a place in their economic and judicial dealings at the city gate. This makes it unlikely that he would so massively misinterpret their intentions. The violent reaction of the Sodomites to his counter-offer, furthermore, is more likely the response of those whose overtures were understood and rejected rather than of those whose demands were comically misunderstood. Another unwarranted conclusion of Doyle is that the men of Sodom knew that the two visitors were angelic beings. Given Lot's apparent ignorance of their identity, though he had greeted and dined with them in his home, there is little reason to think that the Sodomites, who had avoided any personal contact with the visitors to this point, would have been conscious of their supernatural character. Doyle rightly notes the theme of Sodomite pride, as developed in Ezekiel 16, but this can be understood

17. Brian Doyle, "'Knock, Knock, Knockin' on Sodom's Door': The Function of דלת/ פתח in Genesis 18–19," *JSOT* 28, no. 4 (2004): 435-38.

convincingly without reinterpreting the Sodomites' quest in nonsexual terms, as I discuss below.

Scott Morschauser has offered another nonsexual reading of the Sodomites' intentions, and a more plausible one in my judgment. Morschauser argues that "to know" should be understood in a judicial sense. Lot had welcomed the angelic visitors in his role as keeper of the city gate. The men of Sodom came to Lot seeking to ascertain why the visitors had come to the city (perhaps they were spies), and Lot's counter-offer was that his daughters be held in protective custody until these visitors would leave the city. By mentioning his daughters' virginity he emphasized their value (in that cultural context), and demonstrated his good faith and seriousness as gatekeeper. The Sodomites, however, rejected Lot's proposal and proved themselves to be violators of the rule of law.[18] Morschauser raises a number of interesting exegetical arguments, and his view of the judicial dimensions of this story (and of the Sodomites' rejection of the rule of law) is potentially friendly to my broader arguments about the character of natural law. Nevertheless, it is difficult to see why a temporary suspension of legal procedure would warrant the unique and devastating judgment that Sodom received, or how it would accord with Scripture's initial comment about the city in Genesis 13:13: "Now the men of Sodom were wicked, great sinners against the Lord." Furthermore, it is implausible that the Sodomites would have granted Lot the honor and responsibility of guarding the city gate in the first place but then have distrusted and dishonored him in this manner. For such reasons, I find Morschauser's case ultimately unpersuasive.

That Genesis 19 views the *homosexual* character of their conduct, and not simply its violent nature, as exacerbating the general wickedness of the men of Sodom deserves further comment. Many recent writers, even if not denying that the Sodomites intended to gang-rape the visitors, have argued that Scripture itself subsequently interprets the sin of Sodom as something other than specifically sexual. According to some, the emphasis is not upon individual misdeeds but social misdeeds, either in terms of a general breakdown of social order or more specific problems such as oppression of the poor and needy.[19] Many of these arguments have appropriately called attention to

18. Scott Morschauser, "'Hospitality,' Hostiles and Hostages: On the Legal Background to Genesis 19.1-9," *JSOT* 27, no. 4 (2003): 461-85.

19. Along these lines see e.g. Walter Brueggemann, *Genesis* (Atlanta: John Knox, 1982), p. 164; Lyons, *Canon and Exegesis*, pp. 234-35; Hamilton, *Genesis*, p. 21; Fretheim, *Genesis*, p. 474; and J. A. Loader, *A Tale of Two Cities: Sodom and Gomorrah in the Old Testament, Early Jewish and Early Christian Traditions* (Kampen: Kok, 1990), p. 37.

various OT texts that could easily be overlooked and have served to warn against a myopic identification of the "sin of Sodom" as homosexual conduct in the abstract. Several considerations, however, also warn against making the homosexual dimension of the story an unimportant or indifferent matter.

First, the story in Genesis 18–19 cannot be read without the Adamic, Noahic, and Abrahamic covenants in the background. In each of these covenants the concept of *fertility* is prominent. The original covenant of creation commanded human beings to "be fruitful and multiply" (Gen. 1:28), the Noahic covenant repeated this universal precept (9:1, 7), and the Abrahamic covenant revolved around the promise of a son to an infertile couple (12:2; 15:3-6; 17:2-8, 15-21; 18:9-15). The concept of fertility also lies behind the primordial promise of a Messianic offspring for Eve, who will continue to bear children after the fall, albeit painfully (3:15-16). In this context, the Sodomites' pursuit of an inherently infertile form of sexual activity stands in contrast to the tenor of God's laws and promises in these different contexts.[20]

Second, both the Adamic and Noahic covenants make the image of God prominent (1:26-27; 9:6). The people of Sodom were among the mass of humanity sustained as image-bearers according to the provisions of the Noahic covenant. One significant feature of the original creation of human beings in God's image is that God made them "male and female" (1:27). Otherness and difference, rather than uniformity — particularly with respect to sexual identity — characterizes humanity in the image of God. Below I discuss other (xenophobic) problems that the Sodomites had with otherness and difference, but for now I simply note that their desire for union with those who are the same *(homo)* as they are stands again in contrast to prior biblical teaching about the natural order of human relations. This concern is related to a third point, which also seeks to read Genesis 19 in the broader context of the Genesis narratives. In many stories in Genesis, both prior and subsequent to Genesis 19, the treatment of women is a significant issue. As I argue below, two of the stories that raise questions about natural law most poignantly — concerning Abraham and Abimelech in Genesis 20 and Dinah in Genesis 34 — involve sexual sin against women. Leon Kass makes the intriguing observation that Sodom is actually the ultimate misogynist society, relegating women neither to the harem (as in Egypt) nor to concubinage (as in the rural tribe), but treating them with utter disdain.[21] The Sodomites' homosexual desire is such that they

---

20. For similar comments, see Alter, "Sodom as Nexus," p. 33.

21. Leon R. Kass, *The Beginning of Wisdom: Reading Genesis* (Chicago: University of Chicago Press, 2003), p. 330.

not only seek to violate the male visitors in the first place, but have absolutely no interest in the female substitutes Lot offers.[22] If this suggestion accurately reflects the implications of the biblical text, then the homosexual intention of the men of Sodom exemplifies a basic moral problem highlighted in various ways through Genesis: the failure of males to honor females properly, especially in matters of sex and family.

A fourth reason to believe that the homosexual element is meant to be read as an exacerbating factor in the condemnation of Sodom in Genesis 19 arises from the fact that Genesis was written for OT Israel and that homosexual conduct had negative associations for this original audience. The Mosaic law twice condemns homosexual intercourse explicitly (Lev. 18:22; 20:13). It even indicates that the former inhabitants of Canaan, who were to be totally destroyed by the Israelites (evoking memories of Sodom's destruction), were expelled from the land precisely for committing such sins (18:24; 20:23).[23] It is therefore doubtful that the narrator would have written, or the original audience read, the story in Genesis 19 without the homosexual element evoking negative overtones. Finally, Jude 7, which points to the "other flesh" aspect of the Sodomites' conduct as explaining their punishment, offers NT support for seeing the homosexual aspect of the Sodomites' conduct as an exacerbating factor in their judgment.

In summary, instead of adhering to the natural law norm for image-bearers — procreatively fruitful sexual relations between men and women — the men of Sodom pursued violent and inherently nonprocreative sexual

22. Lot himself displays appalling conduct toward women in offering his own daughters to be raped. It is difficult not to agree with Calvin's statement: "He does not hesitate to prostitute his own daughters, that he may restrain the indomitable fury of the people. But he should rather have endured a thousand deaths, than have resorted to such a measure." See *Commentaries on Genesis*, pp. 499-500.

23. See comments in Sarna, *Genesis*, p. 135. This raises some interesting and interrelated issues about homosexuality among the Canaanites and whether Sodom should be understood as a Canaanite city. Noah's curse upon Ham and his son Canaan is perhaps a response to Ham's homosexual rape of his drunken father (Gen. 9:20-27). See Gagnon, *The Bible and Homosexual Practice*, pp. 63-68; and Wold, *Out of Order*, chap. 4. This would associate the Canaanites with homosexuality from the first we hear of them. Wold notes, however, that there is no extra-biblical evidence for widespread homosexual practice in Canaan; see *Out of Order*, p. 60. But given the biblical link between homosexuality and the Canaanites, should we see Sodom as a Canaanite city? Genesis 10:19 may suggest it, but it is ambiguous. Wold asserts that Genesis 10:19 does make Sodom a Canaanite city; see *Out of Order*, pp. 78-79. Loader argues the opposite conclusion; see *A Tale of Two Cities*, pp. 49-51. Genesis 13:12 lends support to Loader's view, since it seems to distinguish Sodom from the land of Canaan.

conduct. This was one aspect of their violation of even the minimalist ethic of the Noahic natural law.

The Abuse of Justice in Sodom

The second great sin of Sodom, and a further violation of the bare minimum of the Noahic natural law, is its radical abuse of justice. The Sodomites' attempted gang rape, of course, is itself an act of injustice. But the theme of injustice is worth considering in its own right, and it comes into particular focus in Genesis 19:7-9. The theme is prominent not only in Genesis 18–19 but also in later biblical interpretation of the Sodom story, and it is important for the biblical theology of natural law being developed in this book. In this subsection I look first at how Genesis 18–19 itself describes the abuse of justice in Sodom and then consider how broader biblical-theological considerations enrich the interpretation of this theme, in connection with a theology of natural law.

The first reference to Sodom in Genesis 18–19 is when God informs Abraham that "the outcry against Sodom and Gomorrah is great and their sin is very grave" (18:20). This statement has strong judicial overtones. The term "outcry" (זעקה) and cognates are used frequently in the OT to describe the response of those suffering great injustice. For example, it is the response of Abel's blood after his murder (Gen. 4:10), of the oppressed Israelites in Egypt (Exod. 2:23; 3:7, 9), and of the mistreated widow and fatherless (Exod. 22:22-23). In Isaiah 5:7 the term serves as the antonym of justice and righteousness: God "looked for justice, but behold, bloodshed; for righteousness, but behold, an outcry!"[24] Even before the angels reach Sodom, therefore, readers are primed to expect some great breach of justice.

The account of what takes place within Sodom (19:1-11) meets these expectations. The immediate failure of the Sodomites to offer hospitality to the visitors is perhaps itself a violation of justice and reciprocal exchange.[25] Following the shocking demand of the Sodomites in 19:4-5, Lot makes an interesting appeal that alerts them to their breach of justice and attempts to

---

24. Among scholars interpreting "outcry" as a response to injustice, see Gerhard von Rad, *Genesis: A Commentary*, rev. ed. (Philadelphia: Westminster, 1972), p. 211; Brueggemann, *Genesis*, p. 164; and Fields, *Sodom and Gomorrah*, pp. 176-77. For an extended study of the term, see Hamilton, *Genesis*, pp. 20-21.

25. For a discussion of this idea, see Thomas M. Bolin, "The Role of Exchange in Ancient Mediterranean Religion and Its Implications for Reading Genesis 18–19," *JSOT* 29, no. 1 (2004): 37-56.

prick their consciences: "I beg you, *my brothers,* do not act so wickedly" (19:7). In a number of places in Scripture, reference to a *common humanity* either magnifies the gravity of an injustice performed or serves as a defense against a charge of injustice. For example, when confronting Cain about his murder of Abel, whose blood was "crying" out, God never calls Abel by name but three times refers to him as "your brother" (Gen. 4:9-11).[26] Chapter 4 will consider Tyre's violation of a covenant of brotherhood and Edom's pitiless pursuit of his brother (Amos 1:9, 11). Positively, Job defends himself by noting how he recognized the humanity he shared with social inferiors: "If I have rejected the cause of my manservant or my maidservant, when they brought a complaint against me, what then shall I do when God rises up? . . . Did not he who made me in the womb make him? And did not one fashion us in the womb?" (Job 31:13-15).[27] Lot's appeal in Genesis 19:7 seems to be a similar tactic for piquing concern about just relations.

The most explicit mockery of justice per se, however, is the Sodomites' response to Lot's appeal in 19:9: "This fellow came to sojourn, and he has become the judge! Now we will deal worse with you than with them." They simply ridicule Lot's appeal. That a sojourner would speak to them about justice is an outrage. In contrast to Abraham, who had acknowledged God as the "judge" of all the earth and called upon him to do what is right (Gen. 18:25), the Sodomites reject the very idea of standing accountable before a judge.[28] Whatever "justice" the men of Sodom might recognize seems based upon raw power and domicile. What is right in Sodom is defined by *Sodomites,* and neither overnight visitors nor even the resident alien is afforded a voice to question the violence of their will. As noted above, the men of Sodom failed to honor otherness and difference with regard to their sexual conduct. Here they manifest a similar problem in xenophobic form.[29]

Later biblical references confirm that abuse of justice was a central sin of Sodom. Isaiah likens Judah to Sodom a couple of times in the early chapters of his prophecy (1:10; 3:9), in both contexts condemning Judah for injustice and oppression, particularly toward the widow, fatherless, and poor (see 1:17;

---

26. See related discussion in David Novak, *Natural Law in Judaism* (Cambridge: Cambridge University Press, 1998), pp. 31-36.

27. See discussion in Markus Bockmuehl, *Jewish Law in Gentile Churches: Halakhah and the Beginning of Christian Public Ethics* (Grand Rapids: Baker Academic, 2003), pp. 94-95.

28. See related comments in Alter, "Sodom as Nexus," p. 32.

29. See also James K. Bruckner, *Implied Law in the Abraham Narrative: A Literary and Theological Analysis* (Sheffield: Sheffield Academic Press, 2001), p. 135; and Kass, *The Beginning of Wisdom,* pp. 328-29.

3:14-15). In a similar vein, Ezekiel states that Sodom is Jerusalem's younger sister and that Jerusalem has walked according to her "ways" and "abominations," and even become "more corrupt" (16:46-47). Among the sins of Sodom mentioned shortly thereafter is that she had "excess of food, and prosperous ease, but did not aid the poor and needy" (16:49). It is interesting, in light of my earlier evaluation of the Sodom narrative, that this statement comes in the midst of a larger passage in which Jerusalem's sins are described through sexual imagery.[30] In the NT, the same texts condemning Sodom's sexual sins also mention sins pertaining to justice. Sodom exemplifies those kept "under punishment until the day of judgment": "especially those who indulge in the lust of defiling passion and *despise authority*" (2 Pet. 2:9-10). Similarly, the people of Sodom are the exemplar of sinners punished with eternal fire, as those who "defile the flesh, *reject authority,* and blaspheme the glorious ones" (Jude 7-8). Throughout Scripture, therefore, Sodom's sins regarding sex and injustice are interrelated.

The flagrant abuse of justice in Sodom confirms certain claims about natural law in the previous chapter. Sodom did not stand in any redemptive covenant relationship with God, but God held it accountable to himself through the natural law, as originally given in the covenant of creation and refracted for a fallen world through the Noahic covenant. As the Sodomites' sexual misconduct ran counter to the fundamental tenor of the image of God under both Adam and Noah, so did their perversion of justice. The heart of image-bearing at creation was a commission to exercise a righteous royal-judicial task in imitation of the creator, and the Noahic covenant appealed to the image of God to explain humanity's ongoing responsibility to maintain proportionate justice in intrahuman affairs. But instead of defending the rights of the vulnerable and wronged, the Sodomites trampled on them and mocked pleas for justice. As the paragon of rebellion against God, it is no surprise that Sodom's citizens radically fail even at this basic requirement of the Noahic moral order.

Conclusion

The story of Sodom exposes the dark side of life under the Noahic covenant. Though God generously preserves this world in his common grace, it is a world

---

30. See Fields, *Sodom and Gomorrah,* p. 176; Wold, *Out of Order,* p. 88; and Gagnon, *The Bible and Homosexual Practice,* pp. 79-86.

full of wicked people who fall into terrible sins. The account of Sodom reminds readers that the Noahic covenant postpones final judgment, but cannot ultimately prevent it, and Sodom's destruction was a harbinger of this ominous event. God singled out Sodom, as we will see him single out other locales in the next chapter, not for falling short with respect to remote implications of the Noahic moral order that promote holistic human flourishing, but for violating its bare minimum standards necessary for the basic sustenance of human society. What is the moral root of this flagrant contempt for the natural law? Perhaps it can be summarized as a self-centered hubris, or as Calvin put it, an "indomitable haughtiness."[31] Genesis 19:1-11 describes the men of Sodom as completely callous toward the other, and Scripture later condemns them as proud and haughty (Ezek. 16:49-50) and as blasphemers of angelic beings (Jude 8). Living under the natural law is about being the *image of God*, and this, if nothing else, should inject a fundamental humility into one's moral life. The significance of this issue will grow in the next section and the following chapter.

Abraham, Abimelech, and Natural Law in Gerar

Following the Sodom narrative and the sad events of Lot's later life in Genesis 19, the text of Genesis resumes the story of Abraham. In the account of Abraham in Gerar in Genesis 20, we find a much brighter side of life under the Noahic covenant. Like the Sodomites, the people of Gerar were not in redemptive covenant with God, as was Abraham; but unlike Sodom, Gerar exhibited a considerable respect for sexual propriety and the norms of justice. Gerar gives evidence of the power of God's common grace in maintaining human society and instilling a basic recognition and honor of the minimal norms of the Noahic natural order among the nations of the world. Not all are like Sodom. Genesis 20 even indicates a different root attitude in Gerar: instead of the hubris of Sodom is a remarkable humility.

In Chapter 6, I reflect in more detail on the significance of Abraham, God's covenant partner, interacting with King Abimelech of Gerar on the basis of natural law. In the present section my main concern is with the presence and effect of natural law in the pagan city of Gerar. I argue that the expressions used by Abraham and Abimelech — "things that ought not to be done" and "the fear of God" — function as appeals to the natural law. The former points to moral

31. Calvin, *Commentaries on Genesis*, p. 501.

boundaries that all people should honor at every time and place, and the latter represents a sense of moral accountability that transcends one's own personal interests and perspectives. In Genesis and the early parts of Exodus these two concepts seem to be specially related to two central aspects of the minimalist ethic of the Noahic moral order: sexual propriety and the promotion of justice. In this section I first consider the context of the narrative and then discuss the things that ought not to be done and the fear of God.

The Context of Natural Law in Genesis 20

While Genesis 18–19 portrayed Abraham in direct interaction with God and as an observer of human affairs from afar, Genesis 20 returns to a theme important since the reader's first introduction to Abraham in 11:31: he is a sojourner among the scattered human communities of the ancient Near East. By this time Abraham has already left Ur of the Chaldeans, traveled to Haran, migrated to Canaan, sought shelter from famine in Egypt, and lived at various times in the Negev, Bethel, and Mamre. Genesis 20:1 reports that he sojourned in Gerar. Thus far Genesis has said nothing about this city. Abraham, for reasons the text does not explain, claims that his wife Sarah is his sister. Perhaps he has concern about personal safety, as when he pulled the stunt in Egypt years before (Gen. 12:10-20), or perhaps he has other diplomatic reasons in mind.[32] Whatever his motives, Abimelech, king of Gerar, takes Sarah into his home (20:2).

The rest of the story unfolds in two scenes. First, God appears to Abimelech in a dream and confronts him about what he has unwittingly done (20:3-7). Next, Abimelech gathers his servants and confronts Abraham about his deception, and the two of them work out proper reparations (20:8-18). This narrative marks a sharp turn of plot from the previous two chapters. Genesis 18 and 19 portray Abraham as the righteous covenant partner of God who successfully intercedes for Lot (to be considered further in Chapter 6) and portrays the pagan city of Sodom as a paragon of wickedness. Genesis 20, however, presents Abraham's conduct as fundamentally unjust and lifts the pagan king Abimelech onto the higher moral ground.

I first consider the text's presentation of Abimelech and Gerar, strangers

---

32. For a discussion of some of the possible diplomatic issues involved, though I do not necessarily endorse his conclusions, see James K. Hoffmeier, "The Wives' Tales of Genesis 12, 20 & 26 and the Covenants at Beer-Sheba," *Tyndale Bulletin* 43, no. 1 (1992): 87-93.

to the redemptive covenant of grace made with Abraham. When Abimelech later challenges Abraham to explain his behavior, Abraham replies: "I did it because I thought, There is no fear of God at all in this place" (20:11). It seems fair to surmise that Abraham, as he approached Gerar, was worried that its moral sensitivities might bear some resemblance to Sodom's and that its king might act as the kings whose behavior prompted the great flood: "the sons of God saw that the daughters of man were attractive. And they took as their wives any they chose" (6:2).[33] Both scenes in Genesis 20 make clear that Abraham significantly misjudged the situation. Abimelech is not the kind of king who would take just any woman to be his wife.

The first scene begins with God's legal arraignment and indictment of Abimelech: "Behold, you are a dead man because of the woman whom you have taken, for she is a man's wife" (20:3).[34] Abimelech responds without questioning the basic moral and legal issue at stake, namely, the impropriety of taking another man's wife. He acknowledges the justice of God's claim.[35] He defends his innocence, instead, by noting that both Abraham and Sarah lied to him and that he therefore acted out of ignorance (20:5). The question Abimelech asks God in 20:4 — "Lord, will you kill an innocent people?" — is noteworthy in a couple of respects. For one thing, Abimelech expresses concern not just for himself but for the city he rules.[36] Also interesting is the word Abimelech uses to describe his people, צדיק, which might be more helpfully translated "righteous" rather than "innocent." Abimelech's language recalls Abraham's words to God in 18:25: "Far be it from you to do such a thing, to put the righteous (צדיק) to death with the wicked, so that the righteous (כצדיק) fare as the wicked!" Abimelech, in effect, makes the same appeal to God's justice that Abraham did.[37] Unlike Abraham, Abimelech has no redemptive covenantal relationship with God, yet as John Calvin notes about 20:4, "Nature itself dictates, that God preserves a just discrimination in inflicting punishments."[38] God responds in 20:6 by sustaining Abimelech's appeal. God knows that Abimelech acted "in the integrity of your heart," and thus he has

---

33. I concur with Novak's conclusion that Genesis 6:2 refers to kings taking common women, in what amounts to "politically sanctioned rape." See *Natural Law in Judaism*, p. 36. See also Meredith G. Kline, *Kingdom Prologue: Genesis Foundations for a Covenantal Worldview* (Overland Park, KS: Two Age Press, 2000), pp. 185-89.

34. See Bruckner, *Implied Law*, p. 172.

35. See Bruckner, *Implied Law*, p. 175.

36. See Gordon J. Wenham, *Genesis 1–15* (Waco, TX: Word, 1987), p. 72.

37. See relevant discussion in Alter, *Genesis*, p. 93; and Fretheim, *Genesis*, p. 482.

38. Calvin, *Commentaries on Genesis*, p. 524.

kept Abimelech from touching Sarah. He instructs him to return Sarah so that Abraham might pray for him, lest he die (20:7).

The second scene describes Abimelech's confrontation of Abraham. Again, a number of narrative details place the pagan king in a positive light. Abimelech rose "early in the morning," indicating his diligence in righting the wrong, and when he informs his servants they are "very much afraid," suggesting that others in Gerar share his concern for rectifying injustice (20:8). When he approaches Abraham in 20:9, furthermore, he does not use his superior political power to dispose of matters unilaterally, but initiates a legal proceeding to resolve their dispute.[39] Accordingly, after making his charge he solicits a response from Abraham and gives him opportunity to speak. In beginning a legal inquiry and allowing the accused to make a defense, Abimelech mirrors God's actions toward him in the first scene. The very purpose for which God had chosen Abraham and his household, "to keep the way of the Lord by doing righteousness and justice" (18:19), is actually reflected in Abimelech.[40] Finally, the exchange between Abimelech and Abraham in 20:9-11 raises two ideas considered below — the things that ought not to be done and the fear of God — and both reflect well on Abimelech and his city. First, Abimelech is conscious of the fact that certain moral boundaries exist beyond which people should not proceed, even if they are foreigners to each other. Second, Abraham's quasi-defense of his conduct — that he thought there was no fear of God in Gerar — is basically an admission that he had misjudged the town. Abimelech and his servants "were very much afraid" when they realized they had done something displeasing to God and they acted immediately to rectify it. Though not in redemptive covenant with him, this city had some sense of the fear of God.

Neither Abimelech nor the people he ruled were perfectly upright. In fact, this text and a couple of later narratives provide subtle details that display their own failures. For one thing, Genesis presents Abimelech as unaware of many important things going on around him, first that Abraham and Sarah were husband and wife and later that his servants had seized Abraham's well (21:25-26) and that Isaac and Rebekah were married (despite his having been fooled by Abraham in the same way Isaac fools him here) (26:6-11). A model king is not constantly ignorant about the affairs of his realm. The surprise

---

39. On the judicial tenor of this scene, see Bruckner, *Implied Law*, p. 173; and Fretheim, *Genesis*, p. 482.

40. These considerations show the inadequacy of the claims of Tzvi Novick that Abimelech's actions toward Abraham are unkingly and reflect an exaggerated sense of his own righteousness; see Novick, "'Almost, at Times, the Fool': Abimelekh and Genesis 20," *Prooftexts* 24 (2004): 278-80.

ending of Genesis 20, in which readers learn that God had closed the wombs in Abimelech's house because of Sarah, seems to highlight this concern.[41] Abimelech was apparently unable to connect the sudden barrenness of his women with the presence of Sarah, the kind of deduction Pharaoh had no problem making in Genesis 12.[42] There is also reason to read Abimelech's later behavior — when he peeks out his window and watches Isaac and Rebekah in an intimate moment — as distinctly inappropriate for a man of his standing.[43] His own servants, though afraid of God's judgment in 20:8, are not above seizing Abraham's well (21:25), and other Gerarian citizens treat Isaac poorly (26:17-21, 27).[44] Abimelech and his citizens are sinful, but the biblical narrative presents them in a very different light from the men of Sodom. As one writer observes, "The reader finds goodness and a keen sense of justice among the outsiders. . . . The text functions with a sense of natural law as a part of the created order of things that can be discerned and observed apart from faith."[45] We return to these matters below.

The narrative not only portrays Abimelech in a positive light but also portrays Abraham in a negative light. The announcement that Abraham is again going to pass Sarah off as his sister is probably intended to make readers roll their eyes or slap their foreheads with amazement. His previous attempt did not come off well, with Pharaoh rebuking Abraham and sending him off shamed before he could offer a word in defense (12:18-20).[46] The initial negative impression of Abraham that readers receive in 20:2 is exacerbated by the fact that this occurs immediately after the account of Lot impregnating his daughters (19:30-38). Abraham, like pitiful Lot, confuses one kind of female family relationship for another.[47]

---

41. Meir Sternberg, *The Poetics of Biblical Narrative: Ideological Literature and the Drama of Reading* (Bloomington: Indiana University Press, 1985), pp. 316-17, argues that the revelation of Abimelech's impotence at the end of the narrative changes readers' perspective on the entire story, by reducing Abimelech to being only technically innocent. Sternberg's analysis is not wholly convincing. Abimelech did not, after all, defend himself to God on the basis of his not touching Sarah but on the basis of Abraham's and Sarah's deception. Furthermore, God states that he had kept Abimelech from Sarah (presumably through impotence) because of Abimelech's integrity of heart.

42. Novick makes relevant comments on this point, though like Sternberg takes too negative a view of Abimelech, in my judgment; see "'Almost, at Times, the Fool,'" pp. 278-79.

43. See Novick, "'Almost, at Times, the Fool,'" pp. 281-82.

44. Similarly, see Waltke, *Genesis*, p. 299.

45. Fretheim, *Genesis*, p. 483.

46. See Westermann, *Genesis*, pp. 166-67.

47. See Laurence A. Turner, *Genesis* (Sheffield: Sheffield Academic Press, 2000), p. 91.

Our impression of Abraham does not improve when we read of his interaction with Abimelech in 20:9-13. Abimelech begins by expressing the same moral outrage against Abraham as Pharaoh showed against him in 12:18 (and that God showed toward Eve in 3:13 and toward Cain in 4:10): "What have you done to us?" (20:9). After he then accuses Abraham of things that ought not to be done, the text proceeds in a way that might seem at first to be an awkward gaffe on the part of the biblical writer. Abimelech speaks and, without any intervening speech by another character or comment by the narrator, the text reads, "And Abimelech said . . ." (20:10). Why reintroduce Abimelech when he has just been speaking? This is likely a skillful and subtle maneuver by which the narrator indicates that Abimelech has paused after his initial comments, presumably waiting for Abraham to speak since he has asked him a question. Abraham, however, has nothing to say. Abraham apparently just stands there without having a good excuse for his actions.[48] So Abimelech speaks again and poses the question in a different way. Abraham, finally persuaded to respond, does not defend the morality of his act per se. He can only plead for understanding since he feared for his life.[49] He thought there was no fear of God in Gerar, but obviously was wrong (20:11). Even assuming that Abraham tells the truth about misjudging Gerar he does not evoke much sympathy. In Genesis 18 God sought to train Abraham in the divine way of righteousness and justice, and God displayed his justice in part by investigating the conduct of Sodom before rendering judgment. Abraham, in contrast, did not investigate the moral character of Gerar before acting as he did. In fact, when he goes on to say that Sarah is actually his (half) sister (20:12-13) — another lame move, giving a judicially meaningless explanation of why, technically speaking, he did not lie to Abimelech — it is not entirely clear that we should believe him.[50] If Abraham is speaking the full truth, and he did in fact have Sarah call Abraham her brother "in every place to which we come," readers are still left with the unflattering impression that the matriarch of Israel may have provided nocturnal pleasure to a large number of local magistrates.[51]

In the big picture, therefore, Abimelech, stranger to the redemptive

---

48. See Alter, *Genesis*, p. 94. For a different interpretation, see Novick, "Almost, at Times, the Fool,'" pp. 279-80.

49. A number of writers describe Abraham's response as "lame"; see e.g. David W. Cotter, *Genesis* (Collegeville, MN: Liturgical, 2003), p. 133; and Wenham, *Genesis*, p. 72. According to Alter, *Genesis*, p. 94, Abraham is "floundering for self-justification."

50. Turner, *Genesis*, pp. 65-66, argues that Abraham is indeed lying.

51. For discussion of this point, see again Turner, *Genesis*, pp. 92-93.

covenant of grace, stands on higher moral and legal ground in comparison to Abraham, the justified believer in the one true God (Gen. 15:6; cf. Rom. 4:2-5; Gal. 3:11). Abraham was God's special covenant partner, who ended up interceding for Abimelech (20:14-18) as he had done for Lot, but this did not mean he would necessarily excel his neighbors in all civil and legal affairs.[52] The relative righteousness of Abimelech testifies to the power of God's common grace in preserving human society through the Noahic covenant, and the recognition of at least some minimal baseline of the natural law among the nations of the world.

Things That Ought Not to Be Done

It is very difficult, I suggest, to understand this civil interaction between Abraham and his pagan neighbors adequately without some conception of natural law. The first evocation of natural law in Genesis 20:9-11 is Abimelech's statement that Abraham has "done to me things that ought not to be done." As Claus Westermann puts it, "Abraham has violated an unwritten ordinance which exists among men."[53] Abraham is a sojourner, a stranger to Gerar and its ways. Yet when he enters the bounds of Gerar its king understands that

---

52. This is an important point that is lost among Christian commentators who feel the need to vindicate Abraham's behavior; e.g., see Chrysostom's comments in *Genesis 12–50*, Ancient Commentary on Scripture, Old Testament II, ed. Mark Sheridan (Downers Grove, IL: InterVarsity, 2002), pp. 84, 87: "Despite such wonderful promises and guarantees given him by God, he saw himself beset by such imposing difficulties and encountering such varied and differing trials. Yet he stood unshaken like some piece of steel, showing his godly attitude and proving no less resolute in any of the problems surrounding him. See in the present instance too, dearly beloved, the kind of trial that befell him at Gerar and the wonderful caliber of the just man's virtue. What everyone else found unbearable and could not bring themselves to accept he put up with without complaint and without demanding from the Lord explanation of what happened, as many people do, even though weighed down with countless burdens of sin. . . . Notice at this point, dearly beloved, the just man's noble purpose in presenting them with a lesson in the knowledge of God under the guise of an explanation. 'I said to myself, "Surely there is no respect for God in this place, and they will kill me on account of my wife." ' I was concerned, he is saying, that as a result of being still held in ignorance you would have no regard for justice, and so I made allowance for the fact that when you discovered she was my wife you would, out of lust, have wanted to kill me — that was the reason I did it. See how in a few words he takes them to task and at the same time teaches them that the person who has God uppermost in mind ought to commit no crime but rather fear that unsleeping eye and in view of the heavy judgment impending from that source have regard for justice."

53. Westermann, *Genesis*, p. 325.

certain mutual expectations should exist among people, regardless of their national origin or religion. Presenting one's wife as his sister, so that another man takes her into his house, transgresses such expectations. Though Abraham and Abimelech do not share religious, ethnic, or national identities, they share at least one thing, a common humanity. This is a source of moral appeal across social and cultural boundaries throughout the OT (e.g., Gen. 4:9-11; 19:9; Job 31:13-15; Prov. 22:2; Amos 1:9, 11). To put this in terms of previous chapters, to be a human being is to be an image-bearer of God, to be made in a certain way, with common attributes and responsibilities. Certain human relations are a given, a product of the divinely established order of nature rather than human will. As Kass puts it with respect to Abraham and Pharaoh in Genesis 12, but equally apropos here, "The attentive reader may learn from this story that though one may choose a wife, one cannot choose what 'wife' means, that a wife is not transmutable into a sister or a concubine when it serves one's purposes."[54]

The story of Jacob's first wedding in Genesis 29 provides an illuminating comparison. Having fled from Esau, Jacob has taken residence with his uncle Laban. He falls in love with Laban's daughter Rachel and agrees to work for him for seven years in exchange for her hand in marriage. On the wedding day, unbeknownst to Jacob, Laban switches his daughters and Jacob ends up marrying the older sister, Leah, and spending the night with her. In the morning Jacob awakes to quite a surprise and confronts his uncle with the same outrage that Abimelech and Pharaoh expressed when they were duped about a woman's true identity: "What is this you have done to me?" (29:25). Nonplussed, Laban responds: "It is not so done in our country, to give the younger before the firstborn" (29:26). Laban's language (in the Hebrew text) is quite similar to Abimelech's when he accuses Abraham of doing something that ought not to be done. But how should we evaluate Laban's moral claim? Jacob elicits little sympathy from the reader, for he deceived his father Isaac (Genesis 27) and thus ultimately his uncle gives him what he deserves. But Laban's defense to Jacob is still not morally satisfying, precisely because of the way it differs from Abimelech's claim. While Abimelech states simply that Abraham has done something that should not be done, Laban speaks of what is not to be done "in our country." Not giving a younger sister in marriage before an older sister is a local custom, not a universal norm. While Abimelech could rightly expect any visitor within his borders to know the difference between a wife and a sister, Laban could not expect a visitor to Haran to know their custom. Abimelech

54. Kass, *The Beginning of Wisdom*, p. 275.

appeals to universal natural law; Laban does not.[55] Laban has paid back Jacob for his unjust deception of Isaac by unjustly deceiving him.[56]

Also illuminating is the appeal to things that ought not to be done in Genesis 34. This chapter reports that Shechem, the prince of a local Hivite territory, raped Jacob's daughter Dinah (or at least that he illicitly seduced and exploited her).[57] When her brothers hear about it, they are "indignant and very angry, because he had done an outrageous thing in Israel[58] by lying with Jacob's daughter, for such a thing must not be done" (34:7).[59] The situation resembles that of Abimelech and Abraham rather than that of Jacob and Laban. As in both other cases, this one deals with what foreigners and their local hosts should expect from each other morally, but the complaint here alleges

55. For additional discussion see Novak, *Natural Law in Judaism*, pp. 50-52.

56. For further reflections on how the text of Genesis 29 pushes readers toward disapproval of Laban's response, see Sternberg, *Poetics*, p. 243.

57. The understanding that Shechem's actions toward Dinah — "he seized her and lay with her and humiliated her" (34:2) — describe rape is the most convincing to me. Among those defending this interpretation, see Yael Shemesh, "Rape Is Rape Is Rape: The Story of Dinah and Shechem (Genesis 34)," *Zeitschrift für die Alttestamentliche Wissenschaft* 119, no. 1 (2007): 2-21; and Sternberg, *Poetics*, p. 446. A number of recent writers have argued instead that Shechem seduced Dinah, who consented to sexual relations; e.g., see David Noel Freedman, "Dinah and Shechem: Tamar and Amnon," *Austin Seminary Bulletin* 105 (Spring 1990): 54; Ellen Van Wolde, "Does 'INNÂ Denote Rape? A Semantic Analysis of a Controversial Word," *VT* 52, no. 4 (2002): 528-44; and Lyn M. Bechtel, "What If Dinah Is Not Raped? (Genesis 34)," *JSOT* 19 (1994): 24-31. Important to note is that the language of the text portrays what Shechem did (whether or not Dinah resisted or consented) as a wicked and illicit deed, particularly given his royal status; for relevant comments see Wenham, *Genesis*, p. 311; Waltke, *Genesis*, p. 462; Sarna, *Genesis*, p. 234; and Kass, *The Beginning of Wisdom*, p. 483. In light of this, my general conclusions about Genesis 34 hold true whether or not 34:2 technically describes rape.

58. The phrase "in Israel" appears anachronistic, but seems best understood as "against Israel" in this context; see Alter, *Genesis*, p. 190.

59. It is not entirely clear whether the statement that Shechem's deed was outrageous and a thing not to be done is presented here as a fact that explains the brothers' reaction or as the brothers' judgment. Either way, the narrator presents this declaration as an accurate verdict. See discussion in Wenham, *Genesis*, p. 312; and Shemesh, "Rape Is Rape Is Rape," pp. 18-19. Two brothers end up moving the story forward by slaughtering the entire city, taking advantage of a treaty under which all the male residents were suffering the after-effects of circumcision. Whether they were in the right is a disputed question. Genesis 34 is a literary masterpiece that provokes a number of interpretive questions. Among those who believe that the narrator ultimately favors Simeon and Levi, see especially Sternberg, *Poetics*, pp. 445-75; and also Ronald T. Hyman, "Final Judgment: The Ambiguous Moral Question That Culminates Genesis 34," *Jewish Bible Quarterly* 28 (April-June 2000): 98-100. For contrary arguments, see Danna Nolan Fewell and David M. Gunn, "Tipping the Balance: Sternberg's Reader and the Rape of Dinah," *JBL* 110, no. 2 (1991): 193-211; and Freedman, "Dinah and Shechem," pp. 57-59.

a violation of universal norms rather than local custom. Sexually exploiting girls is wrong everywhere. Prince Shechem is like the prediluvian kings who took any women they chose and provoked God into sending the flood (6:2).[60] What he has done, the narrator informs us, is "an outrageous thing." Scripture often uses this term, נבלה, with respect to sexual transgression,[61] and the term refers to offenses that threaten to rip apart the fabric of the social order.[62] As the covenant with Noah associated appropriate procreative sexuality and proportionate justice with the image of God and thus with natural law, and as the story of Sodom in Genesis 19 inextricably linked sexual deviancy and social injustice, so in Genesis 34 the reference to a thing that is not to be done (the abuse of a girl by a local magistrate) connects sexual misdeed with a fundamental breach of just social order. Returning to Genesis 20 and the thing Abraham ought not to have done, we see concerns about sex and justice again. Whereas Sodom incurred divine wrath for despising the baseline natural obligations of the Noahic covenant, Abimelech and Gerar recognize them and, to some degree, submit to them.

The Fear of God

In Chapter 2, I argued that Genesis 9:1-7 focuses upon a few basic moral obligations that constitute a kind of bare, minimalist natural law ethic, and we have seen these obligations at the center of attention with respect both to Sodom's judgment and Abimelech's relative righteousness. But the previous chapter also noted that Genesis 9:1-7, in context, suggests that these basic obligations are not isolated rules but prominent aspects of a broader moral order. Earlier

---

60. Waltke notes that the same sequence of verbs ("saw" and "seized") is used in both Genesis 34:2 and in 6:2, further strengthening this association of Shechem with the prediluvian tyrants; see *Genesis*, p. 462. Another link between these stories is that the term used to describe God's grief in response to prediluvian human wickedness (ויתעצב) is not used again in Genesis until 34:7, which describes Dinah's brothers' reaction to Shechem's act; see Westermann, *Genesis*, p. 538.

61. See e.g. Deut. 22:21; Judg. 19:23-24; 20:6; 2 Sam. 13:12; and Jer. 29:23. For further discussion see Brueggemann, *Genesis*, p. 276; Hamilton, *Genesis*, p. 357; Fields, *Sodom and Gomorrah*, pp. 119-20; and Shimon Bar-Efrat, *Narrative Art in the Bible* (Sheffield: Almond, 1989), p. 262.

62. See Sarna, *Genesis*, p. 234; and Anthony Phillips, "NEBALAH," *VT* 25, no. 2 (April 1975): 241. Bar-Efrat, *Narrative Art*, p. 262, notes that everywhere the term is used in the Bible the culprit pays with his life. Novak, *Natural Law in Judaism*, p. 51, mentions the traditional Jewish belief that this was a communal, not just an individual, crime against Dinah.

I observed some reasons to think that Sodom's sexual impropriety and disregard for justice were rooted in a deeper attitude of hubris. Here in Genesis 20 we find the converse: the sense of sexual propriety and judicial rectitude in Gerar is rooted in a humility expressed in the phrase, "the fear of God" (Gen. 20:11). Like "things that ought not to be done," the "fear of God" here should be understood in natural law terms. In short, the fear of God refers to a respect for basic moral obligations toward other people, particularly in the context of civil justice and the treatment of outsiders, rooted ultimately in a sense of accountability to someone greater than oneself.

An initial consideration for understanding "the fear of God" in 20:11 is the clear impression created by the narrative that though Abraham originally thought there was no fear of God in Gerar, *he was mistaken.* All the indications suggest that Gerar was not a place where people did the thing that worried Abraham, that is, kill husbands in order to give their wives to local magistrates. When confronted by God in a dream, Abimelech did not defend his right to Sarah, only his ignorance of what he had done (20:3-5). When Abimelech's servants heard the truth of the situation, they "were very much afraid" (20:8). *Fear* was precisely their response before God. If there is anyone in the story who does not fear God, it is, ironically, Abraham, who compromises the integrity of his marriage out of the fear of his fellow human being. If Abimelech, who stands outside the redemptive covenant between God and Abraham, is portrayed as a God-fearer, then the fear of God referred to in 20:11 is not confined within a single religious community.

The way in which many subsequent biblical texts use the fear of God idea corroborates this conclusion. As in Genesis 20:11, a number of later stories portray the fear of God as relevant when members of Abraham's line, who are in redemptive covenant with God, interact with those outside, particularly regarding basic matters of justice. A first example is Genesis 42:18. When the sons of Jacob come to Egypt to buy grain, their brother Joseph, a powerful Egyptian magistrate who conceals his identity, says: "Do this and you will live, for I fear God." Joseph is ultimately one of them, a circumcised member of the covenant with Abraham. But he speaks here not as covenant member to covenant members. Hiding his true identity, he speaks as an Egyptian ruler, through a translator (see 42:23), seeking to assure these foreigners that he will treat them justly.[63] His fear of God is a guarantee that these politically powerless outsiders will not be treated unjustly while in a foreign land. Ironically, in a way analogous to Genesis 20, this Egyptian ruler manifests the fear of God

63. See similar comments in Kass, *The Beginning of Wisdom,* p. 578.

more than did the sons of Jacob, God's covenant partners, who sold Joseph into slavery.[64]

Another interesting example takes place in Egypt. Exodus 1 relates how a subsequent Egyptian regime threw off constraints of justice and ordered the killing of male babies born to their Israelite guests. Yet the "Hebrew midwives" — who are best understood as Egyptians who served Hebrew women[65] — "feared God and did not do as the king of Egypt commanded them, but let the male children live" (1:17). Here the fear of God indicates a hearty concern for justice, displayed by people outside the Abrahamic covenant of grace, that makes them willing to defy a tyrant's orders and rescue the innocent from destruction. A third example comes from Exodus 18, when Jethro, Moses' father-in-law, pays a visit to Israel after their departure from Egypt, shortly before they reach Mount Sinai. It is not certain how readers should understand Jethro's relationship to the one true God. He is not an Israelite and not a participant in the covenant made with Abraham, but he is described as the "priest of Midian" (3:1). Whatever the case, the only divine covenant in which Jethro and the Israelites clearly participate in common is the Noahic, and thus they are foreigners to one another ethnically and religiously. Yet when Jethro hears about the Israelites' judicial procedure, which put the entire burden on Moses, he offers advice that Moses heeds. Jethro the Midianite tells Moses to share the load with other judges, "men who fear God, who are trustworthy and hate a bribe" (18:21). Here again, the concept of the fear of God serves to communicate basic concerns about justice across particular religious and ethnic divides.[66]

God's instructions to Israel about the Amalekites at the end of Deuteronomy 25 are also illuminating. Exodus 17 reports that Israel fought a battle with Amalek while traveling through the wilderness. Deuteronomy 25:17-19 provides additional information about this encounter, relating how Amalek attacked them "when you were faint and weary, and cut off your tail, those who were lagging behind." For this behavior Israel is to "blot out the memory of Amalek from under heaven" after they settle in the promised land. The explanation for the Amalekites' inhumane conduct was that they "did not

---

64. See Fretheim, *Genesis*, p. 629.

65. I find Novak's arguments convincing. He notes especially that it is more likely that Pharaoh would have entrusted Egyptian, rather than Hebrew, women with the task of exterminating Hebrew babies and more likely that Egyptian women would have cast a slur upon Hebrew women in 1:19 (though the nature of the slur is obscured in most English translations). See *Natural Law in Judaism*, pp. 49-50.

66. See again the discussion in Novak, *Natural Law in Judaism*, pp. 55-60.

fear God." Again, this cannot refer to the heart of true religious devotion that Israelites were to render as participants in the covenant with Abraham. The Israelites confronted many hostile peoples during their wilderness sojourn who were foreigners to the covenant, but Amalek is singled out as lacking the fear of God and condemned to radical destruction (analogous to the annihilation of Sodom). Simply being a foreigner to the covenant with Abraham did not itself mean that one lacked the fear of God, in the sense used here. Conducting warfare in a particularly barbaric way — targeting civilians, we might say, rather than directly facing the armed men — is what earned the Amalekites their verdict.

This evidence demands the conclusion, I believe, that two distinct notions of the fear of God inhabit the Scriptures.[67] One of them — sometimes termed "the fear of God (אלהים)" but often "the fear of the Lord," using God's unique covenant name, יהוה — describes the heart of true religious devotion exhibited by participants in the redemptive covenants of grace. The other notion, present in Genesis 20:11 and the other texts discussed above — usually termed the "fear of God" rather than "the fear of the Lord" — may be found among people of various ethnic and religious origins. It refers not to a right religious relationship with God in the deepest sense, but a humane respect for just norms of decency and civility.[68] This fear of God should be understood in natural law terms because it does not depend upon special prophetic revelation but upon a universal knowledge of God and his law. Different people who have this sort of fear of God may not be able to worship together, but they can live together peacefully in civil society and, when they have disputes, resolve them according to basic standards of justice that they commonly acknowledge.

Many different terms might have been used for this humane sense of civility and justice, but referring to it as the fear of *God* indicates that it entails more than simply a horizontal respect for fellow human beings. People who have this fear of God refrain from unjust conduct — *even when they could get away with it in terms of human repercussions,* as Abimelech, Joseph, and the midwives presumably could have — because they perceive a moral accountability that transcends what the eye can see.[69] As I suggested above, this is

---

67. See the similar conclusion and discussion in Waltke, *Genesis*, pp. 287-88.

68. Among commentators who interpret the fear of God in Genesis 20:11 in a similar (though not necessarily identical) way, see Westermann, *Genesis 12–36*, pp. 325-26; von Rad, *Genesis*, p. 229; E. A. Speiser, *Genesis* (New York: Doubleday, 1964), p. 149; Hamilton, *Genesis*, p. 67; Sarna, *Genesis*, p. 43; Novak, *Natural Law in Judaism*, p. 48; and Calvin, *Commentaries on Genesis*, p. 529.

69. Psalm 36:1-2 confirms such an understanding of "the fear of God": "Transgression

the opposite of a Sodom-like hubris. It represents an impressive humility that recognizes that one's own self is not at the center of the universe.

This idea of the fear of God confirms and enriches the previous chapter's conclusions about natural law in the fallen world. As those preserved in the image of God under the Noahic covenant, human beings know more than just the minimalist ethic upon which Genesis 9:1-7 focuses. They also retain a sense of accountability before their creator. And as the texts considered here indicate, the strength of this sense of accountability to the divine is intimately connected to an appreciation for the demands of justice. In every example of the "fear of God" discussed above, justice was at the center of concern. Abimelech exhibited the fear of God in his concern for procedural and substantive justice. Joseph appealed to the fear of God as a magistrate assuring suspects of fair treatment. The fear of God emboldened the midwives to defy Pharaoh's legal decree to murder innocents. Jethro recommended judges who feared God in refraining from falsehood and bribery. Finally, the Amalekites rejected the fear of God in committing war crimes (to use today's parlance). These "fear of God" texts suggest, therefore, that concerns about bribery, just war, judicial procedure, and treatment of foreigners are part of the broader natural moral order that underlies the basic obligations explicit in Genesis 9:1-7.

Conclusion

This chapter has provided an initial opportunity to observe concretely how God governs the nations of the world, under the Noahic covenant and through the natural law, in light of my conclusions about Genesis 8:20–9:17 in the previous chapter. To conclude, I reflect upon three respects in which this study confirms and enriches the conclusions suggested in Chapter 2.

First, Genesis 19–20 concretely corroborates the conclusion that through the common grace Noahic covenant God *preserves* the world in *fallen* form. Genesis 19 illustrates the shocking depravity that inhabits the human heart after the fall while Genesis 20 describes an apparently decent and civil human community — and both of these examples are from peoples who do not participate in God's redemptive covenant of grace with Abraham. Neither the depths of sinfulness nor the capacity for righteous conduct should be underestimated in the present world under God's government. By his common grace God pre-

---

speaks to the wicked deep in his heart; there is no fear of God before his eyes. For he flatters himself in his own eyes that his iniquity cannot be found out and hated."

serves the witness of the natural law among all his fallen image-bearers, but it does not work the same effects in each one's life. Concerning the affairs of civil life, Genesis 20 demonstrates that those not participating in the Abrahamic covenant of grace might morally excel those who do. Yet, despite the evident power of divine common grace, Genesis 19 gives sober reminder that a final judgment still awaits that will call the world to account for its sin.

Second, this study of Genesis 19–20 confirms the tentative conclusion of Chapter 2 that the explicit moral obligations communicated in Genesis 9:1-7 constitute a minimalist natural law ethic that corresponds to God's main concern in the Noahic covenant, that is, the basic sustenance of human society. When God enters into premature judgment with Sodom, as it were, he does so because of egregious, fundamental violations of the natural law concerning matters of sex and justice, matters highlighted in Genesis 9:1, 6-7. Gerar's relative righteousness, on the other hand, is displayed in their proper handling of these same issues. Yet Genesis 19 and 20 also confirm that a richer moral order underlies these basics of the Noahic natural law. These chapters show that the bare obligation to "be fruitful and multiply" (Gen. 9:1, 7) needs to be pursued in the context of marriage and family structures and through recognition of proper distinctions between men and women (and proper treatment of the latter by the former). These chapters (and related texts in Genesis and Exodus) also show that the bare obligation to administer proportionate retributive justice (Gen. 9:6) tests a society's attitude toward bribery, just war, judicial procedure, and treatment of foreigners. The broader natural moral order demands recognition of a *common humanity* — that is, recognizing the humanity of the other — that restrains the wrongs one person might do to another.[70] At an even deeper level, these chapters indicate that a destructive hubris is what provokes violation of the minimalist natural law ethic while a measure of humility, even a fear of God, undergirds adherence to this ethic.

Third and finally, Genesis 19–20 and surrounding narratives confirm and enrich my preliminary suggestions in Chapter 2 regarding the implications of natural law, understood through the Noahic covenant, for civil law and social life. At a basic level, these texts illustrate the inevitable connection between a society's stance toward the natural law and the health of its civil relations. Where the "things that ought not to be done" (Gen. 20:9) are shunned, dif-

---

70. As Nicholas Wolterstorff notes, people have tended to see "natural rights" as the rights belonging to their particular in-group. Thus he argues that the recognition of natural *human* rights, applicable to all people, has been a hard-wrought achievement. See *Justice: Rights and Wrongs* (Princeton: Princeton University Press, 2008), p. 318.

ferent and unequal parties resolve their civil disputes peacefully (Genesis 20). Where they are embraced, the powerful terrorize the vulnerable (Genesis 19). These texts also support my preliminary claim that an understanding of natural law through the lens of the Noahic covenant suggests the propriety of honoring rights to religious freedom. Genesis 20 demonstrates the possibility of peaceful relations among people who are religious strangers to one another and even the goodness of seeking such relations. One must be careful about drawing quick moral lessons from such narrative texts. But the text itself casts Abraham (who dealt with the religious other in a sneaky and deceptive way) in a negative light and Abimelech (who dealt with the religious other in a peaceful and civil way) in a positive light. And Abraham seems to learn something from this experience, for sometime later he enters into a formal covenant relationship with Abimelech to ensure and regulate future peaceful relations (Gen. 21:22-34). This intrahuman covenant-making also provides some support for the suggestion in Chapter 2 that it may be fitting for human beings, who image the God who entered covenant with human beings for the sake of sustaining society, to fulfill their responsibilities to promote the welfare of society through entering covenants with their fellow human beings.[71] This idea has a long pedigree in the legal and political thought of my own Reformed tradition.[72]

We will spend much more time considering the significance of natural law for those in redemptive covenant with the God of Abraham, Isaac, and Jacob in Chapters 6-9. In the next chapter, however, we continue this look at how God governs the nations of the world through the Noahic covenant and its natural law, chiefly by examining the oracles of the OT prophets against the foreign nations.

---

71. I follow here the suggestions in David Novak, *The Jewish Social Contract: An Essay in Political Theology* (Princeton: Princeton University Press, 2005), pp. 45-46.

72. The early experience of Reformed settlers in New England offers a good example; see e.g. David A. Weir, *Early New England: A Covenanted Society* (Grand Rapids: Eerdmans, 2005); and John Witte, *The Reformation of Rights: Law, Religion, and Human Rights in Early Modern Calvinism* (Cambridge: Cambridge University Press, 2007), chap. 5.

CHAPTER 4

Crimes against Humanity: Natural Law in the Prophetic Judgments against the Nations

In Chapter 2 I argued that God, after the fall into sin, preserved the original creation, though in a fallen condition. Since the great flood he does so through the covenant with Noah (Gen. 8:20–9:17), a covenant of common, preservative grace, not redemptive grace. Through this covenant, God upholds human nature and the broader natural order, and thereby continues to communicate natural law to all human beings. This natural law exists in organic continuity with the natural law of the original creation, but as refracted in ways fit for the preservation of a fallen world. Chapter 3 then afforded the opportunity to test and enrich these conclusions by observing God's concrete governance of the nations of the world through the Noahic covenant, as described in later biblical texts in Genesis, especially Genesis 19–20. Here we got a glimpse of two human communities that were strangers to the redemptive covenant with Abraham, but with very different experiences: one of them flagrantly violated even the bare minimalist ethic of the Noahic natural order and received God's judgment for it (Sodom), and the other showed a basic respect for this ethic and thus provided a hospitable place for Abraham to sojourn (Gerar).

Chapters 6-9 will consider the significance of natural law for participants in the redemptive covenants of grace, but this present chapter continues the investigation of God's government of the nations of the world by turning to the Old Testament (OT) prophets. These prophets primarily ministered to Israel, who enjoyed redemptive covenantal relationship with God, not only through the covenant with Abraham but also through God's covenant with them at Sinai through Moses. But many of the OT prophetical books also contain series of oracles addressed to foreign nations, who were strangers to these covenants but continued to stand accountable to God and his judgment through the covenant with Noah. A few things about these oracles are worth keeping in mind. The oracles themselves were delivered to Israel (and perhaps only on rare occasion to the foreign nations themselves) and often (though not always) concerned Israel's salvation directly or indirectly. The oracles also at times include promises of salvation for the foreign nations themselves, in which cases the oracles are not so much statements of judgment as prophecies of a coming worldwide redemption. But whatever the many nuances and complexities of these oracles, they deal with nations standing outside the covenant and law of Sinai and in many places display what God holds them liable for and how he brings them into judgment.

As discussed in the previous chapter, God promised after the flood not to bring another universal judgment by water upon the world, but to preserve it. Yet he did not foreclose his right to bring smaller-scale judgments upon particular places. These judgments, like the flood itself, would be harbingers of the final judgment yet to come upon the world at the end of history. As God exercised this right toward Babel (Genesis 11) and Sodom (Genesis 19), so he exercises it toward many of Israel's neighbors, as recorded in the prophetic oracles.

I argue in this chapter that these prophetic oracles against foreign nations provide further confirmation and enrichment of my conclusions about natural law and the Noahic covenant. One noteworthy thing evident in the oracles is that God never judges the foreign nations on the basis of the Torah, God's specially revealed law to Israel in the Mosaic covenant, but always on the basis of natural moral knowledge common to all human beings. Furthermore, these oracles support my provisional conclusion that the moral obligations explicit in Genesis 9:1-7 constitute a kind of minimalist natural law ethic indicating that God's primary concern under the Noahic covenant is the preservation of human society. The prophetic oracles do not condemn the nations for violations of remote implications of the Noahic natural order, but for atrocities, that is, basic injustices that fundamentally compromise humane social life. Remarkably, these oracles never judge the foreign nations for idolatry or other kind of false worship[1] — not that the sin of idolatry is unknowable through the natural

---

1. I am only able to identify two possible exceptions to this claim. The one that seems most obvious is Daniel 5:23, which is not among the judgment oracles per se but an account of the prophet Daniel's words to the Babylonian king Belshazzar. I will explain later in the chapter why this is not ultimately a condemnation for idolatry per se, but for Belshazzar's arrogance toward the true God and his holy things. The most plausible exception, in my judgment, is Habakkuk 2:18-19. These verses fall at the end of a larger text spoken against the Chaldeans and ridicule and pronounce woe on them as idolaters. Even here, the Chaldeans' idolatry is hardly the center of attention, which in previous verses is their arrogance and violence (1:5-11; 2:6-17). Their most

law (Romans 1 indicates otherwise), but that God's concern in bringing these intrahistorical judgments against humanity focuses upon their evil deeds, in intrahuman affairs, that promote the destruction of human society. Nevertheless, these oracles also further confirm my suggestion that a broader moral order must undergird the bare ethic explicit in Genesis 9:1-7. Specifically, like Sodom (but unlike Gerar), these nations display an overweening hubris before God that is apparently the deep root of their unjust ways toward fellow human beings.

To make this case I examine the foreign nation oracles in Amos 1–2 and Isaiah 13–23. Though such oracles occur throughout the OT prophetic writings, the oracles do not all take the same form or serve the same purposes.[2] Sometimes they foretell Israel's deliverance from her enemies and thus serve for her consolation.[3] Other times they warn Israel of foolish action in her international relations (a primary purpose of Isaiah 13–23[4]). Elsewhere they instruct Israel about similar judgments coming upon her (the key strain in Amos 1–2).[5] Or they serve multiple purposes or none of these. In what follows I am not so concerned about the particular purpose of each oracle in its

---

prominent sin here is not that they worship idols, but themselves (see especially 1:11). Other texts in the prophetic oracles refer to the nations' idols, to be sure, but none of them actually condemn the nations because they worship them. Looking beyond these prophetic oracles, we do find one occasion in the midst of history in which Scripture speaks of God judging foreign nations on account of false religious practice: the expulsion of the inhabitants of Canaan from the Promised Land (Deut. 18:9-14) (though this was not the only reason for their expulsion; cf. Lev. 18:24-30). In this case it seems significant that they were expelled from the *Promised Land,* a place God set apart as holy, in which he required his people Israel to avoid idolatry, at the pain of their own expulsion. The idea that God would deal differently with foreign nations within the bounds of the Promised Land from how he deals with them elsewhere is consistent with the fact that he dealt with his own redeemed people differently in the Promised Land from how he dealt with them elsewhere. See Chapters 7 and 10 for more on the natural law and the Mosaic covenant; also see David VanDrunen, *Living in God's Two Kingdoms: A Biblical Vision for Christianity and Culture* (Wheaton, IL: Crossway, 2010), pp. 89-91.

2. See e.g. the helpful comments in Brian C. Jones, *Howling Over Moab: Irony and Rhetoric in Isaiah 15–16* (Atlanta: Scholars, 1996), p. 58. For a concise survey of scholarly debate over the origin and genre of the oracles, see Shalom M. Paul, *A Commentary on the Book of Amos* (Minneapolis: Fortress, 1991), pp. 7-11.

3. That the foreign nation oracles can be generally classed as a form of salvation prophecy for Israel has come under strong and justified criticism in recent years. E.g., see G. R. Hamborg, "Reasons for Judgement in the Oracles against the Nations of the Prophet Isaiah," *VT* 31, no. 2 (1981): 148.

4. See e.g. Jones, *Howling Over Moab,* p. 60; and John Goldingay, *Isaiah* (Peabody, MA: Hendrickson, 2001), p. 92.

5. See e.g. Paul, *Amos,* p. 10; Jörg Jeremias, *The Book of Amos: A Commentary,* trans. Douglas W. Stott (Louisville: Westminster John Knox, 1998), p. 19; James Luther Mays, *Amos:*

context in the canonical books of Amos and Isaiah as I am about the ways in which the prophets hold the foreign nations morally responsible before God and call them to account. After examining Amos and Isaiah we will explore the court scenes in Daniel and consider how that prophetical book deals with the foreign nations of Babylon and Persia.

The Oracles of Amos (1:1–2:3)

Amos was an eighth-century prophet who labored during a window of prosperity for the northern kingdom of Israel.[6] Many scholars have believed the biblical book bearing his name is only partially attributable to Amos himself and is the product of a long history of formation. According to them this diversity of authorship extends to the oracles against the nations in 1:3–2:3.[7] In keeping with my custom I treat the oracles and the book as a unified whole in their received canonical form, written by Amos. Many recent critical scholars now believe there are few compelling reasons to affirm authors other than Amos himself.[8]

Though I make occasional references to material later in the book, my primary focus here is on the oracles against the foreign nations in 1:3–2:3. This extended text consists of six separate oracles, each of them quite short (two or three verses) and directed against a next-door neighbor of either Israel or Judah. Each follows a similar pattern, beginning with the phrase "For three transgressions of [foreign nation/city] X, and for four, I will not revoke the punishment,"[9] followed by the identification of a particular wicked act, and concluding with the announcement of punishment, which in every case involves fire. Each oracle shares distinctive features with the oracle(s) immediately adjoining it, giving evidence of a finely crafted and carefully planned

A Commentary (Philadelphia: Fortress, 1969), pp. 26-27; and David Allan Hubbard, *Joel and Amos: An Introduction and Commentary* (Downers Grove, IL: InterVarsity, 1989), p. 129.

6. See e.g. Paul, *Amos*, pp. 1-2.

7. See e.g. Hans Walter Wolff, *Joel and Amos: A Commentary on the Books of the Prophets Joel and Amos*, trans. Waldemar Janzen, S. Dean McBride Jr., and Charles A. Muenchow (Philadelphia: Fortress, 1977), pp. 106-13; Mays, *Amos*, pp. 13, 25; Jeremias, *Amos*, p. 9; and John Barton, *Understanding Old Testament Ethics: Approaches and Explorations* (Louisville: Westminster John Knox, 2003), pp. 95-96.

8. See e.g. Paul, *Amos*, pp. 6, 16-27; and Francis I. Andersen and David Noel Freedman, *Amos: A New Translation with Introduction and Commentary* (New York: Doubleday, 1989), pp. 143-44.

9. What is here translated as "the punishment" reads literally in Hebrew as "it."

larger text.[10] Some writers have offered ingenious proposals for the reason Amos put the oracles in their particular order,[11] but there seems to be no major interpretive issue at stake for present purposes. Much more important than the order of the foreign nation oracles is that they are followed immediately by an oracle against Judah (2:4-5) and, climactically, against Israel (2:6-16), the original recipient of Amos's prophecy. Amos apparently intended to draw his readers into a false sense of agreement with him, as he railed against the sins of their neighbors and predicted divine judgment upon them, before shocking them with an extended indictment for their own sins against God.

The Nature of the Sins

As mentioned, each of the oracles against the foreign nations exposes a particular sin or two that Amos identifies as basis for the judgment he announces immediately thereafter. In this first section of our study of Amos I survey these sins and make initial observations about them. Then I draw some general conclusions about the nature of these sins and reflect on their relevance for natural law.

Amos first addresses the sins of Damascus (1:3): "Thus says the Lord: 'For three transgressions of Damascus, and for four, I will not revoke the punishment, because they have threshed Gilead with threshing sledges of iron.'" Here the prophet uses agricultural imagery to describe Damascus's sin that provokes divine judgment. Amos probably does not intend to describe literally the use of threshing instruments on the people of Gilead but rather utilizes a stark and well-known image to portray the savage brutality of Damascus's treatment of their Israelite neighbors.[12] Other biblical writers use similar language to describe strong and violent acts of conquest (see 2 Kgs. 13:7; Isa. 41:15; Mic. 4:13; Hab. 3:12).[13] As Hans Walter Wolff puts it, "The technique by which grain was cut up and crushed gives this metaphor its brutal cogency. Grain was threshed by drawing over it a heavy sledge, the boards of which were curved upward at

---

10. See e.g. Paul, *Amos*, pp. 11-13; and Andersen and Freedman, *Amos*, p. 29.

11. Among interesting proposals see Karl Möller, *A Prophet in Debate: The Rhetoric of Persuasion in the Book of Amos* (Sheffield: Sheffield Academic Press, 2003), pp. 194-95; Douglas Stuart, *Hosea-Jonah* (Waco, TX: Word, 1987), pp. 290-91; and especially Andrew E. Steinmann, "The Order of Amos's Oracles against the Nations: 1:3–2:16," *JBL* 111, no. 4 (1992): 683-89.

12. See comments in Anderson and Freedman, *Amos*, p. 239; and Stuart, *Hosea-Jonah*, p. 310.

13. Noted, e.g., in Paul, *Amos*, p. 47.

the front and the underside of which was studded with prongs; the use of iron knives, rather than flint-stones, for these prongs in the iron age significantly increased the efficiency of the sledge."[14] Amos does not mention what exactly Damascus did, but its appalling violence leaves a mark on the reader's mind.

Amos's second target is the Philistines[15] (1:6): "Thus says the Lord: 'For three transgressions of Gaza, and for four, I will not revoke the punishment, because they carried into exile a whole people to deliver them up to Edom.'" This language lacks the brutality of the threshing imagery discussed above, but the indictment is strong nevertheless. Many scholars believe Amos is referring to the slave-trade, a crime against humanity which other OT prophets associate with their Philistine neighbors (see Joel 3:6).[16] Any hand in slave-trading is likely to appall modern readers, but Amos adds weight to the offense by claiming they acted against a *whole* people.[17] Presumably the Philistines could only pull this off against a relatively small population, but the fact that they destroyed an entire people group speaks to the extreme and inhumane character of their action. Unlike the previous indictment, Amos does not name the victim here. Perhaps it was a clan in Israel, perhaps not. The *gravitas* of the crime itself, rather than the identity of the victim, is Amos's concern.[18]

The third condemned city is Tyre, and their indictment is one of the most intriguing (1:9): "Thus says the Lord, 'For three transgressions of Tyre, and for four, I will not revoke the punishment, because they delivered up a whole people to Edom, and did not remember the covenant of brotherhood.'" Initially the indictment sounds similar to that against Gaza, for Tyre too acted against a "whole people," apparently selling them into slavery to Edom. The Phoenicians were international merchants and notorious slave-traders (see Ezek. 27:13; Joel 3:6). But Amos's condemnation of Tyre is complicated by the fact that Tyre had a special relationship with its victim. In selling this people, Tyre failed to remember "the covenant of brotherhood [ברית אחים]." The term "covenant of brotherhood" is unknown elsewhere in the OT or ancient

---

14. Wolff, *Joel and Amos*, p. 154. Compare Jeremias, *Amos*, p. 26; and John H. Hayes, "Amos's Oracles Against the Nations," *Review and Expositor* 92 (1995): 156.

15. Though only the city of Gaza is mentioned in 1:6, the following two verses name three of the other four major Philistine cities: Ashdod, Ashkelon, and Ekron.

16. E.g., see Paul, *Amos*, p. 56; Hubbard, *Joel and Amos*, p. 133; and Jeremias, *Amos*, p. 27.

17. On this point see comments by Anderson and Freedman, *Amos*, p. 258; Donald E. Gowan, *The Book of Amos: Introduction, Commentary, and Reflections*, in *The New Interpreter's Bible*, vol. 7 (Nashville: Abingdon, 1996), p. 361; Stuart, *Hosea-Jonah*, p. 312; and Hayes, "Amos's Oracles," p. 159.

18. See similar comments in Paul, *Amos*, pp. 56-57; and Wolff, *Joel and Amos*, pp. 157-58.

Near Eastern literature, but seems to refer to some kind of political treaty between peoples. International covenant partners did refer to themselves as "brothers" (e.g., in 1 Kgs. 9:13; 20:32), and "to remember" is common language for observing the terms of a covenant (e.g., in Gen. 9:15; Exod. 2:24; 6:5; 32:13; Lev. 26:42, 45).[19] As far as the text indicates, Gaza sold into slavery a people with whom they had no special bond, but Tyre violated an oath-sealed alliance in doing so, hence exacerbating its guilt. Commentators have invested much effort trying to identify Tyre's victim. Israel herself is an immediately plausible candidate, since Israel and Tyre had been treaty partners in the days of David and Solomon (1 Kgs. 5:1-12; cf. 2 Sam. 5:11; 1 Chron. 14:1; 2 Chron. 2:1-16) and since mentioning a sin against Israel would be the tactic most likely to win the attention of Amos's readers.[20] But this is only conjecture. If we focus on the text itself — rather than speculating on what is not in the text — it is evident that Amos's concern is once again not the identity of the victim, but the crime. Amos was perfectly capable of naming victims, and does so on several other occasions. But here he directs attention to Tyre's treacherous act itself.[21]

In passing, I also note the significance of God condemning Tyre for breaking what was apparently a *voluntary human* political arrangement. Unlike all the other sins Amos mentions in 1:3–2:3, this one is not a pure, *per se* violation of God's moral law, but a crime only possible because of sworn commitments that human beings took upon themselves in the course of history. I suggested in Chapters 2 and 3 that since God governs the postdiluvian world by means of covenant, perhaps it is appropriate for his image-bearers, commissioned to administer justice in the world under him, to order their mutual affairs by means of covenant as well.[22] Amos 1:9 provides another small piece of corroborating evidence for this proposal. God himself looks upon human covenant-making as an activity of profound significance and enters into judgment against its despisers.

19. See Paul, *Amos,* pp. 61-62; Jeremias, *Amos,* p. 30; Wolff, *Joel and Amos,* p. 159; Andersen and Freedman, *Amos,* p. 261; Mays, *Amos,* p. 34; John Priest, "The Covenant of Brothers," *JBL* 84 (December 1965): 400-401; and Hayes, "Amos's Oracles," p. 160.

20. Writers who believe Amos was certainly or likely referring to a treaty with Israel include Priest, "Covenant of Brothers," pp. 402-6; Jeremias, *Amos,* p. 30; and Stuart, *Hosea-Jonah,* p. 313. More hesitant are Andersen and Freedman, *Amos,* p. 261; and Gowan, *Amos,* pp. 361-62.

21. See especially Paul, *Amos,* pp. 59-61 (including n. 172); and also Hubbard, *Joel and Amos,* p. 134. Other writers also note the uncertainty in identifying Tyre's victim; see e.g. Mays, *Amos,* p. 34; and Barton, *Understanding,* p. 93.

22. Here I picked up on some suggestions in David Novak, *The Jewish Social Contract: An Essay in Political Theology* (Princeton: Princeton University Press, 2005), pp. 45-46.

Amos has already mentioned Edom twice, as a purchaser of slaves, but in 1:11 Edom takes center-stage as the prophet's fourth target: "Thus says the Lord: 'For three transgressions of Edom, and for four, I will not revoke the punishment, because he pursued his brother with the sword and cast off all pity, and his anger tore perpetually, and he kept his wrath forever.'" This accusation does not so much identify a specific crime as it highlights the context and mode in which Edom waged war. In terms of context, 1:11 follows 1:9 in speaking of actions against a "brother." This time Amos does not mention a covenant, and thus refer to a fraternal relationship created by voluntary agreement. Instead, Amos seems to speak of a natural kin relationship. Since the OT often terms Israel and Edom "brothers" (see Num. 20:14; Deut. 2:4; 23:7; Obad. 10, 12), in light of their common lineage from Isaac (Gen. 25:19-26), many scholars believe Israel is Edom's victim. This is plausible, but again Amos does not identify the victim, focusing attention on the act itself. Just as a brotherly relationship established by treaty formed a bond that was not to be violated (1:9), so also kinship creates a special bond that exacerbates the heinousness of offense.[23] But the nature of Edom's relationship with its victim is not Amos's only concern. He speaks of the mode of Edom's warmongering in terms suggesting its excessiveness or, we might say, its over-the-top character. Edom stifled all his pity or compassion [רחמיו],[24] his anger burned without ceasing [לעד], and he maintained his wrath forever [נצח].[25] There was no restraint or moderation (which, I argued in Chapter 2, the dynamic of the Noahic covenant seems to prescribe even for lawful pursuit of justice). Though Amos does not deal explicitly with the pride theme that we will observe frequently in Isaiah, Edom's extreme behavior suggests more than a little hubris. Edom's crime, therefore, involves both its scorn for the bonds of kinship and its excessive brutality, callous to humane sentiments.[26]

23. See discussions in Paul, pp. 63-64; Andersen and Freedman, *Amos*, p. 264; Jeremias, *Amos*, p. 30; Mays, *Amos*, p. 35; Gowan, *Amos*, p. 362; Stuart, *Hosea-Jonah*, p. 313; and Hayes, "Amos's Oracles," p. 160. Some scholars argue that 1:11 makes a veiled reference to a treaty relationship, similar to what 1:9 refers to; see especially Michael Fishbane, "The Treaty Background of Amos 1:11 and Related Matters," *JBL* 89 (September 1970): 313-18; also considered in Hubbard, *Joel and Amos*, p. 134; and Barton, *Understanding*, p. 94.

24. This phrase would perhaps be better translated as "destroyed the women." See e.g. Paul, *Amos*, pp. 64-65. If so, it would not change the sense of excessiveness present in this verse.

25. For further remarks pertinent to Edom's excessive conduct, see also Andersen and Freedman, *Amos*, p. 264.

26. As Calvin put it, they threw "aside all regard for humanity." See John Calvin, *Commentaries on the Twelve Minor Prophets*, vol. 2, trans. John Owen (Grand Rapids: Baker, 2003), p. 167. He describes the Moabites' act in the next oracle as "inhuman" and "wholly barbarous,"

The next verses bring the reader to Ammon, whose sin probably tops the list for its sheer raw and revolting character (1:13): "Thus says the Lord: 'For three transgressions of the Ammonites, and for four, I will not revoke the punishment, because they have ripped open pregnant women in Gilead, that they might enlarge their border.'" Sad to say, ripping open pregnant women was not an uncommon act in this time and place. Scripture mentions this atrocity on several occasions (2 Kgs. 8:12; 15:16; Hos. 13:16) and it also appears in extra-biblical literature.[27] Still, all the other biblical references present the deed as horrific, and its shock value in Amos 1:13 is evident. The character of the act speaks for itself, but the effect is only heightened when Amos mentions Ammon's motivation: a border war. Ammon perpetrated such a grotesque deed for the sake of nothing more profound than extra territory. Pregnant women were obviously not military threats to the Ammonites, and perhaps the Ammonites wanted to send an intimidating message to their encroaching neighbors. But such conduct likely entailed an even more sinister desire to exert control over future relations, insofar as it eliminated both the fertile women able to raise up the next generation and the next generation itself.[28] In any case, here we see how the perpetration of injustice is tied up with the destruction of ordained patterns of family and reproduction; Genesis 9:6 is not unrelated to Genesis 9:1, 7.[29]

Amos's final foreign nation oracle opens the next chapter (2:1): "Thus says the Lord: 'For three transgressions of Moab, and for four, I will not revoke the punishment, because he burned to lime the bones of the king of Edom.'" The variety of despicable conduct exposed in these oracles is remarkable. All of Amos's previous accusations involve trampling what we today would call human dignity or human rights: there are some things that one person should simply not do to another person, and everyone can recognize these things and be held accountable for them, with or without the Mosaic law. Here this sense of inviolable dignity extends even to the human body after death. The

---

proving "that they had forgotten all humanity and justice." See *Commentaries on the Twelve Minor Prophets,* 2.172.

27. See e.g. Wolff, *Joel and Amos,* p. 161; Paul, *Amos,* p. 68; Gowan, *Amos,* p. 362; and Hayes, "Amos's Oracles," p. 161.

28. See related claims in Daniel L. Smith-Christopher, "Engendered Warfare and the Ammonites in Amos 1.13," in *Aspects of Amos: Exegesis and Interpretation,* ed. Anselm C. Hagedorn and Andrew Mein (New York: T. & T. Clark, 2011), pp. 15-40.

29. Perhaps the oracle against Edom also makes veiled reference to violence against women; see the argument for double entendre in 1:11 in James R. Linville, *Amos and the Cosmic Imagination* (Aldershot, UK: Ashgate, 2011), p. 55.

precise nature of Moab's atrocity remains elusive. Perhaps Moab desecrated the Edomite king's grave or, as some scholars have persuasively argued, burned his bones to obtain raw material for plastering or whitewashing.[30] Whether the motivation was revenge, humiliation, economic gain, or something else, Amos excoriates Moab for a deed widely condemned across cultures throughout history, the abuse of a human corpse.[31]

Yet another matter in this final oracle is nearly as significant for present purposes as the character of the crime itself: Amos condemns *Moab* for sins against *Edom*. Two of the previous oracles condemned foreign peoples for sins explicitly against Israel, and the three others concerned sins for which Israel was at least arguably the victim. But this final oracle confirms my previous claim that Amos's silence about the victims of Gaza's, Tyre's, and Edom's aggression highlights the heinousness of the crime and downplays the significance of the victims' identity. Amos has not portrayed Edom positively in previous verses: Edom happily purchased slaves from Gaza and Tyre and mercilessly slaughtered its own kin. But it was still despicable for Moab to burn the bones of Edom's king. Amos's oracles are not a patriotic rant driven by parochial Israelite bias. Amos addresses *human* moral obligations not limited to specific ethnic allegiance or religious affiliation.

Noahic Natural Law in Amos's Oracles

What do these observations about the oracles of Amos 1:3–2:3 have to do with natural law? Amos does not speak about natural law explicitly and obviously does not develop a natural law *theory*. But the question remains whether Amos was working with an implicit understanding of natural law relevant to the concerns of this book. I conclude that Amos did indeed presume the existence of a natural law, and one consistent with what I have proposed in previous chapters. This is evident both from the absence of other sufficient explanations for the substance of 1:3–2:3 and from positive evidence emerging from this text and Amos as a whole.

One possible explanation for what we find in Amos 1:3–2:3 is that God judged these foreign nations on the basis of Israel's law, the Mosaic Torah.

---

30. This is argued by Paul, *Amos*, p. 72; Wolff, *Joel and Amos*, pp. 162-63; and Gowan, *Amos*, p. 362.

31. I must note that on a day I am editing this chapter a widely disseminated video showing American soldiers urinating on the corpses of slain Afghan militants has provoked international indignation.

But this proposal fails on numerous grounds and, with good reason, is not defended in the scholarly literature. Not only does this proposal raise the serious moral problem of God judging people on the basis of a law he never revealed to them,[32] but also none of the six indictments themselves focuses on explicit violations of the Mosaic law. To be sure, most of the sins exposed are at odds with principles promulgated in the Torah — breaking a covenant of brotherhood is a form of bearing false witness, for example, and splitting open pregnant women is murder — but this hardly proves that the Torah was the basis for the condemnations. None of the indictments says anything that sounds uniquely Mosaic. As if to underscore this point, Amos's indictment of Judah, immediately following the foreign nation oracles, begins this way (2:4): "Thus says the Lord: 'For three transgressions of Judah, and for four, I will not revoke the punishment, because they have rejected *the law of the Lord,* and have not kept *his statutes. . . .*" The Torah-focus of the judgment against Judah stands in contrast with the previous judgment oracles.

Even if responsibility under the Mosaic law per se is ruled out as the basis for the indictments in 1:3–2:3, however, one might still propose that a unique connection to Israel explains God's interest in the nations mentioned in these verses. Michael Barré, for example, has proposed that all the places mentioned in 1:3–2:3 were part of the ideal kingdom of David and Solomon and thus these foreign peoples were in covenant with, and vassals of, Israel's God. As fellow vassals, they should not have attacked one another and, on this basis, were condemned by Amos.[33] This proposal has an abstract plausibility, but textual evidence for it in Amos is extremely scanty, and ultimately it seems to assume more than it proves. Other items in Amos, furthermore, militate against the idea. Amos strongly asserts God's authority over Egypt, which was not part of the Solomonic empire (see 2:9-10), and claims he had authority over the Philistines long before a monarch sat over Israel (see 9:7).[34] As many commentators note, a prominent theme running through Amos is that Israel's God is the universal God.[35] The reason why Amos singled out *these* nations/cities may be no more complicated than that these were the communities with which he and his readers were most familiar. Undoubtedly Amos could have

---

32. Romans 2:12 says that God will not do this. See Chapter 5 for discussion of this text.

33. Michael L. Barré, "The Meaning of *l' 'sybnw* in Amos 1:3–2:6," *JBL* 105, no. 4 (1986): 611-31.

34. These points, and other critiques of Barré, are to my mind persuasively made in Paul Noble, "Israel Among the Nations," *Horizons in Biblical Theology* 15 (June 1993): 56-62.

35. See e.g. Andersen and Freedman, *Amos,* p. 89; Wolff, *Joel and Amos,* p. 101; Mays, *Amos,* p. 6; Hubbard, *Joel and Amos,* p. 110; and Gowan, *Amos,* p. 347.

(theoretically) identified similar atrocities in any number of other peoples scattered around the globe, but condemning Philistines and Moabites was surely a better rhetorical strategy for his Israelite audience than condemning a Celtic clan in Britain or a Native American tribe in Wisconsin.

A better, but I believe still insufficient, explanation is to locate the basis for the condemnations of 1:3–2:3 in (international) customary law, which God himself then enforces.[36] This is plausible. The transgressions Amos recounted may well have been regarded by those cognizant of such things as violations of some ancient Near Eastern common law. Yet again, as far as I am aware, there is little concrete evidence for such, certainly in the text of Amos or even in extra-biblical sources. The very nature of customary law — being unwritten — makes proving its substance several millennia later rather precarious.

If such a customary law existed, Amos 1:9 ("the covenant of brotherhood") suggests that God would have taken its violation seriously, and this may well have been an aspect of why these nations were condemned. But something more also seems necessary to make good sense of Amos 1:3–2:3. These oracles make most sense, I suggest, if the actions condemned are not merely customarily wrong but also, and most significantly, inherently wrong. For one thing, Amos is addressing and trying to arouse not diplomats readily familiar with international conventions of warfare but "the people of Israel," "the whole family that I brought up out of the land of Egypt" (3:1). His rhetorical strategy, as mentioned above, seems gauged to evoke a visceral reaction of the people against the deeds of their neighbors, thereby luring them into agreement with him before he tightens the clamp against them beginning in 2:6.[37] Presumably, breaches of international protocol in skirmishes between Moab and Edom did not rouse the ire of these materialistic Israelites; instinctive moral revulsion to slashing open pregnant women and defiling corpses probably would. One may also doubt whether God would be so profoundly angry about breaches of merely *arbitrary* conventions of ancient Near Eastern common law.[38]

If this text deals with universally known moral standards, established

---

36. For various expressions of this idea, see e.g. Barton, *Understanding*, pp. 78, 109-14; Mays, *Amos*, p. 28; Hubbard, *Joel and Amos*, p. 128; Gowan, *Amos*, p. 357; and Hayes, "Amos's Oracles," p. 166.

37. On the idea that Amos's hearers must have agreed with him on the validity of the charges against the foreign nations, see the related comments in Barton, *Understanding*, pp. 79-81; and John B. Geyer, "Mythology and Culture in the Oracles Against the Nations," *VT* 36, no. 2 (1986): 135-36.

38. See the related argument in Noble, "Israel Among the Nations," pp. 62-65.

by God himself, apart from written law revealed in a redemptive covenantal relationship, then some version of natural law is the only plausible explanation for what grounds the condemnations.[39] Other evidence in Amos supports this conclusion.[40] For one thing, the prophet indicates elsewhere the presence of an established natural order that permeates the world and constrains human conduct. For example, "Do horses run on rocks? Does one plow there with oxen? But you have turned justice into poison and the fruit of righteousness into wormwood . . ." (6:12). As John Barton puts it, this illustrates the natural law idea of "cosmic nonsense."[41] The world is configured in a certain way and some things simply violate the order of reality. Rocks being what they are, it makes no sense to run horses there, and trying to harvest a crop on such ground is vain and bizarre. But this is similar, says Amos, to people turning justice and righteousness into poison and wormwood. It overturns the order of reality. It makes no sense.

Amos reasons in similar fashion in 3:3-6: "Do two walk together, unless they have agreed to meet? Does a lion roar in the forest, when he has no prey? Does a young lion cry out from his den, if he has taken nothing? Does a bird fall into a snare on the earth, when there is no trap for it? Does a snare spring up from the ground, when it has taken nothing? Is a trumpet blown in a city, and the people are not afraid? Does disaster come to a city, unless the Lord has done it?" The prophet again assumes that the world operates in established ways. Certain behavior rightly and expectedly follows from certain causes. This applies to inanimate objects (snares), to animate creatures (lions and birds), to human beings (walking together and blowing trumpets), and even to God himself in his dealings with the world (bringing disaster against cities). Human

39. Among writers taking various natural law approaches to this text, see Andersen and Freedman, *Amos*, pp. 27-28, 91; Barton, *Understanding*, pp. 34-35; Wolff, *Joel and Amos*, p. 152; Jeremias, *Amos*, p. 31; Noble, "Israel Among the Nations," pp. 62-65; and Möller, *A Prophet in Debate*, pp. 189-90.

40. One piece of evidence I am not using is the claim that Amos was influenced by the Israelite wisdom tradition, which, if true, might further strengthen claims that Amos operated with implicit natural law assumptions, in light of my arguments in Chapter 8. Among commentators who have argued for a close tie between Amos and so-called wisdom circles, see Wolff, *Joel and Amos*, pp. 91, 95, 97. But the evidence for this seems too tenuous to be conclusive; see e.g. Paul, *Amos*, p. 4; and Stuart, *Hosea-Jonah*, p. 295. It may nevertheless still be the case, and not insignificantly for my present argument, that "peculiar affinities existed between Amos and the wise"; see Samuel Terrien, "Amos and Wisdom," in *Israel's Prophetic Heritage: Essays in Honor of James Muilenburg*, ed. Bernhard W. Anderson and Walter Harrelson (New York: Harper & Brothers, 1962), p. 114.

41. See Barton, *Understanding*, p. 38.

behavior falling outside this established order would be, at a fundamental level, incomprehensible and irrational. The idea of a natural moral order, accessible to all people and superintended and enforced by God himself, is evidently not foreign to Amos.

This natural law presumed in Amos, I suggest, confirms aspects of my proposal regarding natural law in the Noahic covenant. I have argued that Genesis 9:1-7 indicates that God's chief concern in the Noahic covenant is with the preservation of human society and a minimalist ethic concerning the basics of human survival and relationships. Accordingly, God comes in judgment here, in the midst of history, to condemn extreme breaches of intrahuman justice (cf. Gen. 9:6), one of which cases entails a shocking assault on procreative fruitfulness (Amos 1:13; cf. Gen. 9:1, 7).[42] But God does not condemn any nation for its idolatry. We will see in Chapter 5 that idolatry is indeed contrary to the natural law (see Rom. 1:21-25), but ensuring right worship is not God's real concern under the Noahic covenant in the midst of history; the preservation of human society is. The lack of interest in idolatry here is remarkable, especially when one thinks of the polemics elsewhere in the OT against Israel's fascination with foreign gods such as Baal and Molech (gods worshiped by nations mentioned in 1:3–2:3), as well as the harm brought upon Israel by the paganism of the Phoenician princess Jezebel. In this context, where Amos does not warn Israel about these foreign nations' seductive influence but explains why these foreign nations themselves are going to experience a temporal divine judgment, idolatry goes unmentioned. Instead, Amos highlights the very sins that triggered the great flood and which the postdiluvian Noahic covenant was designed to constrain: unjust violence and bloodshed. Accordingly, the intrahuman offenses Amos exposes are not misdemeanors but shocking felonies.[43] Perhaps also significant is that Amos 1–2 repeatedly attributes such crimes not to ordinary folks but to rulers, the people especially responsible for enforcing justice, which is the whole point of Genesis 9:6.[44]

A Noahic background to natural law in Amos also helps to make sense of some other features of 1:3–2:3. It may explain, for example, why scholars have heard covenantal overtones in much of the text's language.[45] God acts

---

42. On this point also see Paul, *Amos*, p. 71; and Andersen and Freedman, *Amos*, p. 27.

43. For vivid comments on the magnitude of the sins condemned in 1:3–2:3, see e.g. Andersen and Freedman, *Amos*, p. 277; Wolff, *Joel and Amos*, p. 172; and Jeremias, *Amos*, p. 31.

44. See related comments in Noble, "Israel Among the Nations," p. 63; Möller, *A Prophet in Debate*, p. 185; and Anderson and Freedman, *Amos*, p. 231.

45. See especially Barré, "Meaning," though not all of his evidence is equally compelling. But see also Andersen and Freedman, *Amos*, pp. 91, 231; and Gowan, *Amos*, p. 354.

as though he is in a preexisting relationship with these foreign nations, and the dilemma sensed by many scholars — covenant relationship *or* natural law — is a false one. A natural law grounded in the Noahic covenant explains the apparent presence of universal moral knowledge as well as the seemingly covenant-like relationship between God and nations foreign to the Abrahamic and Sinaitic covenants. Finally, the way Amos treats the particular temporal judgments against foreign nations (and Israel) as anticipations of a cosmic final judgment, followed by a cosmic new creation, fits the larger biblical patterns of judgment identified earlier in this chapter and especially in Chapter 3. In accord with the Noahic covenant, after the flood God delivered only temporal local judgments, which nevertheless foreshadowed the final cosmic judgment. Amos begins with particular judgments against foreign nations, followed by extended particular judgments against his special covenant people Israel, but crescendos to an awesome judgment of universal cosmic scope (9:1-10), before giving way to a scene of new creation that closes the book (9:11-15).[46] The Noahic covenant, I suggest, provides very helpful background to Amos 1:3–2:3, and even to the book as a whole.

The Oracles of Isaiah (13:1–23:18)

I turn now to the oracles against foreign nations recorded in Isaiah 13:1–23:18. These chapters do not only concern foreign nations (Israel itself is addressed in Isaiah 22), and some other foreign-nation oracles appear elsewhere in Isaiah, but chapters 13–23 constitute the main block of material in Isaiah directed against other peoples. There is wide consensus that someone (whether Isaiah or another) has arranged Isaiah 13–23 together into a unified whole and, as I note again below, that chapters 24–27 are also a unified text that come purposefully after 13–23 and are meant to shape readers' interpretation of them. I too treat these chapters as a unified composition, and as the product of Isaiah himself.

Unlike the oracles in Amos 1–2, which are uniformly concise and bear many similarities of form and terminology, the oracles of Isaiah 13–23 are quite different from one another. Some are very long, others very short. Some include extensive charges identifying which sins have provoked judgment, and

---

46. On the cosmic dimensions of the judgment described in Amos 9:1-9, even as a reversal of creation described in Genesis 1, see the helpful remarks in Linville, *Amos's Cosmic Imagination*, pp. 6-7, 168.

others identify no sin at all. Some describe the coming punishments; others do not. Some prophesy a future salvation for the foreign nation, while others foretell only judgment. Given the greater bulk and diversity of material here in Isaiah, I follow a somewhat different procedure from what I followed for Amos. I first examine the nature of the sins that trigger judgment against the foreign nations, and do so topically rather than examine each oracle seriatim. Then I examine the nature of the punishments Isaiah announces against these nations, again following a topical order. Next, I offer some preliminary conclusions about the presence of natural law in chapters 13–23. Following this, I look at chapters 24–27 and observe how they enrich the conclusions about natural law drawn in the previous section, particularly with respect to the Noahic context for natural law for which I am arguing more broadly.

The Nature of the Sins Condemned in Isaiah 13–23

The oracles in Amos 1:3–2:3 identify a range of sins committed by foreign nations that provoked the Lord's wrath, but a common thread unites them. They all describe international crimes (one nation against another) that were especially heinous, either in their excessiveness or sheer brutality. The oracles in Isaiah 13–23 are somewhat different. Those that identify the reason for judgment for the most part mention only one sin: pride, or perhaps better, hubris. Whereas Amos seems to focus upon the outward manifestation of rebellion against God (extreme injustice), Isaiah seems to highlight its internal source. Ultimately I believe these prophets hone in on a common problem: people's (especially rulers') rejection of their role as image-bearers of God commissioned to pursue justice (especially for the vulnerable), who instead seek to usurp the place of God and to trample the fellow human beings God appointed them to serve. That the nations' hubris manifested itself in injustice is indeed evident in Isaiah 13–23.

The theme of pride in Isaiah 13–23 is hardly unique to these chapters. Isaiah introduces the theme prominently already in his "day of the Lord" prophecy in chapter 2 (2:11-17), and it continues in texts such as 5:14-16; 9:9; and 10:12-14. Subsequent to chapters 13–23 the theme appears in 25:11; 37:22-29; and especially in chapter 47, which also deals with a foreign nation, Babylon.[47] Many of the other prophets develop the theme in their oracles against foreign

---

47. On the pride motif in Isaiah, see especially Seth Erlandsson, *The Burden of Babylon: A Study of Isaiah 13:2–14:23* (Lund, Sweden: CWK Gleerup, 1970), chap. 6.

nations (e.g., Jer. 48:14, 26-30, 42; 49:4, 16; 50:29-32; Ezek. 28:1-10; 30:6, 18; 31:10; 32:12; Hab. 1:11; 2:4-5; Zeph. 2:10, 15; Zech. 9:6; 10:11). Thus the hubris idea in Isaiah 13–23 taps into a rich motif recurring in the prophetic literature.

The first two oracles, both of them against Babylon (13:1-22 and 14:3-23), work the hubris theme more thoroughly than the rest. The judgment oracle of Isaiah 13 raises the theme first in 13:11, where God associates external injustice (ruthlessness) with their proud attitude: "I will put an end to the pomp of the arrogant, and lay low the pompous pride of the ruthless." When the theme continues shortly thereafter, the prophet analogizes this particular local judgment against Babylon to a great local judgment of old: "And Babylon, the glory of kingdoms, the splendor and pomp of the Chaldeans, will be like Sodom and Gomorrah when God overthrew them" (13:19). When Isaiah's words against Babylon continue in 14:4 after a brief interlude (14:1-3), he immediately reintroduces the hubris theme, again connecting it to abuse of justice: "How the oppressor has ceased, the insolent fury ceased!"

This second oracle against Babylon is not a straightforward pronouncement of judgment but a "taunt" (14:4). It takes the form of a dirge, but with the satirical intent of mockery rather than genuine lament.[48] The pride theme appears in the initial section of this remarkable poem: "Your pomp is brought down to Sheol" (14:11). Following this, at the heart of the dirge, is a sort of mini-dirge in 14:12-15.[49] It draws upon the mythological lore of the ancient Near East[50] to portray Babylon as an exceedingly arrogant tyrant: "How you are fallen from heaven, O Day Star, son of Dawn! How you are cut down to the ground, you who laid the nations low! You said in your heart, 'I will ascend to heaven; above the stars of God I will set my throne on high; I will sit on the mount of assembly in the far reaches of the north; I will ascend above

48. On the use of satire and parody here, see R. Mark Shipp, *Of Dead Kings and Dirges: Myth and Meaning in Isaiah 14:4b-21* (Atlanta: Society of Biblical Literature, 2002), chap. 3; Gale A. Yee, "The Anatomy of Biblical Parody: The Dirge Form in 2 Samuel 1 and Isaiah 14," *CBQ* 50 (1988): 565-86; R. Reed Lessing, "Satire in Isaiah's Tyre Oracle," *JSOT* 28, no. 1 (2003): 103; R. Reed Lessing, *Interpreting Discontinuity: Isaiah's Tyre Oracle* (Winona Lake, IN: Eisenbrauns, 2004), p. 207; Hans Wildberger, *Isaiah 13–27: A Continental Commentary*, trans. Thomas H. Trapp (Minneapolis: Fortress, 1997), pp. 50-52; Jones, *Howling Over Moab*, p. 134; and Brevard S. Childs, *Isaiah* (Louisville: Westminster John Knox, 2001), pp. 125-26.

49. Among many writers recognizing this, see especially Shipp, *Of Dead Kings*, pp. 139-40; and Yee, "The Anatomy of Biblical Parody," pp. 574, 577-59.

50. The most extensive study of the mythological motifs utilized by Isaiah here is found in Shipp, *Of Dead Kings and Dirges*. Also see Wildberger, *Isaiah 13–27*, pp. 62-63; Goldingay, *Isaiah*, pp. 102-3; Joseph Blenkinsopp, *Isaiah 1–39* (New York: Doubleday, 2000), p. 288; and R. E. Clements, *Isaiah 1–39* (Grand Rapids: Eerdmans, 1980), p. 143.

the heights of the clouds; I will make myself like the Most High. But you are brought down to Sheol, to the far reaches of the pit."

I return to these words below to make another point, but I note here a few things regarding Babylon's sin relevant for the argument of this chapter. First, Babylon expresses hubris through failure to recognize its proper place in the order of reality, trying to usurp God's preeminence as the heavenly king. Babylon's king uses a generic name for God, "the Most High," rather than Yahweh, his covenant name revealed to Israel.[51] Since he is a pagan this is not surprising, and it fits with the use of mythological imagery, but it is still interesting that the text condemns him for his general challenge to the Deity (and not, for example, dishonoring the true God through idolatry). Second, this imagery evokes the memory of Babel, which in pride declared its intent to reach the heavens (Gen. 11:4).[52] As Isaiah 13 associates Babylon's judgment with Sodom's, so Isaiah 14 associates its sin with Babel's. Third, Babylon's proud attitude was manifest in tyrannical injustice. The taunt is directed specifically against Babylon's king (14:4), and his attempt to challenge God in heaven was accompanied by cutting down and laying low nations on earth (14:12; see also 14:6). Later the dirge says of the king: "Is this the man who made the earth tremble, who shook kingdoms, who made the world like a desert and over-threw its cities, who did not let his prisoners go home?" (14:16b-17). Babylon's pride is encapsulated in its king, and it drives him to massive abuse of office.

After brief oracles against Assyria and Philistia at the end of Isaiah 14,[53] the hubris motif arises again in the lengthy oracle against Moab in chapters 15–16. This is, in fact, the only sin of which Isaiah accuses Israel's neighbor:[54] "We have heard of the pride of Moab — how proud he is! — of his arrogance, his pride, and his insolence; in his idle boasting he is not right" (16:6). Isaiah does not unpack the hubris of Moab as he did Babylon's in chapter 14, though other OT prophets make similar accusations against the Moabites (see Jer. 48:7, 26, 29-30, 42; Zeph. 2:8-10).[55] Isaiah returns to this theme by describing proud Moab swimming in a heap of excrement in 25:10-11.

---

51. On the use of this title for the Deity, see e.g. Clements, *Isaiah 1–39*, p. 143; and John D. W. Watts, *Isaiah 1–33* (Waco, TX: Word, 1985), p. 211.

52. For evidence of the Babel theme in the larger oracle, see Robert H. O'Connell, "Isaiah XIV 4B-23: Ironic Reversal Through Concentric Structure and Mythic Allusions," *VT* 38, no. 4 (1988): 412-13.

53. Though Isaiah 14:24-27 does not ascribe pride to Assyria, Isaiah 10:5-15 and 37:23-29 do; see Hamborg, "Reasons for Judgement," pp. 153-54.

54. Noted by Jones, *Howling Over Moab*, p. 146.

55. See Hamborg, "Reasons for Judgement," p. 151.

The oracles in chapters 17–21 do not pick up the pride motif, and in fact say little at all about the basis for the judgments they announce. Isaiah 22 concerns Jerusalem, and thus is outside the scope of the present inquiry. But the closing oracle against the foreign nations, concerning Tyre in chapter 23, resumes the theme: "The Lord of hosts has purposed it, to defile the pompous pride of all glory, to dishonor all the honored of the earth" (23:9). The context of Tyre's pride is somewhat different from that of Babylon's in chapters 13–14. Whereas Babylon's pride was incarnate in its tyrannical king, Tyre's is on display among its world-renown merchants (23:2-8). Yet their transgressions run in the same direction. Immediately before the accusation of hubris, Isaiah writes: "Who has purposed this against Tyre, the bestower of crowns, whose merchants were princes, whose traders were the honored of the earth?" (23:8). Though the Phoenicians had established their power through international commerce rather than the sword, its trading prowess evidently brought political influence. As with Babylon, therefore, Tyre's pride was not far removed from issues of rightful rule and administration of justice.

Though hubris, exhibiting itself in injustice, is the central sin Isaiah highlights in chapters 13–23, a couple of other matters deserve brief note. First is the theme of excessiveness. As noted above, Amos accuses several peoples not merely of injustice but of over-the-top injustice. Gaza and Tyre sold *whole* peoples in slavery, and Edom would not let up its oppression or show the least pity. Similarly, Isaiah says that Babylon "struck the peoples in wrath with *unceasing* blows" and "ruled the nations in anger with *unrelenting* persecution" (14:6).

Second, and again resembling Amos's oracles, Isaiah never condemns the foreign nations for idolatry or other kinds of false religious practice. Not even Tyre and Sidon are judged on this score, though their wicked daughters Jezebel and Athaliah brought so much trouble on Israel and Judah through devotion to Baal.[56] Egypt's idolatry and sorcery are mentioned in 19:3, though not as the ground of condemnation but as evidence of their desperate response to the divine curse.[57] Following God's future saving work, people will cast aside their idolatrous altars (17:7-8), but this reference to idolatry is also unrelated to the reasons for judgment in the text.

---

56. See Goldingay, *Isaiah*, p. 133.

57. See Hamborg, "Reasons for Judgement," p. 147. Blenkinsopp sees 19:3 as an attack on Egypt's sorcery and wisdom; see *Isaiah 1–39*, p. 315. In a sense it surely is, but more as a way of ridiculing Egypt's plight under God's judgment than as the reason assigned for the judgment.

The Nature of the Punishments Threatened in Isaiah 13–23

Also relevant for the present study is the nature of the punishments Isaiah 13–23 decrees against the foreign nations. Though Isaiah mentions a variety of specific curses, two broad themes pervade these chapters: the idea that the punishment fits the crime (expressed through the *lex talionis* or poetic justice) and the idea of de-creation. Both themes anticipate the final judgment (see Rev. 16:6; 18:6-7, 21-23). And as I explain, both themes are appropriate if the Noahic covenant indeed underlies God's dealings with these nations.

First, Isaiah 13–23 states many curses in ways emphasizing that the punishment fits the crime. One way is through variations of the *lex talionis*, considered at some length in Chapter 2. Whether applied literally or not, the "eye for an eye" formula captures the idea of proportionality and equivalence: crime and punishment are balanced on the scales of justice. Isaiah 13–23 also expresses this idea through poetic justice. In poetic justice an ironic fate befalls the wrongdoer, such that the kind of mischief he perpetrated ricochets back on his own head. These themes of *lex talionis* and poetic justice appear in many other prophetic oracles against the nations (see e.g. Jer. 49:2; 50:15, 29; Ezek. 25:12-14, 15-17; Joel 3:4-8; Obad. 15; Hab. 2:8, 15-17). Such examples communicate that God repays according to merit and is perfectly impartial.

This theme of punishment fitting the crime in a proportionate or ironic way is prominent in the oracles against Babylon. It first emerges subtly in 13:19, where the excessively exalted Babylon is brought to the utter depths of degradation: "And Babylon, the glory of kingdoms, the splendor and pomp of the Chaldeans, will be like Sodom and Gomorrah when God overthrew them." Then the interlude between the Babylon oracles speaks of what Israel will one day do to her enemies in explicitly talionic terms: "They will take captive those who were their captors, and rule over those who oppressed them" (14:2). The theme is most poignant in the satirical dirge of 14:4b-21 mentioned above.[58] The king of Babylon, for example, suffers the same fate he has imposed upon others: "How you are cut down to the ground, you who laid the nations low!" (14:12) The repetition of vocabulary also highlights the ironic equivalence between crime and punishment: in his boast the king says, "I will sit on the mount of assembly in the far reaches [ירכתי] of the north" (14:13), and in response the prophet states, "you are brought down to Sheol, to the

---

58. O'Connell even argues that the concentric structure of the poem itself demonstrates the justice of the judgment imposed, showing that "his debasement corresponds in extent to his arrogance." See "Isaiah XIV 4B-23."

far reaches [ירכתי] of the pit" (14:15).[59] Later verses heighten the irony. His brazen arrogance reached so high that even Sheol is too good for him. While the other departed kings of the earth are at least buried in state with a certain honor, he who was their superior in life is denied a proper burial and ejected from their presence in death (14:18-20).[60] A radical and entirely fitting reversal of fortunes awaits the proud tyrant.[61]

The oracle against Moab in Isaiah 15–16 arguably also drips with satire. Many commentators do not adopt a satiric reading but believe that Isaiah expresses true sympathy for the plight of Moab when she is judged.[62] Others of late, however, have reembraced the reading of Martin Luther and John Calvin and persuasively argued that Isaiah's words of sympathy are actually biting ridicule.[63] If this latter reading is correct, poetic justice is patent in the oracle. Consider the statement about Moab's pride conjoined with the words of "lament" that immediately follow: "We have heard of the pride of Moab — how proud he is! — of his arrogance, his pride, and his insolence; in his idle boasting he is not right. Therefore let Moab wail for Moab, let everyone wail. Mourn, utterly stricken, for the raisin cakes of Kir-haresheth" (16:6-7). Few things humiliate a person like ridicule. Mockery is itself a weapon and means of punishment.[64] And what is more fitting punishment for insolent boasting than biting mockery? The one who sought to humiliate others is himself humiliated.

Finally, the oracle against Tyre also communicates that punishment fits the crime. This oracle too is most likely satirical, in form resembling a lament but in fact mocking the fall of this prosperous city.[65] Thus, as with Moab, heaping humiliation on the proud is rich poetic justice. Poetic justice also emerges in the details. As Reed Lessing notes, 23:1-3 portrays Tyre in the best of circumstances: it has the world's most honored ships, transporting the most famous crop (wheat), from the most famous land (Egypt), to itself, the world's

---

59. Noted, e.g., in Watts, *Isaiah 1–33*, p. 211; and Edward J. Young, *The Book of Isaiah*, vol. 1 (Grand Rapids: Eerdmans, 1965), p. 443.

60. See Shipp, *Of Dead Kings*, pp. 149-50.

61. On the reversal of fortunes theme here, see Csaba Balogh, *The Stele of YHWH in Egypt: The Prophecies of Isaiah 18–20 concerning Egypt and Cush* (Leiden: Brill, 2011), p. 88.

62. See e.g. Wildberger, *Isaiah 13–27*, p. 153; and Young, *Isaiah*, 1:458.

63. See especially Jones, *Howling Over Moab*; see also Lessing, "Satire in Isaiah's Tyre Oracle," p. 103.

64. See Jones, *Howling Over Moab*, pp. 240-41; and Lessing, *Interpreting Discontinuity*, pp. 200-201, 238.

65. See Lessing, "Satire in Isaiah's Tyre Oracle"; and *Interpreting Discontinuity*, chap. 8. He points to parallels with Ezekiel 27 and Jeremiah 48; see *Interpreting Discontinuity*, pp. 204-6.

most famous harbor.[66] Yet now she is barren and brought to shame (23:4). Lessing also points out the irony that Tyre, the wealthiest of merchants, would be dismissed as a prostitute, one who sells herself cheaply (23:16).[67] Such ironic reversal is exquisite poetic justice.[68]

The other key theme characterizing the punishments in Isaiah 13–23 is de-creation. By this I mean that the fate of the nations under judgment involves the reversal and disintegration of the natural order. This theme is related to the theme of poetic justice. Whereas the latter involves the humiliation of proud tyrants, for example, in the de-creation motif civilized cities are returned to disordered chaos. What is high — whether ruler or society — is brought low.

A prominent example of the de-creation theme is when Isaiah 13–23 describes civilized nations being stripped of human inhabitants and overrun with wild animals. The proper order described in the creation account, in which God created animals first and then formed human beings to rule and subdue them (Gen. 1:24-28), crumbles. The oracles against Babylon provide vivid examples. Isaiah 13:20-22 declares: "It will never be inhabited or lived in for all generations; no Arab will pitch his tent there; no shepherds will make their flocks lie down there. But wild animals will lie down there, and their houses will be full of howling creatures; there ostriches will dwell, and there wild goats will dance. Hyenas will cry in its towers, and jackals in the pleasant palaces. . . ." Babylon will become "a possession of the hedgehog" (14:23). Likewise, the oracle against Damascus asserts: "The cities of Aroer are deserted; they will be for flocks, which will lie down, and none will make them afraid" (17:2). The final oracle is similar: "Behold the land of the Chaldeans! This is the people that was not; Assyria destined it for wild beasts" (23:13). The theme appears elsewhere in Isaiah (see 5:17; 27:10; 34:11-15) and among other OT prophets (e.g., Jer. 50:39; 51:37).[69]

Different hues of the de-creation theme also arise in these oracles. Given the prominence of human reproduction in the original creation account (Gen. 1:28) and the Noahic covenant (Gen. 9:1, 7), for instance, the curse of barrenness proclaimed against Tyre suggests dissolution of the natural order: "I have neither labored nor given birth, I have neither reared young men nor brought up young women" (23:4). Genesis 1 also emphasizes how God put the waters

---

66. Lessing, *Interpreting Discontinuity*, p. 214.

67. Lessing, *Interpreting Discontinuity*, pp. 227-28.

68. For discussion of a similar theme in an earlier foreign nation oracle, also see Michael Chan, "Rhetorical Reversal and Usurpation: Isaiah 10:5-34 and the Use of Neo-Assyrian Royal Idiom in the Construction of an Anti-Assyrian Theology," *JBL* 128, no. 4 (2009): 717-33.

69. See Blenkinsopp, *Isaiah 1–39*, pp. 280, 311.

in their proper place, and Genesis 8 how God reestablished their boundaries after the flood. Thus the promised curse upon the Nile in 19:5-10 is not only entirely fitting for Egypt, whose livelihood was so tied to the ebb and flow of that river, but also sounds hauntingly like the dissolution of the fragile boundaries of the natural world.[70]

Preliminary Conclusions about Natural Law in Isaiah 13–23

I now offer some preliminary conclusions about natural law in the oracles of Isaiah 13–23. In the following section I reflect upon Isaiah 24–27 and argue that these chapters confirm and enrich this preliminary conclusion. In brief, I conclude that Isaiah must have been working with some conception of natural law to say the things he did in chapters 13–23, and a conception consistent with my earlier conclusions about natural law and the Noahic covenant.

A first question is whether something other than natural law can explain how, why, and for what Isaiah condemns the foreign nations and foretells their punishment. It cannot be the Mosaic law, for Isaiah never appeals to the Torah when judging these nations, who were not in special covenant relationship with God through Sinai. When discussing Amos I also considered whether the prophet might have judged the foreign nations because of a special tie with Israel through residence within the bounds of the Solomonic empire. That idea is entirely implausible here, since many of the nations addressed in Isaiah 13–23 were outside even its most ideal boundaries. Another theme I considered in Amos was that international customary law was the basis for the prophet's words of judgment. I suggested above that though these nations might indeed have breached customary law and that this may well have been part of the basis for God's indictment (see Amos 1:9), it could not have been the sufficient basis, for violating merely arbitrary human conventions hardly seems sufficient ground for arousing such great indignation in God. This concern holds here as well. In addition, one of the chief sins highlighted in Isaiah 13–23, hubris, is an attitude or disposition, whereas customary law concerns concrete external conduct.

Given the insufficiency of these options for explaining the basis of judgment in Isaiah 13–23, is it the case that Isaiah operated in natural law

---

70. For interesting proposals regarding the prophet's use of Egypt's own culture and literature in 19:5-10, see Hilary Marlow, "The Lament over the River Nile — Isaiah xix 5-10 in Its Wider Context," *VT* 57 (2007): 229-42.

categories? Dan Johnson, commenting on Isaiah 24:5, claims that the idea of natural law "runs completely contrary to the Hebrew mind which knows no law except the revealed law."[71] Such sentiments, I believe, betray a modern prejudice that gives too little credit to the depth of OT theology. I will offer additional evidence in subsequent chapters, but even in Isaiah there are many reasons to reject Johnson's claim. The work of Barton is especially helpful on this issue. Barton admits that Isaiah does not explicitly develop a natural law theory, but asserts that he "already had a developed understanding of the basis of morality — one which has more affinities with Western theories of natural law than has usually been thought and less in common with the notion of moral imperatives as 'revealed' or positive law, given by God as the terms of a 'covenant' or contract with the people of Israel, than is supposed by many Old Testament specialists."[72] Key to appreciating Barton's insight is a point I have already made and will defend further in later chapters: the natural law should not be conceived as a series of discrete rules but as a moral order pervading the created world and obligating human beings to live within its bounds.

To put the case concisely, we might say that Isaiah saw the world as an ordered whole, in which each aspect of reality has its proper place, and according to which order human beings are obliged to conform. For human beings to subvert this natural order is foolish and nonsensical. It is ultimately rebellion against God, who established this order and rules as its head. This idea is implicit at the very outset of Isaiah, when he calls heaven and earth to witness against his rebellious people (1:2): "The ox knows its owner, and the donkey its master's crib, but Israel does not know, my people do not understand" (1:3; cf. Jer. 8:7). God's world is ordered. Even oxen and donkeys — reputedly stupid animals — can recognize their place within it. By contrasting Israel's rebellion against its Lord with these animals' submission to their masters, Isaiah characterizes Israel's sin not in terms of violation of a written law per se but as foolish and utterly nonsensical behavior that flips the order of reality.[73]

---

71. Dan G. Johnson, *From Chaos to Restoration: An Integrative Reading of Isaiah 24–27* (Sheffield: Sheffield Academic Press, 1988), p. 43.

72. Barton, *Understanding,* p. 130; see also pp. 138-40.

73. See Barton's comments in *Understanding,* p. 37. Calvin recognized this point, commenting: "Nor ought we to wonder at this; for the beasts frequently observe the order of nature more correctly, and display greater kindness, than men themselves." Later he polemicizes against Roman Catholic writers for allegorizing this text and writes: "here the Prophet does not speak of miracles, but of the order of nature, and declares, that those who overturn that order may be regarded as monsters." See John Calvin, *Commentary on the Book of the Prophet Isaiah,* vol. 1, trans. William Pringle (Grand Rapids: Baker, 2003), pp. 41, 42. Despite the

This sort of perspective emerges frequently as the book of Isaiah unfolds. For example, 5:20 states: "Woe to those who call evil good and good evil, who put darkness for light and light for darkness, who put bitter for sweet and sweet for bitter!" Confusing things opposite by nature stands at the heart of moral rebellion. Light and darkness have objective characteristics and one can hardly mistake one for the other; the same holds for sweetness and bitterness. As one who confuses light and darkness or sweet and bitter is utterly out of touch with the ways of the world, so is one confusing good and evil.[74] Isaiah 10:15 is similar: "Shall the axe boast over him who hews with it, or the saw magnify itself against him who wields it? As if a rod should wield him who lifts it, or as if a staff should lift him who is not wood!" The prophet again presumes an order permeating the world. Tools are just that: instruments of another's will. To think that an axe would lord it over the one using it is ridiculous, and ridiculous because so blatantly disordered. But such chaotic rearranging of reality characterizes Assyria: it considers itself God rather than his tool (see 10:5-11). This idea of rearranging the natural order is perhaps most explicit in 29:15-16: "Ah, you who hide deep from the Lord your counsel, whose deeds are in the dark, and who say, 'Who sees us? Who knows us?' You turn things upside down! Shall the potter be regarded as the clay, that the thing made should say of its maker, 'He did not make me'; or the thing formed say of him who formed it, 'He has no understanding'?" The point of the potter and clay analogy is similar to that of workers and their tools in 10:15: rebellion against God is a flipping of reality and a ridiculous attempt to put things out of place. It is indeed a turning of things "upside down."[75]

Isaiah's conception of a natural order helps to explain — and is further illuminated by — the importance of hubris and punishment-fits-the-crime in the oracles of chapters 13–23. What is hubris, after all? It is not something

---

strong tendency of early Christian commentators to allegorize texts like these, some recognize something of the natural law dimension of Isaiah 1:3. For example, Basil the Great writes: "If the love of children for their parents is a natural endowment and if this love is noticeable in the behavior even of brute beasts, as well as in the affection of human beings in early infancy for their mothers, let us not appear to be less rational than infants or more savage than wild beasts by alienating ourselves from him who made us by being unloving toward him. . . . This gratitude is characteristic not only of humans, but it is also felt by almost all animals, so that they attach themselves to those who have conferred some good upon them." See *Isaiah 1–39*, Ancient Christian Commentary on Scripture, Old Testament X, ed. Steven A. McKinion (Downers Grove, IL: InterVarsity, 2004), p. 4.

74. As Calvin puts it, the folly of such people "would tend to confound and destroy all the principles of nature." See *Commentary on Isaiah*, 1.187.

75. Barton discusses some of these verses in *Understanding*, pp. 37, 137.

readily prohibited by positive law, but rather a radical confusion about one's proper place in the world. To anticipate significant themes in Chapter 8: a key virtue for living well within the natural moral order is wisdom, and wisdom requires humility grounded in the fear of God. Hubris is the opposite of humility, a foolish exalting of oneself above God. The pride of the Babylonian king who tries to ascend to heaven and take the place of the Most High (Isa. 14:4b-21) is heinous because it is so ridiculous, bizarre, and absurd — a person created in the *image* of God who thinks he is God![76] The sin of hubris coursing through Isaiah 13–23 is a fundamental violation of the natural moral order.[77]

The theme of punishment fitting the crime in chapters 13–23 merits the same conclusion. The *lex talionis* principle presumes that things have an established nature and inherent value. When there is wrongdoing, equivalence must be maintained and balance restored. The idea of poetic justice depends upon the reality of a natural moral order even more strongly. Poetic justice derives its power from the widespread and instinctive recognition that a certain sort of punishment is deliciously fitting. One does not need to read a law code to perceive the ironic appropriateness of, say, a king who tries ascending to the far reaches of heaven being thrown down to the far reaches of Sheol. In chapters 13–23 and elsewhere God presents himself as visiting sin in a way humans can recognize as eminently appropriate, for it just fits the way the world hangs together.[78]

The conclusion is compelling, I believe, that God deals with the foreign nations in Isaiah 13–23 not on the basis of the Mosaic law, a special relationship with Israel, or customary law, but on the basis of natural law. In emphasizing the folly of hubris and the fitting justice of their punishments, Isaiah relies upon a universally knowable natural moral order rather than upon any written or conventional source of morality.

Furthermore, Isaiah's working presumptions about natural law seem consistent with the conclusions I have been developing about natural law and the Noahic covenant. Reflecting God's larger purposes in the Noahic covenant, the moral obligations explicit in 9:1-7 focus upon basic issues fundamental for the preservation of human society. One of these obligations is that human beings, as image-bearers of God, administer justice on behalf of victims (Gen. 9:6). Accordingly, Isaiah condemns foreign nations for hubris (making oneself

---

76. Compare here also the discussion in Chapter 1 concerning how Adam, an image-bearer, flips the creation order in his submission to the serpent and rebellion against God in Genesis 3; see also Ezekiel 28:1-19.

77. Relevant here are Barton's comments in *Understanding*, pp. 135-36.

78. Along these lines see Barton, *Understanding*, pp. 40-43.

a god rather than recognizing one's identity as the *image* of God), especially as exhibited by their rulers, those entrusted with the administration of justice who instead commit excessive acts of injustice. Isaiah 13–23, furthermore, does not condemn foreign nations for idolatry or other sorts of sinful worship or religious ritual. This does not mean that natural law is indifferent to such conduct, but reflects the fact that God's chief purpose in the Noahic covenant is not to expunge idolatry from the world but to sustain the existence of human society within it. Yet Isaiah's presupposition about a natural moral order also comports with my suggestion that Genesis 9:1-7 itself hints at a broader moral order that must undergird the minimalist ethic on the surface of these verses. In addition, the prominent theme of punishment-fitting-the-crime in Isaiah 13–23 lies at the heart of Genesis 9:6, which formulates the *lex talionis* as a model for human justice in the image of God. Finally, God's punishing rebellious nations through de-creation in Isaiah 13–23 also taps Noahic themes. As argued in Chapter 2, Genesis 8 is a scene of re-creation, in which God re-forms the world he consigned to chaos through the flood. The Noahic covenant promises the maintenance of cosmic structures (8:21-22; 9:11, 15) and ordains the continuation of human society in part through subordinating animals under the lordship of human beings (9:2-4). The de-creation curses of Isaiah 13–23 roll this back, leaving animals free to roam in depopulated cities and upsetting the regular patterns of nature, in anticipation of the final judgment when God will bring the Noahic order to an end.

Isaiah 24–27 and Noahic Natural Law

The immediately following chapters in Isaiah support this preliminary conclusion. Isaiah 24–27 presents an awesome eschatological scene of a final, universal judgment followed by the establishment of a glorious new creation. What is striking for present purposes is that this description of final judgment draws richly upon the substance and imagery of the particular local judgments pronounced in chapters 13–23, indicating the organic connection between them: the particular local judgments within history are anticipatory foretastes of the universal cosmic judgment to come. In this universal judgment, God will condemn the *whole* world for *covenant* violation, specifically violation of the *Noahic* covenant. This further justifies reading the earlier inchoate judgments in a Noahic light.

Some of these claims are controversial, so I offer a brief defense. The organic connections between the oracles of Isaiah 13–23 and chapters 24–27 (especially 24) are evident and numerous, and widely recognized. Though many commentators believe that chapters 24–27 are a later composition, there is strong consensus that they come purposefully after chapters 13–23 and are designed to shape our reading of the latter.[79] The oracles against Babylon in chapters 13–14 offer perhaps the most anticipations of 24–27.[80] Among common themes are references to the day of the Lord, the destruction of sinners, the desolation of land and city, the dimming of cosmic bodies, the reduction of population, and imagery of the pit. Among motifs in the Moab oracle (Isaiah 15–16) that echo in chapters 24–27 are the languishing of the earth, human grief, destruction of vineyards, lack of wine, and reduction of population. The oracle against Damascus (Isaiah 17) anticipates the desolation of the city, reduction of population, and the analogy of beating an olive tree. The Cush oracle (Isaiah 18) anticipates divine wrath against the whole earth, destruction of vineyards, lack of wine, and reduction of population. The oracle against Egypt (Isaiah 19) foreshadows the languishing of the earth, human grief, and the staggering of drunkards. The later oracle against Babylon (Isaiah 21) anticipates the betrayal of traitors. Finally, the Tyre oracle (Isaiah 23) foreshadows the end of joyous singing and the city's desolation.[81] Too much information, perhaps, but it demonstrates the intimate tie between chapters 13–23 and 24–27.

But what exactly is going on in chapters 24–27? With many commentators, I believe they portray a universal and eschatological judgment followed by the establishment of a new creation.[82] This is not the unanimous view, but the evidence supports it. A first piece of evidence is the universal cosmic language at work from the outset of Isaiah 24. In 24:1-6 "the earth" is described as emptied, desolate, depopulated, withered, and devoured, even "utterly" so. The Hebrew term for "earth" (ארץ) could simply mean a particular "land," but the combination of this word with the global term "world" (תבל) in 24:4

---

79. See e.g. Blenkinsopp, *Isaiah 1–39*, p. 347; Wildberger, *Isaiah 13–27*, pp. 446-47; Childs, *Isaiah*, pp. 172-73; Clements, *Isaiah 1–39*, p. 196; and Edward J. Young, *The Book of Isaiah*, vol. 2 (Grand Rapids: Eerdmans, 1969), pp. 146-47.

80. This is claimed by Blenkinsopp, *Isaiah 1–39*, p. 346; and Christopher R. Seitz, *Isaiah 1–39* (Louisville: Westminster John Knox, 1993), pp. 118, 127.

81. For a sampling of discussions identifying such connections, see Donald C. Polaski, "Reflections on a Mosaic Covenant: The Eternal Covenant (Isaiah 24.5) and Intertextuality," *JSOT 77* (1998): 61-62; and Young, *Isaiah*, 2:146.

82. E.g., Wildberger, *Isaiah 13–27*, p. 446, refers to this as "a *universal*, eschatological-apocalyptic *turn of events*." Another example is Childs, *Isaiah*, p. 173, who sees this as the eschatological and cosmological judgment and restoration, which creates an "extreme tension" between the old age that dies and the new age that enters, a tension not characteristic elsewhere in the OT prophets.

makes this translation unlikely.[83] Confirming this conclusion, the effects of God's judgment are felt, and response to it offered, from the "coastlands of the sea" and "the ends of the earth" (24:15-16). The windows of heaven open and the foundations of the earth tremble, causing the earth to be "utterly broken," "split apart," and "violently shaken" (24:18-19). God's judgment even extends to "the host of heaven, in heaven, and the kings of the earth, on the earth" (24:21). The heavenly bodies themselves will be struck (24:23).

Some have noted, however, that Isaiah sometimes uses such cosmic and universal language in previous chapters to describe particular local judgments.[84] This is true, though the pervasiveness of such imagery in Isaiah 24 is unmatched elsewhere, and one wonders how else the prophet could have identified a final universal judgment if he wished to do so. Not only does the language of "earth" and "world" suggest a judgment of universal extent, but also the generic reference to "the city," whose destruction is described in 24:10-12, strikingly contrasts with chapters 13–23, which identify specific locations even when using cosmic language.[85] As one writer puts it, the nameless and general description of "the city" seems to make it "a type of 'Vanity Fair.'"[86]

If a specific local judgment is prophesied here, which location is it? Johnson has made the strongest case for a local judgment, and he believes it refers to Jerusalem.[87] But I have already noted that Isaiah 24–27 pulls imagery from most of the foreign nation oracles of chapters 13–23, especially those against Babylon. The opening verse, in which God promises to scatter the earth's inhabitants (24:1), sounds like the curse on Babel. Much of the language, furthermore, seems designed to reflect an every-person quality rather than anything specifically Israelite. Isaiah 24:2 states: "And it shall be, as with the people, so with the priest; as with the slave, so with his master; as with the maid, so with her mistress; as with the buyer, so with the seller; as with the lender, so with the borrower; as with the creditor, so with the debtor." This could describe the breakdown of any civilized human society.

Finally, the description of judgment and redemption in chapters 25–27 confirms a universal and eschatological reading. God will destroy Leviathan, the great dragon (27:1). A great banquet on the mountain of the Lord will be

---

83. See e.g. Young, *Isaiah*, 2:149, 154.

84. E.g., Johnson, *From Chaos to Restoration*, p. 26.

85. Among those arguing for this as a reference to a symbolic or typological city, see Seitz, *Isaiah 1–39*, pp. 173-75; Clements, *Isaiah 1–39*, pp. 202-3; and Blenkinsopp, *Isaiah 1–39*, p. 347.

86. Clements, *Isaiah 1–39*, p. 202.

87. See his argument in Johnson, *From Chaos to Restoration*, pp. 29-35.

prepared for "all peoples" (25:6). Most powerfully, 25:7-8 prophesies the destruction of death itself, something rather inconceivable in an intrahistorical event. In the New Testament, Revelation associates all of these happenings with the last day.

The interpretation of this broader text is bound up with interpretation of its most fascinating and debate-provoking verse, 24:5: "The earth lies defiled under its inhabitants; for they have transgressed the laws, violated the statutes, broken the everlasting covenant." *Therefore,* continues 24:6, a curse devours the earth. What, in particular, is this covenant the earth's inhabitants have broken? Some have argued for the Mosaic covenant,[88] most see a reference to the Noahic covenant,[89] others have traced the reference back to an original Adamic covenant,[90] and some see multiple references, such that no single covenant alone is in view.[91] The terms of the most common debate — between a Noahic and Mosaic reference — are readily understandable. On the one hand, 24:5 refers to an "everlasting covenant" (ברית עולם), a term explicitly used for the Noahic covenant (Gen. 9:16) but not for the Mosaic covenant. On the other hand, 24:5 also mentions transgression of "laws" (תורת) and "statutes" (חק), which is typically Mosaic terminology. And while the OT indicates that the Mosaic covenant could be broken by human rebellion, Genesis 8:20–9:17 suggests that the Noahic covenant could not. Though it is understandable how someone persuaded that chapter 24 predicts the judgment of Jerusalem would conclude that 24:5 must refer to the Mosaic covenant, I believe this verse's broader context much favors a reference to the Noahic covenant, and the *prima facie* objections to a Noahic covenant view are more easily explained than the *prima facie* objections to a Mosaic covenant view.

88. Most thoroughly, see Johnson, *From Chaos to Restoration,* pp. 27-28. See also John Calvin, *Commentary on the Book of the Prophet Isaiah,* vol. 2, trans. William Pringle (Grand Rapids: Baker, 2003), p. 170.

89. E.g., see Childs, *Isaiah,* p. 179; Seitz, *Isaiah 1–39,* pp. 179-82; Steven D. Mason, "Another Flood? Genesis 9 and Isaiah's Broken Eternal Covenant," *JSOT* 33, no. 2 (2007): 177-98; Daniel R. Streett, "As It Was in the Days of Noah: The Prophets' Typological Interpretation of Noah's Flood," *Criswell Theological Review* 5 (Fall 2007): 42-46; Watts, *Isaiah 1–33,* p. 318; Blenkinsopp, *Isaiah 1–39,* pp. 351-52; Goldingay, *Isaiah,* p. 138; and Clements, *Isaiah 1–39,* p. 205.

90. E.g., Meredith G. Kline, "Death, Leviathan, and Martyrs: Isaiah 24:1–27:1," in *A Tribute to Gleason Archer,* ed. Walter C. Kaiser Jr. and Ronald F. Youngblood (Chicago: Moody, 1986), pp. 234-35.

91. In some very different ways, see e.g. Young, *Isaiah,* 2:157-59; Wildberger, *Isaiah 13–27,* pp. 480-81; Polaski, "Reflections on a Mosaic Covenant"; and Robert B. Chisholm, "The 'Everlasting Covenant' and the 'City of Chaos': Intentional Ambiguity and Irony in Isaiah 24," *Criswell Theological Review* 6, no. 2 (1993): 248-52.

In terms of the broader context of 24:5, the universal cosmic ethos of chapter 24 and the interest in the foreign nations in Isaiah 13–23 (chapters organically linked to chapter 24), overwhelmingly favor a Noahic over Mosaic interpretation. A simple, but to my mind decisive, observation is that all the earth's inhabitants and all the nations are in covenant with God through Noah, but not through Moses. For God to judge all the world for violating the Mosaic covenant would be unprecedented in Scripture, and seemingly unjust. The cosmic dissolution of Isaiah 24 (filled with de-creation themes) corresponds to the Noahic promise of cosmic regularity in Genesis 8:22. The curse on the earth consequent upon violation of the covenant (Isa. 24:5-6) corresponds to withdrawal of the curse in the Noahic covenant (Gen. 8:21). The windows of heaven opened in Isaiah 24:18 correspond to the windows of heaven shut at the conclusion of Noah's flood (Gen. 8:2; see 7:11).[92] Even the call for God's people to enter their chambers and shut the door behind them for a little while until his fury has passed (Isa. 26:20) evokes memory of God shutting Noah and his family in the ark when the rains came upon the earth (Gen. 7:16).[93] And why do God's people need to hide themselves? Because God is coming to judge the earth's inhabitants for their bloodshed (Isa. 26:21), the very thing that precipitated the flood (Gen. 6:11-13) and that the postdiluvian Noahic covenant was designed to suppress (9:5-6).[94]

There are two plausible objections to a Noahic interpretation of 24:5. First, the terminology of "laws" and "statutes" is typically Mosaic. This is true, but the terms are not universally Mosaic. God called Abraham to obey his "laws" and "statutes" (Gen. 26:5) long before he gave his law on Sinai, for example. Jeremiah also uses the term "statute" to describe God's fixing the order of sun, moon, and stars to give their light at proper times (Jer. 31:35-36), a text with strong covenantal overtones when read alongside Jeremiah 33:20-21. In short, these terms can refer to covenantal relationships — with people or the larger cosmic order — other than the Mosaic.

The second plausible objection is that the covenant of 24:5 could be broken, which seems inconsistent with a Noahic reference. In response, I note first that *any* "everlasting covenant" being broken presents a certain dissonance in the text. Perhaps, as one writer notes, the fact that the earth's inhabitants have broken an apparently unbreakable covenant is precisely the point; it highlights

---

92. See e.g. Clements, *Isaiah 1–39*, p. 205; Young, *Isaiah*, 2:175; Streett, "As It Was in the Days of Noah," p. 43.

93. See e.g. Childs, *Isaiah*, p. 192; and Streett, "As It Was in the Days of Noah," pp. 45-46.

94. See Chisholm, "The 'Everlasting Covenant,'" pp. 246-47.

how corruptly they have acted.[95] Ultimately I concur that the Noahic covenant was not truly bilateral and thus not breakable, strictly speaking, as argued in Chapter 2.[96] But this covenant did communicate (natural law) obligations to the human race and provided hints that a termination day of God's own choosing was built into its purpose (per Gen. 8:22, "while the earth remains"). Thus there is nothing unseemly about God, at termination day, calling attention to humanity's gross violation of this covenant's precepts and holding them accountable. If Isaiah 24–27 describes the end of history, then God indeed has kept his Noahic promise to maintain the natural cycles of nature as long as the earth endures and never again to destroy the earth with a flood.

The evidence, I conclude, suggests a reference to the Noahic covenant in Isaiah 24:5. Yet the idea that there is a hint of vagueness in the identity of this "everlasting covenant" is intriguing. Perhaps the Mosaic overtones present in Isaiah 24 are intentional. If, as I argue at length in Chapter 7, the Mosaic law made OT Israel a microcosm, displaying in bright colors the predicament of the whole sinful world under obligation to God, then God's judgments upon Israel under the Torah, like his judgments upon the foreign nations under the natural law, were foretastes of the final judgment described in Isaiah 24. And if both the Noahic and Mosaic covenants are incomprehensible apart from the reality of an original creation covenant that Adam broke (as argued in Chapter 2 and Chapter 7), and if breaking the creation covenant merited a final cosmic judgment that was postponed but not canceled, then this original covenant must not lurk far out of the picture in 24:5.

I conclude that Isaiah 24–27 supports and expands my preliminary conclusions about chapters 13–23. God deals with the foreign nations by means of the natural law, that is, a natural moral order pervading the world he created, knowable by all human beings, and holding them accountable to him. God now promulgates this natural law through the covenant he made with all creation through Noah after the flood. According to the terms of this covenant, God refrains from bringing any universal cosmic judgment upon the world until the last day. But he brings small-scale local judgments upon particular people in particular places, at times he alone knows, and does so on the basis of the Noahic natural law. These local judgments foreshadow and anticipate the final judgment, at which time God will bring radical dissolution — an eschatological de-creation — upon the present natural order. All of this, of

95. Seitz, *Isaiah 1–39*, p. 182.

96. And thus contra Mason, "Another Flood?" in his defense of a Noahic reference in Isaiah 24:5.

course, is only one aspect of the larger story of biblical history, which includes at its center a plan of redemption that culminates in a glorious new creation. That is evident too in Isaiah 13–27, though it is not our focus here.

Natural Law and Noahic Covenant in the Court Scenes of Daniel

Daniel 2–6 does not consist of prophetic oracles against foreign nations along the lines of Amos 1–2 or Isaiah 13–23, but of famous narratives recounting the experience of Daniel and his three friends in the Babylonian and Persian royal courts. As such, Daniel 2–6 allows us to test the conclusions drawn to this point in the chapter. These stories describe an Israelite prophet directly addressing foreign monarchs, interpreting their conduct, and at times announcing God's judgment upon them.[97] Do the words and behavior of Daniel and his friends corroborate the claims about natural law I have drawn from Amos and Isaiah?

This inquiry is useful for broader reasons too. It permits us to observe not only the basis upon which God holds the nations of the world accountable to himself but also the way in which believers in this one true God conducted themselves in the midst of such nations. Daniel and his friends find themselves away from theocratic Israel and in the center of pagan social and political life. Given that contemporary Christians have no theocratic homeland but are called to live in many nations and many social settings, we might suspect that the stories of Daniel 2–6 provide much relevant grist for reflection about how Christians today ought to undertake faithful engagement in and service to their societies. The NT confirms this suspicion when it portrays the Christian's identity in the world in terms of "exile" (1 Pet. 1:1, 17) and uses the ancient city of Babylon as an image for describing the cities in which Christians live today (1 Pet. 5:13; Rev. 18).[98] The fact that Christians are not OT prophets and live under the new covenant means that we must be careful about drawing simplistic one-to-one correspondence between Daniel's conduct and what God expects

---

97. It is interesting to note that Daniel 1, which deals with the intra-Jewish matter of fidelity to the Torah's dietary laws while in exile, is written in Hebrew, while Daniel 2–7, which concerns genuinely international issues and the conduct of foreign rulers, is written in Aramaic, the *lingua franca* of that day. See relevant discussion in Bill T. Arnold, "The Use of Aramaic in the Hebrew Bible: Another Look at Bilingualism in Ezra and Daniel," *Journal of Northwest Semitic Languages* 22, no. 2 (1996): 1-16.

98. For further development of this theme, see also VanDrunen, *Living in God's Two Kingdoms*, Part 2.

of contemporary Christians, but this is valuable material for developing a holistic biblical theology of Christian engagement in public life. I will therefore offer some constructive suggestions along these lines at the end of this section and will return to such issues in Part 2.

I argue that Daniel 2–6 does indeed confirm the conclusions about natural law drawn from Amos and Isaiah. These chapters treat the Babylonian and Persian monarchs not as those in redemptive covenantal relationship with God and obligated to him under the Mosaic law, but as those commissioned to rule nations under God's sovereign authority as established under the covenant with Noah. Their chief sins concern injustice and especially pride, and the chief thing they need to learn is to exercise just rule with humility, founded upon a general fear of God. To advance this argument I first mine data from each of the five stories and then bring this material together in a systematic way, suggesting how Daniel 2–6 supports a theology of natural law grounded in the Noahic covenant.

The Sins, Judgments, and Responses of the Foreign Monarchs

Daniel 2 is the first of three stories dealing with Babylonian king Nebuchadnezzar. In it he sees a dream and demands that his wise men tell him not only the dream's meaning but also the content of the dream itself. Through divine revelation, Daniel describes Nebuchadnezzar's dream of a multilayered statue destroyed by a giant rock, identifies Nebuchadnezzar as the statue's head, and identifies subsequent world empires as the rest of its body. Finally, he defines the rock as an everlasting kingdom of God that obliterates the statue.

Daniel 2 provides the least relevant material for present purposes. It does not condemn Nebuchadnezzar for any sin or present him in a particularly negative light at all. Consistent with this, it also pronounces no judgment against him (except in the general sense that one day God will bring all world empires to an end). Of some note, however, is Nebuchadnezzar's response to Daniel's description and interpretation of his dream. Nebuchadnezzar first offers expressions of worship to Daniel himself (2:46) and then makes this confession: "Truly, your God is God of gods and Lord of kings, and a revealer of mysteries, for you have been able to reveal this mystery." The text offers no evaluation, but we can observe that his statement acknowledges God's sovereignty only generally, and is not even a monotheistic confession (at best placing Daniel's God as supreme among the gods). Daniel, in fact, refers to God by a generic and nonspecifically Israelite name, "the God of heaven" (2:28, 37, 44), and does not press any claim for monotheism. The idea that Nebuchadnezzar converts to "the Jewish faith" goes far beyond what the text itself says.[99]

Daniel 3 tells the famous story of how Daniel's fellow Jews and civil servants, Shadrach, Meshach, and Abednego, refuse to worship an enormous statue Nebuchadnezzar constructs. Nebuchadnezzar has them thrown into a fiery furnace, from which God rescues them through an angel. As in the previous story, the text does not condemn Nebuchadnezzar for any sin or pronounce any judgment against him. But it does describe sinful acts of Nebuchadnezzar. Among them are constructing an idol and requiring its worship (3:1, 5-7), arrogantly asserting his incredulity that any god could deliver Shadrach, Meshach, and Abednego "out of my hands" (3:15), and condemning them to death in the furnace. Coloring all of this is the subtle suggestion in 3:1-7 that Nebuchadnezzar, by gathering a host of peoples, nations, and languages to him in Babylon, is attempting to reverse God's judgment at Babel (thoughts of Babel having already been conjured when 1:2 locates Babylon in the "land of Shinar"; cf. Gen. 11:2).[100] Nebuchadnezzar, however, does not condemn the three Jews for worshiping their God, but only for refusing to worship his gods (plural) and the image (3:12).

Nebuchadnezzar's confession at the end of this chapter (3:28-29) resembles his confession at the close of the previous story. First he acknowledges that their God has delivered the three men (without mentioning that he has delivered them out of *his* hands) and recognizes their right to disobey him in order to worship their God alone (3:28). Then he issues a decree prohibiting anybody from speaking against their God, in light of his unique ability to rescue (3:29). Thus Nebuchadnezzar again makes no move toward monotheism but simply notes a certain superiority of "the God of Shadrach, Meshach, and Abednego." And he legislates no positive requirement that others worship him, but simply prohibits anyone from opposing him.

The third story from the Babylonian court is Daniel 4. This narrative

99. This claim is made in Louis F. Hartman and Alexander A. di Lella, *The Book of Daniel* (Garden City, NY: Doubleday, 1978), p. 150. It reflects the judgment of many older interpreters; e.g., see the comments of Chrysostom in *Ezekiel, Daniel,* Ancient Christian Commentary on Scripture, Old Testament XIII, ed. Kenneth Stevenson and Michael Glerup (Downers Grove, IL: InterVarsity, 2008), p. 173. Calvin, however, takes a fairly cynical view of Nebuchadnezzar's profession; see John Calvin, *Commentaries on the Book of the Prophet Daniel,* vol. 1, trans. Thomas Myers (Grand Rapids: Baker, 2003), p. 195. Ernest Lucas rightly notes that Nebuchadnezzar's confession does not even embrace monotheism; see *Daniel* (Downers Grove, IL: InterVarsity, 2002), pp. 77, 80.

100. See John E. Goldingay, *Daniel* (Dallas: Word, 1989), p. 72.

describes how God judges Nebuchadnezzar by expelling him from human society and reducing him to a beast-like state for seven years, after which time God restores his kingship. A good deal of the story is a first-person account from Nebuchadnezzar himself (4:1-18, 34-37). Like Daniel 3, this story depicts Nebuchadnezzar in sin, but unlike both Daniel 2 and 3 the text explicitly condemns and judges him. First, then, what was Nebuchadnezzar's sin? The short answer is *hubris*. Daniel's prophecy of the coming judgment (delivered as an interpretation of Nebuchadnezzar's dream about the felling of a great tree) portrays Nebuchadnezzar's greatness as having grown "to heaven" (4:22), again evoking memory of Babel (see Gen. 11:4).[101] The punishment itself is triggered by Nebuchadnezzar's boast over Babylon, which he hails as his own creation, for the glory of his own majesty (4:30). Nebuchadnezzar was supposed to learn that "the Most High rules the kingdom of men and gives it to whom he will" (4:25, 32). Forsaking his pride, Nebuchadnezzar needed to recognize God's sovereignty rather than his own. Furthermore, he was to express humility through the right administration of justice, by "practicing righteousness . . . [and] showing mercy to the oppressed" (4:27). Hubris, which exalted him over God and made him callously unjust toward his subjects, was the sin that brought down Nebuchadnezzar.

The nature of the punishment imposed on Nebuchadnezzar is also worth noting. To borrow language used above, Daniel 4 describes a judgment of de-creation. Nebuchadnezzar represents the height of human civilization. He rules a magnificent city and also spreads his "dominion to the ends of the earth" (4:22), language evocative of humanity's original commission as image-bearer of God (Gen. 1:26, 28). Yet God reduces his portion to that of "the beasts in the grass of the earth" and changes his mind from a man's to a beast's (4:15-16). Instead of eating animals like a human being (Gen. 9:3) he eats grass like an animal (Dan. 4:32-33). This punishment also carries a sense of ironic reversal. As Isaiah 14 portrayed the king of Babylon as arrogantly grasping the heights of heaven and being cast down to the depths of Sheol, a case of rich poetic justice, so Daniel 4 presents Nebuchadnezzar's fall from god-like world dominion to animal-like groveling, a punishment whose fittingness is readily evident.

Finally, like the previous two chapters, Daniel 4 concludes with a response of Nebuchadnezzar to preceding events (4:34-37; cf. 4:1-3). He begins by acknowledging that God's dominion is everlasting, that earth's inhabitants are as nothing before him, that God does his will both among the host of heaven

101. See Goldingay, *Daniel*, p. 94.

and the inhabitants of earth, and that no one can stay his hand or question his ways (4:34-35). In a final confession Nebuchadnezzar praises God, acknowledges the justice of his ways, and recognizes that he can humble the proud (4:37). Nebuchadnezzar's words about God are most effusive here, though he still makes no explicit commitment to serve God *alone*. Daniel never demands this and God never punishes him for failing to do so.[102] Also interesting is that Nebuchadnezzar, unlike in chapters 2–3, issues no law to his subjects about their relation to this God.

Daniel 5 keeps us in Babylon but tells the tale of a successor to Nebuchadnezzar, king Belshazzar. Daniel is still around, and his reputation current, but he appears not to have the prominent place in court that he enjoyed under the Nebuchadnezzar regime (see 5:10-12). The story begins with Belshazzar in Dionysian revelry, bringing out vessels from the Lord's temple to help him enjoy his wine and honor his idols. A hand appears and writes a few words on the wall, Daniel is summoned to interpret their meaning, and that night Babylon falls to the Medes and Persians and Belshazzar is slain. For what sin is Belshazzar condemned? Unlike the apparently competent Nebuchadnezzar before him (whatever his many moral shortcomings), Belshazzar comes across as an incompetent idiot. While his kingdom teeters on the brink of collapse, he regales himself with wine and women. This sets a powerful tone for how readers view Belshazzar, but this is not exactly why judgment is coming upon him. Daniel later points to his big problem as hubris: though he knew about the judgment upon Nebuchadnezzar and what it taught about the sovereignty of the "Most High God," Belshazzar refused to humble his heart but instead lifted himself up against "the Lord of heaven" (5:18-23). This exhibited itself in three ways: he and his coterie drank wine from the Lord's temple vessels, he praised his idols, and did not honor "the God in whose hand is your breath" (5:23).

This triad raises an interesting issue. None of the material I have surveyed thus far from Amos, Isaiah, and Daniel 2–4 has announced temporal judgment against a foreign nation for idolatry or other offense related to religious ritual. Yet here Belshazzar's praise of "the gods of silver and gold, of bronze, iron, wood, and stone" is part of the charge against him. Is this an anomaly? Does Belshazzar alone suffer temporal judgment for this sin? Looking at the indictment of 5:23 as a whole suggests that God is not singling

---

102. Calvin is less skeptical about Nebuchadnezzar's confession here than in previous chapters, but concludes that we are unable to determine from the text whether this represented genuine repentance; see *Commentaries on Daniel*, 1.245.

out Belshazzar for a sin that he forbore in others. The text gives no reason to think that if Belshazzar had engaged in typical idolatry in the ordinary course of events — as Nebuchadnezzar did — he would have endured the judgment Daniel pronounces in 5:25-28. Belshazzar does not commit three separate sins but one threefold sin: in a drunken stupor he defiles the vessels of God's temple, using them for the worship of idols and not honoring the God whose vessels they are. In this sacrilege Belshazzar has done something that apparently Nebuchadnezzar himself, in all his arrogance, never did. Idolatry per se is not the charge. Dishonoring the Lord in wanton hubris by using his holy things for pagan worship — that is the ground of Belshazzar's judgment.

One other dynamic in Daniel 5 deserves mention. Belshazzar is the only one of the three kings in Daniel 2–6 who loses his kingdom and his life. He is also the only one who fails to render any honor or confession to God. Perhaps the latter is ground for the former, though the fact that Daniel announces God's verdict before Belshazzar has any opportunity to respond may indicate instead that Belshazzar's hubris has outstripped that of the other kings. On the other hand, there is nothing in Daniel — or in the prophetic oracles against the nations, or in the Noahic covenant — suggesting that God brings temporal judgments in any strict and predictable correspondence to the weight of the crimes.

We come finally to the story of Daniel 6, with Daniel in the court of Persian king Darius. Daniel quickly attains high standing in Darius's inner circle, and the king's other advisors enviously devise a plot against him. Unable to find any lawful charge against Daniel, they trick Darius into making a decree requiring prayer only to himself for thirty days. When Daniel does not comply, Darius, full of regret, is compelled to cast Daniel into the lions' den. To the king's relief God delivers Daniel, and Darius offers his devious advisors as repast for the hungry beasts.

Darius is perhaps the most difficult of the three monarchs to evaluate. Nebuchadnezzar comes off as exceedingly arrogant, though in a somewhat understandable way given his impressive credentials. Belshazzar is also full of hubris, though not for any noteworthy accomplishment but as a foolish child playing with a fire far beyond his power to handle. Darius, on the other hand, comes across as a generally good man, albeit one who falls prey to flattery in a moment of weakness. This may be a surprising evaluation, given that Darius's decree actually goes beyond anything done by Nebuchadnezzar or Belshazzar, in that he not only promotes worship of a false god but also prohibits worship of the true God. But his virtues in the text are many. He wisely recognizes

Daniel's worth as an advisor (6:1-3), is immediately distressed when he realizes the unintended consequence of his decree (6:14), wishes Daniel well in seeking the help of his God (6:16), fasts all night while Daniel is in the den (6:18), rejoices at his deliverance (6:23), executes the *lex talionis* against Daniel's enemies (6:24),[103] and ends with a confession of God's greatness (6:26-27). As one commentator puts it, Darius is a "sympathetic figure" throughout.[104] He is subject to vanity, to be sure, but unlike a typical person of hubris promptly repents and humbles himself. Daniel never condemns him for anything and God brings no judgment upon him.[105]

Daniel 6 concludes with a record of Darius's confession, which resembles those of Nebuchadnezzar. He proclaims that God's kingdom endures forever and marvels at his great works (6:26b-27).[106] Before this, Darius issues legislation requiring more than Nebuchadnezzar's in chapter 3. Whereas Nebuchadnezzar prohibited his subjects from speaking anything against Daniel's God (3:29), Darius positively requires his people "to tremble and fear before the God of Daniel" (6:26a). It is difficult to know how to evaluate this. Darius's previous decree trying to regulate religious devotion did not go well, and though his intentions here are certainly nobler, one might wonder whether he again dips into matters beyond his competence. In contrast, Nebuchadnezzar, in what seems to be his keenest moment of insight into his place in the universe under God's sovereignty, makes a personal confession about God's dominion but issues no legislation (see Daniel 4). Whatever its wisdom, Darius's decree remains at a very general level. It requires no adherence to the Mosaic law or observance of any specific religious ritual, but a fear and trembling that sounds more like awe-filled fright than loving worship.

---

103. Darius does to them what they unjustly plotted to do against Daniel. Hartman and di Lella compare Darius's action to the punishment prescribed against false witnesses in Deuteronomy 19:18-21, where it is put explicitly in terms of the *lex talionis*; see *Daniel*, p. 200. See also Lucas, *Daniel*, p. 152. John J. Collins describes the punishment of Daniel's enemies as "poetic justice"; see *Daniel, First Maccabees, Second Maccabees* (Wilmington, DE: Michael Glazier, 1981), p. 66.

104. Collins, *Daniel*, p. 66.

105. At the same time, the text has some fun at Darius's expense. It is richly ironic that the king who requires everyone to pray only to him becomes a slave to his own statute — which could not be changed, "according to the law of the Medes and the Persians" — and was powerless to bring about his own deepest desire, Daniel's deliverance. On these points, see Lucas, *Daniel*, p. 151.

106. Here again Calvin is skeptical that this is a true conversion; see *Commentaries on Daniel*, p. 388.

Implications of Daniel 2–6

My observations about Daniel 2–6 in the previous pages have raised many issues pertinent for this chapter. I now bring these observations together and present the implications I see for my claims about natural law under the Noahic covenant. I conclude that Daniel 2–6 provides strong support for my claims in that they portray the three foreign kings as accountable to God in ways consistent with the portrayal of foreigners in Amos and Isaiah and entirely compatible with the expectations created in the Noahic covenant of Genesis 8:20–9:17. I also make some tentative suggestions about the normativity of Daniel's conduct in a pagan court for contemporary Christians in civil society today.

First to note is the correspondence between the foreign nation oracles in Amos and Isaiah and the narratives of Daniel 2–6. Amos indicts the foreign nations for heinous sins — crimes against humanity — and Isaiah condemns them primarily for hubris, expressed through acts of injustice. So also hubris is the great sin of which Daniel charges foreign kings (in the two chapters where he levels charges), and Nebuchadnezzar's hubris is manifest in failure to act justly. In most of Amos's oracles, and some of Isaiah's, the chief target of condemnation is the ruler or others with power. So also Daniel always deals with monarchs. Isaiah describes punishments with two characteristic themes: *lex talionis* (often expressed as poetic justice) and de-creation. Besides Belshazzar's loss of kingdom and life, Daniel 2–6 announces only one punishment, Nebuchadnezzar's transformation into a beast, and this is an act of both de-creation and poetic justice. Finally, in Amos and Isaiah God never judges a foreign people for idolatry or other offense involving religious ritual. Likewise, Daniel never condemns the Babylonian monarchs for their evident idolatry or pagan worship per se (ultimately even in the case of Belshazzar).

The stories in Daniel 2–6 also help to clarify a difficult issue. If God does not bring temporal judgment upon foreign monarchs for idolatry and matters germane, what exactly is their relationship to God? Though Amos focuses solely upon intrahuman relationships, Isaiah's emphasis upon hubris makes clear that "religion" in a broader sense is not an indifferent matter for God's governance of foreign nations, particularly with respect to their kings. In Daniel 2–6 this issue is heightened, and the foreign monarchs' relationship to the true God is a central theme throughout. What becomes evident in these texts is that God does not — *in terms of his temporal governance and temporal judgments* — require relinquishment of idols, specific rituals of worship, or any kind of conversion to the Mosaic covenant. Rather, he requires kings to recognize humbly his ultimate sovereignty over the course of history and to keep their hands off his holy things and those who worship him.[107] Nebuchadnezzar and Belshazzar are condemned precisely for failing on these points. Likewise, the confessions of Nebuchadnezzar and Darius hail the sovereign power and prerogative of God, without embracing any specific form of worshiping him and without forswearing other gods.[108] They acknowledge no "salvation," in terms of forgiveness of sins or eschatological life. As I mentioned above, it is difficult to evaluate the legislation of Nebuchadnezzar in Daniel 4 and of Darius in Daniel 6. Nebuchadnezzar prohibits speaking against God, and Darius requires fearing and trembling before him. The text never says whether they act righteously, and in any case they legislate differently. Even if we view their decrees in a positive light, they pertain to respect for God and his power only at a general level. To utilize an idea discussed in Chapter 3, the Lord seems to hold these foreign monarchs responsible for humbly exhibiting a basic "fear of God" (which is not the same as saving faith).

This is, I conclude, evidence of God's governance of the world through the Noahic covenant. As interpreted in Chapter 2, Genesis 9:6 calls human beings, as image-bearers of God, to administer (retributive) justice in response to bloodshed. This means that human beings ought to recognize their place in the grand order of things, as originally established at creation and preserved in fallen form. They have a noble place, having a certain authority over the animals (9:2-3) and a unique relationship with God, but they are only the *image* of God. Hubris is fundamentally at odds with this reality. Accepting one's place as a servant under a sovereign God also entails the responsibility to serve others through pursuit of justice, symbolized by the *lex talionis*. Genesis 9:6 thereby draws attention to the duties of civil authorities (those in a privileged position to execute justice), especially toward the vulnerable (exemplified in the victim of bloodshed). Along these lines, Daniel 2–6 (and the foreign nation oracles of Amos and Isaiah) take special interest in kings and hold them liable

---

107. As mentioned above, many OT prophetic oracles condemn foreign nations for wicked actions toward Israel (though this is not a prominent emphasis in Amos or Isaiah). This is probably not simply a charge of general injustice; treating Israel unjustly is like exalting oneself over God himself. Israel is the "apple of his eye" (Zech. 2:8). This is also a significant theme in Revelation (e.g., see 16:5-7; 18:20, 24; 19:2). In light of Daniel and the prophetic oracles, it seems fair to conclude that the humility toward God required in the Noahic covenant entails respect for those who worship him exclusively.

108. This fact should have tempered the tendency among many earlier commentators to use such texts as rallying cries for civil magistrates to take action against heretics and the like; see e.g. Calvin, appealing to Augustine, in *Commentaries on Daniel*, p. 246.

particularly for hubris toward God and breaches of justice toward weaker fellow human beings. Furthermore, while the Noahic covenant commissions human beings to pursue justice with humble recognition of their place under God's ultimate authority, it imposes no specific demands for worship or religious ritual and makes no reference to a Messiah or plan of salvation, nor does it grant authority to human beings to impose worship practices or specific theological doctrines upon others. As suggested earlier, this covenant provides foundation for recognizing rights to religious liberty. Accordingly, Daniel 2–6 (and the foreign nation oracles of Amos and Isaiah) do not prosecute foreign nations and their kings for idolatry per se.

As argued in Chapter 2, the Noahic covenant deals with God's *temporal* government of the world, aimed at the *preservation* of the cosmic and social orders, and encompassing *all human beings,* whatever their specific religious profession. Following the judgment oracles of Amos and Isaiah, Daniel 2–6 deals with foreign nations and their rulers along precisely these lines.

Natural law itself is not explicitly prominent in Daniel 2–6. The kings condemned and punished — Nebuchadnezzar and Belshazzar — were not judged on the basis of the Mosaic law. They did receive some special prophetic revelation (the former directly, the latter indirectly through observing Nebuchadnezzar's experience), which they failed to heed before God imposed judgment. Nevertheless, the basic content of this revelation — that they had sinned through injustice rooted in hubris — was hardly novel. Through prophetic revelation God warned and judged these kings for what they already knew. The important point for present purposes is that the natural moral order of the Noahic covenant governed these foreign kings, though it was also reinforced by prophetic revelation.

Finally, what might we observe about the conduct of godly saints in the courts of a pagan kingdom? For context it is worth remembering that Daniel and his friends were pious Israelites, evidently trained under the law of Moses (see 1:8) and zealous for the welfare of Jerusalem and the prophetic promises (see 9:1-19). Yet they were thrust into exile and conscripted into the service of a pagan king. And this was not just any pagan king, but the very one who had demolished Jerusalem, taken them into exile, and imposed his violent will upon much of the known world.[109] But Daniel and friends serve this king and his empire willingly and loyally. They put their abilities to work for the

---

109. As Seitz remarks with respect to Isaiah 13–14, Babylon had made an "unprecedented assault on humanity and common codes of justice," seeking to rule the world at all costs; see Seitz, *Isaiah 1–39,* pp. 135-36.

benefit of what Scripture portrays so often as the archetypally proud city. As some commentators have noted, the grand vision of history depicted in Nebuchadnezzar's dream in Daniel 2 might have been reasonably interpreted as a call to resist Gentile authority and to fight for reestablishment of the Israelite theocracy. But instead Daniel and friends remain faithful servants of a king and empire doomed to pass away.[110] Daniel 2 does put the Noahic covenant in eschatological perspective: this covenant will come to an end in the kingdom of God's ultimate triumph. But Daniel 3–6 encourages submission to its structures while it remains in force.

The message of Daniel thus corresponds to Jeremiah's response to the exiles wrestling with similar issues (Jer. 29:1-14). Hope ultimately lies in the restoration of the fortunes of God's special covenant people, not in Babylon, which lies under judgment. But that day will come in God's timing, and until then the saints must live ordinary lives in exile and seek the welfare of this city. A further observation is that Daniel and friends rendered this service to Babylon within the structure of its own laws and customs. Though careful not to transgress the law of God when there was irremediable conflict (as in 1:8-16; 3:8-18; 6:10), they excelled in their Babylonian higher education (1:4, 17-20) and managed to function within the pagan court and even to prosper and be honored within it. Daniel made an impressive transition to the customs of the Persian court in Daniel 6. In fact, when his envious colleagues tried to find something against him, they were unable to find any viable charge "with regard to the kingdom" (6:4) — he was a model of fidelity to Persian law.

Depending upon one's views of Christianity and the public square, much of this may seem surprising. But it is consistent with God's promise to preserve and govern the world through the Noahic covenant. God continues to make his moral will known in the fabric of creation and maintains order in part through human instrumentality (Gen. 9:5-6). Human authority structures and systems of justice, even when riddled with serious flaws, should not be despised. If Daniel could serve the archetypally proud city in his exile, then contemporary Christians should at least give careful thought before refusing faithful service to their own communities and governments in the midst of their exile. Romans 13:1-7 seems to confirm this suggestion. Even the Roman magistrate — like the Babylonian regime, no paragon of just authority — was established by God and served as his minister in accomplishing real good in the world. Paul called the early Christians to be submissive to it. I realize that this raises many difficult practical questions, to some of which I will return in

---

110. E.g., see Collins, *Daniel*, pp. 34-35.

later chapters of this book. Here I simply note that the larger story of biblical revelation suggests the normative significance of Daniel's public service, a public service characterized by remarkable deference to the authority and laws of a pagan people.

Conclusion

In this chapter I have continued the biblical examination, begun in the previous chapter, of how God dealt with foreign nations that stood outside the Abrahamic and Mosaic covenants and to whom he had not delivered the Torah. I have argued that Amos 1–2, Isaiah 13–23, and Daniel 2–6 demonstrate God's continuing revelation of himself and his law to these nations through the natural order, as sustained by the Noahic covenant, under whose authority all people exist.

These biblical texts confirm earlier arguments that the moral obligations explicit in Genesis 9:1-7 focus upon a minimalist ethic that reflects the primary concern of the Noahic covenant, that is, God's temporal preservation of the world and human society within it. The OT prophets judge foreign nations not for remote moral implications of the Noahic covenant or for idolatry or other misplaced religious worship, but for heinous acts of injustice. Yet the prophets' attention to hubris and to a broader order of created reality that ought not to be breached also confirms that the thin Noahic ethic of Genesis 9:1-7 is ultimately undergirded by a thicker natural moral order at whose root should be a humble fear of God. As God sustains human society through his common grace, some nations of the world evidence a relative respect for this natural moral order, as our previous study of Gerar (Genesis 20) displayed. Yet others fall into shocking disregard for it, and on some occasions God wills to bring temporal judgments upon them, as seen in the story of Sodom and the prophetic oracles. These judgments foreshadow the final judgment to come upon the whole world at the last day, yet God executes such intrahistorical judgments according to the expectations and standards of his universal government through the Noahic covenant. These prophetic texts also support my previous suggestions that the Noahic covenant supports a positive view of religious liberty and of forming social communities through intrahuman covenants.

This study of God's universal government of the nations of the world continues, and concludes, with our consideration of Romans 1–2 in the next chapter. Here we see Scripture's most detailed and focused discussion of the natural law and how God, through natural law, holds accountable to himself even those who are foreigners to the redemptive covenants and without special prophetic revelation. After this we will turn in Part 2 to the significance of natural law for those who participate in the economy of redemptive grace through the Abrahamic, Mosaic, and new covenants.

CHAPTER 5

Universal Accountability before the Impartial Judgment of God: Natural Law in Romans 1:18–2:16

In Chapters 2-4 I presented an interconnected series of arguments about natural law in the fallen world, drawn from a number of texts in the Old Testament (OT). After the primordial human rebellion in Genesis 3, God preserved the original creation, though in fallen form. Since the great flood he has done so through the covenant with Noah (Gen. 8:20–9:17), a covenant of common grace established with the entire human race and even the whole order of nature. By maintaining human beings as divine image-bearers, situated in the broader created order, God continues to make known a natural law, by which he holds them morally accountable to him and commissions them to exercise a modified form of that benevolent dominion over the world to which he originally called them at creation. The explicit moral obligations in Genesis 9:1-7 represent a minimalist ethic focused upon the basic necessities for the preservation of human society, in line with the general purposes of the Noahic covenant. Yet these verses themselves, in context, also hint at the existence of a broader natural moral order that underlies the minimalist ethic. Genesis 19–20 and the prophetic oracles against the foreign nations confirm that there is universal moral knowledge, even apart from special prophetic revelation. They also confirm that God, in his temporal governance of the nations of the world under the Noahic covenant, has special interest in human performance of its basic obligations. These texts furthermore provide additional evidence of a broader natural moral order known to all human beings.

This chapter turns to a biblical text with a special place historically in Christian thinking about natural law, Romans 1:18–2:16. The relevance of this text for Christian natural law theory is not difficult to gather, given its references to a knowledge of God acquired through creation, to sins that are against nature, to the things of the law written upon the heart, and to the operations of conscience. Yet in recent decades theologians and biblical scholars have wrestled with this text in debates on the validity of natural theology, the moral status of homosexual conduct, and the so-called "Paul and the law" issues, debates calling into question many aspects of the traditional interpretation.

I argue in this chapter that the Apostle Paul, in Romans 1:18–2:16, does indeed teach the existence of a natural law, and that this text further confirms and enriches the conclusions of previous chapters. I deal with Romans 1:18–2:16 at this point in my study because this text provides New Testament (NT) reflection on the specific topic considered in the previous three chapters: God's government of the nations of the world through the Noahic covenant and its natural law. Paul does not make explicit reference to the Noahic covenant here, but it is significant that he focuses upon the moral accountability of all human beings before a just God, not upon salvation in Christ or the distinctive moral life of the church as God's new covenant people. Therefore Paul speaks precisely about human life as it stands in relationship to God through the Noahic covenant. Echoing the OT prophets before him, but with more detail and clarity, Paul affirms the universal moral knowledge of the human race. He roots it in an understanding of God and his law understood through nature itself. Consistently with the idea that natural law is communicated through a divinely enacted covenant, Paul speaks of this communication of the law in nature as God's *revelation*. We also see in Romans 1:18–2:16 the continuing significance of the minimalist ethic explicit in Genesis 9:1-7, as well as the reality of a broader natural moral order. Genesis 19 and the prophetic oracles focus upon God's temporal government and his judgments upon particular nations of the world (in anticipation of the final judgment), and hence highlight their egregious violations of the minimalist Noahic ethic necessary for the sustenance of human society. In comparison, Paul thinks especially of the guilt of all individuals before God, to be exposed ultimately at the final judgment of the last day. Thus he probes to the bottom of their rebellion and identifies perversion of the natural knowledge of God himself as the core and source of their many other failures under the natural law. Given the place of 1:18–2:16 in Paul's larger argument in Romans, we also see here that understanding God's impartial judgment under the natural law is a crucial foundation for understanding the Christian gospel, even though it is not to be confused with it.

To explore Romans 1:18–2:16 and its teaching about natural law, I first examine 1:18-32 and then turn to 2:1-16. I conclude the chapter with a general summary of the argument in Part 1 and my proposal regarding natural law and God's preservation (but not redemption) of the entire world, through common grace, under the Noahic covenant.

Knowing but Rebelling: Natural Law in Romans 1:18-32

Christian commentators have classically interpreted Romans 1:18-32 as foundation Paul lays for the explanation of the gospel of salvation in Christ that he begins to unfold in 3:21. Specifically, in 1:18-32 Paul explains that all human beings have a natural knowledge of God and his will but, because of sin, they twist and corrupt it. Thus God holds the entire human race accountable before him and the human race therefore needs a new initiative of grace in order to escape the divine judgment.[1] A number of debates have arisen in recent decades questioning whether Paul really affirms such natural knowledge and, if so, what exactly it is. Such debates include (sometimes tortuous) exchanges about "natural theology" conducted in the shadow of Karl Barth's famous clash with Emil Brunner[2] and about Paul's conception of sex in terms of "nature" and the "natural" in light of changing views in much of the Western world about same-sex relationships. One scholar has even argued that Paul is not explaining his own views in 1:18-32 but those of others he intends to refute.[3]

---

1. As the editor of a compilation of patristic comments on Romans 1:18-32 summarizes, "God can be known by the human mind, and every form of wisdom is due to divine revelation of one kind or another. The Fathers generally believed in the possibility of coming to a true, albeit limited, knowledge of God by using the resources of the human mind to contemplate the mysteries of the universe. To their way of thinking, this did not open the door to a form of salvation by works. Rather it merely increased the horror of the condemnation that humanity incurred for having turned away from God." See Gerald Bray, ed., *Romans,* Ancient Christian Commentary on Scripture, New Testament VI (Downers Grove, IL: InterVarsity, 1998), p. 34.

2. For a reprint of their famous exchange, see Emil Brunner and Karl Barth, *Natural Theology: Comprising "Nature and Grace" by Professor Dr. Emil Brunner and the reply "No!" by Dr. Karl Barth* (Eugene, OR: Wipf & Stock, 2002). An example of a discussion that strikes me as tortuous, which tries mightily to read Romans 1 without finding any "natural theology" or any natural knowledge of God apart from Scripture, is found in C. E. B. Cranfield, *The Epistle to the Romans,* vol. 1 (Edinburgh: T. & T. Clark, 1975), pp. 113-16. One prominent debunker of Barthian attempts to expunge natural theology from Romans 1 and all of Scripture was James Barr, especially in *Biblical Faith and Natural Theology* (Oxford: Clarendon, 1993). On page 50 he makes the amusing comment: "The kind of exegesis which will refuse any openness to natural theology in Romans 1-2 is the kind of negative exegesis which will also deny a doctrine of incarnation in John or a doctrine of the Trinity in Paul." Though a helpful corrective in many respects, Barr's treatment of Romans 1 and other texts has not gone unchallenged by competent exegetes; e.g., see Francis Watson, *Text and Truth: Redefining Biblical Theology* (Grand Rapids: Eerdmans, 1997), pp. 242-67. There is surely much wisdom in Joseph Fitzmyer's comment that "preoccupation with the problem that the Enlightenment introduced" has tended to obscure what Paul is really trying to say; see Joseph A. Fitzmyer, S.J., *Romans: A New Translation with Introduction and Commentary* (New York: Doubleday, 1993), p. 274.

3. See Douglas A. Campbell, "Natural Theology in Paul? Reading Romans 1.19-20,"

Without being able to engage all the details of such debates, I argue in this section in support of the classical view that Paul does indeed teach a universal natural knowledge of God and his moral will, and hence the reality of natural law. Paul indicates that God objectively reveals this natural law through the created order and that human beings subjectively know the natural law, but sinfully distort it. Though he states his indictment here in universal terms, Paul seems to focus upon sins of the Gentiles (offering an indictment with which his Jewish readers would probably agree), before turning his focus upon Jews at some point in Romans 2, where he includes the latter under the same indictment as the Gentiles. This strategy resembles that of Amos 1–2. As in all the prophetic oracles examined in the previous chapter, Paul here condemns the Gentiles on the basis of their universal natural knowledge of God, not on the basis of the Torah.[4] I consider here a number of interrelated issues Paul addresses in 1:18-32 and reflect upon their implications for the biblical theology of natural law I am developing in this book.

The Revelation of Wrath

The opening of the text presents a bleak background for Paul's teaching about natural law: "For the wrath of God is revealed from heaven against all ungodliness and unrighteousness of men" (1:18). Despite a brief hint in 2:14-15 about a positive role natural law plays in this world, the overwhelming burden of 1:18–2:16 (indeed, through 3:20) is to establish the judgment of God against a sinful world, and Paul's statements relative to natural law contribute to that thesis. A basic, but critically important, point in this text is that natural law makes no positive contribution to the attainment of salvation.

If one associates Paul's statement in 1:18 too closely with what he has

---

IJST 1 (Nov. 1999): 231-52. Campbell has subsequently expanded this argument in a massive innovative interpretation of Romans and Pauline thought generally; see Douglas A. Campbell, *The Deliverance of God: An Apocalyptic Rereading of Justification in Paul* (Grand Rapids: Eerdmans, 2009). The initial reviews of this work seem generally to reject Campbell's claim that Romans 1:18–3:20 represents primarily the voice of someone other than Paul whom Paul was attempting to refute and embarrass. For one example, see R. Barry Matlock, "Zeal for Paul but Not According to Knowledge: Douglas Campbell's War on 'Justification Theory,'" *JSNT* 34 (Dec. 2011): 139-44.

4. On the resemblance to Amos, see Arland J. Hultgren, *Paul's Letter to the Romans: A Commentary* (Grand Rapids: Eerdmans, 2011), p. 86. Later Hultgren comments that Paul would "have shared the traditional [Jewish] view that God can be known in part through general revelation" (p. 92).

just written in 1:17, there is risk of obscuring the negative backdrop for natural law that permeates 1:18–2:16. Paul opens 1:18 with "For" (γάρ), which raises an interesting question about the relation of 1:17 and 1:18. Paul's words in 1:17 are full of light: "For in it [the gospel] the righteousness of God is revealed from faith for faith, as it is written, 'The righteous shall live by faith.'" According to some commentators, Paul begins 1:18 with "for" because the wrath of God is of one piece with the righteousness of God revealed in the gospel.[5] Other writers, taking "for" to indicate a contrast between God's righteousness and his wrath, have grasped Paul's larger point more accurately, I believe.[6] Romans 1:18 begins a lengthy section that extends to 3:20. Paul's concern with God's wrath and judgment continues through the entire section and culminates with these words: "Now we know that whatever the law says it speaks to those who are under the law, so that every mouth may be stopped, and the whole world may be held accountable to God. For by works of the law no human beings will be justified in his sight, since through the law comes knowledge of sin" (3:19-20). Then in 3:21 Paul's argument makes a decisive shift, as he returns to the theme announced in 1:17 but left undeveloped in subsequent verses: "the righteousness of God" by faith. This theme, reintroduced in 3:21 and following, stands in contrast to what has gone before and is the solution to the problem that 1:18–3:20 has announced. The law has left all people condemned as unrighteous, "*But now* the righteousness of God has been manifested *apart from the law* . . . the righteousness of God through faith in Jesus Christ for all who believe" (3:21-22). The righteousness of God, in this section of Romans at least, is something that brings salvation and thus contrasts with God's wrath against sin.

Therefore, when Paul begins 1:18 with "for," he likely does not indicate that the wrath of God is an aspect of "the righteousness of God" but that he is beginning an exposition of essential background material for understanding what this righteousness is and why his gospel announces it as good news.[7]

---

5. E.g., see Cranfield, *The Epistle to the Romans*, 1:109-11; and Robert Jewett, *Romans: A Commentary* (Minneapolis: Fortress, 2007), pp. 151-52. Somewhat similar is Mark A. Seifrid, "Unrighteous by Faith: Apostolic Proclamation in Romans 1:18–3:20," in *Justification and Variegated Nomism*, vol. 2, *The Paradoxes of Paul*, ed. D. A. Carson, Peter T. O'Brien, and Mark A. Seifrid (Grand Rapids: Baker, 2004), pp. 109-13.

6. E.g., see James D. G. Dunn, *Romans 1–8* (Dallas: Word, 1988), p. 154; Charles H. Talbert, *Romans* (Macon, GA: Smyth & Helwys, 2002), pp. 58-59; John Murray, *The Epistle to the Romans* (Grand Rapids: Eerdmans, 1968), p. 35; and Luke Timothy Johnson, *Reading Romans: A Literary and Theological Commentary* (New York: Crossroad, 1997), p. 30.

7. See e.g. Douglas J. Moo, *The Epistle to the Romans* (Grand Rapids: Eerdmans, 1996),

Later in this chapter I discuss further the purposes of 1:18–3:20 in the larger scheme of Romans, but suffice it to say for now that Paul's predominant (if not exclusive) purpose in this section is the negative one of placing all people under the wrath and judgment of God due to sin. This is the context in which Paul delivers his most extensive comments pertaining to natural law.

In light of the OT material examined in previous chapters, it is no surprise to find natural law expounded in the context of God's wrath and judgment. Under the covenant of creation in Genesis 1–2 natural law presented God's moral standard and threatened judgment, without promise of mercy, if the first humans did not render perfect obedience. Under the Noahic covenant natural law continues to make known God's retributive justice, though tempered by forbearance, in his present government of the world. In Genesis 19 and the prophetic oracles against the nations God poured out temporal judgments upon people who egregiously violated the natural moral order.[8] Here in Romans 1:18–2:16, likewise, Paul forces his readers back behind the façade of God's temporary forbearance and makes them peer into the abyss of divine judgment against sin, hints of which are already being revealed (Rom. 1:18, 24, 26, 28) and whose full brunt is coming (cf. 2:5, 8-9).[9] As we will see, natural law continues to exist, but not in order to save or even to provide positive preparatory aids along the way to salvation.[10] Whatever provisional good natural law does for the maintenance of human society, with respect to salvation Paul assigns it no positive function. It serves to leave every person "without excuse" (1:20).

---

pp. 92, 99; and Richard H. Bell, *No One Seeks for God: An Exegetical and Theological Study of Romans 1.18–3.20* (Tübingen: Mohr Siebeck, 1998), pp. 16-17.

8. Contra Campbell, "Natural Theology in Paul?" p. 238, the fact that the so-called traditional reading of Romans 1:18–3:20 works with "a god of retributive justice" is not an argument against it. In light of the various retributive and talionic themes observed in previous chapters, what Paul says in Romans 1 does not seem at all out of accord with his OT background.

9. There is some exegetical debate about whether the revealed wrath mentioned in 1:18 refers to the final judgment or to present manifestations of divine anger. Bell, *No One Seeks for God*, pp. 14-18, e.g., believes that the reference is to the final judgment, despite the present tense "is revealed." On the other hand, e.g., Bernadette J. Brooten sees the wrath of 1:18 as manifest in God's present "giving them up" (1:24, 26, 28); see *Love Between Women: Early Christian Responses to Female Homoeroticism* (Chicago: University of Chicago Press, 1996), p. 221. S. J. Gathercole says that Romans 1 concerns a transcendent model of divine wrath active in the present, while Romans 2 offers a similar picture in the eschatological sphere; see "Justified by Faith, Justified by his Blood: The Evidence of Romans 3:21–4:25," in *Justification and Variegated Nomism*, 2:170.

10. See the comments along these lines in Moo, *Romans*, pp. 105-6, 108. See also Thomas R. Schreiner, *Romans* (Grand Rapids: Baker, 1998), p. 86.

In the Things That Have Been Made: Nature as Divine Revelation

Strikingly, Romans 1:18-32 teaches that the theological and moral truth communicated through nature puts a person in relationship to *God*. As noted in the Introduction, many recent works on natural law emphasize the need to abandon the tendency (often imprecisely associated with the Enlightenment) to conceive of nature and natural law as an autonomous sphere that can be understood apart from theological commitment. Romans 1:18-32 amply supports the rejection of such views.

One feature of Paul's initial indictment that strips the natural order of any pretension to autonomy is his portrayal of God as creator and the world as creation.[11] God is not an abstract and distant being, but one who has entered into relationship with this world from its outset. Correspondingly, this world has always manifested the one true God. In 1:20 Paul asserts that God's "invisible attributes, namely, his eternal power and divine nature, have been clearly perceived, *ever since the creation of the world.*" Paul immediately adds that this knowledge of God comes "in the things that *have been made.*" This world is *created* and has continually served as a means through which human beings know their *creator*. Nature has no autonomous existence. The natural order is a theater for divine communication and response to it. Paul uses the language of "creature" and "creator" again in 1:25.

The creator-creation overtones introduced in 1:20 are perhaps strengthened in the following verses through imagery of Adam and Eden. Scholars have disputed whether and to what extent Paul refers to Adam and the opening chapters of Genesis in this text,[12] but the evidence for allusions to Genesis 1,

---

11. See similar comment by James D. G. Dunn in *The Theology of Paul the Apostle* (Grand Rapids: Eerdmans, 1998), p. 91.

12. Among those seeing rich Adamic imagery in Romans 1, see M. D. Hooker, "Adam in Romans 1," *NTS* 6 (1959-60): 297-306; M. D. Hooker, "A Further Note on Romans 1," *NTS* 13 (1966-67): 181-83; Robert A. J. Gagnon, *The Bible and Homosexual Practice: Texts and Hermeneutic* (Nashville: Abingdon, 2001), pp. 236, 289-94; Cranfield, *The Epistle to the Romans,* 1:125; Dunn, *Romans 1–8,* pp. 53, 60-61-62, 69, 72-73, 76; Dunn, *The Theology of Paul,* pp. 91-93; N. T. Wright, *The Letter to the Romans,* New Interpreter's Bible 10 (Nashville: Abingdon, 2002), p. 433; Schreiner, *Romans,* p. 81; Richard B. Hays, *The Moral Vision of the New Testament: Community, Cross, New Creation* (New York: HarperSanFrancisco, 1996), pp. 386, 404 n. 21; Jewett, *Romans,* p. 161; Bell, *No One Seeks for God,* pp. 48-49; Johnson, *Reading Romans,* p. 33; and Niels Hyldahl, "A Reminiscence of the Old Testament at Romans i.23," *NTS* 2 (1955-56): 285-88. Others are more restrained in seeing Adamic imagery here, including Stanley K. Stowers, *A Rereading of Romans: Justice, Jews, & Gentiles* (New Haven: Yale University Press, 1994), pp. 83-91; Seifrid, "Unrighteous by Faith," pp. 117-18; Martti Nissinen, *Homoeroticism in the Biblical*

and likely to Genesis 3 as well, is rather strong.[13] Whatever objections might be mustered against one or another of the proposed allusions, the overall effect is weighty. The corruption of present humanity reflects the transgression of its first parents. Contemporary rebellion against what it means to be human is ultimately rebellion against the God who made us human. The natural order in which humans live and act is the *created* order. Natural law concerns human beings in relation to God.

Another way Paul strips nature of any pretension to autonomy early in Romans 1:18-32 is through reference to *revelation* and *manifestation*. Though created things mediate knowledge about God and his law, this communication is ultimately God's own action.[14] It is interesting that Paul, when announcing the gospel in 1:16-17, says that the righteousness of God "is revealed," and then immediately, when turning to the bad news, says that the wrath of God also "is revealed" (1:18). The things that can be known about God, Paul goes on to say in 1:19, are "plain to them, because God has *shown* it to them." Since, Paul continues, what may be known about God is communicated through "the things that have been made" (1:20), this communication-via-nature is God's own communication.

Therefore, if by "natural theology" one means attaining the knowledge

---

World: A Historical Perspective (Minneapolis: Fortress, 1998), p. 107; Moo, *Romans,* pp. 109-10; and Fitzmyer, *Romans,* p. 274.

13. The corruption of *knowledge* described in Romans 1:21 hearkens back to the primordial temptation through the tree of the knowledge of good and evil (Gen. 2:17; 3:1-7). The description of sinful human beings — "claiming to be wise, they became fools" (Rom. 1:22) — recalls the desire of Eve to become "wise" by eating of the forbidden tree (Gen. 3:6). The ludicrous exchange of "the glory of the immortal God for images resembling mortal man and birds and animals and reptiles" (Rom. 1:23) presents humanity's sinful condition as a parody of the original situation, when human beings were the image of God and the overlord of birds, animals, and reptiles (Gen. 1:26-28, 30). The "lusts of their hearts" (Rom. 1:24) and "dishonorable passions" (1:26), though referring immediately to sexual immorality, perhaps reflect the initial disordered passions manifested by Eve when the serpent instigated her to see the tree as "good for food, and . . . a delight to the eyes" (Gen. 3:6). The use of "females" and "males" in Romans 1:26-27, rather than the more expected "women" and "men," may reflect the language of Genesis 1:27, which declares "man," the image of God, to be "male and female." The reference to shame in Romans 1:27 recollects the reaction of Adam and Eve to their nakedness in Genesis 3:7-10. Even the final statement of the chapter — "they know God's decree that those who practice such things deserve to die" (Rom. 1:32) — brings to mind the original Edenic threat of death (Gen. 2:17).

14. Among commentators noting Paul's emphasis upon divine activity in this communication of knowledge, see Moo, *Romans,* p. 104; Dunn, *Romans 1-8,* p. 54; and Jewett, *Romans,* p. 154.

of God as "the consummation of an upward ascent of the rational mind" or through "the observation of nature and/or unaided reason alone," then Paul is indeed not promoting natural theology here.[15] Nor, if my observations in the Introduction to this book are correct, is he speaking of the kind of knowledge of God allegedly garnered through Thomistic natural theology.[16] At the same time, Paul indicates that there is an empirical aspect to this natural revelation.[17] God does not communicate simply by placing ideas immediately in the human mind, but through the testimony of the "things that have been made" (Rom. 1:20). As Psalm 19:1 says, "the heavens declare the glory of God."[18] Human beings know God through apprehension of the external world, though Paul does not explain *how* in more detail. Thus, attempts to downplay the empirical character of this communication (because revelation is miraculous) or to downplay its revelatory character (because it is based upon empirical reflection) are both unconvincing.[19] Paul makes clear that "invisible" divine attributes (1:20) are made known to human beings through their confrontation with the visible creation, which is God's own manifestation of himself.

15. See, respectively, Talbert, *Romans,* p. 62; and Hultgren, *Romans,* p. 91.

16. As noted in the Introduction, Romans 1 makes problematic the Thomistic idea that a person only comes to know something about God from nature at the end of a process of metaphysical speculation. As Thomas Joseph White, O.P., writes of Thomas, "The primary being, for Aquinas, has an ontological priority with regard to all others, but *for us* this is discovered last." See *Wisdom in the Face of Modernity: A Study in Thomistic Natural Theology* (Ave Maria, FL: Sapientia Press of Ave Maria University, 2009), p. 160.

17. See the discussion, e.g., in Murray, *Romans,* pp. 37-41; and Ben Witherington III, *Paul's Letter to the Romans: A Social-Rhetorical Commentary* (Grand Rapids: Eerdmans, 2004), p. 67.

18. Many patristic writers appreciated this point; see e.g. the comments of Ambrosiaster and Chrysostom in *Romans,* Ancient Christian Commentary, pp. 37-39. Ambrosiaster writes, "although the power and majesty of God cannot by themselves be seen by the eyes of the creature, they may be known by the work of the structure of the world." John of Damascus states: "The very creation, by its harmony and ordering, proclaims the majesty of the divine nature"; see *Romans,* Ancient Christian Commentary, p. 40. Augustine writes: "They did not hear the prophets, nor did they receive the law of God, yet God spoke to them silently through the very operation of the world"; see *Romans: Interpreted by Early Christian Commentators,* ed. and trans. J. Patout Burns Jr. (Grand Rapids: Eerdmans, 2012), p. 28.

19. For an example of the former, see Bell, *No One Seeks for God,* pp. 40-41, who says it is nonempirical because as revelation it is mediated and miraculous. For an example of the latter, see Fitzmyer, *Romans,* p. 273, who says that Paul is not thinking of an act of revelation, but uses a word other than "reveal" (i.e., "shown"). For Fitzmyer, God reveals the gospel, but people can come to an awareness of him through reflection upon the material creation.

Paul's description of God as *creator* and his natural *revelation* indicates that interaction with nature is an encounter with the living God. In such encounter, fallen human beings possess genuine knowledge about God (Rom. 1:19, 21) and his righteous judgment (1:32). As sinners they "suppress the truth" (1:18), but the very act of suppression presupposes knowledge. One of Paul's chief points, that God's revelation has left all people "without excuse" (1:20; cf. 3:19), likewise makes sense only if they have acted disobediently with something they possessed.[20] To put this Pauline teaching in the broader biblical context explored in previous chapters: the created natural order continues to exist due to God's covenantal promises to Noah. All people by nature are in covenant with God, and thus the truth revealed in nature is *covenantal* knowledge. As creatures in covenant, human beings cannot be confronted with God in nature without the obligation to respond appropriately. Accordingly, the issue for Paul is not whether people have knowledge of God and his law but what they do with it: "although they knew God, they did not honor him as God or give thanks to him" (1:21). The idea that people might know God's law in nature without knowing that it is *God's* law fails to capture the burden of Paul's argument.[21]

The Content of the Natural Law (1): Idolatry

At this point we begin considering the moral substance of the natural law Paul discusses in Romans 1:18-32. This text is consistent with the conclusions tentatively offered in Chapter 2 and confirmed in Chapters 3-4, and further enriches these conclusions. In earlier chapters I argued that there is a minimalist ethic explicit in Genesis 9:1-7, which reflects the basic necessities for the preservation of human society. Such preservation is God's primary concern in his temporal governance of the world through the Noahic covenant. When God brought temporal judgments against particular peoples who were strangers to the covenants with Abraham and Israel, therefore, he condemned them primarily for egregious violations of these basic obligations. But the texts examined in previous chapters also hinted at a broader moral order that

20. As Augustine stated: "Paul does not call them ignorant of the truth but says that they held the truth in iniquity." See *Romans,* Ancient Christian Commentary, p. 39.

21. Contra Bell, *No One Seeks for God,* p. 101. Early in his work, Bell denies any distinction between knowledge of God and acknowledgment of God in this text and argues that no ongoing knowledge of God exists in the people described in Romans 1 precisely because they do not acknowledge him; see *No One Seeks for God,* pp. 49, 92-97.

undergirds these core obligations of the natural law. In Romans 1:18-32 we find a striking acknowledgment of the two core obligations that often come into focus in Genesis 19 and the prophetic oracles against the foreign nations: proper sexual morality and the administration of justice. But we also see here extensive acknowledgment of the broader natural moral order, which Paul opens up at length for readers' consideration. The first specific moral issue he deals with is idolatry, which he identifies as the root of other natural law violations perpetrated by sinful humanity.

Paul writes: "For although they knew God, they did not honor him as God or give thanks to him, but they became futile in their thinking, and their foolish hearts were darkened. Claiming to be wise, they became fools, and exchanged the glory of the immortal God for images resembling mortal man and birds and animals and creeping things" (Rom. 1:21-23). Here Paul identifies idolatry as rejection of the true knowledge of God they possessed through natural revelation. Idolatry is a symptom of hypocritical foolishness. He also portrays this idolatry as the root cause of other sins against the natural order he identifies later in Romans 1, for he begins the next verse: "*Therefore* God gave them up in the lusts of their hearts to impurity . . . , because they exchanged the truth about God for a lie and worshiped and served the creature rather than the Creator . . ." (1:24-25).

These verses broaden the biblical conception of natural law developed in previous chapters. The account of the Noahic covenant itself expresses no interest in prohibiting idolatry, and in the later biblical judgments against the foreign nations God does not condemn them for idolatry or other matters of religious ritual. As I suggested in Chapters 2-4, this reflects God's primary interest in his temporal government of the world under the natural law of the Noahic covenant, namely, the preservation of human society and the baseline conduct necessary to sustain it. But even these earlier biblical texts treated human beings as divine-image-bearers and addressed matters of the "fear of God" and its opposite, hubris, indicating that behind the bare ethic necessary for the maintenance of human society lie crucial issues concerning the divine-human relationship.

In Romans 1:21-23 Paul asserts what these OT texts did not: human beings know the folly of idolatry through natural revelation. In other words, the natural law prohibits idolatry.[22] When biblical texts (such as those studied in

---

22. As Mark A. Seifrid puts it, Paul "charges that idolatry entails the unjustified suppression of God's self-manifestation through the created order. His language makes it clear that he has in view a knowledge of God as creator which is full and sufficient for the creature

Chapters 2-4) concern God's temporal government of the world, they focus upon matters of natural law in terms of the minimalist ethic necessary for sustenance of human society. Here in Romans, conversely, where Paul's concern is exposing the sinfulness of all individuals and their inability to save themselves from divine judgment, Paul looks deeper into natural revelation to unveil the most fundamental problem with human response to the natural law. In fact, Paul suggests that other violations of the natural law, apparently including matters of sexual morality (1:24-25), are symptoms of the root sin of worshiping created things rather than the creator (though he presumably understands that not all idolaters fall into all the sins listed later in the chapter). Paul's teaching that the natural law sin of idolatry tends to lead to further natural law violations raises interesting questions in light of the fact that certain OT texts considered earlier, such as Genesis 20 and Daniel 2–6, suggest that some idolaters also exhibit the fear of God and thereby honor basic norms of justice. Paul does not explain how this works, but if we are to take all of these texts seriously, and not myopically focus on some to the exclusion of others, it seems necessary to conclude that the subjective response of sinners to God's natural revelation is complex and varied, and thus not to be portrayed simplistically.

The Content of the Natural Law (2): Homosexual Conduct as "Against Nature"

The second issue of moral substance Paul relates to the natural law concerns sex, namely, "the lusts of their hearts to impurity, to the dishonoring of their bodies among themselves" (Rom. 1:24). As Paul unpacks this matter in 1:26-27, it becomes evident that he has same-sex relationships particularly in mind.

Few issues have provoked more ecclesiastical controversy in previous decades, particularly in mainline Protestant denominations, than the issue of homosexuality. As often noted, Scripture only rarely speaks about homosexual conduct explicitly. But readers have traditionally taken what Scripture does say as unambiguous. Two statements in the Mosaic law (Lev. 18:22; 20:13) condemn male homosexual activity as an "abomination,"[23] two OT stories appear to condemn it implicitly (Genesis 19 and Judges 19), and here Romans 1:26-27 speaks

---

to worship him rightly." See "Natural Revelation and the Purpose of the Law in Romans," *Tyndale Bulletin* 49, no. 1 (1998): 119.

23. For a detailed discussion of the OT's teaching related to homosexual conduct, see Gagnon, *The Bible and Homosexual Practice*, chap. 1. On page 229 he summarizes: "The Old Testament is unanimous in its rejection of homosexual practice."

of gay and lesbian conduct as "contrary to nature." Though three other NT verses make apparent references to homosexual conduct as immoral (1 Cor. 6:9; 1 Tim. 1:10; Jude 7),[24] the relative paucity of biblical discussion has made the stakes high for debates about texts that do mention it. This has certainly been the case with Romans 1:26-27.

Beginning with John Boswell's much-discussed 1980 study, *Christianity, Social Tolerance, and Homosexuality,* a number of studies appeared in a relatively brief space of time arguing, in various and sometimes contrasting ways, that Romans 1 does not actually condemn all same-sex relationships as sinful. Boswell, for example, argued that Paul only condemned heterosexuals who pursue homosexual relations, while Robin Scroggs claimed that Paul only had pederastic relationships in mind and L. William Countryman reasoned that Paul saw homosexual conduct as impure rather than sinful.[25] Many recent studies, on the contrary, have agreed with the opinion of Douglas Moo — even if they do not put it so bluntly — that such works are "vain attempts to

---

24. For a recent scholarly argument that 1 Corinthians 6:9 and 1 Timothy 1:10 unequivocally condemn homosexual activity, see Gagnon, *The Bible and Homosexual Practice,* pp. 303-36. See also Hays, *The Moral Vision of the New Testament,* pp. 382-83.

25. See John Boswell, *Christianity, Social Tolerance, and Homosexuality: Gay People in Western Europe from the Beginning of the Christian Era to the Fourteenth Century,* 8th ed. (Chicago: University of Chicago Press, 2005); Robin Scroggs, *The New Testament and Homosexuality: Contextual Background for Contemporary Debate* (Philadelphia: Fortress, 1983), pp. 114-17; and L. William Countryman, *Dirt, Greed, and Sex: Sexual Ethics in the New Testament and Their Implications for Today* (Philadelphia: Fortress, 1988), chap. 6. Boswell has garnered support for certain conclusions; e.g., see Nissinen, *Homoeroticism in the Biblical World,* p. 109. One significant complaint about Boswell's thesis has been his anachronistic importation of contemporary categories of sexual orientation into the structure of Paul's thought; e.g., see Hays, *The Moral Vision of the New Testament,* pp. 388-89. Scholars have also refuted Boswell's contention that παρὰ in 1:26 does not mean "contrary to" or "against" but simply "beside" or "alongside of," thus indicating that Paul found homosexual acts to be extraordinary or peculiar; e.g., see Fitzmyer, *Romans,* p. 286. Critics have countered Scroggs's claims at several points. Brooten, for example, argues from the Leviticus background that lack of mutuality or consent had nothing to do with Paul's reasoning; see *Love Between Women,* pp. 257, 293-94. Mark D. Smith compiles evidence that there was great diversity in Greco-Roman homosexual activity, of which Paul was surely aware, and that Paul used irresponsibly vague language if he was indeed attempting to condemn only one form; see "Ancient Bisexuality and the Interpretation of Romans 1:26-27," *JAAR* 64 (Summer 1996): 223-56. Perhaps the most basic difficulty with Countryman's argument is its failure to reckon with Paul's own understanding of what he is doing in Romans 1:18–3:20: "we have already charged that all, both Jews and Greeks, are under the power of *sin*" (3:9). For detailed critique of Countryman, see, e.g., Gagnon, *The Bible and Homosexual Practice,* pp. 273-77.

avoid the obvious."[26] A number of writers, while arguing that Paul teaches the immorality of all homosexual activity, encourage the church either to reject what Paul says or to transcend his ethical conclusions in one way or another.[27] Other writers have explored the difficulties of analyzing contemporary debates in terms of Paul's discussion, since the idea of sexual orientation, so important to present debates, was unknown to Paul.[28] Many other scholars — and not simply from predictably conservative provenance — have embraced traditional readings of Romans 1 and argued for their continuing normativity.[29]

Thus, though there are various opinions about the application of Paul's ethical conclusions for the church today, a significant number of commentators agree that Paul condemns same-sex relations broadly in Romans 1. In my judgment the exegetical evidence does indeed support the idea that Paul considered all homosexual activity to be inherently immoral — in his own words, "contrary to nature." Without trying to discuss all the exegetical debates surrounding Romans 1:26-27, I now offer some reflections on Paul's natural law assessment of homosexual conduct and its place in the biblical theology of natural law developed in this book.

Perhaps the key questions here are why Paul associates the concepts of "nature" and the "natural" with questions about homosexual conduct and what he means by these terms. Many studies of Romans 1 have discussed possible sources for and influences upon Paul's language and reasoning. A number of options seem plausible, such as Greek philosophical (especially Stoic) sources, Hellenistic Judaism, and of course the Hebrew Scriptures (especially Levit-

26. Moo, *Romans*, p. 115 n. 118. Among other prominent commentators who believe that Paul condemns all homosexual conduct in Romans 1:26-27, see Dunn, *Romans 1-8*, p. 65; Wright, *Romans*, pp. 433-35; Johnson, *Reading Romans*, p. 34; Talbert, *Romans*, pp. 65-67, 74-77; and Jewett, *Romans*, pp. 173-81.

27. Perhaps most notably, see Brooten, *Love Between Women*, chapters 8-10, whose thorough exegesis of Romans 1 adopts an essentially traditional reading of Paul but urges the church to reject his prescriptions because they were based upon notions of female subordination. See also Dale B. Martin, "Heterosexism and the Interpretation of Romans 1:18-32," *Biblical Interpretation* 3 (October 1995): 332-55; Brian K. Blount, "Reading and Understanding the New Testament on Homosexuality," in *Homosexuality and Christian Community*, ed. Choon-Leong Seow (Louisville: Westminster John Knox, 1996), pp. 28-38; Smith, "Ancient Bisexuality," pp. 223-56; Karl A. Kuhn, "Natural and Unnatural Relations between Text and Context: A Canonical Reading of Romans 1:26-27," *Currents in Theology and Mission* 33 (August 2006): 313-29; and Margaret Davies, "New Testament Ethics and Ours: Homosexuality and Sexuality in Romans 1:26-27," *Biblical Interpretation* 3 (October 1995): 315-31.

28. E.g., see Hultgren, *Romans*, pp. 616-20.

29. See e.g. Hays, *The Moral Vision of the New Testament*, pp. 379-406; and Gagnon, *The Bible and Homosexual Practice*, pp. 229-339.

icus).[30] Given Paul's background and training — and the very language he utilizes — all of these may have played a role in shaping Paul's thought and terminology. But biblical teaching would presumably have preeminence for him. The broader argument in 1:18-32 points to one aspect of the Hebrew Bible as having special importance for his assessment of homosexual activity as against nature: the creation accounts of Genesis.[31] He speaks of "the creation," "the things that have been made" (1:20), "the creature," and "the creator" (1:25). He also refers to the orders of created animals and to the image of God (1:23) and, as noted, seems to allude several times to the stories in Genesis 1–3 (1:21-25). By 1:26 the ordered world of God's creation is in the foreground. For Genesis and for Paul himself, furthermore, the image of God is a thoroughly moral reality. Previous chapters have considered this with respect to Genesis 1–2 and 9, and Paul enlists the image to ground ethical exhortations in Ephesians 4:24 and Colossians 3:10.

In light of these things, for Paul to refer to "nature" and the "natural" in Romans 1:26-27 in terms of the creation described in Genesis 1–2 makes sense of his developing argument. For Paul, sin entails acting contrary to the created order. Like Genesis 1–3, Paul presents sin not simply as the violation of positive divine commands but as thinking and acting out of accord with what it means to be a human being situated in a divinely created world. Though the terminology of "nature" and the "natural" may well be of Greek rather than Hebrew origin, Paul was not thinking about nature independent of his biblical doctrine of creation.

Objections to this conclusion may arise from Paul's other use of such terminology. Later in Romans, for example, he speaks of "nature" with reference to the organic life of a tree (11:21, 24). But this is in an obviously different context. It is biologically descriptive without having moral connotations. More difficult is 1 Corinthians 11:14, where Paul does refer to "nature" to make a moral point — the perhaps puzzling point that "nature itself" teaches men not to wear long hair. Some claim that this is a reference to social convention rather than to the universal nature of reality, and at least one writer has argued that nature-

---

30. The secondary literature on this issue is extensive. For a detailed consideration of many possible sources, see e.g. Brooten, *Love Between Women,* chaps. 9-10.

31. Among the many writers who see a primarily Jewish background to this text, and in many cases a specific reference to the creation order, see Cranfield, *The Epistle to the Romans,* 1:126; Dunn, *Romans 1–8,* p. 64; Hays, *The Moral Vision of the New Testament,* p. 387; Moo, *Romans,* pp. 115-16; Fitzmyer, *Romans,* p. 276; Bell, *No One Seeks for God,* pp. 63-89; and Stephen Westerholm, *Perspectives Old and New on Paul: The "Lutheran" Paul and His Critics* (Grand Rapids: Eerdmans, 2004), pp. 409-11.

as-social-convention is also what Paul must have had in mind in Romans 1:26-27.[32] Whatever the correct interpretation of 1 Corinthians 11:14 — I briefly consider this text in a later chapter — an obscure verse in a quite different context contributes little to understanding Romans 1:26-27, where Paul's references to nature have a creation-order context.[33] Paul himself tells us what his main concern in 1:18–3:20 is: to charge "that all, both Jews and Greeks, are under sin" (3:9). He begins his brief not with the weak observation that certain people act contrary to social convention (which, with respect to homosexual activity in the Greco-Roman world, would not really have been true).[34] He begins by identifying activities that violate universally valid norms — universal because they corrupt what it means to be human and as such are "contrary to nature."

But why, many have asked, does Paul single out *this* issue among so many examples of immorality he would have observed in the surrounding culture? Some claim it is because Paul thought homosexual conduct to be more egregious than other sins,[35] while others propose different explanations.[36] I do not believe Paul provides a definite answer. But reading this text in light of the creation-order context of the preceding verses and in light of my conclusions about natural law drawn from the OT in previous chapters may be helpful for interpreting Romans 1:26-27 as part of the larger biblical canon. Though not a theme in the Pauline epistles, in Genesis 1 and 9 bearing the divine image entailed the obligation of the human race to be fruitful and multiply, in likeness to the abundantly fruitful God who created the world and then re-created it after the flood. From this perspective, homosexual conduct not only overturns the complementary male-female structure that defined the image of God and was foundational for the human social order (Gen. 1:27; 2:23-24) but also diverts sexual activity from its procreative context. As argued in Chapter 3, such conduct in Sodom becomes emblematic of a disordered society. Along these lines, Paul's understanding of nature and natural law in Romans 1:26-27

32. See Nissinen, *Homoeroticism in the Biblical World*, pp. 105-7.

33. On this point, see Fitzmyer, *Romans*, p. 287.

34. Or, as Hultgren puts it, the social convention view "seems too weak at this point, following upon the moral tone of 'degrading passions' in the previous clause." See *Romans*, p. 97.

35. E.g., see Gagnon, *The Bible and Homosexual Practice*, p. 268; and Murray, *Romans*, p. 47.

36. I mention two examples. Stowers, *A Rereading of Romans*, pp. 93-97, has pointed to the overlap of the Jewish concern for purity with the Gentile ethic of self-mastery. Brooten suggests that this reflects a traditional anti-Gentile Jewish polemic with special attention to the situation in Rome (where same-sex relations had greater visibility); see *Love Between Women*, pp. 261-62.

follows the trajectory of Genesis and thus of the biblical theology of natural law developed thus far in this book.[37]

The Content of Natural Law (3): The Broader Moral Law

Paul's natural law indictment of (Gentile) humanity continues in Romans 1:28-31, where he mentions a host of sins that further darken his portrayal of human corruption. In previous chapters I have repeatedly suggested that the natural law of the Noahic covenant must involve a broader moral order, and not merely the minimalist ethic explicit in Genesis 9:1-7. Romans 1:28-31 seems to affirm this suggestion most clearly. Whereas Romans 1:21-25 points beyond the minimalist ethic by identifying the fundamental root of its rejection (idolatry), 1:28-31 sweeps around various points of the moral compass and chronicles detailed consequences of the inhumane conduct that the Noahic covenant aims to curtail. In this subsection I reflect briefly on three matters arising in 1:28-31 relevant to my larger argument.

First, 1:28-31, read in conjunction with previous verses, may corroborate the popular Christian idea that the Decalogue is a useful summary of the moral content of the postlapsarian natural law,[38] a point I made in Chapter 1 with respect to natural law before the fall. This is not to say that Paul is explicitly alluding to the Decalogue, but simply that Christian theologians' inclination to see the Decalogue as encapsulating the substance of the natural law finds some justification here. Paul identifies people as "disobedient to parents" (1:30), describing violation of the fifth commandment (using traditional Reformed numeration of the Decalogue) and indicating a fundamental disrespect for legitimate authority structures in society (a subject to which Paul returns in Rom. 13:1-7). Paul

---

37. It is interesting to compare the way Paul seems to reason in Romans 1 with the reasoning of contemporary writers who defend same-sex marriage through natural law arguments. E.g., Jean Porter sees procreatively fruitful heterosexual unions as the paradigmatic form of marriage, but supports same-sex unions (and argues against the inherent immorality of homosexual conduct) by highlighting how such unions embody some, though not all, of the purposes served by heterosexual marriage. See "The Natural Law and Innovative Forms of Marriage: A Reconsideration," *JSCE* 30 (Fall/Winter 2010): 79-97. In contrast, in Romans 1 Paul focuses on the ways in which homosexual conduct deviates from the norm and thus manifests human rebellion against the natural order.

38. E.g., see Thomas Aquinas, *Summa Theologiae* 1a2ae 100.1; 100.3; Martin Luther, "How Christians Should Regard Moses," in *Luther's Works,* vol. 35, ed. E. Theodore Bachmann (Philadelphia: Fortress, 1960), pp. 172-73; and John Calvin, *Institutes of the Christian Religion,* 2.8.1.

addresses the sixth commandment with his reference to "murder" in 1:29, and perhaps also by mentioning "malice" and "maliciousness" in the same verse (cf. Matt. 5:21-22). He treats the ninth commandment explicitly with his charge of "deceit" in 1:29 and implicitly by writing of gossip, slander, and boasting in 1:29-30. Sinners violate the tenth commandment through the "covetousness" and "envy" described in 1:29. When combined with the violations of the first, second, and third commandments entailed in Paul's earlier description of corrupt worship, and with the violation of the seventh commandment entailed in his earlier condemnation of homosexual activity, these charges in 1:28-31 bring almost all ten of the commandments within the purview of the natural law.

Second, in Romans 1:28-31 Paul does not simply describe a random list of individual sins but portrays the general breakdown of healthy social relationships.[39] In previous chapters I observed that humanity's social nature is a prominent feature of the image of God in Genesis 1 and 9 and that God's temporal judgments on the basis of natural law consistently target extreme anti-social behavior. Thus, in this respect also, Paul's analysis in Romans 1:28-31 follows the biblical trajectory for natural law established in the OT. Skewing the image and acting against nature result not only in disordered individuals but also in disordered societies.

Third, Paul's statement that God has given them up to do "what ought not to be done" (1:28) has interesting natural law resonance. Scholars, with good evidence, typically take this phrase to be a technical expression in Stoic philosophy referring to actions that are against nature.[40] Yet it is intriguing that a similar phrase appears in Genesis 20:9 and 34:7, in contexts that demand a natural law interpretation, as argued in Chapter 3. The pagan king Abimelech accused Abraham of doing "things that ought not to be done" (Gen. 20:9) and Stoics, independently and many years later, apparently recognized that certain conduct "ought not to be done" (Rom. 1:28). Perhaps it is no surprise that Paul, in turn, might find the phrase useful when presenting an indictment based upon natural law.

The Content of Natural Law (4): Knowing the Judgment of God

By the time Paul reaches Romans 1:32 he has already provided a broad-ranging indictment of pagan humanity based upon the witness of natural revelation, but

---

39. On this point see Dunn, *Romans 1–8*, p. 76.
40. E.g., see Brooten, *Love Between Women*, p. 259; and Dunn, *Romans 1–8*, pp. 66-67.

his portrayal of the content of natural law is only complete with this final verse of the chapter: "Though they know God's decree that those who practice such things deserve to die, they not only do them but give approval to those who practice them." Many commentators find this statement puzzling, for reasons I consider momentarily. In fact, it makes good sense to interpret Paul again as reflecting the OT teaching about natural law explored in previous chapters.

Paul continues to speak in natural law mode in 1:32.[41] Beginning with 1:18 he has made many explicit and implicit appeals to the will of God known through nature, but he never calls upon the OT law or other explicit biblical precept in order to justify his indictment in 1:18-32. As Paul presents pagan humanity as knowing (γνόντες) God through the natural order in 1:21, so in 1:32 he describes them as knowing (ἐπιγνόντες) God's righteous judgment.[42] By nature human beings not only know God and the basic requirements of the moral life but also the penalty for disobeying those terms: death. This indicates an organic continuity with the prelapsarian natural law, whose sanctions as well as its requirements were naturally known by human beings made in God's image, as argued in Chapter 1.

Many interpreters of Romans 1:32 have been puzzled about why Paul speaks as if giving approval to those who act contrary to nature is just as bad as, if not worse than, committing the actions themselves.[43] The covenant of creation and the Noahic covenant provide helpful background. In these covenants, rendering right judgments was one of the fundamental natural law responsibilities for those bearing the image of God. In Genesis 1–2 God spoke and rendered just judgments about the goodness of creation. His image-bearers in turn were to speak and to make right judgments about the animals and about the intrusion of evil into the world. Genesis 9:6, furthermore, appeals to the image of God in commissioning human beings to execute judgment against wrongdoers. This is a central plank of the minimalist ethic explicit in the account of the Noahic covenant (Gen. 9:1-7). Judicial procedure was also a central concern in the stories in Genesis 19–20 considered

---

41. Among patristic commentators who recognized this, Ambrosiaster wrote: "Those who knew by the law of nature that God requires righteousness realized that these things were displeasing to God"; see *Romans,* Ancient Christian Commentary, p. 50. On this point also see Brooten, *Love Between Women,* p. 263.

42. On the need to interpret 1:32 in the light of previous statements about the natural knowledge of God, see e.g. Brooten, *Love Between Women,* p. 263; and Dunn, *Romans 1–8,* p. 69. Bell, *No One Seeks for God,* p. 61, expresses a contrasting opinion, arguing that what people know in 1:32 is simply the principle of retribution, and not its divine origin.

43. E.g., see Cranfield, *The Epistle to the Romans,* pp. 133-35; Schreiner, *Romans,* pp. 99-100; Moo, *Romans,* p. 122; and Jewett, *Romans,* p. 191.

in Chapter 3. The OT indicates, therefore, that human beings, as part of their natural obligation to exercise dominion in the world, must maintain justice by identifying and naming what is right and what is wrong, what is socially beneficial and what is socially destructive. Commentators misunderstand the climactic character of 1:32 by overlooking this. The term συνευδοκέω can have a strong forensic flavor;[44] thus giving "approval" to those who do wicked deeds may have special reference to perverting the judicial task. When sinners fail to make just judgments about conduct that destroys human society — declaring good what is evil — they violate a fundamental obligation of the natural law and do just the opposite of what God's likeness requires.

The Lex Talionis: The Natural Law Standard of Judgment

The final issue to consider in Romans 1:18-32 also connects Paul's understanding of natural law with the OT texts studied in previous chapters: God's judgment under the natural law is fitting and proportionate, reflecting the principle of the *lex talionis*. While Paul uses no explicit version of the talionic formula (such as "eye for an eye"), commentators often recognize themes of proportionality and fittingness in these verses and some actually adopt the *lex talionis* terminology to describe what is going on.[45] There is "measure for measure justice" and "correspondence between the sin and the retribution inflicted."[46] Three times Paul speaks of an "exchange" made by sinful human beings: of the glory of God for creaturely images (1:23), of the truth of God for a lie (1:25), and of natural relations for those contrary to nature (1:26). In each case God "gave them up" in response. He gave them up to impurity in their lusts (1:24), gave them up to dishonorable passions (1:26), and gave them up to a debased mind (1:28). These human acts of sin, therefore, provoke corresponding divine acts of judgment.[47] The last of these "gave them up"

---

44. Though this word is not used frequently in the NT, see, e.g., the courtroom or generally judicial context of its use in Luke 11:48; Acts 8:1; 22:20.

45. E.g., see Jewett, *Romans*, p. 167; Seifrid, "Natural Revelation," p. 119; and Bell, *No One Seeks for God*, p. 51.

46. See, respectively, Stowers, *A Rereading of Romans*, p. 100; and Murray, *Romans*, p. 48.

47. For scholarly comment on this threefold exchange/give over structure, see e.g. Gagnon, *The Bible and Homosexual Practice*, p. 251; and Dunn, *Romans 1–8*, p. 53. Hooker says that by saying the same thing three times in 1:24-28 Paul seems purposefully to have chosen language to make the punishment fit the crime; see "A Further Note on Romans 1," p. 182.

expressions is especially noteworthy. Paul turns to wordplay in 1:28 that many English translations do not capture.[48] As sinners did not see *fit* (ἐδοκίμασαν) to acknowledge God, he says, so God gave them over to an *unfit* (ἀδόκιμον) mind. This is the same poetic justice observed in Isaiah in Chapter 4: a sinful action elicits an ironically appropriate penalty in return. Something similar is present in 1:22-23, where God gives those who exchange his *glory* over to the *dishonoring* of their bodies.[49]

The end of 1:27 also highlights the proportionality of God's judgment. Paul states that men who commit shameful acts with men receive in themselves "the *due penalty* for their error." A more protracted translation of the italicized words (ἀντιμισθίαν ἣν ἔδει) might read: "the payback which was necessary." The ἀντι- prefix tends to convey a sense of reciprocity, and it is no coincidence that the Greek NT's way of stating the *lex talionis,* following the Septuagint (LXX), used ἀντι as a preposition: ὀφθαλμὸν ἀντὶ ὀφθαλμοῦ καὶ ὀδόντα ἀντὶ ὀδόντος (Matt. 5:38; in the LXX cf. Exod. 21:24; Lev. 24:20; Deut. 19:21). The only other Pauline use of ἀντιμισθίαν is 2 Corinthians 6:13, which speaks of a tit-for-tat kind of exchange. To say that a reciprocal action on God's part was *necessary* in Romans 1:27 is striking. Delivering a proportionate payback is what a just God must do.

Romans 1:18-31 describes God as dealing out this proportionate justice in the ordinary course of human history.[50] Yet Romans 1:32 most likely refers to the final judgment and thus to the penalty of *eschatological* death rather than to capital punishment which puts an end to life in this present world. Can *both* judgments — the intrahistorical payback and the final judgment — really be perfectly proportionate when they are punishments for the same sins yet are so different from each other?

Interpreting Romans 1 against its OT background, and specifically through the dual lens of the covenant of creation and the covenant with Noah, may provide an answer. The covenant of creation implicitly presented eschatological death as the fitting penalty for disobedience to God's original mandate. If Adam and Eve did not keep the commandment designed to bring eschatological *life,* God would hand them over to eschatological *death.* This was talionic justice in its ultimate sense, *coram Deo.* Yet the Noahic covenant

---

48. On this point see Wright, *Romans,* p. 434.

49. For more on this point, see Bell, *No One Seeks for God,* pp. 53-54.

50. For discussion of God's active role in what may otherwise seem to be a mechanistic decline from bad conduct to worse, see e.g. Gagnon, *The Bible and Homosexual Practice,* pp. 262-63; Cranfield, *The Epistle to the Romans,* 1:120-21; Schreiner, *Romans,* p. 93; Moo, *Romans,* p. 111; and Murray, *Romans,* p. 44.

revealed the principle of retributive justice mingled with forbearance. God simply could not impose ultimate talionic justice upon a sinful world if he intended to preserve human society for a time. The human justice that God commended in the Noahic covenant, therefore, expresses the talionic principle, yet operates on a penultimate level, focusing upon recompense for significant harm *to fellow humans*.[51] The eye-for-an-eye principle is operative, yet not on an ultimate level at which every sin is reckoned as wrongdoing *against God,* a rejection of eschatological life and thus deserving of eschatological death (cf. Rom. 3:23; 6:23).

Although Paul does not explicitly refer to the covenant of creation or Noahic covenant, his argument in Romans 1:18-32 seems to presume this foundational OT background. The wrath of God is revealed from heaven (1:18) and one day it will result in eschatological death (1:32; cf. 2:5-10, 16). Until then, God also deals with sinners according to the *lex talionis* on a penultimate level. Through the seemingly natural course of history God inflicts temporal penalties as a fitting response to the sins committed. Civil magistrates play a special mediating role in bringing these temporal penalties (see Rom. 13:1-7). They do not settle ultimate accounts, but they give a foretaste of the standard of judgment to be applied on the last day.

It is therefore illuminating to read Genesis 9 in conjunction with Romans 1. Human beings are to reflect the image of God by administering talionic justice tempered by forbearance (Gen. 9:6). Romans 1 describes how God himself administers talionic justice tempered by forbearance in this world. God gives people over to subsequent sins as a fitting and reciprocal response to their prior sins, yet this concerns only the present life. This justice is proportionate, but mixed with forbearance through the postponement of final judgment. The very act of giving sinners something less than their ultimate due, while just and proportionate on one level, is simultaneously an act of forbearance on another level.[52] Human justice, as administered by those who bear God's image, ought to reflect this divine justice (though human beings can never determine from God's providential governance of the world the perfect balance between talionic justice and forbearance, and this leaves much room for flexibility and prudence in concrete cases).

---

51. As noted in a previous chapter, I will discuss in Chapter 10 how the *lex talionis* can account for concerns of restorative justice as well as retributive justice.

52. In addition, though Paul does not explore the point here, God also shows forbearance in withholding even this penultimate retributive justice for so many sins.

Conclusion

Though the importance of Romans 1:18-32 for a Christian theology of natural law has long been recognized, reading it in light of the OT background established in Chapters 1-4 provides helpful insight for its interpretation. This background illumines aspects of the text commentators have found puzzling — such as the meaning of "nature," the attention to homosexual conduct, and the climactically wicked character of approving evil deeds. I conclude that Paul, in Romans 1:18-32, confirms my earlier conclusion that God sustains the natural law in the present, postlapsarian world, in organic continuity with the natural law of the original creation but as refracted in ways fit for its fallen condition. Paul also confirms, and enriches, earlier claims about the substance of this natural law and its standard of judgment. I will further summarize these conclusions at the end of the chapter, after examining Romans 2:14-15.

The Work of the Law Written on the Heart: Natural Law in Romans 2:14-15

Romans 2:14-15 has long been the biblical proof-text for natural law *par excellence*,[53] for understandable reasons: "For when Gentiles, who do not have the law, by nature do what the law requires, they are a law to themselves, even though they do not have the law. They show that the work of the law is written on their hearts, while their conscience also bears witness, and their conflicting thoughts accuse or even excuse them." If these verses do refer to natural law, they deserve close attention in developing a biblical theology of natural law, due to their explicit use of the term "law" and their references to the Mosaic law and the function of conscience. But there has always been an undercurrent of dissent from this common Christian view that Paul speaks about natural law here. According to some interpreters, the "Gentiles" referred to in 2:14 are *Christian* Gentiles who by nature did not have the (Mosaic) law but now have the law of God written on their heart by the redemptive work of the

---

53. For a few examples, see the appeals to Romans 2:14-15 in support of natural law in Aquinas, *Summa Theologiae*, 1a2ae 91.2; Martin Luther, "Lectures on Romans," in *Luther's Works*, vol. 25, ed. Hilton C. Oswald (St. Louis: Concordia, 1972), pp. 186-87; John Calvin, *Commentaries on the Epistle of Paul the Apostle to the Romans,* trans. John Owen (Grand Rapids: Baker, 2003), pp. 96-99; and Francis Turretin, *Institutes of Elenctic Theology,* vol. 2, trans. George Musgrave Giger, ed. James T. Dennison Jr. (Phillipsburg, NJ: Presbyterian and Reformed, 1994), p. 4.

Holy Spirit. Augustine took this view, and it has gained considerable traction in contemporary scholarship.[54] To put this in perspective: a biblical theology of natural law does not depend upon Romans 2:14-15. As I am arguing in this book, the reality of natural law permeates Scripture. If Paul speaks of Christian Gentiles rather than pagan Gentiles here, then he simply addresses a different issue from the one we are considering.

There are some challenging exegetical issues in these verses, especially when read in their larger context and considered in light of complex issues surrounding debates about the so-called new perspective on Paul.[55] I believe, however, that a natural law interpretation of Romans 2:14-15 remains the strongest option. Many competent scholars continue to take this view.[56] In this section, therefore, I first argue that Paul indeed refers to natural law in Romans

54. Augustine presented a Christian Gentile interpretation in *De Spiritu et Littera* 26.43–28.49; see also *Romans: Interpreted by Early Christian Commentators,* pp. 51-53. Among recent defenders of a Christian Gentile position, see Cranfield, *The Epistle to the Romans,* 1:155-63; S. J. Gathercole, "A Law unto Themselves: The Gentiles in Romans 2.14-15 Revisited," *JSNT* 85 (2002): 27-49; Stowers, *A Rereading of Romans,* pp. 109-17; and Wright, *Romans,* pp. 441-43.

55. A seminal work often considered the inspiration for the new perspective on Paul was E. P. Sanders, *Paul and Palestinian Judaism: A Comparison of Patterns of Religion* (Philadelphia: Fortress, 1977). Perhaps the two most prominent names associated with this movement are James Dunn and N. T. Wright. Among their important works on Paul, see Dunn, *The Theology of Paul;* and Wright, *Paul: In Fresh Perspective* (Minneapolis: Fortress, 2005). For critical evaluations of the new perspective on Paul with respect to issues such as law, justification, and Jew-Gentile relations, see Simon J. Gathercole, *Where Is Boasting? Early Jewish Soteriology and Paul's Response in Romans 1–5* (Grand Rapids: Eerdmans, 2002); Guy Prentiss Waters, *Justification and the New Perspective on Paul: A Review and Response* (Phillipsburg, NJ: Presbyterian and Reformed, 2004); A. Andrew Das, *Paul, the Law, and the Covenant* (Peabody, MA: Hendrickson, 2001); and Westerholm, *Perspectives Old and New on Paul.* While the new perspective has generated important discussions about Pauline thought and has helped to correct overgeneralized stereotypes of first-century Judaism, I agree with these latter scholars that traditional Protestant interpretations of Paul are still fundamentally sound. For a helpful statement from a critic of the new perspective about how the new perspective has positively advanced Pauline scholarship, see Westerholm, *Perspectives Old and New on Paul,* p. 445.

56. Among recent defenders of this view see Dunn, *Romans 1–8,* p. 98; Schreiner, *Romans,* p. 117; Moo, *Romans,* pp. 148-51; Bell, *No One Seeks for God,* pp. 152-53; John W. Martens, "Romans 2.14-16: A Stoic Reading," *NTS* 40 (1994): 55-67; Fitzmyer, *Romans,* pp. 309-10; William J. Dumbrell, *Romans: A New Covenant Commentary* (Eugene, OR: Wipf & Stock, 2005), p. 33; Talbert, *Romans,* pp. 83-86; Das, *Paul, the Law, and the Covenant,* pp. 180-82; Westerholm, *Perspectives Old and New on Paul,* p. 410; Murray, *Romans,* pp. 72-76; Herman Ridderbos, *Paul: An Outline of His Theology,* trans. John Richard de Witt (Grand Rapids: Eerdmans, 1975), p. 107; C. John Collins, "Echoes of Aristotle in Romans 2:14-15: Or, Maybe Abimelech Was Not So Bad After All," *Journal of Markets and Morality* 13 (Spring 2010): 123-73.

2:14-15. Here I present largely a contextual argument, not even utilizing certain internal evidence that further bolsters the case.[57] Then I identify several things Paul says about natural law in these verses that contribute to the broader biblical theology of natural law I am developing in this book. I conclude that Paul again confirms and elucidates several of my earlier conclusions about natural law drawn from the OT and also that he brings to light some aspects of natural law not previously considered, in particular its relation to the law of Moses and to conscience.

An Argument for a Natural Law Interpretation of Romans 2:14-15

As noted, the chief issue facing the natural law question in Romans 2:14-15 is whether "the Gentiles" are pagans or Christians and, therefore, whether the internal operations described in these verses should be associated with a universal natural law or with the Holy Spirit's sanctifying power in believers. Simply examining the statements in 2:14-15 does not produce a convincing answer. Paul rarely uses the bare term "Gentile" to refer to Christians (thus suggesting a natural law interpretation of 2:14-15), but there is at least one place even in Romans (9:30) where he seems to do just this.[58] Though Paul's reference to the work of the law written on the heart sounds similar to the blessing of the new covenant described in Jeremiah 31:33 (thus suggesting a Christian Gentile interpretation), it seems strange that Paul would describe a person whose sins God remembers no more (Jer. 31:34) as plagued by conflicting thoughts that accuse him.[59] But though it seems reasonable that Paul would describe a pagan's thoughts as accusing him (again commending a natural law interpretation), the idea that a pagan's conscience might also *excuse* him — especially in the light of Romans 1:18-32 — requires explanation. In short, Paul's description of the Gentiles in 2:14-15 provides plausible arguments for and against both positions.

Many writers have probed another question internal to 2:14-15 to resolve

---

57. For instance, the presence of possible allusions to Aristotle in these verses; e.g., see Collins, "Echoes of Aristotle in Romans 2:14-15."

58. See the contrasting claims in Martens, "Romans 2.14-16," p. 61; and Gathercole, "A Law unto Themselves," p. 31.

59. See Seifrid, "Natural Revelation," p. 122. Gathercole, "A Law unto Themselves," p. 41 n. 72 comments: "Reference (or not) to Jer. 31 on Paul's part in Rom. 2.15 is the key boundary-marker dividing those who see the Gentiles as Christian and those who do not." Gathercole argues that Paul does make this reference. I will explain below why I do not believe he does.

this issue: Does the short phrase "by nature" — a single word in Greek (φύσει) — refer to what comes before it or after it in the sentence? In other words, are these Gentiles who did not *have* the law by nature or who *do* the law by nature? Those favoring the former tend to support a Christian Gentile view and those who support the latter a pagan Gentile (and hence natural law) view. But this route of inquiry cannot resolve the question. For one thing, though scholars have mounted numerous arguments on both sides as to why one answer is to be preferred as a grammatical and literary matter, most admit that both options are possible grammatically.[60] Thus their respective arguments are largely a dispute about which option is more probable. Furthermore, even if one adopts the former interpretation, Paul could still be referring to Gentile pagans rather than Gentile Christians. Gentile pagans also do not have the law by nature, and Paul could perhaps be referring to some instinctual conduct of theirs that conforms to the demands of the (Mosaic) law.

In the end, the identity of "Gentiles" and "nature" must be determined from the relation of Romans 2:14-15 to its broader context. Specifically, what argument is Paul making in 2:1-13, and how does 2:14-15 advance that argument as it proceeds through 3:20 and beyond? Does the context suggest or even demand a natural law or a Christian-Gentile reading of 2:14-15? A key question that consumes much of the exegetical debate about Romans 2:1-13 is Paul's vivid description of the final judgment by works in 2:6-10, 13. Does Paul envision Christians as those who will receive glory (2:7, 10) and be justified (2:13) by works on the last day, or is his larger purpose to establish that *no one* can meet this standard at the final judgment?[61] Though interpreters' opinions about whether Paul is speaking literally about Christians' experience in the final judgment in 2:7, 10, or 13 do not perfectly correlate to their views of 2:14-15, those who believe he is speaking about Christians' experience tend to adopt a Gentile-Christian view and those who believe he is not tend to adopt a natural law view.

In what follows I argue that Paul is *not* describing the literal experience

---

60. Among those arguing that it makes more sense grammatically with what precedes, see Stowers, *A Rereading of Romans*, pp. 115-16; and Gathercole, "A Law unto Themselves," p. 37. Among those arguing that it makes more sense grammatically with what follows, see Dunn, *Romans 1–8*, p. 98; and Fitzmyer, *Romans*, p. 310.

61. Some early Christian writers thought that Paul was thinking of righteous Gentiles before Christ's coming; Chrysostom, e.g., points to Melchizedek, Job, the Ninevites, and Cornelius. See *Romans*, in Ancient Christian Commentary, p. 62. Given Paul's belief that God required perfect obedience to meet this judgment and that all people on their own merits stand condemned before God, as argued below, I believe this interpretation fails.

of Christians on the last day in 2:7, 10, and 13. Instead, throughout 2:1-16 Paul seeks to demonstrate that God is impartial in judging every person according to the works they have performed. He likely even has in mind perfect obedience as the standard for judgment. Paul's argument reminds readers how things operate under the law as originally imposed under the covenant of creation. In pressing this case, Paul has no interest in saying anything about Christians per se. Paul explains the Christian message of salvation later in his epistle, where he is at pains to show that Christians are not under the law and not justified by works, and hence how they escape the judgment described in Romans 2. Christians no longer exist under the reign of death and condemnation brought by the covenant of creation through the sin of Adam. Instead they are under grace and are justified by faith through the righteousness of Christ. Accordingly, Paul does not speak of Gentile Christians in 2:14-15 but of Gentiles considered apart from Christ. These verses elucidate how God can be impartial in judging Gentiles according to their works though they do not have the law of Moses. For Paul, the existence of natural law vindicates God's justice and answers an objection to his larger argument that arises in 2:12-13.

Romans 2:1-16 unfolds structurally in three main sections or paragraphs: verses 1-5, verses 6-11, and verses 12-16.[62] In considering 2:1-5 first, and then 2:1-16 as a whole, it is important to keep in mind the thematic unity — and perhaps even structural unity[63] — of these verses with what has preceded in 1:18-32. Paul begins Romans 2 with a strong causal connector, διò ("therefore"). He wishes to continue and advance the indictment that commenced in 1:18. That indictment, in Paul's own words, is that "all, both Jews and Greeks, are under the power of sin" (3:9).

Romans 2 begins with a sharp and pointed statement: "Therefore you have no excuse, O man, every one of you who judges. For in passing judgment on another you condemn yourself, because you, the judge, practice the very same things." How does this follow from what he has just said at the end of Romans 1? It seems unlikely that Paul draws an immediate conclusion from 1:32, which identifies people who not only do wicked things but give approval (judicial approbation) to others who do them. In 2:1, in contrast, Paul speaks of those who pass judgment on other people. The people he targets in 2:1, therefore, seem very different from those targeted in 1:18-32, in at least one important respect: while the latter give judicial approbation to those who do

---

62. For helpful comments about this structure, see Moo, *Romans*, p. 127.

63. Das argues that 1:18–2:11 forms a chiasm; see *Paul, the Law, and the Covenant*, pp. 172-75.

wicked things, the former condemn them. Initially, then, the people addressed in 2:1 appear to be righteous, since by condemning the wicked they act according to God's image as set forth in the covenant of creation and the covenant with Noah. The key twist in Paul's argument — a dramatic shift in focus that provides an initial clue as to how to read 2:1-16 as a whole — is that those targeted in Romans 2:1-16 are just as guilty and liable to divine judgment as the degenerate people described in 1:18-32. Paul makes this surprising claim because these people who judge others have "practiced" the very same wicked deeds as those they condemn. Though technically more righteous than the others because they condemn rather than condone the wicked, their externally correct judgments about others are sinfully hypocritical. They do not apply their keen judicial eyes to their own conduct. The wicked of 1:32 give approval to those who "practice" (πράσσουσι) evil deeds and the hypocrites of 2:1 "practice (πράσσεις) the very same things." In 2:2, Paul says explicitly what is implicit in his move from 1:32 to 2:1: "We know that the judgment of God rightly falls on those who do (πράσσοντας) such things." Judging other people (even correctly) will not spare a person from God's judgment if that person performs wicked deeds such as those described in 1:18-32.

These considerations suggest that Paul's "therefore," which begins 2:1, does not draw a direct conclusion from 1:32 but extracts and reformulates a principle running through 1:18-32 as a whole: the wrath and judgment of God comes against those who suppress the truth and perform wicked deeds.[64] The emphasis upon *doing* and *practicing* (through various uses of the root words ποι- and πρασσ-) begins in Romans 1 and continues prominently in Romans 2. Paul is developing a larger case that God judges on the basis not of external appearances but of the true quality of people's work. Most likely he indicts primarily Gentiles in 1:18-32 and then turns primarily to Jews in 2:1-16, though this is somewhat disputed. The precise identity of his target in 2:1-16 is not crucial for the exegetical and theological questions we are pursuing here. Paul explicitly addresses Jews beginning in 2:17, and many clues throughout 1:18–2:16 indicate that his charges should make all people, whatever their background, uneasy about their standing before God's judgment.[65]

---

64. Among commentators seeing "therefore" in 2:1 as drawing a conclusion but referring back beyond 1:32, see Bell, *No One Seeks for God*, pp. 137-38; Moo, *Romans*, p. 129; and Dunn, *Romans 1–8*, p. 79.

65. Most interpreters see a primarily Gentile target in 1:18-32 and a primarily Jewish target beginning in 2:1; e.g., see Moo, *Romans*, pp. 93, 96-97, 126; Talbert, *Romans*, p. 80; Schreiner, *Romans*, pp. 78-79; Dunn, *Romans 1–8*, p. 51; Gathercole, *Where Is Boasting?*, pp. 197-99; and Murray, *Romans*, pp. 54-56. Some see a Gentile audience in 2:1-11 (or at least primarily so); e.g.,

As noted, in Romans 2:1-2 Paul denounces those who condemn others because they perform the very same evil works as those they condemn, for God's judgment falls upon all who do such works. Paul proceeds in 2:3 to ask a rhetorical question that underscores his point: "Do you suppose, O man — you who judge those who do (πράσσοντας) such things and yet do (ποιῶν) them yourself — that you will escape the judgment of God?" He asks another rhetorical question in 2:4 that both reinforces this same point and implicitly responds to a potential objection: "Or do you presume on the riches of his kindness and forbearance and patience, not knowing that God's kindness is meant to lead you to repentance?" Implicitly, Paul responds to an objector who appeals to the past display of God's forbearance as evidence that God will never call them to account for their sin. It is intriguing that Paul does not mention God's forgiveness in 2:4, but only divine attributes that characterize God's posture toward the world under the covenant with Noah. Under this covenant God is kind, patient, and forbearing toward the world but does not offer forgiveness of sins. The Noahic covenant means the *delay* of final judgment, not its elimination.[66] Paul does not refer or allude to this covenant here, but his argument reflects this OT background. Those who experience God's kind forbearance here and now should not conclude that they will escape judgment but should see it as opportunity to mend their ways. Paul does not point readers to rest in Christ's forgiveness (as he does later in Romans) but instructs them to examine their own conduct.

With 2:5, Paul brings the initial paragraph of 2:1-16 to a close. His target group, instead of repenting, has a "hard and impenitent heart." For this reason, he says, "you are storing up wrath for yourself on the day of wrath when God's righteous judgment will be revealed." He continues by summarizing the theme initiated in 2:1-3: they commit wicked deeds and therefore will be condemned under God's judgment. He mentions "wrath" twice in 2:5. The wrath of God revealed out of heaven (1:18) will strike one (those condemned thus far in 2:1-

---

see Wright, *Romans*, p. 429; Stowers, *A Rereading of Romans*, pp. 101-5; and Johnson, *Reading Romans*, pp. 35-36. Other interpreters see a general audience in view in 2:1-11; e.g., see Das, *Paul, the Law, and the Covenant*, pp. 172-75; Bell, *No One Seeks for God*, pp. 137-38; and Seifrid, "Unrighteous by Faith," pp. 120-21.

66. If Paul is addressing Jews here I do not think it changes this observation. As I explain more in Chapter 7, the exile and fall of Jerusalem was a recapitulation of Adam's banishment from Eden and a foretaste of the final judgment. Israel under the Mosaic law was a microcosm disclosing the predicament of the whole world under the natural law. But as God now shows forbearance in delaying the final judgment, so God for many years showed forbearance in delaying the exile. But eventually accounts had to be settled for Israel's corporate rebellion.

5) as well as the other (those condemned in 1:18-32). In 2:5, furthermore, he specifically refers to the final judgment for the first time. His references to *the day* of wrath and the *revelation* (ἀποκαλύψεως) of God's righteous judgment are rich with eschatological overtones.

Romans 2:6 begins a new subsection that extends through 2:11. This paragraph has an overtly chiastic structure.[67] At the outer points of the chiasm Paul states his main point. To begin he asserts that God "will render to each one according to his works" (2:6) and to end he pithily claims that "God shows no partiality" (2:11). In between, Paul asserts twice that God will give good things to those who do good things (2:7, 10) and twice that God will give bad things to those who do bad things (2:8-9). Paul's point seems obvious in light of the indictment articulated in 2:1-5. In 2:1-5 he placed people under God's wrath and judgment because of their evil works and concluded with a reference to the final eschatological manifestation of divine wrath. Now in 2:6-11 he vividly describes that final judgment. It is completely impartial with respect to external appearances and is based upon a strict accounting of a person's works.

As suggested above, understanding whom Paul has in view when he describes this final judgment is crucial for interpreting 2:14-15. Identifying those who "do evil" (2:9), who are "self-seeking and do not obey the *truth,* but obey *unrighteousness*" (2:8), seems simple enough: the wicked people he has been describing in 1:18–2:5, who have "truth" and "unrighteousness" problems (see 1:18). The difficulty comes with interpreting the positive verdicts of 2:7, 10. Paul has said nothing to this point in his argument (beginning in 1:18) to prepare us for them. To this point everything has been negative. All the people Paul discusses are evildoers who can expect wrath and condemnation. So who are these people, hitherto unknown to the reader of this section of Romans?

One obvious candidate is *Christians,* and many commentators have chosen this route.[68] In many places Paul identifies Christians as those who will enjoy honor, immortality, glory, and peace in the age to come. This seemingly

---

67. Among those who discuss it, see e.g. Jewett, *Romans,* p. 194; and Moo, *Romans,* p. 136.

68. Among them (some of them also seeing Christians in view in 2:13, others not) are Wright, *Romans,* pp. 438-40; Kent L. Yinger, *Paul, Judaism, and Judgment According to Deeds* (Cambridge: Cambridge University Press, 1999), pp. 150-51, 165, 175-78; Fitzmyer, *Romans,* p. 297; Ridderbos, *Paul,* pp. 178-79; Richard B. Gaffin Jr., *By Faith, Not by Sight: Paul and the Order of Salvation* (Waynesboro, GA: Paternoster, 2006), pp. 96-99; Seifrid, "Unrighteous by Faith," pp. 124-25; Schreiner, *Romans,* pp. 114-15; Murray, *Romans,* pp. 62-64; Ernst Käsemann, *Commentary on Romans,* trans. and ed. Geoffrey W. Bromiley (Grand Rapids: Eerdmans, 1980), p. 57; and Talbert, *Romans,* pp. 82-83.

simple answer, however, runs up immediately against a formidable — and in my judgment insurmountable — objection. A reference to Christians in 2:7, 10 does not make sense in light of Paul's particular argument in 2:1-16, of his broader argument in 1:18–3:20, or of what he says about Christians later in Romans. The alternative option is that Paul does not have anyone in particular in mind in 2:7, 10, for the basic reason that he does not think anybody could possibly meet the standard of divine judgment he describes. This view also has many advocates, and has been a particularly popular view in traditional Protestant exegesis.[69] Many label this position the "hypothetical" view — hypothetical in the sense that people would earn these eschatological blessings *if* they render the requisite obedience, but in fact no one can. A more felicitous way to describe this view, in my judgment, is that in 2:5-11 Paul explains how things operate according to the law and its strict standard of justice.[70] I now present a brief case for this position.

An initial argument looks ahead to how *Paul himself* summarizes his argument in 1:18–3:8: "we have already charged that all, both Jews and Greeks, are under the power of sin" (3:9). When an author states his intentions it is wise to listen, yet commentators often overlook the significance of 3:9. If, in 1:18–3:8, Paul is driving toward the conclusion that *all* people are in bondage to sin, then there would be something awkward about asserting — so positively and confidently, and right in the middle of the argument — that some people actually do good works and by them earn eternal life. This awkwardness is exacerbated if we consider where Paul goes after summarizing his conclusion in 3:8: to a litany of OT verses showing that there is *no one* who is righteous, understands, or seeks for God (3:9-18). Then he speaks of *every mouth* being stopped and the *whole world* being accountable (ὑπόδικος) to God (3:19). This is forensic language, and Paul says clearly that every person without exception fails to meet the standard of God's judgment. For him to assert in 2:7, 10, then, that some people actually do meet the standard of God's judgment because of their righteous deeds would be to detract from his thesis and to provide evidence against it. The awkwardness of seeing Christians in view in 2:7, 10 is most apparent in how Paul climactically concludes the entire section stretching from 1:18–3:20: "For by works of the law no human being will be

69. E.g., see Moo, *Romans*, pp. 139-44, 147-48, 155-56; Bell, *No One Seeks for God*, pp. 142-44, 162, 253-54; and Waters, *Justification and the New Perspective*, pp. 176-77. With particular respect to 2:13, see also Westerholm, *Perspectives Old and New on Paul*, pp. 274, 411-12; and Cornelis P. Venema, *The Gospel of Free Acceptance in Christ* (Edinburgh: Banner of Truth, 2006), pp. 282-84.

70. This follows the suggestion in Moo, *Romans*, p. 142.

justified in his sight, since through the law comes knowledge of sin" (3:20). To be justified means to be pronounced righteous by a judicial act.[71] For Paul to assert in 2:6-7, 10 (and 2:13) that some people will be successfully judged on the basis of their works, as a link in his argument meant to demonstrate that no one will be justified by works, is awkward indeed.

Reflecting upon Paul's larger purpose in 1:18–3:20 is not the only thing that exposes problems with seeing Christians in view in 2:7, 10. Comparing what Paul unquestionably says about Christians later in Romans — specifically with respect to their works and justification — also presents serious difficulties with inserting them into the earlier argument. After Paul's repeated and emphatic conclusion that *all* people are guilty before God's judgment and that *no one* can be justified by their works — it would be difficult to know how Paul could have said this more clearly — he makes a dramatic transition in 3:21: "But now. . . ." Paul presents Christians as justified by grace and through faith, *in contrast to works (and the law)* (3:21-22, 27; 4:2-6, 13-16; 6:14-15; 9:30–10:6; 11:6). Their righteousness is not inherent, but imputed (4:6), and he goes on to explain that this imputed righteousness is the obedience of Jesus Christ (5:17-19).[72] Because of this justification by faith they have peace (5:1) and confidence in the face of God's wrath on the day of judgment (5:8). The things Paul sets forth as crucial for understanding how the Christian escapes unscathed through the judgment of God and enjoys peace with him are entirely absent in 2:5-11. With respect to the people who come through the judgment in 2:5-11 Paul says absolutely nothing about faith, grace, imputed righteousness, or the obedience of Christ. Paul's description of the people who survive the judgment in 2:7, 10 sounds entirely opposite to his description of Christians beginning in 3:21. As he comes to 3:20, Paul intends to leave every reader with the foreboding sense that they must find some way of escape from the judgment described in 2:5-11. The answer he

71. The biblical and theological definition of justification has of course been a point of contention in the broader Christian church. I believe the historic Protestant understanding is correct. I will not defend it here, although I will address the issue of justification, particularly with respect to the law, in Chapter 9. For a recent defense of the historic Reformed view of justification, see J. V. Fesko, *Justification: Understanding the Classic Reformed Doctrine* (Phillipsburg, NJ: Presbyterian and Reformed, 2008).

72. For my defense of the idea that Paul teaches justification by the imputed righteousness of Christ in Romans, see David VanDrunen, "To Obey Is Better Than Sacrifice: A Defense of the Active Obedience of Christ in the Light of Recent Criticism," in *By Faith Alone: Answering the Challenges to the Doctrine of Justification,* ed. Gary L. Johnson and Guy Prentiss Waters (Wheaton, IL: Crossway, 2006), pp. 127-46.

goes on to unpack is that the gospel of Jesus Christ provides this escape, such that they are "not under law but under grace" (6:14). Paul's larger point in Romans, therefore, as explored further in Chapter 9, is that all people are subject to the judgment of the law described in Romans 2:6-13, *unless* they escape it through justification by Christ.

These considerations present major obstacles to reading Romans 2:7, 10 as a description of Christians' experience at the final judgment. In contrast, it makes sense, in the context of Paul's developing argument, to conclude that 2:6-11 enunciates the basic principles of justice by which God judges the world, even though no sinner can successfully meet this standard. Again we must heed Paul's own clues about his intentions. Paul has constructed 2:6-11 in chiastic fashion, and he announces his main point in 2:6, 11: God will render to each according to his works (2:6) and shows no partiality in his judgment (2:11). The intervening verses, 2:7-10, are meant to illustrate this point. The whole dynamic underlying an impartial judgment according to works is that people who do good works are rewarded with good things and people who do bad works are punished with bad things. If God did not reward the good with good things, he would not be an impartial judge. This is why Paul speaks as he does in 2:7, 10.

Even many writers who think 2:7, 10 describes Christians recognize the attraction of the interpretation of 2:5-11 I have just presented. They understand the need to convince their readers that there is no tension between Christians being justified by works at the final judgment and Paul's later portrayal of Christians as justified by grace. Among popular attempts to make this case, I believe one has a certain plausibility and the other does not.

The implausible suggestion points to the preposition used to describe divine judgment in 2:6: God "will render to each one *according to* [κατὰ] his works."[73] The argument is that Paul points to works not as the strict basis upon which judgment is rendered but as something that bears rough correspondence to the judgment, which is rendered, strictly speaking, upon another basis (most plausibly the righteousness of Christ identified later in Romans). This argument is implausible because it creates a radical *distinction* between the judgments that God renders to two different groups when Paul's very point is to demonstrate the *evenhandedness* of God's judgment to every person without distinction. Surely Paul is not claiming in 2:6 that the wicked will be condemned because of some rough correspondence between their evil

---

73. E.g., see Yinger, *Paul, Judaism, and Judgment,* pp. 175-78; Gaffin, *By Faith, Not by Sight,* pp. 98-99; and Talbert, *Romans,* pp. 82-83.

works and the judgment they receive upon some other basis.[74] Paul has been saying as clearly as possible that God condemns people *because of* their wicked deeds. In 2:6 he borrows common OT language, and the OT precedents hardly suggest a "rough correspondence" interpretation: "Give to them according to their work and according to the evil of their deeds; give to them according to the work of their hands; render them their due reward" (Ps. 28:4). Paul's point in 2:5-11 is that God's judgment according to works is *the same* for every person. He is not saying that the righteous receive glory and honor because of a general *correspondence* of (some of) their works with God's righteous judgment while the wicked receive wrath, fury, tribulation, and distress as the *due reward* of their works.

Another attempt to defend the view that Christians are described in 2:7, 10 is more plausible. Though popular, it too ultimately fails. This argument reasons that Paul, on several other occasions, speaks of Christians being judged by works on the last day. Far from being a foreign element to Paul's thought, therefore, the idea that Christians will be judged by works, with a positive result, is a standard part of Pauline theology that must be accounted for. Paul evidently did not see Christians' judgment by works as inconsistent with his soteriology. Thus it is illegitimate to deny that Romans 2:7, 10 refers to Christians on the grounds of inconsistency with the rest of Romans.[75]

This argument is plausible because Paul does indeed refer to Christians being judged by works elsewhere in his epistles (see 1 Cor. 3:12-15; 2 Cor. 5:10). But this fact itself does not prove that Paul is talking about a judgment by works for Christians *in Romans 2:7, 10*. For one thing, Paul never speaks about such a judgment in a context in which he labors to demonstrate that *no one* can be justified by works and that Christians are justified by grace through faith *in contrast to justification by works*. Paul's arguments and purposes are different in 1 and 2 Corinthians from what they are in Romans. Another significant

---

74. A possible objection to this claim is that Paul, in Romans 5:12-19, portrays the whole human race as condemned in Adam, and thus it is plausible to say that people will be judged on the last day not on the basis of their own works but according to a rough correspondence of their works to their preexisting condemnation in Adam. While I believe that Paul does teach the condemnation of the whole human race in Adam, which means that people are not born into the world as blank slates with no standing before God, neither he nor any other biblical writer rests upon this idea to deny that God will hold all people accountable for their own actions. Paul's emphasis in Romans 2, in fact, is on the individual: God will render *to each one* according to *his* works (2:6).

75. Among those making such an argument are Yinger, *Paul, Judaism, and Judgment,* pp. 175-78; Schreiner, *Romans,* pp. 114-15; Gaffin, *By Faith, Not by Sight,* pp. 96-97; Ridderbos, *Paul,* pp. 178-79; Käsemann, *Romans,* p. 57; and Murray, *Romans,* pp. 62-64.

consideration is that when Paul speaks of Christians being judged by works in other epistles he never conflates their judgment with that of unbelievers.[76] The judgment by works in Romans 2:6-11, on the contrary, is the *same* for all people who undergo it, without distinction or partiality on God's part. In 1 Corinthians 3:12-15 and 2 Corinthians 5:10 Paul speaks of God judging *believers* on the last day and does not mention what will transpire with respect to unbelievers. In fact, in 1 Corinthians 3:12-15 Paul explicitly speaks of believers being saved and escaping through the fire of judgment even if (some of) their work is burned up. Paul never says anything of the sort about unbelievers, and it sounds quite dissimilar to the strict judgment by works — to glory or damnation — set forth in Romans 2:6-11. Furthermore, on both occasions when Paul relates a person's works to possession of the kingdom of God he speaks of works *disqualifying* a person from the kingdom rather than of works qualifying a person for it (see 1 Cor. 6:9-10; Gal. 5:19-21). In the broader context of both these passages Paul would not have wished the latter to be inferred from the former. In 1 Corinthians 6:11 the great alternative to being disqualified from the kingdom because of wicked works is being washed, sanctified, and justified "in the name of the Lord Jesus Christ and by the Spirit of our God" — nothing like what Paul describes in Romans 2:6-11. By the time Paul gets to Galatians 5:19-21 he has labored at length to contrast justification by works and law with justification by faith and grace. Earlier in Galatians 5 he has not only explained that coming under the law means that a person must render *perfect* obedience (5:3)[77] but also that those who advocate coming under the law should emasculate themselves (5:12). Christians earning the kingdom of God by their own good works according to the law is nowhere in the equation.

In short, the Pauline texts that clearly describe Christians being judged by works on the last day should not be conflated with the texts that describe a judgment by works on the last day for unbelievers. As 1 Corinthians 3:12-15 explains, Christians' judgment on the final day will not be according to the strict standard of works *portrayed in Romans 2:6-11 (and 2:13),* because their salvation is already assured on other grounds. To use another NT writer's words, Christians will not face "judgment without mercy" (what is described in Rom. 2:6-13) but will be "judged under the law of liberty" (James 2:12-13; cf. 2:10-11).

---

76. See Bell, *No One Seeks for God,* pp. 253-54.

77. For a detailed defense of the claim that Galatians 5:3 teaches that the law requires perfect obedience, see S. M. Baugh, "Galatians 5:1-6 and Personal Obligation: Reflections on Paul and the Law," in *The Law Is Not of Faith: Essays on Works and Grace in the Mosaic Covenant,* ed. Bryan D. Estelle, J. V. Fesko, and David VanDrunen (Phillipsburg, NJ: Presbyterian and Reformed, 2009), pp. 259-80.

To this point we have considered the first eleven verses of Romans 2:1-16. Romans 2:12-13 puts us on the threshold of our ultimate concern, 2:14-15, and interpretation of the former verses is crucial for understanding the purpose and meaning of the latter. I argue that Paul continues the theme of God's strict and impartial judgment by works he has been developing in previous verses and that his claims in 2:12-13 create a strong presumption in favor of a natural law interpretation of 2:14-15.

Romans 2:12-13 states: "For all who have sinned without the law will also perish without the law, and all who have sinned under the law will be judged by the law. For it is not the hearers of the law who are righteous before God, but the doers of the law who will be justified." The preceding chiastic paragraph, 2:6-11, has just demonstrated that God will render to each according to his works in an impartial manner, and 2:12-13 elaborates on this theme, applying its insight to a heretofore unaddressed issue: the Mosaic law. Romans 2:12 is Paul's first reference to "law" in this epistle, though he uses the term frequently hereafter. Many contemporary Pauline scholars assert that Paul almost invariably refers to *the law of Moses* when he mentions "the law." This is indeed usually the case and constitutes an essentially accurate general rule, though Paul in fact uses the term with a variety of nuances, and νόμος does not simply *mean* "Mosaic law."[78] Romans 2:14-15, in fact, is a good case in point, as considered below. In 2:12, however, there is little question that "law" refers generally to the law of Moses. Paul has just mentioned "the Jew first and also the Greek" (2:10) as part of his proof for God's impartial justice. Of all the things that distinguished Jew and Gentile, probably nothing would come to mind more prominently for Paul and his audience than the Mosaic law. Given that Jews understood divine justice so thoroughly in terms of the Mosaic law, the fact that they possessed and adhered to it, while the mass of Gentile humanity did not, raises obvious questions about how God can maintain his impartial justice toward all in light of this obvious disparity.

Paul therefore addresses this issue in Romans 2:12-13 by stating that Gentiles, who sin ἀνόμως (lawlessly, or apart from the law),[79] will be judged in a

---

78. See Westerholm, *Perspectives Old and New on Paul*, p. 261, and chap. 16; and Moo, *Romans*, pp. 149-51.

79. See Stowers, *A Rereading of Romans*, pp. 134-39, for an argument that ἀνόμως means "evil" or "wicked" rather than "apart from the law," as nearly all other interpreters take it. Though Stowers offers evidence that the word was commonly used this way in Jewish literature, it only makes a degree of sense in 2:12 if one follows Stowers's idiosyncratic interpretation of Romans, which includes the claim here that Paul saw Jews and Gentiles as equally under the Mosaic law.

corresponding and appropriate manner — that is, apart from the law. Jews, on the other hand, who sin by breaking the law, will be judged by that law. Paul's larger point is that God's impartiality is served by not judging people according to a legal standard they do not possess and under whose terms they are not living. As some commentators note, certain extant Jewish traditions held that God gave (or at least offered) the Mosaic law to all nations and thus that all nations were in some sense accountable to this publicly accessible standard.[80] Romans 2:12, however, indicates that Paul did not see things in this way. Gentiles did not live under the Mosaic law, which God gave to Israel through a special covenant relationship. Jews and Gentiles both will be judged impartially, but God will hold Jews accountable under the Mosaic law and Gentiles in some other way, thus far not yet identified.

The pithy statement Paul adds to this claim in 2:13 — "For it is not the hearers of the law who are righteous before God, but the doers of the law who will be justified" — is at once unexceptional and puzzling. It is unexceptional in that the emphasis upon *doing* (οἱ ποιηταὶ) has been a common theme in preceding verses, going back at least to 1:32. In this larger section of Romans Paul teaches that judgment is based upon a person's works, so for him to say that the doers of the law will be justified (that is, declared righteous) sounds very much like a repetition of previous claims. Though there are new issues raised implicitly in 2:13 that advance the broader argument (such as the folly of relying upon possession of the law — see 2:17-29), to say that the doers of the law will be justified seems to state the same theological principle asserted in 2:6, that God "will render to each one according to his works." There are indeed several reasons to believe that Paul is still explaining how things operate according to a strict standard of justice and does not have the actual experience of Christians on the last day in mind in 2:13.

First, I have noted how 2:12-13 logically develops Paul's argument from 2:6-11 and earlier. Paul has been reiterating a principle — that God judges impartially according to a person's works — and he offers no obvious clue that he has significantly changed the focus of his argument in 2:12-13. Second, the larger context of the book of Romans — which provides evidence against the claim that Paul has the actual experience of Christians in mind in 2:7, 10 — provides even more compelling evidence for the same conclusion with regard to 2:13. In 2:13 Paul explicitly speaks of *justification*. Paul subsequently teaches in Romans that *no one* is justified by works of the law (3:20). Anyone who is justified is justified as one "who does not work," as "the ungodly" (4:5),

---

80. E.g., see Stowers, *A Rereading of Romans,* p. 114.

by a free gift of grace through Jesus Christ that saves people from the wrath of God's strict judgment by works on the last day (see 5:6-11).

Third, the fact that 2:13 provides further explanation of 2:12 indicates that Paul intends the principle enunciated in 2:13 to prove only that the impartial strict justice of the last day will condemn all (not that it will actually ensure the justification of some). It is interesting that after Paul's even-handed description of God's impartial strict justice in 2:7-10 (i.e., good things will come to those who do good and evil things to those who do evil), in 2:12 he speaks only negatively. He does not describe those who act righteously with or without the law, but only those who *sin* with or without the law. The principle of 2:13 (the doers of the law will be justified) is meant to prove that *all sinners* will be judged and will *perish*. To reason in this way — that is, from strict impartial justice to the lost estate of all people — is precisely the way Paul wants his readers to think as he drives them toward the final conclusion of this section (3:19-20).

Finally, a couple of considerations suggest that when Paul speaks of the doers of the law being justified in 2:13 he is thinking of *perfect obedience*, which would rule out the idea that a future justification of sanctified but imperfect Christians is in view. One consideration suggesting this is the similarity of 2:13 to Leviticus 18:5, "You shall therefore keep my statutes and my rules; *if a person does them,* he shall live by them." For Paul to have this verse in mind would not be surprising, given the fact that Leviticus 18 (which condemns homosexual conduct) was on his mind in Romans 1 and that he quotes Leviticus 18:5 later in Romans (10:5). In Romans 10:5-6 Paul places the Leviticus 18:5 principle *in contrast to* the righteousness of faith that he has been at pains to explain. He does precisely the same thing when quoting Leviticus 18:5 in Galatians 3:10-12, where his point depends upon an implied premise in 3:10 that the law demands *entire* obedience, such that any transgression brings condemnation.[81] Comparison with Galatians 5:3 also suggests that Paul, in Romans 2:13, believes that perfect obedience is necessary for justification. In the context of Galatians 5:3 Paul again refers to those who are "under the law" (in contrast to those who are not under the law because they are justified through faith in Christ), and speaks of them in terms of doing (ποιῆσαι) the law. Those who present

81. For defense of the idea that Paul sees the law as demanding perfect obedience in Galatians 3:10, see e.g. Das, *Paul, the Law, and the Covenant,* pp. 145-70; A. Andrew Das, "Galatians 3:10: A 'Newer Perspective' on an Omitted Premise," in *Festschrift,* ed. Christopher Skinner et al. (Atlanta: Society of Biblical Literature, forthcoming); and Bryan D. Estelle, "The Covenant of Works in Moses and Paul," in *Covenant, Justification, and Pastoral Ministry: Essays by the Faculty of Westminster Seminary California,* ed. R. Scott Clark (Phillipsburg, NJ: Presbyterian and Reformed, 2007), pp. 124-33.

themselves to God as doers of the law, he explains, are obligated to complete performance of the entire law (ὀφειλέτης ἐστὶν ὅλον τὸν νόμον ποιῆσαι).[82] For Paul, those who stand before God's final judgment on the basis of doing the law must present a perfect dossier.[83]

Thus Paul in 2:13 continues to teach his ominous theme of strict impartial judgment by works without the actual future experience of Christians in view. But this is where 2:12-13 becomes puzzling. The claim that God will judge Jews by the Mosaic law (which they possess) and Gentiles not by the Mosaic law (which they do not possess) is precisely what we would expect in an argument for God's impartial justice (2:11). Likewise, the claim that God looks at *doing* the law, rather than merely possessing the law, is fully expected in light of the fact that God judges *according to works* (2:6). Even the idea that the doing which God requires is the same for both Jew and Gentile is a reasonable application of the impartiality thesis. Where Paul's argument may seem to get off track is his assertion in 2:13 that it is the doers *of the (Mosaic) law* who will be justified. Paul has just said that those who do not have the law will not be judged by the law (2:12), yet in the very next verse he indicates that the law is still what all people must perform. How can this be? How could Gentiles be held accountable for doing the Mosaic law when they do not possess it and are not judged by it? Has Paul not undercut the very point that he emphasizes in 2:12?

These questions finally take us to Romans 2:14-15. Upon finishing 2:13 Paul has left his readers with an obvious and serious question outstanding. If Paul speaks in 2:14-15 of the sanctified heart, mind, and conscience of Gentile Christians he speaks off point and does not address the question provoked by 2:13. If, instead, Paul speaks about pagan Gentiles and the operation of natural law in 2:14-15, then he speaks exactly on point and addresses the pending

---

82. See Baugh, "Galatians 5:1-6," pp. 259-80.

83. The standard of obedience that first-century Judaism and Paul believed the Mosaic law requires has been a disputed question in recent Pauline scholarship. Many have claimed that first-century Jews, including Paul, did not believe that the law requires perfect obedience, particularly in light of provisions for repentance and sacrifice that were built into the law itself. The evidence seems to suggest that first-century Judaism had mixed views on this topic. As noted above, Galatians 3:10 and 5:3 indicate that Paul, in an apparent attempt to correct overly lax views about the stringency of the law's requirements, perceived the law ultimately to demand perfect obedience. With respect to Romans 2, Bell defends the idea that perfect obedience is in view (albeit with some provision for repentance, though not cultic sacrifice); see *No One Seeks for God*, pp. 144-45, 239-51. Among those arguing specifically against seeing perfect obedience in 2:13 are Stowers, *A Rereading of Romans*, p. 140; Yinger, *Paul, Judaism, and Judgment*, pp. 166-69; and Jewett, *Romans*, p. 212.

question. The context, in other words, compels a natural law interpretation of 2:14-15.

Why does a natural law interpretation of 2:14-15 fit the context? In short, the reality of natural law explains how God can impartially judge Gentiles apart from the Mosaic law. God can *judge* Gentiles because, though they do not have the Mosaic law, they have some knowledge of the requirements of the law. They do the things of the law, they are a law to themselves, and the work of the law is written on their hearts. When Paul speaks of those "who do not have the law" and of "what the law requires" (or, "the things of the law" — τὰ τοῦ νόμου) he evidently speaks of "law" in terms of the Mosaic law (or a part thereof — I will address this interesting issue below). But when he speaks of "a law to themselves," he cannot be referring to the Mosaic law. Paul's use of "law" is not invariably uniform. Some other "law" exists that governs the Gentiles. This law somehow functions internally, through the testimony and judgments of the heart, conscience, and thoughts. This internal law is associated with a "doing" (ποίη) of the (Mosaic) law on the part of those who do not have God's law in written form. Depending on the resolution of the grammatical question mentioned above, Paul may even be saying that they do this internal law "by nature." In any case, Paul affirms that these Gentiles have an internal knowledge of (at least the moral core of) the Mosaic law and sometimes follow its requirements. Thus calling this law the "natural law," as so much of the Christian tradition has done, seems entirely appropriate. By speaking here of this natural law Paul is not introducing something brand new in Romans, for we have already considered at length how the reality of natural law, manifest through natural divine revelation, underlies much of Paul's argument in 1:18-32. But reintroducing this concept in 2:14-15 allows Paul to explain, generally, how God can judge the Gentiles and, specifically, how Jews and Gentiles can be judged according to the same basic standard of *doing* as substantively specified in the Mosaic law. This resolves the problem provoked by 2:13.

But why precisely would speaking of the sanctified conscience of Gentile Christians in 2:14-15 be out of place in context? Paul has been speaking about God's impartial strict judgment according to works, *apart from the reality of salvation in Christ, which liberates people from this judgment.* It is simply off point for Paul to appeal to the internal mechanisms of Gentile Christians to demonstrate that God is just in judging pagan Gentiles according to their doing of the Mosaic law which they do not possess. At this stage of Paul's argument, such an appeal would also be irrelevant. If my previous arguments concerning 2:1-13 are sound, then Paul is concerned to describe the situation of all people — Jew and Gentile — apart from Christ. They are under God's impartial strict judgment by works, they are sinners, and therefore they are unable to be justified by works and are subject to divine wrath. Appeal in 2:14-15 to a law universally known by human beings — i.e., the natural law — helps to explain this and thus advances Paul's argument. Reference to the sanctified consciences of Gentile Christians would not help to explain this and would distract from his argument.

This lengthy discussion has built a case for a natural law interpretation of 2:14-15 largely from contextual considerations. Two popular objections to this line of exegesis also depend upon the larger context of Romans. I now address these objections briefly.

The first contextual objection arises from 2:16, where Paul immediately follows up 2:14-15 with another reference to the final judgment. In and of itself this would raise no problems for a natural law interpretation of 2:14-15, but Paul says that this judgment takes place "according to my gospel" and "by Christ Jesus." If the final judgment takes place according to Paul's *gospel,* then how can a reader of 2:1-15 claim that Paul does not have Christians in view when he writes about the final judgment? This claim may have an initial attraction, especially for readers (such as myself) who embrace the legacy of the Protestant Reformation, with its clear distinction between law (what God requires) and gospel (what God graciously promises). Crucial as I believe this distinction is theologically, however, Scripture does not always use the terms "law" and "gospel" in the precise sense that we use them to construct our systematic theological categories. This does not make the theological categories incorrect, but it does mean that each biblical occurrence of a term cannot be assumed to match the technical theological definition. Part of Paul's larger "gospel" message — and that of the NT generally — is that there is a final judgment and that Christ presides over it. This is true whether or not Paul refers to the experience of Christians in 2:7, 10, 13-15.[84]

The second contextual objection is perhaps the weightiest argument against my conclusion that Paul speaks of the final judgment for those apart from Christ in 2:6-13. This objection points to Romans 2:25-29, which is within the larger section of Romans under consideration here (i.e., 1:18–3:20), yet allegedly refers to Christians, who are circumcised in heart by the Spirit. According to this objection, Paul speaks about Christians' experience in

---

84. Others adopt a narrower understanding of the "gospel" in 2:16 yet do not feel compelled to see the experience of Christians described in previous verses. E.g., Bell, *No One Seeks for God,* pp. 160-61, says that it is not strange for Paul to relate the gospel to judgment since the full knowledge of sin only comes through the gospel.

2:25-29, as part of his larger argument placing all people under sin, and this undermines my argument that reference to Christians' actual experience on the last day would be out of context in 2:7, 10, 13. Furthermore, this objection continues, Paul refers to Christians in 2:25-29 through language that parallels 2:14-15, which suggests that 2:14-15 itself must describe Christians rather than pagans.[85]

The constraints of space prohibit a full consideration of this issue, but I mention two things in response. First, as some exegetes have noted, the claim that Paul refers to Christians in 2:25-29 is not as clear-cut as sometimes suggested.[86] Everything in 2:25-29 indicates that Paul continues his micro argument (from 2:17) that merely possessing the law is no guarantee of God's favor, and also that he continues his macro argument (from 1:18) that all people apart from Christ are under the power of sin and therefore condemned under God's impartial justice based upon works. As he asserted in 2:12-13 that the doers of the law (rather than mere possessors of the law) will be justified, so here he explains that internal conformity to the law (not mere outward conformity) is what really matters. The idea of circumcision of the heart is not new to Christian proclamation, for the Mosaic law itself commanded its hearers to circumcise their hearts (see Deut. 10:16). Simply being circumcised outwardly is hardly sufficient conformity to the law. A full-orbed, internal obedience — loving God with all of one's heart, soul, mind, and strength — is what the law requires. It is therefore plausible, even likely, that in 2:29 Paul, by reminding them of circumcision of the heart, which the Mosaic law made the duty of the people themselves, is rounding off his argument from previous verses. The Mosaic law requires a holistic obedience, including internal purity, that none of his readers can honestly claim to exercise.

A possible difficulty with this exegesis is that Paul uses the phrase ἐν πνεύματι in 2:29 to refer to circumcision of the heart, in contrast to circumcision "by the letter." Paul uses the term πνεῦμα to refer both to the Holy Spirit and to a person's soul, so the phrase could either mean "in the spirit" or "by the (Holy) Spirit." The entire context of 1:18–3:20, and the particular purpose

85. Among those defending a Gentile Christian interpretation of 2:25-29, generally as evidence for seeing reference to Gentile Christians earlier in Romans 2 (though not necessarily in 2:13-15), see Schreiner, *Romans*, pp. 139-45; Seifrid, "Unrighteous by Faith," p. 125; Wright, *Romans*, pp. 448-49; Gaffin, *By Faith, Not by Sight*, p. 95; and Murray, *Romans*, pp. 85-86.

86. Among writers who have denied that Paul speaks of Gentile Christians in 2:25-29, or at least that he makes anything more than a passing allusion to them, see e.g. Moo, *Romans*, pp. 168-75; Bell, *No One Seeks for God*, pp. 193-200; Waters, *Justification and the New Perspective*, p. 177; and Venema, *The Gospel of Free Acceptance*, pp. 283-84.

of 2:25-29 to elucidate the true meaning of adherence to the Mosaic law, may suggest support for "in the spirit," in that Paul emphasizes that circumcision is ultimately about a person's internal state rather than his external ("by the letter") state. If Paul in fact is referring to the Holy Spirit (along the lines of his Spirit-letter contrast in Rom. 7:6 or 2 Cor. 3), then he evidently makes an allusion to Christians in 2:29. Even so, this hardly demands a re-exegesis of 2:6-13 in the face of all the evidence to the contrary.[87] Reminding his readers that circumcision of the heart transpires only by the Holy Spirit, while the Mosaic law required the people themselves to do it (Deut. 10:16), further serves to expose the folly of seeking justification by the law. Furthermore, brief allusion in 2:29 to what *radically distinguishes* Christians from non-Christians hardly requires that in 2:6-13 Paul must have placed Christians and non-Christians under the *same* impartial judgment by works. Finally, even if 2:29 alludes to Christians, the differences between the Christian's circumcision of the heart by the Spirit and the workings of the Gentile's heart and conscience in 2:14-15 are significant enough to suggest that Paul is not referring to the same thing in both passages. I will revisit this point below.

The Content of the Natural Law in Romans 2:14-15

If a natural law interpretation of Romans 2:14-15 is indeed appropriate, the question arises how these verses contribute to our understanding of the substantive content of the natural law. As considered earlier, Romans 1:32 corroborates the conclusion of earlier chapters that a basic task of the human race under the natural law is to render right judgment. Romans 2:14-15 further confirms this teaching through its portrayal of the judicial activity of thoughts and conscience. The reality of natural law prompts conscience to "bear witness" and thoughts to "accuse or even excuse."

The real contribution of Romans 2:14-15 to this issue, however, is how it identifies the content of natural law with the content of the Mosaic law. The relationship of the natural and Mosaic laws is the principal topic of Chapter 7, and the following comments anticipate and prepare for that later discussion. As argued above, in 2:12-13 Paul portrays Jews alone as being under the law but describes both Jews and Gentiles as liable to judgment based upon their (not) doing of the law. Paul's appeal to natural law in 2:14-15 explains how this is consistent with God's justice, and in doing so he implies that the natural law

---

87. On this point see especially Moo, *Romans*, pp. 174-75.

obligates Gentiles to pursue (approximately) the same moral life as binding upon the Jews under Moses.

Two related questions arise: Why add the term "approximately" when Paul's reasoning in 2:12-15 seems to require a strict identity between the Mosaic and natural laws, and is it not ridiculous to think that Paul (or anyone else who has read, for example, Leviticus) would identify the natural law with the Mosaic law? In response, I added "approximately" because I believe that Paul did not think that the natural and Mosaic laws have exactly equivalent content. Romans 2:14-15 virtually demands the conclusion that Paul did not consider all of the sacrificial and ritual elements of the Mosaic law to be universally known through natural revelation. Whether Paul is speaking about pagan or Christian Gentiles, the Gentiles in view in 2:14-15 were *not* keeping the various ritual elements of the Mosaic law. Pagan Gentiles were obviously not keeping them, and Paul, with the other NT writers, defended the right of Christian Gentiles not to be circumcised or to adhere to the Mosaic law. Yet in 2:14-15 Paul says that Gentiles at times do the requirements of the law and have thoughts that excuse their behavior. Paul evidently regarded Gentiles, insofar as they followed the matters of the law written on their hearts, as keepers of the Mosaic law in a general sense, even though they did not follow many of its particular precepts. By saying that these Gentiles do τὰ τοῦ νόμου (literally, "the things of the law") Paul seems to find a way to describe this general keeping of the law by those who did not know all of its individual commandments.[88] The reference to "the work of the law" written on the heart is also an unusual Pauline expression (whereas "the law" or "works of the law" is common), and perhaps this too is a way by which Paul hints that he is not referring to the substance of the Mosaic law exhaustively.

This leaves the question as to how Paul, given his commitment to establishing the absolute impartiality of divine justice, can speak of an approximate identity of the natural and Mosaic laws without cheating his argument. I develop a detailed answer in Chapter 7, but Romans 2:25-29 offers an initial indication of how Paul would have justified his reasoning. In 2:25-29 Paul claims (probably surprisingly to Jewish ears) that a physically uncircumcised person can be counted as "circumcised" and as "a Jew" if he actually keeps the law. On the face of things Paul's claim seems oxymoronic. Somebody who is not circumcised has by that very fact not kept the law. Paul's argument presumes

---

88. According to Gathercole, on the contrary, "the things of the law" does not suggest that only some of the precepts of the law are in view (though it does not refer to perfect obedience either); see "A Law unto Themselves," pp. 32-34.

that truly *doing the law* (even perfectly) is not equivalent to keeping *each and every Mosaic commandment*. Perfect obedience to the law in 2:13 evidently does not mean, for Gentiles, perfect obedience to *every individual precept* of the law (including circumcision). To capture Pauline thinking some distinction must be made between the essential and universally obligatory aspects of the law and the nonessential aspects that Gentiles can fail to perform and yet be reckoned righteous in God's impartial justice. Applying this insight to Romans 2:14-15 establishes the basic coherence of Paul's argument. If the natural law is substantively identical to the essential and universal aspects of the Mosaic law (and is thus "approximately" equivalent to the Mosaic law as a whole), then any Gentile who obeys the natural law is in fact just as much a "doer of the law" in Paul's mind as a Jew who obeys the Mosaic law.

What I have just claimed indicates that the old Christian idea that the permanent "moral" aspects of the Mosaic law need to be distinguished from nonpermanent aspects (the "ceremonial" and "judicial") grasps something important and finds some textual basis in Romans 2.[89] Furthermore, Romans 2 also confirms the common Christian idea that the moral aspects of the Mosaic law are substantively equivalent to the natural law.[90] We will return to these issues.

Natural Law and Conscience

The linking of conscience and natural law in Romans 2:15 has had significant influence upon Christian moral theology, but Paul does not provide a precise or technical discussion. His references to "heart," "conscience," and "thoughts" do not seem to demarcate distinct aspects of the internal human constitution, and his references to the work of the law, witness-bearing, and accusing/excusing do not seem to be entirely separate functions. Rather, Paul speaks in general ways about the internal moral operations of human beings as they exist in their fallen-but-preserved condition, apart from redemption in Christ.[91] Accordingly, I do not draw overly specific conclusions about the

89. See e.g. Aquinas, *Summa Theologiae*, 1a2ae 99.4; Calvin, *Institutes*, 4.20.14; and Turretin, *Institutes*, 2:145.

90. See e.g. Aquinas, *Summa Theologiae*, 1a2ae 100.1; 100.3; Martin Luther, "How Christians Should Regard Moses," in *Luther's Works*, vol. 35, ed. E. Theodore Bachmann (Philadelphia: Fortress, 1960), pp. 164, 168; Calvin, *Institutes*, 4.20.15-16; and Turretin, *Institutes*, 2:12.

91. In a number of other places Paul speaks about the conscience in ways that are unique to Christians, due to their experience of God's grace in Christ.

relationship between natural law and conscience. What Paul does say about these internal moral operations, however, has bearing on several aspects of a biblical theology of natural law. I mention three.

First, Romans 2:14-15 complements the teaching of Romans 1:18-32 with respect to how people know the natural law. Romans 1:18-32 teaches that people know God and the just verdict that sin deserves. This text does not explain in detail how people attain this knowledge, but the one indication it gives points to an *external* source. The invisible attributes of God "have been clearly perceived . . . in the things that have been made" (1:20). God has "shown" people the things that "can be known about" him (1:19) through the witness of the created order around them. Given these statements, it may be presumed (though perhaps not definitively asserted) that when Paul speaks of homosexual acts as "contrary to nature" a few verses later (1:26) he thinks of them as actions out of accord with the objective reality of what male and female are and what God intended their mutual relation to be.[92] Romans 2:14-15, on the other hand, focuses upon *internal* things. Here Paul speaks not of the objective structure of the world but the subjective apprehension of God's law and self-judgment about one's conformity to it.[93] Their hearts show the work of the law, their consciences bear witness, and their conflicting thoughts accuse and excuse.

In earlier chapters I presented OT evidence that human beings, as image-bearers of God situated in an ordered world, know their moral obligations by nature, but I also noted that these chapters do not provide a natural law epistemology. Romans 1:18–2:16 does not either, but gives a little more help in that direction. This text as a whole teaches that God has made the human person's internal faculties to correspond to the broader natural order. The created world offers testimony to God and his law, and the human heart and conscience perceive them, respond to them, and make moral judgments accordingly. The natural order objectively communicates moral knowledge, and human beings are equipped to understand it subjectively (though they sinfully distort it). This may be as much as we can safely conclude for now.

Second, the judicial overtones of Paul's description of the mind and heart in Romans 2:14-15 confirm earlier conclusions about the character and limitations of natural law. As I argued from Genesis, the prophetic oracles,

92. This is Gagnon's general understanding, though perhaps he presses the point too far in stressing visual observation of male-female bodily complementarity with respect to Romans 1:26-27; e.g., see *The Bible and Homosexual Practice*, pp. 254-58, 264.

93. See comments comparing Romans 1 and 2 along these lines in Murray, *Romans*, pp. 37-41.

and Romans 1:18-32, natural law — both as originally promulgated in creation and as refracted for the fallen world through the Noahic covenant — required image-bearing human beings to render righteous judicial decisions and created expectation for just sanctions (but not forgiveness) from God in response to obedience or disobedience. Romans 2:14-15 confirms both of these points. With respect to rendering righteous judgments, Paul says that the internal witnessing, accusing, and excusing demonstrate that the work of the law is written on the heart.[94] To be an image-bearing human being is to make judgments — for better or for worse — and here it is the presence of natural law that provokes such judgments. With respect to the expectation of just sanctions (but not forgiveness), Paul writes that people's conscience and thoughts render judgment upon their own conduct in anticipation of the final judgment (cf. 2:16) — accusing or acquitting. This is consistent with the teaching of 2:1-13 regarding God's strict, works-based justice.

This is a very important point, I believe, in light of recent debates about natural law in 2:14-15. Many writers believe that the similarity of 2:14-15 to various OT descriptions of the *redemptive* internalizing of God's law — most notably Jeremiah 31:33 ("I will put my law within them, and I will write it on their hearts") — is key proof that Paul is *not* talking about a universal natural law here.[95] Romans 2:14-16, however, speaks of an internalized law that renders verdicts about a person's conduct in anticipation of the final judgment. Jeremiah 31:33, in contrast, says nothing about an internalized law provoking self-judgment. In context, rather, Jeremiah teaches that God "will remember their sin no more" under the new covenant, such that "I will be their God, and they shall be my people" (31:33-34). Jeremiah 31:33, in other words, describes an internal embrace of God's law in response to salvation from God's merciless final judgment described in Romans 2:5-13, while Romans 2:14-15 describes an internal knowledge of God's law that evokes self-judgments and anticipates that merciless divine judgment yet to come. Romans 2:14-15 speaks of a universal natural law whose testimony God preserves for all fallen human beings. Jeremiah 31:34 and similar OT verses do not.

Third, Paul's description of the conscience and the internal moral operations of the human person further confirms earlier conclusions about natural law in a fallen world by hinting at a (limited) positive function of natural law. The function of natural law in Romans 1:18-32 is pervasively negative. It pro-

---

94. On the forensic nature of these acts, see e.g. Bell, *No One Seeks for God*, p. 149; and Murray, *Romans*, p. 52.

95. E.g., see Gathercole, "A Law unto Themselves," p. 41.

vides knowledge of God and his moral will, but sinful human beings suppress this knowledge (1:18), act contrary to nature (1:26), fail to acknowledge God (1:28), refuse to render right judgments about sin (1:32), and know that they deserve to die (1:32). The negative tone continues through Romans 2. The general context of 2:1-16 demands that natural law in 2:14-15 be viewed primarily as a means by which God justly condemns sinful people. But 2:14-15 does not have a wholly negative cast, for Paul says that these sinners' thoughts not only accuse them but also *excuse* them. If their thoughts both accuse and excuse they must be performing both good and evil deeds.

Reading Romans 2:14-15 in the light of the OT background established in earlier chapters provides an explanation for these "excusing" thoughts without downplaying the pervasive human depravity emphasized elsewhere in Romans (cf. 3:9-20; 6:20-21; 7:13-24; 8:7-8). According to Genesis 8:20–9:17 God preserves this present world for a time and upholds the social order. Image-bearing human beings, though corrupt and still liable to the final judgment, render partial, though nothing like complete, obedience to their natural obligations. Paul's principal point in Romans 1:18–3:20 is to put human corruption on display and to demonstrate the consequent inevitability of divine condemnation. Yet anybody looking at Paul's world could see that God's covenant with Noah was still in effect. Despite the corruption of sexual and judicial conduct (1:26-27, 32), most Roman adults continued to reproduce within the confines of marriage and the Roman law was one of the great cultural achievements of Western civilization. Paul himself understood this. It is hardly unreasonable to think that a pagan's conscience would have responded in different ways to his rendering a just verdict in court on the one hand and to his visiting a boy lover on the other. The moral life of most people is indeed a mixed bag, from a penultimate perspective, and within the boundaries of a fallen but preserved world Paul understandably portrayed pagans as having "conflicting thoughts" that both accuse and excuse — even while the excusing thoughts themselves could never give them ultimate confidence for the day of judgment.[96] These

---

96. Calvin put it as follows: "They prove that there is imprinted on their hearts a discrimination and judgment by which they distinguish between what is just and unjust, between what is honest and dishonest. He means not that it was so engraven on their will, that they sought and diligently pursued it, but that they were so mastered by the power of truth, that they could not disapprove of it. For why did they institute religious rites, except they were convinced that God ought to be worshipped? Why were they ashamed of adultery and theft, except that they deemed them evils? . . . Nor can we conclude from this passage that there is in men a full knowledge of the law, but that there are only some seeds of what is right implanted in their nature, evidenced by such acts as these — All the Gentiles alike instituted religious

considerations may shed further light on my earlier observation that Romans 1, read in conjunction with OT texts studied in previous chapters, suggests that the same person might be both a natural law-breaking idolater and a natural law-keeping God-fearer with a (very imperfect) respect for norms of justice.

In a fallen world, the natural law cannot provide a way of attaining eschatological life. Ultimately the moral judgments it provokes anticipate God's condemnatory verdict on the day of judgment. But as a penultimate matter it also provides a means for knowing and partially performing the requirements of God's moral will for as long as God preserves the present world. This penultimate function, prominent in the Noahic covenant (Gen. 8:20–9:17) and in the story of Abimelech (Genesis 20), is largely out of Paul's purview in Romans 1:18–2:16. He nevertheless seems to give a passing nod to its existence even as he prosecutes his case that one's ultimate standing before God's judgment is of much more pressing concern than the temporal affairs of this life.

Summary of Part 1

With this study of Romans 1:18–2:16 I conclude Part 1. These chapters have focused upon the character and role of natural law insofar as it governs the human race generally and universally, first in the original creation and then in the fallen world as preserved by God through the covenant with Noah. But these chapters have not considered the significance of natural law specifically for the moral life of those with whom God has entered into redemptive covenant and revealed his work of eschatological salvation: with Abraham and his household, with Israel at Sinai, and with the NT church. Before addressing this latter topic in Part 2 I offer the following summary of Chapters 1-5.

Fundamental to the larger argument in Part 1 is that a distinction must be made between natural law as it existed in the original creation and as it exists in the world as fallen, though there is also an organic continuity between them. God preserved the created natural order upon its fall into sin, but preserves it in a fallen condition. This affects both the moral substance and the purpose of the natural law.

In his work of creation, I argued in Chapter 1, God as the great king ordered the world in a display of his bounty and justice and then entered into a triumphant rest, having finished his work. As the climax of his creative labor

---

rites, they made laws to punish adultery, and theft, and murder, they commended good faith in bargains and contracts." See *Commentaries on Romans*, 97-98.

he made human beings in his own image and likeness, thereby commissioning them to exercise a just, benevolent, and fruitful dominion in the world and then to join him in his eschatological rest in a consummated creation. The image of God consisted of both essential attributes and a royal task, and thus by their very nature human beings were oriented to righteous conduct and a glorious destiny, meaning that they knew both the substance of the natural law and the consequences of their response to it. In likeness to God, who revealed himself to them in the covenant of creation by requiring perfect obedience to attain this destiny, their natural commission to just and benevolent dominion included the responsibility to make right judgments but not to show mercy toward evildoers.

With the fall into sin the human race disqualified itself from joining God's eschatological rest. God brought judgment upon the world, but it was not final judgment. God put the world, including the human race, under a curse, but also initiated a twofold work inchoately manifest already at the end of Genesis 3. Through common grace God would preserve the world and through a special saving grace God would bring the world one day to its original eschatological destiny. To use traditional Reformed terminology, (common) grace preserves nature and (saving) grace consummates nature. Since the great flood God has exercised his common grace through the covenant with Noah, and this work has been the focus of Chapters 2-5.

Through the Noahic covenant God preserves the natural cosmic order as well as the human social order, and even preserves human beings in his own image. In its fallen condition human nature retains its essential attributes (e.g., being body and soul, having rationality and volitionality), but in corrupted form, such that humans no longer use their natural gifts righteously. Due to this corruption, human beings by nature have no true expectation of attaining their original destiny. The Noahic covenant preserves humanity and the world around, but provides no eschatological hope. In this world, image-bearing human beings retain their basic commission bestowed in the covenant of creation, but in a form refracted for a fallen world through the Noahic covenant. Genesis 9:1-7 sketches a bare, minimalist ethic, indicating that fallen humanity's natural law obligations focus upon conduct necessary to maintain the existence of the human community, reflecting God's general preservative purposes in this covenant. Among these basic obligations is the responsibility to enforce retributive justice (Gen. 9:6). Yet to reflect the image of God as he revealed himself in the Noahic covenant, such justice must be tempered by forbearance (though not forgiveness). Genesis 9:1-7 and its larger context also indicate that a broader natural moral order undergirds the minimalist ethic.

The initial conclusions drawn in Chapter 2 about natural law in the fallen-but-preserved world suggested some significant conclusions relevant to historic Christian natural law theory as well as to Western political and legal thought. They suggested, for one thing, that natural law is indeed to serve as the basic standard for the development of civil law as it governs the human community. But it should do so not in ways meant to enforce natural law morality comprehensively but in ways best designed to promote human survival and even a measure of imperfect human flourishing in various social circumstances. In addition, these initial conclusions suggested that these human communities governed by God under the Noahic natural law ought to respect the religious liberty of all of its members.

Subsequent parts of Scripture examined in Chapters 3-5 — from the Abraham narratives, the OT prophets, and the Apostle Paul — confirm and enrich these initial conclusions about natural law in the fallen world as upheld through the Noahic covenant. The OT texts describe local judgments God brings against certain peoples, in anticipation of the talionic justice of the final judgment, and these judgments show both God's special interest in upholding the minimalist natural law ethic in his temporal government of the world and also the reality of a broader natural moral order underlying this minimalist ethic. These texts also describe the benevolent effects of God's common grace in the relative flourishing of other human societies, through a genuine (though very imperfect) recognition of the basic natural law ethic. Romans 1:18–2:16 confirms both the significance of the minimalist natural law ethic and its broader moral order, pointing notably to idolatry as a root sin from which other violations against the natural order tend to spring. This text also clarifies that natural law is objectively manifest through creation itself as God's natural revelation and that it is subjectively apprehended (though constantly distorted) through the internal workings — heart, thought, and conscience — of the human person.

These texts considered in Chapters 1-5 provide significant material for developing a biblical theology of natural law. They provide repeated evidence that Christians should consider natural law a moral standard given and enforced by God, not an autonomous moral standard. They indicate that God reveals the natural law through a covenant relationship with the entire human race, by which he makes known humanity's continuing moral obligations before him and the consequences of their response. Part 1, therefore, has offered a rich *theological* account of natural law, but without making natural law a *distinctively Christian* ethic, for the natural law ethic obligates all human beings and is grounded in God's work of preservation, not his work of redemption.

But as the place of Romans 1:18–2:16 in the larger context of Romans attests, understanding the natural law is foundational for understanding the Christian gospel and its moral call.

In Part 2 we consider God's work of redemption and what the significance of natural law is for the beneficiaries of this great work.

PART 2

CHAPTER 6

Natural Law for Sojourners: The Abrahamic Covenant

Chapters 1-5 considered the meaning and significance of natural law for all human beings in the original state of creation and under God's providential government of the world in its fallen condition. God entered the covenant of creation with Adam, the representative of the human race, placing moral obligations upon him in accord with his nature as an image-bearer of God living in the midst of a broader created order, and holding out for him the prospect of life in an eschatological new creation should he prove obedient to his commission. One of God's two great works in response to Adam's fall was the preservation of the natural order for a time, in a fallen state. After the great flood God entered a covenant with Noah and all living creatures, and through this covenant God now regulates the affairs of the present world for as long as it endures, in accord with its nature as he preserves it.

Chapters 6-9 consider the second, and greater, work of God following Adam's fall: the accomplishment of redemption from sin and evil, ultimately through the coming of the Lord Jesus Christ and the consummation of the present world in the new heaven and new earth, the original goal of the human race. In the terminology I previously borrowed (with important modifications) from Thomism and neo-Calvinism, *(common) grace preserves nature, (saving) grace consummates nature.* In accord with much of historic Christian theology, I view the accomplishment of redemption as a unified work of God through the whole of history, from the *protevangelium* of Genesis 3:15 to Christ's second coming, but accomplished through a progressively unfolding series of saving acts.[1] I also continue to make special use of the traditional Reformed

---

1. I think, for example, of the incipient biblical theologies in the fourth book of Irenaeus's *Against Heresies* or the second part of Augustine's *The City of God.*

emphasis on the divine covenants. Reformed theology has ordinarily seen a single, unified "covenant of grace" throughout biblical history by which God accomplishes salvation and gathers a redeemed people for himself. Reformed theology has also taught that God has called and governed his covenant people through a series of distinct "administrations," particularly with Abraham and his household, with Israel at Sinai, and with the New Testament (NT) church.[2] As I explain in the Introduction, I agree that these are properly understood as a unified covenant of grace with distinct administrations, though for the sake of clarity I refer to them here as the "covenants of grace."[3]

The next four chapters address the significance of natural law for these three covenants. Though touching upon many familiar themes that contribute to the broader biblical theology of natural law developed in preceding chapters, I focus especially upon the distinct roles that natural law plays in these covenants of grace and the distinct ways in which natural law is meant to shape the moral and social lives of God's people in them. Under each of the covenants of grace God has called his people to live in this present world, governed by the Noahic covenant, and thus natural law has always played a crucial role in determining their moral obligations. Yet the covenants of grace, as progressively revealed through history, are ultimately concerned with liberating God's people from this present cursed world and granting them citizenship and eschatological life in the heavenly kingdom of the age-to-come. God's redemptive work in the covenants of grace brings a *new creation*, through which the order of nature and the natural law as we now know it pass away in their present form and are brought to consummation. Old Testament (OT) believers looked forward to the blessings of the new creation, but did not enjoy a foretaste of them in as profound a way as NT Christians do today.

This chapter focuses upon the Abrahamic covenant. In this covenant God made promises of salvation to Abraham and his household that pointed to a special land, a coming Messianic seed, and the blessing of redemption for all peoples. Though God distinguished Abraham's household from the rest of the world through his gracious election, he called them to continue living in and interacting with the pagan societies all around, as sojourners in lands not

---

2. I do not mean to disregard the importance of the covenant with David. It falls within the larger story of God's dealings with Israel under the Mosaic covenant, however, and I do not believe it makes a significant new contribution to a biblical theology of natural law per se.

3. Thus, as also noted in the Introduction, my use of "covenants of grace" terminology does not reflect any disagreement with the closing sentence of the *Westminster Confession of Faith*, 7.6: "There are not therefore two covenants of grace, differing in substance, but one and the same, under various dispensations."

truly their own (Gen. 12:10; 15:13; 20:1; 21:34; 23:4). As such, Abraham and his household needed to understand the natural law on multiple levels. A knowledge of natural law was necessary for them to understand the common life they shared with their pagan neighbors under the Noahic covenant, and also to comprehend God's just judgment of this world, a judgment in which God called Abraham, his covenant partner, to participate. In light of Christians' identity as *sojourners* (1 Pet. 2:11) — that is, active residents of this world who are ultimately citizens of heaven (Phil. 3:20), who have no lasting city here but await the city to come (Heb. 13:14) — these Abraham narratives provide some initial grist for reflection on the significance of natural law for contemporary Christians' moral life, in anticipation of the detailed consideration of that topic in Chapter 9.

In this relatively brief chapter I first provide an overview of the classic Reformed view of the covenants of grace in their historical development and describe some distinctive aspects of the Abrahamic covenant. Second, I focus on the conversation between God and Abraham in Genesis 18:16-33 and observe God's desire to instruct Abraham, as his covenant partner, in his ways of governing and judging the world through the natural law. Finally, I reflect again on some of the texts considered in Chapter 3 and explore the implications of God's government of the world, through natural law and the Noahic covenant, for the moral life God called Abraham to pursue as sojourner in this world.

The Covenants of Grace

These next four chapters utilize traditional Reformed teaching about the covenants of grace as an organizing structure to explain the organically unified progress of redemptive history throughout Scripture. Since this covenant theology will be unfamiliar to many readers, I now explain it in a little detail and discuss some of its basic biblical foundation.

The Westminster Confession of Faith (WCF), product of the Westminster Assembly in the 1640s, represents a consensus expression of the tenets of Reformed Christianity during the mature flourishing of Reformed orthodox theology, and has subsequently served as a secondary standard for Presbyterian churches worldwide. Chapter 7 of the WCF treats the biblical doctrine of the covenants. After describing the covenant of works at creation in 7.2, which I discussed in Chapter 1, WCF 7.3 states: "Man, by his fall, having made himself uncapable of life by that covenant, the Lord was pleased to make a second, commonly called the covenant of grace; wherein he freely offereth unto sinners life and salvation by Jesus Christ; requiring of them faith in him, that they may be saved, and promising to give unto all those that are ordained unto eternal life his Holy Spirit, to make them willing, and able to believe." This affirms the basic unity in God's covenantal dealings with his people through history. Faith in Jesus Christ has been the one way of life and salvation for all people at all times.

WCF 7.5-6 then explains that this covenant, though in essence one through all of history, is administered in distinct ways during different periods. WCF 7.5 begins: "This covenant was differently administered in the time of the law, and in the time of the gospel," and WCF 7.6 concludes: "There are not therefore two covenants of grace, differing in substance, but one and the same, under various dispensations." "Christ, the substance" (WCF 7.6), has been savior of believers at all times. Under the law, however, God administered the covenant through "promises, prophecies, sacrifices, circumcision, the paschal lamb, and other types and ordinances delivered to the people of the Jews, all foresignifying Christ to come" (WCF 7.5). Under the gospel, with the coming of Christ, the covenant is administered through the preaching of Scripture, baptism, and the Lord's Supper. These are simpler and less outwardly glorious than the ordinances of Moses, yet hold forth the covenant "in more fullness, evidence, and spiritual efficacy, to all nations, both Jews and Gentiles" (WCF 7.6).

Though the WCF, with concision fitting a confessional document, speaks specifically only of the Mosaic covenant ("the law") and the new covenant ("the gospel"), Reformed theologians have believed that the origins of this covenant of grace pre-dated Moses. They point especially to the *protevangelium* of Genesis 3:15 and the covenant with Abraham (Genesis 15 and 17).[4]

Reformed theologians have seen evidence of this covenant theology throughout the Scriptures, but have often referred to Galatians 3 as a clear and concise presentation of a unified covenant of grace administered differently in various eras of redemptive history. In 3:1-9 Paul declares that Abraham heard the gospel proclaimed in God's promises to him and was justified through faith in God. Those who believe today are children of Abraham and share in his blessings. Christians' covenant relationship with God today is substantially one with Abraham's. The same gospel, the same blessings, and the same response of faith animate both.

---

4. For treatment of this early OT development of the covenant of grace, in an important Reformed work on covenant theology, see Herman Witsius, *The Economy of the Covenants between God and Man: Comprehending a Complete Body of Divinity,* 2 vols., trans. William Crookshank (1822; reprint, Phillipsburg, NJ: Presbyterian and Reformed, 1990), 2:108-62.

Paul recognized, however, that this affirmation raises acute questions about the law of Moses and how it governed God's people. The law required perfect obedience, and thus placed all people, as sinners, under a curse (Gal. 3:10; quoting Deut. 27:26). By promising life through obedience to its precepts, the law stands in contrast to the message of faith, which promises life and justification to those who believe (Gal. 3:11-12; quoting Hab. 2:4 and Lev. 18:5). Christ has redeemed his people from the curse of the law and thus brought to fulfillment the blessings of Abraham that come by faith (Gal. 3:13-14). Yet the long reign of the law may cast doubt on the consistency and coherence of God's purposes in history, and thus Paul unpacks the larger divine plan.

Paul's first point is negative: the law did not annul the promises made 430 years earlier to Abraham, such that the inheritance would come by obedience to the law rather than by promises received through faith. Even in human affairs, a covenant cannot be annulled once it is ratified. God made covenant promises to Abraham and his offspring (ultimately Christ himself), and the coming of the law could not change their terms (3:15-18). Thus, God did not give the Mosaic law as an alternative to attaining salvation by faith, as if his great purposes of redemption had changed. "Why then the law? It was added because of transgressions, until the offspring should come to whom the promise had been made" (3:19). Hence Paul vigorously denies that the law was a competitor to God's promises, for the law, which brought everyone under condemnation (3:10), could not bring life and righteousness (3:21). "But the Scripture imprisoned everything under sin, so that the promise by faith in Jesus Christ might be given to those who believe" (3:22). The law held people captive and imprisoned them, serving as "our guardian until Christ came, in order that we might be justified by faith" (3:23-24). Upon Christ's coming, God's people are no longer under a guardian but, united to Christ by faith, are Abraham's offspring and heirs of the promise, whether they are Jew or Gentile (3:25-29).

In summary, the same promises, blessings, faith, and Christ have been in view at all times for God's people, and the way of life and salvation has always been by faith rather than by obedience to the law. The law was "added" for a time, however, for pedagogical purposes that made sin manifest and directed Abraham's descendants to the coming Messiah.[5] Thus the Reformed

---

5. Not only the Reformed have appreciated these basic points. Among patristic theologians, Ambrosiaster, for example, wrote concerning Galatians 3:17: "Once the promise had been established, the law was given subsequently, not so that it could undermine the promise but so that it might point to what was to be fulfilled and when it would come." On Galatians 3:19 Augustine commented: "Here arises a rather pertinent question: if faith justifies and even

have affirmed that these covenants of grace are one in substance but have been administered in different ways. The promises were given to Abraham. The law was given to Moses, and this law was intended to direct Israel to faith in the coming Christ. And with the coming of Christ the promises have been fulfilled and thus through Abraham all nations have been blessed.

Though some Reformed theologians have regarded the postdiluvian covenant with Noah (Gen. 8:20–9:17) as an administration of this unified covenant of grace, I agreed with other Reformed theologians in Chapter 2 that this covenant with Noah is a distinct covenant of *common* grace. The material surveyed above confirms this conclusion. An organic continuity binds the Abrahamic, Mosaic, and new covenants together in terms of the making and fulfilling of promises that culminate in salvation from sin and attainment of the eschatological new creation. The Noahic covenant made different promises and thus stands outside of this line of organic continuity, though its promises ensured the continuation of a human race from whose members God would choose a special covenant people. Neither Galatians 3 nor any other biblical text treats the postdiluvian Noahic covenant in organic continuity with the later covenants of grace. Thus it is important to keep in mind in Chapters 6-9 that God's maintaining the witness of natural law for the human race at large through the Noahic covenant is a fundamentally different work from his entering into the covenants of grace with a chosen people. The covenants of grace themselves do not promulgate the natural law, but they do raise important questions about how participation in the unique blessings of God's redemptive grace relates to the ongoing obligations of the natural law shared in common with the entire human race. This is the key inquiry that unites Chapters 6-9.

This overview of the covenants of grace in redemptive history provides background for Part 2 as a whole. But for purposes of this present chapter, I close this section with a few reflections on the Abrahamic covenant specifically.[6] God's initial call to Abraham appears in Genesis 12:1-3. Though this

---

the former saints, who were justified before God, were justified through it, what need was there for the law to be given? . . . The law was given to a proud people, but the grace of love cannot be received by any but the humble. Without this grace the precepts of the law cannot possibly be fulfilled. Israel was rendered humble by transgression, so that it might seek grace and might not arrogantly suppose itself to be saved by its own merits; and so it would be righteous, not in its own power and might but by the hand of the Mediator who justifies the ungodly." See *Galatians, Ephesians, Philippians,* Ancient Christian Commentary on Scripture, New Testament VIII, ed. Mark J. Edwards (Downers Grove, IL: InterVarsity, 1999), pp. 44-46.

6. With many interpreters, I speak of a single Abrahamic covenant, revealed in several stages. The later, explicitly covenantal, promises in Genesis 15 and 17 are anticipated in the

text does not use the term "covenant," ברית, it anticipates important aspects of the later covenantal promises. God summons Abraham out of his native country to a promised land and pledges to make him into a great nation, to bless him, to make his name great, and to bring blessing to all the families of the earth through him. Many years later God repeats these promises in the formal enactments of his covenant with Abraham. God declares that Abraham would have innumerable descendants, and Abraham responds with faith (Gen. 15:5-6). Furthermore, God promises that his descendants would possess the land of Canaan, a promise he confirms and explains in a dream (15:7-16). A smoking fire pot and flaming torch pass between the pieces of a sacrificial animal; "On that day the Lord made a covenant with Abram" (15:17-18). God repeats and expands these covenant promises to Abraham in Genesis 17:1-8, where he again pledges to give his descendants the land of Canaan and states that he will be the father even of a multitude of nations. On this occasion God commands Abraham to circumcise himself and all males in his household, as a sign of the covenant, for all future generations (17:9-14).

In the Introduction I noted that while all the divine covenants in Scripture share some common features, other characteristics vary from covenant to covenant, especially with regard to the obligations assumed by the parties and the conditions (or lack thereof) that need to be met to receive the covenant's blessings. It is noteworthy that though God places obligations upon Abraham in this covenant (see Gen. 12:1; 17:1, 9-13), Abraham's fulfilling them was not the ultimate basis for the attainment of the covenant promises. God took a self-maledictory oath upon himself that he would do for Abraham as he promised (Gen. 15:17-21). In other words, God's own action would ensure his promises' fulfillment. As Paul explained, the work of the coming Messiah (to whom Abraham looked in faith), rather than Abraham's works, won the covenant's blessings (Romans 4; Galatians 3). Conversely, while individual members of Abraham's covenant household could be expelled for failure to be

---

initial blessing God pronounces in 12:2-3, and the promises in chapters 15 and 17 are mutually overlapping. Among interpreters who stress the differences between the covenant terms in Genesis 15 from those in Genesis 17, there is still disagreement about how exactly to understand their relationship. Paul R. Williamson, for example, says there are "two distinct, but related covenants"; see *Sealed with an Oath: Covenant in God's Unfolding Purposes* (Downers Grove, IL: InterVarsity, 2007), p. 89. Scott W. Hahn, on the other hand, concludes that "while there is essentially one covenant relationship with Abraham, this covenantal relationship undergoes development"; see *Kinship by Covenant: A Canonical Approach to the Fulfillment of God's Saving Promises* (New Haven: Yale University Press, 2009), pp. 102-3.

circumcised (Gen. 17:14), God pronounces no curses upon disobedience that would terminate the covenant itself.

In both respects this is quite different from the covenant of creation, which promised a blessing — life in an eschatological new creation — dependent upon *Adam's* own obedience to the (natural law) commission to exercise royal rule as divine image-bearer, and which threatened a curse for disobedience that terminated any hope that someone could attain the blessing through the terms of that covenant. As we will examine in considerable detail in the next chapter, the Abrahamic covenant also differs in this respect from the Mosaic covenant with Israel. Its promised blessing of temporal prosperity in Canaan was contingent upon obedience to the extensive regulations of the Mosaic law, and its curse upon disobedience threatened to drive the entire people from their promised land and make it unattainable again by the terms of that covenant.[7] That covenant could, and did, become "obsolete" (Heb. 8:13). Israel's experience under the Mosaic covenant, therefore, in part recapitulated the covenant of creation and reminded of the natural law, in order to serve God's ultimate redemptive purposes.

Also significant for the present study is that the Abrahamic covenant did not directly regulate Abraham's broader social life, in its various political, legal, or economic aspects. God made promises that Abraham was to believe, and Abraham was to keep the covenant through living a blameless life and observing the rite of circumcision (Gen. 17:1, 9-14), but God gave no novel or specific instructions about his interaction with the human society surrounding him. As argued in Chapter 2, God's covenant with Noah in Genesis 8:20–9:17 was to encompass all human beings for as long as the earth endures. God gave

---

7. The temporal blessings and curses in the promised land were far from the only things going on in the Mosaic covenant. The next chapter will explore these issues more thoroughly, but my comments here already indicate that the Mosaic covenant is a covenant of grace, which pointed to and administered God's salvation that would be fully accomplished through the coming Messiah, and yet as part of its complex terms it promised temporal blessings in the land contingent upon obedience to the law, a condition that, from the outset, God said they would be unable to satisfy. Thus this conditional aspect, which echoed the conditionality of the covenant of creation, served the larger purpose of pointing the covenant people away from trust in their own accomplishments and toward trust in their Messiah. Thus, as many Reformed theologians have synthesized these strands of teaching within the Mosaic covenant, "At Sinai it was not the 'bare' law that was given, but a reflection of the covenant of works [i.e., the covenant of creation] revived, as it were, in the interests of the covenant of grace continued at Sinai." This was Geerhardus Vos's summary of a common Reformed view; see *Redemptive History and Biblical Interpretation: The Collected Shorter Writings of Geerhardus Vos,* ed. Richard B. Gaffin Jr. (Phillipsburg, NJ: Presbyterian and Reformed, 1980), p. 255.

Abraham no guidelines to the contrary, and thus the commands of Genesis 9:1-7 apparently still bound Abraham and his house, in common with his pagan neighbors who were strangers to the covenant God had made with him. Thus Abraham, presumably, was to participate in a variety of pursuits alongside of and in conjunction with his fellow human beings around him, under God's moral governance through the Noahic covenant. The Abraham narratives in Genesis confirm this theological hypothesis. With his pagan neighbors Abraham waged war (14:1-16), engaged in judicial disputes (20:8-13; 21:22-31), entered into covenants (21:32), and pursued economic transactions (23:3-16).

If Abraham was indeed to pursue his broader social life under the governing framework of the Noahic covenant, then, given my conclusions in Part 1, we would expect the natural law to have been normative for his social interaction with those who lived near him. We have already considered, in Chapter 3, some of the rich natural law themes in the Abraham narratives (and the rest of Genesis). These narratives probe how believing sojourners might faithfully and peacefully interact with those who do not share their religious faith and how learning God's ways of justice in governing the broader world is important for their distinctive identity as his chosen people. Genesis 18:19 states, in the context of Sodom's imminent destruction, that God chose Abraham in order to instruct his offspring "to keep the way of the Lord by doing righteousness and justice." God wishes his covenant partners to know and to adhere to his just paths in this world, and thus reflecting again upon the significance of natural law and the Noahic covenant in the Abraham narratives should be a profitable task for contemporary Christians.

Divine Justice and Natural Law: God's Covenant Partner in Training

I now examine the account of God's interaction with Abraham in Genesis 18:16-33, immediately prior to the destruction of Sodom. Though in Chapter 3 I considered separately the following scene inside the walls of Sodom (19:1-11), Genesis 18–19 as a whole displays an artful narrative unity.[8] Genesis 18:16-33,

---

8. For arguments defending the narrative unity of Genesis 18–19, see Nachman Levine, "Sarah/Sodom: Birth, Destruction, and Synchronic Transaction," *JSOT* 31, no. 2 (2006): 131-46; and especially Robert Ignatius Letellier, *Day in Mamre, Night in Sodom: Abraham and Lot in Genesis 18 and 19* (Leiden: Brill, 1995), chap. 2. Some commentators, however, believe Genesis 18–19 is a compilation of disparate material; e.g., see Walter Brueggemann, *Genesis* (Atlanta: John Knox, 1982), pp. 166-77; and Claus Westermann, *Genesis 12–36: A Commentary,* trans. John J. Scullion, S.J. (Minneapolis: Augsburg, 1985), p. 292.

however, is of particular interest in revealing how God's dealings with Sodom pertain to his special covenant relationship with Abraham, the nature of divine justice and mercy, and the anticipation of the final judgment.

The famous dialogue between God and Abraham in Genesis 18:23-32 transpires only after a prior sequence of events that gives little clue that God is planning a catastrophic judgment against several wicked cities. In Genesis 18:1-15, God and two angels, apparently taking human appearance, come to Abraham and Sarah at their tent in Mamre. After Abraham and Sarah prepare them a meal, the Lord declares that he will return in a year, at which time Sarah will bear a son, in fulfillment of God's earlier covenant promises. The attention shifts in 18:16, when the visitors get up to go. God makes a series of statements, apparently first speaking to himself, wondering whether he should make his plans known to Abraham (18:17-19). Deciding to do so, God reveals his intent to investigate Sodom (18:20-21). At this point the two angels head to Sodom while Abraham remains standing before God (18:22). Here their dialogue occurs (18:23-32), following which the Lord goes on his way and Abraham returns to his tent (18:33).

Genesis 18 as a whole makes clear that God has come to earth in human appearance for two primary purposes, to promise a son to Abraham and Sarah and to deal with Sodom and Gomorrah. The prelude to Abraham's dialogue with God indicates that these two seemingly disparate events are intimately interconnected. God initially asks himself: "Shall I hide from Abraham what I am about to do, seeing that Abraham shall surely become a great and mighty nation, and all the nations of the earth shall be blessed in him? For I have chosen him, that he may command his children and his household after him to keep the way of the Lord by doing righteousness and justice, so that the Lord may bring to Abraham what he has promised him" (18:17-19). Whatever God's reasons for calling Sodom to account, he wishes Abraham to be privy to his intentions, precisely because of their covenant relationship that originally prompted the promise of a son. Through this insight Abraham will understand "the way of the Lord" and be better equipped to train his offspring in its righteousness and justice. With good reason some writers portray this interaction between God and Abraham as part of God's education of Abraham as his covenant partner.[9]

9. E.g., see William John Lyons, *Canon and Exegesis: Canonical Praxis and the Sodom Narrative* (Sheffield: Sheffield Academic Press, 2002), pp. 182-83; Leon R. Kass, *The Beginning of Wisdom: Reading Genesis* (Chicago: University of Chicago Press, 2003), pp. 320-21; and Jonathan Burnside, *God, Justice, and Society: Aspects of Law and Legality in the Bible* (Oxford: Oxford University Press, 2011), pp. 87-88.

The larger text, in fact, suggests that Abraham actually participates in God's judgment against Sodom. Not only does Abraham raise a series of judicial concerns that allow God to clarify the character of his justice,[10] but the narrator also indicates that God rescues Abraham's nephew Lot from the destruction of Sodom because he "remembered Abraham" (19:29). Abraham's intercession for the righteous — he pleads that they not be swept away with the wicked (18:23) — is instrumental in Lot's salvation. This biblical interest in how God's covenant partner participates in God's judgment against the wicked (and salvation from it) is not limited to this particular text. Paul speaks of Christians judging the world with God on the last day (e.g., 1 Cor. 6:2-3) and throughout the Scriptures the prayers of prophets, and ultimately of all believers, are instrumental in bringing salvation to sinners.

In light of my broader purposes in the present book, such matters highlight one important reason for Christians to have interest in the natural law. If natural law is one of God's chief means for holding all people accountable before his judgment on the last day, as already seen in Romans 1:18–2:16, then an understanding of natural law must be prerequisite for his people to fulfill their covenant responsibility as co-adjudicators of the great assize. Similarly, when God instructs Abraham in his righteousness and justice with respect to Sodom, whose judgment would be a harbinger of the final judgment (see Chapter 3), he educates him in the ways of natural law. The ways of natural law, though certainly not the only thing, or even the most important thing, that Abraham must learn and teach his offspring, are an essential part of his covenant education.

Following his internal deliberation (18:17-19), God speaks in Abraham's hearing: "Because the outcry against Sodom and Gomorrah is great and their sin is very grave, I will go down to see whether they have done altogether according to the outcry that has come to me. And if not, I will know" (18:20-21). God initiates an inquest, an investigation into the charges against Sodom that have reached his ears.[11] Why does the almighty God — able to make ninety-year-old Sarah bear a son — portray himself as generally ignorant of

10. James K. Bruckner, *Implied Law in the Abraham Narrative: A Literary and Theological Analysis* (Sheffield: Sheffield Academic Press, 2001), pp. 131-34, identifies four concerns raised by Abraham: detailed discovery of the facts, the innocent bearing the consequences of the actions of the guilty, the community in which the innocent live, and the Lord acting and being known as a just judge.

11. On the following text as a judicial inquiry, see Terence E. Fretheim, *The Book of Genesis*, in *The New Interpreter's Bible*, vol. 1 (Nashville: Abingdon, 1994), p. 467; Bruckner, *Implied Law*, p. 125; and Letellier, *Day in Mamre*, p. 133.

the affairs of Sodom except for some rumors that have reached him, and in need of making a journey to ascertain the facts? The Scriptures often utilize anthropomorphic language to describe God, and by such language God accommodates himself to human language and human conceptions for the sake of his covenant partners. God has decided to open the doors of his courtroom to Abraham so that he might understand his ways of justice. To aid Abraham's comprehension, God portrays himself as a human judge who must hear charges and gather concrete evidence in order to rule justly. Charges have arisen in terms of the "outcry against Sodom and Gomorrah" and God himself, with his angelic servants, will garner eyewitness testimony by going "to see" what is happening there. Through this openness and transparency, God observes due process and thus displays to Abraham a crucial aspect of his righteousness and justice. (It also prepares readers to perceive the utter disregard for due process in Sodom in Genesis 19:1-11, which is one aspect of their moral degeneracy.)[12]

After God alerts Abraham to his purposes and the angels head for the city, Abraham remains standing before God and initiates one of the most familiar divine-human exchanges in Scripture. At the highest level, Abraham confronts God about his own reputation and character, asking famously, "Shall not the Judge of all the earth do what is just?" (18:25). This question about divine justice was prompted by the earlier question whether God would "sweep away the righteous with the wicked" such that "the righteous fare as the wicked" (18:23, 25). Abraham's concern seems to be the basic Aristotelian maxim that each person should receive his due. But squeezed between these two expressions of justice is Abraham's question whether God would "sweep away the place and not spare it for the fifty righteous who are in it" (18:24), a line of thought God allows Abraham to pursue until God agrees to spare the city for the sake of ten (18:27-32). With this question Abraham turns his focus away from whether each individual will receive his due reward and inquires whether God might be *merciful* to the whole city for the sake of a small minority of righteous persons. Ironically, and puzzlingly, Abraham in effect pleads for God to treat the wicked as the righteous (by sparing the whole city for the sake of the righteous) in the midst of asking that God not treat the righteous as the wicked (by destroying the whole city for the sake of the wicked).[13]

12. For similar reflections on this anthropomorphic presentation of God, see Bruckner, *Implied Law*, pp. 145-46, 156-57.

13. For discussion of Abraham's shifting rationales in these verses, see e.g. Lyons, *Canon and Exegesis*, pp. 187-203; Nahum Sarna, *Genesis*, in *The JPS Torah Commentary* (Philadelphia:

A couple of other puzzling issues about this dialogue are worth noting. One is whether Abraham is concerned more about principle (justice and/or mercy) or about attaining a desired result. Abraham clearly raises important questions of principle, but his single-minded focus upon "the city," that is, Sodom, in 18:23-32, when God had announced his plan to investigate Sodom *and Gomorrah,* raises suspicion that Abraham was really only concerned about the fate of a certain resident of Sodom, his nephew Lot, who had gone to live there some years earlier (13:10-12; 14:12).[14] Another disputed question is whether God or Abraham is the lead figure in the dialogue. Is Abraham the driving force, exposing the danger of unjust behavior on God's part and instructing God of his duties, or is God the driving force, setting up and using this conversation to educate Abraham and to make manifest the justice of the course of action he has already set in motion?[15]

To address these questions, I argue first that God, rather than Abraham, is the driving force in this dialogue and that he is the one providing moral instruction. An initial reason for this conclusion is the unpersuasive character of certain assumptions about the origins of Genesis 18:23-32 that support the opposite case. The first assumption is that 18:23-32 is a late addition into the earlier surrounding text and provides a different theological perspective. According to this view, 18:23-32 presents a perspective of grace that softens and broadens the narrow, conventional view of retributive justice at work in the description of Sodom's destruction in Genesis 19.[16] Thus Abraham widens God's horizons. As noted above, the evidence for the narratival unity of Genesis 18–19 belies this claim and disallows the easy option of explain-

---

Jewish Publication Society, 1989), p. 133; and B. Jacob, *The First Book of the Bible: Genesis,* trans. Ernest I. Jacob and Walter Jacob (New York: Ktav, 1974), pp. 121-22.

14. Among those thinking that general concerns of justice move Abraham, see Bruce K. Waltke (Cathi J. Fredricks), *Genesis: A Commentary* (Grand Rapids: Zondervan, 2001), p. 270; among those seeing his focus on Sodom as betraying his real concern for Lot, see Kass, *The Beginning of Wisdom,* p. 322.

15. Among those seeing Abraham as directly challenging and rebuking God, see Brueggemann, *Genesis,* pp. 166-77; and R. N. Whybray, " 'Shall Not the Judge of All the Earth Do What Is Just?' God's Oppression of the Innocent in the Old Testament," in *Shall Not the Judge of All the Earth Do What Is Right? Studies on the Nature of God in Tribute to James L. Crenshaw,* ed. David Penchansky and Paul L. Redditt (Winona Lake, IN: Eisenbrauns, 2000), p. 6. For counterarguments, see e.g. Robert Eisen, "The Education of Abraham: The Encounter between Abraham and God over the Fate of Sodom and Gomorrah," *The Jewish Bible Quarterly* 28 (April-June 2000): 80-86; and Letellier, *Day in Mamre,* p. 134.

16. E.g., as cited above, see Brueggemann, *Genesis,* pp. 167-77; and Westermann, *Genesis 12–36,* p. 292.

ing a difficult text by positing different authors with different purposes. The second assumption, not necessary for the argument but bolstering it, is that an old Hebrew scribal tradition is the preferred reading of 18:22: instead of "Abraham . . . stood before the Lord," the text should read "the Lord stood before Abraham." This modification of the text, which ascribes the superior position to Abraham, is not supported by the extant textual evidence and scholars widely reject it.

A number of positive considerations in 18:16-33 and 19:12-29 support the conclusion that God is the leading figure in the dialogue and uncover some important, if not easily comprehensible, attributes of God's justice and mercy. First, in 18:17-19 God reveals his intention to inform Abraham about his plans for Sodom. If the larger text is indeed uniform and coherent, then the dialogue that follows must be God's way of providing this instruction for Abraham. Second, the scattered nature of Abraham's appeals in 18:23-25 does not support the idea that the narrator meant to present Abraham as the superior pedagogue. Third, God himself chooses which of Abraham's various lines of appeal to take up, and though he accedes to all of Abraham's requests he uses the dialogue for his own purposes, not Abraham's. As noted, Abraham appeals both to the concept of due justice for each individual, such that the righteous not be destroyed with the wicked (18:23, 25), and to the concept of mercy for the whole city because of the righteousness of a few (18:24). God picks up the latter strain without explicitly dealing with the former.[17] He agrees to Abraham's terms for how many righteous are needed to save the city, beginning with fifty and working all the way down to ten (18:26-32). The result, however, is not the salvation of the city, as Abraham sought. Instead, Abraham's extended negotiation with the Lord serves to highlight the purposes of God in this narrative, namely, to show the extent of Sodom's depravity and thus to silence any objection that God has acted precipitously in judging the city.

Fourth, and following upon this last point, is that the way in which God finally acts toward Sodom in 19:12-29 transcends the options as Abraham saw them. For Abraham the options seemed to be either that God separate the righteous from the destruction of the wicked and thus "do what is just" (18:23, 25) or spare the whole city for the sake of the righteous (18:24), in which case presumably God would not give the wicked what they justly deserve but show them mercy. What God does in the end is to "remember Abraham" by delivering Lot from the overthrow of Sodom (19:29). God does not show mercy to the wicked by sparing the city. But he does not exactly follow Abraham's

17. On this point, see Lyons, *Canon and Exegesis*, pp. 208-9.

first option either. God indeed separates the righteous from the wicked, but not by giving out just deserts. God is "merciful" to Lot in bringing him out of Sodom (19:16). Lot's character is not simple to judge.[18] On the one hand, Lot is *not* just another man of Sodom. He alone shows hospitality to the angelic guests who come to the city (19:1-3) and faces the violent mob alone with rather admirable courage (19:6). The NT refers to Lot as a "righteous" man who was deeply disturbed by his neighbors' conduct (2 Pet. 2:7-8). Yet Lot is also willing to sacrifice his daughters to the mob (19:8) and the next morning lingers in leaving the city even after all that had transpired (19:16). Furthermore, Lot's character comes across badly in his moving toward Sodom in the first place (see 13:8-13) (perhaps even taking a woman of Sodom for his wife)[19] and in letting himself become drunk and haplessly siring his daughters' sons (19:30-38). Lot is a righteous man, but imperfectly righteous and thus requiring mercy. God's actions in this story cannot be reduced to either justice or mercy alone.

God's treatment of Lot, I suggest, is incomprehensible in terms of either the original covenant of creation or the covenant with Noah. In the covenant of creation God dealt with human beings in terms of a strict retributive jus-

---

18. As one commentator puts it, "Lot is a complex character." See Laurence A. Turner, *Genesis* (Sheffield: Sheffield Academic Press, 2000), p. 90. For various assessments of Lot, see e.g. Lyons, *Canon and Exegesis,* pp. 222-24; Weston W. Fields, *Sodom and Gomorrah: History and Motif in Biblical Narrative* (Sheffield: Sheffield Academic Press, 1997), p. 60; Letellier, *Day in Mamre,* pp. 142-44; J. A. Loader, *A Tale of Two Cities: Sodom and Gomorrah in the Old Testament, Early Jewish and Early Christian Traditions* (Kampen: Kok, 1990), pp. 36-37; T. Desmond Alexander, "Lot's Hospitality: A Clue to His Righteousness," *JBL* 104, no. 2 (1985): 289-91; and David W. Cotter, *Genesis* (Collegeville, MN: Liturgical, 2003), p. 122. John Calvin frequently calls Lot "the holy man"; see *Commentaries on Genesis,* trans. John King (Grand Rapids: Baker, 2003).

19. Kass makes this claim, though he does not defend it; see *The Beginning of Wisdom,* p. 327. The claim is plausible, and I believe even probable. No mention is made of Lot having a wife during the time he travels with Abraham. The fact that he has daughters coming to marriageable age in Genesis 19 indicates that he may have married about the time he moved into Sodom. Furthermore, the text makes no mention of Lot's wife helping with the hospitality in 19:3, which makes her similar to the inhospitable Sodomites who offered no lodging to the city guests in 19:1 and dissimilar to Sarah, who is hospitable to these guests in 18:6. Finally, Lot's wife proves her love for Sodom by looking back toward the city during their flight to safety (19:26). As a tangential note: if Lot's wife was a Sodomite, then, following the thread of the biblical story, the bloodline of Sodom continued through Lot's daughters, through their descendants the Ammonites and Moabites, through Ruth the Moabitess, and through King David the descendant of Ruth, meaning also that the blood of Sodom coursed through the veins of Jesus of Nazareth, the Son of David.

tice, such that one act of disobedience would bring judgment. In the covenant with Noah God maintained the principle of proportionate retributive justice, but only as tempered by forbearance, and without promise of forgiveness or ultimate deliverance from final judgment on the last day. Yet read in larger biblical perspective, the rescue of Lot from Sodom was not a manifestation of God's forbearance through *postponement of* final judgment for him, but a picture of *deliverance from* final judgment. As discussed in Chapter 3, later biblical texts portray the judgment against Sodom, like the great flood, as a foretaste of the cataclysmic judgment at the end of history (e.g., Deut. 29:23; Isa. 1:9-10; 13:19; Jer. 49:18; 50:40; Lam. 4:6; Hos. 11:8; Amos 4:11; Zeph. 2:9; Luke 17:28-30; 2 Pet. 2:5-9; 3:5-7; Jude 6-7). Read in larger biblical perspective, therefore, the rescue of Lot foreshadows the eschatological salvation of the godly (2 Pet. 2:5-9), a blessing attained through participation in the covenants of grace, not the Noahic covenant. God rescues Lot because he is associated with Abraham, the one with whom God has entered this special covenant relationship in which he graciously reckons sinners to be righteous by faith (Gen. 15:6). *This* mode of God's dealings with human beings cannot be understood in terms of natural law, either of the original unfallen world or in refracted form under Noah.

In summary, in Genesis 18:16-33 God gives Abraham inside access to his purposes in the upcoming events in Sodom, as part of the education of this man with whom God had entered a special covenant of grace. God unfolds to him ahead of time what he is about to do because he has chosen Abraham and his house "to keep the way of the Lord by doing righteousness and justice" (18:19). As considered in Chapter 3, Sodom and its neighboring cities were not in redemptive relationship with God and were not recipients of special prophetic revelation. God held them accountable to himself through the Noahic covenant, and thus through the natural law whose testimony it maintains. This means that Abraham's education into God's ways with Sodom must have been, in significant part, instruction about his just government of the world through the natural law, which in turn was to shape Abraham's own practice of righteousness and justice. As a privileged participant in God's judgment of the world (Gen. 18:23-32; cf. 1 Cor. 6:2-3) — and, as considered below, as a collegial participant in human society alongside those who were strangers to God's special covenant with him — it was necessary for Abraham to understand the natural law. At the same time, God's miraculous rescue of Lot from the flames of Sodom also informed Abraham about the redemptive mercy bestowed in his special covenant relationship, a redemptive mercy unknown in the covenant with Noah.

Natural Law in Practice: Abraham's Sojourn in Human Society

Following its account of the judgment against Sodom and its aftermath, the text of Genesis returns to the peregrinations of Abraham. Genesis 20 tells of Abraham's experience with king Abimelech of Gerar. As considered in Chapter 3, Abraham presented his wife Sarah as his sister, and Abimelech took her into his house. After learning the truth, Abimelech confronted Abraham in a judicial procedure, which resulted in a peaceful resolution of the crisis. I suggested in the previous section that God's training Abraham in the ways of righteousness and justice — which entailed training in the natural law — was necessary not only that he might participate in God's judgment against Sodom but also that he might live properly in the human societies around him. Genesis 20 provides good evidence for that conclusion.

The first thing to note is that the natural law serves as basis for the judicial exchange between Abraham and Abimelech in Genesis 20:9-11. In terms of God's covenant with Abraham in Genesis 15 and 17, and the special revelation that accompanied it, these two men are strangers to one another. They do not share a common religious faith or worship. But they do share a common existence in the fallen world preserved by God under the Noahic covenant, and with it common human responsibilities regarding sex and procreation, eating, and administration of justice (Gen. 9:1-7). God gave Abraham no special instructions in the covenant of Genesis 15 and 17 regarding his common life in human society. But this indicates no flaw in that covenant, for God already required Abraham, as a member of the fallen human race, to live under the natural law ethic of the Noahic covenant. Accordingly, as argued at length in Chapter 3, Abimelech charges Abraham with doing "things that ought not to be done" (Gen. 20:9), which presumes a universally shared knowledge of basic moral truth and thus serves as an appeal to the natural law. Likewise, Abraham, not defending the morality of his action per se so much as explaining his motivations, responds by recalling his doubt that there was any "fear of God" in Gerar (Gen. 20:11). This is another natural law concept, indicating a general respect for the divine judge, which in turn constrains unjust human action. Abraham and Abimelech interact, in short, in terms of the natural law, the objective moral foundation they share in common under God's ordination. God did not give Abraham special instructions for his social life; if he was to be a just participant in the human communities in which he sojourned, he would have to adhere to those "things that ought [to] be done," which he, like Abimelech, knew by nature.

A second observation is that Abraham did surprisingly poorly in this obligation, and Abimelech surprisingly well — another point noted in Chapter 3. Abraham's poor conduct is surprising not only in light of the rebuke he received from Pharaoh for similar behavior many years earlier (Gen. 12:10-20) but also because God had just recently given him a private tutorial on the ways of justice and righteousness (Gen. 18:16-33). Abimelech's civility is surprising — obviously to Abraham (Gen. 20:11) and probably also to readers of Genesis — in light of the radical incivility of other pagan cities (Sodom and Gomorrah) in whose environs Abraham had previously sojourned.

This observation too is instructive regarding the relationship of God's special covenant partner to the natural law. For one thing, this story offers a sobering reminder that being God's special covenant partner did not, in Abraham's common social interaction with strangers to the covenant, ensure his moral superiority over them. Genesis 20 does not suggest that Abimelech understood the requirements of the natural law better than Abraham, but it does indicate that, in this instance, he showed a heartier moral fiber than Abraham. This encounter ought to have instilled a significant humility in Abraham with respect to how he evaluated his personal righteousness. It also should have inspired a more fair and open-minded outlook for future decisions about how to engage his pagan neighbors. A certain caution toward his neighbors seems entirely appropriate, but not a hostile suspicion. God's purpose in the Noahic covenant of preserving human society would have its beneficial effects. Genesis 21:22-34 indicates that Abraham may have learned at least the latter lesson, for he became willing to enter an oath-bound covenant with Abimelech to govern their future relations. Subsequent stories, such as his purchase of a field from the Hittites (Genesis 23), seem to attest to a measure of good faith, mixed with a certain aloofness, in Abraham's interaction with his neighbors. Later generations of his covenant household continue to struggle with questions about how close to get to their neighbors, perhaps displayed most clearly in the story of Dinah and Shechem in Genesis 34, considered briefly in Chapter 3, in which such questions internally divide members of Jacob's household.

Conclusion

This chapter has initiated Part 2 and its consideration of the relationship of natural law to the covenants of grace. In Part 1 we explored how God established the testimony of the natural law in the original creation and then, after the fall, sustained its testimony in refracted form through the Noahic covenant. God holds the entire human race accountable to him by this natural law. But while God preserves the world and postpones the final judgment through the Noahic covenant, God has also enacted a plan of redemption through the covenants of grace, particularly the Abrahamic, Mosaic, and new covenants. Through these series of organically united covenants God gathers a chosen people from among the members of the preserved human race, delivers them from the coming final judgment, and will ultimately bring to fruition the eschatological new creation that was the original destiny of the human race. *(Common) grace preserves nature; (saving) grace consummates nature.* God's work of promulgating natural law, through the natural revelation maintained under the Noahic covenant, is a distinct work from this work of redemption through the covenants of grace. The question before us in Part 2, therefore, is the significance and role of natural law for participants in the covenants of grace, who also remain members of the human race and participants in the covenant with Noah.

I have identified in this chapter two main areas for which natural law was crucial for Abraham and his household. Knowledge of the natural law was necessary for understanding God's ways of righteousness and justice, so that he could both participate in God's judgment of the world and interact rightly with his neighbors in broader human society. With respect to the latter, God did not give Abraham any new and distinctive instructions for his political, legal, or economic life. Abraham remained obligated, in common with all his fellow human beings, under the natural law of the Noahic covenant. As a sojourner in lands not his own, Abraham was to seek to live justly and peacefully with his pagan neighbors as those jointly bound by the natural moral order.

The Mosaic covenant, with its extensive legal requirements and bestowal of a theocratic promised land, opens a great many new questions about the relationship of natural law to God's work of redemption among a chosen people. This is the focus of Chapter 7, which considers the relationship of natural law and Mosaic law, and of Chapter 8, which explores the significance of natural law for the OT wisdom literature. With the coming of Jesus Christ and the new covenant, the chosen people would no longer have an earthly homeland and would thus return to the status of sojourner. Though the life of the NT church is different in so many significant ways from that of Abraham's household, with profound implications for its relationship to the natural law, we will see in Chapters 9 and 10 how Abraham's responsibility to pursue just and peaceful cohabitation with the surrounding human society, under the natural law that obligates them all, echoes strongly in the New Testament.

CHAPTER 7

Natural Law and Mosaic Law: The Sinai Covenant

Many centuries after the Abrahamic covenant, God remembered his promises to Abraham, Isaac, and Jacob, brought Israel out of their bondage in Egypt, and made a covenant with them at Mount Sinai. At the center of this covenant was the Law — the Torah. When God covenanted with Abraham he made great promises but gave no specific instructions about his moral life in broader human society. God expected him to pursue a just and peaceful coexistence according to the norms of the natural law, which bound all humanity in common through the covenant with Noah. But at Sinai God constituted Abraham's descendants, now a great people, as a theocratic nation, destined to live in a promised land all their own, and he gave them a law that set forth detailed regulations about their lives before him and one another. Entrusted with such a law, what need did the Israelites have of the natural law? What relationship did God's law revealed in nature bear to God's law revealed on Sinai? How do the answers to these questions contribute to a Christian understanding of God's larger purposes in establishing the Mosaic covenant?[1]

This chapter explores such questions and proposes a thesis about the relationship of the natural law and Mosaic law important for the broader theology of natural law being developed in this book. In short, I argue that *one* of the chief purposes of the Mosaic covenant was to make Israel's experience a recapitulation of the creation, probation, and fall of Adam. In so

---

1. I refer throughout this chapter to a single Mosaic covenant, though God delivered the terms of this covenant to Israel in different stages, especially at Sinai (recorded in Exodus) and later on the plains of Moab (recorded in Deuteronomy). Though there are certain differences between what transpires on these two occasions, there are many points of organic unity among them, and it seems evident that the requirements, promises, and threats of each one remain binding upon Israel through their subsequent history.

doing, Old Testament (OT) Israel made manifest the basic predicament of the whole human race and thus served as a microcosm of fallen humanity. In this scenario, the law of Moses played a special role. The Mosaic law served, *in part,* to govern Israel's existence in a way that mirrored how the natural law governs all the peoples of the world in their identification with Adam. The Mosaic law did this in a way that respected the unique situation of Israel as God's covenant people, and the Mosaic covenant did some very important things that the natural law has never done, such as proclaiming the forgiving grace of God, in part through establishing a priestly and sacrificial system that, the New Testament (NT) explains, foreshadows the atoning work of the coming Messiah. But though its distinctives should be recognized, the Mosaic law also regulated Israel in many ways functionally and substantively similar to the natural law's regulation of Israel's pagan neighbors. In so doing it manifested the justice and righteousness of God, the promise of blessing and life that obedience to God's law would bring, the ultimate futility of Israel's efforts in light of the curse and death that would follow her inevitable disobedience, and the need for a Messiah who would bear this curse and win the blessing. The terms of the unwritten natural law were displayed in concrete forms in the law of Moses. In this respect, the Mosaic law was a *protological* moral standard (and thus distinct in important respects from an *eschatological* moral standard).

As I unpack this in the present chapter and especially in Chapter 9, I mean the following by *protological* and *eschatological.* A protological law is designed for people living in this present, nonconsummated creation who are under a state of probation, and thus going to be judged (justified or condemned) on the basis of their (dis)obedience to this law. An eschatological law is designed for those who have already passed successfully through God's judgment (as justified) and made citizens of the new creation, and thus obey the law as a response to God's judgment already rendered. The natural law, as expounded in previous chapters, I take to be a protological law; it arises out of and governs life in the natural order of the present creation and communicates that God will judge people on the basis of their obedience or disobedience to it. The Mosaic law, I argue here, is in part, though not entirely, a protological law. People of faith under Moses were justified and heirs of the new creation (e.g., see Rom. 4:6-8; Heb. 11:23-40), and there would be no Mosaic law at all apart from this fact. Yet one of its crucial purposes was to take Israel through a recapitulation of Adam's probation and thus display the ultimate (negative) outcome of life under protological law, as a way of preparing God's people for their coming Messiah.

I realize that my claim that the Mosaic covenant has *both* protological and redemptive aspects may be puzzling to many readers, especially in light of my defense of the crucial distinction between God's protological work of creation and preservation (particularly through the Adamic and Noahic covenants) and his redemptive work through the covenants of grace, the latter of which overcome the evil introduced into the original creation by the fall into sin and achieve the eschatological new creation. But while I recognize the attractiveness of a simple view that affirms *either* the protological *or* redemptive character of the Mosaic covenant, the overall biblical description of the Mosaic covenant, I believe, makes both of the either/or options oversimplified. On the one hand, provisions of the Mosaic covenant itself declare forgiveness of sins for the people of Israel, particularly through the priestly and sacrificial system (e.g., Lev. 1:4; 16:21). Based upon NT teaching, Christians believe that this system was not efficacious in and of itself for the forgiveness of sins and reconciliation with God, but only insofar as it typified and foreshadowed the truly efficacious work of the Lord Jesus Christ as the perfect priest and perfect sacrifice (see especially Hebrews 7–10). On the other hand, Scripture also presents the Mosaic covenant as taking Israel through a recapitulation of Adam's probation and fall (see evidence below) and as resulting inevitably in Israel's curse and exile (Deut. 30:1), such that God's people needed a "new covenant" that would both accomplish what the Mosaic covenant could not and make the Mosaic covenant obsolete (Jer. 31:31-34; Hebrews 8). I noted in the previous chapter that the human obligations of the Abrahamic covenant did not serve as conditions, the violation of which could terminate the covenant itself. On the contrary, the Israelites under Moses, through disobedience to their covenant obligations, could terminate any hope of blessing through the Mosaic covenant. And, like Adam before them under the covenant of creation, they did so. As argued below, Paul teaches that the Mosaic law confirms fallen Adamic humanity in its sin under God's judgment, from which the redemptive grace of Christ provides liberation.

In light of these things, I affirm that the Mosaic covenant has both protological and redemptive aspects, both of which served important roles in God's larger purposes in redemptive history. Theologians in the Reformed tradition have long discussed and debated how exactly to understand the nature of the Mosaic covenant, and many of these debates have revolved precisely around the challenge of expressing its protological and redemptive features in a properly balanced way. As evident from previous chapters, I consider the Mosaic covenant a covenant of grace (or, specifically, as an administration of the one covenant of grace spanning redemptive history), along the lines of the Westminster Confession of Faith (7.5-6). And as part of this gracious work, and in service to it, God also provided his people with a stark reminder of the plight of fallen humanity by attaching the threat and imposition of curse sanctions to the Mosaic law. This sort of position has been a prominent one in the Reformed tradition,[2] and is summarized perhaps nowhere more precisely and concisely than by Geerhardus Vos: "At Sinai it was not the 'bare' law that was given, but a reflection of the covenant of works [i.e., the covenant of creation] revived, as it were, in the interests of the covenant of grace continued at Sinai."[3]

In this chapter I focus upon the protological aspect of the Mosaic covenant. This is not because I view the redemptive aspect as unimportant or even as secondary, neither of which is true. Rather, I focus on the protological aspect because this is a book on natural law, not a book seeking to provide a comprehensive study of the Mosaic covenant, and the protological aspect of this covenant is key for understanding the relationship of the natural and Mosaic laws, or so I argue. I will frequently employ phrases such as "in this respect" or "in part" in order to remind readers that my claims about the protological aspect of the Mosaic covenant are not meant to be an exhaustive description of it.

One of my assumptions in this chapter is that the legal material in Exodus through Deuteronomy is divine revelation, given by God to regulate his covenant relationship with Israel. As such, it is a canonically unified whole, ultimately free of contradictions despite the diversity of material and its composition through human instrumentality. I constantly interact with modern critical scholarship on the exegesis of the texts I consider, but I do not engage its debates and theories about the various sources underlying the different parts of the Mosaic law.

Another assumption is that the NT is a faithful interpreter of the meaning and purposes of the Mosaic law. This book is a work of Christian theology and considers the NT to be the climactic prophetic revelation. From the standpoint of the Messiah's life, death, and exaltation the NT looks back upon the entirety of God's work through history and interprets it authoritatively. I

---

2. For recent essays supportive of this general view, including discussion of some important historical sources, see *The Law Is Not of Faith: Essays on Works and Grace in the Mosaic Covenant,* ed. Bryan D. Estelle, J. V. Fesko, and David VanDrunen (Phillipsburg, NJ: Presbyterian and Reformed, 2009).

3. Geerhardus Vos, *Redemptive History and Biblical Interpretation: The Collected Shorter Writings of Geerhardus Vos,* ed. Richard B. Gaffin Jr. (Phillipsburg, NJ: Presbyterian and Reformed, 1980), p. 255.

explained this assumption in the Introduction, and it has been operational in previous chapters, but it becomes particularly patent here in light of the extensive interpretation of the Mosaic law in many NT writings. Christian theologians must read the OT law itself, in its original context, but I believe a proper Christian understanding of the law also requires reading the law in light of the NT's commentary on it. The epistles of the Apostle Paul will play a particularly important role in this chapter. Paul's interpretation of the law, especially in Galatians and Romans, has been of decisive influence through the history of Christian theology, and a revival of interest in "Paul and the Law" has been one of the most vibrant areas of biblical scholarship in the past several decades. The nature and role of the Mosaic law is such an important matter in the Pauline epistles, in fact, that many writers have plausibly claimed that Paul's broader theology cannot be well understood without coming to grips with his theology of the law.[4] I take Paul as a faithful expounder of the purposes and functions of the Mosaic law as entrusted by God to his people.[5] I also assume that Paul's theology was fundamentally harmonious within and among his epistles, though he used various arguments and modes of expression.[6] In fact, I suggest that some features of Paul's thought that most often provoke the charge of internal contradiction make a great deal of sense when

---

4. Such claims appear across the theological spectrum. E.g., a critic of the cogency of Paul's thought writes, "'One can hardly understand his theology, if one does not grasp his theology of the Torah', says G. Eichholz with respect to Paul. This is probably true." See Heikki Räisänen, *Paul and the Law* (Philadelphia: Fortress, 1983), p. 1. A prominent conservative scholar, on the other hand, writes: "The vast amount of effort being expended is defensible since Paul's theology of the law constitutes an essential part of his gospel, for we cannot grasp Pauline theology without explaining his understanding of the law and justification. If we want to understand Paul we cannot suspend judgment on his view of the law and leave it as a perpetual question mark in our thinking. Grasping Paul's theology in this area is essential for understanding his soteriology, the death of Jesus, Christian ethics, the relationship between Jews and Gentiles in the new community, and the continuity and discontinuity between the Testaments." See Thomas R. Schreiner, *The Law and Its Fulfillment: A Pauline Theology of Law* (Grand Rapids: Baker, 1993), p. 13.

5. A number of recent Pauline scholars, though writing from Christian backgrounds, have concluded that Paul imposed his views on the OT or asserted a continuity between old and new covenants that did not really exist. E.g., see Kari Kuula, *The Law, the Covenant and God's Plan*, 2 vols. (Göttingen: Vandenhoeck & Ruprecht, 1999), 1:204; 2:370; and Udo Schnelle, *Apostle Paul: His Life and Theology,* trans. M. Eugene Boring (Grand Rapids: Baker, 2005), pp. 517-18.

6. Many prominent Pauline scholars have claimed to find significant internal tensions or even contradictions in Paul's theology of the law, perhaps within particular epistles themselves or at least between Galatians and Romans. See generally Räisänen, *Paul and the Law;*

the relationship of the Mosaic law and natural law is understood along the lines argued in this chapter.

To explain and defend my claims about the relationship of the Mosaic and natural laws I first examine three texts from the Mosaic law: Exodus 20:23–23:19, Leviticus 18 and 20, and Deuteronomy 4:1-8. Then, in the second half of the chapter, I explore Paul's teaching on the Mosaic law and argue that it confirms my conclusions drawn from the OT and also provides a deep theological explanation of God's purposes in establishing the Mosaic law's resemblance to the natural law.

Natural Law in Exodus, Leviticus, and Deuteronomy

In this first main section of the chapter we primarily consider three texts from the Mosaic law — the so-called Covenant Code of Exodus 20:23–23:19, Leviticus 18 and 20, and Deuteronomy 4:1-8. I choose these texts for several reasons. For one thing, they represent three distinct parts of the Pentateuch — each of which has a different origin according to modern historical criticism — and so my sampling cannot be dismissed as reflecting just one perspective of OT law among others. In addition, each of these texts implicitly raises fascinating questions about natural law. My chief argument here, first, is that these three sections of the law, each from a different angle, indicate that the foreign nations around Israel had knowledge of the natural law, to which they submitted to some degree but through which they also stood accountable under God's judgment. This conclusion further supports my general claims in Part 1 about natural law and the nations of the world. Second, I argue that these three texts demonstrate that the Mosaic law reflects the substance and the sanctions of the natural law (in ways appropriate to Israel's peculiar historical situation). For all of its distinctiveness, the Mosaic law bore significant similarities to the natural law that obligates the entire human race in common. To close this first section of the chapter I will briefly examine a theme that appears in the Mosaic law itself and elsewhere in the OT: by bringing Israel into the promised land under the authority of the Mosaic law, God intended to take Israel through a recapitulation of Adam's creation, probation, and fall. This discussion will provide an initial explanation for why God gave Israel a law with such substantive similarities to the natural law.

---

also see Hans Hübner, *Law in Paul's Thought,* trans. James C. G. Greig (Edinburgh: T. & T. Clark, 1984); Kuula, *The Law;* and Schnelle, *Apostle Paul,* pp. 514-15.

The Covenant Code (Exod. 20:23–23:19)

The so-called Covenant Code (CC) falls immediately after the account of God's giving the Ten Commandments to Israel from Mount Sinai and Moses' approach to God in thick darkness. It consists primarily of case laws regarding interpersonal disputes, though it also includes various sacrificial and ceremonial regulations. Following the CC, Exodus records God's promise about Israel's future entrance into Canaan (23:20-33) and then resumes the narrative of Israel's experience at Sinai (beginning at 24:1).

As long recognized, the CC bears many striking resemblances to extant non-Israelite legal material from the ancient Near East (ANE), in regard to substance, form, and sometimes even structure. Of special interest to many over the past century have been fascinating similarities between the CC and the Babylonian Laws of Hammurabi (LH), which, even on a traditional early dating of Exodus, is older than the CC by hundreds of years. In the first part of this study of the CC I survey some of the significant similarities and many of the numerous differences between the CC and other ANE legal texts, especially the LH. My first major conclusion is that the CC's resemblance to, and apparent utilization of, ANE legal material with regard to substance and form indicates that there must have been significant civil justice achieved through these foreign laws. Otherwise, the inspired divine law would not have made use of it. This confirms the idea that the nations of the world had access to a universal moral standard — the natural law — that shaped their conduct in significant ways (though very imperfectly). My second major conclusion is that the CC's borrowing of material from the law of pagan nations (though always for its own distinctive purposes) indicates that important aspects of the CC's civil justice were not parochial and unique, but addressed common human concerns. The CC, in other words, reflects the moral substance of the natural law.

*Similarities to and Differences from Other
Ancient Near Eastern Law*

First, I survey some of the similarities and differences between the CC and ANE legal texts, particularly the LH. In the end, I identify more differences than similarities, and the differences, I believe, are ultimately more important. But the similarities, hardly insignificant, are in many respects theologically profound.

The scholarly literature often remarks that the CC is part of a long ANE legal tradition.[7] This does not prejudge the question of what the CC does with older material, but simply recognizes that the CC shares many characteristic features with other ANE legal collections. The CC could not be mistaken for a legal code of a twenty-first-century American state. It uses forms, language, and cases familiar to its time and place in history. Even where the OT texts promulgate law in ways that reflect a critical posture toward the ANE legal tradition, comments Raymond Westbrook, "they continue to share its basic concepts and assumptions."[8] As Tremper Longman puts it, "The true and wise God of the Bible articulated his will in a manner that was recognizable to his people. . . . The uniqueness of biblical law is not based on the fact that its ethic and formulation cannot be found elsewhere."[9]

A first similarity between the CC and the LH is that they recognize the same basic civil law categories. With respect to fundamental moral questions, the CC and the LH are in agreement: disrespect for proper authority, murder, adultery, theft, and lying are wrong and should be redressed. The Decalogue almost immediately precedes the CC in the text of Exodus, and it may well be proper to read the CC as applications of the Decalogue to Israel's unique historical situation.[10] The LH does not address the issues raised in the first four commandments, but it generally embraces the commandments of the so-called second table.[11] There are, to be sure, important differences between the CC and LH as to what exactly constitutes each of these moral offenses, how they should be punished, and perhaps even the order in which they are considered.[12] And the second table itself bears marks of Israel's unique relationship

7. To highlight the length and breadth of this tradition, it may be helpful to note that while the Hebrew-language CC sounds very similar in many ways to the Akkadian-language LH of centuries before, the LH itself often sounds very similar to Sumerian-language legal texts that are centuries older than it. See comments in J. J. Finkelstein, *The Ox That Gored* (Philadelphia: The American Philosophical Society, 1981), p. 18.

8. Raymond Westbrook, *Studies in Biblical and Cuneiform Law* (Paris: J. Gabalda, 1988), p. 1.

9. Tremper Longman III, *How to Read Exodus* (Downers Grove, IL: IVP Academic, 2009), p. 62.

10. See Longman, *Exodus*, p. 126; and John I. Durham, *Exodus* (Waco, TX: Word, 1987), pp. 336-37.

11. See Longman, *Exodus*, p. 59: "In general we can say that the laws of the ancient Near East are not all that different from the biblical laws when we consider the general principles that regulate human interaction as expressed by the fifth to the ninth commandments. They too have laws that protect parents' authority over children and prohibit murder, adultery, theft, and lying."

12. Steven A. Kaufman argues that commandments 6-9 of the Decalogue were the major classificatory categories of law for ANE jurists, but that the LH deals with them in reverse

to God (e.g., "Honor your father and your mother, that your days may be long *in the land that the Lord your God is giving you*" — Exod. 20:12). But the CC and LH hold in common generally that the offenses included in the second table should be discouraged through civil penalties. With other ANE codes, the LH recognized that, at some level, protection of legitimate authority, life, marriage, and property was essential for a well-ordered society.

A second similarity between the CC and the LH involves how these offenses are punished: both bodies of law embrace the *lex talionis*. Again several qualifications are in order. For example, the CC and LH do not always identify the nature of a particular harm in the same way, and thus sometimes differ on what the proportionate penalty should be.[13] Also, it is not certain that the two texts take the same view of when monetary compensation can or should be substituted for literal enforcement of the *lex talionis* in cases of bodily harm.[14] But though they may apply the *lex talionis* in different ways, both the CC and LH embrace it as a general paradigm for determining the just resolution of disputes. The talionic principle is evident throughout the LH, even from the outset: "If a man has accused a man and has charged him with manslaughter and then has not proved (it against) him, his accuser shall be put to death" (LH 1).[15] The CC states the principle in Exodus 21:23-25: "But if there is harm, then

---

order. He believes this reveals a major difference in moral perspective between Israel and its ANE predecessors. See "The Second Table of the Decalogue and the Implicit Categories of Ancient Near Eastern Law," in *Love and Death in the Ancient Near East: Essays in Honor of Marvin H. Pope,* ed. John H. Marks and Robert M. Good (Guilford, CT: Four Quarters, 1987), pp. 111-13, 116.

13. For instance, the LH at times imposes talionic punishment vicariously, on a person who did not commit the crime. An example is LH 230, which states that if a house collapses and kills the owner's son, the son of the house's builder must be put to death. The logic of this penalty depends on the assumption that the harm done was to the adult owner of the house, not to the boy who was killed. The CC, on the other hand, never imposes vicarious talionic punishment, evidently because it always views bodily injury as harm done to the person injured.

14. See further discussion of this issue below.

15. Quotations from the LH are taken from *Ancient Codes and Laws of the Near East,* vol. 2, *The Babylonian Laws,* ed. G. R. Driver and John C. Miles (Oxford: Clarendon, 1955). On the importance of the *lex talionis* in the LH, see Hans Jochen Boecker, *Law and the Administration of Justice in the Old Testament and Ancient East,* trans. Jeremy Moiser (Minneapolis: Augsburg, 1980), pp. 81, 132. Boecker, however, also reacts strongly against the idea that the *lex talionis* is central for OT jurisprudence; see pp. 172-75. This seems to me something of an overreaction, depending upon an unnecessarily literal reading of the *lex talionis*. If one takes the *lex talionis,* as Boecker himself puts it at one point, as representing a "legal principle" on the basis of which judicial decisions were to be made, then the *lex talionis* seems quite fundamental for understanding the Mosaic law.

you shall pay life for life, eye for eye, tooth for tooth, hand for hand, foot for foot, burn for burn, wound for wound, stripe for stripe" (cf. Deut. 19:16-21 for an even closer analogy to LH 1). As discussed again below, in embracing the *lex talionis* the CC and LH were not necessarily advocating physical mutilation as a general practice, but were alike promoting a foundational principle of justice: punishments should be proportionate and balanced; that is, punishments should fit the crime.[16]

A third similarity between the CC and the LH is that they use the same casuistic form for presenting their laws. "Casuistic" simply refers to the use of concrete cases. A random example is this: "If fire breaks out and catches in thorns so that the stacked grain or the standing grain or the field is consumed, he who started the fire shall make full restitution" (Exod. 22:6). Instead of giving long lists of definitions and abstract rules like a typical contemporary Western legal code, the CC, like the LH, describes what ought to happen when a particular situation arises.[17] The ramifications are far-reaching, though perhaps not immediately obvious. Contemporary Western codes tend to aim at comprehensiveness; hence their propensity to offer precise definitions and be exceedingly long.[18] A chief goal is to ensure that legislators alone make the law and that judges, as far as possible, simply apply the law as it stands in the books. In contrast, the CC, LH, and other ANE legal "codes"[19] are full of gaps and holes that leave many areas of life unaddressed.[20] What they provide are

16. In the CC we find a related statement (Exod. 23:6-8) about the need for purity of judgment, uncorrupted by biases or personal factors: "You shall not pervert the justice due to your poor in his lawsuit. Keep far from a false charge, and do not kill the innocent and righteous, for I will not acquit the wicked. And you shall take no bribe, for a bribe blinds the clear-sighted and subverts the cause of those who are in the right."

17. See Jonathan Burnside, *God, Justice, and Society: Aspects of Law and Legality in the Bible* (Oxford: Oxford University Press, 2011), p. 5; and Longman, *Exodus*, p. 60.

18. The 2006 edition of the United States Code, for example, is 27,000 pages, somewhat longer even than the present chapter.

19. Finkelstein notes that the first editor of the LH, more than a century ago, labeled it a "code," and thus instilled a bias in subsequent discussion about the nature of this legal text. See *The Ox That Gored*, p. 15.

20. Longman, *Exodus*, pp. 59-60, mentions the similarities among these texts on this issue. For helpful discussion of particular areas where the Mosaic law is far from exhaustive, see Joe M. Sprinkle, '*The Book of the Covenant': A Literary Approach* (Sheffield: Sheffield Academic Press, 1994), pp. 84-87, 122, 137-48, 143, 157-58, and 164. Shalom M. Paul comments on the general lack of family law in the CC (in contrast to other ANE legal texts); see *Studies in the Book of the Covenant in the Light of Cuneiform and Biblical Law* (Leiden: Brill, 1970), pp. 43-44. Westbrook notes that the CC has no laws about adultery (and Deuteronomy covers only some adultery cases); see *Studies*, p. 6.

"paradigmatic illustrations" or "typical cases" that are hardly designed to be exhaustive of life's possibilities.[21] Even in areas they do address, the representative cases describe only a few particular situations, where even small changes in circumstance would seem to demand a very different legal outcome.[22] From a contemporary perspective in which codes are to be comprehensive, legislators the sole lawgivers, and judges specialized technicians who identify and apply the correct code provision, texts like the CC and LH must seem exceedingly substandard.

Yet it is hardly self-evident that the contemporary perspective is better. At least it must be said that these ancient texts were not striving toward contemporary goals and cannot be straightforwardly judged by contemporary norms. The CC and LH presuppose a legal system in which most institutions, procedures, and rules were not prescribed by written codes. One way or another, the ancient Israelite and Babylonian communities had practical mechanisms for filling in the many gaps in their legal collections, and they evidently did not look upon their collections as failures because of this.[23] This has significant implications for the natural law questions before us, and I return to these matters below.

Fourth and finally, the CC and LH often deal with precisely the same cases, sometimes even the same odd and peculiar cases. The overlap in particular cases they consider would be too tedious to recount in detail, and perhaps there is nothing especially striking about the fact that the CC and LH both deal, for example, with the case of a person causing fire in another's

21. I draw these quotes, respectively, from Sprinkle, *Book of the Covenant*, p. 122; and Bernard S. Jackson, *Wisdom-Laws: A Study of the* Mishpatim *of Exodus 21:1–22:16* (Oxford: Oxford University Press, 2006), p. 27.

22. Arguably the CC does attempt to be more comprehensive than the LH (and other ANE codes) at some points. Jackson, e.g., makes this claim with respect to the goring ox rules in Exodus 21:28-32, 35-36; see *Wisdom-Laws*, pp. 285-86. Yet this only raises the further question as to why use *this* as a representative case evidently meant to guide other situations in which one's animal injures a person or another animal. Goring oxen were surely not everyday phenomena in the ANE; see Finkelstein, *The Ox That Gored*, p. 21. How should the case of a vicious dog be handled in comparison?

23. Burnside observes that the Pentateuch itself describes several situations in which the Israelites had to resolve legal problems that the law of Moses did not address, citing Numbers 27:1-11; 9:6-14; 15:32-36; and Leviticus 24:10-23. See *God, Justice, and Society*, pp. 18-19. Granted, Moses resolved these cases by directly consulting the Lord, rather than by referring them to ordinary judges without such supernatural resources at their disposal. But these examples do support the general claim that gaps in the Mosaic law were not perceived as flaws.

field (Exod. 22:6; LH 105-6), probably a regular problem in relatively hot and dry agricultural communities. But it is quite striking to see the CC and LH (and other ANE texts) deal with the case of an ox that fatally gores a human being (Exod. 21:28-32; LH 250-52).[24] As J. J. Finkelstein observes, we lack any historical evidence that goring oxen were a perennial problem in the ANE. It is thus exceedingly doubtful that numerous legal texts from various communities over the span of many centuries would independently and coincidentally choose *this* case as the representative example for how to deal with other people's dangerous animals. This example alone provides strong evidence for an organic link among the CC, LH, and other ANE legal collections.[25] In other words, in its goring ox rules the CC apparently adopted a *locus classicus* of ANE jurisprudence, further illustrating that we should view the CC as part of a larger legal tradition.

There are other points of similarity beyond the four just mentioned. David P. Wright, for example, has argued recently that the casuistic laws of the CC "display the same or nearly the same topical order as the laws in the last half of Hammurabi's collection," corresponding in fourteen specific points.[26] This is key (though not the only) evidence Wright musters in reviving the claim that the CC is directly dependent upon the LH. I have no technical competence, nor present motivation, to judge whether Wright's thesis or some other theory about the relationship of the CC to the LH is preferable (perhaps the general content and form of the LH were simply in the air, so to speak, and the human author of the CC, as a well-educated person, had them in mind when writing the text).[27]

24. Longman uses this example to make a similar point; see *Exodus*, pp. 60-61. Boecker notes that the CC, LH, and Code of Eshnunna all handle this case in terms of negligence and that all require compensation for death of a slave; see *Law and the Administration of Justice*, p. 164. For further comparison of the CC and LH on this point of law, see David P. Wright, *Inventing God's Law: How the Covenant Code of the Bible Used and Revised the Laws of Hammurabi* (Oxford: Oxford University Press, 2009), pp. 206-13.

25. See Finkelstein, *The Ox That Gored*, pp. 19-21.

26. Wright, *Inventing God's Law*, p. 8.

27. Many scholars offer caveats about an "overzealous pressing of ANE collections as source and parallel versions," to borrow the words of Durham, *Exodus*, p. 317. In critique of an earlier article by Wright, Raymond Westbrook speaks of material in the CC that resists "Hammurabification"; see "The Laws of Biblical Israel," in *The Hebrew Bible: New Insights and Scholarship*, ed. Frederick Greenspahn (New York: New York University Press, 2008), p. 107. Yet neither of these writers, or other critics of Wright, questions the general utilization of the ANE legal tradition by the CC. For another critique of Wright's earlier work on the CC-LH relationship, see Bruce Wells, "The Covenant Code and Near Eastern Legal Traditions: A Response to David P. Wright," *Maarav* 13, no. 1 (2006): 85-118.

Whatever the case, the CC and LH are evidently part of a common legal tradition and have profound similarities.[28]

Before addressing the implications this raises for natural law, I mention a number of differences between the CC and LH, to help keep matters in perspective.[29] As with my list of similarities, this list highlights some noteworthy matters but is not comprehensive.

First, a significant difference emerges when comparing how the CC and LH place value upon human life. Though some have disputed the claim, the cumulative evidence indicates that though the CC did not create an egalitarian society, it values each individual human life as human life. It refuses to deal with any case of murder as though it merely concerned a property interest and refuses to treat people guilty of property crimes as if they are guilty of murder, in distinction from the common practice of the LH. To mention several examples in which the CC differs from the LH: the CC holds the negligent owner of a goring ox accountable for murder in every case and possibly subject to the death penalty (Exod. 21:29-32), it does not prescribe the death penalty for thieves unable to pay the prescribed restitution, and it never imposes the *lex talionis* vicariously, as if the murder of a boy is an offense against the property interests of his father rather than against the life of the boy himself.[30]

A second notable difference is the heightened concern for the poor and oppressed in the CC. Norbert Lohfink insightfully notes that though the epilogue of the LH invites oppressed people to come and read its laws and set their minds at ease, the laws themselves make no actual mention of the poor

---

28. The idea that the CC's human author utilized the ANE legal tradition, and perhaps the LH specifically, may sound like a problematic idea to some with a conservative view of biblical authority. I note in passing, however, that the idea in general, if not in all its specific forms, is not inconsistent with traditional ideas about the divine inspiration of Scripture or even the Mosaic authorship of Exodus. Though God is the ultimate author of Scripture, he used individual human beings, with their particular aptitudes and skills, to produce the biblical texts. As the biblical wisdom writers borrowed preexistent non-Israelite genres to write their literature, and as Paul used Greco-Roman conventions to pen his epistles, without thereby compromising the divine inspiration of their texts, so the human author of the CC could utilize the ANE legal literature to compose his work. In fact, when one considers Moses' upbringing in the Egyptian court it is entirely plausible — even likely — that he would have been familiar with the ANE legal tradition. Longman, *Exodus,* p. 53, makes a similar point.

29. For other lists of differences, see e.g. Burnside, *God, Justice, and Society,* pp. 9-10; and Longman, *Exodus,* p. 63.

30. For a few relevant discussions, see Burnside, *God, Justice, and Society,* pp. 264-65; Paul, *Studies,* pp. 61, 65, 87; Longman, *Exodus,* pp. 128-29; and John H. Walton, *Ancient Israelite Literature in Its Cultural Context: A Survey of Parallels Between Biblical and Ancient Near Eastern Texts* (Grand Rapids: Zondervan, 1989), p. 79.

or oppressed. In contrast, the CC explicitly mentions many vulnerable groups — slaves, sojourners, widows, the fatherless, and the poor — and defends their interests (see Exod. 21:1-11, 20-21; 22:21-27; 23:6).[31] The subject of slavery in the Mosaic law is a bigger issue than I can deal with here, but it seems that without abolishing slavery the CC makes it more humane,[32] particularly for Israelite slaves (who, according to the Jubilee legislation in Leviticus 25, would have become "slaves" only as a way to pay off debts and only for a set period of time). A good example of this more humane perspective is Exodus 21:20, which holds a master guilty of murder for killing his own slave, an idea absent from other ANE legal texts.[33]

A third difference between the CC and the LH is that Exodus sets the CC in the context of the history of God's covenant-making with Israel. There are all sorts of literary ways in which the text of the CC is connected to the surrounding narrative about Israel at Sinai.[34] Thus the CC must be interpreted as the law given by God to Israel through a covenant, rather than as an independently existing legal code inserted into an independently existing historical narrative.[35] In contrast, Hammurabi identifies *himself* as the lawgiver, and though he acknowledges that he legislates with the wisdom granted him by his god Shamash, the law is his own product and serves to vindicate Shamash's election of him as king.[36]

The divine covenantal character of the CC helps to explain a number of its other differences with the LH. For example, the CC not only uses casuistic

---

31. Norbert Lohfink, S.J., "Poverty in the Laws of the Ancient Near East and of the Bible," *TS* 52 (1991): 36-42. See also relevant discussion in Boecker, *Law and the Administration of Justice*, pp. 166-67; and Paul, *Studies*, pp. 40, 76.

32. E.g., see Sprinkle, *Book of the Covenant*, p. 102; and Finkelstein, *The Ox That Gored*, p. 42.

33. See Paul, *Studies*, p. 69; and Boecker, *Law and the Administration of Justice*, pp. 162-63.

34. For extended defense of this idea, see Sprinkle, *Book of the Covenant*, chap. 1; and Assnat Bartor, *Reading Law as Narrative: A Study in the Casuistic Laws of the Pentateuch* (Atlanta: Society of Biblical Literature, 2010), chap. 1. See also briefer comments in Burnside, *God, Justice, and Society*, p. 14; Durham, *Exodus*, p. 318; and Jackson, *Wisdom-Laws*, p. 6. Taking a different view, Boecker asserts there is no doubt that the CC already existed before incorporation into the Sinai narratives; see *Law and the Administration of Justice*, p. 136.

35. For related comments on the decisiveness of the covenant for understanding the law, see Burnside, *God, Justice, and Society*, chap. 2; Paul, *Studies*, pp. 31, 36; and Finkelstein, *The Ox That Gored*, p. 42. Also relevant is Bartor's discussion of how, in contrast to the LH, in the CC the lawgiver frequently inserts himself into the text of the laws themselves, his laws being "communicative texts"; see *Reading Law as Narrative*, chap. 2.

36. Discussed, e.g., in Paul, *Studies*, pp. 6-7, 25, 36; and Wright, *Inventing God's Law*, p. 13.

laws (discussed above) but also so-called apodictic laws. Apodictic laws are general or abstract rules that do not mention particular cases or circumstances. For instance, Exodus 23:1 commands: "You shall not spread a false report." It is not as though apodictic laws were entirely absent from ANE literature, for they did appear in treaty (covenant) and wisdom literature, for example. But ANE legal texts rarely utilized them.[37] The fact that the CC is both legal literature and an account of a treaty/covenant, therefore,[38] helps to make sense of its combination of casuistic and apodictic laws. Also rooted in the CC's covenantal character is the fact that it includes both "civil" and "cultic" material. Though ANE societies did not attempt to keep civil and religious matters separate as do contemporary Western democracies, they generally did not regulate their cultic practices in the same legal documents that set forth their mundane civil laws.[39] Being in a special, holistic covenant relationship with God, Israel was a truly theocratic nation in which civil and cultic matters alike were divinely dispensed and organically related.

A final difference between the CC and LH is the presence of motivation clauses in the former. That is, the CC at times offers reasons for its laws that provide motivation for performance (though motivation clauses appear more frequently in other places in the Mosaic law). For example, "You shall not wrong a sojourner or oppress him, *for you were sojourners in the land of Egypt*" (Exod. 22:21). In comparison, motivation clauses are very infrequent in the LH and other ANE legal texts.[40] In part, the motivation clauses in the CC tie in to the previous point: Israel was in covenant with God who rescued them from Egypt and was bringing them into a promised land; this was why Israel must obey.[41] Furthermore, motivation clauses in OT law constitute a point of similarity with biblical wisdom literature and in both cases serve a didactic function.[42] In other words, motivation clauses make manifest that the Mosaic law was meant to do more than simply regulate a legal system. It was also to teach and train the people as a whole in the way to walk before God. This point too has implications for thinking about natural law.

---

37. See Burnside, *God, Justice, and Society*, p. 10; Paul, *Studies*, pp. 122-24; and George E. Mendenhall, *Law and Covenant in Israel and the Ancient Near East* (Pittsburgh: The Biblical Colloquium, 1955), p. 7.

38. As observed by Burnside, *God, Justice, and Society*, p. 46.

39. See Paul, *Studies*, p. 9; and Walton, *Ancient Israelite Literature*, pp. 76, 90.

40. See Rifat Sonsino, *Motive Clauses in Hebrew Law: Biblical Forms and Near Eastern Parallels* (Chico, CA: Scholars, 1975), pp. 223-24.

41. Sonsino, *Motive Clauses*, p. 174.

42. See Sonsino, *Motive Clauses*, p. 175; and Burnside, *God, Justice, and Society*, pp. 9-10.

There are several possible reasons why, in any particular instance, the Mosaic law apparently utilizes material from the ANE legal tradition, but changes it. It may do so because an ANE provision was fundamentally unjust, from the standpoint of the natural moral order under which all people live. Or the CC might change it because Israel's unique status in redemptive history as God's theocratic covenant people made a different rule more fitting, without thereby implying that there was anything unjust about the ANE rule for its own society. There may even be a third possibility: the ANE provision was just, but Israel's different geographical or economic situation — in matters not determined by its distinctive covenantal identity — suggested a different application of that provision. I do not claim it is easy to determine which possibility is the correct choice in each case. In some cases the ANE rule may have been unjust *and* Israel required a rule distinctively geared for its covenantal identity. Determining to what degree Israel's civil laws are unique and to what degree they are more broadly applicable has been a perennially vexing problem for Christian theology and ethics.[43] One thing that seems clear is that the Mosaic law's civil provisions are so organically intertwined with Israel's identity as God's covenant people and with their obligation to worship him in their distinctive way that any sweeping claim that the Mosaic civil laws should be imposed by civil communities today (who are not in relationship to God through the covenant at Sinai) is fundamentally misguided.[44] Applying the Mosaic civil laws as a whole only makes sense within the context of the Mosaic covenant, and it is presumptuous for any nation other than OT Israel to act as if it is in covenant with God through Moses.

The famous goring ox case provides a good example of the organic intertwining of civil provisions and the broader Mosaic covenantal context. Why is it that the CC requires the offending ox to be killed (earlier ANE laws said nothing about the ox's fate) and why was the ox to be killed by stoning? That the ox was to be slain might be explained as ensuring a universal point of justice, namely, that grave threats to public safety should be removed. The text itself does not explain why the ox should be *stoned*, but quite possibly the provision is meant to keep this judicial animal-killing properly distinct from ritual sacrificial animal-killings.[45] In any case, untangling the universal

43. For a helpful consideration of this topic, see David Skeel and Tremper Longman III, "The Mosaic Law in Christian Perspective," in *The Bible and the Law*, ed. Robert F. Cochran Jr. and David VanDrunen (Downers Grove, IL: IVP Academic, 2013), pp. 80-100.

44. A representative work defending such a broad imposition of Mosaic civil law is Greg L. Bahnsen, *Theonomy in Christian Ethics* (Nutley, NJ: Craig, 1979).

45. This is the argument of Westbrook in *Studies*, p. 88.

natural justice communicated in the Mosaic law from its unique covenantal hue is a difficult endeavor. I do not pursue this task here, though I address the issue again in Chapter 10.

Implications of These Similarities and Differences

Despite these caveats, I believe there are at least two major implications of this comparison of the CC and LH for matters of natural law. First, this comparison of the CC and LH provides evidence that the natural moral order was constraining and shaping the pagan jurists who constructed them, however imperfectly. The reason is this: the CC intentionally utilized much of the ANE legal tradition (as argued above), and if the CC communicated genuine, divinely approved justice (as follows from my assumptions throughout this book regarding the divine inspiration and authority of Scripture), then there must have been a significant degree of justice achieved through these ANE codes. Second, and following upon the first, if the CC indeed utilized some of the just provisions captured in the LH and if the justice captured in the LH indeed reflected the lingering influence of the natural law, then the CC too must have reflected and applied the moral substance of the natural law. Recalling some of the similarities between the CC and LH identified above should help to solidify these conclusions.

First, I discussed above the general similarity in moral substance underlying the CC and the LH. Despite many differences in detail, both legal texts embrace the basic principles expressed in the fifth through ninth commandments of the Decalogue. In several previous chapters I concluded that biblical evidence supports Christian theology's traditional view of the Decalogue as a useful general summary of the universal moral truth revealed in the natural law (though the Decalogue itself contains material unique to Israel). Insofar, then, as these pagan ANE nations understood in some elementary way that respect for the so-called second table of the law was necessary for an orderly and prosperous social life, the presence and effect of the natural law among them is secretly manifest.[46] Furthermore, this point of similarity between the CC and LH indicates that when God inspired the promulgation of the CC

---

46. In somewhat different terms, but I believe making a similar point, Longman writes, regarding the other nations: "while they were not the recipients of God's special grace that would restore a relationship with him, God still demonstrated his common grace toward them." See *Exodus*, p. 62.

he was not giving his people something brand new or entirely unfamiliar (though some of it surely was new and unfamiliar). In a great many ways it must have confirmed and clarified what they already knew simply by being human persons with experience of this world and with functioning (though sinful) consciences.[47]

A second similarity between the CC and LH identified above concerns the standard for just punishment and restitution. Though again they differed in multiple ways regarding details, both texts embraced the principle of *lex talionis*. It is crucial to note that elevating the *lex talionis* as a principle of justice cannot simply be taken as a prescription of literal physical mutilation in all cases of bodily injury. In the CC, LH, and many other legal systems through history, the *lex talionis* represented a foundational principle of justice, namely, that a punishment should fit the crime and thus must be proportionate to the harm done.[48] Retribution should be neither too lax nor too stern, but must maintain a balance that the talionic formula so tautly expresses. "Eye for an eye" — what better captures the proper price for loss of an eye than another eye? As Reformed theologian Wolfgang Musculus put it, "Nothing can be fairer than the law of equivalence *(lex talionis)*."[49] Many scholars have observed that the "eye for an eye" formula itself, with a moment's thought, demonstrates why the *lex talionis* really cannot be interpreted in a woodenly literal way. What if a two-eyed man takes out the remaining eye of a one-eyed man? Would removing one eye from the former really be commensurate to the harm he caused by totally blinding his victim?[50] In addition, it seems evident from the CC, LH, and many other legal systems that monetary compensation was regularly substituted for physical mutilation.[51] These and many other factors demonstrate that the *lex talionis* was an ideal, a principle of proportionate (and poetic) justice.[52]

That the pagan ANE nations understood this at a basic level (notwith-

47. For similar statements, with appropriate sensitivity also to the uniqueness of the Mosaic law, see Burnside, *God, Justice, and Society,* pp. 81-82; and Longman, *Exodus,* pp. 56-57.

48. For a scintillating study of this general topic, see William Ian Miller, *Eye for an Eye* (Cambridge: Cambridge University Press, 2007).

49. See *Genesis 1-11,* Reformation Commentary on Scripture, Old Testament I, ed. John L. Thompson (Downers Grove, IL: IVP Academic, 2012), p. 295.

50. See discussions, for example, in Burnside, *God, Justice, and Society,* p. 12; and Finkelstein, *The Ox That Gored,* p. 34 n. 22.

51. See discussions in Sprinkle, *Book of the Covenant,* pp. 94-95; and Burnside, *God, Justice, and Society,* pp. 276-77.

52. See e.g. Westbrook, *Studies,* p. 46; Sprinkle, *Book of the Covenant,* p. 92; and Burnside, *God, Justice, and Society,* p. 275.

standing their many failures to apply and maintain this standard of justice) offers further testimony to the presence and power of natural law among them. I have argued in previous chapters that the natural law communicates not only the *requirements* of God's moral law but also the *sanctions* of the law. When wrong is done, the natural law demands proportionate retribution. Genesis 9:6 demonstrates most memorably that this principle is appropriately captured in the *lex talionis*. God, communicating the universal commission of image-bearing human beings to pursue justice, in the context of his covenant to sustain the postlapsarian natural order, states the proper response to murder in talionic form: "whoever sheds the blood of man, by man shall his blood be shed." This is a key part of the minimalist natural law ethic identified in Chapter 2. Thus we would expect any basically functional society to have some rudimentary appreciation for the *lex talionis* principle. That is indeed the case in the LH and many other legal systems through history.

These matters concerning punishment and retribution also tell us something important about the relationship of natural law and Mosaic law. In promulgating the *lex talionis,* the CC was not giving Israel something brand new or unfamiliar. Again, it confirmed and clarified a legal principle that Israelites already knew something about thanks to the natural revelation they received in common with the rest of humanity. Yet we should also note that Exodus further impressed this natural law principle of just retribution upon Israel through placing the CC in the context of the demands and sanctions of the Mosaic covenant generally. For example, prior to the CC, as a prologue of sorts, God says: "if you will indeed obey my voice and keep my covenant, you shall be my treasured possession among all peoples, for all the earth is mine; and you shall be to me a kingdom of priests and a holy nation" (Exod. 19:5-6).[53] Then, as a sort of epilogue to the CC, God warns Israel that he will not forgive their disobedience to his law but promises to bless them abundantly as they enter the promised land, upon condition of their obedience (23:20-33).[54] The ultimate concern of the Mosaic law was not to regulate intrahuman affairs but to regulate Israel's relationship to their covenant Lord. This too reflects the broader dynamic of the natural law observed in previous chapters: though its minimalist ethic explicit in Genesis 9:1-7 focuses upon intrahuman conduct, it ultimately concerns a broader moral order at whose center is every human being's relationship to God (Rom. 1:21-23, 32; 2:14-16).

A third similarity between the CC and LH discussed above concerns

53. See Paul, *Studies*, pp. 31-32.
54. See Sprinkle, *Book of the Covenant*, p. 34.

their casuistic form and their corresponding noncomprehensive nature. Form is important, because a just legal system needs not only substantively just laws but also effective procedures and institutions to administer these laws properly. Therefore, the mere fact that the CC adopted the same form for stating laws, with the kind of procedures and institutions they presuppose, indicates that the legal procedures and institutions of the Babylonian society regulated by the LH must have been able to administer justice in significantly effective ways. And this again points to the presence and power of the natural law in this pagan community. To extend the point: the casuistic form, with its noncomprehensive character, presupposes a wisdom able to fill in the many gaps in the written law.[55] This wisdom would express itself through an unwritten common law and through discerning judges able to perceive the just resolution of particular cases.[56] All of this, in turn, presupposes the presence of a natural moral order that exists independently of the written law, for, as we will consider in the next chapter, perception of the natural moral order gets precisely to the heart of what wisdom is. Israel, therefore, having this sort of law (noncomprehensive and to a considerable degree casuistic), was required to interpret and apply it against the background of their ongoing life within the natural moral order. They could not achieve justice in real-life concrete circumstances without this. Therefore the CC must have been, at a basic level, harmonious with the natural law. This further corroborates the thesis that the Mosaic law was, in part, an application of the natural law designed for Israel's particular situation.

55. Jackson's analysis of the CC in terms of "wisdom laws" is relevant here. He distinguishes the legal system obviously at work in Israel with a Western "rule of law" model, and argues, concerning the CC, that its linguistic rules are to be read not literally but in their narrative and contextual sense, and that third-party adjudication is to be avoided in favor of private resolution against the background of custom; see especially *Wisdom-Laws*, pp. 23-24. Burnside makes this related observation: "Practical reasoning depends upon 'a never fully articulable' background consensus. Biblical law addresses this by offering rules that are limited in number but which are designed to promote wisdom. . . ." See *God, Justice, and Society*, p. 19. Though I cannot utilize her work in detail here, the proposed narrative reading of biblical law by Bartor in *Reading Law as Narrative* seems very relevant and often quite helpful in thinking through these matters. See also Sonsino, *Motive Clauses*, p. 175.

56. For related discussion, see e.g. Westbrook, *Studies*, pp. 4-6; Burnside, *God, Justice, and Society*, pp. 11-12; and Jackson, *Wisdom-Laws*, p. 31. Jackson also argues that the CC must have developed in a context in which wisdom teachings were known, and offers a number of examples of similarities between the CC and material in Proverbs; see *Wisdom-Laws*, pp. 41-42. While Jackson's analysis presumes views of the dating of Exodus with which I disagree, the similarities in content between the CC and Proverbs are highly suggestive.

Sex and the Nations (Leviticus 18 and 20)

Leviticus 18 and 20 are evidently meant to be read together. Though each chapter has distinctive features, both deal with worship of false gods and, most prominently, with a host of sexual offenses that Israel must shun. Leviticus 18 is structured around general warnings (18:1-5, 24-30), with numerous exhortations, mostly about sex, sandwiched in between (18:6-23). Leviticus 20 deals with other matters first (20:1-9), then proceeds to mention many of the same sexual offenses, but does so by prescribing proper punishments (20:10-21). It concludes with general warnings similar to those in Leviticus 18.

These two chapters are illuminating to read alongside the CC of Exodus. Whereas the CC borrows significant legal material from elsewhere in the ANE (though always for its own purposes), Leviticus 18 and 20 explicitly reject the practices of other ANE peoples and thereby seek to differentiate Israel radically from pagan nations. Yet despite that outward difference between these two sections of the Mosaic law, I believe consideration of Leviticus 18 and 20 compels a conclusion similar to my claims about the CC: the pagan nations were held accountable to God via the natural law, and the Mosaic law applied the natural law in a way appropriate for OT Israel.

In this section I explore these issues and develop my conclusions in three parts. First I reflect on how Leviticus 18 and 20 are substantively similar to the natural law. Next I observe how these chapters proclaim just sanctions for violations of the law, in a way that again reflects the law of nature. Finally, I note how Leviticus 18 and 20 situate Israel under the Mosaic law in a way analogous to the condition of the Canaanites under the natural law, with respect to both substance and sanctions.

Leviticus 18 and 20 and the Substance of the Natural Law

First, then, what can be said about the *substance* of the sexual morality expressed in Leviticus 18 and 20 in comparison with the sexual morality communicated in the natural law? This is a significant question for the present volume, since, as repeatedly observed in previous chapters, where Scripture says things related to natural law sex is often in view. Investigation of Mosaic teaching about sex, therefore, is a good test of this chapter's claims about the relationship of natural law and Mosaic law.

Some previous chapters have explored biblical texts that set forth natural sexual morality in positive terms, particularly as encapsulated in the Adamic and Noahic commission to be fruitful and multiply. In these texts, Scripture portrays human beings as constituted by nature to express their sexual capacities in heterosexual marriage relationships that are procreatively fruitful. But other texts deal with sex and natural law negatively, portraying various sorts of sexual relationships as contrary to the natural law. Though it is probably not possible to construct a strict hierarchy of sexual offenses against natural law from the texts considered in previous chapters, some of these texts do seem to suggest that certain kinds of sexual offenses deviate further from the norm than others.[57] A couple of prominent passages, for instance, highlight homosexual conduct as a serious transgression of the natural moral order. In the case of Sodom it was especially problematic because nonconsensual and violent. Another example is Genesis 2:18-25, which emphasizes that a human being's proper sexual/marriage partner is another human being, not an animal, implicitly identifying bestiality as radically contrary to the sexual order of creation.

How does the sexual morality of Leviticus 18 and 20 compare with the natural law sexual morality explored in previous chapters? Leviticus 18 and 20 do not put things positively by defining the sexual norm to which people should conform, but only list sexual practices to avoid. It takes little effort to see, however, that one does not run afoul of any of these prohibitions by having intercourse within a heterosexual marriage (provided that one's spouse is not a close relative or having her monthly period). And while the same might be said about intercourse between two unmarried people of the opposite sex, other parts of the Mosaic law disapprove of this behavior. Thus, a heterosexual marriage relationship between those not too closely related, which would ordinarily be procreatively fruitful, is evidently the implied norm in Leviticus 18 and 20.

A cynical reader of these chapters might observe that they could be much shorter if they simply prohibited any deviation from the norm, rather than compiled a long list of specific prohibitions. But the fact that it was composed in this way requires investigation of the order of presentation and what it may communicate about the offenses. Jonathan Burnside has recently made a compelling argument about the structure of Leviticus 20 (with reference

---

57. One of the reasons to be cautious about hierarchically ranking sexual offense by their degree of deviation from the natural norm is that while some offenses — say, consensual heterosexual adultery — may be per se less removed from the norm than a homosexual affair or especially homosexual rape, they may also be far more prevalent than offenses that are per se further removed from the norm, thus making them cumulatively more damaging to the social order.

also to chapter 18).[58] He claims that the structure reflects the content; this is similar to Jacob Milgrom's comment regarding a later section of Leviticus: *"structure is theology."*[59] What then is the structure, and what are its theological implications? Burnside believes that the nature of the penalties is key for the passage's organization, which is arranged chiastically. He argues that Leviticus 20, following the Decalogue, makes the simple case of adultery the paradigmatic sexual offense and presents other offenses as forms of adultery. As the baseline sexual violation, adultery is presented first (20:10). Then, from verse 10 to verse 16, offenses get progressively worse, further removed from the norm of heterosexual marriage. The decline culminates with the case of female bestiality (20:16).[60] Its penalty is described in peculiar fashion (both the woman and the animal are to be both "killed" and "put to death"), highlighting the serious character of the offense.

I find Burnside's case persuasive. If he is correct, the sexual morality of Leviticus 18 and 20 is at least consistent with, and even confirmatory of, my conclusions about natural law sexual morality. I argued in previous chapters that the natural law commends the norm of sex within heterosexual marriage relationships that ordinarily produce children. This is part of the minimalist natural law ethic explicit in the Noahic covenant (Gen. 9:1, 7). I also suggested that the nature of the image of God — which entails being created in community, as "male and female" (Gen. 1:27) — may help to explain why homosexual conduct is sometimes singled out as a significant violation of this norm: it involves uniting oneself to a person who is one's own reflection, rather than an "other." The hierarchy of offenses in Leviticus seems to operate with these perspectives.[61] The case of simple adultery is bad (20:10), yet is least removed from the ideal of being united to an other in a fruitful relationship. What the relationship lacks is the permanence of marriage, while also damaging an existing marriage. Cases of incest (20:11-12) are worse. Though they might take the cover of "marriage," they compromise the otherness principle. The

---

58. Burnside, *God, Justice, and Society,* chap. 11.

59. See Jacob Milgrom, *Leviticus 23–27: A New Translation with Introduction and Commentary* (New York: Doubleday, 2001), pp. 2129-30 (italics his).

60. On this point compare John E. Hartley, *Leviticus* (Dallas: Word, 1992), p. 289, who sees a progression in the order of sexual offenses in Leviticus 18, from distortions of normal sexual practice to unnatural practices. This progression also culminates with female bestiality.

61. Note also Jacob Milgrom's argument that Leviticus 18's basic rationale is procreation within the patriarchal structure, with verses 6-18, 20 pertaining to seed destructive of the family and verses 19, 21-23 pertaining to relationships that produce no seed; see *Leviticus 17–22: A New Translation with Introduction and Commentary* (New York: Doubleday, 2000), pp. 1530-31.

sexual partner is of the opposite sex, but he or she is a close relative, not quite different and other enough. In addition, by being united to the wife of one's father or son (the specific cases in 20:11-12), one comes to have, in effect, a twofold family relationship with the same person,[62] a situation that hearkens back to Abraham's identification of Sarah as his sister, which was so strongly condemned by two pagan monarchs and implicitly condemned as a violation of universal moral norms by the narrative in Genesis. Also, at least from our modern scientific perspective, incestuous relationships indirectly compromise the commission to be fruitful and multiply, since in some cases they bring heightened risk of genetic deformity. In light of these things, the progression in Leviticus 20 thus far seems to match the portrayal of natural law sexual morality discussed in previous chapters.

The next offense condemned is (male) homosexual conduct (20:13).[63] In terms of natural law considerations, this offense ratchets up the deviation from the norm in at least two respects. It involves a relationship with one who is not an other in the very important respect that both are males. In this respect the otherness principle is more seriously violated than in the previous incest cases. It also results in a union that is inherently unfruitful, unlike a heterosexual incestuous relationship. The ordering of homosexual conduct further down the road from simple adultery and two kinds of incestuous practice, therefore, seems again to match the perspective of Genesis and Romans on homosexual conduct as a paradigmatic deviation from the natural law norm.

But only with two additional offenses do readers reach the denouement. The first is the man who takes both a woman and her mother (20:14). I am not certain why this offense falls where it does. The final case is bestiality, first as committed by a male and then by a female (20:15-16). At first glance bestiality seems to honor the principle of otherness. But according to Genesis 2:18-25, in creation God established other human beings, rather than animals, as the proper human sexual partner. Bestiality violates the natural sexual order in at least a couple of respects. For one thing, as a cross-species union it is the nonfruitful relationship *par excellence* (Greek myth notwithstanding). Furthermore, while one's partner in bestiality is indeed other, the sexual relationships commended for image-bearers of God are a *human* activity. Taking an animal as a lover does not confuse otherness

---

62. See related comments in Adrian Schenker, "What Connects the Incest Prohibitions with the Other Prohibitions Listed in Leviticus 18 and 20?" in *The Book of Leviticus: Composition and Reception*, ed. Rolf Rendtorff and Robert A. Kugler (Leiden: Brill, 2003), pp. 166-67.

63. Most of the offenses in Leviticus 18 and 20 are described as if males are the audience.

within the human species but, even worse, constitutes an essential denial of one's humanness altogether.[64]

This analysis leads to the conclusion that the substance of the sexual morality expounded in Leviticus 18 and 20 is consistent with the substance of the natural law sexual morality identified above.[65] Though Leviticus 18 and 20 deal with more types of sexual relationships than do texts considered in my previous chapters, their basic perspective on what the ideal is and what kinds of offenses deviate from the norm, and to what degree, moves in the same direction as the natural law. Below I will argue against the assumption that each and every particular offense condemned in Leviticus 18 and 20 is a universal offense against the natural moral order; as with the CC, some things are best interpreted as specifically applicable to OT Israel. But even with this caveat, Leviticus 18 and 20 further corroborate my thesis that the Mosaic law, in part, communicates the moral substance of the natural law in a way appropriate for God's OT people.

Leviticus 18 and 20 and the Sanctions of the Natural Law

In the second part of this section I move from the *substance* of the sexual morality of Leviticus 18 and 20 to the *sanctions* or *consequences* of its violation. A theme in previous chapters is that the natural law communicates not only the requirements of God's law but also its just sanctions, holding out life and blessing for obedience and death and curse for disobedience. As in the CC of Exodus, I also argue that in Leviticus 18 and 20 the Mosaic law preaches the message of retributive justice to be administered to Israel, according to people's deeds, in response to God's law. This adds more sup-

---

64. The question may arise as to why in 20:16, alone in Leviticus 18 and 20, the text specifically addresses females, and seems to make female bestiality even worse than male bestiality. Burnside insightfully notes that in the case of female bestiality the woman and the animal receive the same punishment. He argues that males are ordinarily viewed as the proper instigators of sexual activity. In the case of female bestiality the woman must take that role (she "approaches" the animal), and thus she commits yet another degree of offense beyond that of the male perpetrator of bestiality. Therefore, says Burnside, the woman and the animal receive the same penalty, for there really remains no way to tell the two apart. See *God, Justice, and Society*, p. 366.

65. Perhaps also worthy of consideration is how Leviticus 20 moves from consideration of idolatrous practices to violations of sexual propriety, a similar movement to Paul's argument beginning in Romans 1:18, where he condemns the nations for their rebellion against the natural moral order.

port to the idea that the Mosaic law in part reflects the natural law, in a way fitting for OT Israel.

The issue of sanctions or consequences of the law arises on both smaller and larger scales. On a smaller scale, Leviticus 20 describes the penalties for individuals who commit any of the prohibited sexual acts. Sanctions on a larger scale — concerning Israel as a corporate body and their holistic obedience — appear at both the beginning and end of Leviticus 18.[66] It is these larger-scale sanctions upon which I focus now. Leviticus 18 opens with warnings not to follow the practices of the Egyptians or Canaanites but to adhere to God's statutes, and this introductory section of the chapter concludes by stating the sanctions of the law in terms of a positive outcome: "You shall therefore keep my statutes and my rules; if a person does them, he shall live by them: I am the Lord" (18:5). At the end of the chapter is another warning about following other nations (18:24-30), but here the sanctions are stated negatively: "you shall keep my statutes and my rules and do none of these abominations . . . , lest the land vomit you out when you make it unclean, as it vomited out the nation that was before you. For everyone who does any of these abominations, the persons who do them shall be cut off from among their people" (18:26, 28-29). Leviticus 20:22 offers a similar warning. The focus is whether Israel will "do" (עשׂה) the things God commands (18:5, 26). If so, they will live; if not, they will be cut off from the people (as individuals) or vomited out of the land (as a nation). As God intervened in history periodically to bring devastating judgment against pagan nations for their egregious violations of the natural law, in anticipation of the final judgment of the last day (as considered in Chapters 3 and 4), so also God would send devastating judgment against Israel for their disobedience of the Mosaic law.

It is not as though Leviticus (and the Mosaic law) as a whole do not speak of God's gracious redemption for sinners, for they clearly and extensively do. But Leviticus 18:5 itself operates at a *protological* rather than *redemptive* level. It propounds the principle of justice that a person (or nation) must render obedience to God in order to receive the proffered reward; it does not propound the gracious redemptive principle that the proffered reward is given to those who are disobedient but forgiven (a contrast to be considered

66. Though there is probably nothing crucial to my argument at stake with this issue, I believe it is plausible to take "a person" (or traditionally, "the man") in 18:5 as corporate reference to Israel as a whole, especially in light of the use of the plural "you" earlier in the verse, as well as the threats of national expulsion from the land later in the chapter. For an argument along these lines, see Douglas C. Mohrmann, "Making Sense of Sex: A Study of Leviticus 18," *JSOT* 29 (Spring 2004): 75.

at length in Chapter 9). In the big picture God has graciously redeemed Israel from Egypt and given the entire Mosaic law subsequent to this event. Yet if my argument later in this chapter is correct, one of God's purposes in giving the law to redeemed Israel was to enable her to recapitulate the original probation of Adam and his protological experience of needing to be obedient in order to attain the blessing of life. The ultimate purpose of this was to show Israel, and through her the nations, that such obedience was impossible and that justification by faith in Christ was the only way. We should not be surprised, therefore, to find expressions of this protological principle of justice lodged within Israel's law, and in Leviticus 18:5 we find a classic example. This is how Paul interpreted Leviticus 18:5 (Gal. 3:10-12; Rom. 10:5): not as an expression of his gospel of salvation by grace alone but as an expression of the protological dynamic of the law in which obedience brings blessing and disobedience brings curse.[67] Paul's interpretation of Leviticus 18:5 was not novel, but followed that of Nehemiah 9:29 and Ezekiel 20:11, 13, 21.

67. Later in the chapter I will discuss Paul's use of Leviticus 18:5, particularly in Galatians 3:10-12. There Paul interprets "if a person does them, he shall live by them" as a statement of the law in distinction from his gospel message summarized by Habakkuk 2:4, "the righteous shall live by his faith." According to Paul these two OT statements express contrasting methods of justification: by one's own works or by faith, respectively. It is not uncommon, however, for Christian exegetes, even those who adhere to Paul's doctrine of justification (understood along Reformation lines), to see Leviticus 18:5 itself, in original context, as teaching precisely the same thing as the Pauline gospel of justification by faith and not by works. Gordon Wenham, for example, does this by writing as if Paul himself used Leviticus 18:5 to teach that obedience to the law is a fruit of justification rather than its cause; see Gordon J. Wenham, *The Book of Leviticus* (Grand Rapids: Eerdmans, 1979), p. 261. Yet Paul clearly appealed to Leviticus 18:5 (in Rom. 10:5 as well as Gal. 3:12) as an illustration of the way of justification to be rejected, as considered further below. John Murray's approach accurately recognizes this latter fact. But he regards this as something of a problem to be solved, since he reads Leviticus 18:5 itself as expressing the same dynamic as Paul's gospel: in the context of his gracious redemption of Israel from Egypt, God calls them to obey his law as a grateful response and to live in this path. Paul has used Leviticus 18:5 out of context, in other words. But Murray defends the apostle's use of the OT by explaining that Paul, for his own polemical purposes, cited the verse as his Pharisaic opponents were using it, not as Moses originally intended. See *The Epistle to the Romans* (Grand Rapids: Eerdmans, 1968), 2:249-51. I argue below that Paul does not intend to use Leviticus 18:5 as misinterpreted by his opponents, but in a way consistent with its original context. And since Leviticus 18:5, in original context, emphasized that blessing and curse are strictly tied to one's obedience or disobedience, Paul accurately contrasted its message with the message of his gospel of justification by faith, which is a justification of the *ungodly* (see Rom. 4:5). While Leviticus 18:5, in context, did not advocate a way of attaining *eschatological* life through obedience to the law, but a way of blessed life in the promised land of Canaan, Paul and other NT authors considered Israel's life in the promised land as a picture of life in

Leviticus contains much beautiful teaching about God's redemptive grace, which Christians believe points to Christ's work of atonement, especially in the sacrificial system described in its opening chapters. But Leviticus 18 offers not a single word of consolation that promises forgiveness upon disobedience. Only two outcomes are described: life for obedience, and being cut off from the people and expelled from the land for disobedience. One aspect of the text that supports this conclusion is that in holding out these options to Israel God analogizes their situation to the situation of the Canaanite inhabitants of the promised land, as discussed below. The Canaanites in the land violated God's will, and so they were vomited out; the Israelites are coming into the land, and if they violate God's will they will be vomited out (or if they obey it, they will live). Leviticus 18 wants Israel to see itself not as the recipients of a sweet forgiveness but as a people subject to severe temporal retribution if they disobey God's law. Leviticus has much comfort to offer, but chapter 18 is not the place to find it.

Neither is (most of) chapter 26, which unpacks in detail the offer of life and threat of curse from chapter 18. Leviticus 26:3-12 provides a list of blessings that will come "if you walk in my statutes and observe my commandments and do them" and then 26:14-39 provides a much longer, and frightening, list of curses God will impose "if you will not listen to me and will not do all these commandments." All of this, again, falls in a protological context: obedience must be rendered, and then blessing will ensue. The curses even have a talionic ring: they will be "sevenfold" (26:18, 21, 24, 28), that is, perfectly proportionate to the wrongs done. The protological cast of this chapter is heightened by the way the curses describe the dissolving of the creation order upheld by God after the fall (similar to the de-creation theme observed in Chapter 4). After the fall God promised Adam that he would eat from the ground through the sweat of his brow (Gen. 3:17-19), but here the ground turns to bronze and iron and yields nothing (Lev. 26:19-20). In the Noahic covenant God placed the animals in subjection to human beings and gave them as food (Gen. 9:2-3), but here the animals rise up against the Israelites and the Israelites end up eating

---

the original Edenic paradise and of eschatological life in the new creation. Hence Paul does not use his opponents' misinterpretation of Leviticus 18:5, but accurately interprets Leviticus 18:5, in light of its ultimate referent in God's larger purposes in the Mosaic covenant. In short, Leviticus 18:5 reminded Israel of Adam's original probation: Israel would enjoy temporal life in the land through obedience to God's law, as Adam would have enjoyed eschatological life in the new creation through obedience to God's law. Paul contrasts his gospel with Leviticus 18:5 in this sense; they represent two fundamentally different ways of attaining eschatological life, by faith in Christ or by one's own obedience.

each other (Lev. 26:22, 29). It is as if in Israel's rebellion the rightful curses of Adam's original rebellion are finally coming to fruition.

But Leviticus 26 also offers some helpful perspective for interpreting such passages and understanding how they fit into God's larger redemptive purposes in history. For one thing, 26:3-39 speaks only of curses and blessings in regard to earthly things of this present life. This is also the case in Leviticus 18.[68] What is being promised and threatened, therefore, is not eschatological life and death, but enjoyment or deprivation of earthly blessings in the land of Canaan.[69] This is why the NT can speak of sinful Mosaic-era saints as recipients of the same eschatological salvation by faith as NT believers (e.g., Rom. 4:6-8; Heb. 11:23-40), without contradicting the fact that the former at times endured earthly curses triggered by their disobedience. Leviticus 26 is also helpful for putting things in bigger perspective by holding out hope for forgiveness after Israel has suffered these earthly curses (26:40-45). The basis for this forgiveness, however, is not found in the Mosaic law itself, but in the covenant with Abraham, Isaac, and Jacob long before.[70] Here is more confirmation of Paul's sweeping interpretation of OT history in Galatians 3. The coming of Christ and justification by faith in him is the ultimate fulfillment of the Abrahamic covenant, and the Mosaic law came in between not to annul this larger plan but to bring his people for a time under the bondage of the protological law, part of whose purpose was to expose their guilt and self-helplessness.

---

68. See discussion in Wenham, *Leviticus,* p. 253; and Hartley, *Leviticus,* p. 293. As discussed in a previous footnote, this does not mean that Paul misuses Leviticus 18:5 when he quotes it in his argument about individuals' eschatological salvation. The earthly life and blessings promised under the Mosaic law were meant, in NT terminology, to be types and shadows of eschatological blessings to be won by Christ.

69. The significance of the land of *Canaan* is highlighted by the fact that though the Egyptians and Canaanites are both mentioned in 18:3 as bad role models for Israel, only the Canaanites get vomited out of their land as punishment for their sins (18:25, 28). This particular land was set aside for Israel, and the expulsion of its native inhabitants for their sins was prophesied long before (see Gen. 15:16). Insofar as Canaan was a type of the eschatological promised land, the judgment upon the Canaanites was a foreshadowing and sneak preview of the final judgment.

70. As Burnside puts it, when commenting on Exodus 32:13, "Moses apparently understands that any basis for resolving the breach between God and Israel must lie beyond the Sinaitic covenant." See *God, Justice, and Society,* p. 55. There is some question whether Leviticus 26:45 refers to the covenant at Sinai when it speaks of God remembering "the covenant with their forefathers, whom I brought out of the land of Egypt." Considered by itself, the phrase could be read that way, though I take it that this is not making a different point, or referring to a different covenant, from 26:42. For an argument that both the Abrahamic and Mosaic covenants are in view here, see Milgrom, *Leviticus 23–27,* pp. 2338-39.

This consideration of the sanctions of obedience and disobedience to the law in Leviticus 18 adds further confirmation of this chapter's thesis about the Mosaic law and natural law. The natural law promulgates not simply the requirements of God's will but also the just consequences of people's response. Chapter 4 considered how God occasionally sent pagan nations striking reminders of this, by bringing temporal local judgments against them for their egregious violations of the natural law, in anticipation of the final judgment. The Mosaic law likewise announces for Israel both God's demands and how he will bring temporal blessing or curse upon them based upon their obedience or disobedience. The law of Moses, in other words, in part echoes the protological dynamic of the natural law: obedience, then blessing; disobedience, then curse. This corroborates the claim that God designed the Mosaic law in part to reflect the natural law, in a way appropriate for the situation of OT Israel.

Israel under the Mosaic Law, the Nations under Natural Law

The third and final issue this study of Leviticus considers is the way chapters 18 and 20 analogize Israel's accountability to God under the Mosaic law with other nations' accountability to God apart from the Mosaic law. This is, perhaps, the most interesting natural law-related matter in these chapters. This provides further evidence that the natural law was actively at work among all people (the main focus of Part 1) and also that Israel's life under the Mosaic law, in part, resembled that of humanity in general under the natural law.

Leviticus 18 begins by warning Israel not to follow the ways of the Egyptians and Canaanites. Later it explains that God expelled the Canaanites from the land before Israel, for they became unclean "by all these" (18:24) — that is, by the sins recounted in previous verses. The land vomited them out because they "did all of these abominations" (18:27). These Canaanites suffered a fate similar to that of Sodom and the pagan nations judged in OT prophetic oracles (considered in Chapters 3-4), who stood condemned under the natural law. In this case, however, we know exactly why *these people* suffered a drastic recompense for their sin, in anticipation of the final judgment, rather than continuing to enjoy God's forbearance under the Noahic covenant: they inhabited the land God had set aside for his people Israel (see Gen. 15:13-21) in order to advance his special purposes in the history of salvation (see Gal. 3:15-29).[71]

---

71. An often-troubling moral question arising from the Mosaic law and the fate of the Canaanites is *cherem* warfare, that is, God's commands to Israel to exterminate the native

In this final section of Leviticus 18 God says he will bring the very same judgment upon Israel if they commit the same sins as the Canaanites: "lest the land vomit you out when you make it unclean, as it vomited out the nation that was before you" (18:28). Leviticus 20:22-23 presents a similar, though more concise, analogy between Israel and the Canaanites.[72] The judgment that will befall Israel for their sins is like the judgment that befell the Canaanites for their similar sins (which in turn was like the judgments against Sodom and the pagan nations condemned by the OT prophets, which in their turn anticipated the final judgment coming upon the whole world). Israel, in falling into the sins described in Leviticus 18 and 20 and being judged for it, was a kind of microcosm of the nations under the natural law.

Leviticus 18:3 gives a general warning not to do as the Egyptians and Canaanites do. Clearly this cannot be taken as absolute. The borrowing of ANE legal material I considered in the previous section offers one clear reason not to believe that Israel was to reject their neighbors' customs holistically.[73]

---

inhabitants of Canaan. I offer a few comments here, and revisit the issue in Chapter 10. God's judgment against the Canaanites, I believe, ought to be seen in a similar light to God's judgment against Sodom and the pagan nations condemned in the OT prophetic oracles. These nations *were* very sinful and deserved divine judgment. The fact that these nations suffered God's devastating temporal judgment does not mean they were necessarily the most sinful of peoples. Unpleasant as it is to consider, in the final equation *all* peoples deserve God's wrath because of their sin (see Romans 1:18–3:20 and Chapter 5) and will in fact endure this wrath at the final judgment unless reconciled with God. God's choosing to bring catastrophic judgment against some particular peoples (even while forbearing with their sinful neighbors) does these peoples no injustice. In light of these considerations, and my arguments in Chapter 2, it should be evident that God's commands to Israel to exterminate the Canaanites can in no way be used as a model for Christians (or Americans, or anyone else) today to wage holy war on those perceived as enemies. God's forbearance with the world under the Noahic covenant, not his occasional devastating anticipations of the final judgment, is normative for public life. Israel received a unique command from God — dependent upon their distinctive covenantal status, the unique status of their land, and God's purposes for this era of redemptive history — that does not apply to any people or nation today.

72. In light of such evidence, Burnside writes: "Leviticus 20 does not present a purely ritual understanding of the harm that results from certain forms of sexual behavior. Nor is this understanding limited to the internal cult of Israel. Instead, it is presented as a universal understanding of harm that applies to all." See *God, Justice, and Society,* p. 359. Compare also Schenker, "What Connects," p. 177: this text "implies that these rules are known to all people" — the author regarded these rules as "common sense" and "obvious" and thus "compulsory for all men."

73. Regarding Leviticus 18:30 Milgrom comments: "Perhaps the laws and norms of the nations are described as *huqqot*, not as *mispatim* 'jurisprudence', because obviously much of the latter is acceptable." See *Leviticus 17–22,* p. 1583.

Apparently there is something about the Egyptians' and Canaanites' sexual practices that triggers this exhortation to reject their ways. There seems to be good reason for this. Biblically speaking, Egypt had a reputation for sexual licentiousness, evident in texts like Ezekiel 16:26, and there is biblical precedent for homosexual conduct among the Canaanites (Gen. 19:5-8; and perhaps 9:20-26). Extra-biblical evidence does not give an entirely clear picture of the sexual customs of Israel's neighbors, but we know that marriage between siblings occurred in the Egyptian royal family and other consanguineous marriages happened outside royal circles.[74] Other ANE societies banned some acts of sodomy, though the absolute ban of Leviticus 18 and 20 seems unusual.[75] There is also evidence of bestiality found in Egyptian, Canaanite, and Hittite sources. The Hittite laws, in fact, prohibited some forms of bestiality while permitting others (with horses and mules).[76] This provides at least some basic evidence that important concerns of Leviticus 18 and 20 — incest, homosexual conduct, and bestiality — were practiced among Israel's neighbors.

But these chapters do more than say that Israel's neighbors committed sexual sins that Israel should not follow. They also assert, in the case of the Canaanites, that they were held accountable for these practices and therefore judged. This implies that they knew what they were doing was wrong. Such a conclusion seems necessary if we are to avoid the implication that God was unjust in condemning and expelling the Canaanites. I do not believe Leviticus 18 and 20 intended, at least as their primary concern, to vindicate God's ways with the Canaanites, but indirectly they offer a hint in this direction.[77] Since the Canaanites had no access to the Mosaic law, God must have judged them on the basis of their knowledge of the natural law. They disobeyed the natural law, but at some level were not ignorant of their sin. They *knew* "God's decree that those who practice such things deserve to die" (Rom. 1:32). The Canaanites had fair warning, if only through the silent testimony of conscience. The Israelites now had more than fair warning. God supplemented the testimony of conscience with clearer instruction from his word. And if they do as the Canaanites did they will receive exactly the same penalty: get vomited from the land.

At this point a qualification seems to be in order: though Leviticus 18 and 20 at least teach that God held the Canaanites accountable for committing all

---

74. See Milgrom, *Leviticus 17–22*, pp. 1518-20; and Wenham, *Leviticus*, p. 251.

75. See Milgrom, *Leviticus 17–22*, p. 1566.

76. See Wenham, *Leviticus 17–22*, p. 252; and Hartley, *Leviticus*, p. 297.

77. Schenker, on the other hand, does see Leviticus 18 and 20 as a defense of the Canaanite expulsion; see "What Connects," p. 177.

the *kinds* of sins prohibited in these chapters, they should not necessarily be read as teaching that God held the Canaanites accountable for committing all the *particular* sins prohibited here. These chapters assert the universal character of sexual immorality, and some writers' attempt to limit the scope of the prohibitions very narrowly does not do justice to the text.[78] On the other hand, God gave Leviticus uniquely to Israel, and as I observed with respect to the CC in Exodus, even matters legislated in the Mosaic law that seem most universally relevant are shaped by Israel's particular circumstances.[79] Without sensitivity to this fact readers can all too easily universalize Leviticus 18 and 20 in questionable ways.[80]

In defense of this claim I offer a few reasons for taking the statement that the Canaanites "did all of these abominations" as general rather than as a reference to each and every action condemned in Leviticus 18 and 20. One reason is the interesting fact that the patriarchs of Genesis violated a number of the incest provisions of Leviticus 18 and 20 — obvious examples being Abraham marrying his half-sister and Jacob marrying women who were sisters.[81] Not only does the text of Genesis not condemn them for this, but it even indicates approval of their general practice of marrying close relatives. It is Esau, from one perspective seeming to do best by marrying Hittite women, whom the text portrays as sinning. Furthermore, they practiced this incest in the promised land, precisely the focus of action in Leviticus 18 and 20. I do not assert this dogmatically, but there seems to be something relative about the prohibited character of incest. That people should not marry those who are too closely related to them seems a sound universal rule in accord with the natural moral order. But how close is too close? Not marrying one who is

---

78. I think here of Milgrom's comments pertaining to homosexual conduct in Leviticus 20; see *Leviticus 17–22*, pp. 1750, 1786-88.

79. As noted, in Chapter 10 I discuss again the significance of natural law for difficult questions concerning the general applicability of the Mosaic law.

80. Hartley may provide an example in *Leviticus*, pp. 300-301, where he concludes his comments on Leviticus 18 by stating that people today need to be ecologically responsible or the lands in which we live will vomit us out. Ecological abuse of any land is indeed bad, but Leviticus 18 speaks of expulsion from a *holy* land by a *supernatural* judgment of God, for *sexual* sins. It is not at all clear what this teaches about the consequences of environmental degradation in contemporary societies.

81. For studies of the connections between Leviticus 18 and 20 and the Genesis narratives, and theories about the implications for interpreting the former (with which I do not always agree), see Gershon Hepner, "Abraham's Incestuous Marriage with Sarah: A Violation of the Holiness Code," *VT* 53 (2003): 143-55; and Calum M. Carmichael, *Law, Legend, and Incest in the Bible: Leviticus 18–20* (Ithaca, NY: Cornell University Press, 1997), chaps. 1-2.

too close presupposes the availability of spouses who are not near relatives. Such spouses are sometimes unavailable, and the patriarchs' situation offers an example: they needed to procreate, but marrying pagan neighbors would compromise the integrity of their own community. In many social-political circumstances, in fact, there may be need to balance marrying too close and marrying too far away. When Israel entered the promised land, Leviticus 18 and 20 set boundaries for what was too close, but other passages set limits upon what was too far away (e.g., Num. 25:1-9; 36:5-12). While God apparently held the Canaanites generally accountable for incest through the natural law, the balance struck in the Mosaic law may not have been the precise standard to which God held them.

A second reason for taking the condemnation of the Canaanites as general rather than precise is the connection between 18:24-30 and 18:1-5. Structurally these passages belong together, as an epilogue and prologue framing the chapter. We have been reflecting on the way 18:24-30 announces the accountability of the Canaanites for doing "all of these abominations," referring back to the list of sexual offenses in 18:6-23. But in doing so we should compare how 18:1-5 speaks of the Egyptians and Canaanites and says to Israel: "You shall not do as they do." As noted above, this latter warning cannot be interpreted as comprehensive. The Egyptians and Canaanites ate, slept, and plowed their fields, but Israel was not thereby prohibited from these acts. This was a general warning, requiring some further reasoning to put into practice responsibly. But if this warning in the prologue is to be interpreted generally, rather than technically and precisely, we have good reason to read the epilogue in the same way. In sum, I believe we should not automatically identify each prohibited practice in Leviticus 18 and 20 as a natural law offense, without further argument. God held the Canaanites accountable for the kinds of things prohibited in these chapters, not necessarily each and every act.

I also take it that the Canaanites were held accountable for not enforcing the kinds of penalties required in Leviticus 18 and 20. It must be noted that in these chapters, when read together, God does not simply say he will destroy Israel for one individual person's violation of these requirements. Otherwise there would be no point in recording the civil penalties the people themselves were to impose upon perpetrators. It seems, instead, that God would expel Israel from the land if they not only practiced these things but also failed to punish the people who did so. By exercising individual judgment themselves on the guilty they would avoid corporate judgment from God. Presumably the same dynamic was at work in God's dealings with the Canaanites. This would be consistent with Genesis 9:6, in which administering judicial penalties for intrahuman wrongs is a key part of the minimalist ethic of the natural law, reflecting God's Noahic purpose to maintain the existence of human society, not to create a perfect society. This would also be consistent with Romans 1:32, where Paul condemns the nations for not only doing things they knew were against the natural order but also for approving those who do so. Yet if the Israelites' accountability under the prohibitions of Leviticus 18 was of a general nature, presumably this was also the case for the penalties of Leviticus 20. That is, the fact that Israel was to impose the *death penalty* on those who broke these commands does not necessarily mean God held the Canaanites responsible for this.[82]

These reflections on the analogy between the Israelites and the Canaanites lead to a twofold conclusion. First, we have further confirmation of the reality of natural law operative in the fallen world and accessible to all people, along the lines argued in Part 1. This is because the Canaanites were held accountable for violations of sexual propriety that were inconsistent with the natural law, yet they had no knowledge of the Mosaic law. Second, Leviticus 18 and 20 also confirm my claim that the Mosaic law was, in part, an application of the natural law in a way fit for Israel's unique situation. Israel's moral situation under the Mosaic law in many ways reflected the situation of their pagan neighbors under the natural law.

The Law and Wisdom: Deuteronomy 4:1-8

This section turns to a third and final text from the Mosaic law. Deuteronomy 4:1-8 is a helpful selection to consider alongside the CC of Exodus and Leviticus 18 and 20 because it deals with many of the same issues yet approaches them from a very different angle. If the CC involved the *borrowing* of legal material from the pagan nations, and Leviticus 18 and 20 called for Israel to *reject* many of the practices of the pagan nations, Deuteronomy 4:1-8, we might say, exhorts Israel to *impress* the pagan nations by their obedience to the law. Yet in the end the implications for the natural law questions being considered in this chapter are remarkably similar. I look first at the exhortations and promised consequences in 4:1-5 and then at the impact of their obedience upon the foreign nations in 4:6-8. I argue that this text adds supplemental evidence to the idea that the natural law was at work among all people (as discussed in Part 1)

---

82. Again, see Chapter 10 for more discussion of natural law and the general applicability of the Mosaic law.

and to the claim that the Mosaic law served, in part, to republish the content and sanctions of the natural law in a way fitting for OT Israel.

The Exhortations and Consequences in Deuteronomy 4:1-5

Deuteronomy 4 begins by calling Israel to obey God's commands in anticipation of their long-awaited entrance into the promised land and by clearly stating the consequences of obedience. In these opening verses, 4:1-5, I highlight the protological justice expressed here, in echo of the natural law, and how, in light of Deuteronomy as a whole, Israel's experience of this justice resembled that of the pagan nations.

One of the most striking things about this text when one comes to it after studying Leviticus 18 and 20 is the similarity between Deuteronomy 4:1-5 and Leviticus 18:1-5. As in the latter passage, the former calls Israel to listen to God's "statutes" (חק) and "commands" (משפט) and to "do" (עשה) them in order to "live" (חי). Deuteronomy 4:1-5 also emphasizes that Israel should pursue this course in order to enter the "land" (4:1) and as their standard in the "land" (4:5), as in Leviticus 18:24-30, where tenure in the land was the focal point of the sanctions recounted there. Additionally, the "life" promised for obedience in Leviticus 18:5 was earthly life and blessing. So too Deuteronomy 4:4 states, "you who held fast to the Lord your God are all alive today," indicating that the promise to "live," if they are obedient, directly concerns the extension of this present life. What we seem to find, therefore, is another clear statement of the principle of protological justice explored throughout the present volume and expressed so forcefully in Leviticus 18:5: obey first and then receive a fitting reward. Deuteronomy indeed also reminds Israel that they would not even be in this relationship with God in the first place had it not been for his grace toward them as a stubborn people (9:4-6), and it promises a new initiative of grace after their inevitable failure and endurance of divine curse (see 30:1-10). But here in 4:1-5 the point is not for Israel to take comfort from God's forgiveness but to learn the connection between obedience and life and between disobedience and death. This protological principle of justice, as argued in Part 1, is precisely what the natural law propounds.

As the concise statement of this principle in Leviticus was emphatically confirmed later in that book (particularly in Leviticus 26), so also its concise affirmation in Deuteronomy 4:1-5 is constantly repeated throughout this final book of the OT law. To quote all the examples would be tedious and unnecessary; to cite all the examples (by my fallible reckoning) should make the point:

4:25-27, 40; 5:16, 29, 33; 6:1-3, 13-18, 24-25; 7:4, 9-15; 8:1, 19-20; 10:12-13; 11:8-9, 13-28; 12:25, 28; 13:17-18; 15:4-6, 10; 16:20; 17:18-20; 25:15; 26:14-15; chapters 27–28 as a whole; 29:9, 24-25; 30:9-10, 16-20; 31:18, 29; 32:46-47. With a touch of poetic justice that should be appreciated by readers of the present volume, God even announces a talionic punishment to be inflicted upon his disobedient people (32:21). In short, Deuteronomy tells Israel: obey God's law and enjoy previously unimaginable blessings of prosperity, fertility, peace, and international domination; disobey God's law and suffer hideous curses of famine, infertility, war, subjection to enemies, and ultimately expulsion from the land. In *these* texts God does not instruct Israel to find their peace and security in his merciful grace, but in their obedient conduct. As Deuteronomy 6:24-25 memorably puts it, doing the Lord's statutes and fearing him "will be righteousness for us." Or in some of Moses' final utterances, the word they must be careful to do will be "your very life" (32:46-47).[83]

It is perhaps necessary to emphasize the point again: their obedience was not their way to eschatological life (that is never promised), but to blessed life in the land. In broader perspective, we will see shortly, their probation in the land was in part a recapitulation of Adam's probation in Eden. By administering this probation the Mosaic law prepared Israel for the coming of their Messiah.

Also relevant here is that Deuteronomy itself, with brash insensitivity to the Israelites' self-esteem, predicts Israel's failure to obey and the inevitable triggering of the curses (30:1). In NT perspective (e.g., Galatians 3) God never intended the Mosaic law to be the end of the story. The law fulfilled its divine purpose not in Israel's obedience but ultimately in its disobedience. It locked them up and held them captive until the revelation of Christ and the clear manifestation of justification by faith. This makes sense in the bigger picture explored later in this chapter. For Israel to recapitulate the experience of Adam effectively, the result of their probation under God's law must be failure, not success.

It is also significant that Israel's experience of God's curse following disobedience was to resemble the experience of rebellious pagan nations. With a scent of Leviticus 18 and 20 in the air, Deuteronomy 8:20 predicts: "Like the

---

83. I speak here in broad terms about how the curses and blessings function in Deuteronomy. Sometimes they function in somewhat different ways, when God has different motivations for bringing Israel into certain circumstances; e.g., God's humbling Israel in the wilderness not as a punishment but as a means of testing (Deut. 8:2). For a discussion (with which I do not entirely agree) of some of this complexity in Deuteronomy, see John G. Gammie, "The Theology of Retribution in the Book of Deuteronomy," *CBQ* 32 (1970): 10-11.

nations that the Lord makes to perish before you, so shall you perish, because you would not obey the voice of the Lord your God." Perhaps even more penetrating is the later comparison of God's judgment upon Israel to his judgment upon Sodom. After God judges Israel, people will see "the whole land burned out with brimstone and salt, nothing sown and nothing growing, where no plant can sprout, an overthrow like that of Sodom and Gomorrah, Admah, and Zeboiim, which the Lord overthrew in his anger and wrath" (29:23). In the eyes of Deuteronomy, Israel's experience under God's law appallingly resembles that of pagan nations under the natural law. As Sodom's overthrow was a foretaste of the final judgment coming upon the whole earth (2 Pet. 2:6), so apparently was Israel's.

In short, by echoing the natural law's standard of protological justice and thereby securing Israel's resemblance to the nations under natural law, Deuteronomy 4:1-5, in the context of Deuteronomy as a whole, corroborates two important aspects of this chapter's conclusions about the relationship of natural law and Mosaic law.

Impressing the Nations: Deuteronomy 4:6-8

The next part of the text, Deuteronomy 4:6-8, raises intriguing questions about natural law because it associates obedience to the Mosaic law with wisdom, and not merely a parochial Israelite wisdom but one recognizable by the pagan nations. God calls Israel to impress foreign nations through their adherence to his law. By investigating these verses I argue that one purpose of the Mosaic law was to instill a universally perceptible wisdom in the Israelites, and that this presupposes an organic similarity between the effects of the Mosaic law in Israel and the effects of the natural law among the pagan nations.

These verses begin: "Keep them [God's statutes and rules] and do them, for that will be your wisdom and your understanding in the sight of the peoples, who, when they hear all these statutes, will say, 'Surely this great nation is a wise and understanding people'" (4:6). A quick read of this verse may leave the impression that the *law itself* is their wisdom, but it actually says that their wisdom will consist in their *doing* of the law.[84] The thing that will be their

---

84. Most commentators make the same point. See e.g. Peter C. Craigie, *The Book of Deuteronomy* (Grand Rapids: Eerdmans, 1976), p. 131; J. Ridderbos, *Deuteronomy*, trans. and ed. Ed M. van der Maas (Grand Rapids: Regency Reference Library, 1984), p. 83; S. R. Driver, *A Critical and Exegetical Commentary on Deuteronomy* (Edinburgh: T. & T. Clark, 1895), p. 65; Duane L. Christensen, *Deuteronomy 1:1–21:9*, rev. ed. (Nashville: Thomas Nelson, 2001), p. 80;

wisdom is referred to in the singular ("*that* [הוא] will be your wisdom"), which would be inappropriate if the "statutes and rules" (4:5) themselves were in view. This point is reinforced by the fact that wisdom is something subjective. Though Proverbs 1-9 famously anthropomorphizes wisdom, it is ultimately a virtue characterizing those who have proper perception of the natural moral order and have the skill to live successfully within it. Thus, it makes much more sense to identify learning the law and living in obedience to it as "wisdom" than to identify the law itself as "wisdom." Yet this distinction between the law and obeying it should not be overdrawn. Deuteronomy 4:6 indicates that the foreign peoples will in fact "hear all these statutes," not simply observe Israel's behavior, and this prompts their words of wonder about Israel's wisdom and understanding. Israel would hardly become wise through obeying God's law if the content of the law was not righteous and instructive about wisdom's ways.

Deuteronomy 4:6-8 concludes with two rhetorical questions: "For what great nation is there that has a god so near to it as the Lord our God is to us, whenever we call upon him? And what great nation is there, that has statutes and rules so righteous as all this law that I set before you today?" (4:7-8). Though these are Moses' questions to Israel, the way they follow 4:6 indicates that they provide rationale for the nations' conclusion about Israel and her law. In other words, the nations will marvel at Israel's wisdom and understanding because they will see God's nearness when Israel cries to him and will recognize the righteousness of Israel's laws. These two rhetorical questions, then, confirm the interpretation of 4:6 above. The nations will observe Israel's conduct and the astounding blessings it brings (4:7) and will be compelled to conclude that their law is righteous (4:8).

My claim about 4:6-8 amounts to the following. When Israel obeys the law, God will bless them consistently and abundantly. The nations will look on, knowing that a wise and understanding life ought to bring prosperity, but also recognizing that so often in life things do not turn out as one would expect. But they watch Israel and notice that when they observe their law they flourish consistently and exceedingly. Israel, they conclude, must be *really* wise and understanding, and their law must be perfectly calibrated to bring

---

Patrick D. Miller, *Deuteronomy* (Louisville: Westminster John Knox, 1990), p. 55; and Georg Braulik, *The Theology of Deuteronomy* (Richland Hills, TX: BIBAL, 1994), p. 9. Moshe Weinfeld associates the law itself with wisdom in this verse, but tellingly notes this is "somewhat paradoxical," since the laws were given by God but were identified with Israel's wisdom; see *Deuteronomy and the Deuteronomic School* (Oxford: Clarendon, 1972), pp. 255-56. Weinfeld appears to have changed his view somewhat in his later commentary; see *Deuteronomy 1–11: A New Translation with Introduction and Commentary* (New York: Doubleday, 1991), p. 202.

success. The nations do not sit down in a library and study the Mosaic law in the abstract. They see it in action — in Israel's faithful performance and God's faithful blessings in response — and face the inevitable conclusion that this law must be very righteous.

The soundness of my claim rests in some measure on the interpretation of "a god so near" in 4:7. It may seem a strange thing, at first thought, that what would initially strike the foreign nations about Israel is that their God is very near them. What exactly is this nearness and how exactly would the nations recognize it? Presumably they would not recognize it through the miraculous deeds God performed in bringing Israel out of Egypt. This did impress and intimidate foreign nations for a while (e.g., Josh. 2:9-11), but the nearness of God at issue in Deuteronomy 4:7 concerns what is going to happen after Israel is in the land and their relationship to God then. It seems unlikely, in addition, that this nearness of God refers to what we might call "spiritual" blessings — an inner joy produced by piety or the presence of God in their worship.[85] Israel would surely experience such blessings if they obeyed the law, but it is doubtful that foreign nations would have the ability to perceive these things. What the foreign nations would be able to perceive are outward blessings, the sort of earthly prosperity that Deuteronomy repeatedly promises for obedience.[86] Pagan peoples would be no judge of God's secret nearness to Israel in worship, but they would have little trouble seeing and appreciating bountiful harvests, fertile wives, vibrant health, and success in warfare — and these are precisely the benefits that accompany obedience, according to Deuteronomy. These things, I suggest, constitute the nearness of God that Israel's neighbors would perceive.

There may be two subtle hints in the language of 4:6-8 that reinforce this conclusion. First, Walter Brueggemann has observed that the phrase "wise and understanding" in 4:6 is unexpected in Deuteronomy, for it is the language of "pragmatic, prudential ethics, the ethics of those who are wise in the use of power."[87] These are traits displayed by Joseph in ruling pagan Egypt (Gen. 41:33, 39) and by Solomon in ruling Israel (1 Kgs. 3:12) — the latter in a way that the nations indeed admired (1 Kgs. 10:1-13, 24; cf. 2 Chron. 2:12). What the nations seem to be hailing, therefore, is Israel's economic and geopolitical

---

85. Something along these lines seems suggested by Craigie, *Deuteronomy,* p. 131; Weinfeld, *Deuteronomy,* pp. 1-11, 202; and Driver, *Deuteronomy,* p. 65.

86. Among those favoring this sort of interpretation, see e.g. Walter Brueggemann, *Deuteronomy* (Nashville: Abingdon, 2001), p. 52; Miller, *Deuteronomy,* p. 55; and Braulik, *The Theology of Deuteronomy,* p. 17.

87. Brueggemann, *Deuteronomy,* p. 52.

success, not the wisdom of an ivory-tower sage or a pious monk. The second hint confirming my interpretation regards Lohfink's observation about Israel's *calling* to God in 4:7. Lohfink notes that the only other times in Deuteronomy when people cry out (קרא) to God are when the poor appeal to him when mistreated by the more prosperous, who are then held "guilty of sin" (15:9; 24:15).[88] Deuteronomy 4:7 may suggest, therefore, that God will be swift to uphold the justice of his law, particularly in defense of the vulnerable prone to slip into poverty. If there would be massive flouting of rules concerning the poor (which there was), then massive judgment would come upon Israel (which it did), and the nations obviously would not be admiring their wisdom, per 4:6. But perhaps 4:7 indicates that, within a setting of widespread obedience to the law, God will be quick to remedy even the small beginnings of poverty — he will be near when the vulnerable call to him. Ideally there was to be no poverty in Israel (15:4), and one can only imagine how amazed the nations would be in seeing this.

And yet, is it really plausible to think that the foreign nations could make the connection between earthly prosperity and wisdom? A complete answer requires the consideration of Proverbs offered in the next chapter. Suffice it to say for now that though there are unique aspects of the wisdom of God's chosen covenant people, Scripture also portrays wisdom as an international phenomenon. And since wisdom in a general sense involves the ability to forge a flourishing life within the bounds of the natural moral order, if there is one thing about their observation of Israel that should have made sense to the nations it would have been that extreme earthly flourishing manifests magnificent wisdom. What the nations looking on would likely not fully understand is that Israel's wisdom and prosperity in obeying her laws could not be ultimately explained by their having masterfully figured out the natural moral order per se. Rather, their experience of obedience and blessing was the result of the covenant at Sinai in which God promised to guarantee the connection between good living and earthly flourishing in a way that only roughly and unevenly holds true in the world at large, as sustained under the Noahic covenant.

To return to broader themes of this chapter, Israel's moral experience under Moses was meant, in part, to resemble that of the nations under the natural law: obedience to God's law truly is to bring blessing, and disobedience to his law is to bring curse. It is interesting that the nations appear again in Deuteronomy 29:24-28, wondering why Israel has suffered a fate like Sodom's.

88. Lohfink, "Poverty in the Laws," p. 46.

This time the nations really are confused. Israel has acted as they themselves have acted (indeed, that is much the point), yet Israel has suffered harm far worse than they have experienced. What 29:24-28 does is explain to the nations the covenantal system under Moses. Both blessing for obedience and curse for disobedience will be exaggerated in Israel's experience (in comparison to how things tend to work under Noah), but this strict connection between works and consequences is not ultimately an exaggeration, for it makes manifest ahead of time the judgment of the last day that was earned, though not imposed, on the day of Adam's rebellion.[89]

Natural Law Implications

What are the implications for natural law of this interpretation of Deuteronomy 4:6-8? I mention two, the first regarding the work of natural law among the nations and the second concerning the relationship of natural law and Mosaic law.

First, as just discussed, the pagan nations, for all their sinfulness, had enough moral insight to recognize — had Israel been obedient — that something magnificent was going on in Israel. As explored in the next chapter, wisdom entails the perception of the natural moral order and the connection between right living and earthly flourishing. And this reality was not completely unfamiliar to the other nations. They had insight to realize that there was something profoundly righteous in the laws of Israel. Even while it served ultimately to condemn them, the testimony of the natural law evidently had some positive effects among the pagan nations, as argued in Part 1. Along these lines, Deuteronomy 4:6-8 provides further appreciation for why the Covenant Code of Exodus could utilize the laws of ancient Near Eastern peoples.

In addition to the nations' insight into the natural law, Deuteronomy also reminds readers of the nations' accountability before God under the natural

---

89. If this analysis is correct, then Ridderbos's claim that Deuteronomy 4:6-8 involved Israel's "missionary task" to the nations, albeit in a veiled way, seems misguided unless seriously nuanced; see *Deuteronomy,* p. 83. Deuteronomy 4:6-8 is about the law, not the gospel. In light of arguments below, it was to show the nations how things work under the covenant with Adam, not how things work under the covenant of grace with Christ. But there is indirect missionary service that Israel's actions before the nations could display. Israel's experience could, and ultimately did, manifest the need for obedience to God's law and the impossibility of people rendering it by their own efforts, and hence pointed to the good news of Christ's work on their behalf.

law. In Deuteronomy 25 God encourages the Israelites to remember how the Amalekites attacked them in the wilderness (cf. Exod. 17:8-16), so that when they enter the promised land they might "blot out the memory of Amalek from under heaven" (Deut. 25:19). Moses justifies this severe commission by noting how Amalek fought them in an egregiously immoral fashion, "when you were faint and weary, and cut off your tail, those who were lagging behind you." What could explain this breach of, we might say, international law? Amalek "did not fear God" (25:18). It is remarkable (though consistent with my broader argument) that while Deuteronomy exhorts Israel numerous times to fear "the Lord" — using his special covenant name יהוה — only here is the fear of *God* mentioned. Israel must fear Yahweh, but the foreign nations are expected to fear God. The object of fear is one and the same, but Israel and the nations are in different kinds of relationship with him. Here, then, we find another example of that "fear of God" observed in Genesis and Exodus that signals a kind of basic respect for universal moral norms among pagan peoples (see Chapter 3).[90] The Amalekites did not display this fear of God, and they would be held accountable for it.

Second, my analysis of Deuteronomy 4:6-8 has implications for understanding the relationship of Mosaic law and natural law. The fact that the Mosaic law is able to instill a wisdom in Israel as they respond in obedience has serious ramifications for the overall claims of this chapter. If the Mosaic law instills a wisdom that is recognizable by the foreign nations, then whatever its distinctive aspects, this wisdom must not have been wholly unique but bore significant organic similarities to the wisdom that pagans were able to gain (however partial and corrupted) through their observation and experience of the natural moral order. In this way we see still further corroboration of the thesis that a purpose of the Mosaic law was to promulgate the substance of the natural law, in a way distinctively geared for OT Israel.

Legitimate questions may arise at this point. If, as I argued above, what the nations would particularly recognize were the extreme blessings consequent upon Israel's obedience, then is it perhaps overreaching to conclude that the substance of the wisdom instilled through the Mosaic law is organically related to the substance of the wisdom instilled through the natural law? Might it not be, rather, that Israel through obedience would gain a unique wisdom, though its blessed consequences would be parallel to the consequences of a natural law wisdom? Ultimately I believe that such questions, though fairly posed, do not dislodge the conclusion of the previous paragraph. For one

90. See also Weinfeld, *Deuteronomy and the Deuteronomic School*, pp. 274-76.

thing, the very fact that pagan nations could recognize that Israel's blessings — good crops, numerous offspring, etc. — were wonderful things, and the evidence of wise living under righteous laws, says something significant. Recognition that things like eating well and having children are truly good is itself an insight into human nature and the purpose of human existence in a world like ours. The mere ability to make meaningful connections between behavior, consequences, and laws is evidence of the power of the natural law at work among human beings generally (despite their sin).

One other important factor, however, seems to demonstrate the organic connection between gaining wisdom under the natural law and gaining wisdom under the Mosaic law: the remarkable similarities between Deuteronomy and Proverbs, with respect to both their purpose and substance. The genres of the books — legal literature and wisdom literature — are quite different. Yet some very interesting studies have identified numerous points of correspondence between the two books.[91] This evidence, which I can only summarize, indicates that both how Deuteronomy trains people to live and the moral substance of Deuteronomy resemble what we find in Proverbs. (I am assuming here that one of the main purposes of the canonical book of Proverbs is to instruct God's people how to understand the natural moral order.)

In regard to how people acquire wisdom, Deuteronomy has a strong didactic character. Though it is a book of law, and even functions as a quasi-constitution for the people of Israel, it is not the typical constitution or law code, insofar as it encourages parents to instruct their children, seeks to instill "discipline," uses motivation clauses, and like matters.[92] Furthermore, as Assnat Bartor argues, Deuteronomy (and other parts of the Mosaic law to some degree) has a powerful way of drawing readers into situations that mimic those of everyday life, thereby compelling readers to identify with what is described.

91. See especially Weinfeld, *Deuteronomy and the Deuteronomic School,* Part 3; and William P. Brown, "The Law and the Sages: A Reexamination of *Tora* in Proverbs," in *Constituting the Community: Studies on the Polity of Ancient Israel in Honor of S. Dean McBride Jr.,* ed. John T. Strong and Steven Shawn (Winona Lake, IN: Eisenbrauns, 2005), pp. 251-80. Both of these sources include extensive citations of verses from Deuteronomy and Proverbs.

92. S. Dean McBride Jr. has argued against ascribing a strong didactic character to Deuteronomy, preferring instead to see it as Israel's constitution; see "Polity of the Covenant People: The Book of Deuteronomy," in *Constituting the Community,* pp. 17-33. Patrick D. Miller offers a balanced and persuasive argument that the choice between Deuteronomy as constitution or didactic instruction is a false one, and that part of its genius lies in powerfully combining both elements; see "Constitution or Instruction? The Purpose of Deuteronomy," in *Constituting the Community,* pp. 125-41.

It also has a powerful way of provoking interest in the interior life, thereby challenging readers to reflect on the connection between the inner life and exterior behavior. All of this, she says, draws Deuteronomy's readers more deeply into the human situation. Deuteronomy does not simply recite a cold list of legal rules.[93] In all of these respects Deuteronomy has striking similarities to the way that Proverbs goes about its task, evidence of which the next chapter explores. The substantive similarities between Deuteronomy and Proverbs are even more striking. Both commend the need for wisdom for those with political or judicial authority and have strong doctrines of retribution. The "fear of the Lord" motif pervades each book. Both speak about moving landmarks and carrying unjust weights, the relationship of masters and slaves, treatment of the poor, the significance of vows, and justice, including themes of bribery, credibility of witnesses, and impartial judgment.

In many matters concerning method and substance, therefore, Deuteronomy and Proverbs bear remarkable similarities. This provides confirmation that the wisdom Deuteronomy hoped to instill in Israel through the law is organically connected to the wisdom that Proverbs aimed to instill in Israel through guiding its experience and observation of everyday life under the natural moral order, through which experience and observation it was encouraged to learn even from non-Israelite sources. In this we have further evidence that one purpose of God in giving the Mosaic law to Israel was to republish the natural law in a form appropriate for his OT covenant people.

Israel's Recapitulation of Adam's Experience

From these texts in Exodus, Leviticus, and Deuteronomy, I have argued that God designed the Mosaic law, in part, to communicate the substance and the sanctions of the natural law, in a way fitting for the unique identity of OT Israel. In doing so, I have noted that the Mosaic law reflects a protological moral standard and ensures that Israel's moral experience resembles that of its pagan neighbors in many respects. But to this point I have not offered theological explanation for this. Before turning to Paul's interpretation of the Mosaic law, which will provide a great deal of such theological explanation, I address one issue emerging from within the books of the Torah themselves: in bringing Israel under the Mosaic law God intended Israel to recapitulate the experience of Adam's creation, probation, and fall. Under the Mosaic law, in other words,

---

93. See especially Bartor, *Reading Law as Narrative*, chaps. 3-4.

Israel exemplified the great predicament of the whole human race, namely, the condition of being sinners liable to the judgment of God.

This recapitulation is evident in the many ways in which the pattern of Israel's history mimics Adam's story in Genesis 1–3.[94] First, God brought forth Israel through the waters in order to bring them to a good and prosperous land, as he had brought forth Adam from the original watery chaos (Gen. 1:2) and placed him in the Garden of Eden (Gen. 2:8). The OT looks back to the Exodus as the time of Israel's birth as a nation, when God heard his people's cry from bondage and remembered his promises to Abraham. God brought them out of Egypt and led them through the waters of the Red Sea while the Egyptian armies were deluged behind them (Exod. 14). God appointed Canaan, the promised land, as their destination. Deuteronomy describes this land as well watered, abundant in food (from which they were to eat their fill), and full of precious metals (8:7-10; 11:10-11), descriptions strikingly like that of Eden (Gen. 2:9-14). In various places the OT explicitly likens Canaan to the Edenic garden (see Gen. 13:10; Isa. 51:3; Ezek. 36:35; Joel 2:3). Even the law's instructions for the building of the tabernacle (Exodus 35–40) and the ordination of the priests (Leviticus 8) are filled with creation imagery and provide echoes of Eden.

Second, God put Israel on probation, giving them his law, with promises and threats attached to their response, as he had put Adam on probation, giving him legal commands and hinging life or death upon his response (Gen. 1:27-28; 2:16-17). Though God reminded Israel that he had not chosen them or brought them into the land because of their own righteousness, but because of the wickedness of the land's former inhabitants and his own promises sworn to Abraham, Isaac, and Jacob (e.g., Deut. 9:4-6), he not only gave them his law but also made clear they were on probation. As already considered, God promised abundant blessing in every aspect of life in the land if they would "faithfully obey the voice of the Lord your God, being careful to do all his commandments" (Deut. 28:1-14). He also threatened to curse them holistically within their land and then to "scatter . . . [them] among all peoples" in a degrading exile if they would "not obey the voice of the Lord your God or be careful to do all his commandments and his statutes" (Deut. 28:15-68). God asserted: "You shall . . . keep my statutes and my rules; if a person does them, he shall live by them . . ." (Lev. 18:5). As God established Adam as a king and priest with

---

94. For another treatment of this issue, which has aided my own presentation, see G. K. Beale, *The Temple and the Church's Mission: A Biblical Theology of the Dwelling Place of God* (Downers Grove, IL: InterVarsity, 2004), pp. 116-17.

the probationary commission to exercise royal dominion and priestly service in the Garden (Gen. 1:26, 28; 2:15; see Chapter 1), so God declared Israel "a kingdom of priests and a holy nation" if they would "indeed obey my voice and keep my covenant" (Exod. 19:5-6).

Finally, God exiled Israel from Canaan because of their disobedience to his law, as he had banished Adam from Eden for his rebellion (Gen. 3:22-24). God explicitly threatened to expel Israel from Canaan if they disobeyed his law, and the northern tribes' banishment from their land and Judah's exile to Babylon are major themes in the subsequent OT story. As the fall of Adam was the decisive turning-point in the primeval history of the human race, so the fall of Jerusalem "was an event without precedent in the history of Israel, and it would become a turning point in Jewish religious development. The destruction of Jerusalem is the event in which the long narrative from Genesis through Kings culminates. . . ."[95] Yet God also promised Israel a gracious eschatological deliverance from the curse of exile, a reminder and focusing of his great promise of a Messianic deliverer to Adam and Eve following their fall (Gen. 3:15). These Adamic and Israelite storylines differ in some important respects, to be sure. Adam and Eve were expelled from Eden after one act of rebellion while Israel and Judah were expelled from Canaan after centuries of rebellion and God's longsuffering forbearance. Likewise, Israel entered its probation already sinful and thus inevitably destined to fail (see Deut. 31:24-29), unlike originally upright Adam whose compliance with God's commands was evidently possible. Nevertheless, the terms of their probations (obedience to God's commands) and the rationale for their exiles (disobedience to the commands) are remarkably similar. Furthermore, as God promised a messianic deliverer to Adam and Eve in the very midst of pronouncing judgment upon them, so God promised Israel that he would restore them and sanctify them through a new initiative of his grace, in the very context of predicting their inevitable sin and judgment (e.g., Deut. 30:1-14; cf. Rom. 10:6-9). Redemption and eschatological blessing awaited both Adam and Israel on the other side of their exile, in God's own timing.

In short, by recapitulating the story of Adam, OT Israel showcased the plight of the fallen human race under the judgment of God. Here is an initial clue as to why the Mosaic law, in part, republished the natural law and hence reflected a protological moral standard. The natural law in original form was what Adam violated; the natural law in refracted form is what binds human-

---

95. Adele Berlin, *Lamentations: A Commentary* (Louisville: Westminster John Knox, 2002), p. 1.

ity fallen in Adam. Thus it was fitting for Israel to display the predicament of Adamic humanity by living under a law that, in many respects, promulgated the substance and sanctions of the natural law.

Mosaic Law and Natural Law in Pauline Perspective

In the first main section of this chapter I examined several texts in the Mosaic law and argued two main conclusions: first, that these texts demonstrate the ongoing testimony of the natural law at work among Israel's pagan neighbors (consistent with my claims in Part 1) and, second, that God designed the Mosaic law, in part, to apply the substance and sanctions of the natural law in a way fitting for Israel's unique historical situation. Thus the Mosaic law reflected a protological ethic, and Israel's moral experience under the Mosaic law resembled that of their pagan neighbors under the natural law, in important respects. At the end of this initial section I presented a basic theological explanation for these things evident in the books of the Torah themselves: Israel's life under the Mosaic law in the promised land brought them through a recapitulation of Adam's creation, probation, and fall in Eden. Israel under the Mosaic law thus showcased the predicament of the entire world as fallen sinners in Adam. Given the significance of the natural law for Adam in his original state and for all of humanity in its fallen state (as argued in Chapters 1-5), therefore, it seems appropriate that the substance and sanctions of the Mosaic law would reflect those of the natural law.

In this latter half of Chapter 7 we consider the Apostle Paul's theology of the Mosaic law, particularly in Romans and Galatians. I argue that Paul confirms the conclusions drawn earlier in the chapter and also adds theological depth to the explanation of why the natural and Mosaic laws bear the relationship they do. Paul helps us to see this issue in broader perspective, in light of God's grand purposes in the history of redemption. I consider first Paul's account of the substantive and functional similarities between the natural and Mosaic laws. Then I explore the deeper rationale for these similarities in Pauline theology. Specifically, Paul, following the OT, sees Israel's experience under the Mosaic law as a recapitulation of Adam's experience, and in light of this treats OT Israel as a microcosm. Israel's plight under the (Mosaic) law and judgment of God encapsulated the plight of the whole of Adamic humanity under the (natural) law and judgment of God — though the Mosaic law also showed a way forward, in a coming Messiah, that the natural law never could.

The Mosaic Law and the Natural Law

One aspect of Paul's teaching about the Mosaic law is that it resembles the natural law that once bound Adam and continues to bind all human beings. Thus Paul confirms one of the key claims earlier in the chapter, as argued from Exodus, Leviticus, and Deuteronomy. By God's design, the Mosaic law is functionally and substantively similar to the natural law. It played a role in the life of OT Israel similar to the role natural law played among the Gentile nations, and the moral content of the Mosaic law resembles the moral content of the natural law. To be sure, this resemblance is not identity. As noted earlier, the Mosaic law played other roles within Israel's life that the natural law did not play among the Gentiles (e.g., prophesying of the work of the coming Messiah through its priestly and sacrificial system), and even some of its most universal-sounding elements bear clear marks of Israel's unique status as God's theocratic covenant people. Nevertheless, God gave the Mosaic law in order to reflect the functions and substance of the natural law in significant respects. What natural law does inaudibly and more weakly the Mosaic law does audibly and more strongly.[96]

Functional Similarity: Providing Knowledge, Instigating Sin, and Pronouncing Judgment

Functional similarity between natural law and Mosaic law is evident from the parallel roles they play in Paul's theology. In a number of striking statements, Paul asserts that the Mosaic law gives knowledge of God's will (and thus of sin), instigates or catalyzes sin, and imprisons and pronounces judgment upon people. Elsewhere, particularly in Romans 1–2, Paul ascribes the same or very similar roles to the natural law. (See Chapter 5 for defense of my interpretation of Romans 1–2 below.)

---

96. Nicholas Wolterstorff discusses the OT law and universal standards of justice in ways very relevant, and in many respects congenial, to my treatment here; see *Justice: Rights and Wrongs* (Princeton: Princeton University Press, 2008), pp. 85-90. He comments: "The Torah formulates in the mode of commandment the universal requirements of justice." Later he argues that God commands what is in the Mosaic law because it is just; it does not become just simply because God commands it there. He comments, for example: "Bribing judges does not become a case of perverting justice because Yahweh commands Israel that it not be done; bribing judges was already that." Wolterstorff avoids using the term "natural law" here because he thinks this goes beyond the way the writers of Scripture were thinking, but he holds open the possibility that this is the proper way in which we should flesh out their thinking.

First, both the Mosaic and natural laws provide knowledge of God's will and thus of sin. Regarding the Mosaic law, for example, Paul claims that no one will be justified by works of the law; instead, "through the law comes knowledge of sin" (Rom. 3:20). More expansively, he writes in Romans 7:7: "if it had not been for the law, I would not have known sin. For I would not have known what it is to covet if the law had not said, 'You shall not covet.'" For Paul, however, the natural law provides a similar knowledge of God's moral will, though this sounds initially contradictory to his statement in 7:7.[97] After mentioning the Gentiles' perception of God and his attributes in the created order (Rom. 1:20), Paul writes: "although they knew God, they did not honor him as God or give thanks to him" (1:21). The natural knowledge of God entailed the obligation to respond with proper worship. Paul then prosecutes an extended case against these Gentiles for twisting their natural knowledge and falling into a multitude of sins. He concludes the indictment by noting that they "know God's decree that those who practice such things deserve to die" (1:32). In 2:14-15 Paul explains that Gentiles, ignorant of the Mosaic law, are "a law to themselves," "show that the work of the law is written on their hearts," and have consciences that accuse and excuse. This implies a knowledge of God's will by virtue of the natural law. Paul did not see the Mosaic law as the only source of knowledge of God's will and of sin, and did not view those to whom the Mosaic law testified as otherwise completely ignorant of these things. Instead, Paul teaches that the Mosaic law communicates a more clear and complete knowledge of what the natural law already reveals.

Second, the natural and Mosaic laws both instigate or catalyze sin, in that sin uses both laws to stir up rebellion in human hearts. With respect to the Mosaic law, Paul writes in Romans 7:5 of those living in the flesh, whose "sinful passions, aroused by the law, were at work in our members to bear fruit for death." Shortly thereafter he says: "sin, seizing an opportunity through the commandment, produced in me all kinds of covetousness. For apart from the law, sin lies dead. . . . For sin, seizing an opportunity through the commandment, deceived me and through it killed me" (7:8, 11). First Corinthians 15:56 presents the same idea, in compressed form: "The sting of death is sin, and the power of sin is the law." Paul likely intends a similar point in Romans 5:20 ("the law came in to increase the trespass")[98] and in Galatians 3:19 (the law was

---

97. See below for further discussion of Romans 7:7 and its context.

98. For arguments that this refers to the law truly bringing about an increase in sin, see Schreiner, *The Law and Its Fulfillment*, pp. 73-74. For further discussion on the negative role of the law expressed here, see also N. T. Wright, *The Letter to the Romans*, New Interpreter's Bible 10 (Nashville: Abingdon, 2002), p. 530; and James D. G. Dunn, *The Theology of Paul the*

added "because of transgressions").[99] The evidence that Paul sees the natural law playing the same role is not as clear. Nevertheless, his indictment of the Gentiles in Romans 1:21-32 describes their sinful rebellion as a response to receiving knowledge of God's will through natural revelation. Paul does not explicitly say that the natural law provokes sin, but he makes clear that their sin is characterized by rebellious reaction to the natural law's testimony. For example, failure to worship God and futility in mind and heart follow upon knowing God through the things that have been made (1:20-21). Perhaps most strikingly, three times Paul characterizes their sin in terms of "exchange": they knew and possessed what was good and natural, but exchanged it for lies and perversion (1:23, 25, 26-27). When the Mosaic law stirred up sin in Israel, therefore, this was at least analogous to the dynamic already at work with the natural law.

Third and finally, both the Mosaic and natural laws reveal God's judgment against sin. Paul says this about the Mosaic law toward the end of the first main section of Romans: "Now we know that whatever the law says it speaks to those who are under the law, so that every mouth may be stopped, and the whole world may be held accountable to God" (3:19). Romans 4:15 is similar: "the law brings wrath." The Mosaic law, in other words, ensures the just condemnation of sinners and thus brings God's wrath against them. Paul may make a similar point in Galatians 3:22 when he speaks of the Mosaic law imprisoning everything under sin. Once again, Paul assigns to natural law the same roles he assigns to the Mosaic law. He begins his discussion of the

---

Apostle (Grand Rapids: Eerdmans, 1998), p. 146. Along different lines, C. E. B. Cranfield does not see here a negative view about the law itself, but simply a statement of historical fact; see *The Epistle to the Romans*, vol. 1 (Edinburgh: T. & T. Clark, 1975), p. 292.

99. For arguments that this refers to an *increase* of sin, see In-Gyu Hong, *The Law in Galatians* (Sheffield: Sheffield Academic Press, 1993), pp. 150-51; Jason C. Meyer, *The End of the Law: Mosaic Covenant in Pauline Theology* (Nashville: Broadman & Holman, 2009), pp. 166-71; Schreiner, *The Law and Its Fulfillment*, pp. 75-76; J. Louis Martyn, *Galatians: A New Translation with Introduction and Commentary* (New York: Doubleday, 1997), p. 354; Hübner, *Law in Paul's Thought*, p. 26; Herman Ridderbos, *Paul: An Outline of His Theology*, trans. John Richard de Witt (Grand Rapids: Eerdmans, 1975), p. 150; and (cautiously) Graham Stanton, "The Law of Moses and the Law of Christ: Galatians 3:1–6:2," in *Paul and the Mosaic Law*, ed. James D. G. Dunn (Grand Rapids: Eerdmans, 2001), p. 112. Among those who see a positive purpose for the law here, see Dunn, *Theology of Paul the Apostle*, pp. 139-43; and James D. G. Dunn, *The Epistle to the Galatians* (Peabody, MA: Hendrickson, 1993), pp. 188-90; Richard B. Hays, *The Letter to the Galatians: Introduction, Commentary, and Reflections*, in *New Interpreter's Bible*, vol. 11 (Nashville: Abingdon, 2000), p. 267; and Don Garlington, *An Exposition of Galatians: A New Perspective/Reformational Reading*, 2nd ed. (Eugene, OR: Wipf & Stock, 2004), p. 179.

Gentiles' natural knowledge of God and his law by claiming that "the wrath of God is revealed from heaven against all ungodliness and unrighteousness of men" (Rom. 1:18), and such wrath comes because everyone knows God through the testimony of creation and thus is "without excuse" (1:19-20). All people are aware of this just verdict against them through natural revelation: "Though they know God's decree that those who practice such things deserve to die, they not only do them but give approval to those who practice them" (1:32). This theme continues through 2:15, where Paul explains that the Gentiles render judgment upon themselves through their knowledge of the natural law: "They show that the work of the law is written on their hearts, while their conscience also bears witness, and their conflicting thoughts accuse or even excuse them."

The epistles of Paul, therefore, present natural law and Mosaic law as performing several similar tasks. Both natural and Mosaic laws provide knowledge of God's will and thus of sin, instigate and catalyze human rebellion, and pronounce a just verdict against sinners. The sorts of things the Mosaic law did for Israel were already being done for all nations by the law of nature, in a silent and more obscure, yet nevertheless decisive, way.

Substantive Similarity: Romans 1–2 Revisited

In addition to functional similarity between the Mosaic and natural laws, Paul also saw substantive similarity. Paul's language and logic in 1:32 and 2:12-15, and then again in 2:19-20, indicate that he saw the natural and Mosaic laws as moral standards that were, for purposes of God's universal judgment, substantively equivalent. This present section again presupposes my exegetical conclusions in Chapter 5.

Though the strongest evidence for substantive similarity comes from Romans 2, Paul gives an intriguing hint about where he's heading as he brings Romans 1 to a close. Since 1:18 he has offered an extended indictment of Gentile humanity for lapsing into a morass of sin. All human beings understand through nature that their actions are unrighteous, yet pursue them anyway. At the end of this indictment Paul writes: "Though they know God's decree [δικαίωμα] that those who practice such things deserve to die, they not only do them but give approval to those who practice them" (1:32). Paul's reference to God's "decree" is intriguing. While the context of Romans 1:18-32 indicates that this knowledge Gentiles possess is a natural knowledge, perceived "in the things that have been made" (1:20), what they know — God's decree — has strong Mosaic overtones. When the NT uses this word, δικαίωμα, in a similar judicial context, it refers to the Mosaic law, including two examples later in Romans (2:26; 8:4). Perhaps also relevant is that the primary sins highlighted in previous verses — idolatry and homosexual intercourse — were not capital crimes in Roman law but were under the Mosaic law.[100] It seems likely that Paul is imputing to Gentiles knowledge of something stated explicitly only in the law of Moses. The penalty communicated by the natural law corresponds to the penalty imposed by the Mosaic law.

This conclusion requires nuance. According to 1:32, the natural law teaches that those who do "such things" deserve to die, and "such things" refers back not only to Mosaic capital crimes such as idolatry and homosexual conduct (1:22-27) but also to all the sins listed in 1:29-31. Though these sins include other Mosaic capital crimes — murder and disobedience to parents — the Mosaic law did not punish most of them by death, and did not punish some of them at all. Indeed, sins such as covetousness and envy are inherently outside the purview of civil law. In 1:32 Paul is evidently not thinking about the death penalty as imposed by civil law, but indicates that natural law pronounces a death sentence upon sinners at a more ultimate level. While the Mosaic law could sentence sinners to no more than physical death, the destination of Paul's argument suggests that the natural law sentences sinners to an eschatological death (cf. 5:17, where condemnation in death is conquered by justification in *resurrection* life). The Mosaic law reflects at a penultimate level what the natural law proclaims to be true at an ultimate level: sin deserves death. In Romans 1:32, therefore, Paul hints that the natural and Mosaic laws are substantively similar (not identical) with respect to their sanctions.[101]

Shortly thereafter Paul more than hints. The logic underlying his argument in 2:12-15 presumes that the natural and Mosaic laws bear a substantive similarity. In 2:12 Paul states a basic principle of justice: "For all who have sinned without the law will also perish without the law, and all who have sinned under the law will be judged by the law." In other words, only those (Jews) who have received the Mosaic law will face judgment under its auspices. Gentiles will be judged by some other standard. Yet Paul seems to draw himself

---

100. Among those who discuss these points, see Frank Thielman, *Paul and the Law: A Contextual Approach* (Downers Grove, IL: InterVarsity, 1994), p. 169.

101. As I touch upon below, and discuss again in Chapter 10, the fact that the natural law decrees, at an ultimate level, that all sin deserves eschatological death before God does not mean that natural law decrees that civil law should inflict the death penalty for all sin. Neither do I believe that the Mosaic law's civil penalties should be the standard for civil penalties in contemporary law (though they may inform our thinking about such).

into a contradiction in the following verse: "For it is not the hearers of the law who are righteous before God, but the doers of the law who will be justified" (2:13). If Gentiles who do not have the Mosaic law will not be judged by it, how can Paul say that only doers of the law will receive justification? The next two verses, 2:14-15, point to the natural law and thus provide the answer. Gentiles will not, indeed, be judged by the Mosaic law, but they would be justified as doers of the (Mosaic) law were they to render the requisite obedience to the natural law. Paul's logic demands a fundamental substantive similarity (if not formal identity) between the Mosaic and natural laws. Only in this way would obedience to the latter make a person a doer of the former.[102]

This fundamental substantive similarity between the Mosaic and natural laws may also be background to Paul's argument in the verses that immediately follow. Paul first surveys a number of boasts that Jews of his day were making based upon their possession of the law (2:17-20). Then he condemns them for their hypocrisy, for they break the law even while teaching it and boasting about it (2:21-24). The last of the Jewish boasts is that they have "in the law the embodiment [τὴν μόρφωσιν] of knowledge and truth" (2:20). This statement explains why Jews think they can be moral teachers of Gentiles. Because they have the law as the embodiment of knowledge and truth they are "a guide to the blind, a light to those who are in darkness, an instructor of the foolish, a teacher of children" (2:19-20). Apparently these Jews, in teaching their law to Gentiles, believed that it embodied something relevant even to them.[103] It is possible that Paul is here thinking of Jewish efforts to proselytize Gentiles and hence to make them Jews, in which case these teachers may have been promoting distinctively Jewish practices like circumcision. Yet the things Paul mentions as the content of their teaching — no stealing, adultery, idolatry (2:21-22) — are universal matters of the natural law. It seems unlikely, furthermore, that God's name was blasphemed among the Gentiles (2:24) because of Jewish hypocrisy on parochial issues like circumcision. Thus, Paul was probably thinking of Jewish teachers instructing "blind" and "foolish" (2:19-20)

---

102. Thielman draws similar conclusion in *Paul and the Law,* p. 173: "God has given even to Gentiles a rudimentary form of the Jewish law."

103. Some interpreters believe that this opinion described by Paul reflects the Jewish tradition correlating law and wisdom, as developed in many inter-testamental works. See especially Eckhard J. Schnabel, *Law and Wisdom from Ben Sira to Paul: A Tradition Historical Enquiry into the Relation of Law, Wisdom, and Ethics* (Tübingen: Mohr Siebeck, 1985), pp. 227-34. The relationship of law and wisdom is a difficult, but important, question. I believe both the OT and Paul handle the subject differently from the inter-testamental literature. Chapters 8 and 9 consider these issues at more length.

Gentiles, from the Mosaic law, about universal moral obligations they were breaking. And Paul evidently agreed with his compatriots' view of the Mosaic law at this point: it was the embodiment of knowledge and truth even for Gentiles.[104] He himself has asserted the correspondence between the Mosaic and natural laws in preceding verses (see 2:12-15) and does not here condemn these Jews for what they teach, but for not doing what they teach others to do. The Jews' claim in 2:19-20 actually supports Paul's larger point.

1 Corinthians 9: Mosaic Law and Natural Law in Practice

While Romans 1–2 is pivotal for understanding Paul's view of the substantive similarity between the natural and Mosaic laws, another place in his epistles illustrates its practical relevance for the church. In 1 Corinthians 9 Paul asserts his rights as an apostle and also says that he has not utilized them, lest he "put an obstacle in the way of the gospel of Christ" (9:12). Verses 6-10 focus on why he has the right to receive a living from preaching the gospel and thus to refrain from other employment. After raising this issue in 9:6, he states: "Who serves as a soldier at his own expense? Who plants a vineyard without eating any of its fruit? Or who tends a flock without getting some of the milk?" (9:7). This is an implicit appeal to natural law.[105] He calls upon readers to use their common sense and to observe the natural order of things. Civil magistrates simply cannot rely upon self-supporting soldiers to staff their military. People will not expend the hard work necessary to plant a vineyard if they expect to eat none of its grapes. Shepherds do not ordinarily tend a flock if they cannot derive some advantage from it. Paul essentially says to the Corinthians: you know how the world works. People can resist this natural order, but they will not get along very well if they ignore these basic truths.

---

104. Among the many interpreters agreeing with this conclusion, see Stephen Wester-holm, *Perspectives Old and New on Paul: The 'Lutheran' Paul and His Critics* (Grand Rapids: Eerdmans, 2004), pp. 411-12; Joseph A. Fitzmyer, S.J., *Romans: A New Translation with Introduction and Commentary* (New York: Doubleday, 1993), p. 317; Wright, *Romans*, p. 447; Cranfield, *Romans*, pp. 166-67; and Ridderbos, *Paul*, p. 134. Others, however, believe that Paul means to contrast his own view with that of the Jews; e.g., see James D. G. Dunn, *Romans 1–8* (Dallas: Word, 1988), p. 113; and C. Marvin Pate, *The Reverse of the Curse: Paul, Wisdom, and the Law* (Tübingen: Mohr Siebeck, 2000), pp. 137-38.

105. Or as John Calvin puts it, "natural equity"; see *Commentary on the Epistles of Paul the Apostle to the Corinthians*, vol. 1, trans. John Pringle (Grand Rapids: Eerdmans, 1948), p. 293.

In what way Paul believes this natural law should regulate the life of the church is a very important question, but one that must wait until Chapter 9. Here I comment only on one point: Paul confirms his appeal to natural law by a quotation and explanation of the Mosaic law. In 9:8 Paul begins: "Do I say these things on human authority?" Paul knows that some of his readers may not take his natural law appeals very seriously (some things apparently never change). So Paul offers a second line of proof: "Does not the Law say the same? For it is written in the Law of Moses, 'You shall not muzzle an ox when it treads out the grain.' Is it for oxen that God is concerned? Does he not speak entirely for our sake? It was written for our sake, because the plowman should plow in hope and the thresher thresh in hope of sharing in the crop" (9:8-10). The Mosaic law, according to Paul, reflects the same sort of common sense he has derived from the natural order in previous verses. Paul seems to find what Reformed Christians have referred to as the "general equity" of the Mosaic civil regulations.[106] He does not seek to impose the Mosaic law upon the Corinthians in a woodenly literal way, but finds a basic principle of justice motivating this Mosaic regulation, a basic principle also communicated by the order of nature: people who work on something have a right to derive material gain from the things they produce. Very interestingly, Paul does not begin by assuming the literal applicability of a Mosaic law and then wonder if it might correspond with something in the natural law. Instead, he begins with the natural law and then looks for the natural-law principle in the Mosaic law, finding it in a not-so-obvious place.[107]

Paul and the Mosaic Recapitulation of Adam

I have argued that Paul confirms my earlier claim that part of God's intention for the Mosaic law was that it reflect the natural law. Accordingly, Israel's experience under Moses resembled the experience of the nations of the world

---

106. The Westminster Confession of Faith 19.4 reads: "To them [OT Israel] also, as a body politic, he gave sundry judicial laws, which expired together with the state of that people; not obliging any other now, further than the general equity thereof may require."

107. As explained further in Chapter 10, Paul's argument here provides helpful insight for Christians today thinking about natural law and the applicability of the Mosaic law. The natural law is generally applicable for Christians' social life today. The precepts of the Mosaic law are applicable today not simply because they are precepts of the Mosaic law, but the Mosaic law is applicable insofar as it reflects the natural law, which it illustrates and exemplifies. Again, this seems to be precisely what the Westminster Confession of Faith 19.4 commends.

under the natural law in significant respects. Now I argue that Paul also confirms my earlier theological explanation for this reality: Israel's life under the Mosaic law was meant to take Israel through a recapitulation of the experience of Adam's creation, fall, and probation. This provides initial Pauline insight on why natural law and Mosaic law, by God's ordination, bear such resemblances: Israel's condition under Moses showcased the plight of the whole of humanity fallen in Adam.

Romans 5:13-14

The first two Pauline texts I consider in support of Israel's recapitulation of Adam are, admittedly, very difficult and controversial passages. The case for this recapitulation does not depend on these texts, but I believe they bolster the case. The first text is Romans 5:13-14: "For sin indeed was in the world before the law was given, but sin is not counted where there is no law. Yet death reigned from Adam to Moses, even over those whose sinning was not like the transgression of Adam, who was a type of the one who was to come." Though the nature of the Mosaic law is not Paul's principal focus here, his reasoning seems to depend upon a fundamental similarity between the original situation of Adam and the situation of Israel under Moses, with particular respect to the law.

Paul begins 5:13 with the conjunction "for" (γὰρ), indicating that 5:13-14 offers explanation of 5:12, where he writes: "Therefore, just as sin came into the world through one man, and death through sin, and so death spread to all men because all sinned. . . ." Understanding Paul's explanatory point in 5:13-14, therefore, demands appreciation for his claim in 5:12. The first part of 5:12 is straightforward and derived from Genesis 3: sin entered the world through Adam's fall and this sin introduced death. The second part of the verse is less clear. At a basic level, interpreters must choose between a "Pelagian" or "Augustinian" trajectory. Either Paul teaches that death has come to all because all people individually have sinned in a way analogous to Adam or that death has come to all because Adam's first sin was, in some way, the corporate sin of the human race. Despite the attempted rehabilitation of Pelagius among some exegetes of 5:13-14,[108] the Augustinian trajectory still commends itself in context.[109] Most importantly, Paul's point in the following verses (especially 5:15,

---

108. E.g., see J. C. Poirier, "Romans 5:13-14 and the Universality of Law," *NovT* 38 (1996): 244-58.

109. A generally Augustinian interpretation of Romans 5:12-19 does not depend upon

17) is decidedly *not* that all people's own sinning has brought them death but rather that the sin of the one man Adam is death's origin.[110] When Paul finally resumes the comparison that he begins in 5:12 ("just as") but leaves hanging until 5:18, he is focused upon Adam's one sin and its effects ("one trespass led to condemnation for all men"). The point of this focus is to analogize Adam's corporate representation to Christ's corporate representation in 5:18-19, a subject previously addressed in Romans (see 3:25; 4:25; 5:6-8). Adam is, as Paul puts it in 5:14, "a type of the one who was to come," that is, Christ.[111] The Pelagian reading also stumbles over 5:14, where Paul affirms the dissimilarity between Adam and his immediate posterity. Those living between the time of Adam and Moses did *not* sin in a way analogous to their primal father. Paul does indeed say in 5:12 that death came to all because *all* sinned, but this is precisely the kind of language Paul uses elsewhere in a corporate or representative way. For example, he writes concerning Christ in 2 Corinthians 5:14: "one has died for all, therefore all have died."

Paul's larger point in this section of Romans, 5:12-21, is to bring his explanation of justification by faith to a dramatic conclusion, particularly by expounding the representative righteous obedience of Jesus Christ. But Paul accomplishes this by highlighting the similarities and dissimilarities between Adam and Christ, who is the "Last Adam" (cf. 1 Cor. 15). Adam was "a type of the one who was to come" (Rom. 5:14). To establish his claims about Christ he must present some basic truths about Adam from which to work, and this he does in 5:12: death came to all people because all sinned corporately through Adam.

Paul, understandably, seems to anticipate that this bold claim requires defense, which he provides in 5:13-14. He makes two claims in 5:13. First he states that sin was in the world before the giving of the (Mosaic) law. In light of the Genesis accounts of the days of Noah, the tower of Babel, and the conduct

---

reading the text in exactly the way I do here. For other generally Augustinian approaches that differ from mine, see e.g. Arland J. Hultgren, *Paul's Letter to the Romans: A Commentary* (Grand Rapids: Eerdmans, 2011), pp. 221-25; and Charles A. Gieschen, "Original Sin in the New Testament," *Concordia Journal* 31 (October 2005): 366-70.

110. See John Murray, *The Imputation of Adam's Sin* (Grand Rapids: Eerdmans, 1959), p. 11.

111. Robin Scroggs makes the interesting suggestion that the "one who was to come" is Moses rather than Christ. Given the way Paul develops at length the Adam-Christ comparison in the following verses, which includes similarities as well as dissimilarities, it is much more likely that he refers to Christ than to Moses in 5:14. See Robin Scroggs, *The Last Adam: A Study in Pauline Anthropology* (Philadelphia: Fortress, 1966), pp. 80-81.

of Sodom, this statement seems uncontroversial. Then he notes that sin is not counted, or imputed (ἐλλογεῖται), where there is no law. This claim is not quite so obvious, but it is helpful to interpret it in light of what Paul said earlier: "the law brings wrath, but where there is no law there is no transgression" (4:15). For Paul, "transgression" is a certain kind of sin, a kind that involves the breaking of a "law." But it must be "law" in the sense of an explicit divine command, because it is specifically Adam (5:14) and Israel (4:15) that could commit transgressions. Sin is not "imputed" where there is no law, apparently, because there is no explicit or public reckoning of sin without the kind of explicit divine-human relationship within which transgression is possible.

However, by mentioning these two basic facts — that sin was in the world before the Mosaic law and that sin is not counted where there is no law — Paul has triggered a logical conclusion that should trouble his readers' minds. If sin was in the world before the Mosaic law and yet sin is not imputed where there is no law, then it would seem that the sin of the pre-Mosaic people should not have been counted against them, and if their sin was not counted against them, then presumably they should not have suffered the penalty of death. Yet the spread of death to all is precisely what Paul has just asserted in 5:12, and the point would have been obvious even had Paul not said it. The apostle, therefore, seems to have generated a contradiction between his claims in 5:12 and 5:13.

The way to come to grips with Paul's argument is not to try to tamp down the apparent tension between these two verses. Paul, I suggest, intended to create the tension. This is evident by the way he begins 5:14. He uses a strong adversative conjunction, ἀλλὰ ("yet"), indicating that he now makes a point that contrasts with, or is at least unanticipated in the light of, 5:13. And the point he makes ("death reigned from Adam to Moses") reflects the very thing he asserted at the end of 5:12 ("death spread to all men").[112] Thus in 5:12 and 5:14 he claims that death has come to all people, including those living between Adam and Moses, while he also claims in 5:13, apparently in opposition to the first point, that sins were not counted against those living between Adam and Moses. Paul has constructed a seemingly incongruous state of affairs in which death, the penalty for sin, has come upon people whose sins were not counted against them.

112. Douglas J. Moo, e.g., recognizes and defends this adversative and the consequent contrast between 5:13b and 5:14; see *The Epistle to the Romans* (Grand Rapids: Eerdmans, 1996), pp. 329-33. Among writers who see less significance in the adversative and tend not to see a contrast between 5:13b and 5:14, see Cranfield, *Romans*, pp. 282-83; Wright, *Romans*, p. 527; and T. L. Carter, *Paul and the Power of Sin: Redefining 'Beyond the Pale'* (Cambridge: Cambridge University Press, 2002), pp. 172-73.

The reason for this apparent tension, however, is to offer evidence for his main point in 5:12, namely, that death has come to all because of Adam's corporate act of sin. During the Adam-to-Moses period people's own sinning cannot fully explain their death, so there must be some explanation outside themselves. Someone else's sin must have served as the legal ground for their death, and Adam's transgression is precisely this. Paul has thus offered evidence in 5:13-14 for Adam's identity, which in turn undergirds his explanation, in the following verses, of Christ the Last Adam's identity and his corporate act of redemption.

Paul's argument in 5:13-14 presumes an important difference between the situation of Israel under Moses and the situation of those living between Adam and Moses. Under Moses it was evidently easy to understand why people died. God gave them the Mosaic law and threatened to hold them guilty and to strike them with curse and death if they disobeyed it. In light of their constant rebellion death was the expected outcome.

Paul's argument in 5:13-14 makes another presumption, and this gets to the heart of my present case. Paul presumes that Israel under Moses was similar to Adam at the very point where Israel under Moses was dissimilar to those living between Adam and Moses. Unlike the pre-Mosaic people, Israel had the law, and therefore their sins were transgressions (see 4:15), that is, their sins were counted against them. But being in this situation, Israel under Moses was similar to Adam, for his sin too was a "transgression" (παράβασις) (5:14) and thus God brought death upon him as a consequence (5:12).[113] By stating that the pre-Mosaic people sinned in a way unlike Adam (5:14), Paul implies that Israel under Moses sinned in a way similar to Adam. In this way, the situation of Israel under the Mosaic law reflected the situation of Adam under the law that God imposed upon him. Thus Israel's sin and consequent guilt and death recapitulated the experience of Adam's probation, fall, and condemnation.[114]

My interpretation of 5:13-14 provokes a significant question: How can Paul reason in 5:13-14 on the presumption that pre-Mosaic people were not under law and their sins were not counted against them when he has already

113. For helpful comment on the parallel use of παράβασις in 4:15 and 5:14, and how Paul thereby describes Israel and Adam as both under law, see Chris A. Vlachos, *The Law and the Knowledge of Good and Evil: The Edenic Background of the Catalytic Operation of the Law in Paul* (Eugene, OR: Pickwick, 2009), p. 114.

114. Among many writers seeing this or a similar Israel-Adam analogy in Romans 5:13-14, see Otfried Hofius, "Adam-Christ Antithesis and the Law: Reflections on Romans 5:12-21," in *Paul and the Mosaic Law*, pp. 195-96; Wright, *Romans*, p. 527; Fitzmyer, *Romans*, p. 418; and Vlachos, *The Law*, p. 116.

argued at length (1:18–2:16) that all people know God's law and the judgment sin deserves, because of God's natural revelation?[115] The solution, I suggest, is to affirm both poles and to recognize that Paul is trying to make different points at these stages of his larger argument in Romans.[116] There is a sense in which those not living under Moses have the law and are accountable to it in ways similar to Israel, and there is also a sense in which those not living under Moses are very different from Israel who has the Mosaic law. In Romans 1–3 Paul is concerned to demonstrate the universal sinfulness and accountability of the human race, in part to silence Jews who boasted about possessing the law of Moses. For this argument, pointing out the ways in which Jews and Gentiles alike know and violate God's moral requirements is an effective tactic. In Romans 5:12-21 Paul seeks to explain Christ's corporate work of redemption, in order to further his argument that justification is by faith in Christ's work and not by their own works. For this argument, comparing and contrasting Christ and Adam is an effective pedagogical tool, and the dissimilarity of Israel to the pre-Mosaic people, who had no law verbally revealed to them by God, helps readers to understand that Adam's corporate sin is necessary to explain the reality of death between the times of Adam and Moses.[117] There are important similarities between Gentile nations under the natural law and Israel under the Mosaic law, but in Romans 5:13-14 Paul is concerned to set forth Israel as a recapitulation of Adam.

115. Similar questions are raised by some of the authors mentioned above who use this apparent conflict as evidence of the tension or even contradiction within Paul's thought; e.g., see Hübner, *Law in Paul's Thought,* p. 81; and especially Räisänen, *Paul and the Law,* pp. 145-47.

116. Along similar lines is Westerholm, *Perspectives Old and New,* pp. 424-25. Dunn, *Romans 1–8,* p. 275, also helpfully notes that Paul is making a different point here from his argument in Romans 1–2 concerning the universality of law, though Dunn does not see the emphasis upon Adam as corporate representative along the lines I have argued above.

117. For these reasons I reject Poirier's proposal (in "Romans 5:13-14") that Paul is furthering the argument of 1:18–2:16 here in 5:13-14. It is possibly attractive, at first glance, to think that if Paul speaks of sin and death being in the world from Adam to Moses and claims that sin is not imputed where there is no law, he reinforces the idea of the universality of law. This conclusion, however, makes 5:13-14 totally disconnected from Paul's larger point in 5:12-21 concerning Adam and Christ in their corporate capacities. Also problematic is that it reads 5:13-14 as stressing the virtual identity of all people in their experience of individually sinning and dying, whereas Paul in fact highlights the particular situation of the pre-Mosaic people in distinction from Israel's experience under the law. Finally, this conclusion is inconsistent with the strong adversative Paul uses to begin 5:14. Were Paul trying to teach the universality of law in these verses, the idea that death reigned from Adam to Moses would be the natural conclusion following what he wrote in 5:13 rather than an assertion that stands in tension with it.

Romans 7:7-12

Romans 7:7-12 also treats OT Israel's experience as a recapitulation of Adam's. Like 5:13-14, these verses have stirred considerable debate among scholars. I cannot come close to interacting with all the voluminous literature on the subject, but the weight of the evidence, I conclude, suggests that in 7:7-12 Paul makes a dual allusion to the experience of Adam receiving God's commands at creation and to the experience of Israel receiving the law at Sinai.[118]

Romans 7:7-12 falls after a lengthy passage triggered by an antinomian sort of objection Paul anticipates in 6:1. Having set forth his doctrine of justification by faith, from 3:21 to 5:21, Paul seeks to answer the charge that his theology promotes a lax attitude toward sin. He explains that believers have died to sin and are no longer enslaved under its power, since they have died with Christ and died to the law. Paul concludes this section emphasizing that believers have been released from the law and that this is the very reason why they now walk in the ways of the Spirit and bear fruit to God (7:4-6). With this strong conclusion Paul has answered his imagined critic: the freedom from the law granted in justification, far from promoting antinomianism, actually results in holy conduct generated by the Spirit. This conclusion, however, provokes Paul to address another troubling objection. If the law represented a sort of bondage, and dying to it means sanctification by the Spirit, then is the law itself sin (7:7)? Paul vigorously denies that conclusion, and in the following verses explains that the law itself is good, but sin (personified) has used the law to stir up disobedience in those who hear it.

A key exegetical question concerns the identity of the "I" whom Paul describes as being alive apart from the law but then hearing the law (specifically the command not to covet), being deceived by sin, and dying. Most interpreters do not think that Paul is simply relating his own personal experi-

---

118. Among writers who defend parallel references to Adam and Israel in these verses, many of whom use the very language of "recapitulation," see Dunn, *The Theology of Paul the Apostle*, pp. 98-100; Wright, *Romans*, pp. 553, 562-63; N. T. Wright, *The Climax of the Covenant: Christ and the Law in Pauline Theology* (Minneapolis: Fortress, 1992), p. 197; N. T. Wright, *Paul: In Fresh Perspective* (Minneapolis: Fortress, 2005), p. 31; Dennis E. Johnson, "The Function of Romans 7:13-25 in Paul's Argument for the Law's Impotence and the Spirit's Power, and Its Bearing on the Identity of the Schizophrenic 'I,'" in *Resurrection and Eschatology: Theology in Service of the Church: Essays in Honor of Richard B. Gaffin Jr.*, ed. Lane G. Tipton and Jeffrey C. Waddington (Phillipsburg, NJ: Presbyterian and Reformed, 2008), pp. 31-36; and Ridderbos, *Paul*, pp. 143-44.

ence.[119] There is no evidence that Paul especially struggled with covetousness in his early life. More importantly, that Paul believed he once lived "apart from the law" and then was suddenly confronted by it (7:9) is highly unlikely for one who identified himself as "circumcised on the eighth day . . . , a Hebrew of Hebrews" (Phil. 3:5).[120] Instead, Paul likely adopts some sort of rhetorical technique by which he uses the first person singular to assume the role of another.[121] But who is this other? Two popular candidates are Adam in Eden and Israel at Sinai.[122]

The arguments for Adam and for Israel both seem to line up well with many of the specific statements in Romans 7:7-12. In 7:7-8 Paul isolates the tenth commandment, "you shall not covet," as the law that confronts the "I." On the one hand, this is a direct quotation from the Decalogue given to Israel on Mount Sinai. On the other hand, the fact that Paul chose this particular commandment from the Mosaic law is strikingly appropriate were Paul trying to allude to the sinful desires emerging in Eve as described in Genesis 3:6.[123] Then, in 7:9, Paul states that the "I" was alive apart from the law, but that when the commandment came he died. This could be a fitting description of Israel at Sinai. Prior to Sinai they were in possession of the life-giving promises to

119. Though for a recent defense of an autobiographical interpretation, see Hultgren, *Romans*, pp. 685-88.

120. And as noted by A. Andrew Das, there is no evidence for the practice of the bar mitzvah in Paul's day; see *Paul and the Jews* (Peabody, MA: Hendrickson, 2003), p. 215.

121. One suggestion is that Paul uses the rhetorical technique of impersonation, or *prosopopoeia,* which involves the assumption of a role. See Ben Witherington III, with Darlene Hyatt, *Paul's Letter to the Romans: A Socio-Rhetorical Commentary* (Grand Rapids: Eerdmans, 2004), pp. 179-89. He argues that Paul is impersonating Adam.

122. Writers believing that Paul refers to Israel in these verses include Moo, *Romans,* pp. 428-29; Fitzmyer, *Romans,* pp. 462-65; and Paul W. Meyer, "The Worm at the Core of the Apple: Exegetical Reflections on Romans 7," in *The Conversation Continues: Studies in Paul and John in Honor of J. Louis Martyn,* ed. Robert T. Fortna and Beverly R. Gaventa (Nashville: Abingdon, 1990), p. 75. Among writers defending a reference to Adam, see Ernst Käsemann, *Commentary on Romans,* trans. Geoffrey W. Bromiley (Grand Rapids: Eerdmans, 1980), p. 196; Witherington, *Paul's Letter to the Romans,* pp. 179-89; and Carter, *Paul and the Power of Sin,* pp. 186-87. L. Ann Jervis, " 'The Commandment Which Is for Life' (Romans 7.10): Sins' Use of the Obedience of Faith," *JSNT* 27 (2004): 214, strongly rejects seeing a reference to Adam. A. Andrew Das, *Solving the Romans Debate* (Minneapolis: Fortress, 2007), chap. 5, argues for a reference to Gentile Christians who became aware of the law.

123. That the prohibition against coveting was viewed as a summation of the entire law and that Adam and Eve committed this sin were popular opinions in early Jewish exegesis; see Dunn, *Theology of Paul the Apostle,* pp. 98-99; and Witherington, *Paul's Letter to the Romans,* pp. 188-89.

Abraham and had just been released from the suffocating bondage of Egypt, but after receiving the law at Sinai they were soon condemned for disobedience and consigned to death in the wilderness. Yet this description in 7:9 could also fit Adam. He was given the breath of life (Gen. 2:7) and was then sentenced to death after the giving and violation of God's commandment (Gen. 3:19). Furthermore, Romans 7:10 states that "the very commandment that *promised life* proved to be death to me." Again, this description fits both the Israelite and Adamic contexts. One of Paul's favorite OT verses for describing the Mosaic law is Leviticus 18:5: "if a person does them [God's statutes and rules], he shall *live* by them." (See Gal. 3:12; Rom. 10:5.) Yet the promise of life also attached implicitly to the commandment given to Adam in Genesis 2:17, since the threat for disobedience was death and the tree of life beckoned nearby (Gen. 2:9).

Various other considerations point to Israel while others favor Adam. In support of Israel, for example, is the simple fact that the chief concern initiating 7:7-12 is a serious question about the law of Moses in light of Paul's seeming disparagement of the law in previous verses. Were Paul not addressing the law of Moses at some basic level in 7:7-12 then he would fail to address his interlocutor's concern. Furthermore, N. T. Wright may be correct that a "new exodus" theme pervades Romans 5–8 and that in 7:7-12 Paul arrives with his readers at Sinai.[124] Other aspects of the text have an Adamic flavor. Romans 7:11, for example, says that sin used the law to "deceive," the word with which Eve described her own experience of temptation (Gen. 3:13, LXX) and which Paul uses elsewhere when alluding to Genesis 3:13.[125] There may also be allusions to the story of Cain (Genesis 4) in the very next verses, 7:13-20,[126] which would add further reason to see reference to Adam in the immediately preceding text.

In the end, I find it compelling to see simultaneous reference to Israel at Sinai and Adam in Eden, whichever reference might be primary. I am not refusing to make a difficult choice, but recognizing the weight of evidence on both sides.[127] It is telling that many commentators who argue for either an Israel-focused or Adam-focused interpretation of 7:7-12 also concede that

124. Wright, *Romans*, p. 550.

125. Cranfield, *Romans*, p. 352, comments: "In LXX Gen 3.13 the woman says . . . ἠπάτησέν . . . , but the compound verb ἐξαπατᾶν, which is used here, is also used by Paul in 2 Cor 11.3 (cf. I Tim 2.14), where he is quite definitely echoing Gen 3.13."

126. Wright, *Climax*, pp. 228-29.

127. Not surprisingly, serious arguments have also been made against each position. E.g., see Das, *Solving the Romans Debate*, pp. 216-21 (though Das himself does not think these arguments preclude the possibility of allusions to Adam and/or Israel at Sinai).

Paul may also make allusions to the other. The conclusion that Paul makes a dual reference becomes even more plausible in light of his larger argument in Romans, since he has already associated the experiences of Adam and Israel in the verses considered above, 5:12-21. Romans 7:7-12 continues in the same vein and thus adds additional evidence that Paul, following the OT's own perspective, viewed Israel's experience in receiving and responding to the law as a recapitulation of Adam's probation and fall in Genesis 1–3.

The Mosaic Law and Paul's Two Adams Paradigm

The claim that Paul saw the experience of Israel under the Mosaic law recapitulating the experience of Adam in Eden finds further support from his "two Adams" doctrine. In both Romans 5 and 1 Corinthians 15 Paul compares the work of Adam in bringing death into the world with the work of Christ in bringing salvation. He associates Adam with sin, death, and condemnation while he associates Christ with righteousness, resurrection life, and justification. In 1 Corinthians 15:45 Paul refers to the two as the "first Adam" and "last Adam." They represent, as it were, two humanities: protological humanity and eschatological humanity. To be identified with the first Adam is to be under the sway of sin and decay while to be identified with the last Adam is to be liberated from these enemies and to have hope of eternal life. This striking Pauline framework is important for present purposes because in the only two places where Paul explicitly compares the two Adams he also discusses the Mosaic law, and on both occasions he places the Mosaic law on the side of the *first* Adam.[128] Romans 5:20 and 1 Corinthians 15:56 thus bolster the case for seeing Israel's experience under the Mosaic law as a recapitulation of Adam's experience in Eden. They portray the law as confirming and strengthening the Israelites' identity with protological humanity fallen in Adam and in bondage to sin and death.

I comment first on Romans 5:20. As discussed above, Romans 5:12-19 speaks of Adam's corporate sin, through which sin and death enter the world and leave all human beings condemned. It compares Christ to Adam insofar

---

128. Though Romans 5 and 1 Corinthians 15 are the only explicit presentations of the Two Adams paradigm, the idea may lurk behind some other Pauline texts. One candidate is Galatians 4:4-5, where Paul describes Christ as "born of a woman," a possible allusion to the proto-Messianic promise of Genesis 3:15. Among commentators who see Paul's Two-Adams theology at work in Galatians 4:4-5, see Dunn, *Galatians*, pp. 215-16; and Garlington, *Galatians*, p. 194.

as the former's redemptive work overcomes Adam's deadly work and brings justification and life. Immediately after a series of verses that place Adam and Christ side-by-side, Paul writes, "Now the law came in to increase the trespass, but where sin increased, grace abounded all the more, so that, as sin reigned in death, grace also might reign through righteousness leading to eternal life through Jesus Christ our Lord" (5:20-21).

Though Paul does not mention Adam's name again in 5:20-21, he continues to think in the same Adam-Christ terms that have structured the previous verses.[129] As does each verse from 5:15 to 5:19, both 5:20 and 5:21 compare one set of realities to another, and these realities are associated in 5:15-19 with Adam on the one hand (trespass, sin, and death) and with Christ on the other (grace, righteousness, and life). Paul thinks in the same dual terms in 5:20-21 as in 5:15-19. In this context Paul reintroduces the Mosaic law, and places it explicitly on the Adam side of the ledger. The law serves to increase the trespass. I discuss later what exactly this "increase" refers to, but suffice it to say for now that Paul handles the law in a way distinctly at odds with the views of his contemporary Jewish compatriots.[130] Contrary to their opinion, Paul speaks of the law not as God's remedy for the problems of fallen humanity but as something that confirms and exacerbates the problems. As one writer puts it, for Paul the law does not bring a new era of blessing but "actually entrenches man in death."[131] According to 5:20, the law "came in," and that was not good news per se.[132]

While Paul's reference to the Mosaic law in Romans 5:20 is not unexpected in context, 1 Corinthians 15:56 has been an enigma to many interpreters. Paul gives little attention to the Mosaic law through the first fourteen chapters

---

129. For helpful remarks on this point, see Hofius, "Adam-Christ Antithesis," p. 170.

130. See Wright, *Romans,* pp. 524-29, 529-30; and Wright, *Climax,* p. 39.

131. Scroggs, *The Last Adam,* p. 82. For similar comments, see e.g. Dunn, *Romans 1–8,* p. 286; Carter, *Paul and the Power of Sin,* p. 174; and Thielman, *Paul and the Law,* p. 192. Among patristic commentators, Ambrosiaster comments: "It stole in, because, once willingly received, it showed the guilt of those who had already sinned. For they recognized that God would demand the fruit of the seed of righteousness, which had been sown in nature. To steal in, therefore, is to enter without attracting notice and then to dominate. Once the law entered, sin flourished, because the law exposed both the older sinners from the time before the law and those sinning after the law." See *Romans: Interpreted by Early Christian Commentators,* trans. and ed. J. Patout Burns (Grand Rapids: Eerdmans, 2012), p. 128.

132. Commentators are divided on whether "came in" (παρεισῆλθεν) is simply a neutral term, meaning something like "was added," or carries negative connotations. For a defense of the former, see Hofius, "Adam-Christ Antithesis," pp. 198-99; for a defense of the latter, see Moo, *Romans,* pp. 346-47.

of 1 Corinthians, and says not a word about the law in his lengthy treatment of the resurrection earlier in chapter 15. Then, seemingly out of nowhere, Paul states: "The sting of death is sin, and the power of sin is the law." An older opinion, still occasionally defended today, is that this verse does not make sense in context because it is an interpolation and not a genuine part of the original epistle.[133] But not only is there no textual evidence in support of this, but 15:56 actually makes a great deal more sense in context than commentators usually appreciate. The force of Paul's statement is very similar to his point in Romans 5:20: the Mosaic law confirms people in their identity with fallen Adamic humanity.

An initial point suggesting that Paul's (negative) reference to the law in 15:56 is not really out of place in 1 Corinthians is the fact that places where Paul previously mentions or alludes to the Mosaic law have negative connotations.[134] In 7:19 Paul comments that neither circumcision nor uncircumcision counts for anything, thereby relativizing the Mosaic requirements. Likewise, in 9:20 Paul claims he is not "under the law," even though he willingly acts as he does sometimes "in order to win Jews." Beyond these brief clues from earlier in the epistle is the more significant point that the statements in 15:56, read in context, sound so entirely Pauline.[135] That sin brings death and that sin (personified) uses the law as its tool are themes already observed in Romans 5 and 7 and that also appear in Galatians. In addition, Paul raises these themes in 1 Corinthians 15:56 when the Two Adams are in his thoughts, which is precisely what he does in Romans 5 (and to some extent in Romans 7). The Mosaic law may initially seem to come out of nowhere in 15:56, but to Paul's theological mind it must have been an obvious topic to raise. In fact, that Paul would mention the law here, where no specifically law-focused controversy was at issue, may indicate just how thoroughly entrenched in Paul's thought was the connection between

133. A recent writer taking this view is Carter, *Paul and the Power of Sin*, p. 79.

134. Some interpreters do not believe Paul is referring to the *Mosaic* law in 15:56. Vlachos, e.g., believes that Paul refers to law in general, "law qua law"; see *The Law*, pp. 75-79. H. W. Hollander and J. Holleman argue that Paul is not thinking in terms of Judaism or the Mosaic law but adopts the ideas of Philo and many Hellenistic philosophers who viewed human laws as a feature of the degeneration of humanity; see "The Relationship of Death, Sin, and Law in 1 Cor 15:56," *NovT* 35 (1993): 270-91; see also Harm W. Hollander, "The Meaning of the Term 'Law' (Νόμος) in 1 Corinthians," *NovT* 40 (April 1998): 131-34. The fact that Paul has spoken of the Mosaic law with negative overtones in 7:19 and 9:20, and the fact that the statements in Romans 5 and 7 similar to 1 Corinthians 15:56 speak explicitly of the Mosaic law and not simply of law(s) in general, suggest that in 15:56 Paul has the Mosaic law at least primarily in mind.

135. See the helpful comments in Thielman, *Paul and the Law*, pp. 106-8.

the Mosaic law and the forces of sin and death among people identified with the First Adam.

Understanding how Paul connects Adam and the law in 1 Corinthians 15 requires going back at least to 15:22, where Paul makes a programmatic statement that gives focus to the rest of the chapter: "As in Adam all die, so also in Christ shall all be made alive."[136] The First Adam brings death for those identified with him and the Last Adam brings resurrection life for those united to him. In 15:23-44 Paul proceeds to discuss various truths about the resurrection of Christ and his people, and then in 15:45-50 returns explicitly to the Two Adams theme. As in Romans 5:15-19 he sets the Two Adams side-by-side in an extended comparison, attributing opposite characteristics to each. He associates Adam and Christ, respectively, with death and resurrection, with the natural and the spiritual, with dust and heaven, and with perishability (flesh and blood) and imperishability/the kingdom of God. Paul then describes the day of resurrection at Christ's return, when death will be decisively defeated (15:51-55). At this point Paul speaks of sin as the sting of death and the law as the power of sin (15:56). The Mosaic law confirms and strengthens the reign of death under the First Adam. As in Romans 5:20, the law per se here serves a negative function. And as also in Romans 5:20-21, Christ the Last Adam rescues people from the forces of death with which he associates the law: "But thanks be to God, who gives us the victory through our Lord Jesus Christ" (1 Cor. 15:57). The Mosaic law stands explicitly on the First Adam side of the Two Adams ledger.

Romans 5:20 and 1 Corinthians 15:56, therefore, add further weight to the claim that the experience of Israel under the Mosaic law served, in part, as a recapitulation of Adam's experience of probation, fall, and condemnation in Eden. Even while prophetically anticipating Christ in various ways, the Mosaic law also served to bind the people ever more tightly to the powers of sin and death ushered into the world by the rebellion of Adam. Living under the law confirmed OT Israel in their protological Adamic identity, from which God would rescue them through the coming of Christ and his eschatological blessings.[137]

---

136. Joseph A. Fitzmyer Jr. helpfully comments that 15:56 explains what Paul presupposes in 15:20-28; see *First Corinthians: A New Translation with Introduction and Commentary* (New Haven: Yale University Press, 2008), p. 607. The most thorough study to date on the importance of the Two Adams material earlier in 1 Corinthians 15 for understanding 15:56 is Vlachos, *The Law*.

137. Among early Christian interpreters to recognize this point, see e.g. Cyril of Alexandria on Romans 5:20: "The law entered in so that the many-sided nature of the fall of those

The Sanctions of the Mosaic Law according to Paul

When considering the three texts from the OT in the first half of this chapter, I noted how the Mosaic law, especially Deuteronomy, attached sanctions of blessing or curse to Israel's response to the law. In terms of the Adam-Israel parallel, Israel recapitulated Adam's probation and, on account of their disobedience, Adam's condemnation and exile. This idea is also present in Paul. The apostle, understanding Israel's experience as a recapitulation of Adam's, describes the Mosaic law as demanding (perfect) obedience and bringing a curse because of Israel's failure to render it. This pattern in Paul's thought is most clearly evident in Galatians.

In Galatians 3:10 Paul says that those who are of the "works of the law"[138] are under a curse, and proves it by quoting Deuteronomy 27:26: "Cursed be everyone who does not abide by all things written in the Book of the Law, and do them." Paul follows the Septuagint in adding the word "all" to the Hebrew text of Deuteronomy, hence emphasizing the entirety of the obedience that the Mosaic law demands. For this verse to prove his point (namely, that all ¯people who are under the law are also under a curse), Paul must be working with an implied premise: no one actually keeps the law perfectly.[139] Such an

---

who were under the law might be made clear. Nobody could ever be made righteous because of the weakness of human nature. Rather, everyone condemned themselves by their crimes of transgression. The law came as the revealer of our common weakness, so that the human race would appear even more clearly to need the aid of the medicine of Christ." See *Romans,* Ancient Christian Commentary on Scripture, New Testament VI, ed. Gerald Bray (Downers Grove, IL: InterVarsity, 1998), p. 150.

138. I take "works of the law" as a reference to the Mosaic law as a whole. For defense of this position, see e.g. Moisés Silva, "Faith Versus Works of Law in Galatians, in *Justification and Variegated Nomism,* vol. 2, *The Paradoxes of Paul,* ed. D. A. Carson, Peter T. O'Brien, and Mark A. Seifrid (Grand Rapids: Baker Academic, 2005), pp. 221-26; Guy Prentiss Waters, *Justification and the New Perspectives on Paul: A Review and Response* (Phillipsburg, NJ: Presbyterian and Reformed, 2004), pp. 158-70; Moo, *Romans,* pp. 206-10; A. Andrew Das, *Paul, the Law, and the Covenant* (Peabody, MA: Hendrickson, 2001), chap. 7; Pate, *The Reverse of the Curse,* pp. 194-99; and Hong, *The Law in Galatians,* pp. 134-35.

139. For arguments that Paul presumes the premise of sinful inability, and hence teaches the requirement of perfect obedience, see e.g. Das, *Paul, the Law, and the Covenant,* chap. 6; A. Andrew Das, "Galatians 3:10: A 'Newer Perspective' on an Omitted Premise," in *Unity and Diversity in the Gospels and Paul: Essays in Honor of Frank J. Matera,* ed. Christopher W. Skinner and Kelly R. Iverson (Atlanta: Society of Biblical Literature, 2012), pp. 203-23; Seyoon Kim, *Paul and the New Perspective: Second Thoughts on the Origin of Paul's Gospel* (Grand Rapids: Eerdmans, 2002), chap. 4; Bryan D. Estelle, "The Covenant of Works in Moses and Paul," in *Covenant, Justification, and Pastoral Ministry: Essays by the Faculty of Westminster*

implied premise is eminently consistent with Paul's view of human depravity outside of Christ (see Rom. 3:9-21; 8:7-8). The apostle expands his point in the following verses. In 3:11 he quotes Habakkuk 2:4 ("the righteous shall live by faith") to show that no one can be justified by the law. The law, he adds in 3:12, "is not of faith." He proves this by quoting from the law itself: "The one who does them shall live by them" (Lev. 18:5). While faith promises life by believing, the law promises life by doing.[140] Paul's larger point in Galatians 3:10-12, therefore, is that the Mosaic law demands perfect obedience and promises life for it, but inevitably brings a curse because sinful human beings disobey it. Paul echoes these sentiments in Galatians 5:2-4, where he says that those seeking to be justified by the law are "obligated to keep the whole law" — a strong demand for perfect obedience[141] — and find no benefit from Christ. In context, Paul obviously does not consider this a viable option, but one ending inevitably in failure.

Recent footnotes have acknowledged interpreters (many associated with the so-called New Perspective on Paul) who take a different view of Galatians 3:10-12 and 5:3 and deny that Paul is really setting up a contrast between faith and obedience to the law and teaching that the law requires perfect obedience. Some recent Reformed commentators acknowledge that Paul is sharply con-

---

Seminary California, ed. R. Scott Clark (Phillipsburg, NJ: Presbyterian and Reformed, 2007), pp. 124-33; Schreiner, *The Law and Its Fulfillment,* pp. 44-49; and Richard N. Longenecker, *Galatians* (Dallas: Word, 1990), p. 118. Other recent commentators reject the claim that Paul teaches perfect obedience here; e.g., see Martyn, *Galatians,* pp. 309-11; Hays, *Galatians,* p. 247; and Dunn, *Galatians,* p. 171.

140. For arguments that Paul intends to make a sharp contrast between Leviticus 18:5 and Habakkuk 2:4 in Galatians 3:11-12, see e.g. Meyer, *The End of the Law,* pp. 161, 217; Martyn, *Galatians,* pp. 332-33; and Longenecker, *Galatians,* p. 119. That Paul makes a similar contrast between Leviticus 18:5 and Deuteronomy 30:14 in Romans 10:5-8, see Guy P. Waters, "Romans 10:5 and the Covenant of Works," in *The Law Is Not of Faith,* pp. 210-39; and Meyer, *The End of the Law,* pp. 224-25. Despite the antithetical language Paul uses, some argue that he sees a fundamental harmony between Leviticus 18:5 and Habakkuk 2:4; see e.g. Dunn, *Theology of Paul the Apostle,* pp. 152-53; Dunn, *Galatians,* pp. 175-76; and Garlington, *Galatians,* pp. 161-63. Garlington acknowledges that 3:12 "poses a problem" for his reading.

141. For an extended argument that Paul teaches the law's demand for perfect obedience in Galatians 5:3, see S. M. Baugh, "Galatians 5:1-6 and Personal Obligation: Reflections on Paul and the Law," in *The Law Is Not of Faith,* pp. 259-80; see also Hans Dieter Betz, *Galatians: A Commentary on Paul's Letter to the Churches in Galatia* (Philadelphia: Fortress, 1979), pp. 260-61; and Schreiner, *The Law and Its Fulfillment,* pp. 63-64. Among writers arguing instead that Paul simply holds out the task of fulfilling the law as a never-ending process or a total way of life, see Martyn, *Galatians,* pp. 470-71; Garlington, *Galatians,* pp. 238-39; Hays, *Galatians,* p. 312; and Dunn, *Galatians,* p. 266.

trasting faith and works of the law in these and parallel passages, yet deny that the Mosaic law itself can be contrasted with faith (in this sense adopting a similar conclusion to many New Perspective proponents). Instead, these Reformed commentators believe that when Paul quotes Leviticus 18:5, or elsewhere refers to the law in contrast to faith, he thinks not of the Mosaic law itself but of the law as legalistically misinterpreted by his Jewish contemporaries.[142] In my judgment this line of interpretation should also be rejected.[143] Undoubtedly Paul dealt with people whom he judged to have misinterpreted the purposes of the Mosaic law, but the idea that the *law itself* stood in contrast to faith, in certain respects, was Paul's own view. For one thing, it is implausible that Paul would concede the interpretation of Leviticus 18:5 to his opponents both in Galatians 3:12 and Romans 10:5 (where he introduces his quote by saying, "*Moses* writes" about the righteousness of the law). Furthermore, in Galatians 3:19 Paul asks a rhetorical question, understandable in light of the contrast of law and faith in previous verses: "Why then the law?" His explanation in 3:19–4:7 is that *God's own purpose* in giving the Mosaic law was to keep his people imprisoned under sin for a time, a condition from which Christ released those who believe in him. In this same section of Galatians Paul speaks of Christ himself being "born of the law, to redeem those who were under the law" (4:4-5). As Israel was under the Mosaic law so Christ came under the Mosaic law. Yet Paul could hardly have been asserting that Christ, who he says elsewhere "knew no sin" (2 Cor. 5:21), lived under a subjective misinterpretation of the law. Christ, like the Israelites, came "under the law" in an objective sense that reflected God's own purposes in giving it.

Despite these considerations it may still be difficult to think that Paul really believed that the Mosaic law itself, in some significant respect, stands in contrast to faith. After all, Paul considered OT saints to be people of faith and he required obedience on the part of NT saints, sometimes even in terms of the law (see Chapter 9). But Paul's contrast of faith and the Mosaic law is readily understandable if we remember that he believed that

142. Two prominent examples are Herman Ridderbos and John Murray. See e.g. Herman N. Ridderbos, *The Epistle of Paul to the Churches of Galatia* (Grand Rapids: Eerdmans, 1953), pp. 123-25; Ridderbos, *Paul*, pp. 134-42, 153-58; and Murray, *Romans*, 2:50-51, 249-51. The legalistic misinterpretation idea is also common in Cranfield's Romans commentary, which is sometimes regarded as a standard Reformed exposition of this epistle. Räisänen, with justification, dismisses Cranfield's frequent recourse to the misinterpretation idea as "an eloquent bit of special pleading." See *Paul and the Law*, p. 43.

143. For a more expanded argument, along the same lines as my own, see Westerholm, *Perspectives Old and New*, pp. 330-33.

one central purpose of the Mosaic law was to establish Israel as a recapitulation of Adam. God intended the Mosaic law to function for Israel in a way analogous to how God's primordial law to Adam functioned in Eden: promising life for obedience and threatening death for disobedience. But God sent his Son as the last Adam, who redeemed those under the law (Gal. 4:5) so that by faith alone his people might no longer be united to the First Adam. God intended life under the Mosaic covenant, in part, to mimic the experience of the First Adam; God did not intend life under the new covenant to do this at all.

These observations should help to provide a response to Heiki Räisänen's assertion that Paul, inconsistently, held Jews to a higher standard than Christians, for he condemned Jews for failure to render perfect obedience to the Mosaic law while not expecting such performance from Christians.[144] Räisänen makes a valid observation, but this feature of Paul's thought reveals the depth of his Two Adams theology rather than an inherent tension. For Paul, Christians had escaped the bondage of the Mosaic law insofar as it associated people with Adam and his failed probation. Not being condemned for lapses in obedience is part of the glory of the gospel that Paul preached "apart from the law" (see Rom. 3:21). Along similar lines, Räisänen also falsely accuses Paul of contradiction for teaching both that the Mosaic law promised life (e.g., Gal. 3:12; Rom. 7:10) and that it could not lead to life, even in principle (e.g., Gal. 3:21).[145] Insofar as the Mosaic law was designed to replicate the probationary status of Adam, it held out life as the consequence of obedience, and nowhere does Scripture indicate that perfect obedience would *not* have produced this promised blessing. Yet the Mosaic covenant was not a simple do-over. The Israelites were sinners and already condemned in Adam before arriving at Sinai. They would inevitably disobey the law (Deut. 30:1). God's ultimate purpose for the Mosaic covenant was not to replicate the Adamic covenant *simpliciter* but to highlight the miserable state of Adamic humanity so that grace might abound "all the more" through the work of Christ in the last days (Rom. 5:20-21). In this sense, according to Paul, God never intended the Mosaic law to be his people's vehicle to life (Gal. 3:21).

I have argued that Paul confirms OT teaching that the Mosaic covenant made Israel's experience a recapitulation of Adam's experience under the covenant of creation in Eden. In this covenant the law played a special role,

---

144. Räisänen, *Paul and the Law,* p. 149.
145. Räisänen, *Paul and the Law,* p. 152.

prescribing Israel's required obedience and announcing the just sanctions that would follow their response to God's commands. One purpose of the Mosaic law was to echo the law originally revealed to Adam. The Mosaic law is thus, *in part,* a protological moral standard, teaching about God's moral relationship to human beings in their created and fallen condition. This provides basic theological explanation for the similarities of the Mosaic law and natural law. To enable Israel to recapitulate the experience of Adam, its law resembled the natural law that bound Adam under the covenant of creation.

The Mosaic Law and Israel as Microcosm

In the previous section I argued, from Paul, that one of God's chief purposes in placing Israel under the Mosaic law was to make his people's experience a recapitulation of Adam's probation, fall, and condemnation. The Mosaic law exposed and clarified the protological moral relationship of God and humanity. This section presses a distinct but related point. For Paul, Israel under the Mosaic law was a *microcosm,* "a paradigm case of what has happened with all human beings. . . ."[146] Israel was a world-in-miniature, exemplifying the situation of all peoples, who have knowledge of God's law and are obligated to it, yet live in fundamental rebellion against it and stand under its judgment. Given my previous argument about the Adamic character of the Mosaic law, combined with Paul's insistence in Romans 5 and 1 Corinthians 15 that the entire human race lies in the grip of sin and death under Adam, this conclusion should not be surprising. In the very thing that most evidently set Israel apart from the world — having God's law specially revealed at Sinai — Paul thought Israel was destined to manifest the basic human plight they shared with their pagan neighbors. This provides a deeper theological explanation of why the Mosaic law resembles the natural law in significant respects: the Mosaic law's resemblance to the natural law that continues to bind the entire human race helps to ensure that Israel's experience can be, in part, representative of the experience of the world as a whole. To make this argument, I consider two interesting phenomena in the Pauline epistles: Paul reasons as if Gentiles share the Israelite condition of being under the Mosaic law, and he treats Israel's situation under the law as resembling the situation of pagan Gentiles living within the natural order.

146. In the words of Westerholm, *Perspectives Old and New,* p. 333.

Gentiles under the Law

First I consider several Pauline texts that speak of being "under the [Mosaic] law," or something similar, as a condition that extends beyond OT Israelites and encompasses Gentiles as well. In these texts Paul uses a seemingly parochial description of Israel under Moses as a way of describing both the plight of all humanity under sin and the character of salvation for all people in Christ.

Two relevant texts are Romans 6:14 and 7:4-6. In Romans 6:14 Paul tells readers that sin will not lord it over them "since you are not under law but under grace." In Romans 7:4-6 Paul says that they have "died to the law" and been "released from the law" through the work of Christ. Paul presumes that his readers at one time were under the law. He does not say this explicitly in 6:14, but this verse follows an extended explanation of the radical transition effected for believers through their identification with Christ's death and resurrection. Romans 6:14 is a climactic assertion describing the effects of moving from one realm of existence to another. Being under the law characterized the old realm. In 7:4-6 this is explicit. Paul's readers "have died to the law" and "are released" from it, "having died to that which held us captive." The context indicates that Paul refers to the Mosaic law specifically.[147] This is evident, first, from the fact that the entire section of Romans in which these verses fall was triggered by a hypothetical objection in 6:1. This objection was instigated by Paul's strong statements at the end of Romans 5 about the justification in Christ that rescued people from the reign of sin and death, whose reign was solidified by the law which "came in" (at Sinai). If Romans 6–7 addresses how Christians overcome a law other than the Mosaic law, then Paul fails to address the specific objection. Furthermore, in the verses immediately following 7:4-6 Paul defends the law against the slander of another imagined objector, and, as argued above, makes some reference in 7:7-12 to the law as given at Sinai.

147. A number of interpreters note that Paul is referring first and foremost to the *Mosaic* law, as given by God, yet with a universal application in view, as I argue. See e.g. Moo, *Romans,* pp. 387-88, 416-17; Das, *Paul, the Law, and the Covenant,* pp. 227-28; Witherington, *Paul's Letter to the Romans,* p. 164; and Fitzmyer, *Romans,* p. 447. Murray argues, on the other hand, against a reference to the Mosaic law as given by God; see e.g. *Romans,* 1:228-29, 239. This conclusion, driven by his (correct) presupposition that OT saints also enjoyed the benefits of salvation by faith, is closely related to his embrace of the Jewish legalism/misinterpretation view discussed in a previous footnote. In my judgment, Murray allows a valid Pauline doctrine (salvation by grace in the OT) to override another valid Pauline doctrine (justification as being liberated from the Mosaic law). By invalidating the second doctrine *a priori* he has eliminated a point of dramatic tension in the text and — at least from the perspective of the present study — banished one of the most interesting features of Paul's argument in both Galatians and Romans.

But while Paul proclaims the liberation of his readers from the bondage of the Mosaic law, his readers include Gentiles. I do not wish to engage the ongoing debates about whether Paul wrote to a primarily Jewish or Gentile audience. I note only that Paul had at least some Gentile readers (see e.g. 11:13-24) and that a chief concern of Paul when discussing humanity's condemnation under sin and its salvation in Christ was to unite Jew and Gentile in a common experience. In Romans 6–7 Paul's announcement of release from being under the Mosaic law is good news for *all* his readers.

Several verses in Galatians from the middle of chapter 3 to the beginning of chapter 4 use the phrase "under the law" (or close equivalents) in a way similar to Romans 6:14 and 7:4-6. The first example is Galatians 3:13-14, where Paul writes that "Christ redeemed us from the curse of the law." Who is this "us" whom Christ has redeemed? In the larger section of Galatians we are now considering, Paul's use of first and second person plural pronouns has divided interpreters.[148] In 3:13-14, however, Paul's reference seems clear. Immediately after stating that Christ has redeemed "us" from the curse of the law by becoming a curse for us he indicates the result: "so that in Christ Jesus the blessing of Abraham might come to *the Gentiles*. . . ." Though obviously not excluding Jews, Paul's focus is upon the Gentiles' enjoyment of Abraham's blessing.[149] They are no longer under curse. Somehow the curse of the law, imposed through the sanctions of the Mosaic covenant (3:10), reveals the state in which Gentiles also found themselves when they were outside of Christ.

Shortly thereafter Paul asks a question that naturally rises in light of the negative-sounding things he has been saying about the law of Moses: "Why then the law?" (Gal. 3:19). His explanation through the rest of the chapter points to the temporary functions of the law while God's people were under age: the law was never meant to overturn the promises to Abraham but to keep the covenant people under supervision in anticipation of the Messiah's coming. Within this explanation Paul again uses language seemingly unique to Israel that in fact applies to Gentiles as well. First, he says: "the Scripture imprisoned everything under sin" (3:22). In context this statement indicates that the Mosaic law imprisoned all people, Gentiles included. Paul has been explaining the purposes and functions of the Mosaic law in the preceding verses, in answer to the "why the law" question of 3:19. Thus Paul is still speaking of the law's work though he uses "Scripture"

---

148. For further argument that Gentiles are in view throughout the texts in Galatians 3–4 I consider here, see Das, *Paul and the Jews*, pp. 120-28.

149. For further argument that this "us" refers to Gentiles, see Räisänen, *Paul and the Law*, pp. 19-20.

instead of "law" in 3:22. Any doubt about this conclusion is eliminated by the next verse, where Paul speaks again of imprisonment and associates it explicitly with the law. Whom does the Scripture/law imprison in 3:22? Again we would expect a parochial reference to Israel, who stood at Sinai to receive the law through angels (3:19). But Paul uses the neuter "everything" (τὰ πάντα), which suggests that the law's work has a universal effect that encompasses Gentiles as well.[150] Furthermore, the purpose of this imprisonment is that "the promise by faith in Jesus Christ might be given to those who believe." Given Paul's larger point that Jews and Gentiles alike are called to faith, this statement adds further evidence of the universal relevance of the law at this point in his argument.

Galatians 3:24-25 is similar. Paul begins by stating that "the law was our guardian until Christ came." To whom does "our" refer? Again we would expect a particularistic focus upon Jews who belonged to the old covenant people, but the scope of Paul's thought is broader here as well. The purpose of the law's guardianship is that "*we* might be justified by faith" (3:24), such that with the coming of faith "*we* are no longer under a guardian" (3:25). Paul provides proof for all this in 3:26: "for in Christ Jesus you are all sons of God, through faith." As believing Jews and Gentiles share a common adoption as God's children, they look back and confess that they are "no longer" under a guardian. The guardianship of the law somehow applied to Gentiles too, such that their redemption can be described as a liberation from it.[151]

Finally, in Galatians 4:4-5 Paul declares that in the fullness of time "God sent forth his Son, born of woman, born under the law, to redeem those who were under the law." Who were those under the law and redeemed by Christ? Again Paul's reference extends beyond Israel. In 4:5-6 Paul explains that Christ redeemed those under the law "so that *we* might receive adoption as sons. And because *you* are sons, God has sent the Spirit of his Son into our hearts." Paul's chain of reasoning encompasses his Gentile audience. These Gentile believers are sons, because they have been adopted, because they have been redeemed from being under the law. Hence in 4:7 Paul can also say: "So you are *no longer* a slave, but a son, and if a son, then an heir through God." The slavery that being under the law entailed was a condition Gentile Christians once endured, though technically they were never bound by the Mosaic covenant.[152]

---

150. See further comments in Longenecker, *Galatians*, p. 144; and Dunn, *Galatians*, p. 194.

151. For further defense that Paul refers here to Gentiles as under the law's guardianship, see Räisänen, *Paul and the Law*, p. 20.

152. For further argument on the Gentile reference in 4:5-6 see again Räisänen, *Paul and the Law*, pp. 20-21.

The upshot of these texts is that Gentiles too have experienced salvation in Christ as a release from being under the Mosaic law, though they were never joined to God's old covenant people Israel. Kari Kuula looks at the same evidence examined above and describes Paul's reasoning as "tortuous, incoherent or even contradictory."[153] Paul's thought may be complex and layered, but there is nothing tortuous about it. The explanation is that he saw Israel as a microcosm of the nations. The experience of Israel was paradigmatic of the lost estate of the whole human race under sin. Microcosmic Israel so displayed the basic predicament of humanity at large that Paul can describe the pre-Christian state of the Gentiles in terms seemingly reserved for Israel under Moses. Jews and Gentiles alike can look back at their former state as one "under the [Mosaic] law."

Israel under the Stoicheia of the World

In this subsection I continue to reflect upon the idea of Israel as microcosm, but from the opposite direction. In Galatians 4:3 and 4:9 Paul speaks of the στοιχεῖα τοῦ κόσμου, which I refer to as the "*stoicheia* of the world," since the meaning, and thus the proper translation, of the first word in the Greek phrase is disputed. Paul speaks in these verses of the experience of Israel under the Mosaic law as similar (though not identical) to the experience of pagans living within the confines of the natural order. Thus, Paul reveals the microcosmic identity of Israel not only by making Israel's experience of the law paradigmatic for the situation of Gentiles before Christ (considered in the previous subsection) but also by making the situation of such Gentiles paradigmatic for Israel's experience under the Mosaic law. Initially shocking though it may sound — and it is all the more startling coming from a trained Pharisee — Paul saw life under the Mosaic law as analogous to the life of Gentile pagans in certain respects.[154]

First, what is the immediate reference of "*stoicheia* of the world" in 4:3

153. Kuula, *The Law*, 1:202.
154. Some remarks by commentators help to capture the astounding character of Paul's claims. Hays (*Galatians*, p. 287) states: "This is perhaps the most stunning sentence in this entire confrontational letter. Paul is suggesting that Judaism's holy observances are, in effect, no different from paganism's worship of earthly elements." J. Louis Martyn comments: "His charge that the Law is one of the cosmic powers that enslave human beings . . . will certainly have been considered monstrous [to Paul's Galatian opponents]." See *Theological Issues in the Letters of Paul* (Nashville: Abingdon, 1997), p. 38.

and 4:9? In 4:3 Paul identifies the *stoicheia* with the Mosaic law and hence with the experience of Israel, as several factors indicate. For one thing, 4:1-7 is in many respects a recapitulation of 3:23-29. In both cases Paul describes the condition of being under age and under close supervision and then being liberated from that condition.[155] In 3:23-29 he refers specifically to the giving of the Mosaic law, in answer to the question posed in 3:19. Paul uses a series of virtually identical expressions in 3:23-29 that refer to the experience of OT Israel: under the law, under sin, and under a guardian. Paul uses a similar phrase in 4:3 — enslaved under (ὑπὸ) the *stoicheia* of the world — and then promptly moves back to "under the law" in 4:5 to describe the same people who were under the *stoicheia*. Though Paul has universal application in mind in 3:22-29, as we saw in the previous subsection, he speaks in the language of Israel under the Mosaic law. Thus, since 4:1-7 recaps and elaborates the argument of 3:22-29, Israel under the Mosaic law must again be the immediate reference in 4:3. Jews under Moses were children enslaved under the *stoicheia*.

The immediate reference shifts, however, in 4:9. Paul's statement in 4:8 switches focus to his Gentile audience's pre-Christian condition: "Formerly, when you did not know God, you were enslaved to those that by nature are not gods." Despite the generally negative cast of Paul's teaching about the Mosaic law in Galatians 2–4, he obviously did not think it provided no knowledge of the true God or enslaved people to false gods. The Mosaic law was anything but atheistic or polytheistic. Paul speaks in 4:8, therefore, of Gentile believers' former life in paganism. He continues to address these Gentiles' situation when he proceeds to write in 4:9: "But now that you have come to know God, or rather to be known by God, how can you turn back again to the weak and worthless elementary principles [*stoicheia*] of the world, whose slaves you want to be once more?" The Gentiles had evidently been enslaved to the *stoicheia* during their life as pagans, else Paul would not have written "again" or "once more."[156] Thus the phrase "*stoicheia* of the world" can refer both to the Mosaic law that bound OT Israel and to something that bound pagans.

---

155. See Hays, *Galatians*, pp. 280-81.

156. Contra the conclusion of Jonathan F. Bayes, *The Weakness of the Law: God's Law and the Christian in New Testament Perspective* (Carlisle: Paternoster, 2000), chap. 3, who argues that Paul identifies the *stoicheia* with the Mosaic law but not with pagan principles or practices. Though Bayes understandably wishes to protect Mosaic religion from the taint of paganism, I judge that his conclusion about the *stoicheia* involves letting a valid theological concern override one of the most interesting features of this particular text. The poignant exegetical question is not whether Paul analogizes life under the Mosaic law to pagan existence in Galatians 4, but why and how he did.

It is important to note, furthermore, exactly how Paul reasons in 4:9. If the Gentile believers were in danger of turning back to the *stoicheia* then they must have been under the *stoicheia* as pagans. But the particular threat that Paul is addressing throughout Galatians is the danger that these Gentile believers would submit to the Mosaic law. He is not concerned that they would return to paganism. What Paul says implicitly in 4:9, therefore, is that by submitting to the Mosaic law these Gentile believers would be putting themselves into the same pitiful condition they experienced as pagans. Both life under the Mosaic law and life under paganism can be described as "under the *stoicheia* of the world." As far as Paul is concerned, it would not make any material difference whether a Gentile Christian returned to paganism or submitted to the Mosaic law. Both constituted a rejection of the redemptive riches found in Christ.[157]

But what then exactly does "*stoicheia* of the world" mean? Scholars debate a number of possibilities. Some believe it refers to demonic forces, and Paul's statement in 4:8 concerning the false gods the Gentile believers used to worship gives the claim some initial plausibility.[158] Several considerations militate against it, however. First, though worship of false gods obviously was part of the Gentiles' pagan experience under the *stoicheia*, it is not clear from 4:8-9 that Paul means to equate being under the *stoicheia* with being idolatrous. Second, living under the dominion of demonic forces would not be an accurate way to describe life "under the [Mosaic] law," yet being under the Mosaic law was one way of being under the *stoicheia* (as evident in 4:3). The Mosaic law was rigorously monotheistic, and Paul's concern about a return to the Mosaic law in Galatians did not involve fear of polytheism or demon worship. Finally, there is no extant evidence for this meaning of the phrase anywhere else in Greek literature until a century later than Galatians was written.[159]

Two other possibilities for translating "*stoicheia* of the world" are much more plausible. One is that the phrase refers to the world's elemental substances (air, fire, water, earth). The principal evidence for this view is that it

---

157. See comments in Meyer, *The End of the Law,* p. 174; and Thielman, *Paul and the Law,* p. 134.

158. Defenders of this view include Hong, *The Law in Galatians,* pp. 162-65; and Clinton E. Arnold, "Returning to the Domain of the Powers: STOICHEIA as Evil Spirits in Galatians 4:3,9," *NovT* 38 (January 1996): 55-76; see also Clinton E. Arnold, *The Colossian Syncretism: The Interface between Christianity and Folk Belief at Colossae* (Grand Rapids: Baker, 1996), pp. 183-84.

159. See Hays, *Galatians,* p. 282; Ben Witherington III, *Grace in Galatia: A Commentary on St Paul's Letter to the Galatians* (Grand Rapids: Eerdmans, 1998), pp. 284-85; and Longenecker, *Galatians,* p. 165.

is very well attested in the Greek literature of the time, and important aspects of Paul's message in Galatians also make sense of this interpretation.[160] The other plausible option is that the *stoicheia* are basic principles.[161] This view is not well attested in the extant Greek literature of Paul's day, though many factors in the text of Galatians make it attractive. In my judgment, making a definitive decision between these last two options is not crucial for the issues under consideration here. Whichever interpretation one finds persuasive, it is crucial to recognize that Paul speaks of the *stoicheia* of the world in Galatians 4:3, 9 in order to refer both to a moral standard that obligates humanity and to the things of this present created order. Paul wishes to affirm that the Mosaic law and natural law alike are *protological* moral standards tied to the original creation that God continues to preserve.

First, then, Paul's reference to the *stoicheia* of the world has strong moral overtones (which gives the translation "basic principles of the world" its appeal). For example, in Galatians 6:16 Paul writes: "And as for all who walk [στοιχήσουσιν] by this rule, peace and mercy be upon them. . . ." Instead of using a more familiar and expected word for "walk," such as περιπατέω (as in 5:16), Paul uses an unexpected term that evokes memory of the phrase "*stoicheia* of the world" earlier in the epistle. That he indeed wishes readers to recall 4:3, 9 when reading 6:16 is bolstered by the fact that in 6:14 he declares that he has been crucified to "the world" and "the world" to him. He no longer belongs to the world, with its *stoicheia,* but now walks [*stoichēsousin*] according to a new rule that corresponds to the new creation (6:15-16). Here in 6:16, significantly, Paul refers to a way of life for believers, whose basic principles are not boasting in the flesh or clinging to circumcision (6:12-15). Moral overtones to the phrase "*stoicheia* of the world" also emerge from a few features of Paul's argument in 4:1-10 itself. In 4:1-3, for instance, he refers to the *stoicheia* in a way meant to parallel the Mosaic law, as something fitting for children but not adults. In 4:10, furthermore, Paul describes what a return to the *stoicheia* (through embracing the Mosaic law) would look like, and it involves observing rituals according to the movement of the calendar.

Second, "*stoicheia* of the world" in Galatians 4:3, 9 also points to the

---

160. This view is taken, e.g., in Dunn, *Theology of Paul the Apostle,* p. 108; and Martinus C. de Boer, *Galatians: A Commentary* (Louisville: Westminster John Knox, 2011), pp. 252-56.

161. A good case for this view is offered in Witherington, *Grace in Galatia,* pp. 285-86; see also Linda J. Belleville, "'Under Law': Structural Analysis and the Pauline Concept of Law in Galatians 3:21–4:11," *JSNT* 26 (1986): 53-78; Longenecker, *Galatians,* pp. 165-66; Garlington, *Galatians,* p. 192; and Ridderbos, *Paul,* p. 149.

things of the present created order. One of the attractions of the phrase for Paul is that it refers to the *world* and thus highlights the *protological* character of the Mosaic law. The "*stoicheia* of the world" refers to a moral standard designed and appropriate for life under the confines of the original creation. Israel's life under the Mosaic law and Gentile existence in paganism, for all their many differences, share this protological condition in common.

One clue supporting this conclusion appears in the verse following Paul's second reference to the basic principles of the world: "You observe days and months and seasons and years" (4:10). This is a layered statement. Most immediately Paul refers to observance of the Mosaic law's calendar requirements. He is concerned about Gentile believers embracing the Mosaic law, and he appeals to these practices as things characteristic of reversion to Moses. Paul likely refers, respectively, to Sabbath days, offerings at the beginning of each month (Num. 10:10; 28:11-15), appointed feasts and festivals (Leviticus 23), and sabbatical and Jubilee years (Leviticus 25).[162] At another level Paul must be evoking recollection of their former pagan practices. If observing the Mosaic calendar bore no similarity to pagan practices then the force of Paul's point would be eviscerated. For Paul, the fact that the OT law contained extensive calendar regulations was evidence for the likeness between life under the law and life under paganism (though these regulations obviously had many distinctive Mosaic features). Paganism typically pays careful attention to the movement and rhythms of the calendar, and so did the Mosaic law. At yet another level, Galatians 4:10 hearkens back to the creation story of Genesis 1.[163] At creation God created the sun, moon, and stars, "for signs and for seasons, and for days and years" (1:14).

Why, of all the many Mosaic laws, did Paul single out these calendar requirements in Galatians 4:10, especially when many of the relevant ceremonies would have been relatively insignificant for Jews living in Diaspora regions such as Galatia? The answer appears to be their basic similarity to Gentile pagan practices (however distorted by sin the latter are) and their rootedness in the original created order. The protological moral standard Paul has in mind is naturally entwined with the movement of days, months, seasons, and years governed by sun, moon, and stars. The Mosaic law thus can be characterized as the basic elements/principles of *the world*.

162. See Garlington, *Galatians*, pp. 201-2; see also Longenecker, *Galatians*, p. 182; and Dunn, *Galatians*, pp. 227-28.

163. See Martyn, *Galatians*, pp. 416-18; and Hays, *Galatians*, p. 288. Though he is not commenting on Galatians 4:9-10, compare relevant comments in Joseph Blenkinsopp, *Wisdom and Law in the Old Testament: The Ordering of Life in Israel and Early Judaism* (Oxford: Oxford University Press, 1983), pp. 107-8.

That Paul was attracted to the phrase *"stoicheia* of *the world"* because the Mosaic law was a moral standard rooted in the present created order finds further support in the conclusion to Galatians. Commentators generally agree that the closing section of Galatians (6:11-18) is of great significance, as Paul recaps his argument and seeks to make it hit home in a striking manner. At the heart of this closing salvo he writes: "But far be it from me to boast except in the cross of our Lord Jesus Christ, by which the world has been crucified to me, and I to the world. For neither circumcision counts for anything, nor uncircumcision, but a new creation" (6:14-15). Paul asserts his break with "the world" that has been effected through Christ's cross. This is evidently the world in which the distinction between circumcision and uncircumcision matters, a world standing in contrast to the new creation. Is this reference to "world" meant to remind readers of the *stoicheia* of the "world" mentioned in 4:3, 9? The very fact that Paul brings together so many of the themes of his letter in this closing section makes an affirmative answer likely. In both chapters 4 and 6, furthermore, "the world" is something from which Paul dissociates himself adamantly. Adding to the evidence is the fact, discussed above, that Paul alludes back to the *stoicheia* of 4:3, 9 through the unusual word for "walk" that he uses in 6:16. Paul evidently wished to bring 4:3, 9 back to special remembrance in his conclusion.

This means that Paul's radical break from the world through Christ's cross (6:14) is of one piece with his being redeemed by Christ from slavery to the *stoicheia* of the world (4:3-5). And since Paul's identification with the "new creation" is the great alternative to belonging to "the world" (6:14-15), Paul must also intend believers' identification with the "new creation" to contrast with slavery to the *stoicheia* of "the world" (4:3, 9). Paul was evidently attracted to the phrase "the *stoicheia* of *the world,*" therefore, because he wished to communicate that the Mosaic law was not a moral standard rooted in the "new creation."[164] In other words, the Mosaic law, in important respects, is a protological, not an eschatological, moral standard. This idea fits well with other eschatologically charged themes throughout Galatians.[165]

---

164. See comments in Meyer, *The End of the Law,* p. 171 n. 188.

165. The reference to "the present evil age" in 1:4 sets the tone. In light of Paul's later references to "the world" (4:3, 9; 6:14) it is interesting to note that Paul elsewhere uses "this age" and "the world" interchangeably (e.g., 1 Cor. 1:20; 3:18-19); see Hong, *The Law in Galatians,* pp. 88-89. Other prominent examples of the eschatological motif in Galatians include the comparison between the earthly and heavenly Jerusalems in Galatians 4 and the Spirit/flesh contrast in Galatians 5. See relevant comments in Dunn, "In Search of Common Ground," in *Paul and the Mosaic Law,* p. 318. On the apocalyptic character of Galatians generally, see especially Martyn, *Theological Issues,* chap. 7.

Further bolstering this conclusion about the significance of "the world" in Galatians 4:3, 9 is the argument of Colossians 2:8-23, which places both the Mosaic law and pagan moral rules under the category of "*stoicheia* of the world" and also contrasts them with a distinctively eschatological, or new creation, identity. I take Paul to be the author of Colossians, and thus his reasoning in this later letter and utilization of the "*stoicheia* of the world" theme can at least shed light upon what he was trying to argue in the earlier epistle to the Galatians.

In Colossians 2:8-23 Paul seems to alternate between references to the Mosaic law and paganism, adherence to both of which he sees as incompatible with Christian faith. He first takes on philosophy and human tradition — presumably pagan — and identifies this with the *stoicheia* of the world (2:8). Shortly thereafter he refers to "the record of debt that stood against us with its legal demands," which Christ canceled through his cross (2:14). This sounds like a reference to the Mosaic law, a suspicion strengthened by the fact that Paul uses a word, δόγμασιν, also used in Ephesians 2:15-16 to speak of the Mosaic law as abolished through the cross of Christ. Paul continues his reference to Moses in Colossians 2:16-17, where he forbids passing judgment about "food and drink, or with regard to a festival or a new moon or a Sabbath." This echoes Paul's extended discussion in Romans 14:1–15:7 about judging other Christians based upon Mosaic rules. The idea that such rules were a "shadow of the things to come" also fits a Mosaic rather than pagan context. Yet in the following verses, specifically Colossians 2:18, 20-23, the focus seems to shift back to paganism, since the asceticism and angel worship it condemns find no place in the Mosaic law, and are condemned as "human precepts and teachings." In this context Paul again refers to the *stoicheia* of the world (2:20). Though Paul obviously recognized many crucial differences between the Mosaic law and pagan teachings, he links them together here in that observing either one is now incompatible with a person's union with Christ. And what exactly is the moral alternative to both the Mosaic law and pagan asceticism? Immediately following Colossians 2:8-23 Paul reminds readers that they have been raised with Christ, who is seated at God's right hand. They are to set their minds on things above, not on earthly things, for they have died and their lives are hidden with Christ in God, while they wait to appear with Christ in glory when he appears (3:1-4). Following this, Paul launches into a detailed series of moral exhortations appropriate for those whose true identity is found with Christ in heaven rather than upon this earth.

According to Colossians 2–3, therefore, Christians are separated from protological things of the present earth and united to Christ in his eschatological heavenly kingdom. This adds further evidence to my reading of the *"stoicheia* of *the world"* in Galatians 4. For Paul, the Mosaic law was a moral standard fit for protological existence in the old creation order, and in this way resembled the moral norms under which all people have lived apart from Christ in this present world created by God.

In this subsection I have argued, particularly from Galatians 4:1-10, that Paul not only saw Israel under the Mosaic law as a microcosmic paradigm for the basic condition of the whole human race but that he also saw the condition of pagan Gentiles, living under the confines of the present creation order, as in some sense paradigmatic for Israel under the Mosaic law. The truth is essentially the same, but Paul viewed it moving in both directions. Israel's plight under the law displayed for all the world its lost estate before God, yet the nations' existence under the natural order of the old creation was replicated in important respects through Israel's existence under the law of Moses. It is important to emphasize, at the same time, that Paul obviously did not view life in the Mosaic covenant and life in paganism as identical in every respect. For Paul the Mosaic law was holy, righteous, and good (Rom. 7:12), unlike pagan religion which perverted the truths known from the natural created order (see Rom. 1:22-25). The Mosaic law also testified to the righteousness to be revealed in the Lord Jesus Christ (Rom. 3:21), a privilege Paul never ascribed to natural revelation, let alone to pagan religion. Paul's point is that the pagan Gentiles, living under the present created order (whose witness to God they distorted in their sin), existed under a protological moral standard, while OT Israel, living under the Mosaic law (whose truth they also sinfully distorted), likewise existed under a protological moral standard.

With this we now have before us Paul's deepest theological explanation for the similarities between the Mosaic and natural laws. Not only did Israel's experience under the Mosaic law recapitulate Adam's experience under God's natural law at creation but also Israel's life under the law showcased the situation of all nations in their existence under the natural order as God preserves it. What the Mosaic law revealed to Israel — that they were accountable to God, condemned before him, and thus in need of a Savior — was also true of their pagan neighbors, as they themselves understood through the natural law. God intended the Mosaic law to resemble the natural law in many respects in order to ensure that Israel's experience under Moses would not be relevant for themselves alone but would be an accurate microcosmic encapsulation of the predicament of the whole world.

Conclusion

This chapter is long but nevertheless far from comprehensive. I have not examined the vast majority of the law of Moses nor the teaching of NT writers other than Paul. I have not explored in any detail the purposes and teaching of the Mosaic law unknown in the natural law and hence unique to Israel, such as the sacrificial system that foreshadowed the atoning work of Christ. I have not discussed the experience of God's redemptive grace the OT saints experienced or the joy they expressed in obeying the law in response to this grace. And I have not reflected on the way the OT prophets pricked Israel's conscience and held them accountable for disobedience to the Mosaic law through appeals to their commonsense knowledge of the broader natural order (e.g., Isa. 1:2-3; 29:16; Amos 3:3-8; 6:12).[166] But in the many passages considered I have set out extensive evidence for several claims of significance for this broader study.

According to Paul and several texts from Exodus, Leviticus, and Deuteronomy, one reason that God gave the Mosaic law to Israel was to bring them through a recapitulation of Adam's original probation and fall. As such, the Mosaic law served, in part, as a protological moral standard. It promised life for obedience and death for disobedience. In so doing, the Mosaic law made Israel a microcosm of the nations, showing forth the ultimate predicament of the whole human race created and fallen in Adam and accountable to the justice of God. The Mosaic law, in playing this role, governed Israel in a way analogous to the way the natural law governed the nations. Functionally and substantively, the Mosaic law did for Israel in audible and more clear ways what the natural law does for the nations in silent and more obscure ways. In displaying the protological connection between response to God's law and divine recompense, the Mosaic law, on the one hand, reinforced the sobering message of the natural law that human sin leaves all people accountable to God and under his judgment. But on the other hand it served the ultimate positive purpose of driving Israel — and finally all people — to forsake reliance on their own works and to find their righteousness in the coming Messiah. This Messiah would satisfy all the just demands of the protological law, earn its promised blessings, and attain the original human eschatological destiny. This final scene of the biblical story of natural law awaits Chapter 9.

166. See the brief discussion of these texts in Chapter 4.

CHAPTER 8

By Me Kings Reign, and Rulers Decree What Is Just: Natural Law in the Wisdom Literature

In Part 2 of this book we have considered the significance of natural law for the moral life of participants in the redemptive covenants of grace. In his covenant with Abraham, God gave little specific instruction about his broader moral life as a sojourner in human society, but expected Abraham to live according to the natural law that obligated the human race in common under the Noahic covenant (Chapter 6). In the Mosaic covenant, God gave to Israel a detailed written law, but the substance and sanctions of this law, in many significant respects, resembled those of the natural law. This furthered God's purpose to make Israel a microcosm, so that Israel could showcase the plight of the whole of fallen Adamic humanity under the judgment of God and display its need for a Messiah. In addition, as detailed as the Mosaic law was, it was far from comprehensive, and the Israelites needed to exercise wisdom in order to obey it faithfully in concrete circumstances (Chapter 7). Picking up this last point, the present chapter continues and enriches this study of natural law for Israel under the Mosaic law by examining the Old Testament (OT) wisdom literature, particularly Proverbs. In addition to illuminating the relevance of natural law for Israel's moral life, Proverbs also solidifies some of the suggestions I made in Part 1 about the character of natural law in general under the Noahic covenant.

From the outset of this book I have presented natural law not as it is sometimes understood, that is, as a series of discrete rules. Instead, I have taken natural law as a moral order inscribed by God in the very structure of the world he created. At the beginning, God made human beings with a particular nature and situated them in the world in a particular way, and this reality entailed a holistic human obligation to be God's royal representatives in the present creation and, by faithful execution of this task, to attain the goal of new creation. After the fall into sin, God preserved the world and human beings' place within it, sustaining the natural moral order in refracted form, eventually through the covenant with Noah. Fallen human beings live under God's judgment and have been stripped of their eschatological destiny of life in the new creation, yet by virtue of their nature and their place in this world God continues to obligate them for as long as the present creation endures. This natural moral obligation has always been subject to summary through a rule or collection of discrete rules: "have dominion" (Gen. 1:26); or, "be fruitful and multiply and fill the earth and subdue it and have dominion" (Gen. 1:28); or, "be fruitful and multiply and fill the earth . . . [and] whoever sheds the blood of man, by man shall his blood be shed" (Gen. 9:1, 6); or the rules enshrined in the Decalogue (Exodus 20; Deuteronomy 5). Yet the natural moral order involves a holistic royal task that can be summarized in rules but never fully comprehended by them.

The present chapter brings the idea of *wisdom* to the fore and highlights, perhaps more explicitly than anywhere else in the book, the reality of a natural moral order able to be apprehended by all human beings through their experience in this world. The OT wisdom literature — particularly Proverbs — presents a marvelously complex, yet orderly, world created by God's own wisdom, in which sinful human beings can thrive to some degree in earthly affairs through the exercise of a wisdom that reflects God's. Human wisdom subjectively perceives the objective moral obligations communicated in the cosmic and social orders as they exist under God's governance. In Proverbs wisdom entails a moral sense of the holistic task incumbent upon all human persons, as creatures of a certain nature situated in the present creation.

With this chapter we explore a genre of biblical literature not previously considered in our investigation of historical narratives, epistles, prophecy, and law. Scholars generally identify three books of the Hebrew Scriptures as wisdom literature: Proverbs, Job, and Ecclesiastes (and occasionally the Song of Songs).[1] These books, however, are representatives of a genre common throughout the ancient Near East. Postcanonical Jewish writers continued to produce wisdom treatises, most famously Ben Sira (also known as Sirach or Ecclesiasticus) and the Wisdom of Solomon. The New Testament Epistle of James also bears certain characteristics of wisdom literature. Of the three OT wisdom books, I focus on Proverbs for two particular reasons: a detailed

---

1. Many scholars also identify "wisdom psalms." For discussion, see e.g. Leo G. Perdue, *The Sword and the Stylus: An Introduction to Wisdom in the Age of Empires* (Grand Rapids: Eerdmans, 2008), chap. 4. Perdue points to Psalms 1, 19, 32, 34, 37, 49, 73, 111, 112, 119, and 127.

exploration of all three books is not feasible if the present study is to remain within reasonable bounds and, of the three, I believe Proverbs provides the most material contributing to a biblical theology of natural law. I am aware that many scholars read Job and Ecclesiastes as offering a fundamental challenge to the theological and moral outlook of Proverbs. Though I believe the tensions between Proverbs and Job/Ecclesiastes are often exaggerated (for many of the complexities of the latter are anticipated in the former, and some of the themes of the former are echoed in the latter), it is certainly true that Job and Ecclesiastes expose difficulties and limitations of the quest for wisdom beyond those acknowledged in Proverbs. I try to take brief account of this in the concluding section of the chapter and place both Proverbs and the OT wisdom literature generally in the larger context of the progress of redemptive history, in its relation to natural law in particular.

Identifying the authors, editors, and dating of Proverbs presents numerous challenges.[2] Among the contested issues are its origins in folk wisdom and/or the royal court, the degree of dependence on non-Israelite wisdom, the role of Solomon in its production, and the date and cultural setting of its final editing. I address some of these issues below as they become relevant for the questions being explored. My general view is that much of Proverbs originated within the ordinary rural life of ancient Israel, that Solomon composed and collected much proverbial material that formed the basis for a great deal of Proverbs as we know it, that royal officials (especially under Hezekiah) undertook important work in preserving and refining Solomon's material, and that later authors and editors, likely during or after the exile in Babylon, brought the Solomonic material and material from other authors (such as Agur and Lemuel) into their final form and sandwiched it between an introduction (Proverbs 1–9) and conclusion (Prov. 31:10-31), which are intimately related to one another. Whatever the exact details of the human process of Proverbs' production, which will never be fully known, I take Proverbs to be divine revelation and I take its own internal clues about authorship, as well as corroborating evidence from 1 Kings, to be historically accurate.

Whatever the uncertainties regarding authors and dates, Proverbs was produced within the era of Israel's existence under the Mosaic covenant. This fact alone is a puzzle to many students of Proverbs, since the book, unlike most

---

2. All of the standard commentaries on Proverbs discuss these issues. For two brief examples, see R. N. Whybray, *Proverbs,* New Century Bible Commentary (Grand Rapids: Eerdmans, 1994), pp. 5-7; and Richard J. Clifford, *Proverbs: A Commentary* (Louisville: Westminster John Knox, 1999), p. 6.

of the rest of the OT, shows little apparent interest in God's dealings with Israel under Moses, or indeed in anything distinctively Israelite. Yet the perceived lack of interest in God's unique relationship may not be quite as thorough as ordinarily thought, and there is much in Proverbs that closely resembles the moral dynamic of Deuteronomy. At the same time, a number of features of Proverbs — not least of them the recognition of genuine wisdom outside the borders of Israel — witness to the ongoing relevance of the covenant with Noah. While I do not aspire to provide any comprehensive account of Proverbs' place within the larger theology of the OT, I do believe the Reformed covenant theology I utilize in this book and the theology of natural law I am developing provide helpful insight for understanding this issue. There is ultimately no conflict between the so-called "creation theology" underlying the OT wisdom literature and the "salvation history" unfolded through most of the rest of the OT.[3] They are organically connected and neither makes good sense without the other. At the end of the chapter I will explain why this is the case.

In this chapter, then, I aim to show how Proverbs confirms and enriches many of the conclusions about natural law drawn in previous chapters. First, I discuss a number of general themes related to natural law. We will see how Proverbs speaks of an objective moral knowledge revealed in the natural order as created by God through his wisdom. Without using explicit terminology of the "image of God," Proverbs exhorts human beings to pursue and appropriate this divine wisdom in order to take up their task of fruitful and productive life in the world under God's authority. Though no human being ever interacts with the world apart from moral predispositions, Proverbs implies a basic epistemology in which moral knowledge is in part obtained through observation of, experience in, and reflection on the world. Furthermore, this moral knowledge is accessible to all human beings and, despite the pervasive sinful distortion of knowledge gained through the natural order, people who do not participate in the covenants of grace have genuine moral insight from which participants in the covenant should learn. Second, I discuss several specific substantive moral themes that appear throughout Proverbs and note how they confirm earlier suggestions that natural law entails both the minimalist ethic

---

3. Nearly every significant study of the OT wisdom literature wrestles at some level with this relation between "creation theology" and "salvation history." Much of the recent debate has taken place in the wake of the work of Gerhard von Rad, as expressed, for example, in his *Old Testament Theology*, 2 vols. (New York: Harper & Row, 1962-65). For just one example of a serious and interesting investigation of the broader relationship between creation and history in the OT, see Rolf P. Knierim, "Cosmos and History in Israel's Theology," in *The Task of Old Testament Theology: Method and Cases* (Grand Rapids: Eerdmans, 1995), pp. 171-224.

explicit in Genesis 9:1-7 and a broader moral order. Among natural law themes prevalent in previous chapters and prominent in Proverbs are justice and matters of sex and family. I also explore the theme of work and the significance of the fear of the Lord.

Law and Wisdom

Before turning to these general themes and specific moral issues, I offer some observations about the relationship between law and wisdom. This is a complex issue, but in light of the topic of my book and the lengthy discussion of the Mosaic law in Chapter 7, the present exploration of Proverbs demands attention to the subject.

The very pairing of the terms "law and wisdom" can breed confusion if not clarified. Biblical scholars are likely to hear "law and wisdom" as a reference to the OT Torah and the OT wisdom literature. Ethicists and lawyers, on the other hand, are likely to take "law and wisdom" as a reference to law in general and the virtue of wisdom. In a study such as mine, both understandings are pertinent and I have both in mind when using this terminology. Since the OT Torah is a particular expression of law, and the OT wisdom literature a particular exploration of wisdom, I believe that the relationship of OT law and OT wisdom is, in important respects, a subset of the more general relationship between law and wisdom.

Generally speaking, I take law to be *objective.* In other words, law represents a web of obligations binding upon a particular group of people. But whether we think of the whole world governed through natural law, God's special covenant people governed through biblical law, or a particular human society governed by its own civil law, the governing law can never be reduced to a series of discrete rules. The world, the covenant community, and an ordinary human society are all too complex to be comprehensively governed by a legal code. No human legislator is able to foresee every possible situation, with all its attending nuances, and promulgate a rule to fit. The omniscient God does know every possible situation, but a collection of rules for each one of them would be too immense to be useful to us; and in any case, God has not provided such an all-comprehensive collection of rules. Thus God's law for human beings and civil law for human societies constitute a web of obligations — that is, an *order*.[4] Rules may be enormously useful as summaries of and

---

4. Here I believe it is important to note that the legal order binding a human society

guideposts to this larger order, but the rules (or what we think of as individual laws) must always be applied to particular situations, and situations constantly arise for which the rules provide no clear and unambiguous answer. The old English common law tradition, I believe, provides a good example of written legislation being consciously utilized only in the context of a larger legal system in which particular disputes were adjudicated in the light of custom and precedent that transcended legislation. The quest for a comprehensive legal code, in my judgment, is a delusion.[5]

Continuing to speak generally, I take wisdom to be *subjective.* Through wisdom people perceive the order that obligates them and conduct themselves accordingly.[6] If life were amazingly simple and law merely a series of rules, wisdom as such would be unnecessary. But wisdom is the ability to perceive the order that underlies the world or a given society and thus to understand what sort of behavior fits and brings good results in a particular situation. Without wisdom a person cannot understand the law — whether divine or human — as it really is and thus will inevitably act in ways that are inappropriate and harmful. Christian theologians have long recognized this truth and promoted, for example, the need for *equity* to temper the wooden application of law in concrete cases.[7]

---

is not simply defined by legislation but by the inscrutable formation of social custom that instills certain expectations for conduct within the society. Were civil law simply legislation, there would be no coherent legal order. A society's legislated rules can only make full sense as interpreted within the broader practices and assumptions embedded in its customs.

5. What is to my mind definitive evidence that the law is primarily about order, and not rules, is the fact that the vast majority of the people you interact with (provided you are not reading this while incarcerated) have little problem leading law-abiding lives, and yet have rarely, if ever, cracked open the governing code of the jurisdiction in which they live. People keep the law without knowing much or any legislation.

6. Oliver O'Donovan puts it well in making a similar point: "The items in a code stand to the moral law as bricks to a building. Wisdom must involve some comprehension of how the bricks are meant to be put together." See *Resurrection and Moral Order: An Outline for Evangelical Ethics,* 2nd ed. (Grand Rapids: Eerdmans, 1994), p. 200.

7. E.g., see Thomas Aquinas, *Summa Theologiae* 2a2ae 120.1: "Since human actions, with which laws are concerned, are composed of contingent singulars and are innumerable in their diversity, it was not possible to lay down rules of law that would apply to every single case. Legislators in framing laws attend to what commonly happens: although if the law be applied to certain cases it will frustrate the equality of justice and be injurious to the common good, which the law has in view. . . . In these and like cases it is bad to follow the law, and it is good to set aside the letter of the law and to follow the dictates of justice and the common good. This is the object of *epikeia* which we call equity." Cf. 1a2ae 96.6. See also John Calvin, *Institutes of the Christian Religion,* trans. Henry Beveridge (Grand Rapids: Eerdmans, 1953), 4.20.16 ("As

This general dynamic is reflected in the particular relationship of Torah and wisdom literature in the OT. Several differences between the Torah and wisdom literature are obvious. The books of the Torah were promulgated explicitly in the context of the Mosaic covenant and as an implication of it, while the wisdom literature has no explicit grounding in the Mosaic covenant, but rather in the reality of God's creation. The Torah, furthermore, propounds rules that are noncomprehensive and in need of application, yet that nevertheless must be followed, often upon pain of severe punishment. The wisdom literature, conversely, provides guidance for viewing the world and responding to others in certain ways. Specific counsels not only may, but must, be rejected in certain situations, for some individual proverbs give contrary advice.[8] Related to the previous point, while the Torah emphasizes obedience, wisdom concerns the skill of navigating through a complicated world with effectiveness and prosperity.[9]

Yet, a great deal of similarity exists between the Torah and the wisdom literature, especially between Deuteronomy and Proverbs (as mentioned in the

---

constitutions have some circumstances on which they partly depend, there is nothing to prevent their diversity, provided they all alike aim at equity as their end"); and Francis Turretin, *Institutes of Elenctic Theology,* vol. 2, trans. George Musgrave Giger, ed. James T. Dennison Jr. (Phillipsburg, NJ: Presbyterian and Reformed, 1994), p. 137 ("equity is the mind of the law").

8. The best example is surely Proverbs 26:4-5: "Answer not a fool according to his folly, lest you be like him yourself. Answer a fool according to his folly, lest he be wise in his own eyes." For discussion of how proverbs get at only a small part of reality, are sometimes contradictory, and are heavily dependent on context, see e.g. Roland E. Murphy, *The Tree of Life: An Exploration of Biblical Wisdom Literature,* 3rd ed. (Grand Rapids: Eerdmans, 2002), pp. 10-11; and Raymond C. Van Leeuwen, *Proverbs,* in *The New Interpreter's Bible,* vol. 5 (Nashville, Abingdon, 1997), p. 23. James L. Crenshaw helpfully notes that biblical wisdom is very much about propriety, finding the right word or deed at the right time; see *Old Testament Wisdom: An Introduction* (Louisville: Westminster John Knox, 1998), p. 11. Ronald E. Clements refers to early wisdom as open-ended and ad hoc; see *Wisdom in Theology* (Grand Rapids: Eerdmans, 1992), p. 42.

9. Of particular interest here is the subtle meaning of *hokmah* (חכמה), the word ordinarily translated "wisdom" in Proverbs. See Stuart Weeks, *Early Israelite Wisdom* (Oxford: Oxford University Press, 1994), pp. 74-75, for discussion of the use of this word in the OT, where it refers variously to shrewd calculation, skill in artisanship, government, and judgment. Scholars offer various suggestions for capturing the nuances of the word most effectively in English. Whybray, for example, defines the word in Proverbs as "life-skill," the ability to conduct one's life in the best possible way to the best possible effect; see *Proverbs,* pp. 32-33. Michael V. Fox suggests "expertise" as the nearest English equivalent, which can manifest itself in craftsmanship, knowledge gained through study, understanding the implications of situations, skill in devising plans, and good judgment, among other things; see Michael V. Fox, *Proverbs 1–9,* vol. 18a, *The Anchor Bible* (New York: Doubleday, 2000), pp. 32-33.

previous chapter). Though the genres and purposes of these two books should not be conflated, their similarities are evident with regard to moral substance as well as purpose and method.

The similarity of moral substance between Proverbs and Deuteronomy is striking. For one thing, Proverbs shows concern for most of the commandments of the Decalogue, as considered again below.[10] In a rich article, William Brown offers extensive and compelling evidence of the similarity between Proverbs and Deuteronomy on a host of issues, including impartiality in judgment, bribery, credibility of witnesses, property rights, respectful relations between neighbors, standardized weights and measures, usury, treatment of the needy, conduct in war, the relationship between the royal office and administration of justice, and sacrifice. He argues that the word *torah,* as used in Proverbs, deals with civil and cultic matters ordinarily associated with Deuteronomy. From the other angle, he argues that Deuteronomy evinces a "sapiential ethos" more commonly associated with Proverbs.[11] Among other similarities are the promises of overflowing barns, the exhortation to bind good things on one's heart or hand, the importance of administering justice, the need to follow the right path, and the expulsion of the wicked from the land.[12] Though Ben Sira's complete identification of OT Torah and wisdom was an innovation (and in my judgment a regrettable one), there is plenty in Proverbs and Deuteronomy that provides understandable seeds for such development.[13]

10. See Tremper Longman III, *Proverbs* (Grand Rapids: Baker Academic, 2006), p. 81, who pairs up specific proverbs with the commandments of the second table.

11. William P. Brown, "The Law and the Sages: A Reexamination of *Tora* in Proverbs," in *Constituting the Community: Studies on the Polity of Ancient Israel in Honor of S. Dean McBride, Jr.* (Winona Lake, IN: Eisenbrauns, 2005), pp. 251-80. Brown explores a number of other interesting and related themes not mentioned above. See also Moshe Weinfeld, *Deuteronomy and the Deuteronomic School* (Oxford: Clarendon, 1972), Part 3.

12. For discussion and texts, see e.g. Katharine Dell, *The Book of Proverbs in Social and Theological Context* (Cambridge: Cambridge University Press, 2006), pp. 172-75; Jonathan Burnside, *God, Justice, and Society: Aspects of Law and Legality in the Bible* (Oxford: Oxford University Press, 2011), p. 25; Clifford, *Proverbs,* p. 51; Harold C. Washington, *Wealth and Poverty in the Instruction of Amenemope and the Hebrew Proverbs* (Atlanta: Scholars, 1994), p. 130; Stuart Weeks, *Instruction and Imagery in Proverbs 1–9* (Oxford: Oxford University Press, 2007), pp. 150-52; and R. N. Whybray, *Wealth and Poverty in the Book of Proverbs* (Sheffield: Sheffield Academic Press, 1990), pp. 80-81.

13. Among significant studies of law and wisdom in Ben Sira, see especially Eckhard J. Schnabel, *Law and Wisdom from Ben Sira to Paul: A Tradition Historical Enquiry into the Relation of Law, Wisdom, and Ethics* (Tübingen: Mohr Siebeck, 1985), chap. 1. For other briefer discussion about his identification of Torah and wisdom, see also Murphy, *Tree of Life,* p. 76;

Proverbs and Deuteronomy also have similarities in purpose and method. Both books aim to mold the life and conduct of God's covenant community.[14] They have similar educational goals, use motivation clauses to stimulate right behavior, and emphasize the need to internalize their teaching.[15]

In short, law and wisdom in general are different yet organically related. Likewise, there are significant differences between the promulgation of the Mosaic law in books like Deuteronomy and the inculcation of wisdom through books like Proverbs, though these biblical books have many similarities in substance and purpose. Proverbs presumes the existence of a moral order — a law — to be perceived and heeded, and Deuteronomy presumes the need for wise application of its statutes. OT Israelites could not keep the law without wisdom, yet they would not be wise without following the law (Deut. 4:6; Prov. 28:7). As Jonathan Burnside notes, "Although biblical law is not complete, its role in the purpose of God is to teach wisdom, which is complete."[16] From the other direction, as we will see, Proverbs aims to instill a wisdom useful for enabling OT Israelites to obey the law of Moses. Proverbs was apparently written for the covenant people of Israel, yet the wisdom it commends is also accessible to some degree to all people as they are confronted by the universal law of nature.

Natural Law in Proverbs: Foundational Matters

In this section I discuss various matters in Proverbs foundational for a theology of natural law. All of these matters have arisen in previous chapters, though they bear a distinctive flavor in Proverbs that enriches our theological understanding. We see here that Proverbs grounds the moral life in the natural order created by God through his wisdom, presents human beings as designed

---

Leo G. Perdue, *Wisdom & Creation: The Theology of Wisdom Literature* (Nashville: Abingdon, 1994), pp. 270-72; and Perdue, *Sword and Stylus*, p. 285. Weeks claims that much of what Ben Sira does is already done implicitly in Proverbs 1–9; see *Instruction and Imagery*, p. 172. Among other OT statements that prepared the way for the total identification of wisdom and law, yet stopped short of it, Schnabel points to Jer. 8:8; Mal. 2:6-7; Ezra 7:6, 10, 25; and Ps. 1; 19; 119; see *Law and Wisdom*, p. 84.

14. See Longman, *Proverbs*, p. 80.

15. See e.g. Joseph Blenkinsopp, *Wisdom and Law in the Old Testament: The Ordering of Life in Israel and Early Judaism* (Oxford: Oxford University Press, 1983), pp. 45-46, 100; and Weeks, *Instruction and Imagery*, pp. 112-13.

16. Burnside, *God, Justice, and Society*, p. 472.

to appropriate God's wisdom and to order the world as rulers under him, calls for learning moral truth through reflective observation and experience of the world, and recognizes the universal accessibility of this wisdom.

The Created Natural Order

Though natural law theories take a variety of forms, close to the heart of nearly every classical theory is that the world has a real, objective, and meaningful nature that, in one way or another, communicates moral obligations to human beings. In a Christian theology of natural law, God has created this world and thus ultimately he is the one who obliges human beings through the testimony of nature. Proverbs, in numerous ways, presents this world as created by God and thus as meaningful, orderly, and morally instructive.

First, Proverbs calls readers to recognize that God's creative work is the foundation of all that exists. As many scholars note, while the OT wisdom literature is virtually silent on God's particular salvific acts toward Israel, it orients readers toward his universal work of creation. "Creation theology and its correlative affirmation, providence, were at the center of the sages' understanding of God, the world, and humanity."[17] It plays a major role in Job, for example, particularly in God's speeches toward the end of the book.[18] In Proverbs, the theme of creation is evident in part through reminders that God is the "maker" of all and that this has moral consequences for dealing with fellow human beings (e.g., Prov. 14:31; 17:5; 22:2). But the most prominent and memorable expressions of the theme appear in 3:19-20 and 8:22-31. If Proverbs 1–9 was indeed authored as an introduction to the rest of the book, as many believe, then these striking references are meant to color the way we read the whole. The entire quest for wisdom occurs against the backdrop of God's work of creation.

Proverbs 3:19-20 states: "The Lord by wisdom founded the earth; by understanding he established the heavens; by his knowledge the deeps broke open, and the clouds drop down the dew." Though there is some debate about the meaning of the preposition "by" in 3:19, it is compelling to take it as instrumental: *through* wisdom, or *by* wisdom, God created the world.[19] This idea is

---

17. Perdue, *Wisdom & Creation*, 20; see also Leo G. Perdue, *Proverbs* (Louisville: Westminster John Knox, 2000), p. 7.

18. E.g., see Job 12:10-25; 36:22–37:24; 38–41; see comments in Murphy, *Tree of Life*, p. 33.

19. See e.g. Roland E. Murphy, *Proverbs*, Word Biblical Commentary, vol. 22 (Nashville: Thomas Nelson, 1998), p. 22.

not unique to Proverbs (see also Ps. 104:24; 136:5; Jer. 10:12; 51:15).[20] What is so remarkable is that the very wisdom commended to human beings throughout Proverbs resides ultimately and prototypically in God himself, exhibited in the way he structures and orders the world. The world from which human beings are to learn wisdom reflects the wisdom of God.[21]

These stimulating ideas briefly encapsulated in 3:19-20 are further unfolded in the remarkable verses, 8:22-31. In this text, wisdom is personified — the famous Lady Wisdom or Woman Wisdom[22] — and ascribed a place of eminence in God's work of creation, though determining her precise role would require untangling several contested exegetical issues. Some general observations must suffice for present purposes. For one thing, Proverbs 8:22-26 indicates that God possessed wisdom prior to his general work of creation, which means that wisdom played a role in God's construction of the entire world we know. "The Lord possessed me at the beginning of his work, the first of his acts of old." The verses that follow, 8:27-29, describe God's creative progress from the heavens above to the seas below to the boundaries of the sea and land. In all this work, says Wisdom, "I was there." Finally, Wisdom claims to be "beside" God, rejoicing or playing in the world and delighting in the human race (8:30-31). Here she is described as אָמוֹן, whose meaning is uncertain, but perhaps refers to a craftsman or artisan.[23] Such a description

---

20. See Perdue, *Wisdom & Creation*, p. 82; and Weeks, *Instruction and Imagery*, p. 109.

21. See Perdue's helpful comments on this dynamic in *Wisdom & Creation*, p. 82; and *Proverbs*, p. 103.

22. The literature on Woman Wisdom is immense. For some general introduction to debates about the origin of this figure, her identification, and other matters, see e.g. Whybray, *Proverbs*, pp. 27-28; Clifford, *Proverbs*, pp. 23-28; and Murphy, *Proverbs*, pp. 278-87. In light of the extensive literary connections between Proverbs 1–9 and the description of the "woman of excellence" that concludes the book in 31:10-31, consideration of the latter figure seems important for determining the meaning of Woman Wisdom; among significant studies exploring this point, see Christine Roy Yoder, *Wisdom as a Woman of Substance: A Socioeconomic Reading of Proverbs 1–9 and 31:10-31* (Berlin: Walter de Gruyter, 2001); and Claudia V. Camp, *Wisdom and the Feminine in the Book of Proverbs* (Sheffield: Almond, 1985), pp. 188-206.

23. For general discussion of the term and the plausible translation options, see e.g. Whybray, *Proverbs*, pp. 134-36; and Clifford, *Proverbs*, pp. 99-101. Among those arguing for a translation of "artisan," "craftsman," or something similar, see Van Leeuwen, *Proverbs*, pp. 94-95; Longman, *Proverbs*, p. 207; and Craig G. Bartholomew, "A Time for War, and a Time for Peace: Old Testament Wisdom, Creation and O'Donovan's Theological Ethics," in *A Royal Priesthood? The Use of the Bible Ethically and Politically: A Dialogue with Oliver O'Donovan*, ed. Craig Bartholomew, Jonathan Chaplin, Robert Song, and Al Wolters (Grand Rapids: Zondervan, 2002), p. 92. For a defense of the translation "ward" or "child," see Fox, *Proverbs 1–9*, pp. 285-88.

of Wisdom corresponds to 3:19-20, where wisdom is God's instrument in creation. God himself displayed wisdom in his masterful crafting of this world.

Not to be missed in both 3:19-20 and 8:22-31 are numerous similarities to the descriptions of God's creation in Genesis 1 and 2. There are waters above and below, for example, and God's initial work brings things into existence and establishes boundaries for the waters' domain.[24] Raymond Van Leeuwen also proposes an interesting connection between Proverbs 8:30 and Genesis 1:26, in that the Akkadian cognate of the word אמון also refers to a counselor or advisor, thereby suggesting the heavenly court scene probably alluded to in the Genesis 1:26 language of "let us make."[25] Though presented in its own distinct ways, Proverbs 3 and 8 portray God's work of creation in a way harmonious with and suggestive of the opening chapters of Scripture.

Proverbs' robust affirmation of God's wise creative work raises important questions about the idea of *order*. Some scholars have wondered whether something like the Egyptian concept of *Ma'at* is at work in Proverbs. Occasionally writers have suggested that Proverbs envisions a pervasive system of cause-and-effect in the cosmic and social realms that operates even apart from direct divine involvement.[26] As most students of Proverbs readily realize, numerous affirmations run counter to the idea that God is not actively involved in this world. Yet extreme proposals sometimes provoke extreme reactions, and Roland Murphy, it seems to me, while rightfully rebuking the proposals of Klaus Koch and others, has overpolemicized against the concept of order in Proverbs.[27] The cosmic and social realms are in no sense autonomous or

---

24. See e.g. Dell, *Book of Proverbs,* pp. 142-43. Other writers point out differences in the creation accounts in Proverbs and Genesis; e.g., see William P. Brown, *The Ethos of the Cosmos: The Genesis of Moral Imagination in the Bible* (Grand Rapids: Eerdmans, 1999), pp. 275-76.

25. Van Leeuwen, *Proverbs,* pp. 94-95. See Appendix 4 for discussion of the divine plural in Genesis 1:26.

26. Most famously and controversially, see Klaus Koch, "Is There a Doctrine of Retribution in the Old Testament?" in *Theodicy in the OT,* ed. James L. Crenshaw (Philadelphia: Fortress, 1983), pp. 57-87 (originally published in German in 1955). Another related view, that the early wisdom material was thoroughly secular and later writers added a religious dimension to it, is considered and critiqued by, e.g., Weeks, *Early Israelite Wisdom,* chap. 4; Dell, *Book of Proverbs,* chap. 4; Perdue, *Wisdom & Creation,* p. 46; Crenshaw, *Old Testament Wisdom,* p. 77; Tomás Frydrych, *Living Under the Sun: Examination of Proverbs and Qoheleth* (Leiden: Brill, 2002), pp. 176-77; and Whybray, *Proverbs,* pp. 7-12.

27. E.g., see Murphy, *Tree of Life,* pp. 115-17. For a study of Murphy's opposition to seeing wisdom as a search for order, see James L. Crenshaw, *Urgent Advice and Probing Questions: Collected Writings on Old Testament Wisdom* (Macon, GA: Mercer University Press, 1995), chap. 20.

independent of God, but it is difficult to escape a sense of regularity and predictability permeating these realms. Certain effects follow from certain causes. Wisdom consists, to a significant degree, in perceiving the resultant order and structuring one's life in conformity to it.[28] A great many exhortations in Proverbs depend upon the expectation that good or bad results are bound to flow from certain actions. "For pressing milk produces curds, pressing the nose produces blood, and pressing anger produces strife" (30:33). There are, to be sure, exceptions to the usual course of things. And yet the very fact that they run counter to the grain of the universe — that is, that they are *exceptions* — testifies to the reality of the regular order. Sometimes snow does come in summer, and rain does fall at harvest, and honor is accorded to a fool (see Prov. 26:1), but such things bear an anomalous and bizarre character that provokes a certain sense of revulsion in the wise.

One of the most interesting aspects of the idea of order at work in Proverbs is the interconnection of the cosmic realm and the human social realm. The natural moral order is such that the regularities of the impersonal natural world and of human society, while not identical, are intimately intertwined.[29] Describing this precisely is difficult, but many kinds of statements in Proverbs work with such an assumption. For example, moral lessons about laziness and its consequences are extracted from observing the life of ants (6:6-11). A bit differently, Proverbs also draws analogies between natural phenomena and human moral phenomena. For example, as a man who carries fire at his chest will burn his clothes and as one who walks on hot coals will get scorched feet, so the man who goes in to his neighbor's wife will get punished (6:27-29). Similarly, Proverbs 25–26 is full of statements comparing certain kinds of behavior with certain objects or events in nature. For example: "Like clouds and wind without rain is a man who boasts of a gift he does not give" (25:14); "trusting in a treacherous man in time of trouble is like a bad tooth or a foot

---

28. Such a conclusion is common among contemporary Proverbs scholars; see especially Leo G. Perdue, "Cosmology and the Social Order in the Wisdom Tradition," in *The Sage in Israel and the Ancient Near East,* ed. John G. Gammie and Leo G. Perdue (Winona Lake: Eisenbrauns, 1990), pp. 458-61; *Sword and Stylus,* p. 12; and *Proverbs,* pp. 11-12. See also Crenshaw, *Old Testament Wisdom,* pp. 11, 55; Clements, *Wisdom in Theology,* p. 45; Dell, *Book of Proverbs,* p. 134; Frydrych, *Living Under the Sun,* p. 100; and Bartholomew, "A Time for War," p. 93.

29. For comment on this theme, see e.g. Perdue, "Cosmology and the Social Order," p. 472; and Crenshaw, *Urgent Advice,* p. 396. Keith W. Whitelam sees this same theme elsewhere in Scripture, such as Psalm 85:2 and 2 Samuel 23:3b-4; see *The Just King: Monarchical Judicial Authority in Ancient Israel* (Sheffield: JSOT Press, 1979), pp. 30-31.

that slips" (25:19). Finally, Proverbs even at times speaks of how the cosmic order will be shaken when the human moral order crumbles. For instance, "Under three things the earth trembles; under four it cannot bear up; a slave when he becomes king, and a fool when he is filled with food; an unloved woman when she gets a husband, and a maidservant when she displaces her mistress" (30:21-23).[30] If contemporary human society is bold enough to think that its irresponsible behavior is changing the physical climate, then perhaps it is no stretch to think that the authors of Proverbs really believed that the overturning of social structures could have ramifications for cosmic structures. But even if they did not take things so literally, the force of such a saying seems lost without a strong sense that the entire natural order — cosmic and human — is an interconnected whole.

In summary, Proverbs teaches that God created the world, and did so by wisdom. God's wise formation of the world has instilled it with an orderly regularity that penetrates both the cosmic and the human social realms. Wise human beings seek to appropriate this divine wisdom and thus to perceive the natural order and to conduct themselves in a way that befits it.

The Image of God

In Chapters 1-2 I grounded natural law in the idea that God created the world (and re-fashioned it after the flood) and immediately commissioned his human image-bearers to take up a royal commission in this world as his representatives. Does Proverbs reflect this dynamic? In the previous subsection we observed how Proverbs 3 and 8 echo the creation account of Genesis 1–2 and emphasize that God created through wisdom, producing a world with an interconnected cosmic and human moral order. Now I explore how Proverbs, without using explicit terminology of the "image of God," also echoes the teaching of Genesis 1–2 with respect to the human task performed in God's likeness.[31] This is evident with respect to how human wisdom reflects divine wisdom, how human wisdom involves the skillful ordering of the world, and the interest of Proverbs in kings and just human rule.

First, Proverbs presents human wisdom as the reflection of divine

---

30. Other places in Scripture speak similarly; e.g., Psalm 82:5.

31. Though he pursues the topic in a way different from how I do, at least one Proverbs scholar sees in the book a high anthropology resembling the perspective on the *imago Dei* in Genesis 1; see Frydrych, *Living Under the Sun*, pp. 127-28.

wisdom, such that in the possession and use of wisdom in their lives human beings mirror the activity of God.[32] Here we turn back to Proverbs 3:19-20 and 8:22-31. Immediately preceding the former text is a reminder of the blessing that comes to human beings who "lay hold" and "hold fast" to wisdom (3:18). Immediately following is a call not to "lose sight" of her (3:21). In the midst of such appeals to pursue wisdom is the grand statement that God himself used wisdom in creating the world (3:19-20). The very same instrument of human flourishing *in* the world served God in his creation *of* the world.[33]

As in Proverbs 3, reading 8:22-31 in its surrounding context also highlights the connection between divine and human wisdom. Preceding these verses, for example, is the statement, to be considered further below, that by wisdom "kings reign, and rulers decree what is just" (8:15). Following 8:22-31 is the exhortation to keep wisdom's ways, not to neglect her, and to listen to her (8:32-34). The wisdom that stood at God's side during creation is the very thing that human beings should use and hold fast. The statement that the Lord "possessed" wisdom at the beginning of his work (8:22) is also relevant. "Acquire," in fact, seems the best translation of the Hebrew word used here. Michael V. Fox helpfully argues that the word choice carries no intention of asserting that wisdom preexisted independently of God, but serves to establish God's relation to wisdom as the prototype of humanity's relation to wisdom. Indeed, Proverbs uses this same Hebrew word repeatedly to call for human beings to acquire wisdom (see 1:5; 4:5, 7; 15:32; 16:16; 17:16; 18:15; 19:8; 23:23). Though God and human beings "acquire" wisdom in ontologically different ways, proper human use of wisdom is an analogy of God's use of her.[34] Finally, Claudia Camp observes a chiasm in the Hebrew of 8:30b-31 in which there is movement from the divine realm to the human realm. In this movement, wisdom serves as the link between God and humanity: God delighted in wisdom, and wisdom delighted in human beings.[35]

---

32. To be clear, Proverbs is not as interested in human beings' *unique* role as God's image-bearers as Genesis 1 is. The ant, after all, can be wise and thus reflect God's wisdom too in a sense. But Proverbs does focus on human beings and implicitly highlights the theme of humanity's divine likeness.

33. On 3:19-20 Clifford writes: "Since the world was created by wisdom, anyone who lives in accord with it lives in accord with the structure and purpose of the universe." See *Proverbs*, p. 55.

34. See Fox, *Proverbs 1–9*, pp. 279-80; see also 355-56; and Dell, *Book of Proverbs*, p. 142.

35. Camp, *Wisdom and the Feminine*, p. 272. She writes: "The first stich presents *Wisdom* as *Yahweh's* 'delight'; the final stich says that *her* 'delight' was with *humankind.* The middle

Second, an implicit image of God theme emerges in Proverbs through the way in which wisdom involves the skillful ordering of the world. This point follows organically from the previous. In Genesis 1, I have argued, the image of God is not primarily about possessing certain attributes but about a royal office for executing a commission. Likewise in Proverbs, human beings do not resemble God through static possession of wisdom but through an active life in the world. Wisdom may be a character trait of sorts, but people gain and utilize it only through engagement in their proper affairs. Again, 3:19-20 and 8:22-31, when read in the context of Proverbs and even the OT as a whole, are instructive. Van Leeuwen remarks that the Hebrew verbs used in 3:19 to describe God's construction of the world by wisdom are commonly used for human labor in constructing a city, house, or temple (e.g., 1 Kgs. 6:37; 1 Chron. 17:24; Ezra 3:12; Isa. 14:32). "Building a house is a human echo of God's wise work of creation."[36] Van Leeuwen also notes, concerning Proverbs 8:27-31, that as God keeps the boundaries of the cosmic realm in place through wisdom, so should wise human beings keep human structures and boundaries fair and stable (e.g., Prov. 22:28; 23:10-11).[37] More generally, the implicit work of God described in 8:27-29 — namely, the suppression of the forces of chaos through the imposition of order — seems very much like the mundane human work envisioned in Proverbs. Children are prone to destructive foolishness, but parents train them and cajole them away from it. Fields spring weeds when left on their own, but farmers work them and produce crops. Societies lapse into injustice, but kings bring just resolution to disputes.[38] The kinds of things that God does by wisdom, human beings are to do by wisdom as well.

Another important facet of the implicit image of God theme in Proverbs concerns the issue of rulers and kingship. In Chapter 1, I argued that the image of God entailed a *royal* office and commission. God, the great king of creation, established those made in his likeness to rule the earth under his authority. The role that Israelite monarchs and their royal courts played in the compo-

---

two stichs correspond to this movement from the divine realm to the human: Wisdom 'plays' both *before him* and *in his inhabited world*. . . . In this poem, Wisdom is the only link between God and humans."

36. Van Leeuwen, *Proverbs*, pp. 53-54.

37. Van Leeuwen, *Proverbs*, p. 93.

38. E. W. Heaton makes the interesting observation that the OT uses a single word — *hokmah* — to describe the wisdom of the craftsman, the king, the royal counselor, and God himself. In each case wisdom concerns expert mastery over raw material, which is shaped to one's own design. See *Solomon's New Men: The Emergence of Ancient Israel as a National State* (New York: Pica, 1974), pp. 18-19.

sition of Proverbs is disputed,[39] but Proverbs clearly shows a keen interest in kings and their functions. Kings should, and apparently often do, model true wisdom. Many of the chief characteristics of the wise life, especially seeking justice but also helping the needy and remaining sexually moral, are of special interest to kings. To be clear, all people are to pursue these things as aspects of wisdom, but Proverbs envisions kings as having particular responsibility in these matters.[40] With some fear of overstatement, but reading Proverbs in light of Genesis 1, I suggest that this organic connection between the wise task of kings and the wise task of all people means that though political office vests only in a few individuals, the people as a whole bear a royal call. Their daily responsibility to promote just relations, to aid the poor, and to guard sexual fidelity is part of the same task that the king performs on a larger scale.

It may be helpful first to consider the general place of kings (or rulers) in Proverbs. Initially striking is the role ascribed to kings in the production of the book. Most prominently, 1:1 associates Proverbs as a whole with King Solomon, 10:1 identifies the collection that follows (through 22:16) as "the proverbs of Solomon," and 25:1 introduces another collection (chapters 25–29) as additional "proverbs of Solomon."[41] Proverbs 25:1 is also interesting be-

---

39. A number of scholars have considered the claim that much of Proverbs originated in the royal court. Among those weighing the arguments at some length (and finding them ultimately unpersuasive), see Weeks, *Early Israelite Wisdom,* chap. 3; and Whybray, *Proverbs,* pp. 45-59. On the other hand, Fox, for example, strongly supports seeing an important role for the royal court; see *Proverbs,* p. 10.

40. In a relevant comment, Perdue refers to an "ethic of results" in the wisdom tradition in which order must be actualized in the world, in response to a divine commission, and "this ethic uses the metaphor of king." See "Cosmology and the Social Order," p. 470.

41. As mentioned above, I take the description of Solomon as a wise king and a collector and composer of proverbs, in both Proverbs and 1 Kings, to be historically accurate, though I leave open the question of just how many of the sayings found in Proverbs 10–22 and 25–29 derive from him personally. Among those writers inclined to trace the origins of Proverbs back to the days of Solomon, see Heaton, *Solomon's New Men,* p. 123; Walter Brueggemann, *In Man We Trust: The Neglected Side of Biblical Faith* (Atlanta: John Knox, 1972), pp. 49-50; Frydrych, *Living Under the Sun,* pp. 213-14 (and see n. 9); Clifford, *Proverbs,* pp. 3-4; Longman, *Proverbs,* pp. 24-25; and André Lemaire, "Wisdom in Solomonic Historiography," in *Wisdom in Ancient Israel: Essays in Honour of J. A. Emerton,* ed. John Day, Robert P. Gordon, and H. G. M. Williamson (Cambridge: Cambridge University Press, 1995), pp. 106-18. On the other hand, many argue that biblical claims about Solomon's wisdom and role in composing proverbs are largely legendary and/or for propaganda purposes; see e.g. Perdue, *Sword and Stylus,* pp. 87-88; Perdue, *Proverbs,* p. 19; Crenshaw, *Old Testament Wisdom,* pp. 37-40; Clements, *Wisdom in Theology,* pp. 111-12; Ronald E. Clements, "Solomon and the Origins of Wisdom in Israel," *Perspectives in Religious Studies* 15 (1988): 23-26; Whitelam, *The Just King,* pp. 156-57, 162.

cause it mentions another king, Hezekiah, whose "men . . . copied" these latter Solomonic proverbs.[42] In addition to these two Israelite kings who played a significant part in the production of Proverbs, 31:1-9 records the words of a king Lemuel. As discussed below, this Lemuel was probably a foreign monarch.

Many individual sayings in Proverbs refer to rulers in one way or another. One writer puts the number at forty.[43] Some larger sections express a special interest in their work, such as chapters 28–29.[44] A handful of proverbs speak of kings in such an exalted way as to suggest that they are endowed with supernatural gifts, perhaps even infallibility in their judgments (e.g., 20:8; 25:3). But these need to be read alongside the many others that urge kings to be vigilant about temptations to injustice or that forthrightly acknowledge the reality of tyranny and its malevolent consequences (e.g., 28:3; 31:2-5). Overall, Proverbs accords rulers a special and crucial role to play in society, which means not only that their deeds have a distinctive God-like character but also that they have a heightened moral responsibility to walk in wisdom through the fear of the Lord.[45] This connection between kings and wisdom is not unique to Proverbs.[46]

I mentioned above that several general characteristics of the wise life pertinent for all people have particular importance for kings. The most prominent is the responsibility to pursue justice. The ruler's throne "is established by righteousness" (16:12; see also 25:5). Kings are to protect the rights of the afflicted (31:5, 9) and to winnow out all evil (20:8). Envisioned ideally, the ruler's "mouth does not sin in judgment" (16:10). A king who acts tyrannically, on the other hand, is an "abomination" (16:12), a "charging bear" (28:15), and a "cruel oppressor" (28:16).[47] Another prominent theme in Proverbs is sexual fidelity.

---

42. Among scholars seeing this reference to Hezekiah's men as historically credible, see Crenshaw, *Urgent Advice*, p. 357; and Fox, *Proverbs 1–9*, p. 10. Others are more skeptical; e.g., see Weeks, *Early Israelite Wisdom*, pp. 41-46.

43. See Frydrych, *Living Under the Sun*, p. 145. For an extensive list of verses dealing with rulers in Proverbs, see Dell, *Book of Proverbs*, p. 70.

44. These chapters have sometimes been called a "mirror for princes." See e.g. Van Leeuwen, *Proverbs*, p. 215.

45. Dell has helpful observations on the frequent close proximity of proverbs about rulers and "Yahweh proverbs," indicating both the importance for kings to obey God and the link between God's role and the role of rulers. See *Book of Proverbs*, p. 111.

46. This is of course particularly evident in the Solomon narratives in 1 Kings 3–10. Among other examples, see Deuteronomy 34:9 and Ezra 7:25. Blenkinsopp asserts that in the Hebrew Bible wisdom belongs *par excellence* to the ruler; see *Wisdom and Law*, p. 5.

47. Among relevant discussions, see Perdue, *Wisdom & Creation*, p. 107; Crenshaw, *Urgent Advice*, p. 394; and Clements, *Wisdom in Theology*, p. 101.

Though not specially associated with kings through most of Proverbs, this idea takes an emphatic and foreboding place in its final, and lengthiest, exhortation to rulers, 31:1-9. Here King Lemuel recounts his mother's appeal — "Do not give your strength to women, your ways to those who destroy kings" (31:3) — in terms reminiscent of the warnings to young men about the forbidden woman in chapters 1–9. Finally, Proverbs' reminder to be kind to the needy is applied in strong terms to the king. This is again particularly evident in the words of King Lemuel (31:6-9), though there are similar statements earlier in the book (e.g., 29:14), and elsewhere in the OT (e.g., Ps. 72:4).[48]

The obligation of kings (and others) to be kind to the poor raises a final issue for this subsection: the idea of a common humanity. Though Proverbs does give a prominent place to rulers and never condemns the fact that some are rich and others poor, it also reminds readers that all people share a common nature and expects this fact to restrain bad behavior toward the vulnerable. I describe this shared nature in terms of a "common human-ity" because Proverbs does not describe human nature in terms of abstract attributes but in terms of being creatures rather than God. There is a basic equality among all people because God is the creator of everyone: "The rich and the poor meet together; the Lord is the maker of them all" (22:2); "the poor man and the oppressor meet together; the Lord gives light to the eyes of both" (29:13). Therefore to oppress the poor is ultimately an insult to God (14:31; 17:5). Whatever heightened privileges and responsibilities prominent people may have, in the big scheme of things they are no better than anyone else.

I have suggested that a balance needs to be maintained when consider-ing Proverbs' anthropology and the place Proverbs assigns to kings. On the one hand, those holding a royal office play an almost larger-than-life role in human society. On the other hand, their work is really not unique, but con-sists of many common human tasks they pursue on a bigger stage and with more profound consequences. Reading Proverbs in the light of Genesis 1–2, as interpreted in Chapter 1, I conclude that the entire human race has a royal task to order this world, in small and large ways, through the same wisdom by which God established the world in the first place. Without using the phrase, therefore, the anthropology of Proverbs views human beings as created in the image of God.

---

48. Also see discussion in Perdue, *Wisdom & Creation*, pp. 102, 107; and Whybray, *Wealth and Poverty*, p. 109.

The Question of Epistemology: Coming to Know the Natural Moral Order

Proverbs presents no explicit epistemology, but its exhortations to acquire wisdom imply many things relevant for the question of how to gain moral knowledge. In this subsection I first identify a basic precondition in Proverbs for the acquisition of all moral knowledge and then explore the various ways in which Proverbs speaks of people gaining such knowledge. I will also suggest several implications for our larger topic of natural law.

Before discussing *how* Proverbs expects human beings to gain moral knowledge I believe it important to identify its precondition: the fear of the Lord. Proverbs begins with the invitation "to *know* wisdom and instruction, to *understand* words of insight" (1:2). A simple statement follows shortly thereafter: "The fear of the Lord is the beginning of knowledge" (1:7). Proverbs gives many clues that some sort of genuine wisdom exists outside the bounds of Israel, among those who do not know *YHWH*, and we will consider this fact below. But wisdom in an ultimate sense comes only by beginning with the fear of the Lord. Proverbs never suggests that some sort of rational or empirical quest precedes this fear of God or can produce it. No one should pretend to approach life from an autonomous stance. Rather, the ways that people grow in wisdom — observing, reflecting, analogizing, learning from others — are to be pursued only in light of the fear of the Lord. Thus, I suggest that this fear of the Lord functions as a precondition of all true, holistic moral knowledge in Proverbs. Believers in the one God have much to learn even from those who worship false gods, but they should undertake their whole pursuit of wisdom wearing God-fearing glasses. Their observations and reflections on the world presume that God governs it and that they are accountable to him. Keeping this in mind should help to guard against seeing the naturalistic fallacy at work in how Proverbs draws moral conclusions from observation of the world.[49]

A first way in which Proverbs envisions people gaining moral knowledge is through empirical means, that is, through observation of and experience in the world. Proverbs presumes that people grow in wisdom through the active life, not an isolated contemplative life. Yet observation and experience are not sufficient for moral growth, for the wise also reflect on their observations and experiences, construct analogies from better-known to lesser-known things, and draw appropriate moral conclusions.

---

49. That is, we are not to derive "ought" from "is" by mechanically examining nature as a neutral observer, but to examine nature through the lens of certain convictions about God and the nature of the world he made. See Chapter 1 for comments on the naturalistic fallacy.

Proverbs repeatedly takes readers through the process of observing the world and learning from it.[50] At times the authors relate their own process of observing, reflecting, and drawing conclusions, and other times they exhort readers to follow the process themselves. A good example is Proverbs' admonition against laziness through the twice-stated saying, "a little sleep, a little slumber, a little folding of the hands to rest, and poverty will come upon you like a robber, and want like an armed man" (6:10-11; 24:33-34). In the latter of these two contexts, the author takes readers through his own thought process. He recounts how he passed by a sluggard's field and looked around. He noticed that it was overgrown with thorns and nettles and that its stone wall had crumbled (24:30-31). That was his observation. Next followed reflection: "Then I saw and considered it; I looked and received instruction" (24:32). Finally, he drew his conclusion that too much sleep leads to poverty.

Proverbs, however, expects readers not to admire the sage's moral reasoning, or even simply to accept his conclusion, but to engage in a similar thought process. This is evident in the first instance of the sleep/slumber saying. Here the author begins with a command: "Go to the ant, O sluggard; consider her ways, and be wise" (6:6). What the sluggard will see if he opens his eyes is that ants have no leader, yet they prepare bread in the summer and gather food at the harvest (6:7-8). In other words, these insignificant creatures do what is necessary to eat, without being told. It is as if the author knows that yelling at the sluggard to get up is not enough; the sluggard needs to see it for himself. Observing the ants and thinking about it for a moment, the sluggard should be struck by the anomaly that he, an intelligent human being, loafs through the day despite warnings. The author asks in a show of disbelief: "How long will you lie there, O sluggard? When will you arise from your sleep?" (6:9). Then follows the sleep/slumber saying.

These are perhaps the most explicit examples in Proverbs of the process of observation-reflection-moral conclusion, and of course most individual proverbs are simply asserted, without background information on how the conclusion was reached. But the fundamental importance of observation, in the midst of ordinary life experience, is evident in many places in the book. An example is Proverbs 7:6-23, an extended account of the hapless youth seduced by the adulteress, like an ox led to slaughter. The account derives from the author's observation, from what he had "seen" and "perceived" when he

---

50. Among helpful discussions of this theme in Proverbs, see Longman, *Proverbs,* pp. 74-76; Perdue, *Creation & Wisdom,* pp. 109-10; Clements, *Wisdom in Theology,* p. 21; Clifford, *Proverbs,* p. 218; and Frydrych, *Living Under the Sun,* pp. 53-56.

"looked out" and saw this young man (7:6-7). Though this passage is highly stylized and surely not to be read in quite as literal a way as the description of seeing the sluggard's field in 24:30-34, one gets the sense that the author is not just making up a story. The author has seen a young man get seduced by a wicked woman and suffer severely for it. He evidently has observed the rage of a betrayed husband (see 6:34-35). As it is not enough simply to tell the one prone to laziness that he should work hard, so it is not enough simply to tell a young man not to commit adultery. He needs to open his eyes and see what happens to one who travels this path. This is how a person gains deep moral knowledge, and the motivation to act upon it.

One important aspect of this process of coming to know, evident in these examples concerning laziness and adultery, is the ability to perceive similarities between different areas of reality and to construct creative analogies to express them.[51] The young man beckoned by an adulteress needs to sense the similarity between his going into a married woman's home and an ox being led unwittingly to the slaughter. The sluggard who ignores his alarm clock needs to recognize the similarity between the results of an ant's work and the results of human work. Analogies of various sorts abound throughout Proverbs. Numerous examples appear in Proverbs 25–26, where human behavior is compared to jewelry, the weather, weapons, body parts, cities, animal conduct, and doors, among other things. The series of "three things . . . four" sayings in 30:18-31 also provide fruitful examples. The author sees profound similarities among eagles, serpents, ships, and men (30:18-19), for example, and among lions, roosters, goats, and kings (30:29-31).

This is not a bare empiricism, as if Proverbs envisions human beings as blank slates that observe the world and automatically deduce proper moral conclusions. As already observed, Proverbs looks to the fear of the Lord as a basic precondition of all practical observation. Furthermore, Proverbs seems to view human beings as prone to foolishness and thus in need of all sorts of prodding and cajoling in order to turn ordinary experience into proper moral knowledge. In addition, the perception of analogies is something of an art, involving both common sense and imagination. The sluggard should gain moral instruction by conforming his life to the industrious ant, not the hibernating bear. How does he know this? Well, further observation might help in part (for example, noticing that bears emerge

---

51. For relevant discussion, see e.g. Crenshaw, *Old Testament Wisdom,* p. 55; Crenshaw, *Urgent Advice,* pp. 250, 295; Clements, *Wisdom in Theology,* pp. 45-46; Perdue, *Sword and Stylus,* p. 11; and Perdue, *Proverbs,* pp. 33-34.

from hibernation doing just fine physically, while recognizing that human beings would not), though there also seems to be at work here a certain sense of what it means to be human, a sense that makes the analogy to ants instinctively plausible and the analogy to hibernating bears instinctively silly. Human beings, not machines, gain knowledge through observation and reflection in the book of Proverbs.[52]

Despite this caveat against a crass empiricism, the importance of observation and reflection as basis for moral knowledge in Proverbs should not be underestimated.[53] Proverbs views the world as created by God and thus as having an objective reality and meaning. The world, furthermore, is an interconnected whole, encompassing the cosmic realm, the animal kingdom, and human society. Proverbs also sees human beings as having basic sensory and rational capacities, which are able to find truth in the world, precisely because it is a meaningful and reliable whole.[54] To observe, to reflect, and to draw conclusions is a crucial part of Proverbs' working epistemology.

A few other matters need to be mentioned in order to fill out the epistemology of Proverbs. One very important issue is that Proverbs does not advocate an individualistic quest for moral knowledge solely through one's personal experience. Rather, it instills a respect for the accumulation of knowledge

52. Related to this topic of Proverbs and empiricism, Frydrych claims that Proverbs' epistemology is flawed, due to its circularity: the writers' paradigm is based on experience, but only experience that fits the paradigm is accepted as valid; see *Living Under the Sun*, p. 68. Frydrych has a certain point, in my judgment, but concluding that their epistemology was flawed is unfair. All acquisition of knowledge inevitably has a circular quality. No one comes to the world as a blank slate. People interpret new experiences in light of past experiences and already-formed conclusions. The authors of Proverbs, I imagine, realized this.

53. Michael V. Fox, for example, may be guilty of such underestimation in his strong polemic against identifying Proverbs' epistemology as empiricist; see Michael V. Fox, *Proverbs 10–31*, vol. 18b, *The Anchor Bible* (New Haven: Yale University Press, 2009), pp. 963-76. He argues that some of the material to which I appealed above, such as exhortations to "go to the ant," is pedagogical in nature and not indicative of an epistemology. He argues for a "coherence theory of truth." Fox offers salutary warnings about seeing empiricism in Proverbs too quickly and easily. But in the end I fear he downplays the significance of gaining moral knowledge through observation. While he is certainly correct to see appeals to observation (of the ant, for example) as pedagogical, surely good pedagogues shape their teaching style to the way in which people come to know. Bartholomew may also underestimate the role of experience and observation in Proverbs, claiming that arguments from them are rare and employed only as a rhetorical strategy. He correctly appeals, however, to an idea I defended above, namely, that Proverbs believes that interpreting the creation order must be done in accord with foundational religious principles, particularly the fear of the Lord. See "A Time for War," pp. 101-3.

54. Compare here Clements, *Wisdom in Theology*, p. 21.

through the observation and reflection of many people over time, and hence urges older people to pass down their wisdom to the younger and younger people to give heed to their elders. This theme emerges immediately following the book's introduction: "Hear, my son, your father's instruction, and forsake not your mother's teaching" (1:8). Chapters 1–8 as a whole, in fact, are addressed repeatedly to "my son." A father is handing down wisdom to his son, just as his father did for him (4:3-9). As evident in 1:8, both fathers and mothers are expected to instruct their offspring. Mothers become especially prominent in Proverbs' final chapter, where we read what Lemuel learned from his mother (see 31:1) and meet the woman of excellence who speaks with wisdom and teaches (31:26) and is in turn blessed by her children (31:28). Failure to discipline one's children is a terrible wrong (e.g., 13:24). Those who have reached an advanced age are worthy of special respect (see 16:31; 20:29). In fact, every person's posture should be one of humility, accepting instruction, and listening to advice (e.g., 10:8; 12:15). To become wise, associate with the wise (13:20). As Van Leeuwen puts it, Proverbs is an entry into a generational circle of life and learning.[55] The book of Job, of course, deals critically with a rote confidence in traditional notions. A crucial part of Proverbs' epistemology, however, is that people can only become wise as humble participants in a multigenerational process of learning.

Another significant aspect of Proverbs' epistemology concerns character or virtue. For Proverbs, the person with deep moral knowledge is not someone with moral factoids floating in her head but one who is the right kind of person, the person of character.[56] Proverbs does not promulgate rules, but inculcates wisdom, a virtue. Gaining moral knowledge in Proverbs is concomitant with becoming a virtuous person.

Finally, the issue of rhetoric seems appropriate to mention when considering Proverbs' epistemology. Building true moral knowledge in others, the kind that sinks in deep and makes one the kind of person who can navigate effectively through a messy world, requires more than communicating pieces of information. It requires persuasion. Proverbs does not simply make authoritative claims, but winsomely persuades those prone to foolishness to follow

---

55. Van Leeuwen, *Proverbs*, p. 19. For other helpful discussion of this aspect of Proverbs' epistemology, see Longman, *Proverbs*, pp. 76-77; Crenshaw, *Urgent Advice*, p. 297; and Frydrych, *Living Under the Sun*, p. 57.

56. On this matter see especially William P. Brown, *Character in Crisis: A Fresh Approach to the Wisdom Literature of the Old Testament* (Grand Rapids: Eerdmans, 1996), particularly the Introduction and chapters 1-2. See also Murphy, *Tree of Life*, p. 15; Crenshaw, *Old Testament Wisdom*, p. 3; Perdue, *Wisdom & Creation*, pp. 73-74; and Perdue, *Proverbs*, p. 9.

a better course.[57] It speaks elegantly and cleverly, luring readers into its own compelling understanding of the natural order and humanity's place within it. Proverbs' authors help readers to see things as they see them, and thus make wisdom's path seem attractive.[58] For Proverbs, therefore, true moral knowledge involves not pieces of information but a perception and appreciation of practical truths as part of a beautiful whole.

I close this subsection with a few reflections on the implications of Proverbs' epistemology for a theology of natural law. First, the moral growth described in Proverbs comes primarily through natural revelation, not special revelation. To be sure, special revelation does not go without mention in the book, through appeal to the importance of vision or revelation (29:18) and perhaps in some references to *torah*. Proverbs itself is a book of special revelation. Yet the testimony of special revelation in Proverbs points readers persistently to the reality of natural revelation. The created order at large is witness to God's creative wisdom, and people should come to share in this wisdom through observing and pondering the ways of the world. This is another example of why any allegedly Bible-based objection to the reality of moral revelation in nature, or to its crucial importance for ethics, meets insuperable obstacles in the Bible itself.[59] Second, Proverbs lends support to a generally realist metaphysics. Most natural law theories teach that the world is objectively meaningful, that things in the world have stable natures, and that human beings have the sensory and rational capabilities to understand them. Proverbs consistently presumes these very things.

Third, Proverbs displays a strong pragmatic and utilitarian strain that provides useful grist for reflection on how one might utilize natural law in practical life.[60] I do not refer to pragmatism or utilitarianism in a technical philosophical sense, but simply to the fact that, in Proverbs, sound moral conclusions are often recognized as such through their eminent practical usefulness. The sluggard should realize that laziness is wrong through recognizing the poverty it brings (6:6-11). The young man should realize that adultery is wrong by anticipating the harm that the cuckolded husband may do to him (6:34-35).

---

57. See Crenshaw, *Urgent Advice*, chap. 19.

58. See helpful discussion in Perdue, *Creation & Wisdom*, pp. 63-64 and chap. 2 generally; and Perdue, *Proverbs*, p. 8.

59. John Bolt makes a similar point in "Bavinck's Use of Wisdom Literature in Systematic Theology," *SBET* 29 (Spring 2011): 17-19.

60. For related discussion, see e.g. Clements, *Wisdom in Theology*, pp. 41-42; Crenshaw, *Old Testament Wisdom*, pp. 11-13; Crenshaw, *Urgent Advice*, p. 265; and Brueggemann, *In Man We Trust*, p. 17.

Good behavior, in other words, tends to bring good results in one's own and others' lives, while bad behavior tends to bring deleterious consequences. This must be kept in perspective, since Proverbs communicates such ideas with nuance. For one thing, the fear of the Lord undergirds the whole book, and the moral life is ultimately about accountability to God, not serving one's own best interest. Also, Proverbs often acknowledges that the righteous sometimes suffer and the unrighteous sometimes prosper (trenchantly explored in Job and Ecclesiastes). Nevertheless, Proverbs repeatedly teaches that hard work generally leads to profit, watching one's words to peaceful relations with neighbors, helping the poor to a good reputation, and the like. The very order of the world instills a natural constraint upon evil conduct. People do not say all the nasty things they would like to say to their neighbors because they want to avoid hostility, and they work harder than they are inclined to work because they want to eat. "A worker's appetite works for him; his mouth urges him on" (16:26). There seems to be a recognition here that God's natural order imposes limits upon the evils people can do, even apart from growth in true virtue. To make a moral appeal to others by pointing out that a certain course of action will lead to bad consequences (poverty, hostility, etc.) is, indeed, pragmatic, but it appears to be a species of natural law argumentation. Because of the interconnected integrity of the natural order created by God, pragmatic arguments can be natural law arguments, which in turn are implicit exhortations to act as God wills.

Finally, the epistemology of Proverbs uncovers the mysteries and ambiguities of gaining knowledge through observation, reflection, or heeding one's elders' advice, which in turn should engender modesty in expectations about what investigation of and appeal to natural law can attain. For Proverbs, observation of the world leads to some very obvious conclusions. The authors of the book certainly had no doubt that adultery is exceedingly foolish and that nothing good follows upon its heels. But they also acknowledged that life is full of puzzles. The wise author of Proverbs 30:18-19 recognized similarities among eagles in the sky, serpents on a rock, ships on the sea, and a man with a maid, but confessed that he did not understand any of these things. Despite all its emphasis on human perception and human decision, Proverbs knows that God has the final, and unpredictable, word (e.g., 16:1, 9; 19:21; 20:24; 21:1, 30).[61] The natural order is intelligible, but it does not itself provide comprehensive knowledge of God, the world, or human behavior. Any responsible Christian theology of natural law must wrestle soberly with this fact.

61. See Murphy, *Tree of Life,* p. 11; Murphy, *Proverbs,* p. xxv; and Clements, *Wisdom in Theology,* p. 167.

In several previous chapters I have raised questions about epistemology and noted that the biblical texts under consideration offer only the most general, and never specific, answers to them. Proverbs too does not provide any epistemological theory, and we must be modest about building a detailed epistemology from what is only implicit. Nevertheless, Proverbs provides perhaps the richest material in Scripture pertaining to an epistemology of natural law, and I return to this material when offering final epistemological reflections in Chapter 10.

The Universal Accessibility of Wisdom

Proverbs identifies the "fear of the Lord" as the beginning of wisdom. Given that this phrase uses Israel's special covenant name for God, it may seem logical to conclude that wisdom exists only among the pious in Israel. Yet Proverbs makes clear this is not the case. Though it seems initially contradictory, Proverbs teaches both that devotion to the one true God is foundational for being wise in an ultimate sense and that genuine wisdom exists among those who worship other gods. Proverbs, in fact, required Israel to recognize the universal dimension of wisdom and to learn from the wisdom of foreigners. In this subsection I consider this universal and international flavor of wisdom found in Proverbs, and conclude again with reflections on how this contributes to a larger biblical theology of natural law.

My first point concerns the fact that the OT wisdom literature was part of an international genre. Though we can only tread on this matter lightly, the main point is both clear and significant. Peoples of the ancient Near East (ANE) were producing wisdom literature long before Proverbs came into existence.[62] The most famous of this literature came from Egypt, and scholars have constructed multiple theories about what and how Israel's sages learned from Egypt's. Other peoples also wrote significant wisdom documents probably familiar to Israelites.[63] Questions about the influence of any particular foreign text upon Proverbs are extremely complex, and I am ill-equipped to navigate the intricacies of these debates. What is clear is that the authors of

---

62. For discussion of other ancient Near Eastern wisdom traditions, see Perdue, *Sword and Stylus,* pp. 13-49; Longman, *Proverbs,* pp. 43-52; and Crenshaw, *Old Testament Wisdom,* chap. 9. On the so-called Instruction genre, see especially Weeks, *Instruction and Imagery,* chap. 1.

63. For a study of the influence of the wisdom literature of other Semitic peoples, see John Day, "Foreign Semitic Influence on the Wisdom of Israel and Its Appropriation in the Book of Proverbs," in *Wisdom in Ancient Israel,* pp. 55-70.

Proverbs were well acquainted generally with foreign wisdom literature, utilized its various genres and styles, and repeated many of its substantive themes (while maintaining independence of thought).[64] As the OT law bears many striking resemblances to other ANE legal codes, so Proverbs bears many striking resemblances to other ANE wisdom literature, though there is nothing like slavish imitation in either case.

Beyond the general borrowing of genre and style, Proverbs acknowledges foreign wisdom and utilizes specific foreign material substantively. The first example returns us to Proverbs 8. Proverbs 8:22-31 (along with 3:19-20) describes God's creation of the world by wisdom, such that all things are suffused with God's wisdom and those who pursue wisdom gain a share in what originally belonged to God. This in itself suggests that wise people exist outside the narrow boundaries of Israel. It is possible that wisdom could be objectively available universally without being subjectively accessible to those without faith in the one true God, but at least verses 15-16 prevent this conclusion. The language speaks of political rule in general: "By me [wisdom] kings reign, and rulers decree what is just; by me princes rule, and nobles, *all* who govern justly." These verses speak of "all" just governors, and the Hebrew word translated as "rulers" ordinarily refers to foreign monarchs.[65] If Proverbs 1–9 was composed in an exilic/postexilic context, as most believe, then the implications of this universal appropriation of wisdom by political authorities is all the more interesting. I return to this issue in the chapter's conclusion.

A second example, plausible but uncertain, focuses upon 22:17–24:22. In the late nineteenth century the text of *Amenemope,* an Egyptian wisdom document, was discovered. This ignited a storm of interest in the relationship between OT and other ANE wisdom literature.[66] Scholars immediately recognized numerous similarities between *Amenemope* and Proverbs 22:17–24:22. They proposed various theories about their relationship, many believing that one document (for some Proverbs, for others *Amenemope*) was directly dependent upon the other. Today the opinion that the author of 22:17–24:22 utilized *Amenemope* is widely embraced.[67] Though direct reliance is impossible

---

64. See Weeks, *Early Israelite Wisdom,* chap. 1; and Murphy, *Tree of Life,* p. 175.

65. On the international setting of 8:15-16, see e.g. Clements, *Wisdom in Theology,* p. 115; and Fox, *Proverbs 1–9,* p. 274. On the foreign connotation of "rulers" in 8:15, see Bartholomew, "A Time for War," p. 105 n. 77.

66. On *Amenemope* generally, see Whybray, *Proverbs,* pp. 323-24; and Murphy, *Proverbs,* pp. 291-94.

67. E.g., see Murphy, *Tree of Life,* pp. 23-24; Murphy, *Proverbs,* p. 291; Fox, *Proverbs 10–31,* pp. 754-55; and Washington, *Wealth and Poverty,* p. 138.

to prove, their points of similarity are remarkable. Close parallels also exist between *Amenemope* and other sections of Proverbs.[68] Even if these resemblances are entirely coincidental (from the human standpoint), the fact that Proverbs can speak so similarly to this pagan document makes it impossible for the devotee of Proverbs to doubt that considerable wisdom resides in *Amenemope*.

Some scholars have also suggested that the authors of Proverbs had knowledge of *Ahiqar,* a wisdom document from Assyria.[69] While the idea that Proverbs directly depends on *Amenemope* is plausible and perhaps likely, theories about *Ahiqar* are less probable. Nevertheless, the similarities between *Ahiqar* and Proverbs again suggest that, from Scripture's own perspective, a pagan document evidently contains an impressive degree of wisdom.

Finally, two sections of Proverbs were likely composed by non-Israelites. The first begins in 30:1, which introduces the words of Agur son of Jakeh, though it is not certain where his words end (perhaps after verse 9 or 14). The second records the words of King Lemuel in 31:1-9. In 30:1 the identification of the author is followed by the word המשא in the Hebrew text, and in 31:1 by משא. The term משא could mean "an oracle," thereby identifying the nature of the sayings by Agur and Lemuel. Or the term could point to the north Arabian tribe called Massa, referred to in Genesis 25:14 and 1 Chronicles 1:30, in which case the text identifies Agur and Lemuel as members of a foreign people. Most commentators see a reference to Massa in one or both of these instances,[70] and the arguments seem considerably stronger in this direction. There is no OT record of any Israelite bearing either the name Agur or Lemuel, and scholars have noted a number of Aramaisms in 31:1-9, suggesting a foreign origin. Furthermore, while reference to an oracle is possible in 30:1, given the content of the verses that follow, it seems an unlikely term to be used in 31:1 to describe the maternal advice Lemuel recounts in the following verses. Given that a number of other places in the OT acknowledge the presence of wise people outside Israel, as I discuss next, there should be no insuperable *a priori* objection to the idea that select words of foreign wisdom would be incorporated into the Scriptures themselves.

---

68. For charts setting forth the similarities of *Amenemope* with 22:17–22:24, see Crenshaw, *Urgent Advice,* p. 362; and Fox, *Proverbs 10–31,* pp. 757-60. On the parallels with other parts of Proverbs, see Washington, *Wealth and Poverty,* p. 135.

69. E.g., see Fox, *Proverbs 10–31,* p. 767; also see Day, "Foreign Semitic Influence," pp. 62-70; and Bryan Estelle, "Proverbs and Ahiqar: Revisited," *The Biblical Historian* 1 (2004): 1-9.

70. E.g., see Dell, *Book of Proverbs,* p. 82; Whybray, *Proverbs,* pp. 407, 422; Clifford, *Proverbs,* pp. 260, 270; Murphy, *Proverbs,* p. 226; Perdue, *Proverbs,* p. 269; Longman, *Proverbs,* p. 518; and Fox, *Proverbs 10–31,* p. 884.

We have seen thus far, despite the imprecise nature of determining the relationship between Proverbs and particular traditions and documents of foreign wisdom, that Proverbs is part of an international phenomenon of wisdom literature and acknowledges the presence of genuine wisdom outside of Israel in a number of ways. Proverbs' perspective is confirmed by many other biblical passages that speak of wisdom residing among foreign peoples. A notable example is 1 Kings 4:30: "Solomon's wisdom surpassed the wisdom of all the people of the east and all the wisdom of Egypt." The point of this statement is to magnify Solomon, but the language of comparison displays respect for eastern and Egyptian wisdom. The statement would not magnify Solomon if the wisdom of the east and of Egypt was not impressive. This language is all the more striking when compared, for example, to the story later in 1 Kings regarding Elijah and the prophets of Baal. The biblical text hardly calls Elijah a *better* prophet; rather, Elijah is the only true prophet and the others were not true prophets at all. But in 1 Kings 4:30 Solomon is not the only wise man, just the wisest among many.[71] This point is underscored by later comments in 1 Kings that people of other nations recognized Solomon's wisdom. His wisdom was not, in other words, some kind of esoteric thing comprehensible only by faithful Israelites. For example, 4:31 notes that "his fame was in all the surrounding nations" and 4:34 adds that people from all nations and from all the kings of the earth came to hear his wisdom. Two specific examples are Hiram, king of Tyre, who professed that God had "given to David a wise son" (5:7), and the Queen of Sheba, who recognized that Solomon's wisdom surpassed the rumors she had heard (10:6-9).

Several other examples deserve brief mention. First, the OT prophets Jeremiah and Obadiah acknowledge the wisdom of the Edomites (Jer. 49:7; Obad. 8), a noteworthy belief given the longstanding tensions between Edom and Israel. Second, Job and his three friends, who engage in a most impressive wisdom conversation, are non-Israelites. Job was a man of "the east" (1:3), not a surprising designation in light of 1 Kings 4:30. Though the "land of Uz" cannot be identified with certainty, some believe it is a reference to Edom.[72] A third example are references to the righteous and wise Daniel in Ezekiel 14:14, 20 and 28:3. A casual reader may instinctively think of the prophet Daniel, especially in Ezekiel 14, which speaks of Daniel alongside

---

71. See similar observations in Crenshaw, *Old Testament Wisdom*, p. 44; and Longman, *Proverbs*, p. 42.

72. See Day, "Foreign Semitic Influence," p. 56; see also Perdue, *Wisdom & Creation*, p. 327.

other prominent biblical figures, Noah and Job. But this seems unlikely, for three reasons: Ezekiel and the book of Daniel spell "Daniel" differently; Ezekiel did not write at a time when the prophet Daniel would have attained an eminent reputation worthy of mention alongside these others; and (in 28:3) this Daniel was apparently known to the prince of Tyre. A more likely interpretation is that this Daniel refers to a non-Israelite figure known from Ugaritic texts and famous as a just judge of widows and orphans.[73] This means that all three righteous men Ezekiel refers to in 14:14, 20 are non-Israelites and that Ezekiel calls the ruler of Tyre to account in 28:3 through appeal to an internationally recognized person rather than through a parochial Israelite example. A final example comes from this same chapter. Ezekiel 28 states that the king of Tyre was "full of wisdom and perfect in beauty" (28:12; cf. 28:4-5), comparing his initial state, before his fall into pride, to that of Adam in Eden (28:13-16).

In this subsection I have argued that Proverbs recognizes that genuine wisdom exists outside the bounds of Israel and indicates that God's people should learn from the wisdom of others. How should we harmonize this with the OT conviction that there is one true God and the gods of the nations are idols? Proverbs itself requires a dual affirmation: there is no truly wise person who does not serve the God of Israel, yet a species of genuine wisdom exists among the pagan nations. Perhaps we might say that those who sincerely fear the Lord (the God of Israel) have a *sanctified* or *ultimate* wisdom, while those who do not may still attain a *common* or *proximate* wisdom.[74] The wisdom ascribed to foreign people in Proverbs and elsewhere in the OT does not concern *saving* knowledge of God (Job seemingly excepted) but a moral insight into the order of this present world.[75] By these distinctions I mean to capture something similar to John Calvin's admiring words about the insight and achievement of ancient pagans in the very same context in which he re-

---

73. See Day, "Foreign Semitic Influence," pp. 57-58.

74. It is difficult to find the perfect terms. Thanks to participants in the Warfield Seminar at Westminster Seminary California for suggesting the terms I use here. John Bolt seems to get at the same basic distinction when comparing "the wisdom of the people and the *sharpened* wisdom of Israel." See "Bavinck's Use of Wisdom Literature," p. 23. See also relevant discussion in the next section.

75. Murphy offers a different perspective on this issue. Working with theological ideas pioneered by Karl Rahner, Murphy speaks about how Israel's openness to the wisdom of its neighbors points to the possibility that non-Israelites have saving faith in the creator. See *Tree of Life*, p. 126. Speaking in Reformed terms, I would respond that the foreign wisdom respected in Proverbs concerns insight into the (natural) law, not knowledge of the gospel.

flected on the depths of their sin and lack of true blessedness before God. How, asked Calvin, "can we deny that truth must have beamed on those ancient lawgivers who arranged civil order and discipline with so much equity? Shall we say that the philosophers, in their exquisite researches and skilful description of nature, were blind? Shall we deny the possession of intellect to those who drew up rules for discourse, and taught us to speak in accordance with reason? Shall we say that those who, by the cultivation of the medical art, expended their industry in our behalf, were only raving? What shall we say of the mathematical sciences? Shall we deem them to be the dreams of madmen? Nay, we cannot read the writings of the ancients on these subjects without the highest admiration. . . ."[76]

These conclusions correspond to and enrich conclusions about natural law in previous chapters. By a universal and common covenant with Noah God preserved the cosmic and social orders, sustaining fallen human beings in the image of God without redeeming them. This Noahic covenant provides theological foundation for the international diffusion of wisdom evident in Proverbs. As Abimelech and other non-Abrahamic people displayed righteousness through the "fear of God" before Sinai, so non-Israelites acquired perceptive insight into the ways of wisdom after Sinai, even though they fell short of the true "fear of the Lord" attained through the covenants of grace (see below for further reflection on this fear of God/fear of the Lord distinction). In Proverbs we gain fuller insight into how those outside the covenant community gain this practical moral knowledge: through being instructed, observing, reflecting, analogizing, and drawing conclusions.

Natural Law in Proverbs: Substantive Matters

In the previous section I examined various foundational matters pertaining to natural law in Proverbs, and here I turn to matters substantive, that is, specific moral issues prominent in Proverbs and important for my larger study of natural law. In Part 1, I identified a minimalist natural law ethic explicit in the text of Genesis 9:1-7, which sets forth basic obligations of the Noahic covenant. I suggested that this minimalist ethic — particularly focused upon procreation, eating, and the administration of retributive justice — reflects God's primary purpose in the covenant with Noah, namely, the *preservation* of human society in the midst of the broader created order. The minimalist ethic requires

---

76. Calvin, *Institutes*, 2.2.15. See his broader discussion in 2.2.12-17.

the basics of what is necessary for the human race to continue. In addition, I presented evidence that this minimalist ethic presumes a broader natural moral order which also obligates the human race and points to a deeper earthly flourishing that is still possible to some degree among fallen human beings. Proverbs, which presents wisdom as gained primarily through natural revelation, is consistent with this reality observed in many other places in Scripture. Proverbs pays close attention to justice and to matters of sex and family, but also recognizes a broader moral order which the wise person understands and by which she achieves a measure of success in this world. I look first at Proverbs on justice and matters of sex and family, and then examine a few issues related to the broader moral order.

Justice

The right administration of retributive justice is a cornerstone of the minimalist natural law ethic (Gen. 9:6), and one of the fundamental necessities for the survival of a sinful human race. Accordingly, concerns about justice have arisen everywhere we have looked thus far in Scripture for insight on the natural law. The same holds true for Proverbs, where perceiving the natural moral order through wisdom is inseparable from understanding and practicing what is just. In this subsection I consider this connection between wisdom and justice, the idea of divine justice in Proverbs, and the implications of Proverbs' teaching that human justice should image God's justice.

The theme of the right administration of justice, in various guises, appears throughout Proverbs as a key mark of wisdom. The work of kings, condemnation of bribery, right treatment of the needy, and rendering judgment with integrity are among many topics in which the theme emerges. Beyond such relatively obvious examples, Proverbs connects wisdom and justice in subtle ways. A good example is the call for wisdom to be exercised at the city gate (see 8:3; 22:22-23; 31:23, 30-31), the place where legal proceedings often transpired in ANE society.[77] Wisdom at the city gate meant wisdom in rendering judgment. Elsewhere in the OT wisdom was associated with the work of judges (Deut. 16:19), of kings (2 Sam. 14:20; 1 Kgs. 3:28), and of heads of smaller social units (Deut. 1:13, 15). Organization of the kingdom's administration required wisdom (1 Kgs. 4:1-28; Ezra 7:25), as did promoting

---

77. Elsewhere in Scripture see 2 Sam. 15:2; 18:24; 19:8; Job 29:7. For discussion see Perdue, *Wisdom & Creation*, p. 86.

diplomatic and commercial relations with foreign nations (1 Kgs. 5:1-6; 9:10-14, 26-28; 10:11-12, 22).[78]

The close association of wisdom and justice has instinctive plausibility. If the natural law is so concerned with justice, and if the objective law of the natural order is discerned through the subjective exercise of wisdom, then acquisition of wisdom must be paramount for the practice of justice. But there is more to be mined about justice from the teaching of Proverbs.

In Chapters 1-2, I argued that God revealed himself as a just God first in the covenant of creation with Adam and then in the postdiluvian covenant with Noah. In these covenants God also commissioned human beings, as his image-bearers, to pursue justice in a way that mirrored his own. Proverbs is similar. It repeatedly highlights the justice of God evident in the natural order and requires human justice to reflect this divine justice. In what follows I first explore Proverbs' teaching about divine justice and then its view of human justice as a reflection of God's.

The retributive justice of God is foundational in Proverbs.[79] God knows all things and will call all to account for their actions. "If you say, 'Behold, we did not know this,' does not he who weighs the heart perceive it? Does not he who keeps watch over your soul know it, and will he not repay man according to his work?" (24:12). In light of this conception of God as the just judge, Proverbs insistently teaches that success and flourishing come to the righteous and death and destruction to the wicked. The principle of retribution "is asserted as a fixed law of life."[80] For example, "the wicked are overthrown and are no more, but the house of the righteous will stand" (12:7). In Proverbs 7, the foreign woman, seducing a young man, tries to persuade him not that adultery is good but that they can get away with it: "For my husband is not at home; he has gone on a long journey; he took a bag of money with him; at full moon he will come home" (7:19-20).[81] Orderly retributive justice, in other words, underlies the entire way of wisdom. Doubting the reality of retributive justice sows the seed of despising the moral order altogether. Of special interest for the present study, Proverbs frequently speaks in terms of the *lex talionis*. Under God's just administration of the world, punishment and reward come to people in fitting ways that correspond to their conduct. God's justice in

78. See Lemaire, "Wisdom in Solomonic Historiography," pp. 109-10 for discussion and references.

79. Perdue writes: "all sapiential teaching . . . is grounded ultimately in the justice of God." See *Proverbs*, p. 46.

80. Clements, *Wisdom in Theology*, pp. 159-60.

81. As noted by Camp, *Wisdom and the Feminine*, p. 117.

Proverbs is poetic and proportionate. "To the scorners he is scornful" (3:34); "I love those who love me" (8:17); "whoever brings blessing will be enriched, and one who waters will himself be watered" (11:25); "whoever digs a pit will fall into it, and a stone will come back on him who starts it rolling" (26:27).[82]

Although Proverbs mentions a number of particular blessings that God gives to those doing particular wise things (e.g., economic prosperity to those who work hard), it highlights *life* as the great general blessing for following the path of wisdom. Proverbs repeatedly offers life for those heeding its call and threatens death for the foolish.[83] Most commentators believe that the life promised is a long and successful earthly life.[84] In light of Proverbs' emphasis upon earthly flourishing, this is a generally sound conclusion. Yet it is interesting that on several occasions Proverbs refers to wisdom herself, or her manifestations, as a "tree of life" (3:18; 11:30; 13:12; 15:4), evoking images of the Garden of Eden (and anticipating the heavenly Jerusalem — Rev. 2:7; 22:2), and hence of "living forever" (Gen. 3:22). To be sure, Proverbs' focus is upon the outcome of a person's conduct in this present world. Yet if Proverbs gives insight into the natural moral order, particularly for OT Israel under the Mosaic covenant, and if the natural and Mosaic laws are both protological and remind human beings of their identity with Adam in his probation and fall, then it is not surprising that Proverbs would also remind readers that the reward for wise obedience in the covenant of creation would ultimately have been eschatological life. From the beginning human beings were destined not for indefinite life in this creation but for everlasting life in a consummated new creation. Under the Mosaic covenant, Israel's experience of blessing and curse in this world, as a recompense for their obedience to God's law, was analogous to the experience of blessing and curse at an eschatological level. However one perceives this dynamic at work in Proverbs, Proverbs' repeated emphasis upon God granting life to those who follow wisdom's path, and death to the foolish, highlights the retributive justice of God in ways similar to what we have observed in previous chapters.

This emphasis upon retributive justice reintroduces the theme of order. As concluded above, the idea that Proverbs envisions just retribution coming

---

82. Other examples of the talionic principle at work in God's government of the world include 1:11, 18-19; 1:25-31; 8:17; 11:27, 31; 13:20; 17:13; 22:8, 9, 23; 27:18; 29:23; 30:17.

83. My informal list of examples, almost all of them explicit, is 1:33; 2:18-19, 21; 3:2, 16-18, 22; 4:1, 10, 13, 22; 5:5-6, 23; 6:23, 26; 7:2, 23, 27; 8:35-36; 9:6, 11, 18; 10:1, 11, 16-17, 21, 27; 11:4, 7, 19, 30; 12:28; 13:14, 21, 22; 14:12, 27; 15:4, 24, 27, 31; 16:17, 22, 25, 31; 18:21; 19:16, 18, 23; 21:16; 22:4.

84. E.g., see Crenshaw, *Old Testament Wisdom*, p. 66; Murphy, *Tree of Life*, pp. 28-29; and Perdue, *Proverbs*, pp. 43-44.

automatically to people in the course of things is far too simplistic. God is the one who established and continues to oversee and guarantee this order of justice and, very significantly, there are plenty of important exceptions to the rule (frequently the righteous suffer and the wicked prosper).[85] Though Job and Ecclesiastes probe the latter theme in detail, Proverbs itself clearly recognizes that retributive justice does not always occur as theoretically expected in an orderly world. I suggest that what Proverbs teaches about this is not only true to life as we all experience it but also true to the covenant theology I have been utilizing in this book. Strict retributive justice was God's way in the original covenant of creation, where he threatened judgment for a single sin on humanity's part, without any offer of mercy. Under the Noahic covenant, however, God continues to display his retributive justice, but only as tempered by forbearance. Were God to treat the present world with perfectly consistent retributive justice, it would consume everyone, for no one can meet its exacting standard. Proverbs exhorts people to become wise, but never indicates that anyone can fully succeed. Foolishness is the constant companion of even the wisest. "Surely there is not a righteous man on earth who does good and never sins. . . . See, this alone I found, that God made man upright, but they have sought out many schemes" (Eccl. 7:20, 29). In Proverbs the "wise" still need to be rebuked (e.g., 17:10). Each person is foolish and thus ultimately worthy of God's condemnation. Some people are wise and righteous and subject to God's favorable verdict — but only relatively speaking, in this or that case. As Proverbs recognizes, God does indeed give real and meaningful glimpses of his retributive justice in the earthly success that often comes to the wise and the hardship that often comes to the foolish. But this is a divine retributive justice mixed with exceptions, ambiguities, and mystery. It is fit for a Noahic world, a fallen world preserved by a forbearing God who will nevertheless continue to testify to his justice.

Consistent with the image of God theme discussed earlier in the chapter and throughout this book, Proverbs envisions wise human justice as a mirror of God's retributive justice. God justly pays back all according to their work, and he expects human judgment to hew the same line: "He who justifies the wicked and he who condemns the righteous are both alike an abomination to the Lord" (17:15). As noted, Proverbs frequently speaks of God's just gov-

---

85. See generally the discussion above. For brief comment on how retribution never becomes automatic in Proverbs, see e.g. Perdue, *Sword and Stylus*, p. 115. On Proverbs' recognition of "aberrations and distortions" in wisdom's ability to bring success, see e.g. Clements, *Wisdom in Theology*, p. 161; and Van Leeuwen, *Proverbs*, p. 25.

ernance of the world through the talionic principle of proportionate retribution. Many of those verses imply that God will use human action to execute
this just payback. Proverbs warns against the evil of twisting justice through
failure to give what is fitting: "do not withhold good from those to whom it is
due" (3:27); "do not contend with a man for no reason, when he has done you
no harm" (3:30); "if anyone returns evil for good, evil will not depart from
his house" (17:13). It is frightening to fall into the hands of someone wreak-
ing disproportionate vengeance (6:34-35). Proverbs 24:29 at first glance does
seem to steer people away from the *lex talionis:* "Do not say, 'I will do to him
as he has done to me; I will pay the man back for what he has done.'" But in
context this exhortation appears to envision a situation in which the alleged
harm done to the speaker was concocted, for the previous verse reads: "Be not
a witness against your neighbor *without cause,* and do not *deceive with your
lips*" (24:28). The general teaching of Proverbs is that people should render
truthful judgment, acquit the righteous, condemn the guilty, and give to each
proportionately according to her due.[86]

Just as Proverbs describes divine justice being manifest in the world
according to the terms of the Noahic covenant — that is, as tempered by forbearance — so also Proverbs commends human justice with a Noahic accent.
The wise must seek justice, but with a measure of forbearance. Many times
the wise person, rather than prosecute a wrong, will just let things go: "The
beginning of strife is like letting out water, so quit before the quarrel breaks
out" (17:14); "good sense makes one slow to anger, and it is his glory to overlook
an offense" (19:11; cf. 12:16). Proverbs does not give detailed instructions for
knowing when forbearance is the better course. As with many other things, it
seems to be something the wise person just knows, without a precise calculus to give him a black-and-white answer. In 17:14 a pragmatic consideration
appears to rule: bringing a lawsuit may well bring more headache than just
forgetting about it.[87] In a different vein, the forbearance urged in 25:7b-8 stems
from humility about one's ability to evaluate situations correctly: "What your
eyes have seen do not hastily bring into court, for what will you do in the end,
when your neighbor puts you to shame?" And when a wise person forgoes
just vengeance, it is against the backdrop that God's justice will nevertheless

---

86. Fox has some interesting related comments on the relation of justice to the concepts
of beauty and balance in Proverbs; see *Proverbs 10–31*, pp. 972-76.

87. In Chapter 2, with respect to the Noahic covenant, I argued that though justice is
necessary for harmonious social relations, pursuing justice for every last wrong in the present
world would destroy human society. Sometimes *not* pursuing justice better leads to peace.
Frydrych, *Living Under the Sun*, pp. 177-78, reflects on some matters related to this concern.

be accomplished in the end: "Do not say, 'I will repay evil'; wait for the Lord, and he will deliver you" (20:22).

There are also a few examples where Proverbs counsels not merely forbearance toward the wrongdoer but even forgiveness: "Hatred stirs up strife, but love covers all offenses" (10:12; cf. 17:9). This is not surprising, given that God gave Proverbs to his covenant people Israel, to whom he also revealed his great love and redemptive mercy in all sorts of ways. But since Proverbs primarily instructs about a wisdom learned from natural revelation, which does not reveal God's redemptive grace, Proverbs tends to emphasize the integrity of retributive justice rather than forgiveness.

Sex and Family

Procreation and the increase of the human race are key aspects of the minimalist natural law ethic (Gen. 9:1-7), because they are foundational for the preservation of human society. Hence many of Scripture's descriptions of human rebellion against natural law involve abuse of the purposes of sex and marriage. In this subsection I argue that Proverbs continues this pattern. For Proverbs, integral to the way of wisdom is living within healthy families marked by mutually supportive husband-wife relationships, sexual fidelity, and diligent childrearing.

It seems safe to claim that Proverbs views the family as *the* foundational social institution. As important as kings and rulers are for understanding the life marked by wisdom, Proverbs looks to the family as the building-block of society.[88] Though a tyrannical ruler can bring great social hardship (e.g., 28:15-16), society is more fundamentally threatened from the bottom up, by disintegration of the marriage relationship and failure to raise wise children. I first identify three aspects of healthy family life in Proverbs and then offer a few reflections on the connection between healthy families and the health of the broader social order.

First, Proverbs envisions the wise as living within mutually beneficial and supportive marriages. Proverbs does not contemplate the wise going through life in an unmarried state. Rather, "he who finds a wife finds a good thing and obtains favor from the Lord" (18:22). Yet marriage is not a good per se, for Proverbs describes bad marriages as a kind of hell: "It is better to live

---

88. E.g., see Clements, *Wisdom in Theology,* p. 126; and Frydrych, *Living Under the Sun,* pp. 140, 183.

in a corner of the housetop than in a house shared with a quarrelsome wife" (21:9); "It is better to live in a desert land than with a quarrelsome and fretful woman" (21:19). The overall movement of the book is noteworthy. It begins with a father's address to his son in an apparently immature and vulnerable state (see 1:8-19) and ends by describing the exemplary wife, the woman of excellence (31:10-31). As his son learns to conform his life to the pattern of the natural order, he moves from immaturity to marriage — but he must marry well. In a good marriage the wife brings honor to her husband in his public affairs (31:23) and the husband trusts his wife completely (31:11), praises her (31:28-29), and rejoices in her (5:18). They also share the task of training their children (e.g., 1:8).

Fundamental to a healthy family, secondly, is sexual fidelity. Through the central sections of Proverbs, consisting mostly of individual sayings, a variety of sins bring trouble to oneself and others. But in the book's extended introduction — chapters 1–9 — sexual misconduct is the epitome of folly. Woman Folly, the nemesis of Woman Wisdom, is personified as an adulteress. The ramifications of learning wisdom are clear: "You will be delivered from the forbidden woman, from the adulteress with her smooth words, who forsakes the companion of her youth and forgets the covenant of her God; for her house sinks down to death, and her paths to the departed; none who go to her come back, nor do they regain the paths of life" (2:16-19). These chapters accentuate the erotic dimension of sexual temptation and fidelity. The adulteress seeks to capture the fool "with her eyelashes" (6:25) and seduces him with kisses and a description of her bed (7:13-18). Instead of embracing "the bosom of an adulteress" the young man must "drink water" from his "own cistern," and his wife's breasts should fill him "at all times with delight" (5:15-20).

Third, a good marriage relationship entails proper training of children. The introductory section of Proverbs frames the whole book in terms of parental instruction to a son: "Hear, my son, your father's instruction, and forsake not your mother's teaching" (1:8). These opening chapters repeatedly appeal to "my son." The section that comprises the bulk of the book, "the proverbs of Solomon," begins along the same lines: "A wise son makes a glad father, but a foolish son is a sorrow to his mother" (10:1). Proverbs speaks often of the regular (though not invariable) course of the natural order, and one aspect of the natural moral order is that faithful parental discipline produces wisdom in children: "Train up a child in the way he should go; even when he is old he will not depart from it" (22:6). In the ideal portrait at the end of the book, the excellent wife and reputable husband have appreciative children in good relationship with them (31:28).

As I noted above, the family is so foundational that Proverbs sees the breakdown of the family as a major threat to the breakdown of the larger society. This displays the connection between the administration of justice on the one hand and sex and family on the other.[89] The natural moral order, here and elsewhere in Scripture, is an organic whole. Already in 1:8-19 failure to raise wise children brings not only tragedy for a single family but also destruction of the common good. The foolish son aligns himself with sociopaths who "lie in wait for blood," "ambush the innocent," and are "greedy for unjust gain" (1:11, 19). Furthermore, Woman Folly is not a private seductress. She "sits at the door of her house; she takes a seat on the highest places of the town" (9:14). Her malicious work among the youth is up for public view (7:6-9). Her adultery destroys not one family, but two. It involves the adulteress's husband (7:19-20) and provokes his vengeance against the young man — a jealous and unbounded vengeance, in fact, that compromises the standard of proportionate justice so crucial to society's stability (see 6:34-35).

In summary, the perspective on sex and family communicated through the natural order as described in Proverbs closely resembles the biblical teaching about natural law considered in previous chapters. From the beginning and continuing after the fall, God has made human beings in his image as male and female meant to be fruitful and multiply and fill the earth. A central facet of rebellion against the nature of things is the breakdown of sound marriage relationships, marked by sexual infidelity and the failure to train the next generation in the ways of wisdom.

The Broader Natural Moral Order

As I argued in Part 1, the minimalist natural law ethic explicit in Genesis 9:1-7 is not the entirety of natural law. Natural law is a natural moral order, and the minimalist ethic itself presupposes the reality of this broader order. Having examined two aspects of the minimalist natural law ethic prominent in Proverbs, we now consider some aspects of the broader moral order addressed in Proverbs and organically related to the minimalist ethic.

A first issue is certainly not a major theme in Proverbs, but I believe worth mentioning briefly: kindness to animals. Part of the minimalist natural law ethic is God's implied command to eat animals and plants, with an explicit prohibition of eating meat with its blood (Gen. 9:3-4). At one level this concern

---

89. See related reflections in Camp, *Wisdom and the Feminine*, pp. 118-20.

about eating reflects the basics of what is necessary to preserve the human race. But the prohibition of blood hints at a broader natural moral order humanity is obligated to honor. In Chapter 2, I interpreted 9:3-4 against the background of God's delivering the animal kingdom into the hands of human beings (9:2). Human dominion over the animals means that we can eat them, but at the same time this dominion must respect certain bounds. We may eat animals, but only in a humane way; we may not pounce on animals and eat them alive, as one beast does to another, but should slaughter them, prepare them, and sit down to dine. Such conduct is rooted in humanity's original creation task as divine image-bearers, commissioned by God to exercise *benevolent* dominion and subdue the other creatures. Hence it is appropriate that kindness toward animals is part of the wise life in Proverbs: "Whoever is righteous has regard for the life of his beast, but the mercy of the wicked is cruel" (12:10).

A second issue is a significant topic in Proverbs: work. The minimalist natural law ethic explicit in Genesis 9:1-7 does not mention work, and it has not been a theme in texts considered in previous chapters. But as I suggested in Chapter 2, the minimalist ethic presupposes the reality of human economic life. Eating plants and animals, for example, requires agricultural labor. Furthermore, the right administration of justice presupposes ongoing human activities in which conflicts arise, and among such activities is gainful employment. Justice demands that those who work make due profit from their efforts.

Work is also grounded in other natural law themes considered in this book. The original responsibility of image-bearing humans to exercise dominion and subdue the earth (Gen. 1:26, 28) is in essence a commission to work. God reveals himself as a working God throughout Genesis 1 as he fashions this world and orders it, and he makes human beings to be workers like him, continuing the task of ordering the world under his sovereign authority. After six days of hard and perfectly executed work, God rested (Gen. 2:1-3). As argued in chapter 1, God destined human beings, as his image-bearers, to attain rest with him upon successful performance of their work. After the fall human work became toilsome, but continued (Gen. 3:17-19). Though stripped of an eschatological hope achieved through their own labor, human beings were to expect earthly compensation for their ongoing work: "by the sweat of your face you shall eat bread" (3:19). This is precisely the perspective of Proverbs.

Matters of work, idleness, wealth, and poverty are prevalent in Proverbs. Harold Washington is surely correct that Proverbs treats these issues more frequently than any other book in the OT.[90] One prominent theme is that

---

90. Washington, *Wealth and Poverty*, p. 1. For extensive treatments of these issues in

industriousness brings profit and laziness brings poverty.[91] Some of the most memorable passages in Proverbs reflect this idea, such as the exhortation to go to the ant (6:6-11) and the account of walking by a sluggard's field (24:30-34). The theme fits comfortably within Proverbs' broader teaching about retributive justice: according to the natural order, walking righteously in the ways of wisdom brings good things in this life. The connection between justice and economic equity can be seen, for example, in comparing Proverbs' statements about what is abominable to the Lord. As a general matter, justifying the wicked and condemning the righteous are both an abomination to him (17:15), but Proverbs also describes "unequal weights," "unequal measures," and "false scales" in the same terms (20:10, 23). Hard work is of genuine value that deserves a reward, while seeking material profit through deception is fundamentally unjust. Laziness, accordingly, is one of the chief threats to attaining life.[92] Conversely, the paragon of wisdom, the woman of excellence of 31:10-31, is breathtakingly industrious and earns great profit.[93]

Yet Proverbs is not naïve about the realities of life. The correlation between work and wealth, and laziness and poverty, is far from absolute.[94] Sometimes the righteous become poor and the wicked get rich.[95] Proverbs recognizes that people can profit through bribes (e.g., 17:8) or other species of "unjust gain" (1:19; 28:16). As considered above, in this world sustained under the Noahic covenant, many ambiguities and mysteries pervade the course of human events. Proverbs also suggests, however, that economic inequities tend to be temporary and get corrected in the end (e.g., 28:8).

Other important themes fill out Proverbs' teaching on economics. For one thing, the wise do not grant too high a priority to material gain. Trying to get rich quickly, for example, is the way of fools, and ironically brings poverty

---

Proverbs, see Washington, *Wealth and Poverty;* and Whybray, *Wealth and Poverty.* For briefer summaries of Proverbs' view of work, wealth, and poverty that are also helpfully balanced, see Murphy, *Proverbs,* pp. 261-63; Perdue, *Wisdom & Creation,* p. 103; and Crenshaw, *Urgent Advice,* chap. 24.

91. See 6:9-11; 8:18, 21; 10:4-5; 12:11, 14, 24, 27; 19:10, 15; 20:4; 21:5, 21, 25; 22:4; 23:21; 24:33-34; 27:18, 23-27; 28:19; 31:13-31.

92. See Crenshaw, *Old Testament Wisdom,* pp. 73-74.

93. For a detailed investigation of the woman of excellence in the context of real-world economic life, see Yoder, *Wisdom as a Woman of Substance.*

94. Whybray identifies sources of poverty other than laziness in Proverbs, though he says they are much less common; see *Wealth and Poverty,* pp. 30-31. Washington, on the other hand, claims that less than a third of the relevant passages in Proverbs imply that the rich and poor deserve their fates; see *Wealth and Poverty,* p. 3.

95. Expressed in various ways in, e.g., 10:16; 11:18; 17:1; 23:6-7; 28:6, 11.

instead (see 28:20, 22). The way of wisdom also requires generosity to those in need.[96] People may not use their just claim to compensation from their labor, in other words, to close their eyes to the poor. This aspect of Proverbs' teaching also corresponds to previous discussion of the natural moral order.[97] Generosity to others should be grounded in recognition of a common humanity under one creator (14:31; 17:5; 22:2; 29:13) and, as argued in Chapters 1-2, the God in whose image humanity was created has revealed himself as a generous God who shares the abundance of his own wealth with the world he made.

Finally, I stated above that discrete rules can summarize, but never comprehend, the natural moral order. In earlier chapters I also suggested that there are good reasons for the traditional Christian notion that the basic principles of the Decalogue constitute at least *a* summary of it. Proverbs provides additional support for this conclusion. Each of the fifth through tenth commandments has many corresponding proverbs.[98] Additionally, in light of the centrality of the fear of the Lord (discussed below) and the (albeit relatively few) sayings about sacrifice, the first through third commandments are also in view, and the frequent exhortations about work remind of the fourth commandment. One could certainly do much worse than to summarize the way of wisdom, in accord with the natural moral order, by means of the Ten Commandments.

The Fear of the Lord

With respect to the natural moral order, I also argued in Part 1 that though issues of religious profession and worship do not appear in the minimalist natural law ethic explicit in Genesis 9:1-7, the Noahic covenant ensures that one's response to natural law is ultimately a response to God, and the presence or absence of a basic "fear of God" has profound ramifications for a person's performance of even the minimalist ethic. Likewise, Proverbs initially identifies the fear of the Lord as the beginning of wisdom (1:7). The theme recurs frequently and plays a foundational character for the book as a whole.[99] In Proverbs' perspective, the entire quest for wisdom demands a pervasive respect for God and sense of accountability to him.

In Chapter 3, I discussed several instances in the pre-Sinai biblical his-

---

96. E.g., see 14:21, 31; 19:17; 22:9; 28:8, 27; see Whybray, *Wealth and Poverty*, p. 21.

97. Or, as Perdue puts it, some such teaching in Proverbs takes "the theological perspective of creation"; see *Wisdom & Creation*, p. 101.

98. See Longman, *Proverbs*, p. 81.

99. E.g., see Perdue, *Proverbs*, pp. 14-15; and Crenshaw, *Old Testament Wisdom*, p. 79.

tory that described people outside the special covenant community as having the "fear of God." I argued that this was a way of identifying those with an inchoate sense of accountability to a divine power above them, which in turn constrained their behavior and instilled a regard for just conduct. There is a notable similarity, therefore, between the way Abimelech's "fear of God" indicated his respect for justice gained through the natural law (Genesis 20) and the way the "fear of the Lord" in Proverbs describes the core of the wisdom acquired through observing and reflecting upon the natural order.

An overt difference between this "fear of God" and "fear of the Lord" concerns use of the divine name. Though the distinction is not strictly observed in every part of Scripture, it is surely not a coincidence that for Abimelech — and other non-Israelite God-fearers considered in Chapter 3 — the generic divine name "God" is used, while Proverbs uses his distinctive covenant name *YHWH,* or "the Lord." Abimelech, living under the natural revelation of the Noahic covenant, did not know God as *YHWH,* while Proverbs was entrusted to Israel, the people to whom God made known his covenant name *YHWH* by special revelation. But the difference is much deeper than nomenclature. The non-Israelites could fear God as one who had temporarily suspended judgment upon them, but the Israelites were to fear the Lord who had also revealed his redemptive grace and provided hope of a coming Messiah. For the former, the "fear of God" resulted in a relatively high regard for earthly justice. For the latter, the "fear of the Lord" represented a profound and heartfelt devotion to the God of their salvation. We must take these different contexts into account, though understanding and practicing the natural law, in the case of *both* pagan and Israelite, was deeply dependent upon recognizing one's place before the divine.

Conclusion

On many fronts Proverbs confirms and enriches the biblical picture of natural law already drawn in previous chapters. God's work of creation again takes center stage, but Proverbs highlights an idea not previously observed: God created the world through wisdom. Through wisdom he formed a universe, in which the various realms of life are integrally related in a holistic natural order. Without using the term, Proverbs reflects and elaborates upon the theological idea of the image of God established in Genesis. The wisdom through which God ordered the world is offered to human beings, and through this wisdom they take up their task in daily life. This task is specifically a royal task, exemplified in the righteous work of earthly kings. Human beings come to understand this task through wise perception of the natural order. By observing the world, reflecting upon it, constructing analogies, drawing conclusions, and putting them into practice, the wise learn to make their way successfully in this life. The natural order includes a natural *moral* order, or natural law, that is accessible to human minds and apprehensible through their sensory and rational attributes. This is true not only of God's special covenant people, but of all human beings as they live under the covenant with Noah. Though the former strive for true and ultimate wisdom by beginning with the fear of the Lord, a common or proximate wisdom is found among many others. Worshipers of the true God are bound to learn wisdom from those outside the bounds of their faith.

Proverbs thus brings into focus something mostly implicit elsewhere in Scripture: God's objective "law" communicated to human beings in natural revelation is not a discrete list of individual rules, but a holistic moral order, and this means that understanding the natural law requires not the ability to memorize a set of rules to be mechanically practiced in life, but a wisdom that can perceive the structure of this order and hence understand what actions are appropriate and beneficial in particular circumstances.

Proverbs also confirms conclusions from previous chapters about the moral substance of this natural law. It frequently highlights aspects of the minimalist natural law ethic, particularly regarding justice and sex and family, but also points to related matters presupposed by the minimalist ethic, such as work and the fear of the Lord, the foundation of natural law morality. It also enriches understanding of natural moral obligations, for example, by helping readers to perceive how profit ordinarily follows hard work and ruin ordinarily follows adultery in the regular course of things. More than memorizing rules is necessary. The wise must understand the fittingness of a certain way of life in the world as God constructed it.

I close this chapter with some additional reflections on the relationship between natural law and Proverbs (and the OT wisdom literature as a whole). Specifically, I suggest how a biblical theology of natural law, as I am developing it in this book, helps to resolve one of the apparent tensions with which scholars of the OT wisdom literature perennially wrestle. I also suggest where the OT wisdom literature fits in the progress of the unfolding covenants as I interpret them in this book, and what this means for a full-orbed biblical theology of natural law.

First, I believe that a biblical theology of natural law, grounded in the biblical covenants, helps to resolve a perennial tension in OT wisdom scholarship. Many contemporary scholars wrestle with whether the wisdom literature really fits into the main theological stream of OT Israel or is a foreign element within it. The perceived problem arises primarily from the fact that the wisdom literature says virtually nothing about the central events of Israel's history — the call of Abraham, the exodus from Egypt, the covenant at Sinai, etc. — that are so central for the rest of the OT. The trend in recent years has been to defend the place of the wisdom literature within the broader OT, often by identifying the former with a theology of creation, and pointing out that creation themes appear in many other places in the OT alongside its interest in salvation history.

This perspective is a move in the right direction, yet I suggest that a biblical theology of natural law can provide valuable resources to strengthen it. There can be no adequate theology of salvation history without a robust doctrine of creation, and one reason for this is that the covenant and law delivered on Mount Sinai, by God's design, caused Israel to recapitulate the experience of Adam's original probation and fall. To be sure, the Mosaic covenant ultimately served to remind Israel that striving to obey the protological ethic of this present world can only lead to condemnation and that something more and new — the coming of the promised Messiah — is necessary for salvation. But without a theology of creation we lose a crucial aspect of the Mosaic covenant. Creation theology is not peripheral to OT theology, but part of its central thread.

With respect to Proverbs, scholars are correct, I believe, to identify its roots principally in a theology of creation, though its emphasis upon the fear of the Lord *(YHWH)*, among other things, reminds readers that Proverbs too was written specifically for Israel living under the Mosaic covenant and not for the world at large. But a sound theology of natural law also helps to show how these two realities — grounded in creation, yet delivered specifically to Israel under the Mosaic covenant — are not in tension but wonderfully coherent. As considered in Chapter 7, the laws of Moses were a particular application of the natural law geared for the unique situation of a theocratic people who had a unique purpose in redemptive history. The wisdom commended in Proverbs, in comparison, consists in the proper perception of the natural law as a moral order, understood through observing and reflecting upon the world. In my own terminology, both the Mosaic law and the wisdom of Proverbs are in many respects a *protological* ethic. The Mosaic law (in part) summarized the natural law in a particular way for a particular community, but it was not comprehensive, and the people needed the perception and insight of wisdom to understand more holistically how to live in the midst of the common affairs of everyday life. To put it differently, the fact that the Mosaic law in significant measure communicated the ethic of the natural law meant that the wisdom of Proverbs, cultivated through experience of the natural moral order, was a perfect fit to provide appropriate guidance for the many areas of the Israelites' ordinary life not explicitly directed by the Mosaic law.

This leads to my second and final suggestion, concerning where the OT wisdom literature fits in the unfolding development of the biblical covenants. Assuming that the bulk of the book of Proverbs (chapters 10–29) derives from the work of Solomon and later preexilic collectors and editors (such as the men of Hezekiah, per 25:1), I believe that the coherence between Proverbs' wisdom and the distinctive life of Israel under Moses and the monarchy can be readily appreciated. Proverbs' concern for just retribution in this life, sexual purity, the work of the king, and many other things echoes the concerns of the Mosaic law, especially during the monarchical period. Even the Proverbs material itself, however, recognizes that things do not always turn out as expected in the world, even under the strict threats and amazing promises of the Mosaic law. In its ordinary mundane affairs, OT Israel experienced the natural moral order that God continued to sustain under the Noahic covenant, with its exceptions, ambiguities, and mysteries. Proverbs also, on occasion, pointed to the reality of forgiveness, to which the Mosaic law also testified through its typological regulations of the priesthood, sacrifices, and festivals, for example.

Taking the beginning and end of Proverbs (chapters 1–9 and 30–31) as deriving from an exilic or postexilic context — composed as an introduction and conclusion to the earlier material preserved in chapters 10–29 — I make a few further suggestions about the place of the wisdom literature in the progress of redemptive history. It is very interesting that chapters 1–9 and 30–31, though substantively similar to chapters 10–29 in so many respects, contain nearly all the material in Proverbs that explicitly highlights the universal and international character of wisdom. Proverbs 3 states that God created through wisdom, Proverbs 8 reiterates this idea and asserts that by wisdom all kings reign, and Proverbs 30 and 31 capture words of wisdom from unknown foreign men. Such things were remarkably appropriate for God's people as he prepared them for an extended period under foreign domination. They were no longer under Davidic monarchs, but Proverbs reminded them that *all* kings have access to the wisdom by which God established the world. No longer living in separation from other nations, Proverbs instructed them that they should not simply view the foreigners with whom they regularly interacted as enemies, but also as those from whom they had much to learn. Furthermore, the collection of the material in Proverbs into final form understandably took on special urgency in this context. Though they much needed wisdom even in the most halcyon days of the Davidic monarchy, the impossibility of adhering to many aspects of the Mosaic law in their exilic/postexilic situation accentuated the need for wisdom. The wisdom of Proverbs, I suggest, served in part to aid the covenant people's transition away from theocratic life under Moses and toward a coming new covenant in which they would be required to live in all the world as exiles and sojourners without a civil polity or civil law to call their very own (see Heb. 11:8-16; 13:14; James 1:1; 1 Pet. 1:1; 2:11).

Job and Ecclesiastes (again assuming an exilic or postexilic context) push this point even further. These books focus relentlessly upon the inscrutability and mystery of divine justice in this world and the consequent frustrations of trying to understand life through a scheme of retribution, a scheme instilled in readers by much of the Mosaic law and Proverbs. Readers, I trust, will forgive me a hit-and-run claim about these two most difficult books: Job and Ecclesiastes exposed the shortcomings of life under the retributive justice theoretically permeating Israel's relationship to God as defined under the Mosaic covenant, and they created a longing for something better, which could provide true hope and confidence. These books ultimately pointed to a coming Messiah whose redemptive work would finally answer Job's struggles with divine justice, and these books pointed to a new creation that would provide the satisfying and meaningful home for God's people that Ecclesiastes' realm "under the sun" could not. At this point we appropriately consider natural law under the new covenant.

CHAPTER 9

The Natural Moral Order Penultimized: Natural Law for a New Covenant People

Part 2 has been examining the significance of natural law for the moral life of participants in the covenants of grace. In the Abrahamic covenant God gave Abraham few special commands, and no specific instructions regarding his responsibilities in broader human society. But God indicated that he wished Abraham to learn his ways of righteousness and justice (exhibited, for example, in the judgment of Sodom for their violation of natural law) and Abraham was responsible for pursuing peaceful relations with his pagan neighbors under the natural law that bound them all through the Noahic covenant (Chapter 6). In the Mosaic covenant God made Israel a holy people and gave them a detailed law that regulated many areas of life. Yet to accomplish God's grander purposes in redemptive history, the substance and sanctions of the Mosaic law reflected those of the natural law, and the noncomprehensive character of the Mosaic law required the Israelites to exercise wisdom in order to put it into faithful practice in life's concrete circumstances (Chapter 7). As evident in Proverbs, such wisdom was acquired to significant degree through observing and reflecting upon the natural moral order (Chapter 8).

In the new covenant God's redemptive plans come to fulfillment through the death, resurrection, and ascension of Christ, the pouring out of the Holy Spirit at Pentecost, and the establishment of the New Testament (NT) church. These events also marked a significant turning-point in the relationship of Christ's covenant people to natural law. Through the humiliation and exaltation of the Lord Jesus Christ as the Last Adam, new covenant believers have passed through God's judgment, become citizens of a heavenly kingdom, and made heirs of eschatological life. Their identity is chiefly defined by the new creation rather than by the original creation as sustained by the Noahic covenant. Yet they continue to live within the confines of the protological natural

415

order and must remain, as a general matter, under its moral authority. This chapter explores this multifaceted relationship between new covenant participants and the natural law.

I argue that Christians, at an ultimate level, have been released from the natural law through their union with the crucified and exalted Christ and yet, at a penultimate level, must continue to live within the structures of this present world that exist under the authority of natural law through the Noahic covenant. Christians exist in a time of eschatological tension, in the overlap of this age and the age to come.[1] The new creation kingdom has already been inaugurated through the life, death, and exaltation of Christ, and Christians are already citizens of this kingdom; yet the new creation kingdom has not yet been fully revealed in consummate form and Christians continue to participate in the ongoing life of the original creation as God sustains it. During this interval between the first and second comings of Christ, Christians' relationship to the natural law is not simplistic and unambiguous.

In short, the NT affirms the abiding validity of the natural created order with respect to its basic moral law (such as the principles embedded in the Decalogue) and its basic institutions (such as the family and the state), but the NT simultaneously identifies Christians with a new covenant and kingdom that belong not to this present created order but to the new creation. This new creation is the original destiny and consummation of the original creation, and thus exists in organic continuity with it. It reflects the same holiness and righteousness of God as did the first creation, and God has destined it as the habitation of embodied human beings. Yet the new creation is not defined by the structures and necessities of the present natural order. It has no need of the basic institutions, such as family or state, that characterize the present order. Christians are dual citizens. Their highest allegiance is to the kingdom of Christ's new creation, to which they belong through the new covenant, and in this sense they have been released from the authority of the Noahic natural law. Yet they also remain participants in the structures of this present creation, to which they belong through the Noahic covenant. In this sense, and by Christ's command, they continue to submit to the natural law's authority. Thus Christians are called to live in ways that honor and support the natural moral order but that also, in subtle

1. As should be evident throughout this chapter, the distinction between "this age" and "the age to come" — which reflects Pauline terminology and is a theological theme pervading the NT — is starkly different from any sort of Platonic distinction between the world of matter and the world of spirit, or the like. As I will often note, the age to come is no less material or social than this age, but constitutes its organic, historical, and eschatological consummation.

and surprising ways, testify that the structures and institutions of this world in its present form are of only penultimate importance in light of the dawn of new creation. As I say again at the end of the chapter, determining how to witness to the moral order of the new creation while also honoring the natural moral order perhaps constitutes the principal challenge for Christian ethics.

To put this in another way, using terms from earlier in the book, new covenant Christians participate in both of the two gracious works of God after the fall into sin. They share in the benefits and responsibilities of *common grace,* by which God *preserves nature,* and they share especially in the benefits and responsibilities of *saving grace,* by which God *consummates nature.* Faithful Christian life demands reckoning with both.

On the one hand, the blessings and experiences of new covenant believers are not unique. The saints living under the Abrahamic and Mosaic covenants were also justified, given the Holy Spirit, and granted an eschatological hope (see e.g. Romans 4; Hebrews 11). They too were never to identify fully with the present creation and its natural law. Yet, on the other hand, Scripture treats new covenant believers as enjoying the blessings of salvation much more richly and hence as being released more profoundly from the natural moral order. God has magnificently ratcheted up the eschatological tension in these last days. Like Abraham, Christians today are sojourners in lands not their permanent home (1 Pet. 2:11; cf. Phil. 3:20; Col. 3:1-3; Heb. 13:14) and share much in common with their pagan neighbors in civil society. But only from a distance did Abraham see the coming of the Messiah and the establishment of a worldwide church as the inchoately realized kingdom of God here on earth (John 8:56; Heb. 11:10, 13-19). The saints under Moses enjoyed much divine grace through types and shadows of Christ's work. But Christians today have access to the realities themselves (Hebrews 9–10) and no longer live under the Mosaic law, which not only pointed to Christ's coming but also imprisoned, incited to sin, and condemned (Rom. 3:19-20; 5:20; 7:5, 7-13; 1 Cor. 15:56; 2 Cor. 3:7-9; Gal. 3:10-12, 19, 22-24; 4:21-24).

To explain and defend these claims I draw material from the Synoptic Gospels and especially the Pauline epistles. In the first section I explore evidence that Christians are to remain living under the authority of the Noahic natural law. Next I discuss a complicating matter, namely, Paul's teaching that with the coming of Christ the law (Mosaic and natural) has been fulfilled and the new creation announced, such that Christians are no longer "under the law" and are called to pursue unique, eschatologically shaped moral lives. Then I describe various ways in which this Christian moral life, oriented toward the new creation, penultimizes[2] Christians' worldly obligations toward the activities and structures of the natural order. I conclude the chapter with an attempt to draw these claims together and to formulate a concise description of the relationship of NT believers and the law of nature.

The Natural Law Ethic of the New Testament

In many respects the NT says nothing revolutionary about the natural law but simply teaches believers to live godly lives under its authority. The NT authors never engage in any independent natural law reasoning detached from their broader theological instruction. Nevertheless, in a variety of direct and indirect ways they recognize an enduring order of nature, the moral claims this order impresses upon human beings, and the knowledge of this order that all people, including unbelievers, possess. As Markus Bockmuehl puts it, the NT authors display a "theologically based presupposition of a universal ontology" that grounds their variegated appeals to natural law.[3] This opening section identifies a number of these appeals through focusing primarily upon the Pauline epistles. Paul, I argue, counsels Christians to honor and participate in the natural structures instituted by God, presupposes an objectively knowable moral order through taking pagans' moral judgment seriously, and places aspects of the church's corporate activity under the constraints of the natural order. It is evident that the Noahic covenant remains operative and that professing Christ has not released Chris-

---

2. I have been advised not to apologize for making a key claim through an invented word. I wrestled with using various real words, but the ones I could think of struck me as inadequate in one way or another and would probably be ammunition for unjust criticism. What I am trying to express with "penultimize" in this chapter is that the natural moral order remains legitimate, God-ordained, and obligatory for Christians, yet in light of Christ's ascension and the anticipation of the new creation in the ministry and life of the church, the activities and institutions of the natural moral order are not of highest importance for Christians. They are important — very important — but not of highest importance. I might also have used the word "relativize," along similar (though not identical) lines to how David H. Kelsey puts it: "The theological upshot of Paul's use of apocalyptic conventions in telling of God's inauguration of the eschaton in the resurrection of the crucified Jesus is that all such principles used to constitute a socially constructed lived cosmos are relativized. They do not have absolute or reality-defining importance." See *Eccentric Existence: A Theological Anthropology*, vol. 1 (Louisville: Westminster John Knox, 2009), pp. 492-93.

3. Markus Bockmuehl, *Jewish Law in Gentile Churches: Halakah and the Beginning of Christian Public Ethics* (Grand Rapids: Baker Academic, 2003), p. 116.

tians from their basic (penultimate) obligation to it.[4] This is one piece of NT teaching about natural law.[5]

Sex and Family

In previous chapters I have often observed the prominent place of sex and family issues in biblical texts where natural law themes arise. This is a key aspect of the minimalist natural law ethic explicit in Genesis 9:1-7. Though I consider below some matters that complicate and deepen the following conclusion, at a basic level the NT exhorts Christians to observe the sexual morality grounded in the natural law, as established in the creation and Noahic covenants: sexual activity is to be enjoyed within heterosexual marriage relationships that are mutually beneficial for husband and wife and that serve as the context for childrearing. This basic feature of the natural moral order is confirmed by Paul and other NT authors.

Paul speaks of basic family structures and obligations in a number of places, most prominently in 1 Corinthians 7, Ephesians 5–6, and Colossians 3. In all three texts Paul treats the husband-wife relationship as the foundational family relationship, in accord with the original creation order (Gen. 1:26-27; 2:22-24). In 1 Corinthians he teaches that sexual relations should be a regular part of marriage, and that marriage is the proper context for expression of sexual desires (7:1-5, 9, 36). The marriage relationship is not strictly egalitarian, for Paul commands wives to be submissive to the authority of their husbands, who are their "head" (Eph. 5:22-24; Col. 3:18). Paul sees this hierarchical rela-

---

4. Compare the conclusions of Bockmuehl in *Jewish Law in Gentile Churches,* which are not identical to mine but similar in important respects. Bockmuehl argues that early Christianity adopted the Jewish tradition of public morality, grounded in Pentateuchal laws for resident aliens and the so-called Noahide commands. I refer to and build upon Bockmuehl's work in a number of places in this chapter.

5. As a point of clarification, I note that the question of the Christian's continuing obligation toward the norms and institutions of the Mosaic law must be handled differently from the way I address their obligation toward the natural law, even though the Mosaic and natural laws are both protological laws with so many similarities. Without question the Mosaic law remains morally relevant for Christians (see 2 Tim. 3:16-17, e.g.). But while the natural law is directly binding upon human beings *as human beings* living in this world, the Mosaic law was directly binding upon people *as OT Israelites.* Christians today remain human beings living in this world, and hence the natural law remains straightforwardly binding upon them. Christians today, however, are not OT Israelites, and thus the Mosaic law does not obligate them straightforwardly, but must always be interpreted through the grid of new covenant reality.

tionship as grounded in the created order, reflecting the Genesis 2 account of God creating the man first and then the woman from the man (1 Cor. 11:8-10). But Paul is also clear that marriage should be mutually beneficial for husbands and wives. Both spouses have a certain authority over the other's body and they have reciprocal conjugal rights (1 Cor. 7:3-4). In addition to the responsibility of wives to submit to their husbands Paul commands all Christians to be submissive to each other (Eph. 5:21). The authority that husbands exercise in marriage is to be conducted with the same sort of self-sacrificial love with which Christ loved his church (Eph. 5:25-33; Col. 3:19). Though Paul's letters never explicitly disallow polygamy, they indicate that the monogamous ideal of the original creation is the Christian's norm (1 Cor. 7:2; 1 Tim. 3:2, 12). Related to this, both Paul and Jesus generally prohibit divorce, though they acknowledge exceptions (1 Cor. 7:11-15; Matt. 5:31-32; 19:3-9; Mark 10:2-12), a teaching that Jesus grounds in the natural created order (Matt. 19:4-6; Mark 10:6-9).

Paul never reiterates the natural law mandate to "be fruitful and multiply" (Gen. 1:28; 9:1, 7) — for theologically weighty reasons considered later in the chapter — but occasional comments present childbearing as a regular and expected part of most Christians' lives (e.g., 1 Tim. 5:10, 14). Fathers are to train their children in the ways of the Lord without provoking them to anger (Eph. 6:4; Col. 3:21). Mothers too are responsible for raising children (1 Tim. 5:10). Children are to honor and obey their parents (Eph. 6:1-3).

Paul condemns a number of sexual practices, all of which are logically incompatible with the basic natural mandate to engage in sex only within heterosexual marriage relationships. Besides his numerous prohibitions of general sexual impropriety (πορνεία) and adultery (μοιχεία), two matters stand out for present purposes: incest and homosexual conduct. In previous chapters I have suggested that the sexual morality of the natural law is grounded in the basic affirmation of otherness and difference ("male and female he created them" — Gen. 1:27). Sexual practices that involve the union of people who are too much alike, such as incest and homosexual conduct, receive negative appraisal. Especially interesting here is that Paul prohibits these practices as naturally and universally immoral. Though in one place he forbids homosexual conduct when speaking specifically to Christians as heirs of the kingdom of God (1 Cor. 6:9), Romans 1:26-27 places such practice outside the natural order. With respect to incest, the opening of 1 Corinthians 5 is noteworthy: "It is actually reported that there is sexual immorality among you, and of a kind that is not tolerated even among pagans, for a man has his father's wife. And you are arrogant! Ought you not rather to mourn? Let him who has done this be removed from among you" (5:1-2). Paul's initial polemic highlights that *even pagans* recognize the egregious character of such behavior (an analogous tactic used in Neh. 5:9) — and for Paul pagans were hardly models of sexual propriety (see e.g. Rom. 1:24-27; 1 Thess. 4:3-5). In other words, this is no parochial Christian taboo but a widely recognized moral violation that makes the church's toleration of such conduct all the more shameful.

In all general matters of sex and family Paul commends not a uniquely Christian ethical standard but the universal norms of the natural law. The same objective standard obligates non-Christians and Christians. Though believers are not to enter marriages with unbelievers (2 Cor. 6:14), believers who are married to unbelievers are to remain in that marriage if possible (1 Cor. 7:12-14), for the legitimacy of marriage does not depend upon the grace of the new covenant. The NT ethics of sex and family are rooted in the creational and Noahic covenants.[6] Yet it is also important to remember that Paul often exhorts Christians to pursue sexual purity in light of the distinctive holiness they enjoy through their union with Christ (e.g., 1 Thess. 4:1-8) and on one occasion encourages them to see a glimpse of the relationship of Christ and his church in their own marriages (Eph. 5:32). Part of Christians' general obligation in Christ is to honor the natural law in matters of sex and family.

Justice and Civil Authority

The issue of justice has arisen frequently in previous chapters, as another aspect of the minimalist natural law ethic explicit in Genesis 9:1-7. The obligation to pursue justice in the world is central to human beings' natural identity as image-bearers of God. Later in the chapter we explore the profound ways in which Christ's coming has transformed Christians' relationship to the retributive justice of God and their obligation to pursue just relationships among one another. In this present section, however, I note how the NT, and Paul in particular, speaks of the legitimacy of justice-enforcing civil authority and the responsibility of Christians to support and submit to their civil magistrates. Though Paul never directly appeals to the Noahic covenant, with this issue

---

6. The decision of the Jerusalem Council in Acts 15:19-21 forbids Gentile converts to engage in sexual immorality. I do not think that this is, per se, instructing Gentile Christians to obey the natural law (perhaps via the Jewish conception of the Noahide commands), and thus I do not discuss this passage here. It seems likely to me that all of the particulars of the decision relate to the forbidding of idolatry (sexual immorality, strangling, and rituals performed with blood all being part of pagan religious rites or their after-parties). James does not seem to make any particular reference here either to Noahic or Mosaic regulations.

we again see the continuing relevance of this covenant and the natural order it regulates.

First, Paul affirms the divinely ordained legitimacy of civil authority. Most famously, Romans 13 states that "there is no authority except from God, and those that exist have been instituted [τεταγμέναι] by God" (13:1). Later Paul speaks of authorities as "appointed" [διαταγή] by God (13:2), as "God's servant" [διάκονός] (13:4), and "ministers [λειτουργοὶ] of God" (13:6). This divine appointment grounds Paul's chief concern in Romans 13:1-7 (cf. Titus 3:1; 1 Pet. 2:13-17): the believer's obligation to be "submissive" (13:1) and "in subjection" (13:5) rather than to "resist" (13:2). This submission extends to paying taxes and rendering proper respect and honor (13:6-7). Jesus' command to "render to Caesar the things that are Caesar's" (Matt. 22:21), in answer to a question about taxation (22:15-17), points in the same direction.

Romans 13 and other NT texts indicate that this God-ordained civil authority is a universal human reality rather than a uniquely Christian one. Neither the legitimacy of the civil office nor the obligation to be in subjection depends upon a person's religious identity. Paul states that there is *no* authority except what is from God (13:1), and the original recipients of his letter would have known no authorities except the pagan magistrates of the Roman Empire. Jesus affirmed the authority of *Caesar* (Matt. 22:21). Christian faith (or any other faith) is not a divine prerequisite for civil office. Likewise, coming to faith does not change one's obligations toward civil authority. Paul speaks of such obligations in universal human terms rather than particular Christian terms in Romans 13:1-7 (in distinction, notably, from his love commands in the following passage, 13:8-14, considered below). "Every person" [πᾶσα ψυχὴ] should be in subjection (13:1), as confirmed by the conscience, a universal human endowment (13:5; cf. 2:15). The Christian's obligations, furthermore, are not merely those of passive resignation. Christians owe magistrates "respect" and "honor" (13:6-7; cf. 1 Pet. 2:17) and should pray for them (1 Tim. 2:1-2). In his own life Paul claimed his rights as a Roman citizen (Acts 16:37-39; 22:25-29), repeatedly testified before Roman courts (Acts 24–26), and utilized the appeal process of the Roman judicial system (Acts 25:11).

Also noteworthy is the nature of the authority exercised by civil magistrates. Paul speaks of their authority generally as "for your good" (Rom. 13:4), enabling Christians to "lead a peaceful and quiet life" (1 Tim. 2:2). Specifically, they have authority to *enforce justice*, through coercive means. Those who resist civil authorities will receive "judgment" [κρίμα] (13:2). That Paul thinks of this primarily as *civil* judgment (in contrast to direct divine judgment) is evident in his next words: "For rulers are not a terror to good conduct, but to bad" (13:3). People who do good "will receive his approval [ἔπαινον]" (13:3). He is "an avenger" who "bears the sword" and "carries out God's wrath" against evildoers (13:4). Paul's description of the magistrate as an avenger [ἔκδικος] indicates that he is thinking specifically in terms of *retributive* justice.[7] He acknowledges no proactive task for magistrates but describes a responsive task of avenging wrongs.[8]

When and how did Paul think God had instituted civil authorities? The Scriptures speak generally of God's providential sovereignty over the rise and fall of kings and their kingdoms (e.g., Isa. 45:1; Daniel 4; John 19:10-11), but this does not explain precisely why believers should submit to them. Though Paul does not explicitly refer to Genesis 9:6, this seems the most plausible theological background of Romans 13:1-7: "whoever sheds the blood of man, by man shall his blood be shed, for God made man in his own image." As interpreted in Chapter 2, Genesis 9:6 is prescriptive; it commands "man" to exercise retributive justice against the wrongdoer. In doing so it appeals to divine image-bearing to confirm that human beings are the kind of creatures made to exercise judicial authority. Furthermore, this prescription appears in the context of a divine covenant, in which God established the terms. Finally, this Noahic covenant was universal, instituting civil justice for believer and unbeliever alike. Genesis 9:6 does not explicitly set apart the office of civil magistrate to be held by some individuals. But the NT idea that civil magistrates have the *authority* (ἐξουσία) (Rom. 13:1) from God to exercise retributive justice for all people is nowhere "instituted" or "appointed" (Rom. 13:1-2) more clearly than in Genesis 9:6. Like the NT commands about sex and family,

---

7. Ἔκδικος is not a common word in the NT or Septuagint, though in ordinary Greek usage it often refers to an *avenger,* and retributive justice is nothing if not the procuring of proportionate vengeance. A few verses before those under consideration here Paul quotes the Old Testament and uses a cognate word, ἐκδίκησις, to say: "Vengeance [ἐκδίκησις] is mine, I will repay, says the Lord" (Rom. 12:19). Thus in Romans 13:4 Paul suggests that the civil magistrate is an instrument of the Lord's vengeance, paying back "evil for evil" (cf. 12:17). Other cognate words ἐκδίκησις and ἐδικέω often appear in the Septuagint and very frequently in the context of vengeance, sometimes specifically in connection with the *lex talionis;* e.g., see Ps. 58:10; Gen. 4:15; Exod. 21:20; Deut. 32:43; 2 Kgs. 9:7. Thus John Calvin is correct to state, regarding Romans 13: "the Lord, by arming the magistrate, has also committed to him the use of the sword, whenever he visits the guilty with death, by executing God's vengeance"; see *Commentaries on the Epistle of Paul the Apostle to the Romans,* trans. John Owen (Grand Rapids: Eerdmans, 1948), pp. 481-82.

8. Just because Paul does not mention a proactive task for magistrates does not necessarily mean they do not have one. Still, Paul's emphasis upon retributive justice is noteworthy. See Chapter 10 for more reflections on natural law and the role of civil government.

therefore, Paul's teaching about the state and civil justice is implicitly grounded in the natural law of the Noahic covenant.

Work and Economics

Issues of sex and justice have received more attention in previous chapters than work and economics. Yet the latter have often been in the background. In the covenant of creation the natural obligation to exercise dominion implied the demand to work and the expectation of a just eschatological recompense. In the natural order divinely sustained after the fall God maintained the human calling to productive and gainful labor, though such work would be painful and constrained by scarcity (Gen. 3:17-18). Appropriately, the protological natural ethic, as reflected variously in the Mosaic law and the Old Testament (OT) wisdom literature, treats hard work as a virtue and worthy of just profit. Paul also commends gainful employment. This provides further evidence of the new covenant believer's obligation to honor the natural law.

One example is 1 Thessalonians 4:11, which commands believers "to work with your hands." Elsewhere Paul warns against "idleness" and tells his readers to imitate him, who "with toil and labor . . . worked night and day" (2 Thess. 3:6-8). Those who are idle should instead strive "to do their work quietly and to earn their own living" (2 Thess. 3:12).[9] He also exhorts the thief to "labor, doing honest work with his own hands" (Eph. 4:28).

My conclusion that these commands represent a call to honor the natural moral order is not just an inference, but derives from two features of these Pauline texts. First, Paul treats work as a universal human practice and obligation. He does not require believers to pursue jobs only in their own

9. Commenting on these very texts in 1 and 2 Thessalonians, Reformed NT scholar Herman Ridderbos writes, in conclusions similar to mine here: "No special 'Christian' standards for the life of work are to be derived from this paraenesis. Paul appeals rather to generally recognized standards of order, tranquility, and propriety. . . . That Paul may be said to renounce every other ordering than that of the coming kingdom, the ordering of love, in which work, too, is a matter of course and work-shyness a sin against the will of God, seems to us in view of the passages that have been handled here an unproven thesis. Rather, the order that is spoken of again and again and which is held before the church with the authority of Christ has reference to the will of God with respect to the natural life. . . . The revelation of Christ does not abrogate the order of the natural and present life, but makes it recognized and practiced, from the viewpoint of Christ, exactly in its divine significance." See *Paul: An Outline of His Theology*, trans. John Richard de Witt (Grand Rapids: Eerdmans, 1975), p. 315. My thanks to Jody Morris for reminding me of this text at a very opportune time.

Christian ghettos, but presumes that they work in the presence of unbelievers (1 Thess. 4:12). This work is apparently ordinary human labor and not eccentric or idiosyncratic, for Paul envisions them doing it quietly and minding their own business (1 Thess. 4:11; 2 Thess. 3:12) and expects unbelievers to approve of Christians' labor (1 Thess. 4:12).

There is a second piece of evidence that Paul's work commands are grounded in the natural moral order: his commands presume that honest labor has its just reward. As considered in Chapter 8, a feature of the natural order illuminated by Proverbs is that hard work ordinarily produces financial gain. When Paul commands Christians to work so as to have something to share with the needy (Eph. 4:28), he assumes that labor is gainful. The same assumption underlies his remark that by working they will be dependent upon no one (1 Thess. 4:12) and underlies his practice of working day and night so he would not burden the church (2 Thess. 3:8). If Christians follow his example they will "earn their own living" (3:12). Elsewhere in the NT James 5:4 strongly affirms the continuing obligation to pay workers their due wages. Negatively, Paul thinks refusal to work deserves no reward: "For even when we were with you, we would give you this command: If anyone is not willing to work, let him not eat" (2 Thess. 3:10). Positively, Paul's reasoning in 1 Corinthians 9:6-7 confirms that honest work deserves a just reward. As argued in Chapter 7, Paul defends his (unutilized) right to receive payment for his gospel ministry through a three-pronged appeal to the natural order. He invites his readers to exercise common sense and recognize that soldiers, viticulturists, and shepherds would not bother to work were there no financial gain. For Paul this is no mere empirical fact, but a moral reality built into the basic structure of the world. It demonstrates that the church's ministers *ought* to be paid for their service.

The Unbelievers' Moral Judgment

Another way in which Paul acknowledges the authority of the natural order is by the respect he shows for unbelievers' moral judgments. My claim is *not* that Paul took pagans' views as proof of what the natural law is. Nor would I deny for a moment that he often exhorted Christians to think in ways radically different from pagans (e.g., Rom. 12:1-2; 2 Cor. 10:5; Col. 2:8). But in various situations he indicates that unbelievers' evaluations of moral issues are legitimate, instructive, and even definitive for Christians' conduct. Unbelievers often make correct moral judgments, and this presumes they have a source of moral knowledge, which in turn presumes the ongoing potency of the natural law.

In one sort of text Paul calls believers to "walk in wisdom toward outsiders" (Col. 4:5) or "to walk properly before outsiders" (1 Thess. 4:12). Paul is concerned that Christians give unbelievers a good impression of Christianity. The context of Colossians 4:5 is noteworthy. In 3:18–4:1 Paul's "household code" instructs Christians to order their homes in ways that reflect conventional Greco-Roman notions, as I discuss again below. Walking wisely toward outsiders apparently includes following conventional social practices that are morally sound, so as not to give unnecessary offense.[10] This idea is explicit in Titus 2. Believers' proper conduct prevents the word of God from being reviled (2:5), keeps enemies of the gospel from having anything bad to say about them (2:8), and "adorn[s] the doctrine of God our Savior" (2:10). Christians should act in ways that meet *unbelievers'* standard of conduct, something unthinkable unless unbelievers are capable of making proper moral judgments. This is all the more striking in 1 Timothy 3:7, which states that the church's overseers (ἐπίσκοπος — 3:1-2) "must be well thought of by outsiders." Here unbelievers' moral evaluation of a Christian's life is actually a qualification for ecclesiastical office. This makes no sense unless unbelievers' evaluations are generally reliable and give accurate insight into a Christian's character.[11]

Several other features of Paul's epistles reflect a similar respect for aspects of unbelievers' morality and moral judgments. Again, Paul would never take the fact of pagan practice as proof of the substance of natural law, but his deference to certain pagan practices presumes an objective moral order that is subjectively knowable — and to some extent heeded — by unbelievers. The household codes in Ephesians 5–6 and Colossians 3–4 provide a good example. As argued above, Paul viewed the family structures embodied in these codes

10. See helpful comments in Andrew T. Lincoln, *The Letter to the Colossians,* vol. 11, *The New Interpreter's Bible* (Nashville: Abingdon, 2000), pp. 653-54.

11. Thus I suspect Paul would not have written what he wrote unless he held a generally higher view of unbelievers' moral judgments, in the ordinary course of events, than what Calvin expresses in his interpretation of this verse: "It seems difficult to think that a godly man should have unbelievers who are most eager to tell lies about us as witnesses to his integrity. The apostle's meaning is that, as far as external behavior is concerned, even unbelievers should be forced to acknowledge that he is a good man. For though they slander all God's children without cause, yet they cannot make a rascal out a man who behaves honorably and innocently among them." See *The Second Epistle of Paul the Apostle to the Corinthians and the Epistles to Timothy, Titus, and Philemon,* trans. T. A. Smail (Grand Rapids: Eerdmans, 1964), p. 228.

(at least with respect to husbands, wives, and children) as grounded in the natural created order described in Genesis 1–2. But the codes themselves bear many formal and material similarities to a long tradition of ethical teaching in the Greco-Roman world. They reflect common notions and received wisdom about properly ordered households. The typical structure of the Greco-Roman home, apparently, reflected the natural moral order well enough to be commended to Christian families.[12]

Another example is how Paul promotes virtues typically associated with contemporary notions of public decorum and social propriety. In Philippians 4:8, for example, he resembles Greco-Roman moral philosophers in reciting a catalogue of virtues and he links together a number of virtues respected in the Hellenistic world but rarely mentioned elsewhere in Scripture. This suggests that Paul intended his readers to think of such virtues and embrace them in something like their commonly accepted sense.[13] Finally, Paul adopted many rhetorical techniques popular in the Hellenistic world to make moral points. As now commonly recognized, mode of communication is not morally neutral. Paul evidently recognized the effectiveness of Hellenistic modes of communication and their ability to convey ideas about good conduct. Here then is further evidence that Paul presumed the existence of an objectively existing and subjectively knowable moral order.[14]

The Church's Governance and Order

My last category illustrating the NT's positive view of natural law involves the ordering of ecclesiastical worship and government. As considered below, the NT church is a unique institution established by Christ and is the present earthly manifestation of the kingdom of heaven. As such, its life and ministry penultimize natural law in crucial ways, in anticipation of the full arrival of the new creation. Yet the church continues to exist within the confines of the present creation and its members retain their nonresurrected bodies with their characteristics and limitations. Thus, as we focus again on Paul, we may

---

12. For discussion of these codes see Lincoln, *Colossians,* pp. 652-54; and Peter T. O'Brien, *Colossians, Philemon* (Waco, TX: Word, 1982), pp. 214-19. See also Bockmuehl, *Jewish Law,* p. 128.

13. See John Reumann, *Philippians: A New Translation with Introduction and Commentary* (New Haven: Yale University Press, 2008), pp. 616-17, 637-40; Gerald F. Hawthorne, *Philippians* (Waco, TX: Word, 1983), pp. 186-88; and Bockmuehl, *Jewish Law,* p. 128.

14. See Bockmuehl, *Jewish Law,* pp. 128-29.

observe several requirements for the church that presume an ongoing respect for the natural law as sustained under the Noahic covenant.

One notable example comes from Paul's previously considered defense of ministers' salaries in 1 Corinthians 9. It is not difficult to surmise why the Corinthian Christians were confused about this: Is it really proper to win financial gain from ministering the gospel of Christ? Paul answers yes, and analogizes the minister's work to that of the soldier, viticulturist, and shepherd who rightfully earn payment from their labor. Despite the many ways in which the church's life and ministry are different from natural economic and political structures (some of which Paul unfolds in 1 Corinthians itself), ministerial salaries are governed according to natural law principles.[15] Constrained by time and material necessities as they labor in this present world, ministers must ordinarily be paid if they are to execute their tasks effectively.

Later in 1 Corinthians Paul offers a programmatic requirement for the church's worship: "all things should be done decently and in order" (14:40). Paul's vocabulary — order (τάξις) — is reminiscent of his statements about God's establishment of civil authority and Christians' duty to submit to it (Rom. 13:1-2). The Corinthian church's divine worship was pervasively supernatural, even involving the exercise of prophetic gifts and revelations of the Spirit. Yet Paul recognizes certain natural human limitations that the church, like any other human assembly, must respect.[16] For one thing, in the church people were to speak "each in turn" (14:27) and "one by one" (14:30). The very purpose of speaking is mutual edification (14:26, 30), yet when many speak all at once others cannot pay attention and be instructed. Multi-tasking may be a twenty-first-century ideal, but human nature is such that people really cannot pay close attention to more than one thing at a time. God himself is not "a God of confusion [ἀκαταστασίας]" (14:33). Perhaps better translated, he is not a God of disorder.

Paul raises another issue at the end of 1 Corinthians 14 that he considers a matter of right order, though it is a controversial matter today: male-female relations. According to Paul, women should generally be silent in these church worship services, be in submission, and, if they have questions, ask their husbands at home (14:33-35). He notes in passing that "the Law" also commends

---

15. Calvin puts it in terms of "natural equity"; see *Commentary on the Epistles of Paul the Apostle to the Corinthians,* vol. 1, trans. John Pringle (Grand Rapids: Eerdmans, 1948), p. 293.

16. As the Westminster Confession of Faith (1.6) puts it, "there are some circumstances concerning the worship of God, and government of the church, *common to human actions and societies,* which are to be ordered by the light of nature, and Christian prudence, according to the general rules of the Word...."

this silence and submission. It is not clear where the OT law actually says this, but Paul likely draws an inference from the description of the original creation order in the opening chapters of Genesis. The evidence for this lies particularly in 1 Corinthians 11:2-16, where Paul deals with the related issue of women praying or prophesying with their heads uncovered. Whatever Paul exactly intended — and whatever its contemporary application — he evidently meant to commend a certain male authority in the church's communal life. He saw biblical warrant in Genesis 2: "A man ought not to cover his head, since he is the image and glory of God, but woman is the glory of man. For man was not made from woman, but woman from man. Neither was man created for woman, but woman for man. . . . As woman was made from man, so man is now born of woman. And all things are from God" (11:7-9, 12). The creation-order theme continues when Paul cryptically appeals to what "nature itself teach[es]" (11:14).[17] First Timothy 2:11-14 is also pertinent. The commands appearing in 2:11-12 are similar to those of 1 Corinthians 14:34-35 — namely, women are not to teach or exercise authority over a man in the church, but should learn quietly and submissively — and, like 1 Corinthians 11, they are grounded in Genesis' description of the original created order: "For Adam was formed first, then Eve; and Adam was not deceived, but the woman was deceived and became a transgressor" (1 Tim. 2:13-14).

In conclusion, this larger section has described many ways in which the NT implicitly affirms the ongoing relevance of the Noahic covenant and its natural law. Paul in particular regularly commands Christians to respect the structures and institutions of the present natural order and to live in accord with its norms, whether in the family, the state, or the marketplace. Christians, as those sanctified by the Spirit, ought to excel in their participation in these forums. In various ways Paul acknowledges the moral insight that unbelievers have, thus presuming an objective moral revelation to which all have access and to which even pagans regularly submit in certain respects. The church itself, though a unique manifestation of the eschatological kingdom, still exists in this world and must conform many of its practices to the exigencies of the natural moral

---

17. Bockmuehl wryly notes that this verse is a "hermeneutical jungle"; see *Jewish Law*, p. 132. Many commentators see this appeal to nature as actually an appeal to the custom or convention of Paul's day, or, as C. John Collins sees it, based upon a perceived analogy from Aristotle's writings, "a matter of common observation"; see "Echoes of Aristotle in Romans 2:14-15: Or, Maybe Abimelech Was Not So Bad After All," *Journal of Markets and Morality* 13 (Spring 2010): 147-48. In *Jewish Law*, pp. 132-34, Bockmuehl defends seeing this verse as an appeal to the natural order and to intrinsic male-female distinctions.

order. God proclaimed the Noahic covenant operative for as long as this world endures (Gen. 8:22), and the NT provides ample corroborating evidence that God continues to keep that promise. No NT ethics, I conclude, can hope to be adequate without a robust conception of natural law.

Justification and New Creation:
The Christian's New Relationship to the Noahic Natural Order

The argument in the previous section deals with *part* of the truth about natural law in the NT. I now turn to the other part of the truth: the coming of Christ, his ascension to glory, and the establishment of the new covenant have effected a momentous shift in believers' relationship to natural law. Participants in the new covenant, having been justified by Christ, are released from the natural law in an important sense. Participants in the new covenant, having been made citizens of a new creation, no longer ultimately belong to the natural moral order of this present creation. Though Christians are obligated to live in submission to the structures and norms of the Noahic natural law in many respects, they are also liberated from its structures and norms with respect to their ultimate destiny and called to anticipate their full liberation through an eschatological ethic permeating the present life of the church.

The final two sections of this chapter unpack and defend these claims. This first section considers two related blessings, justification and participation in the new creation. Chapter 1 discussed the origins of natural law in the original creation. This original natural law set forth God's love and justice and obliged divine image-bearers to pursue this same love and justice in a creaturely way in their rule over the world. Yet the regime of this protological natural order was designed, from the beginning, to be temporary. God destined human beings to fulfill their task of righteous rule in the world and, through their obedience, to attain the eschatological goal of a consummated new creation, in communion with God. The fall into sin prohibited attainment of that goal, though God preserved the world, and with it the natural law in modified form. But God also promised that through the offspring of the woman (Gen. 3:15) he would overcome sin and death and accomplish the original purposes of the first creation, namely, the attainment of a new creation.

One of the central messages of the NT is that Jesus Christ has come as the Last Adam, who bore the curse of the sin earned by the first Adam, was obedient to the commission entrusted to him by his Father, thereby satisfied the claims of God's justice, and thus entered the new creation where he reigns even now. In Christ, therefore, those who believe in him are justified. That is, God declares them righteous, those accounted as fulfillers of the requirements of the protological law and as innocent of any charge of violating it. In Christ, furthermore, believers are given citizenship in the new creation. Because of his guilt under the protological law Adam could not attain the new creation, but through their justification believers in Christ have a right to it. Though still called for a time to live in this present world, they do not ultimately belong to it, nor do its law and claims of justice hold ultimate sway over them. All of this, to be sure, was expected and to some degree enjoyed by the saints of the OT, but, with the coming of the promised Messiah, NT Christians revel in these blessings much more profoundly. As participants in the new covenant they stand at the cusp of the new creation. In their lives in this world they antici-pate the full arrival of the new creation — and anticipate the corresponding consummation of the present natural order.

Thus in this section I discuss justification and new creation and begin to lay out their implications for the moral life. In the final section of the chapter I explore in more detail the consequences for the new covenant believer's relationship to the natural law.

Justification

As explored in Chapter 1, God exercised his royal rule in this world, completed his work, submitted his work to judicial evaluation, and, after simultaneously rendering and receiving a favorable verdict, entered into an eschatological Sabbath rest (Gen. 1:1–2:3). God made his human image-bearers to display his likeness through a similar experience. By the natural law they understood their responsibilities as God's representatives and knew that their work would be justly judged. Because they failed to exercise their royal commission faith-fully, God pronounced a guilty verdict upon them and they failed to attain their eschatological reward in communion with God. If human beings were to attain their original destiny — that is, ruling "the world to come" (Heb. 2:5) — then that guilty verdict must first be reversed. Those who failed their image-bearing commission must somehow be reckoned as having completed it. A verdict of righteous (and not merely innocent) must replace the verdict of guilty. This, according to Paul in particular, is what transpires in justification. Jesus Christ, as the Last Adam, has been obedient to his Father's commission and has reversed the verdict imposed upon the first Adam, such that those with faith in him are declared righteous before God.

The doctrine of justification has been a key point of division between Roman Catholics and Protestants since the Reformation, and still today garners significant attention in ecumenical discussions and Pauline studies. I believe that the so-called old perspective on Paul is essentially correct and that the Protestant doctrine of justification — and particularly the Reformed presentation of it — captures the heart of Paul's teaching on the subject.[18] Furthermore, I believe that Paul's doctrine of justification has profound implications for the relationship of Christians with the natural law. A full treatment of justification in Paul would demand a long volume in its own right. For purposes of this study I now present a brief discussion of justification in Paul that reflects a classic Reformation reading of the relevant texts and builds on previous material in this book. I cannot here offer an innovative defense of this reading in detailed interaction with the recent work of Douglas Campbell[19] or the so-called New Perspective on Paul.[20] Toward the end of this section I provide some initial reflection on the consequences of justification for the Christian's moral life.

18. The traditional Reformed doctrine of justification is concisely summarized in the Westminster Larger Catechism (70): "Justification is an act of God's free grace unto sinners, in which he pardoneth all their sins, accepteth and accounteth their persons righteous in his sight; not for anything wrought in them, or done by them, but only for the perfect obedience and full satisfaction of Christ, by God imputed to them, and received by faith alone." Among many important Reformed treatments of this doctrine, see e.g. John Calvin, *Institutes of the Christian Religion*, 3.11-18; James Buchanan, *The Doctrine of Justification: An Outline of Its History in the Church and of Its Exposition from Scripture* (Edinburgh, 1867). More recently see also J. V. Fesko, *Justification: Understanding the Classic Reformed Doctrine* (Phillipsburg, NJ: Presbyterian and Reformed, 2008).

19. See especially Douglas A. Campbell, *The Deliverance of God: An Apocalyptic Rereading of Justification in Paul* (Grand Rapids: Eerdmans, 2009). Some penetrating critique of this work by R. Barry Matlock and Grant Macaskill, as well as a lengthy response by Campbell, appears in *JSNT* 34 (December 2011).

20. As noted in an earlier chapter, a seminal work often considered the inspiration for the new perspective on Paul was E. P. Sanders, *Paul and Palestinian Judaism: A Comparison of Patterns of Religion* (Philadelphia: Fortress, 1977). Perhaps the two most prominent names associated with this movement are James Dunn and N. T. Wright. Among their important works on Paul, see James D. G. Dunn, *The Theology of Paul the Apostle* (Grand Rapids: Eerdmans, 1998); and Wright, *Paul: In Fresh Perspective* (Minneapolis: Fortress, 2005). For well-informed critical evaluations of the new perspective on Paul with respect to issues such as law, justification, and Jew-Gentile relations, see A. Andrew Das, *Paul, the Law, and the Covenant* (Peabody, MA: Hendrickson, 2001); Simon J. Gathercole, *Where Is Boasting? Early Jewish Soteriology and Paul's Response in Romans 1-5* (Grand Rapids: Eerdmans, 2002); Guy Prentiss Waters, *Justification and the New Perspective on Paul: A Review and Response* (Phillipsburg, NJ: Presbyterian and Reformed, 2004); and Stephen Westerholm, *Perspectives Old and New on Paul: The 'Lutheran' Paul and His Critics* (Grand Rapids: Eerdmans, 2004).

The Bible's most detailed discussion of justification is Romans 3:21–5:21. Paul begins this section of Romans by announcing the manifestation of the "righteousness of God" as the answer to the inability of sinful people to be justified by works of the law due to their own moral unrighteousness (3:21; cf. 1:18; 3:9-20). He ends it with a climactic comparison of the Two Adams, showing how the successful work of Christ has reversed the effects of the failed work of Adam and attained the original human destiny. A few matters arising in Romans 3:21–5:21 are worth noting in a bit more detail.

First, Romans 3:21–5:21 deals with justification as a *soteriological* issue, that is, it pertains to salvation. Some advocates of the new perspective on Paul have argued that justification for Paul is primarily an *ecclesiological* issue, in that it defines who belongs to the church as the covenant community.[21] Though justification indeed has profound ecclesiological implications, some of which I explore below, Paul treats it primarily in soteriological terms. This is evident, first, in the problem Paul identifies in the preceding section of Romans, 1:18–3:20, for which justification provides the great answer. The problem is human "ungodliness and unrighteousness" that provoke the "wrath of God" (1:18). The Gentile masses fall into a morass of sins that they know to be wrong from the testimony of nature (1:19-32). In his justice God judges each person "according to his works" (2:6). God judges all people according to the law — whether Mosaic or natural — and justifies only those who do the law (2:12-16). Jews commit the same kind of sins for which they condemn Gentiles, despite the advantages they have through possessing the oracles of God (2:17–3:8). Thus both Jews and Greeks are "under sin" (3:9), demonstrated by a litany of OT passages describing the absence of any truly "righteous" or "good" people (3:10-18). The result, as Paul draws this section to a close, is that the law stops every mouth and makes the whole world "accountable" (ὑπόδικος) to God (3:19). The law proclaims God's requirements but can only pronounce a guilty verdict against those who are under its authority, because no one can keep these requirements. Thus, "by works of the law no human being will be justified in his sight" (3:20).

This is a disheartening passage of Scripture, left by itself. But Paul immediately makes a transition ("But now" — 3:21) to announce the most encouraging news imaginable. The great human plight is sinful unrighteousness, which leaves all people condemned under the law (Mosaic or natural). So the answer is "the righteousness of God" which comes "apart from the law" (3:21).

---

21. See e.g. N. T. Wright, *What Saint Paul Really Said: Was Paul of Tarsus the Real Founder of Christianity?* (Grand Rapids: Eerdmans, 1997), p. 119.

Whereas the law promised justification for those who are "doers" (2:13), this new initiative of God provides justification "through faith in Jesus Christ for all who believe" (3:22). All have sinned and are disqualified from sharing in God's glory (3:23), the original destiny of the human race, but this justification comes "by his grace as a gift" (3:24). Paul's understanding of justification, therefore, is distinctly soteriological. God provides justification in response to sin and to the curse and judgment sin provokes.

An obvious question that emerges is how God can do what Paul says he does, namely, declare righteous those who are unrighteous, especially in light of his previous insistence on God's impartial justice (2:6-11). Readers face this question perhaps most starkly in 4:4-5. Paul contrasts two scenarios. First, "to the one who works, his wages are not counted as a gift but as his due" (4:4).[22] This sounds very much like how things operate according to Paul's description of the law and God's impartial justice in 2:6-13. But in line with his broader argument, Paul asserts that Abraham was not justified in this way. Rather, "to the one who does not work but believes in him who justifies the ungodly, his faith is counted as righteousness" (4:5). Abraham, the great model of justification by faith in Romans 4, was justified *as the ungodly.* This seems counter not only to the way contemporary Judaism viewed Abraham[23] but also to the ways of the just God described in Romans 2 and the self-description of the just God of the OT, who declared "I will not acquit [justify] the wicked" (Exod. 23:7) and claimed that "he who justifies the wicked" is an "abomination" to him (Prov. 17:15).[24]

Yet a big part of Paul's point in Romans 3:21–5:21 is to explain why this justification of the ungodly, though initially counterintuitive, does not impugn

22. As critics of the new perspective on Paul have noted, Paul here speaks of works generally, in contrast to God's grace in Christ, not to works that merely have to do with Jewish ethnic identity and boundary markers to protect it. See e.g. A. Andrew Das, "Paul and Works of Obedience in Second Temple Judaism: Romans 4:4-5 as a 'New Perspective' Case Study," *CBQ* 71 (October 2009): 795-812.

23. See e.g. Douglas J. Moo, *The Epistle to the Romans* (Grand Rapids: Eerdmans, 1996), p. 256.

24. Despite my appreciation for much of Nicholas Wolterstorff's argument in *Justice in Love* (Grand Rapids: Eerdmans, 2011), his conclusion that God can forgive (and hence justify) without making satisfaction for his retributive justice is a major point at which I must dissent from his project. Contra Wolterstorff's line of thought, I believe the evidence here in Romans and elsewhere is that genuine divine *forgiveness* and substitutionary atonement are not alternatives but can only be understood in light of each other. And while Christ's atonement plays no role in Wolterstorff's understanding of the justice of justification in Romans, I believe it is crucial. See further discussion below.

the justice of God. The answer is Christ, the Last Adam. Justification is not a bald assertion of God that tramples roughshod over his justice through a legal fiction. As representative of his people, Christ has satisfied the requirements of divine justice. Paul offers an initial explanation in Romans 3:25-26. God put forward Christ "as a propitiation by his blood." "Propitiation" [ἱλαστήριον], the quenching of wrath, is an appropriate purpose of Christ's crucifixion, insofar as God's wrath against sin lies at the heart of the human predicament (see 1:18).[25] This work of Christ ensures that God "might be just and the justifier of the one who has faith in Jesus" (3:26). If God is justifying the ungodly and unrighteous, his justice is indeed in question. But Christ secures God's justice in justification.

Also pertinent are the verses immediately following the striking claims of Romans 4:4-5. Paul speaks of God "count[ing] righteousness apart from works" (4:6; cf. 4:11). The whole question of divine justice was instigated by the unrighteousness of the justified. For God to declare righteous the unrighteous seems to be a fundamental breach of justice. But Paul indicates here that God does not in fact justify the ungodly apart from considerations of righteousness. The righteousness that undergirds his people's justification is not their own; instead, it is reckoned or *imputed* [λογίζεται] to them.[26] Justification comes to

---

25. I recognize that "propitiation" is a disputed translation of this term, one favored by some interpreters but rejected by many others. I speak of "propitiation" here, as the word used in the English translation of Scripture I utilize throughout this book. The identification of God's wrath against sin earlier in Romans makes such a translation at least plausible in context. As far as I can tell, nothing crucial to my larger argument hinges on this translation question. For a detailed discussion of this question, which rejects the translation "propitiation," see Arlen J. Hultgren, *Paul's Letter to the Romans: A Commentary* (Grand Rapids: Eerdmans, 2011), pp. 662-72.

26. The notion of imputation in Romans 4 has generated a number of exegetical disputes. One significant issue arises from the fact that Paul uses two different kinds of expression: he not only says that God imputes or counts righteousness (4:6; cf. 4:11) but also that "faith is counted as righteousness" (4:5; cf. 4:9). It seems important to recognize that Paul uses an expression similar to the first when he is describing "sin" (4:8) and "wages" (4:4). The one who works has his wages imputed as his due (4:4); the one who is forgiven does not have his sins imputed (4:8); and the one who believes has righteousness imputed (4:6). These are straightforward judicial transactions in which something is credited to one's account. Paul's second way of speaking — "faith is counted as [λογίζεται . . . εἰς] righteousness" — has different connotations. Paul uses a similar expression to describe uncircumcision being "regarded as" circumcision (2:26) or believers being "regarded as [ἐλογίσθημεν ὡς]" sheep to be slaughtered (8:36). In these cases, Paul does not describe a straightforward judicial transaction, but describes one thing being taken for something else. In Romans 4, therefore, God imputes righteousness (identified in 5:17-19 as Christ's obedience) to the believer and, as it were, sees this righteous-

sinners, but to sinners whose transgressions are forgiven. Rather than imputing their own sins to them, God imputes righteousness (4:6-8).

Paul specifies whose righteousness it is that God imputes to them when he gets to the climactic salvo of this larger section, Romans 5:12-21. It is the righteousness of a true human being, the Lord Jesus Christ, in his earthly ministry. Whereas Adam rebelled against God and brought condemnation and death, Christ was righteous and brought justification and life. Paul's progression of thought in 5:16-19 is noteworthy. Justification in Christ comes as a "free gift" (5:16). This free gift that makes us "reign in life" is a "gift of righteousness" (5:17). Paul clarifies further in 5:18: "justification and life" come as a result of "one act of righteousness." This righteousness that makes the many righteous is, most specifically, "the one man's obedience" (5:19).[27]

In summary, Paul's doctrine of justification is directly related to the matters discussed in Chapter 1 about the origins of the natural law. Natural law set forth Adam's requirements as the image-bearer of God with the expectation of a just response from God. Adam disobeyed his commission and faced God's wrath and judgment. Christ, the Last Adam, came to obey God's law, free his people from divine wrath and judgment, and to provide a perfect righteousness imputed to them to bring justification and life. In Christ's work the original human destiny is achieved for those who believe in him.

If the natural law was communicated to Adam and engrained in the original created order with the goal that Adam complete his image-bearing commission and enter into a consummated new creation, then this gift of justification through Christ provokes serious questions about the justified believer's relation to natural law. If God already reckons believers as those who have completed Adam's commission and are thus already heirs of the new creation, are they still under the authority of that law which tells them they must obey to attain these goals? My answer is: no, *in a certain sense*. Human beings, in whatever covenantal relationship with God, are obligated to the "moral law,"

---

ness when he looks at the believer's faith. For a recent exchange on related questions about imputation, see Robert H. Gundry, "The Nonimputation of Christ's Righteousness," in *Justification: What's at Stake in the Current Debates,* ed. Mark Husbands and Daniel Trier (Downers Grove, IL: InterVarsity, 2004), pp. 17-45; and D. A. Carson, "The Vindication of Imputation: On Fields of Discourse and Semantic Fields," in *Justification: What's at Stake,* pp. 46-77.

27. For elaboration and defense of my exegetical conclusions in this paragraph, see David VanDrunen, "To Obey Is Better Than Sacrifice: A Defense of the Active Obedience of Christ in the Light of Recent Criticism," in *By Faith Alone: Answering the Challenges to the Doctrine of Justification,* ed. Gary L. W. Johnson and Guy P. Waters (Wheaton, IL: Crossway, 2006), pp. 142-46.

summarized in the basic principles of the Decalogue and reflecting the holy character of God, which lies at the core of the natural law.[28] But Christians, as justified citizens of the age to come, are no longer ultimately under the natural law, insofar as it continues to communicate to the present creation that each person must render obedience to God in order to pass successfully through his judgment and attain the new creation.[29] In the remainder of this subsection I offer some initial considerations about the effects of justification upon the new covenant believer's moral life.

Since we have been focusing on Romans 3–5 it may be helpful to see how Paul continues his argument in Romans 6–7, for here he answers explicitly an objection from an imagined interlocutor about the moral life and justification. The objection is this: "What shall we say then? Are we to continue in sin that grace may abound?" (6:1). In other words, if the grace of justification is proclaimed to sinners, should we sin more in order to magnify God's grace? Does Paul's doctrine of justification make holy living irrelevant or perhaps even undesirable? Paul explains his short answer — "By no means!" — from 6:2 through 7:6. He argues that justified believers united to Christ are no longer under the law but under grace, and that having died to the law they are no longer under the dominion of sin but bear good fruit for God and walk by his Spirit. The precise point is striking. Paul does not say that a sanctified moral life is *still possible despite* his doctrine of justification, which would have answered the objection narrowly taken. What he says is that a sanctified moral life is *the necessary consequence* of justification and that justification is *the necessary prerequisite* of the sanctified moral life. Dying to the law in justification somehow results in believers for the first time being able to do holy works truly acceptable before God.

---

28. In the words of the Westminster Confession of Faith (19.5) this moral law "doth forever bind all." For similar treatments of a permanently binding "moral law," see also Thomas Aquinas, *Summa Theologiae*, 1a2ae 100; Calvin, *Institutes*, 2.8; and Francis Turretin, *Institutes of Elenctic Theology*, vol. 2, trans. George Musgrave Giger, ed. James T. Dennison Jr. (Phillipsburg, NJ: Presbyterian and Reformed, 1994), pp. 1-167 (Eleventh Topic). In a review of an article I wrote some years ago, Cornelis P. Venema claims that I rejected the application of the moral law to Christians in the "spiritual kingdom" (in terms of the Reformation two kingdoms doctrine); see "The Mosaic Covenant: A 'Republication' of the Covenant of Works? A Review Article: *The Law Is Not of Faith: Essays on Works and Grace in the Mosaic Covenant*," in *Mid-America Journal of Theology* 21 (2010): 55, 101. This was not my view expressed in that article, nor is it now.

29. To put it another way: insofar as the natural law reflects the covenant of creation (or "covenant of works"), it no longer ultimately holds Christians under its authority. As the Westminster Confession of Faith (19.6) puts it: "true believers . . . [are] not under the law, as a covenant of works, to be thereby justified, or condemned. . . ."

Two snippets from Romans 6:2–7:6 bring into focus how justification, though itself a forensic act, serves as the foundation for the subjectively transformative sanctification of the believer united to Christ in his death and resurrection (6:3-4). The first is 6:12-14. Paul commands his readers: "Let not sin therefore reign in your mortal body, to make you obey its passions" (6:12). He then basically restates this prohibition but also adds a positive prescription to describe the alternative: "Do not present your members to sin as instruments for unrighteousness, but present yourselves to God as those who have been brought from death to life, and your members to God as instruments for righteousness" (6:13). Of special note is that Paul calls believers to sanctification *as those brought from death to life* [ὡσεὶ ἐκ νεκρῶν ζῶντας]. In context, this refers immediately to their union with Christ in his death and resurrection, sealed through baptism (6:3-5, 11), which has been experienced specifically in their justification: through the gift of Christ's righteousness believers are saved from condemnation and (eschatological) *death* in Adam unto justification and (resurrection) *life* (5:17-18). In justification Christ has shattered the reign of death effected through sin and the law (5:20-21; cf. 1 Cor. 15:56). By his obedience Christ has successfully sustained Adam's protological probation and thus those united to him belong to the realm of eschatological life. Since Christians are such people, sin should not and must not reign in them. As Paul continues: "For sin will have no dominion over you, since you are not under law but under grace" (6:14). Being "not under the law" is a favorite way for Paul to describe justification in Christ. To be "under the law" means justification must be attained through doing the law (2:13; cf. Gal. 5:3) and thus also entails the impossibility of justification because of sin (3:19-20; cf. Gal. 3:10-12). Therefore justification comes "apart from the law" (3:21; cf. 4:13) and the justified are "not under the law" (6:14-15; cf. Gal. 4:5, 21; 5:18). In Romans 6:14, a person's justification is proof that she must also be sanctified: "Sin will have no dominion over you, *for you are not under law* but under grace." In the broader argument of Romans "law" refers here immediately to the law of Moses, the law that "came in" (5:20). Yet one of the purposes of the Mosaic law, as considered in Chapter 7, was to recapitulate in OT Israel the experience of Adam under the original law of creation. Being not under the law through justification means ultimately that one is not under the law Adam had to obey as the condition for eschatological life. And an essential aspect of the law given to Adam, as argued in Chapter 1, was the natural law instilled in him as image-bearer of God. According to Paul, therefore, believers are not under the dominion of sin because they are not, in a very important respect, under the protological law of the original created order that brought and continues to bring sin and death. In simple terms, they are sanctified because they are justified.

Romans 7:1-6 also illustrates how justification serves as the necessary foundation for sanctification. Though Paul continues to speak in terms of believers' union or participation in Christ, his repeated reference to their relation to the law indicates that justification remains at the forefront of his argument as well.[30] Paul first offers an analogy from the law of marriage (7:1-3). A woman is bound to her husband by law while he is alive but is "released" and "free" from the law of marriage if he dies; she is able to remarry. Likewise, Paul explains, "you also have died to the law through the body of Christ, so that you may belong to another, to him who has been raised from the dead, in order that we may bear fruit for God" (7:4). Paul offers another way to describe the justification believers receive through their union with Christ. He has already explained that justification is "apart from" the law (3:21) and not "through" the law (4:13), and thus believers are not "under" the law (6:14). Here he adds that justification entails *dying to the law.* This dying to the law in justification has a *purpose:* "in order that [ἵνα] we may bear fruit for God." Sanctification is not justification, but sanctification is one of the *purposes* of God's justifying work. Justification has this foundational role, Paul explains in 7:5, because in the former way of life the sinful passions, "aroused by the law," produced fruit for death. By causing believers to die to the law, justification strips "the flesh" of its fuel. Thus, "now we are released from the law, having died to that which held us captive, so that [ὥστε] we serve in the new way of the Spirit and not in the old way of the written code" (7:6). Here Paul describes sanctification as the result of justification: being released from the law results in service by the Spirit.[31]

---

30. This may be as good a place as any to state what may be obvious by now: in interpreting Paul I do not think we should set the forensic over against the participatory (or, justification over against union with Christ), as sometimes happens in Pauline scholarship. R. Barry Matlock's comments in critique of Douglas Campbell's *The Deliverance of God* are noteworthy here: "The result is a *reductio ad absurdum* of the attempt to construe 'justification' and 'participation' as separate doctrines of redemption, and then to have the latter alone represent the 'real' Paul. There have indeed been Protestant readings that are one-sidedly oriented around 'justification by faith' narrowly conceived; but that does not justify one in committing the equal and opposite error. I suspect this book, against its own intentions, will create renewed interest in a third alternative, the effort to offer a satisfactory account of the interdependence of 'justification' and 'participation.' . . ." See "Zeal for Paul but Not According to Knowledge: Douglas Campbell's War on 'Justification Theory,'" *JSNT* 34 (December 2011): 147.

31. For some examples of how older Reformed theologians described this relationship between justification and sanctification, see e.g. Calvin, *Institutes,* 3.11.1: justification must be

That Paul really does argue such a close relationship between release from the law and the sanctified life is evident from the objection that follows in 7:7, from another imagined interlocutor: "What then shall we say? That the law is sin?" Paul adamantly rejects this conclusion, explaining that the law is good but that sin uses the law as its instrument (7:7-13). The very fact that someone might think to offer such an objection, however, confirms that Paul's previous argument intended to prove that sanctification is a consequence of dying to the law. This argument made necessary a defense of the law's inherent holiness. In this defense of the law Paul likely makes a dual reference to Israel's experience at Sinai and Adam's experience in Eden, as argued in Chapter 7. This is further evidence that though Paul may speak directly about justification as dying to the Mosaic law, he thinks ultimately about justification as death to the protological law of the original created order. The Mosaic law was a window for seeing the prime state of humanity under the natural law. Christians no longer exist under the authority of the protological law, insofar as that law instructs people to obey God perfectly if they wish to be justified and inherit eschatological life. Christ has already obeyed that law, provided believers with the requisite righteousness, and won their claim to life in the eternal kingdom.[32]

---

given such great care and attention because "unless you understand first of all what your position is before God, and what the judgment which he passes upon you, you have no foundation on which your salvation can be laid, or on which piety towards God can be reared"; Turretin, *Institutes*, 2:693: "justification stands related to sanctification as the means to the end"; and Wilhelmus à Brakel, *The Christian's Reasonable Service*, vol. 2, trans. Bartel Elshout, ed. Joel R. Beeke (Grand Rapids: Reformation Heritage, 1993): "Justification is the fountain of sanctification. . . . Since justification is the fountain, it therefore defines the proper manifestation of sanctification and its true essence. . . . He who endeavors to attain to sanctification upon another foundation has gone astray, and will never attain to it, and will never make progress in it. . . . He who wishes to be saved, must first be sanctified; and if he is to be sanctified, such sanctification must necessarily proceed from justification" (pp. 405-6); "All true and pure holiness issues forth from being exercised with justification by faith . . ." (p. 612); "True holiness flows forth out of faith and justification" (p. 615).

32. In making these claims I do not deny the reality of the final judgment, in which Christians too will be judged according to their works. But it is a different judgment from the verdict rendered in justification. Christians will be judged as those already resurrected unto life, as "sheep" placed on God's right hand already distinguished from the "goats" before hearing the verdict (Matt. 25:31-46; see also Rev. 20:11-15). Thus the purpose of the final judgment of Christians is not to determine or effect their final destiny, which is already settled. A primary purpose is to vindicate God's ways and show forth evidence that believers really were the recipients of his grace. This judgment highlights their good works they were not even aware of (and thus clearly not doing in order to earn a reward) (Matt. 25:37-39). Even their evil works do not serve to condemn them (1 Cor. 3:12-15).

New Creation

We have considered how the great blessing of justification has released NT believers from the natural law in an important respect. Insofar as the natural law proclaims that people must obey it in order to obtain a positive verdict from God and enjoy eschatological life, justified believers in Christ are no longer under its sway, for they have already obtained a favorable verdict and been made heirs of the eternal kingdom. Now we consider how a related blessing declared in the NT, *new creation,* also effects and illumines the believer's release from the law of nature. Justified people ultimately no longer belong to this present age, which lies under condemnation, but to the age to come, the realm where the claims of justice have been fully satisfied in Christ.

To appreciate the importance of new creation for our study of natural law it should be helpful to remember some important conclusions from Chapter 1. As a *natural* law, it was inscribed by God in the fabric of the original created order, particularly revealing it through image-bearing human nature. But God did not intend the original created order to endure forever. He created the world, and the human race in particular, to attain an eschatological consummation. This entails that the protological natural law as such, by God's design, was set into place only temporarily. The first Adam failed to exercise proper dominion in the world and thus the world never reached its eschatological consummation. But part of the good news of the gospel is that Christ the Last Adam has *already* attained that eschatological goal, and consequently those united to him by faith have *already* been made heirs and citizens of that eschatological kingdom. "New creation" is a present reality for NT Christians, though their full enjoyment of it awaits Christ's return. Insofar as this new creation has come to define Christians' identity they no longer ultimately belong to this present creation and hence no longer live under the oversight of the natural law. In this subsection I discuss how the NT describes this inbreaking new creation and explore some initial implications of what it means for Christians' moral life and their relationship to the law of nature.

It is wise to be skeptical about any claim that someone has discovered *the* center of Paul's theology, but *new creation* is surely one of the key themes that animate and unify his thought.[33] The apostle uses the phrase καινὴ κτίσις only

---

33. For helpful general discussion of the new creation idea in Paul, see Greg K. Beale, "The Eschatological Conception of New Testament Theology," in *'The Reader Must Understand': Eschatology in Bible and Theology,* ed. K. E. Brower and M. W. Elliott (Leicester: InterVarsity, 1997), pp. 11-52, though I fear he goes too far in seeing new creation as the *center* of Paul's thought.

twice (2 Cor. 5:17; Gal. 6:15), in both cases as a kind of aphoristic slogan that has generated plenty of interpretive dispute. Nevertheless, Paul's emphasis on Christ's exaltation and its radical implications for the life of believers united to him by the Holy Spirit makes "new creation" a handy phrase to capture a decisive element of Pauline theology.

New creation is, in part, about anthropology and soteriology: the believer in Christ is a new creature.[34] But new creation, as I interpret it here, also concerns broader social and cosmological realities. To use my variation of Thomistic and neo-Calvinist slogans, saving grace consummates nature — and not just human nature. Paul views salvation not only as the salvation of individuals, but also as the world as a whole longing for and reaching its appointed end (Rom. 8:18-25; Col. 1:19-23; see also Matt. 19:28; Acts 3:21). He looks forward to the reconciliation of "all things" (Col. 1:19). Alongside these considerations, numerous other biblical texts speak of the everlasting punishment of many creatures in hell (e.g., Matt. 3:12; 8:12; 25:46; Rev. 20:10, 15), the cataclysmic judgment by fire that will burn the present heavens and earth (2 Pet. 3:5-12; see also e.g. Heb. 12:26-28; Rev. 6:12-14), and the passing away of the things of present human culture (e.g., 1 Cor. 7:29-31; 2 Cor. 4:18; 1 Tim. 6:7; 2 Pet. 3:10; Rev. 18). Yet the goal of this present world and its history is the "new heavens and a new earth" (2 Pet. 3:13; see also Isa. 65:17; 66:22; Rev. 21:1), despite the deep discontinuity between the two. For Paul, Christians are new creatures as they participate in this cosmic new creation even now. The new creation already exists and Christians already belong to it. According to Hebrews, Christ has "passed through the heavens" (4:14) and from there exercises his heavenly ministry. Paul speaks of believers being citizens of heaven, from which Christ will return (Phil. 3:20). Christians have been raised up with Christ, where he is seated at the right hand of God, and will one day appear with him in glory (Col. 3:1-4).

In light of this, "new creation" is much more than anthropological-soteriological, but involves profound social and cosmological realities. As we consider below, this new creation is a heavenly kingdom where the resurrected Christ now reigns and which, until its full revelation on the last day, is inchoately manifest in the life and ministry of the church. Believers' participation in the new creation entails a certain liberation from the present created order as sustained in the Noahic covenant, with its distinctive structures, institutions,

---

34. An extensive argument for an anthropological-soteriological interpretation of "new creation" appears in Moyer V. Hubbard, *New Creation in Paul's Letters and Thought* (Cambridge: Cambridge University Press, 2002).

and practices. For Paul, the new creation is not restoring or gradually transforming this present creation.[35] The new creation is the consummation of the present creation, but has been marvelously realized ahead of time, as it were, through Christ's ascension. The present creation still exists, but it is transient, awaiting its consummation and the full manifestation of the kingdom on the day of Christ's return.

Looking at one of Paul's explicit references to "new creation" in its context provides corroborating evidence for interpreting new creation in this broader cosmological perspective. In Galatians 6:15 Paul writes: "For neither circumcision counts for anything, nor uncircumcision, but a new creation." This reference to new creation is likely an allusion to Isaiah's prophecy of the "new heavens and a new earth" (Isa. 65:17-25).[36] The new heavens and new earth is not simply a morally better place, but a new sort of natural order in which many constraints of the present order — "the heavens and the earth" created by God (Gen. 1:1) and fallen into sin — no longer apply. Old age no longer shrivels God's people (Isa. 65:20, 22), the curse upon man's labor and woman's childbearing no longer exists (65:23; cf. Gen. 3:16-19), and animal relationships and diet will be transformed (Isa. 65:25). This is prophetic imagery rather than literalistic description, to be sure, but it communicates the idea of radical cosmological transformation. What "counts" for Paul (Gal. 6:15) is the believer's participation in a new cosmic reality.

35. Compare J. Louis Martyn, *Galatians: A New Translation with Introduction and Commentary* (New York: Doubleday, 1997), p. 565. The view that I defend here is different from those who point to the hope of new creation as a motivation for present environmental stewardship, for instance. For a recent example, see Douglas J. Moo, "Nature in the New Creation: New Testament Eschatology and the Environment," *JETS* 49 (September 2006): 449-88. While I wholeheartedly agree with Moo about the materiality of the new creation, and also agree that there are both continuity and discontinuity between this creation and the new, the idea that our present treatment of the earth is in any way moving it closer to the new creation is, biblically speaking, highly doubtful. See David VanDrunen, *Living in God's Two Kingdoms: A Biblical Vision for Christianity and Culture* (Wheaton, IL: Crossway, 2010), pp. 63-71. Though some have read me here as asserting the annihilation of everything other than human bodies on the last day, I wished rather to say that the human body is the only aspect of the present creation Scripture specifically identifies as the point of continuity with the new creation. If doing sit-ups now presumably will have no effect on the strength of my abdominal muscles in my resurrected body, then caring for the health of the present created order, correspondingly, will have no effect on the final state of the new creation. As I see it, environmental responsibility is a matter of obligation under the natural law of the Noahic covenant.

36. See Don Garlington, *An Exposition of Galatians: A New Perspective/Reformational Reading*, 2nd ed. (Eugene, OR: Wipf & Stock, 2004), p. 312; and James D. G. Dunn, *The Epistle to the Galatians* (Peabody, MA: Hendrickson, 1993), pp. 342-43.

This broad scope of Paul's concern is also evident from the immediately preceding verse: "But far be it from me to boast except in the cross of our Lord Jesus Christ, by which the world [κόσμος] has been crucified to me, and I to the world [κόσμῳ]" (Gal. 6:14). Christ's crucifixion has transferred Paul from the auspices of "the world" to those of the new creation. This world to which Paul no longer belongs is the world of the present natural order with its moral exigencies. It is the world of circumcision and uncircumcision, which concern the male organ of procreation — procreation being of great interest to the old creation (Gen. 1:28; 9:1, 7) but being irrelevant for the new creation (see Luke 20:35). Paul's view of "the world" is further clarified earlier in Galatians, where he refers twice to the "*stoicheia* of the world" [στοιχεῖα τοῦ κόσμου] (4:3, 9). As argued in Chapter 7, by this phrase Paul refers to a protological moral standard tied to the original created order God continues to sustain. Those who cling to the *stoicheia* of the world "observe days and months and seasons and years" (4:10). This is likely an allusion to Genesis 1:14 and the origin of the present cosmos. Through Christ's cross and one's identity with the new creation, the believer in certain respects does not belong to this world and its natural order any longer.

Paul's broadest perspective on new creation in Galatians perhaps appears already in 1:4, where he speaks of Christ delivering us "from this present evil age." "The world" and "this age" are often linked in Paul's thought,[37] and thus in 1:4 he likely hints at his later conclusions. Christ has delivered us from this age, that is, from the *stoicheia* of the world, which concern the first heavens and first earth. For Christians, the era of this world has ended and the era of new creation has begun. Though they continue to live in the old creation in this present age, Christians ultimately belong to the new creation of the age to come.

Another Pauline theme that illumines the apostle's view of new creation is the Two Adams. Both explicit references to "new creation," 2 Corinthians 5:17 and Galatians 6:15, likely have the Two Adams concept in the background.[38] But I wish to focus upon the Two Adams idea through the grid of the image of God, especially as elaborated in 1 Corinthians 15. Here the Two Adams idea is explicit and Paul says many things about the new creation, without using the term.

37. E.g., see 1 Corinthians 1:20; 3:18-19. See discussion in In-Gyu Hong, *The Law in Galatians* (Sheffield: Sheffield Academic Press, 1993), pp. 88-89.

38. With respect to 2 Corinthians 5, see discussion in Hubbard, *New Creation*, pp. 172-73. Seeing the Two Adams in the background of Galatians 6:15 depends upon the connection between Galatians 6:14-16 and the beginning of Galatians 4. On the possible Two Adams background of Galatians 4:4-5, see Garlington, *Galatians*, p. 194. The Two Adams theme likely underlies other Pauline arguments as well; e.g., the "old man" and "new man" contrast in Ephesians (see 2:10, 15; 4:22-24).

The image of God is an important grid for considering the Two Adams idea for the simple reason that all people by nature bear the image of God through the first Adam, and all believers, redeemed by God's grace, bear the image of God through Christ the Last Adam. God originally created Adam in his image (Gen. 1:26-27; 5:1). The son that Adam sired bore Adam's image and likeness (Gen. 5:3), and thus all human beings by nature bear God's image through their likeness to Adam. As Paul says, "as was the man of dust, so also are those who are of the dust" (1 Cor. 15:48), and "we have borne the image of the man of dust" (1 Cor. 15:49). Christ, as the Son of Man, became incarnate so that he might resemble us (Rom. 8:3; Heb. 2:14, 17), and thus he also bore God's image through the mediation of Adam. Yet he was also no mere son of Adam. He was *the* image of God (Col. 1:15; Heb. 1:3) and became the new representative of the human race (Rom. 5:15-19). Having obeyed God "without sin" in place of Adam, he "passed through the heavens" (Heb. 4:14-15) and thereby attained the original human destiny (Heb. 2:5-9). This, as argued in Chapter 1, was precisely what Adam as the original image-bearer was to do: to image God through obedient earthly dominion and then through entrance into eschatological rest. The Last Adam succeeded where the First Adam failed. So now believers are renewed in the image of God (Eph. 4:24; Col. 3:10), specifically through being "conformed to the likeness of his Son, in order that he might be the firstborn among many brothers" (Rom. 8:29). Thus Paul's full statement in 1 Corinthians 15:48-49 reads: "As was the man of dust, so also are those who are of the dust, and as is the man of heaven, so also are those who are of heaven. Just as we have borne the image of the man of dust, we shall also bear the image of the man of heaven."

This displays how closely Paul associates the idea of Christ as eschatological image-bearer with the idea of new creation. Human beings bear the image of God in Adam in terms of the old creation (vis-à-vis dust of the earth), whereas believers bear the image of God in Christ in terms of the new creation (vis-à-vis heaven). This is rooted in Paul's conviction that these Two Adams became prototypical image-bearers, respectively, in God's original creation of humanity and in the resurrection: "Thus it is written, 'The first man Adam became a living being' [Gen. 2:7]; the last Adam a life-giving spirit" (1 Cor. 15:45; cf. 15:20-21, 42-44). Believers bear the image of Christ, the resurrected one. He is the firstfruits of a new humanity (15:20-23). The image of the first Adam is "natural," that of the Last Adam "spiritual" (15:46). The image of the first Adam is "perishable," that of the Last Adam "imperishable" (15:50). As Paul emphasizes, believers will be raised up with *bodies,* but a different sort of body from Adam's, for "flesh and blood cannot inherit the kingdom of

God" (15:50). In summary, bearing the image of God in Christ makes one a participant in the new creation, as defined by resurrection, the Spirit, and God's eschatological kingdom — that is, the same sort of new creation realities identified in Galatians.

I end this subsection by discussing some initial implications of the believer's identification with the new creation. That Paul intends his readers to draw moral conclusions from his appeal to new creation in Galatians 6:15 is evident in the next verse. After saying "neither circumcision counts for anything, nor uncircumcision, but a new creation" (6:15) he writes: "And as for all who walk by this rule, peace and mercy be upon them" (6:16). Paul thinks of new creation as imposing a "rule" by which to walk. In context this rule must stand in contrast to "the world's" moral interest in circumcision and uncircumcision (6:14-15), that is, in contrast to the Mosaic law narrowly considered and the "*stoicheia* of the world" broadly considered. But what is this new creation rule? Earlier in Galatians Paul has already identified a rule that contrasts with circumcision/uncircumcision: "For in Christ Jesus neither circumcision nor uncircumcision counts for anything, but only faith working through love" (5:6). So here is the new creation rule that, to Paul's mind, is somehow distinct from the natural and Mosaic laws: *faith working through love*.

This may seem initially odd, since I argued already in Chapters 1-2 that the natural law concerns love, and the Mosaic law explicitly commands love. But Paul identifies here a particular expression of love as something distinct from the love required in the natural and Mosaic laws. For one thing, when Paul unpacks what "faith working through love" entails later in Galatians 5 and 6 he contrasts it with being "under the law" (5:18) and under the power of "the flesh" (5:13, 16-17, 24), the law being the very thing utilized by the flesh and sin (see Rom. 7:4-14; 8:3). Another consideration is that Paul uses an unexpected word for "walk" when speaking of the new creation rule in 6:16. Instead of using περιπατέω (as in 5:16 to describe walking by the Spirit) he uses στοιχέω. This unexpected word choice hearkens back to "the *stoicheia* (στοιχεῖα) of the world" in 4:3 and 4:9. The new creation rule, therefore, which those who have died to the world (κόσμος) (6:14) walk by (στοιχέω), stands in contrast to the *stoicheia* (στοιχεῖα) of the world (κόσμος), which concerns the protological moral standard reflected in the Mosaic and natural laws. Yet this newness and distinctness of "faith working through love" cannot be understood in total discontinuity with the Mosaic and natural laws, for Paul speaks of this new creation rule as the *fulfillment* of the law and as the *law* of Christ in Galatians 5–6 — to be considered in the final section below.

Another initial moral implication of the believer's identification with the new creation emerges from the preceding discussion about the Two Adams and the image of God. Chapter 1 argued that the protological image of God (that is, of the first Adam) was thoroughly ethical. It entailed a royal commission to exercise dominion in the world, with the goal of achieving an eschatological consummation, in likeness to God's own pattern in Genesis 1:1–2:3. But the NT teaches that Christ, as the true image-bearer and Last Adam, has already attained this eschatological goal through his perfect work. Believers who bear his image, therefore, no longer image God in working toward an eschatological rest but image him in the enjoyment of that rest. In other words, while the protological image concerned working toward a rest, the eschatological image concerns enjoying the rest achieved by the work. (I do not mean to suggest that the eschatological state is one of idleness; though it is a state of "rest" in comparison to the "work" of this age, it involves sharing God's rule over the age to come; e.g., see Heb. 2:5; 2 Tim. 2:12.) Since the eschatological image, like the protological image, is thoroughly ethical (Eph. 4:24; Col. 3:10), it must be characterized by obeying the will of God as a *response* to the rest already won rather than as a *prerequisite* of the rest not yet achieved. Insofar as the natural law represents a protological ethic of working in order to attain the rest, then natural law is, in this respect, fundamentally incompatible with the moral dynamic governing new covenant Christians. As "the law" is the antithesis of the new creation rule in Galatians, it is also the antithesis of bearing the image of the Last Adam in 1 Corinthians 15 (see 15:56). Christians require an eschatological ethic distinct in certain respects from the protological ethic of the natural law. Presumably, this eschatological ethic is the rule of new creation (Gal. 5:6; 6:16) unpacked.

But what exactly is this eschatological ethic, and how precisely is it similar to and different from the protological ethic of the natural law? And given Paul's strong confirmation of the natural moral order discussed in the first section of this chapter, how is Paul coherent when he contrasts the justified life of the new creation with life under the natural law of the old creation? Answering these questions is the task of the final major section of this chapter.

The Eschatological Ethic:
The Christian's (Partial) Release from the Natural Law

What I call the "eschatological ethic" is the ethic of the new creation. In the new creation there is no sin, and thus no need to resolve disputes. Its inhabitants will have resurrected bodies and will not marry or have children. The new creation is a land of abundance, without curse. Thus the eschatological ethic must be significantly different from the protological ethic of the natural law as sustained under the Noahic covenant. Its basic moral law remains the same — love God and neighbor — but the context in which this moral law applies is strikingly changed. The eschatological ethic requires no courts to deal with wrongdoers, no families to channel sexual desires and define bonds of kinship, and no marketplace to determine the just price for scarce goods.

Yet the NT envisions this eschatological ethic as realized *now* in anticipatory manner by new covenant believers. While still living in the old creation, amidst all the constraints of the present natural order, Christians are to manifest the eschatological ethic in remarkable ways that defy these constraints and give wonderful testimony to the heavenly citizenship already theirs. They submit to civil courts, live in earthly families, and labor in worldly commerce according to the law of nature, and by the power of the Holy Spirit should pursue these things with excellence. But they also testify to the fleetingness of such things in light of the penultimization of the claims of justice, family allegiance, and toilsome labor.

In this section I consider the eschatological ethic under three headings: the claims of justice, sex and family, and economics. These correspond to three major topics addressed earlier in the chapter concerning the NT's natural law ethic. After discussing how the eschatological ethic transforms Christians' perspective on each issue, I conclude the chapter by reflecting on how Christians ought to embody both the natural law ethic and the eschatological ethic in their present lives between Christ's comings.

The Eschatological Ethic and the Claims of Justice

The first heading for considering the eschatological ethic concerns the claims of justice. This will also be the longest and most detailed discussion, because I believe it may be the most significant. The background for my argument is a theme established in Chapters 1 and 2 and running through subsequent chapters. The natural law obliges human beings to exhibit a love of benevolence and generosity, though always within the bounds of a proportionate retributive justice in which evildoers receive their due recompense. This dynamic of love and justice is somewhat modified in the postdiluvian covenant with Noah, in which the claims of retributive justice are tempered by forbearance. Yet even this covenant constantly reminds fallen human beings of the ultimate claims of divine justice, though God temporarily withholds its full manifestation.

Because it demands enforcement of retributive justice, the natural law does not commend forgiveness. In both the original covenant of creation and the covenant with Noah human beings know the natural law as image-bearers of God, who reveals his benevolent and generous love alongside his commitment to retributive justice.

The eschatological ethic governing the new creation reflects the satisfaction of all claims of retributive justice and a deepening of the nature of love. It is organically connected to the natural law, for as an *eschatological* ethic it presupposes a *protological* ethic that it brings to fulfillment or consummation. Its basic moral substance is the same as the natural law's. As noted above, there is a "moral law" that binds all human beings in every covenantal context. Part of this unchanging moral law is the responsibility to show love for neighbor through "primary" justice, by respecting the obligations and corresponding rights that people have toward one another.[39]

Yet the eschatological ethic, in significant respects, is also profoundly different from the natural law with respect to love and justice, due to Christ's life, death, and exaltation. In the new creation all the claims of retributive justice are fully satisfied through Christ's redemptive work and there is no more threat of sin to demand subsequent judicial action. The love of one person to another in the new creation is unconstrained and unbounded by the need or potential need for recourse to retributive justice. My chief claim here is that the NT calls Christians to reflect and anticipate this new creation moral dynamic in their present earthly lives, though sin remains ever present in this old creation. This is to be institutionally embodied in the communal life of the church, but also expressed in various ways by individual Christians' conduct in broader human society. Christians should act as if the claims of justice are already put to rest, despite the fact that so much seems to remain outstanding. They do so by exercising a forgiving and merciful love that, rather than pursuing retributive justice against those who wrong them, seeks their repentance, reconciliation, and restoration. The compatibility of justice and forgiveness is a classic moral problem: How can one forgive the wrongdoer without simultaneously ignoring the requirements of retributive justice? Christianity

---

39. As in Chapter 1, I am using here Nicholas Wolterstorff's terminology in *Justice: Rights and Wrongs* (Princeton: Princeton University Press, 2008), where he distinguishes "primary" justice from "rectifying" justice (of which retributive justice is a species). This affirmation of the continuing concern for primary justice is one reason, among many, that I reject Anders Nygren's famous understanding of Christian *agape* in *Agape and Eros,* trans. Philip S. Watson (London: SPCK, 1953). Nygren's work has been critiqued by many writers and I feel no need to do so here.

provides a unique and, I believe, satisfying answer that is unknown by natural revelation. Christ has quelled the claims of retributive justice in his kingdom through his loving work of redemption, showing the most merciful love in bearing the just consequences of others' sins. Thus Christians, as citizens of his kingdom, testify to this ultimate reconciliation of justice and forgiveness by forgiving those who wrong them.[40] Because Christ has died and entered into the new creation, believers too, in union with him, can be self-sacrificial without suffering true loss.[41]

40. Presumed here is that while Christians' forgiving is similar to God's forgiving, they are not identical. For helpful reflections on this issue, see Anthony Bash, "Forgiveness: A Re-appraisal," *Studies in Christian Ethics* 24, no. 2 (2011): 133-46. As I see it, God is the moral governor and judge of the universe, and forgives insofar as he provides atonement and thereby satisfies the claims of retributive justice. Christians, on the other hand, forgive those who wrong them not because they make atonement for them, but through their faith in the God who, in Christ, has reconciled the claims of justice and grace. Among philosophers who have explored bases for forgiveness apart from such theological grounds, see Jeffrie G. Murphy, *Getting Even: Forgiveness and Its Limits* (Oxford: Oxford University Press, 2003); and Charles L. Griswold, *Forgiveness: A Philosophical Exploration* (Cambridge: Cambridge University Press, 2007). Griswold, taking a self-consciously secular approach, sees forgiveness as a noble virtue that is for an imperfect world that longs for reconciliation but will never fully attain it; see especially *Forgiveness*, pp. 211-12. If my claims in this chapter are correct, Griswold's conclusion (drawn apart from Christian theological foundations) about the unattainability of complete reconciliation is not surprising. Murphy, even when discussing aspects of Christianity that might make a person more open to forgiveness, fails to mention Christ's atonement; see *Getting Even*, pp. 91-92. Among Christian theologians, some recent works have helpfully described the foundation of forgiveness in the crucifixion and resurrection of Christ and the coming of his eschatological kingdom. See e.g. L. Gregory Jones, *Embodying Forgiveness: A Theological Analysis* (Grand Rapids: Eerdmans, 1995), pp. 47, 64, 123-25; and Miroslav Volf, *Free of Charge: Giving and Forgiving in a Culture Stripped of Grace* (Grand Rapids: Zondervan, 2005), chaps. 4-5. At the same time, both Jones and Volf affirm the reality of forgiveness outside of Christianity, due to universal human capacities and God's universal work of creation and restoration; see Jones, *Embodying Forgiveness*, pp. 219, 239; and Volf, *Free of Charge*, pp. 222-23. Many writers, I fear, fail to maintain a proper distinction between the character of God's work in creation and the character of his work in redemption and the difference in the ways his love and justice are manifest in each. See e.g. Volf, *Free of Charge*, p. 141, who speaks of the same love propelling God to create as propels him to mend creation through forgiveness.

41. Here I must disagree with Timothy P. Jackson, who claims, contra Paul in 1 Corinthians 15, that an afterlife is unnecessary for charity; see *The Priority of Love: Christian Charity and Social Justice* (Princeton: Princeton University Press, 2009), p. 84. Though people sometimes receive, even in this life, more in return for their acts of charity than they lose through self-sacrifice, that is clearly not always true. In the extreme case, without an eschatological destiny where is the ultimate meaning of one's loving self-sacrifice unto death, however noble it may appear?

I argue my case first by examining material from the Gospels and then by returning to Paul's epistles. Specifically, I begin with Jesus' foundational teaching about love and justice in the Sermon on the Mount (Matthew 5) and then explore the concrete implications for dealing with wrongdoing and conflict within the Christian community (Matthew 18). Next, I examine Paul's foundational teaching about love and justice in Galatians 5–6 and Romans 12–15 and then note the concrete implications for the Christian community that he expounds in 1 Corinthians 5–6. The three texts dealing with foundational material — Matthew 5, Galatians 5–6, and Romans 12–15 — have remarkably similar themes. Either implicitly or (in most cases) explicitly, each deals with fulfillment of the law and with setting aside the OT law in certain respects (especially concerning the demands of retributive justice). They also all take a positive view of the OT love commands and the Decalogue, point to love as the fulfilling or summing up of the OT law and as the prime responsibility of Christians, and discuss Christ's redemptive work and the kingdom of God (or, synonymously, the kingdom of heaven). Likewise, the two texts dealing with concrete implications — Matthew 18 and 1 Corinthians 5–6 — have similar themes and display the particularly poignant application of the eschatological ethic as institutionally embodied in the NT church.

Matthew 5, 16, and 18

I begin with Jesus' teaching in the Sermon on the Mount, particularly in Matthew 5:38-42: "You have heard that it was said, 'An eye for an eye and a tooth for a tooth.' But I say to you, Do not resist the one who is evil. But if anyone slaps you on the right cheek, turn to him the other also. And if anyone would sue you and take your tunic, let him have your cloak as well. And if anyone forces you to go one mile, go with him two miles. Give to the one who begs from you, and do not refuse the one who would borrow from you." Understanding the relevance of these words for the Christian's view of love and justice demands attention to the larger context in Matthew, especially Jesus' claim that he had come to fulfill the law and the prophets (5:17) and the series of so-called "antitheses" in 5:21-48. I argue that Jesus explains how the eschatological ethic of the new creation is to be manifest here and now by his followers. This includes the need to set aside the quest for retributive justice, as represented by the *lex talionis*, in favor of a forgiving and reconciling love that mimics God's redemptive love shown to believers in Christ.

Matthew 4:12-17 records significant events prior to the Sermon on the

Mount: Jesus hears that John the Baptist has been thrown into prison, he goes as a light shining in dark lands, and he begins to preach that the kingdom of heaven is near. John's imprisonment is momentous. Matthew 3 portrays John as an OT prophet, yet John prophesies that one greater than he is about to come (3:11-12). Matthew immediately identifies Jesus as the one greater than John (3:13-17). The sequence in Matthew 4 is striking: John, the OT prophet, is arrested and his ministry ends, and only at that point does Jesus' ministry begin (cf. Mark 1:14-15). John is the last of the OT prophets (11:13-14), and when he passes from the scene a new eschatological era commences.

After John's imprisonment the coming of the kingdom is spectacular. The old era yields to something radically new. Jesus first goes to a land of darkness described as "Galilee of the Gentiles" (4:13-16). Thus begins the Matthean theme of the Gentile inclusion, in accord with OT prophecy (Isa. 9:1-2) but surpassing expectations. Then, after calling his first disciples, Jesus goes around teaching, casting out demons, and healing multitudes of the sick (4:23-24). Israel's prophets had performed miracles, but the sheer variety and intensity of Jesus' work is something never before seen. Huge crowds from all over flock to Jesus (Matt. 4:25).

Matthew's peculiar nomenclature highlights the spectacular newness of the coming kingdom: Jesus proclaimed the kingdom of *heaven*. This "kingdom of heaven" in Matthew does not refer to something different from the "kingdom of God" in Mark or Luke (nor does it, of course, refer to some sort of ethereal Platonic conception of heaven).[42] This kingdom Jesus proclaims is heavenly, not earthly, in the sense that it is an eschatological realm that proleptically breaks into this earth from the age to come. To use language explored earlier, the coming of this kingdom is the dawning of new creation. Readers' impression of the heavenly nature of this kingdom is intensified when Jesus goes up on a mountain to begin his Sermon (5:1). In the OT, the mountain was the place where heaven met earth, the place of God's dwelling.[43]

---

42. The prominence of the themes of "heaven" and "earth" in his gospel, however, suggests that Matthew did not use his distinctive terminology for the kingdom to avoid use of the divine name out of deference to his Jewish readers, as sometimes claimed, but that he had crucial theological purposes in mind. For an extensive argument along these lines, see Jonathan T. Pennington, *Heaven and Earth in the Gospel of Matthew* (Leiden: Brill, 2007).

43. Among many OT examples are Psalms 24, 48, and 87 and Isaiah 2:2-3. This theme clearly continues through Matthew's Gospel, where every mountain scene conveys what the ascended Jesus is presently doing in heaven (see 14:23; 15:29; 28:16). Hence the Sermon on the Mount is a message from heaven to earth. W. D. Davies and Dale C. Allison Jr. call the mount of Matthew 5–7 a symbolic mountain, the mount of revelation; see *A Critical and Exegetical*

This background in Matthew 3–4 prepares readers to recognize that the Sermon on the Mount is all about Jesus and his kingdom.[44] Jesus ascends the mountain to teach as a second and greater Moses (5:1) and at the end of the Sermon the crowds are astounded, not so much at the content of the teaching as at Jesus himself and the unique authority with which he taught (7:28-29).[45] The opening and closing Beatitudes proclaim people blessed precisely because the kingdom is theirs (5:3, 10), and throughout the Sermon Jesus repeatedly points to the kingdom as what is sought and experienced in following his exhortations (5:19-20; 6:10, 33; 7:21). The Sermon on the Mount is for both Jews and Gentiles, but it does not promulgate a universal human ethic for every individual in every circumstance. It sets forth a way of life for those who follow Jesus and possess the kingdom. Though the crowds are evidently within earshot (hence 7:28-29), Jesus actually teaches only his disciples (5:2), those who have already followed him (see 4:18-22). The recipients of these commands already possess the kingdom of heaven (5:3, 10) and are already the salt of the earth and light of the world (5:13-14). Jesus has arrived, the kingdom of heaven has drawn near, and disciples graciously plucked by Jesus from the midst of fallen humanity have been told that they are blessed before receiving a single command.

I turn now to the interpretation of Matthew 5:38-42, in the context of Jesus' words about the law and the prophets (5:17-20) and the so-called antitheses (5:21-48). As befits the character of his coming, Jesus does not give commands meant to clarify the Mosaic law. The commands, in some cases, are new and different from the Mosaic law, yet simultaneously reflect the eschatological fulfillment of the Mosaic law accomplished through his coming. In particular, Jesus abolishes the *lex talionis* from his kingdom (5:38-42) because his own work satisfies its just demands once and for all.

Crucial for understanding 5:38-42 is Jesus' programmatic statement in 5:17 that introduces his subsequent commands: "Do not think that I have

---

Commentary on the Gospel According to Saint Matthew, 2 vols. (Edinburgh: T. & T. Clark, 1988), 1:423.

44. According to Joachim Jeremias, the Sermon has to be read as *didache* (teaching) preceded by something else, namely, the *kerygma* (proclamation) of the gospel. The protasis "Your sins are forgiven" should be added to every command of the Sermon. See *The Sermon on the Mount*, trans. Norman Perrin (Philadelphia: Fortress, 1963), pp. 20-26, 30.

45. Comparing Matthew 5 to the Tractate Avot (from around 200 years after), one can see why. Avot illustrates the Jewish practice of making arguments through appealing to rabbis who support a particular point. Jesus, on the other hand, simply declares what is true on his own authority.

come to abolish the Law or the Prophets; I have not come to abolish them but to fulfill them." A common reading of this verse, among Reformed and other interpreters, is that Jesus intends to clarify the Mosaic law in response to Pharisaical corruption of Moses.[46] While this reading has the virtue of guarding against denigration of the Mosaic law, it is not an adequate interpretation of Jesus' words. Generally, it fails to reckon with the eschatological newness of the coming of Jesus and his kingdom so emphasized in the preceding texts in Matthew. Matthew 5:17 reinforces this sense of eschatological newness. For example, the first use of the key Synoptic phrase, "I have come," hints at Jesus' heavenly origin and authority and indicates that Jesus is about to reveal a central purpose of his ministry.[47] In addition, his denial that he has come to abolish the law or the prophets indirectly offers further evidence of the newness of the kingdom: apparently what has transpired thus far in Matthew's story was so different from past experience that it gave some people the impression that Jesus had come to abolish something in the OT.

More concretely, the way in which Jesus' commands unfold in 5:21-48 is incompatible with reading them as clarification of the Mosaic law in opposition to corrupt Jewish interpretation. For one thing, all six of Jesus' "You have heard" statements either quote or paraphrase the actual teaching of the Mosaic law, not contemporary Jewish interpretation of it.[48] Jesus compares his exhortations to the Mosaic law itself. Second, though the first two antitheses are amenable to the view that Jesus is purifying the interpretation of the law,

46. Among the Reformed, e.g., Herman Ridderbos, *The Coming of the Kingdom,* trans. H. de Jongste, ed. Raymond O. Zorn (Phillipsburg, NJ: Presbyterian and Reformed, 1962), chap. 7, presents an extended argument for the Sermon as interpreting the Mosaic law. Along similar lines, John Calvin says that the scribes and Pharisees confined the law to outward duties only and that Christ intended to correct false interpretation of the law and restore its pure meaning, having no design to alter or innovate anything in the law. See *Commentary on a Harmony of the Evangelists, Matthew, Mark, and Luke,* vol. 2, trans. William Pringle (Grand Rapids: Baker, 2003), pp. 281-83.

47. See Simon J. Gathercole, *The Pre-Existent Son: Recovering the Christologies of Matthew, Mark, and Luke* (Grand Rapids: Eerdmans, 2006). According to Warren Carter, the "I have come sayings" in Matthew are meant to connect to the mission announced in 1:21-23 concerning salvation from sin and the presence of God. See "Jesus' 'I Have Come' Statements in Matthew's Gospel," *CBQ* 60 (2001): 44-62.

48. This claim is not obvious with respect to the last statement, "Love your neighbor and hate your enemy." I take "hate your enemy" to be a paraphrase of Israel's obligation to wage *cherem* warfare against the Gentile occupants of the Holy Land, as well as a sentiment expressed, e.g., in the imprecatory Psalms. See also Davies and Allison, *Matthew,* 1:549-50, who argue that the sentiment of hating enemies is indeed present in the OT.

the last four antitheses cannot reasonably bear such a reading. Jesus shows the inward demands of the prohibition of murder and adultery in the first two antitheses, but whereas the Mosaic law prescribed procedures for divorce, oath-taking, just retaliation, and destruction of enemies, Jesus proscribes them. To say, for example, that what Moses really intended by writing "keep your oaths" was that the Israelites should not swear at all strains the imagination. Furthermore, Jesus' statement about divorce in 5:31-32, which presumes that the death penalty is not applied against adulterers, cannot be an elaboration of the OT law (cf. Deut. 22:22).

A better reading of 5:17 is that Jesus fulfills the law and the prophets by accomplishing all of the things that the OT prophesied. To this point in his Gospel, Matthew has already labored to show that Jesus' actions constitute a turning of the ages and bring to pass what the OT foretold and anticipated (1:22-23; 2:5-6, 15, 17, 23; 3:3; 4:4, 6-7, 10, 14-16), and this theme continues in all sorts of ways subsequent to the Sermon on the Mount.[49] Jesus' words in 5:18 confirm a historical and eschatological interpretation of "fulfill" in 5:17 by saying "until heaven and earth disappear" and "until everything is accomplished" (or "comes to pass"). Jesus, I conclude, indicates in 5:17 that he neither abolishes the Hebrew Scriptures nor simply purifies them from corrupt interpretation. By his deeds and here also by his words, Jesus brings the law and the prophets to historical and eschatological fulfillment.[50]

Thus, since the kingdom of heaven is something new, the Sermon on the Mount, as the ethic of this kingdom, proclaims an eschatologically new way of life. Jesus intended to set forth a way of life different from life under Moses, though it reflects the same divine holiness and accomplishes rather than thwarts God's larger purposes in giving the OT law and the prophets. How, exactly, does this conclusion shape our interpretation of Jesus' handling of the *lex talionis* in 5:38-42?

First to consider is how Jesus' commands in 5:38-42 differ from the Mosaic *lex talionis*. As considered in Chapter 7, the "eye for an eye" formula represented a key legal principle of the Mosaic law: justice was to be proportionate

---

49. E.g., 8:1-4; 8:5-13; 9:14-17; 11:7-14, 20-24; 12:1-8, 18-21, 38-42; 13:16-18; 15:21-28; 16:1-4; 21:33-46; 23:37-39.

50. For a summary of the exegetical options concerning "fulfillment" in 5:17, see Davies and Allison, *Matthew*, 1:485-86. For arguments generally supportive of the interpretation that I offer, see e.g. Davies and Allison, *Matthew*, 1:481-509; Stephen Westerholm, "The Law in the Sermon on the Mount: Matt 5:17-48," *Criswell Theological Review* 6, no. 1 (1992): 52-53; and Thomas R. Schreiner, *The Law and Its Fulfillment: A Pauline Theology of Law* (Grand Rapids: Baker, 1993), pp. 234-35.

and retributive.[51] It encapsulated, on a personal level, the central Mosaic theme that Israel would be justly rewarded in the land if they faithfully obeyed God's law and would be justly punished if they disobeyed. In this sense the Mosaic law echoed the idea of justice underlying the natural law.

Matters of justice and OT judicial life are also raised by most of the other Mosaic commands Jesus mentions in Matthew 5:21-48. The one who murders will be liable to judgment (5:21). A legal bill or certificate is required for divorce (5:31). A central purpose of OT oaths was to secure truthful testimony in court (5:33; see Exod. 22:11; Num. 5:19-21). And the command to hate one's enemy — through *cherem* warfare against the Gentile occupants of the Holy Land — was the most severe expression of judgment under Moses. Jesus even seems to ratchet up the forensic tension as Matthew 5 moves along. Oaths ensured that trustworthy evidence would be presented to the court; the *lex talionis* provided a basic standard of justice for rendering the verdict; and *cherem* warfare was the implementation of judgment on a macro level.

Jesus' commands stand in sharp contrast. Matthew 5:38-42 cannot be construed as instructions about how to impose retributive justice most effectively.[52] Jesus' kingdom is marked by the absence of judgment.[53] Its citizens'

---

51. Among recent studies of the *lex talionis* in the Mosaic law, see James F. Davis, *Lex Talionis in Early Judaism and the Exhortation of Jesus in Matthew 5.38-42* (New York: T. & T. Clark, 2005), chap. 3. For counterarguments to his thesis that the Mosaic *lex talionis* was originally meant to be applied literally, see e.g. Meredith G. Kline, "Lex Talionis and the Human Fetus," *JETS* 20 (1977): 197; and Roland de Vaux, *Ancient Israel: Its Life and Institutions*, trans. John McHugh (New York: McGraw-Hill, 1961), pp. 149-50. On the *lex talionis* as a principle of proportionate retributive justice, see generally William Ian Miller, *Eye for an Eye* (Cambridge: Cambridge University Press, 2006).

52. Charles H. Talbert's comments provide a good example of the sort of strained interpretation of 5:38-42 that results from insisting that Jesus is correcting the Jewish interpretation of the law. See *Matthew* (Grand Rapids: Baker Academic, 2010), pp. 85-86: "Apparently some who continued its [the *lex talionis*'s] strict usage took it as justification for personal acts of vengeance by the one wronged. Such an assumed interpretation seems necessary to make sense of the response by the Matthean Jesus. . . . If Jesus is following the same practice as before, this statement must be understood as his interpretation of the divine intent behind the *lex talionis*. The true intent of the principle, he says, is to limit revenge. So if God's intent is to limit revenge, then that intent is better realized through nonretaliation than literal application of the principle of an eye for an eye. The issue is how to understand the *lex talionis* properly." Talbert's odd conclusion, therefore, is that the *lex talionis* is best interpreted as prohibiting retaliation!

53. Westerholm goes through the antitheses one by one and notes that the things prescribed in the law are foundational and necessary for human society, but Jesus' commands transcend them in ways that human legislation could not accomplish. See "The Law in the Sermon on the Mount," pp. 52-55.

way of life is so pure that there is no ground for judgment against them, and when others wrong them they seek reconciliation, not retribution. The Mosaic law occasionally touched upon internal matters of the heart (e.g., Deut. 6:5-6), but its primary focus was external. It intended to establish a theocratic geopolitical community and to maintain justice within it. But this new kingdom announced by Jesus has a different nature. It does not break into history as a theocratic geopolitical realm or aim to enforce justice in civil affairs.

The disciples of Jesus, indeed, do not murder or commit adultery, but they also shun sinful anger and lustful glances (5:28), matters beyond the jurisdiction of any civil justice system. Instead of seeking legal termination of troublesome marriages, they try to maintain relationships (5:32). Instead of going to court to establish truth by oath, they tell the truth at all times (5:34-37). Instead of implementing just retaliation against the tortfeasor, they themselves bear the proportionate payback (5:44-47). Instead of driving out the foreigner from the holy land, their love extends indiscriminately. Retributive justice was a basic jurisprudential standard of the Mosaic law, and the Mosaic law *required* enforcement of the *lex talionis* in certain circumstances (Deut. 19:16-21). But in Jesus' new and different kingdom there is holistic righteousness and no place for retributive justice.

The way I interpreted 5:17 above, however, indicates that Jesus' commands in 5:38-42 not only are different from the Mosaic *lex talionis* but also reflect the eschatological fulfillment (rather than simple abrogation) of it. It is significant that Jesus does not tell his disciples to ignore and walk away from the person who harms them, but to take a second slap, to give up a second garment, to go a second mile. The *lex talionis* prescribes a second action that is proportionate to the first: the person causing the injury should receive the same injury in return. Matthew 5:38-42 preserves the twofold action and the proportionality of the *lex talionis*. The difference is that his disciples themselves — the injured party — should endure the retaliatory response.[54] Someone still

---

54. A similar point is made by Michael Winger, "Hard Sayings," *ExpTim* 115 (2004): 272: "The principle of proportionate retribution, carefully noted in Matthew, is up-ended: in each of the examples the injured person neatly doubles the injury received, as though following the rule but supplying himself the eye that is to be given for the eye, the tooth for the tooth. The calculation is the same; the price is paid; but the retribution — the thesis and point of the commandment — is cancelled out. Judicial process is acknowledged, yet ignored. . . ." Also relevant may be Westerholm, "The Law in the Sermon on the Mount," p. 46: since the Sermon must be read in light of the coming of the kingdom of heaven, and since the kingdom of heaven is about righteousness, we must remember that Jesus offered his life for the forgiveness of sins (see 1:21; 20:28; 26:28).

bears the proportionate penalty, but it is the victim rather than the wrongdoer. This reflects the larger Matthean theme that Jesus' disciples must imitate Jesus in his suffering at the hand of sinners.[55] Jesus has already told them that suffering is their lot in the present age (5:10-12), and later he explains that as he will go to the cross so also they must bear the cross (16:24-26). Matthew's Gospel alludes to, though does not explain in detail, the substitutionary atonement (see 20:28; 26:28).[56] Human beings, as it were, slapped God in the face through their sin, and God responded with the *lex talionis* — not by justly slapping them back but by bearing that retaliatory slap himself through Jesus. God's saving action in Jesus satisfies the claims of retributive justice once and for all. By bearing in their own bodies the just penalty due to wrongdoers in order to bring healing and reconciliation, Jesus' disciples are privileged to show forth the grace that God shows them in Christ. In this way Jesus' words in Matthew 5 reflect not the abolition but the fulfillment of the *lex talionis*.[57] The eschatological ethic of Jesus' kingdom reflects the consummation of the protological natural order. As manifest in the present world, this eschatological

55. In the early church, Hilary recognized this point: "The Gospels not only warn us away from iniquities but also drive out the latent desire for vengeance. For if we have received a blow, we ought to offer the other cheek. . . . The Lord who accompanies us on our journey offers his own cheek to slaps and his shoulders to whips, to the increase of his glory." See *Matthew 1–13*, Ancient Christian Commentary on Scripture, New Testament I, ed. Manlio Simonetti (Downers Grove, IL: IVP Academic, 2001), p. 118.

56. Note the relation of Mark 10:45 (a parallel to Matt. 20:28) with the *lex talionis,* as discussed in Simon Gathercole, "The Cross and Substitutionary Atonement," *The Southern Baptist Journal of Theology* 11 (Summer 2007): 70-71.

57. Here is another point where I dissent from Wolterstorff's conclusions in *Justice in Love;* see especially chap. 11. My arguments here also militate against the conclusion that Jesus "criticized" the *lex talionis* in Matthew 5, as claimed in Thomas L. Schubeck, *The Love That Does Justice* (Maryknoll, NY: Orbis, 2007), pp. 38, 61. Jesus did not have any intrinsic problem with the principle of justice represented in the *lex talionis*. On the contrary, his coming and redemptive work confirmed this principle, though in a way that left the offender justified rather than condemned. Christopher D. Marshall also fails to appreciate this point sufficiently. Marshall makes a number of points about the *lex talionis* and retributive justice that are similar to mine, but his accompanying critique of the idea of penal substitutionary atonement is unwarranted. I believe Marshall also errs in trying to give 5:38-42 "relevance for a public legal system" in the interests of "genuine justice" (that goes beyond the talionic equivalence principle). See *Beyond Retribution: A New Testament Vision for Justice, Crime, and Punishment* (Grand Rapids: Eerdmans, 2001), chap. 2. Jesus, on the contrary, describes the ethic of his eschatological kingdom based upon his redemptive work, and does nothing to change the state's basic obligation to enforce retributive justice under the Noahic covenant. But I note again that the enforcement of retributive justice should *not* rule out concerns of restorative justice. I discuss this further in Chapter 10.

ethic is marked by refusal to seek just retribution against the wrongdoer and by suffering for the sake of Christ.

My attempt to synthesize the Christian's obligation to obey both the continuing natural law obligation to uphold retributive justice and the eschatological ethic of Jesus' kingdom awaits the final section of this chapter. But for the time being it is useful to consider, elsewhere in Matthew, how Jesus envisioned the eschatological ethic being put into concrete practice. In part he wished this ethic to be manifest in his disciples' response to persecution, as we have seen (5:39-41), and in their detachment from the ways of power politics (see Matt. 20:25-28; Mark 10:42-45; Luke 22:24-27), even as they submitted to political authority (Matt. 22:21).[58] But he especially pointed to the church and its discipline as the corporate embodiment of the eschatological ethic.

The Gospel of Matthew does not equate the kingdom and the church, but it identifies the church as the institutional manifestation of the kingdom in the present age.[59] Matthew 16:18-19 and 18:15-20 are key, the only places in the four Gospels where the word ἐκκλησία ("church") appears. The first of these passages immediately follows Peter's confession of Jesus as Messiah, a crucial turning-point in Matthew's Gospel, leaving little doubt about the importance of the church for the evangelist's larger message.

These passages set forth several aspects of the relationship between church and kingdom. First, in bestowing "the keys of the kingdom of heaven" upon the church through Peter (16:18-19), Jesus houses the authority of his kingdom in the church's ministry. If the use of these keys refers to the work of

---

58. For pertinent comments, see Bockmuehl, *Jewish Law,* pp. 122-23. He writes: "The universal human conventions of power are deeply undermined. . . . The paradox seems to be that loyalty to an existing institution (e.g. giving Caesar his due) can nevertheless go hand in hand with a deep structural distaste for its whole way of operating."

59. Though the position that I defend here is different in some respects from that of Ridderbos, as cited above, his basic summary of the relationship between the kingdom and the church is agreeable to me, as far as it goes: "The ekklesia is the community of those who, as the true people of God, receive the gifts of the kingdom of heaven provisionally now already since the Messiah has come, and one day in the state of perfection at the parousia of the Son of Man" (*The Coming of the Kingdom,* p. 354). A potential objection to the way that I associate the kingdom and the church in what follows is the parable of the weeds (Matt. 13:24-30, 36-43), which identifies "the field" where the good and wicked intermingle as "the world." This is arguably not subject to a church-centered interpretation of the kingdom; see Ridderbos, *The Coming of the Kingdom,* pp. 345-46. For a counter-case, with which I am inclined to agree, see Robert K. McIver, "The Parable of the Weeds among the Wheat (Matthew 13:24-30, 36-43) and the Relationship between the Kingdom and the Church as Portrayed in the Gospel of Matthew," *JBL* 114 (1995): 643-59.

a steward, then the administration of the kingdom's heavenly affairs is executed from earth in the church.[60]

Second, the pregnant words, "whatever you bind on earth shall have been bound in heaven, and whatever you loose on earth shall have been loosed in heaven" (my translation),[61] disclose both the nature of the keys (and hence the nature of the church's ministry) and the relationship between the kingdom in heaven and the church on earth. Given contemporary Jewish use of the expression, "binding and loosing" likely refers to authoritative teaching.[62] Hence the exercise of the keys seems to be the preaching and teaching of God's word. In the context of 18:18, furthermore, "binding and loosing" especially concerns admission to the kingdom and expulsion from it. Hence the exercise of the keys in the church through authoritative teaching and response to it determines kingdom membership. More precisely, the use of the future perfect ("shall have been bound/loosed") indicates that what is first true in heaven becomes manifest on earth. The judgment once and for all rendered in heaven on account of Jesus' vicarious death becomes effective on earth through the exercise of the church's keys.

Third, this sense that the church is the community where the kingdom of heaven manifests itself on earth is confirmed in 18:19-20: "I tell you that if two of you on earth agree about anything you ask for, it will be done for you by my Father in heaven. For where two or three come together in my name, there am I with them." In the humble assembly of the church on earth the power of

60. How to understand the keys and their work is debated. Geerhardus Vos, *The Teaching of Jesus Concerning the Kingdom and the Church* (Grand Rapids: Eerdmans, 1958), p. 81, argues that the keys are those of the house-steward (not gate-keeper) and hence pertain to administration of the affairs of the house in general (cf. Isa. 22:22; Rev. 3:7), which means in turn that the things done on earth are recognized in heaven; thus, it must be possible to call the church the kingdom. Ridderbos, *The Coming of the Kingdom*, pp. 359-60, takes a somewhat different view, that of entry into the kingdom through opening and shutting. Joel Marcus notes the predominance of the halakic interpretation of "binding and loosing" (referring to teaching authority), even among those taking a disciplinary view of 18:18. See "The Gates of Hades and the Keys of the Kingdom (Matt 16:18-19)," *CBQ* 50 (1988): 451. In my judgment, 18:18 should shed light on how we read the same phrase in 16:19, suggesting that administering the house and determining membership are in view in Matthew 16. Perhaps several of the varying interpretations of the keys are aspects of the broader truth, if authoritative teaching in the church (a ministration of the Scriptures) is "the keys" and through this ministration of the Scriptures entry (or nonentry) into the kingdom is secured.

61. In defense of taking this as a future perfect periphrasis, see e.g. Marcus, "The Gates of Hades and the Keys of the Kingdom," pp. 448-49.

62. Again, see Marcus, "The Gates of Hades and the Keys of the Kingdom," p. 451.

God in heaven is revealed. The king of the kingdom of heaven, Jesus himself, is present in this assembly.

Fourth, the nature of the disciplinary procedure outlined in 18:15-17 confirms all of this. I argued above that the antitheses of Matthew 5 describe a kingdom whose ethic is marked not by seeking justice when sin and conflict arise but by seeking reconciliation and forgiveness. Matthew 18:15-17 describes this ethic put into practice in the church. The emergence of sin and conflict provokes not retributive justice but three attempts at reconciliation (and the surrounding parables, in 18:10-14 and 18:21-35, reinforce the centrality of mercy and forgiveness in Jesus' kingdom).[63] The only weapons ever wielded are the keys — the word of God — and never a sword. Even when excommunication is necessary, it does not take the form of punishment or retaliation but of recognizing what has already been decreed in heaven, namely, that a person is simply not a citizen of the kingdom. Additionally, the instruction to "treat him as you would a pagan or a tax collector" indicates that how Jesus' disciples conduct themselves corporately toward each other in the church should be different in at least some respect from how they deal with unbelievers in their broader social relations.

In light of these things I conclude that the church, the present institutional embodiment of the life and power of the kingdom of heaven, should be characterized by the reconciliatory and forgiving — rather than violent and retaliatory — ethic of the Sermon on the Mount. The church in Matthew 16 and 18 focuses not upon the people of God scattered in the world through the week but upon the corporate life of those people, particularly in worship and discipline. Even while Christians should also seek to express the love of the kingdom in other areas of life, this ecclesial community should uniquely embody the eschatological ethic of the new creation, an ethic in which forgiving love transcends the claims of retributive justice.

Galatians 5-6

Having considered one foundational text on the eschatological ethic of love and justice (Matthew 5) and its concrete implications (in Matthew 18), I now turn to two other foundational texts (Galatians 5–6 and Romans 12–15) and their concrete implications (in 1 Corinthians 5–6). Contrary to claims that

---

63. See the helpful observations on this point in McIver, "The Parable of the Weeds," pp. 652-53.

Matthew and Paul had quite different views of the law and its fulfillment in Christ,[64] I find in these Pauline texts an understanding similar to what I found in the first Gospel. I begin with Galatians.

In considering the new creation theme earlier in the chapter I discussed the importance of Galatians 6:14-15 in the context of Galatians as a whole. In the cross of the Lord Jesus Christ Paul was crucified to the world, such that new creation is what now counts. Paul also highlights the decisiveness of Christ's redemptive work in 4:4-5 in identifying his coming as "the fullness of time." Paul no longer belongs to the "world" (6:14; 4:3, 9) or to this "present evil age" (1:4). Instead he belongs to "the kingdom of God" (5:21). He is led by the Spirit and walks by the Spirit (5:18, 25). As in Matthew, therefore, Galatians presents Christ's coming as bringing something wonderfully new. The new creation kingdom of God has broken into this world, and believers in Christ already share in its power and life even as they continue to live in the old creation.

Also like Matthew, Galatians 5–6 presents this new creation reality as having dramatic moral implications. Galatians 6:16 mentions a "rule" by which believers should walk, a new creation rule in which neither circumcision nor uncircumcision "counts for anything" (6:15). Paul does not define that rule in 6:15, but the similarity of language to 5:6 indicates what he has in mind: "in Christ Jesus neither circumcision nor uncircumcision counts for anything, *but only faith working through love.*" In Matthew 5 Jesus capped off his presentation of the law of the kingdom by exhorting his disciples to love (Matt. 5:44); likewise, in Galatians 5:6 Paul summarizes the new creation rule by pointing to love, which flows out of justifying faith.

Paul unpacks the character of faith-working-through-love through the rest of Galatians 5 and the beginning of chapter 6. In 5:13-14, for example, he states: "For you were called to freedom, brothers. Only do not use your freedom as an opportunity for the flesh, but through love serve one another. For the whole law is fulfilled in one word: 'You shall love your neighbor as yourself.'" This highlights both the eschatological newness of faith-working-through-love and its organic continuity with the protological ethic. On the one hand, "freedom" is an important theme earlier in Galatians, where it constitutes a great blessing obtained through justification and through being released from "under the law" and under the covenant at Sinai (see 3:22-23; 4:1-9; 4:21–5:4). On the other hand, the Mosaic law itself (Lev. 19:18) required the love

---

64. E.g., see Heikki Räisänen, *Paul and the Law* (Philadelphia: Fortress, 1983), pp. 86-88; and C. Marvin Pate, *The Reverse of the Curse: Paul, Wisdom, and the Law* (Tübingen: Mohr Siebeck, 2000), chap. 8.

Paul celebrates in 5:14 and describes as the fulfillment of the whole law.[65] This twofold idea — released from the law yet required to fulfill the law's own love command — represents another similarity of Galatians 5–6 to Jesus' teaching in Matthew (cf. 5:43-48; 22:34-40). Shortly after Galatians 5:13-14 Paul again speaks of believers as not "under the law" (5:18). They are no longer controlled by the desires of the flesh, which are incompatible with the kingdom (5:19-21), but produce the fruits of the Spirit, the first of which is love (5:22-23).

Galatians 6:1-2 is of particular interest for the present discussion. Paul writes: "Brothers, if anyone is caught in any transgression, you who are spiritual should restore him in a spirit of gentleness. Keep watch on yourself, lest you too be tempted. Bear one another's burdens, and so fulfill the law of Christ." Paul recaps a number of themes he raised in Galatians 5, including love, mutual service, the Spirit, and fulfillment of the law. The unprecedented phrase, "the law of Christ," adds another dimension to his argument. With these verses, I believe, we can see most clearly the similarity of Paul's concerns to those of Christ in Matthew.

First, Paul addresses an issue similar to what is addressed in Matthew 5:38-42 and 18:15-20: how to respond to another's sins. He also commends a similar resolution: rather than seeking just payback, Christians should seek to *restore* the offender. Like Matthew 18:15, therefore, Paul envisions a process of "gain[ing] your brother." Second, Paul's exhortation to bear each other's burdens shows the lengths to which Christians should go in this quest. In Matthew 5:39-42 Christ commanded his disciples to bear the punishment another deserves. In the two parables sandwiching Matthew 18:15-20, Christ illustrated the love animating his kingdom through the images of a shepherd leaving behind ninety-nine sheep for the sake of recovering one (18:10-14) and of a king forgiving the crushing debt of one of his servants (18:21-35). Likewise, in Galatians 6:2 Paul urges Christians to be proactive and sacrificial as they seek to do everything possible to restore the transgressor. They should be willing to bear any burden that hinders reconciliation. Third, Galatians and the Sermon on the Mount both prescribe self-examination. In Matthew 7:1-5 Jesus commands his disciples to get rid of the logs in their own eyes before judging a brother for the speck in his eye. Likewise, in Galatians 6:1 Paul writes: "Keep watch on yourselves, lest you too be tempted." Finally, as Jesus' own redemptive work

---

65. As I note again below, Leviticus 19:17-18 commands love for one's neighbor, but the neighbor is defined there as one's "brother" or the "sons of your own people," that is, fellow Israelites. And this command lies alongside a stark restatement of the *lex talionis* (Lev. 24:19-20). Paul (and Jesus) utilize the words of Leviticus 19:18 to summarize the moral obligations of the new covenant, but they give them a deeper meaning with revised application.

shapes the moral exhortations in Matthew, the same is true in Galatians.[66] The eschatological ethic of Galatians 5–6 binds precisely those who are no longer under the protological law because Christ loved them and sacrificially bore their burdens. God's very own Son was "born under the law" (4:4), a state of imprisonment (3:22-23). Christ, says Paul, "gave himself for our sins" (1:4); he "*loved* me and gave himself for me" (2:20). "Christ redeemed us from the curse of the law by becoming a curse for us — for it is written, 'Cursed is everyone who is hanged on a tree'" (3:13). The Christian's burden-bearing love for his "brother" reflects the image of Christ, or, in terms used earlier in this chapter, the eschatological image of God.

As Christians bear one another's burdens, Paul explains, they "fulfill the law of Christ." This mysterious phrase, appearing only here in the Pauline corpus (though cf. 1 Cor. 9:21), has generated numerous interpretations.[67] Among

66. Though I do not agree with all aspects of his argument, Richard B. Hays makes this basic point and offers several compelling reasons for it; see "Christology and Ethics in Galatians: The Law of Christ," *CBQ* 49 (1987): 268-90; and *The Letter to the Galatians: Introduction, Commentary, and Reflections,* in *New Interpreter's Bible,* vol. 11 (Nashville: Abingdon, 2000), pp. 314, 333. Similarly, see Ben Witherington III, *Grace in Galatia: A Commentary on St. Paul's Letter to the Galatians* (Grand Rapids: Eerdmans, 1998), pp. 423-25. Schreiner attempts to refute Hays in *The Law and Its Fulfillment,* pp. 157-59.

67. Among writers who see the "law of Christ" as a reference to the OT law, though varying among themselves as to how it is promulgated or redefined by Christ, see A. Andrew Das, *Paul and the Jews* (Peabody, MA: Hendrickson, 2003), pp. 166-73; Schreiner, *The Law and Its Fulfillment,* pp. 157-59; Graham Stanton, "The Law of Moses and the Law of Christ: Galatians 3:1–6:2," in *Paul and the Mosaic Law,* ed. James D. G. Dunn (Tübingen: Mohr Siebeck, 1996), p. 116; John M. G. Barclay, *Obeying the Truth: Paul's Ethics in Galatians* (Minneapolis: Fortress, 1988), pp. 131-34; Frank Thielman, *Paul & the Law: A Contextual Approach* (Downers Grove, IL: InterVarsity, 1994), pp. 140-42; Hong, *The Law in Galatians,* p. 176; and Dunn, *Galatians,* pp. 322-23; but compare also Dunn, *The Theology of Paul,* pp. 653-55. J. Louis Martyn reads Galatians 6:2 in the light of 5:14, where he sees "fulfilled" not as gnomic (that is, as a timeless aphorism) but as a typical Greek perfect, referring to what Christ has done to the law, meaning that "the law of Christ" is the law "taken in hand by Christ"; see *Theological Issues in the Letters of Paul* (Nashville: Abingdon, 1997), chap. 14; and *Galatians,* pp. 489-90, 547, 555-58. Among those who believe that Paul is not referring to the OT law, but to Christ's paradigmatic self-giving, see Hays, "Christology and Ethics in Galatia"; Hays, *Galatians,* pp. 314, 333; and Witherington, *Grace in Galatia,* pp. 423-25; see also similar remarks in Richard N. Longenecker, *Galatians* (Dallas: Word, 1990), pp. 275-76. Along other lines, Hans Dieter Betz argues that "bearing one another's burdens" is borrowed from Hellenistic philosophy; see *Galatians: A Commentary on Paul's Letter to the Churches in Galatia* (Philadelphia: Fortress, 1979), pp. 298-99. Somewhat similarly, Udo Schnelle sees Paul using love as a way to combine the OT law, Hellenistic Judaism, and Greco-Roman culture; see *Apostle Paul: His Life and Theology,* trans. M. Eugene Boring (Grand Rapids: Baker, 2005), pp. 518-21.

other things, commentators wrestle with whether this law of Christ refers to the OT law, the OT law as reinterpreted by Christ, the single rule of love, the law taught by Christ himself, or the law exemplified by Christ. In light of the many similarities between Galatians 5–6 and the eschatological kingdom ethic of Matthew, I believe it is compelling to interpret Paul's "fulfill the law of Christ" along the lines of Jesus' moral exhortations in Matthew 5:21-48, which are obligations that ensue for Jesus' disciples in light of his once-for-all fulfillment of the Law and the Prophets (Matt. 5:17).

Many of the ideas with which commentators wrestle capture an aspect of the truth. The focus of the law of Christ is undoubtedly love, in light of 5:6, 13-14, 22, and the way Paul associates this law with bearing others' burdens. The emphasis upon love must also have something to do with the Mosaic law, since the demand for neighbor-love is found in the Mosaic law (Lev. 19:18) and is the fulfillment of it as a whole (5:14). Yet after several chapters of convincing his readers that they are no longer "under" the Mosaic law, the idea that Paul now commands obedience to this law as Christ's law *simpliciter* is untenable. But Matthew 5 shows the way to resolve the seeming incongruity between the oldness of the Mosaic law and the continuing obligation of its love command. Christ's fulfillment of the Law and the Prophets — that is, his accomplishment of all the purposes for which God gave them — means that the same law continues to bind his disciples, but only insofar as this law is transformed by Christ's work. Christ's work is like a prism, and God's law like light. The same light travels into a prism and comes out the other side, but on the other side it is much more beautiful. "The believer fulfills the Mosaic law as it has been modified by its existence in the era of Christ."[68] Thus the love command of Leviticus 19:17-18 still holds, but it no longer applies only to fellow Israelites ("the sons of your own people" — Lev. 19:18) or alongside an obligation to administer the *lex talionis* (Lev. 24:19-20). Its meaning is deepened and beautified. Because Christ has brought the kingdom by fulfilling the Law and the Prophets and thereby satisfying the claims of retributive justice, his disciples do not seek retributive justice *in their unique identity as citizens of the kingdom*. They bestow the gentle grace of forgiveness and reconciliation upon Jew and Greek, not because the protological demand for retributive justice is abrogated but because Christ has satisfied it.

Thus it is in Galatians 6:2. Christ has given himself for their sins and borne their curse, that they might be no longer under the law (1:4; 2:20; 3:13; 4:4). The holiness demanded in the law still beckons them, and its command of

---

68. Das, *Paul and the Jews*, p. 172.

neighbor-love is highly honored. But this love for neighbor, refracted through the work of Christ, comes in a new context. No longer sitting side-by-side with the *lex talionis,* the love command promulgated by the law of Christ requires wholehearted forgiveness, restoration-seeking, and burden-bearing. As also in Matthew, this eschatological love finds institutional embodiment in the church. Paul writes the entire letter to the Galatian churches (1:2), appeals to his readers in 6:1-2 as "brothers" who are to bear "one another's" burdens, and urges them to do good "especially to those who are of the household of faith" (6:10).[69] Yet this last verse also implies that Christians' eschatological love has application outside the church community too.

Romans 12–15

I now turn, more briefly, to Romans 12–15. In these chapters Paul deals with the same themes observed in Matthew 5 and Galatians 5–6, and sets his exhortations in similar context. The central idea uniting 12:9–15:7 is love. Paul commands that "love be genuine" (12:9). Later he adds that they should owe nothing to anyone, "except to love each other," repeats the neighbor-love command from Leviticus 19:18, and states, "love does no wrong to a neighbor, therefore love is the fulfilling of the law" (13:8-10). In 14:15 he notes that if they grieve their brother by what they eat, they "are no longer walking in love." Other commands speak of love implicitly. For example, Paul commends the self-sacrificial practice of pleasing one's neighbor rather than oneself (15:1-2).

As in Matthew 5 and Galatians 5–6, Paul portrays love as organically rooted in the OT law. He twice describes love as the fulfilling of the law (13:8, 10) and writes that the commandments against adultery, murder, stealing, and coveting, "and any other commandment, are summed up in this word: You shall

---

69. On the church as the eschatological people of God, see Thielman, *Paul & the Law,* p. 135. See also the helpful comments in Martyn, *Theological Issues,* p. 122: "One may ask whether the new creation has an embodiment. In the common sense of the expression, can Paul point to it? In effect, the apostle gives three mutually illuminating answers. The new creation is embodied in Christ, in the church, and thus in the Israel of God. . . . Sent by God, Christ is the descendant whom God promised long ago to Abraham (3:16), the one who is, as it were, the seed of the new creation. . . . At numerous junctures in Galatians, Paul speaks of the church's incorporation in this new-creation Christ. It is by being Christ's — by being baptized into him, by putting him on as though he were their clothes (3:27), by having his Spirit in their hearts (4:6), by having him determine the form of their communal life (4:19), by belonging utterly to him the cosmocrator of the new creation (5:24) — that the Galatians . . . are Abraham's corporate seed and God's new creation in Christ (3:29)."

love your neighbor as yourself'" (13:9). Yet here again this love required for NT believers refuses to pursue retributive justice. In language reminiscent of the *lex talionis,* Paul forbids Christians from repaying "evil for evil" (κακὸν ἀντὶ κακοῦ; cf. Matt. 5:38: ὀφθαλμὸν ἀντὶ ὀφθαλμοῦ) (Rom. 12:17). Love does no "wrong" (κακόν) to a neighbor (13:10). As in the Sermon on the Mount, Christians should bless those who persecute them (12:14) and shun vengeance (12:19). Paul warns them about rendering judgment against fellow believers (14:3-4, 10, 13, 22).

Other themes also echo Matthew 5 and Galatians 5–6. An example is Paul's emphasis on faith in Romans 14, such that "whatever does not proceed from faith is sin" (14:23), which precedes his exhortation to please one's neighbor rather than oneself. This echoes the moral dynamic of faith-working-through-love in Galatians 5:6. Furthermore, Paul grounds this distinctive Christian love — faith-centered, nonretributive, and self-sacrificial — in Christ's redemptive work. Christians have the power to love instead of gratifying the flesh because they have "put on the Lord Jesus Christ" (13:14). Their self-sacrificial love mirrors their Lord's: "Let each of us please his neighbor for his good, to build him up. For Christ did not please himself, but as it is written, 'The reproaches of those who reproached you fell on me'" (15:2-3; quoting Ps. 69:9). He adds shortly thereafter: "welcome one another as Christ has welcomed you" (15:7). Paul implicitly calls readers' minds back to Romans 5:8: "God shows his love for us in that while we were still sinners, Christ died for us." Additionally, Paul makes clear that this ethic of love is, as I have called it, an *eschatological* ethic. He motivates believers to action, for instance, by reminding them of the immanence of Christ's return (13:11). More significantly, he appeals to eschatologically charged themes such as the kingdom of God and the work of the Holy Spirit to demonstrate the fittingness of love-driven lives: "For the kingdom of God is not a matter of eating and drinking but of righteousness and peace and joy in the Holy Spirit" (14:17). On a final note, here in Romans Paul resembles Matthew and Galatians in focusing particularly upon the application of this eschatological ethic in the church. Though love should shine forth also to unbelievers, such as those who persecute them (12:14), it has particularly weighty consequences among "brothers" in Romans 14, among those whom God has "welcomed" (14:3) and "for whom Christ has died" (14:15).

1 Corinthians 5–6

We gain insight from 1 Corinthians 5–6 as to how Paul believed this distinctive eschatological ethic should be institutionally embodied in the church when it faces concrete cases of sin and conflict. Without looking at many of the technical exegetical debates about these chapters, I now consider how they instruct the church to put the eschatological ethic into practice.

In 1 Corinthians 5 Paul reprimands the church for tolerating the practice of incest by one of its members. This is a clear violation of the natural law (a sin even pagans avoid — 5:1) and a severe threat to the church's well-being (5:6). Yet he seeks no remedy from civil magistrates, but tells the church itself to deal with it. The method and purpose of the church's discipline, however, are significantly different from those of civil courts. The church wields no sword, but delivers the sinner over to Satan (5:5). Even more striking, it does so not to give the sinner his just recompense but that "his spirit may be saved in the day of the Lord" (5:5). This weighty discipline flows from redemptive springs. The church is a new lump created by the sacrifice of Christ, the Passover Lamb (5:7), and its corporate life must reflect this. These instructions in 1 Corinthians 5 therefore share the spirit of Galatians 6:1-2 and Matthew 5:38-42 and closely resemble the procedures for discipline noted above in Matthew 18:15-20. Wonderfully, the apostle's exhortation in 2 Corinthians 2:5-11 — to forgive and comfort the repentant sinner — indicates that the church's distinctive discipline had accomplished its intended purpose in a particular instance (whether or not the repentant sinner here is the same man mentioned in 1 Corinthians 5).

A similar dynamic is present in 1 Corinthians 6. Paul rebukes the church for going "to law before the unrighteous" (6:1). Defining the proper scope of Paul's prohibition of intra-Christian civil lawsuits is arduous, but his basic point seems indisputable: Christians should resolve their own problems themselves, on their own terms, in light of their distinctive identity in Christ. Paul evokes the spirit of the Sermon on the Mount (Matt. 5:38-42): "Why not suffer wrong? Why not rather be defrauded?" (1 Cor. 6:7). As in 1 Corinthians 5, dispute-resolution in the church is not driven here by concerns of talionic justice. Furthermore, Paul appeals to the reality of new creation to motivate his readers: "Or do you not know that the saints will judge the world?" (6:2). "Or do you not know that the unrighteous will not inherit the kingdom of God?" (6:9). The realities of the final day must govern the church's present way of life.

First Corinthians 5–6 illustrate Paul's earlier claim that the Christian's true wisdom is not the wisdom of this world, but rather Christ himself (1 Cor. 1:18-31). The Christian's highest wisdom is not even a useful but limited wisdom gained through the natural moral order, because their highest wisdom was "secret and hidden" (2:7) but is now found specifically in "Christ crucified" (1:22-23; cf. 2:8) and revealed by the Holy Spirit (2:9-13). In Christ's crucifixion is a wisdom transcending the wisdom gained through natural law, a Christological wisdom that must mold the church's conduct in wonderfully unique ways.

In this lengthy subsection I have discussed the distinctive nature of the eschatological ethic with respect to justice. The natural law, as a protological ethic, reveals God's perfect justice and demands obedience to that law as a condition for eschatological life. Natural law obliges human beings, as God's image-bearers, to love their fellow human beings, though in a way consistent with and constrained by the commission to administer retributive justice in this world (as properly tempered by forbearance under the Noahic covenant). The NT affirms this ongoing responsibility of the entire human race under the natural law, and thus Christians too must support the administration of justice in civil life. But the NT also reveals an eschatological ethic for believers justified in Christ, and this penultimizes their support of the pursuit of retributive justice. The eschatological ethic springs from the fact that Christ's work has fulfilled the purposes of God's retributive justice revealed in the natural law. The distinctive love of Christians here and now anticipates the ethic of the new creation, in which retributive justice has no more claims. Matthew 5, Galatians 5–6, and Romans 12–15 call Christians to exercise a merciful, reconciling, and restorative love that transcends the claims of retributive justice.[70] In so doing they display the eschatological image of God in Christ, for like their Savior they take the second slap and bear the other's burden for the sake of healing and peace. As Christ has once and for all fulfilled the purposes of the protological law, so Christians fulfill the law in his wake as they practice the same sort of merciful and self-sacrificial love.[71] Such love finds institutional embodiment in the corporate life of the church, but is meant to ripple beyond the church into Christians' broader social relationships. I will offer further comments on the relationship of Christians' protological and eschatological responsibilities at the end of this chapter.

70. Readers of the NT can find a similar dynamic also outside of Matthew and the Pauline epistles. For example, 1 Peter 2:23-24 describes Christ in his redemptive work as refusing to exercise the *lex talionis* ("When he was reviled, he did not revile in return; when he suffered, he did not threaten . . ."), and then 1 Peter 3:9 exhorts Christians to follow the same pattern: "Do not repay evil for evil or reviling for reviling, but on the contrary, bless. . . ."

71. The preceding discussion may raise, in Reformed readers' minds, the issue of the "third use of the law," that is, the law as standard for Christians' moral lives in response to their salvation in Christ. The exegetical evidence I have highlighted gives strong foundation for this doctrine, and also indicates that the law in its third use is not the protological law per se but as refracted and transformed, along the lines argued here.

The Eschatological Ethic and Sex and Family

Having explored questions of justice and love, I now consider more briefly the eschatological ethic as applied to questions of sex and family. In previous chapters we have often encountered issues pertaining to sexual morality. I have argued that part of the minimalist natural law ethic explicit in Genesis 9:1-7, and rooted originally in the covenant of creation (Gen. 1:28), is the general obligation to be fruitful and multiply and, correspondingly, to pursue sexual activity only within heterosexual marriage relationships. As discussed earlier in this chapter, the NT affirms this basic sexual morality. Paul, for example, approves of marriage and condemns, as occasion requires, various extramarital sexual practices as well as the internal desires underlying them. Nevertheless, the NT penultimizes the importance of marriage and procreation. The new creation is a realm in which human beings no longer marry or have children. Thus the eschatological ethic of the NT anticipates that state of existence by teaching a certain detachment from the consuming importance of marriage and family, even while affirming the sexual morality of the natural law.[72]

The Gospels set the tone. On the one hand, Jesus affirms the natural law sexual ethic so rigorously that he forbids lust as well as literal adultery (Matt. 5:28) and prohibits divorce except for sexual infidelity (πορνεία) (Matt. 5:31-32; 19:1-9; Mark 10:2-12; Luke 16:18). On the other hand, he also teaches that the importance of marriage and family pales in comparison to him and his kingdom. In response to prospective followers who wish first to bury their fathers or say farewell to their families Jesus says, "Leave the dead to bury their own dead. But as for you, go and proclaim the kingdom of God," and "No one who puts his hand to the plow and looks back is fit for the kingdom of God" (Luke 9:59-62). Elsewhere he asserts that he comes not to establish peace but "to set a man against his father, and a daughter against her mother, and a daughter-

---

72. Similarly, Bockmuehl comments about the Gospels' teaching: "We are confronted with a deep ambiguity here. Marriage is strongly affirmed as integral to the original design of creation, and yet even marriage clearly takes second place to the requirements of the Kingdom of God and the new creation." See *Jewish Law*, p. 124. Also compare Rémi Brague, *The Law of God: The Philosophical History of an Idea,* trans. Lydia G. Cochrane (Chicago: University of Chicago Press, 2007), p. 67: "Christianity rendered such natural ties as those of the family relative. It reasserted the duty to assist one's parents that is implied in the Decalogue . . . , but flesh and blood kinship cedes to a new type of family (Matt. 10:35-37; 12:48). As has been remarked, this was a revolutionary message. Paul tells the Christian that he is neither Jew nor Greek, neither free man nor slave, neither man nor woman (Gal. 3:28). The point is not to eliminate or deny these differences but to refuse them definitive pertinence."

in-law against her mother-in-law. And a person's enemies will be those of his own household" (Matt. 10:34-36; cf. Luke 12:53). This is because Jesus' disciples must be more committed to him than to their families: "Whoever loves father or mother more than me is not worthy of me, and whoever loves son or daughter more than me is not worthy of me" (Matt. 10:37). A parallel passage puts matters even more starkly: "If anyone comes to me and does not hate his own father and mother and wife and children and brothers and sisters, yes, and even his own life, he cannot be my disciple" (Luke 14:26).

To this point nothing may sound particularly new or distinctive. In the protological natural order as well, commitment to God should supersede commitment to family, a fact on display already in the covenant of creation when Adam sinfully allied himself with his wife rather than God. But the issue at stake here is different from the matter of where one's fundamental commitment lies. In the protological natural order, marriage and procreation were not merely goods to be affirmed but means for fulfilling the central purposes of the covenant of creation and thereby attaining the eschatological goal. As considered in Chapter 1, to be fruitful and multiply in that covenant was a key aspect of image-bearing and of the commission to exercise dominion. Through fidelity in such tasks the human race was to attain the eschatological rest of God's seventh day. Though God established no eschatological goal for the Noahic covenant, being fruitful and multiplying remained central to the purpose of that covenant, the preservation of human society in this world. Even in the OT, the anticipatory and forward-looking aspects of the covenants of grace gave procreation a central place. The Messianic Last Adam would come through the seed of the woman (Gen. 3:15) and through the seed of Abraham (Gen. 15:4-5; 17:1-7; cf. Gal. 3:16), such that a ritual performed on the male reproductive organ was the fitting sign of the Abrahamic covenant (Gen. 17:9-14). Under the Mosaic and Davidic covenants circumcision and the hope of a coming Messiah remained crucial, and each tribe's and family's possession of an inalienable inheritance in the promised land added another reason why procreation was fundamental to religious life and ongoing enjoyment of God's blessings.

Something fundamentally changes when the promised Seed comes and religious life is oriented away from an inheritance in an earthly promised land toward a heavenly inheritance in the new creation. Jesus proclaims the arrival of a new age, an eschatological kingdom, in which there is no more marriage and procreation. "The sons of this age marry and are given in marriage, but those who are considered worthy to attain to that age and to the resurrection from the dead neither marry nor are given in marriage, for they cannot die anymore, because they are equal to angels and are sons of God, being sons of the resurrection" (Luke 20:34-36). Marriage and procreation are activities of protological moral life, and fulfill its purposes. In the eschatological age the reign of the Last Adam makes the hope of a coming seed irrelevant and the absence of death makes procreation unnecessary for sustaining the human race. The NT commends an ethic that anticipates and foreshadows this eschatological life, though its adherents retain protological sexual desires and mortal, nonresurrected bodies. The Gospels not only reinforce the natural law obligation to honor God above family, but also give a glimpse of that day when life will no longer be structured around biological families at all. Jesus says, for example, "My mother and my brothers are those who hear the word of God and do it" (Luke 8:21). The closest and most dear relationships for Jesus' disciples even now should be found in the community of disciples (cf. Matt. 19:28-29).

Paul promotes a similar perspective as he provides concrete guidance for the early church. At the original creation God declared it "not good that the man should be alone" (Gen. 2:18). In contrast, Paul states: "it is good for them [unmarried Christians] to remain single as I am" (1 Cor. 7:8). He concedes that most Christians will not follow this way (for legitimate reasons), yet he wishes it would be true for all (7:7). Those who follow his example have less anxiety and hindrance in their service of God (7:32-35), act "even better" than those who marry (7:38), and may be happier (7:40). Either way, people's marital status makes no difference for their standing in the church (see 7:17). Without de-legitimizing marriage or contradicting natural law sexual morality, Paul, like Jesus, encourages a sense of detachment from the consuming importance of family. He can even make startling statements such as, "Let those who have wives live as though they had none" (7:29). The rationale for such a perspective is "the present distress" (7:26). In context this "present distress" probably refers not to a particular problem in first-century Corinth but to the general trials of life for all Christians living in the eschatological tension between the two comings of Christ. I draw this conclusion because Paul, shortly thereafter, again states the rationale for his perspective on marriage, and this time he speaks about the dawning of new creation: "The present form of this world is passing away" (7:31).

As with matters of justice, the NT eschatological ethic concerning sex and family has particular application for the church as the Christian community. Christians' willingness to forsake family relations for the sake of Christ does not leave them entirely without "family." As evident above, those who lose parents, siblings, spouses, or children for Christ's sake gain a new family in the community of disciples (Matt. 19:28-29; Luke 8:21). Paul's sentiments are similar. He calls the church the "household of God" (Eph. 2:19; 1 Tim. 3:15). All Christians, by faith and the Spirit, are adopted as co-heirs with Christ (Rom. 8:14-17; Gal. 4:4-7). Christ is "the firstborn among many brothers" (Rom. 8:29). Appropriately, barrenness, a perennial crisis in the OT, is never reckoned as a problem in Paul or elsewhere in the NT after Christ's coming. Thus in the intimate fellowship of the church Christians experience a wonderful foretaste of the communion of the age to come — which will be familial without present family structures.

Thus the NT handles matters of marriage and family similarly to matters of justice. It anticipates life in the new creation, when the purposes of marriage and procreation will have been fulfilled and resurrected Christians will no longer marry and reproduce, yet simultaneously guides those who live in the old creation before the resurrection. The NT approves of marriage and procreation and affirms natural law sexual morality while showcasing the fleeting character of sex and marriage. The eschatological ethic in no way denigrates these central aspects of protological existence but penultimizes them by testifying to the coming consummation of protological existence altogether.

The Eschatological Ethic and Economics

The realm of economics provides a final angle for exploring the eschatological ethic of the NT. As noted earlier in the chapter, economics has not been a major focus of this book, yet economic life is in the background of many of my discussions about natural law. Thus Paul's commendation of hard work and gainful employment is important evidence of the NT's interest in honoring the natural moral order. Yet in the new creation the conditions of protological economic life will no longer prevail. Scripture portrays the life of the eschatological age as one of *rest* from work (e.g., Heb. 4:9-10; Rev. 14:13). Residents of the new creation will not be inactive, and will surely continue to "work" in a sense, but they will not labor for a reward, for the reward is already theirs. In the new creation, furthermore, a principle of abundance and ample provision that makes payment unnecessary (see Isa. 25:6; 55:1; Joel 3:18; Rev. 21:6; 22:1-3) will stand unconstrained by the curse of "thorns and thistles" (Gen. 3:18) that make good things scarce and dearly acquired in the present world. Therefore economic reality as we know it now — characterized by toilsome employment for obtaining fragile resources — will be unknown in the coming age. Thus the NT ethic, in calling Christians to live now in a way that anticipates their future life in the new creation, gives certain exhortations that confound the economic constraints of the old creation.[73]

A number of statements in the Gospels emphasize the priority of Christ and his kingdom over material profit. The Sermon on the Mount, for example, famously instructs Jesus' disciples to store up treasure in heaven (Matt. 6:19-20) and to "seek first the kingdom of God" (Matt. 6:33; cf. 6:25-34). This message seems to be confirmed in Luke 10:38-42, where Jesus praises Mary's decision to sit at his feet rather than be consumed with domestic responsibilities like her sister Martha. Jesus also tells a parable about a rich fool who pursued economic profit without thinking about God (Luke 12:13-21).

Such exhortations and warnings, however vigorous, do not really get at anything new or distinctive. The natural law itself requires people to pursue hard work, but always with ultimate allegiance to God. Yet elsewhere in the Gospels the coming of Christ's kingdom demands a truly unprecedented rethinking of economic reality. Jesus, for example, tests the loyalty of a wealthy would-be disciple by commanding him to sell all he has and to give to the poor (Matt. 19:21; Mark 10:21; Luke 18:22). He then speaks of the difficulty with which the rich enter the kingdom of God (Matt. 19:23-24; Mark 10:23-25; Luke 18:24-25). As argued in previous chapters, the natural law (as well as the Mosaic law and the wisdom literature) requires generosity and hospitality. But completely divesting oneself of assets is unknown in protological law; a wise person leaves an inheritance for his children's children (Prov. 13:22). Under protological conditions Scripture often describes wealth as an ordinary result of virtue and divine blessing (though of course there are many exceptions).[74] Christ's kingdom disrupts the disciple's economic moorings. In his kingdom the poor are the blessed ones (Luke 6:20) and the rich enter only with great difficulty (Luke 18:24-27). Jesus observes rich people contributing large sums to the temple treasury and concludes that a poor widow, giving two practically worthless coins, has put in *more* than the rich, for it was all she had (Mark 12:41-44). From the economic perspective of Jesus' kingdom, giving all of one's possessions — whether that

73. See the similar conclusion in Bockmuehl, who writes concerning money and labor in the Gospels: "In each case there is a general affirmation of behaviour in accordance with creational realities, which is then profoundly relativized by the demands of the kingdom of God." See *Jewish Law*, p. 125.

74. For example, wealth was a sign of God's blessing for Abraham (Gen. 13:2), under the Mosaic law (Deut. 28:1-14), and in the Psalms (Psalm 128). As discussed in Chapter 8, in Proverbs wealth is ordinarily a result of a wise moral life, though one is not to trust in riches, seek them as a goal, or sacrifice other good things for their sake.

person is rich or poor and thus whatever the actual monetary amount — is what is valuable.

Embracing Jesus' perspective, the believers in the very early church in Jerusalem who owned investment estates or houses sold them and gave the proceeds to the apostles.[75] They held all things in common and there were no needy people among them (Acts 4:32-35). I take it this was no primitive communism, but a display of generosity from the rich in donating their surplus wealth and a willingness of all to contribute anything they had to the needs of their fellow saints. Here the church's own life was not driven by the natural economic reality that long-term provision for all people in society requires wealth-creation, not simply the transfer of assets. The church also did not operate by the natural law justice principle of "to each his due"; rather, goods were distributed "to each as any had need" (4:35). A scheme that has never worked for any attempted earthly utopia prevailed — with success — within the apostolic church.

Even in the more settled conditions of the Corinthian church, the economic perspective of Jesus' kingdom is evident. In words evoking memory of the widow in the temple, Paul states that the Corinthians' "extreme poverty" had "overflowed in a wealth of generosity" (2 Cor. 8:2). Willingly they "gave according to their means . . . and beyond their means" (8:3). Though giving beyond one's means seems a cardinal violation of natural law wisdom, Paul commends the Corinthians and praises God for such deeds. Somehow their extreme poverty produced an "abundance" that supplied the needs of others (8:14). To explain it Paul quotes Exodus 16:18 ("Whoever gathered much had nothing left over, and whoever gathered little had no lack"), which describes no ordinary economic exchange but God's supernatural provision of manna from heaven. Something indeed is transpiring that the natural moral order cannot explain. "God is able to make all grace abound to you, so that having all sufficiency in all things at all times, you may abound in every good work" (9:8). Somehow, impoverished people giving beyond their means become enriched in the process, so that they can give more in turn: "You will be enriched in every way to be generous in every way" (9:11). The explanation lies not in a theory of earthly economics but in the self-giving of Christ and the extravagant abundance it produced, which could never have been predicted on natural terms: "For you know the grace of our Lord Jesus Christ, that though he was rich, yet for your sake he became poor, so that you by his poverty might become rich" (8:9). When this eschatological transaction is replicated in the

---

75. I refer to "investment estates" at the advice of my colleague Steve Baugh.

church's giving and receiving, it not only provides for the needy but also results in "many thanksgivings to God" (9:12).

As with matters of justice and family, these economic realities are institutionally embodied in the church. Though the NT never limits the Christian's generosity to other Christians, the texts considered above, which describe the eschatological economics, concern the church's internal life. In Acts 4 "those who believed" held everything in common (4:32) and the *apostles* supervised the distribution of goods (4:35). Likewise, in 2 Corinthians 8–9 Paul gives guidance for the Corinthian church's offering for the church in Macedonia. Even the widow in Mark 12, acting before the establishment of the NT church, donated her mark to the *temple* treasury. The church, as the present earthly manifestation of the eschatological kingdom of Christ, displays the life of the coming new creation in special and extraordinary ways.

Concluding Reflections

In this chapter we have observed two ideas common in the NT. On the one hand, the NT affirms the natural moral order and requires Christians to honor the institutions that support it. Many major natural law themes considered in previous chapters appear in a positive light in the NT, such as civil authority and its pursuit of retributive justice, the goodness of marriage and procreation, and the necessity of hard work and gainful employment. On the other hand, the NT penultimizes every one of these natural law themes in a variety of subtle ways. Though it never opposes the requirements of natural law or their supporting institutions, the NT also shows Christians a distinctive way of life that transcends the confines of the natural moral order. In this concluding section I now reflect upon these dual concerns in the big picture and suggest how a satisfactory Christian ethic might account for them both.

While I recognize the danger of exaggeration, I believe it generally accurate to say that many conservative forms of Christianity emphasize the first strain of NT teaching (though, ironically, many conservative Protestants simultaneously think they hold a negative view of natural law) and many liberal forms of Christianity find the second strain particularly attractive. Those on the conservative end often closely associate important natural law themes with Christian commitment, with respect to both individual morality and social ethics. Upholding law and order, fostering traditional sexual morality and family structures, and encouraging hard work and economic conditions that reward it are hallmarks of a conservative Christian moral perspective. In contrast, those on the liberal end tend to see such emphases as oppressive and insufficiently attentive to the needs of the poor or minority groups, and thus they promote alternative forms of justice, sexual expression, and economic organization. For them the true genius of NT ethics lies in how it transcends concerns about retributive justice, monogamous heterosexual marriage, and the "he who does not work shall not eat" principle. Navigating this difference of opinion gets at the heart of many fundamental battles over the identity of Christian ethics.

The solution can only be found, in my judgment, by affirming both the continuing normativity of the natural law and the NT's subtle yet profound penultimizing of its importance for the Christian life. The bigger theological puzzle into which these pieces fit involves matters introduced already in Chapter 1 of this study: God created the natural order not as an end in itself but as a *protological* order meant to give way to an *eschatological* order — a new creation — that would be not its annulment or cancelation but its consummation and fulfillment. The covenant with Noah served to maintain this natural order (in refracted form) after the Fall into sin, and the covenants of grace provided a way of salvation by which the Last Adam would achieve the originally intended eschatological order. In the new covenant, the new creation (or kingdom of Christ) has drawn near and broken into human history, granting believers in Christ a present participation in the eschatological life of the age to come. Yet this presence of the kingdom is, as sometimes described, *already and not yet;* the kingdom is inaugurated but not yet consummated. God has ordained the covenant with Noah, with its natural law morality as adapted for a fallen creation, to endure until the end of this world (Gen. 8:22). Though Christians are "citizens of heaven" (Phil. 3:20) they remain "sojourners and exiles" (1 Pet. 2:11) in this old creation. At the heart of the Christian moral life, then, lie this dual identity and corresponding dual citizenship.

A danger of both conservative and liberal forms of Christianity is that one of these poles is jettisoned for the sake of the other, while each form, in the process, often skews the pole it affirms. On the liberal side a danger is moving from proper recognition of a certain NT relativization of "traditional" moral ideals to the notion that NT ethics changes the very character and purpose of the natural moral order as expressed in the state, family, or marketplace. On the conservative side a danger is moving from proper recognition of the NT's affirmation of the natural moral order to confusing a properly functioning state, family, or marketplace with the coming of Christ's eschatological kingdom, and often losing sight of the eschatological ethic in the life of the church. My conclusion in this chapter, building upon preceding arguments, is that the new covenant does not change the character and purpose of the natural moral order and its supporting institutions. Instead, it brings Christians into fellowship with the eschatological new creation that must never be confused with the natural institutions that God temporarily sustains. Both the protological old creation and the eschatological new creation are divinely established and inherently good, but are also distinct.

Crucial to the argument in this chapter is that the new creation, though organically connected to the old creation, is fundamentally distinct from it. The new creation involves a new cosmological order that will be revealed following the radical conflagration of the present cosmological order (2 Pet. 3:5-7, 10-13; Rev. 21:1-2). God's people, with resurrected bodies of a transformed quality fit for this new order, will inhabit the eschatological kingdom (1 Cor. 15:39-50). For my theology of natural law the next point is key: a consummated new natural order implies a consummated new moral order. Just as those bearing the image of the first Adam received a divine commission fit for life in the old creation, so those bearing the image of the Last Adam are called to live in a way fit for the new creation. The protological moral order was geared toward completing a certain task with bodies "of dust" (1 Cor. 15:47-49). Now that Christ has completed that task and been resurrected with a body "of heaven," a new moral order is required. This new moral order reflects the same "moral law" that undergirded the original moral order — that is, the same basic holiness required of all human beings in all circumstances — yet is fit for life with resurrected bodies on the other side of God's final judgment. The NT ethic provides manifold glimpses and anticipations of that moral life of the new creation for Christians still living in the old creation. Their lives are to reflect a new creation realm in which all claims of justice are already satisfied, in which the resurrected no longer marry or procreate, and in which giving and receiving is unconstrained by any poverty. And yet their conduct must testify to this new creation reality without leaving the old creation or ceasing to honor its natural moral order.

Determining how to witness to the new moral order while honoring the present moral order is perhaps *the* central issue of Christian ethics. Offering a black-and-white blueprint or an infallible flowchart for putting this dynamic into concrete practice is probably impossible; at least it is outside the scope of the present book. I suggest, however, that a key consideration for working through concrete implications emerges from an observation I made several times in this chapter: the eschatological moral order is specially anticipated and institutionally embodied in the corporate life of the church. The church's distinctive discipline expresses the satisfaction of God's justice once and for all in the work of Christ. The familial communion of all believers as brothers and sisters in the church, the household of God, proleptically enjoys the heavenly fellowship of believers apart from present practices of marriage and childbearing. The church's giving and receiving that mysteriously provides for the needs of all, even in the midst of poverty, embodies the abundant generosity of the eschatological kingdom, unconstrained by lack of resources. The NT presents the church as the earthly community that presently manifests the eschatological kingdom, and hence the church's internal life most fittingly embodies the moral life of the new creation. On the other hand, the institutions divinely upheld in the Noahic covenant — whether of the state, family, or marketplace — maintain their fundamental roles and purposes defined by natural law.

Even so, there is nothing absolute about this, as if believers' life in the church reflects the new creation and their life in natural institutions reflects the old creation, without any qualification. The church itself exists in the old creation and is subject to many constraints of its natural moral order. For instance, Paul instructs the church to pay its ministers according to the same natural law principles of compensation that govern farmers and soldiers (1 Corinthians 9). And the NT hardly instructs Christians to leave behind their eschatological bearings when reentering the public square on Monday mornings. For example, believers' response to persecution must reflect Christ's satisfaction of the claims of justice (see Matt. 5:38-42; cf. 5:10-12, 17), and their Spirit-inspired generosity should extend beyond the household of faith (see Gal. 6:8-10). The church is radically different from the natural institutions sustained by the Noahic covenant, yet room must be left for the creative use of Christian prudence for determining, in particular circumstances, a fitting way to show forth the glories of the new creation in an old creation whose time is running short. The challenge remains for Christians to express the forgiveness and generosity of the eschatological ethic in their broader social relations without undermining the legitimacy of the protological institutions.

CHAPTER 10

Conclusion

In this book I have developed a biblical theology of natural law. That being the case, I have not explored in detail certain questions traditionally important in natural law theory, for the simple reason that I judge (correctly or incorrectly) that Scripture itself does not provide detailed answers to these questions. For example, I have offered only general suggestions about significant questions regarding how exactly God objectively communicates his law through "the things that have been made" (Rom. 1:20) and how exactly human beings subjectively perceive this natural revelation. Scripture affirms the reality of these things but does not provide any detailed natural law epistemology. What I have attempted here is not an all-comprehensive natural law theory, but a biblical framework for Christian thinking about natural law that leaves room for — and I hope even invites — further philosophical, biological, and sociological investigation of the subject.

In previous chapters I raised a number of important issues for which I promised more discussion in this concluding chapter. Here I will try to make good on those promises. First, I present an overview of my biblical theology of natural law as a whole by summarizing the case I have built through this book. Second, I offer reasons why Christian faith and life demand a sound theology of natural law (or at least something similar if one objects to the "natural law" terminology). Third and finally, I reflect on the implications this biblical theology of natural law has for Christian thinking about life in civil society and some important questions regarding law, politics, and public policy.

A Biblical Theology of Natural Law: An Overview

In developing a *biblical theology* of natural law, I have traced the character and significance of natural law through many of the major events of biblical history. This has required consideration of the natural moral order as God originally created it and investigation of the natural moral order in its fallen condition as God providentially sustains it (Part 1). I have also explored the role of natural law in the moral life of God's chosen and redeemed people who relate specially to him through the series of organically united covenants of grace[1] revealed through Scripture, and who have thereby become citizens of the eschatological new creation, the goal of the original creation from the beginning (Part 2). Though God relates to people through the natural law in different ways under the covenant of creation, the covenant with Noah, and the covenants of grace (Abrahamic, Mosaic, and new), these distinct works of God are interconnected, and natural law is crucial for the moral life of human beings in each of them.

God created an orderly and meaningful world, culminating in the creation of human beings in his own image and likeness. The image of God entailed not only the possession of constituent attributes, such as rationality, but also a moral commission to exercise benevolent rule in the world and then to achieve a triumphant rest in an eschatological new creation, according to the pattern of God himself, who exercised his royal creative work in this world and then entered the rest of the seventh day. The image of God, and thus human nature, was thus an inherently moral and eschatologically oriented reality. God's specially revealed commands to human beings (Gen. 1:26, 28) were not foreign to them but in accord with the nature with which he made them. Following the pattern of God, as he revealed himself in the original creation, humanity's moral commission involved the obligation to exercise a creatively fruitful and benevolent rule and also to exercise retributive justice toward the wrongdoer. Because the original human commission was both natural and legal, it is rightly termed *natural law*. This natural law could be summarized in discrete rules such as "have dominion" and "be fruitful and multiply," but is best understood as a *natural moral order,* which was perceived through wisdom and which communicated to human beings the way of a

---

1. As noted twice in previous chapters, my use of "covenants of grace" terminology does not reflect any disagreement with the closing sentence of the Westminster Confession of Faith, 7.6: "There are not therefore two covenants of grace, differing in substance, but one and the same, under various dispensations." I refer to the "covenants of grace" to refer specifically to the Abrahamic, Mosaic, and new covenants.

flourishing life in this world toward the achievement of their ultimate goal. As such, the natural law was not destined to endure in original form forever, but to direct human beings to complete their commission in this world and then to attain an eschatological life in a consummated new creation. Human beings were to bear God's *protological* image by working toward a rest, with the expectation that one day they would bear God's *eschatological* image by enjoying that rest as a just reward for their faithful work. But disobedience to their commission carried God's threat of retribution through death. All of this, I argued in Chapter 1, is rightly understood in terms of a "covenant of creation," as traditionally understood in Reformed theology. Natural law was not something abstract, impersonal, or autonomous, but a protological moral standard that God communicated to human beings through the creation itself, in the context of a covenant relationship between them.

Because of the fall into sin the human race did not attain the goal of new creation. Yet God did not bring final judgment at this time, but instituted two great works that would shape the subsequent history of humanity and the broader created order. On the one hand, God's providential work sustains the world, albeit in fallen condition. On the other hand, God's redemptive work rescues human beings from the curse of sin and ultimately brings about the world's original goal, the new creation. To use a variation of language borrowed from Thomism and neo-Calvinism, *(common) grace preserves nature* and *(saving) grace consummates nature.* God maintains the testimony of the natural law, in modified form, through his preservative work of common grace.

After the great flood, God entered into a covenant with Noah (Gen. 8:20–9:17). This was a universal covenant, encompassing the whole world, set into place for as long as the present world endures, and promising preservation of the world but not its redemption. It postpones the final judgment but does not cancel it. In this covenant God still deals with human beings as his image-bearers, as those who retain their constitutive attributes (though corrupted) and a natural moral commission to exercise (a more modest) dominion in the world. Thus natural law is again communicated in a covenantal context, though a covenant designed only to preserve the world and not to bring it to eschatological consummation. This natural law is organically continuous with the natural law of the original creation, but refracted in modified form through the Noahic covenant. Accordingly, the substance of natural law in the fallen world reflects this covenant's preservative purposes. Genesis 9:1-7 explicitly highlights only a few natural obligations of fallen image-bearers, and they concern the most basic requirements for the continuation of human society:

procreation, eating (plants and animals, but not meat with its blood in it), and enforcement of retributive justice. I have referred to this as the minimalist natural law ethic, about which God has special concern to have observed in his ongoing government of the world. But even Genesis 9:1-7, especially when read in context, suggests that the natural law also continues to be a broader moral order, which points beyond the minimalist ethic to a richer way of life that promotes a modest human flourishing in the fallen world, and which also reminds human beings of their ultimate accountability before God and his judgment. One important way in which natural law is modified after the fall is that it requires the administration of retributive justice to be tempered with forbearance (though not forgiveness), in order to reflect the revelation of God's own justice and forbearance in the Noahic covenant.

The rest of Scripture subsequent to Genesis 9 offers many occasions to test and enrich these initial conclusions about natural law as sustained under the Noahic covenant, and thus as it concerns the human race as a whole — human beings as fallen human beings. In general, many biblical texts show that human persons, even apart from special prophetic revelation, have a knowledge of their basic moral obligations and that God has particular concern about violations of the minimalist ethic explicit in Genesis 9:1-7. The story of Abraham and Abimelech in Gerar (Genesis 20) illustrates the positive effects of natural law in broader human society, for here people who were strangers to God's special covenant with Abraham display an impressive interest in justice and the integrity of marriage, and even the fear of God. Negatively, texts describing the temporal judgments God brings upon particular human communities, in anticipation of the final judgment, illustrate sinful humanity's rebellion against the natural law. God never judges these nations for violations of the Torah, God's special law for Israel, or for their idolatry or other matters of religious devotion, but for egregious violations of intrahuman justice, committed with a hubristic spirit. This is consistent with the expectations created by the Noahic covenant.

Romans 1:18–2:16 provides a New Testament (NT) perspective on God's governance of the human race through natural law. Paul states that all people stand accountable and inexcusable before God, for God has made himself known in the things that have been made, that is, through *natural revelation*. Paul highlights humanity's rebellion against the natural law through sexual immorality and injustice, matters pertaining to the minimalist natural law ethic. But he also confirms the idea that the natural law involves a broader moral order, for Paul speaks of a variety of other sins as further evidence of humanity's rebellion against God's natural revelation. And though God in the

Old Testament (OT) did not bring temporal judgments against the nations because of idolatry, Paul indicates that idolatry is actually at the core of their rebellion against the natural order and the source of their other sins, for which they will give account one day. Paul does not provide a detailed natural law epistemology, but does speak of both the objective revelation of the natural law in the things that have been made and the subjective appropriation of this revelation through the human heart and conscience.

While God preserves the world as a whole through his providential common grace by means of the Noahic covenant, he also redeems a people for himself through a series of organically united covenants of grace. The beneficiaries of this covenant continue to live in this fallen but preserved world, but God has also made them citizens of the new creation, the world's original destiny, attained through the life, death, and exaltation of Jesus Christ. Under each of these covenants of grace its participants remain obligated to the natural law of the present world, even while looking ahead to the full revelation of the new creation when the natural law, in its present form, will no longer obligate. But the precise character of their relationship to natural law changes with each successive covenant.

In the Abrahamic covenant God gave Abraham and his family a redemptive hope unknown through natural revelation. Yet he gave them few specific moral commands and none concerning his life in broader human society. God expected Abraham to continue living as a sojourner among the nations of the world and to coexist justly and peacefully with them, under the authority of the natural law that mutually bound them through the Noahic covenant. God's education of his covenant partner also included teaching him the ways of "righteousness and justice," in part through his participation in the divine natural law judgment of Sodom.

In the Mosaic covenant God brought Israel into a complex relationship with him and gave them a detailed law to regulate their individual and corporate lives. This relationship was essentially redemptive, as God graciously rescued them from the bondage of Egypt, renewed promises of a coming Messiah, and gave them a priestly and sacrificial system that symbolized their eschatological reconciliation with God and the Messiah's future work. But in part the Mosaic covenant was also protological. One of God's purposes in giving the Mosaic law to Israel was to take them through a recapitulation of Adam's creation, probation, and fall, in order to make them a microcosm; that is, to display in clear ways the predicament of the entire human race, fallen in Adam and under God's just judgment, and to show the need for the coming Messiah. In this respect, the Mosaic law appropriately reflected the substance and the sanctions of the natural law, though in a way fitting for the unique historical situation of OT Israel.

Though detailed, the Mosaic law was not at all comprehensive, but required the exercise of wisdom to be put into practice effectively. Yet people acquire such wisdom in significant degree through perceiving and reflecting upon the natural moral order. Thus the Israelites' need for wisdom confirms the basic correspondence between the natural and Mosaic laws as well as the continuing significance of the natural law for participants in the covenant of grace at this stage in redemptive history.

With the life, death, and exaltation of Jesus the Messiah, God established the new covenant with his church, a people gathered from around the world from among Jews and Gentiles, in fulfillment of the promises to Abraham. On the one hand, God requires new covenant believers to continue living in this fallen but preserved world, and thus to honor the requirements and institutions of the natural law. Like Abraham, they must live as sojourners among the nations of the world and share a common social life with all people under the Noahic covenant. On the other hand, God has simultaneously released new covenant believers from under the authority of the natural law in significant respects. Through the work of Jesus Christ as the Last Adam, those believing in him have *already* been justified (declared righteous before God's judgment) and *already* been made citizens of the new creation. Christ has attained the original destiny of creation, and though the eschatological new creation has not yet been fully revealed, new covenant believers already have rights to this inheritance. They now bear the *eschatological* image of God through Jesus Christ, who has successfully completed the protological human commission and has thus attained the new creation. As the new creation is the consummation of the original creation, and is thus both distinct from and organically connected to it, so also the eschatological ethic of the new creation is distinct from the protological natural law, yet reflects the fulfillment of the latter's purposes.

In light of their present, but not yet full, enjoyment of these redemptive and eschatological blessings (which the OT saints experienced, but to much lesser degree), God calls new covenant believers to express the eschatological ethic even now, though in ways that do not undermine the legitimacy of present natural law institutions such as family and state. In various ways, and especially as institutionally embodied in the church's corporate life, they testify to the satisfaction of God's retributive justice by forgiving, they testify to the intimate fellowship of the new creation community by regarding their brothers and sisters in the church even more dearly than their natural family, and they testify to the abundance of the eschatological kingdom by giving with lavish generosity. Christians live in a time of eschatological tension, with the new creation having dawned but not yet fully arrived, and one of the great challenges of Christian ethics is the quest to show forth the eschatological ethic in powerful ways in this present world without failing to honor the natural law institutions that continue to exist, for a time, under the Noahic covenant. For Christians the natural law is still binding, but also penultimized.

To use a distinction important to the Reformation, in summary, natural revelation reveals God and his law, but does not reveal his gospel. Nor does natural law, as such, reveal what is distinctive about the Christian's moral life in response to the gospel. In light of these considerations, my account of natural law provides a *theological* approach to natural law without portraying natural law as a *distinctively Christian* ethic, for it places all people under obligation to God not *as Christians* but *as human beings* (though Christians carry out their natural law responsibilities as part of their obedience to Christ).

In historical perspective, this biblical theology of natural law stands in continuity with the broad stream of Christian natural law thought. It shares many commonalities, for example, with Thomas Aquinas's perennially relevant theory of natural law, such as a metaphysical and epistemological realism, an understanding of human nature as ordered beyond itself, a conviction that human beings move from a state of original integrity into a fallen condition and then to a state of grace, a conception of natural law as a natural moral order rather than a set of discrete rules, a belief that human civil law ought to be properly grounded in the natural law, the desire to integrate natural law into a broader biblical moral theology, and several other matters noted throughout this book. Yet I have also attempted to present a theology of natural law that is reformed according to the word of God. In that spirit I have drawn upon many aspects of my own Reformed theological tradition, including its emphasis upon the series of covenants that structure the unfolding biblical story, the distinction between God's preservative common grace and his redemptive saving grace, and a Reformation soteriology, including a doctrine of justification in Christ that comes by faith alone without any meritorious contribution from the redeemed sinner. Hence I have developed not a pan-Western natural law theory,[2] or even a pan-Christian theology of natural law that happens to be

2. I am thinking here of the not-uncommon practice of seeing a single natural law "tradition," which seems to encompass almost every Western thinker who embraced some sort of natural law idea. A recent example is Hadley Arkes, *Constitutional Illusions & Anchoring Truths: The Touchstone of the Natural Law* (New York: Cambridge University Press, 2010), chap. 2, which considers, as apparently part of "the tradition," Pufendorf, Vitoria, Aquinas,

written by a Protestant,[3] but a *Reformed* theology of natural law, having deep continuity with pre-Reformation natural law thought.

In contemporary perspective, my project concurs with the sentiments of many recent writers who argue that theories of natural law should be freed from assumptions about human autonomy and more closely connected to biblical ethics and a rich theology and anthropology. It also contributes to the fledgling renewal of interest among Protestants in the place of natural law in Scripture and in the Reformation traditions. But I have sought to add a much more detailed exploration of the presence and role of natural law in both the broad story of Scripture and in particular biblical texts. I have also proposed an account of natural law more thoroughly integrated into a particular Protestant system of theology than writers have hitherto attempted.

Why We Need a Theology of Natural Law

A claim that Christian theology and ethics requires a robust conception of natural law likely seems obvious to many readers while being a matter of deep skepticism for others. I believe that a theology of natural law is in fact not just possible, or potentially consistent with, a generally Christian or specifically Reformed theology, but is actually *necessary* for a satisfactory, stable, and coherent understanding of Christian faith and life. Or, for those still resistant to the terminology of "natural law," Christian faith and life require at least something similar. In this section I defend this claim, in light of my conclusions in previous chapters, by offering a biblical reason, a historical reason, a theological reason, and finally several practical reasons.

A *biblical* reason why a theology of natural law is necessary is that the Bible itself works with an (at least) implicit conception of natural law consistently and insistently, as I have argued for nine chapters. One does not have to agree with all the details of my exegesis or the way I have pieced together the evidence in this book to agree that the idea of a natural moral order appears

---

Aristotle, Lincoln, Locke, Rousseau, Cicero, Burlamaqui, Hooker, John Paul II, Kant, Finnis, George, and finally Plato and Socrates. While there may be occasions when such an inquiry has value, my own natural law theory is much too theologically specific to be embraced holistically by those who do not share my theological convictions, though I hope it has value in many respects for a broader audience.

3. As I mention in the Introduction, this is what I take the project of J. Daryl Charles to be in *Retrieving the Natural Law: A Return to Moral First Things* (Grand Rapids: Eerdmans, 2008), though Charles himself does not describe it in this way.

throughout the Scriptures. And if it does, it seems to place the Christian natural law skeptic into a difficult — perhaps impossible — situation. The very staunch commitment to Scripture that prompts some contemporary Protestants to cast a wary eye upon natural law theory in fact ought to compel them to affirm the importance of natural law for a full-fledged biblical conception of theology and ethics.

My *historical* reason why a theology of natural law is necessary (or, in this case, at least highly desirable) reflects the interest that any theological tradition or school of thought has in not placing itself totally outside the broader Christian tradition. Speaking as a Reformed theologian, I note that the very terminology of "Reformation" and "Reformed" implies a strong sense of continuity with what came before. The Reformers did not seek to start over or create a new religion, but to reform the Christian church and its doctrine and practice. Contemporary Reformed Christians, while maintaining constant vigilance about the need for ongoing reform according to the Scriptures, surely do not desire to stand fundamentally at odds with the broader Reformed tradition of centuries past. In that light, recognizing the prominence of natural law in the confessions and theology of the Reformed tradition as well as in the theology of the pre-Reformation traditions should at least give skeptics of natural law serious pause. To think about issues such as civil government, Mosaic law, wisdom, and final judgment in light of natural law puts one in organic continuity with catholic (which I do not equate with *Roman* Catholic) theological commitments.

Here I wish to address a potential objection, related jointly to these biblical and historical reasons, that might come from some Protestant readers. What about the Reformation doctrine of *sola scriptura,* and does it not call into question this alleged necessity for a theology of natural law? The answer to this objection is very important: the Reformation doctrine of "Scripture alone" meant that Christians do not need forms of *special revelation* other than the Bible (e.g., they do not need a pope speaking *ex cathedra,* an infallible magisterium, or new prophecies of the Holy Spirit). The doctrine of *sola scriptura* never meant that Christians do not need *natural revelation.* This is evident in the most important Reformed confessions of faith produced in the sixteenth and seventeenth centuries and still widely used today.[4] Scripture itself teaches

4. Westminster Confession of Faith 1.6 describes the doctrine of *sola scriptura* in this way: "The whole counsel of God concerning all things necessary for his own glory, man's salvation, faith and life, is either expressly set down in Scripture, or by good and necessary consequence may be deduced from Scripture: unto which nothing at any time is to be added, *whether by new revelations of the Spirit, or traditions of men.*" In the same section it goes on

the existence of natural revelation and demands believers' attention to it (as it never does regarding a pope or magisterium).

To speak in very general historical terms, many eras of the history of theology have witnessed a struggle between theologians who have tended to seek a synthesis between Christian and pagan thought (perhaps most famously represented by Thomas Aquinas) and theologians who have tended to seek the purification of Christian thought from pagan influence (perhaps most famously summarized in Tertullian's rhetorical question, "What has Jerusalem to do with Athens?"). I believe it is also fair to say that the Reformation, on the whole, represented a shift toward the latter in an attempt to conform Christian theology and practice more thoroughly to the Scriptures.[5] But it is crucial to distinguish the Reformation's desire to reform Christian thought and practice according to the word of God from a mindset that thinks to find in Scripture information about *everything*. This mindset, which might be termed "biblicism," is a parody of the Reformation doctrine of *sola scriptura*. The Reformers and their heirs continued to affirm natural law (and natural revelation more broadly) because they recognized that the quest to rid Christianity of pagan elements that contradicted Scripture was not the same thing as ridding Christianity of attention to God's own natural revelation, which remains necessary since Scripture does not speak comprehensively about every subject.

A *theological* reason why a theology of natural law is necessary is that Christianity is a historical religion proclaiming that Christ came to bring fulfillment to God's original goal for the human race and the entire world. The eschatological new creation is comprehensible only in relation to the protological first creation; the goodness of the gospel presumes a binding but broken law. Without insight into this present creation and its natural law one cannot really understand the character of sin, the foundation of the justice Christ

---

to say: "there are some circumstances concerning the worship of God, and government of the church, *common to human actions and societies,* which are to be ordered by the *light of nature, and Christian prudence,* according to the general rules of the Word, which are always to be observed." And earlier in the same chapter (1.1) the Westminster Confession of Faith teaches the reality of natural revelation and all people's inexcusability before its testimony. Similarly, the Belgic Confession (7), in its explanation of *sola scriptura,* lists many kinds of writings, ecclesiastical decisions, and human opinions that cannot be made equal to the Scriptures, but never speaks of the doctrine of *sola scriptura* making natural revelation unnecessary or unimportant. The Belgic Confession also clearly affirms the reality and authority of natural revelation in an earlier article (2).

5. For Charles Taylor, the Protestant Reformation was one aspect of a larger movement of "Reform" that preceded it, which sought the de-paganization of medieval Christianity. See *A Secular Age* (Cambridge, MA: Belknap Press of Harvard University Press, 2007).

satisfied, the abiding threat of the final judgment, or the newness of the ethic institutionally embodied by the NT church. It is difficult for me to think of *anything* related to the events of the "last days" — Christ's first coming in humility, his exaltation, the establishment of the church, Christ's second coming in glory — that transpires apart from the background of this first creation and the law to which it witnesses. A rich Christian eschatology depends upon a robust protology just as a second half requires a first half, a ninth inning a first inning, a back nine a front nine.

I now mention several *practical* reasons why a theology of natural law is necessary (though these practical reasons are themselves theological). First, a theology of natural law is necessary practically because so many ethical obligations of NT ethics are *natural law obligations,* and we have not really understood those obligations unless we understand them as such. While it is not untrue to say that Christians must, for example, honor civil authority, be sexually pure, and work industriously because the NT commands these things, at a deeper and more fundamental level the NT commands these things because that is the way God designed human beings to live in a world such as ours. In other words, such NT commands are not new obligations proceeding from the arbitrary will of God, but perennial obligations of creatures made in the image of God and thus made by nature to pursue certain kinds of tasks in this world. Without such an understanding it becomes very difficult to understand why such obligations are not uniquely Christian but binding upon all people and of pressing concern for questions of civil law and public life (in distinction, for example, from the command to turn the other cheek and other distinctively Christian obligations in the NT).

A second and related practical point is that a theology of natural law is exceedingly helpful for thinking about the common life God calls Christians to live in this world alongside unbelievers. To be clear, having a biblical theology of natural law is not necessary for a person to know the substance of the natural law, for all people know the substance of the natural law whether or not they have thought about it theoretically. The point is that a theology of natural law provides crucial theological foundation for making sense of Christians' present identity as dual citizens, that is, their membership both in Christ's eschatological kingdom and in various natural human institutions.[6]

6. For such reasons I believe that a Reformed theology of natural law appropriately accompanies a Reformed two kingdoms doctrine, properly understood. For a historical survey of the Reformed two kingdoms doctrine and a constructive reappropriation of it, see, respectively, David VanDrunen, *Natural Law and the Two Kingdoms: A Study in the Development of Reformed Social Thought* (Grand Rapids: Eerdmans, 2010) and David VanDrunen, *Living in*

God calls Christians to live at peace with all people as far as possible (Rom. 12:18). Proclaiming the gospel and standing for what is just and true sometimes provokes persecution, but Christians themselves are to strive for peaceful coexistence with those indifferent toward or opposed to what is most precious to them. Under the Noahic covenant, natural human institutions such as the family and civil government (and I believe others too, by extension) are for all human beings created in God's image, and Christians have no more right to them or authority over them than do their non-Christian neighbors. Yet Christians are also to pursue truth and justice in these natural institutions in which they participate, and this entails persuading their unbelieving neighbors (to at least some degree) of what is true and just and collaborating with them in the pursuit of what is (at least penultimately) good.

But how are Christians to identify what the good is that all people *ought* to pursue, even if they refuse to heed the Christian gospel? Unbelievers' moral obligations cannot be rooted in the eschatological order if they have not been justified in Christ and made citizens of the new creation; they are rooted instead in the protological order. Through the Noahic covenant they continue to be bound as image-bearers to God's moral law, and through the Noahic natural law they continue to know what it requires at a basic level. The Noahic covenant, not the redemptive covenants of grace, grounds this moral obligation. Thus I believe it is correct for Christians to think that controversial social issues such as the identity of marriage, the status of the unborn, and matters of wealth and poverty raise moral questions relevant for all people and are of great concern for public policy. To be sure, Christians must approach such issues with hearts sanctified by the Holy Spirit and with the guidance of Scripture. But the reason why unbelievers have moral obligations in these areas and the reason why there is a common social life among believers and unbelievers is the objective reality of the natural moral order as sustained through the Noahic covenant. Without that recognition, Christians will be prone to misunderstand the nature of their dual citizenship and to misunderstand the moral obligations of all human beings — as human beings — and why they have them.

Third, natural law is practically useful not only for providing theological explanation for the what and why of Christians' common social life with

---

God's Two Kingdoms: A Biblical Vision for Christianity and Culture (Wheaton, IL: Crossway, 2010). For an article-length summary of the argument in both books, see David VanDrunen, "The Reformed Two Kingdoms Doctrine: An Explanation and Defense," *The Confessional Presbyterian* 8 (2012): 177-90. See the last section of the present chapter and Appendix 2 for interaction with certain streams of contemporary thought opposed to a two kingdoms perspective.

unbelievers (examined in the previous paragraph) but also for providing an important means for communicating with unbelievers about this common life. If this common life exists under the auspices of God's covenant with Noah, and if the natural law is promulgated through the created order sustained by this covenant, then it must be proper for Christians to seek to persuade unbelievers and to collaborate with them by means of natural law. Since this book is a *biblical theology* of natural law, and Scripture gives no explicit instructions on how to make natural law arguments, this issue is mostly beyond the scope of my present project, though undoubtedly an important issue. Thus I offer here only rudimentary reflections on it, based upon some implicit considerations in Scripture.

I take it that there are numerous ways to make natural law arguments. If, as argued here, natural law is to be identified with the natural moral order pervading the world, then any appeal to the moral implications of the way this world is structured constitutes a kind of argument from natural law. This could be of a highly philosophical nature or a very pragmatic nature. Many people, I suspect, think that genuine natural law arguments are by definition highly philosophical, though I also suspect that such natural law arguments (however rigorous) may often be least effective. Only a small number of people are able to engage them seriously, and non-Christians who do so are likely to pursue them to their logical core and to expose their deepest presuppositions, which they will likely be inclined to reject. But whereas intellectually refined natural law arguments will be (endlessly) debated mostly in rarefied academic circles, a more pragmatic species of natural law argument may well be more accessible to the common person and also more likely to garner a measure of assent.[7] I say this not to be highly optimistic about the potential effectiveness of natural law arguments, which in reality I am not. But it does reflect my conclusion (mentioned in Chapter 5 with respect to Romans 1–2) that sinners' response to the natural law is apparently complex, involving simultaneously a considerable degree of submission to its requirements and a consistent tendency to rebel against them.

As Chapter 8 explored, in Proverbs sound moral conclusions are often recognized as such through their eminent practical usefulness. Doing good things tends to promote good ends, while doing evil things tends to hinder attainment of these ends (with many exceptions to regular patterns). By God's

---

7. I assume that garnering a measure of assent is in fact the goal of natural law arguments made to promote peace in our common social life; I am not considering here the use of natural law in evangelism or apologetics, whose goals I believe are much different.

common grace there are many important good ends that most people, of different faiths, regularly affirm. Most will agree that peaceful relations among neighbors are better than hostile ones, that orderly children are better than wild ones, that economic prosperity is better than poverty, that protection of life is better than rampant violence. Proverbs indicates that the wise person, who understands the natural moral order, perceives that certain patterns of behavior promote such good ends. All this is to say that any attempt to persuade others that they should pursue these patterns of behavior, by demonstrating how these patterns promote various good ends that most people acknowledge at some level, is necessarily a kind of natural law argument. The natural moral order restrains certain sorts of conduct and compels other kinds. People work harder than they are usually inclined to do because they wish to eat and to pay the mortgage; people say less nasty things about their neighbors than they are inclined to say because they want to maintain a decent level of comity among them; people do not commit adultery whenever they feel inclined because they recognize the benefits of domestic peace for themselves and their children. Impressing the natural connection between conduct and consequences is one way to make natural law arguments. Making and understanding such arguments do not demand intellectual sophistication. Neither do they require moral purity or conversion to Christianity to appreciate at a meaningful level. They do not overlook human depravity but seek ways to mitigate and constrain it for the sake of promoting a measure of peace, justice, and prosperity in the present world. From a Christian perspective these goals are not the *most* important things, but they are important things.

A fourth practical reason to recognize the necessity of a natural law theology concerns interpretation of the law of Moses. The Mosaic law itself constitutes a significant portion of the Bible, and much of the Bible subsequent to the Pentateuch deals with the Mosaic law in one way or another. Interpreting and applying the Mosaic law, particularly in light of the new covenant, is difficult and complex. Yet it is interesting to observe that many Christian traditions have shared a basic approach, grounded in the distinction among the moral, ceremonial, and judicial (or civil) aspects of the Mosaic law.[8] The Mosaic law itself never explicitly makes this distinction — nor, for that matter, does the NT. But the staying power of this distinction — through medieval,

---

8. E.g., see Thomas Aquinas, *Summa Theologiae*, 1a2ae 99; John Calvin, *Institutes of the Christian Religion*, 4.20.14-16; and Francis Turretin, *Institutes of Elenctic Theology*, vol. 2, trans. George Musgrave Giger, ed. James T. Dennison Jr. (Phillipsburg, NJ: Presbyterian and Reformed, 1994), pp. 1-18, 145-67.

Reformation, and post-Reformation theology — suggests that it sheds considerable light on the issue. Indeed, it seems to me that any thoughtful attempt to build a new set of categories, provided it wrestles with all of the relevant strands of biblical data, is likely to come back to something rather close to the traditional threefold distinction. Some aspects of the Mosaic law are of permanently binding moral character (the moral law), other aspects shape the identity and worship of God's people under age, in anticipation of the coming Messiah, and are hence to be set aside after his coming (roughly the ceremonial law), and other aspects concern Israel's identity as a civil community needing to deal with common human issues of social order and may be informative for, but are not immediately applicable to, contemporary civil law (roughly the civil or judicial law). This is not to say that each individual law can be holistically slotted into one of these categories, which seems to me clearly not the case, but it is compelling to see these threads running through the Mosaic law and to account for them in one way or another.

When interpreting and applying the Mosaic law in these terms, recourse to the natural law becomes inevitable. Identifying the moral law — that core of moral obligation binding all people as human beings at all times — is inseparable from asking how we were created and what we are designed to be and to do as image-bearers of God.

Untangling the continuing relevance of the Mosaic civil law requires natural law inquiry at multiple levels. At one level it requires distinguishing what is of universal human concern from what has significance only in a specific social context. The requirement to put a fence around one's roof (Deut. 22:8) provides a helpful example. The concern to protect human life through safety regulations reflects the universal natural law, while the interest in a fence around one's roof makes sense only in a context where people use their roofs for living and entertaining. But even in thinking about the contemporary relevance of the culturally specific aspect of this Mosaic rule, natural law must play an important role. What sorts of health and safety regulations ought civil law to promote today in the interest of protecting life? The Mosaic rule itself provides no specific guidance, but leaves us to the exercise of wisdom, which in turn drives us to the thoughtful examination of the natural moral order and the identification of effects likely to result from certain actions.

At another level, interpretation of the Mosaic law compels us to ask whether particular Mosaic provisions, even if reflecting the natural law, may do so in the context of the Sinai covenant in a way that is different from how the natural law should be applied to civil law today in the context of the Noahic covenant. To put it another way, the purposes for which, and the ways in which, the Mosaic covenant applied the natural law to the people of Israel are not always the same as the way contemporary civil societies existing only under the covenant with Noah are to implement the natural law in their legal systems. The Mosaic law, for example, required the extermination of the Canaanite inhabitants of the Promised Land. I take it that this was a unique application of the natural law: it was a singular foretaste of the final judgment, under God's protological law according to the unyielding terms of the covenant of creation, coming upon all sinners outside of saving relationship with the coming Messiah. But, as I argued in Chapter 2 and elsewhere, this is not God's ordinary way for human beings to administer justice under the natural law, *as refracted through the Noahic covenant* (designed to preserve human society for all people in common). With respect to relations with their neighbors of different religious conviction, NT Christians are bound by the Noahic, not the Mosaic, application of the natural law.

This Noahic/Mosaic distinction also seems necessary with respect to civil penalties against individual evildoers. At several points the Mosaic law explicitly promulgates the *lex talionis* as the standard for punishment and does so implicitly elsewhere. In other places it requires punishments that bear no immediately evident relationship to the *lex talionis;* the death penalty for Sabbath-breaking or for bestiality comes to mind. In cases where the *lex talionis* is the clear standard for punishment, Mosaic penalties are designed to inflict a punishment whose harm to the wrongdoer is proportionate to the harm he inflicted on the victim. In these other cases, the Mosaic law inflicts penalties for what we would today call victimless crimes — at least in terms of *human* victims. Since the Mosaic covenant, as noted, was designed in part to highlight the ultimate penalty that every sin deserves under the protological law of the covenant of creation (and which will be administered at the final judgment), God willed that some sins be met with punishments that cannot be fully accounted for in terms of intrahuman relations. These sins are abhorrent to God even if they may strike people today as insignificant (such as gathering sticks on the Sabbath) or as strange but basically harmless (such as sex with animals). In contrast to the Mosaic covenant, the Noahic covenant explicitly ordains civil penalties only in terms of intrahuman relations, and points to the *lex talionis* as the standard for human retributive justice. Thus the fact that contemporary civil law should rest upon application of the *Noahic* natural law again has significant ramifications for thinking through the contemporary relevance of particular civil penalties under the Mosaic law.

Finally, I mention a practical concern that perhaps does not demonstrate the necessity of a theology of natural law, but (at least for me) its attractiveness. A theology of natural law provides an effective foundation for what I will call, for lack of a better term, a Christian humanism.[9] Despite the ravages of sin and the many truly horrible deeds perpetrated in this world, human beings also do acts of astonishing goodness and have accomplished a host of astounding achievements in various areas of human culture. Some of these are the work of Christians, fewer still the work of Reformed Christians — but so many owe their origins to those without faith in Jesus Christ. Truth, beauty, and goodness continue to shine in the human race as a whole. There is compelling reason to follow John Calvin's advice regarding pagan authors: do not despise the truth wherever it is found, but recognize God as the fountain of all truth.[10] For Christians to enjoy and learn from the cultural achievements of the human race — even of pagan humanity — should not be a guilty pleasure, or something they indulge only with major dissonance in their thought. At the same time, Christians should not compromise the supreme lordship of Jesus Christ or downplay the depths of human depravity or deny the impending final judgment. A doctrine of natural law, grounded in the Noahic covenant, provides just the right foundation for maintaining this difficult but crucial balance. The covenant with Noah accounts for and explains, better than any other way I know, the true state of the human condition under sin ("the intention of man's heart is evil from his youth" — Gen. 8:21) as well as the continuance and even flourishing of human culture. It simultaneously captures the sparkling beauty of human achievement and exposes the great tragedy that all things outside of Christ ultimately stand condemned under divine judgment. It enables Christians to be genuine humanists — loving and enjoying what is humane — while reminding them that from the perspective of Christ's eschatological kingdom, the things for which humanity toils "under the sun" are "vanity of vanities" (Eccl. 1:2-3).

Natural Law and the Public Square

In this final section of the chapter and the book, I reflect upon implications of my biblical theology of natural law for social life in the public square. My use of the word "reflect" is worth emphasizing. There is nothing comprehensive

9. For a recent robust attempt to recover a Christian humanism, with a number of concerns similar to mine here, see Jens Zimmerman, *Humanism and Religion: A Call for the Renewal of Western Culture* (Oxford: Oxford University Press, 2012).

10. Calvin, *Institutes of the Christian Religion,* 2.2.15.

about what follows and my analysis of particular issues is far from technical and rigorous. Furthermore, I do not mean to provide anything that might be mistaken for the outlines of *the Christian* political or legal theory — as if such a thing could ever be established. My claim throughout this book that the natural law involves a natural moral order, rather than a series of discrete rules, offers a cautionary note against seeking *the natural law* political or legal theory, let alone *the Christian* theory. As a natural moral order, the natural law provides objective moral direction and boundaries for the conduct of individual human beings and of human society, but it does not dictate a detailed blueprint for either. The objective natural moral order can only be perceived subjectively through the exercise of wisdom, and such wisdom requires familiarity with concrete circumstances and creativity and imagination for structuring human life fruitfully and productively. Individuals and societies can conform to (and deflect from) the natural law in a variety of ways.[11]

In this section I seek to reflect informally upon how the conclusions drawn in previous chapters about natural law might shape and direct thinking about some perennially important questions of social life. As providence provides opportunity and motivation, I hope to take up this pursuit in more detailed manner in a separate book. Here I offer only initial reflections.

Qualified Support of Natural Institutions

The first issue for reflection is the Christian's support of natural institutions and allegiance to them. By "natural institutions" I refer to institutions governed by God under the Noahic covenant, in which human beings participate as image-bearers of God. The conclusions of previous chapters suggest that all people, Christians included, are obliged to support the maintenance of such institutions while also recognizing their limitations. For Christians this means recognizing not only their natural limitations but also the penultimacy of the allegiance due to them in light of their citizenship in the new creation.

The minimalist natural law ethic, explicit in Genesis 9:1-7, involves procreation ("be fruitful and multiply") and the enforcement of retributive justice ("whoever sheds the blood of man, by man shall his blood be shed"), and

11. As cited in an earlier chapter, Jean Porter explores questions concerning the breadth of the discretionary scope provided by the natural law in "Does the Natural Law Provide a Universally Valid Morality?" in *Intractable Disputes about the Natural Law: Alasdair MacIntyre and Critics,* ed. Lawrence S. Cunningham (Notre Dame: University of Notre Dame Press, 2009), pp. 53-95.

thus I take it that the institutions whose purpose is to support these tasks — namely, the family and civil government — constitute the most basic natural law institutions. Just as the minimalist natural law ethic implies the presence of a broader natural moral order, so also the flourishing of these basic natural law institutions implies the development of other natural institutions. Building upon my argument in previous chapters, however, it would seem that the maintenance of families and civil governments is a bare minimum required for the survival of human society as a whole.

The Noahic covenant indicates that the natural law ethic and its natural institutions obligate all people. God issues the promises of the covenant to Noah's offspring and to "all flesh" (Gen. 9:8-17), and its obligations and protections extend not to a special class, but to all those who bear God's image (Gen. 9:6). Presumably the manner of obedience to the ethic and the mode of participation in its institutions can vary from person to person. Marriage and procreation are not possible for everyone, and thus "be fruitful and multiply" cannot be an absolute requirement for every individual, and civil government would be an odd thing if every person were a judge and executioner. The natural law directs all people to honor, support, and participate in these natural institutions, without necessarily specifying *how* each person should do so. That this must include Christians is not simply a logical deduction from the universal tenor of the Noahic covenant and its establishment "while the earth remains" (Gen. 8:22), but is also the teaching of the NT, as considered in Chapter 9. Different modes of participation are permissible, but supporting and honoring institutions of family and government are not optional for the saints.

An issue not considered in Chapter 9, but a longstanding and troublesome question for the church, concerns Christian participation in violent and coercive measures in the name of justice. Advocates of pacifist or nonviolent positions have found a number of eloquent and influential spokespeople over the past several decades.[12] One of the key convictions of many proponents is that the kingdom of God proclaimed by Jesus is a kingdom of peace and reconciliation that rejects all use of the sword, and that Jesus' disciples must embody these traits. Such a view actually corresponds significantly with the position I defended earlier, especially in Chapter 9, where I argued that the eschatological ethic of the kingdom of heaven eschews violence and the enforcement

---

12. E.g., see John Howard Yoder, *The Politics of Jesus* (Grand Rapids: Eerdmans, 1972); Stanley Hauerwas, *The Peaceable Kingdom: A Primer in Christian Ethics* (Notre Dame: University of Notre Dame Press, 1983); and Richard B. Hays, *The Moral Vision of the New Testament: Community, Cross, New Creation* (San Francisco: HarperSanFrancisco, 1996).

of retributive justice, but seeks restoration and reconciliation through loving forgiveness. The Christian's ethic of the kingdom is and must be distinct from the violence that characterizes the state. For advocates of a pacifist or nonviolent position, this distinctive character of the kingdom calls the legitimacy of civil government into fundamental question, or at least prohibits Christians from participating in its coercive actions even if such actions are deemed necessary to some degree.[13] Appeal to natural law is an impoverished basis for Christian ethics and in fact tends to justify the very violence that the ethic of the kingdom prohibits. As Stanley Hauerwas puts it, "violence and coercion become conceptually intelligible from a natural law standpoint."[14]

Such a view makes a fair deal of sense without a conception that Christians are bound by a dual ethic. A natural law that advertises itself as universally human and as justifying violence under certain circumstances is indeed distinct from the ethics of Jesus' kingdom described, for example, in the Sermon on the Mount. In response to pacifist or nonviolent positions I dispute neither the peaceable character of the kingdom of heaven nor the legitimacy of limited violence in defense of justice under the natural law. The error of the nonviolent perspective, it seems to me, is that it fails to reckon with dual covenants under which Christians live and hence the dual character of their ethics. The Sermon on the Mount showed Jesus' disciples that they were released from use of the sword as regulated by the Mosaic covenant, but it did not strip them of responsibilities under the Noahic covenant. The proponents of nonviolence do well to remind us of that prime responsibility of the church to be the church and therefore to embody the peaceable ways of the kingdom, but this does not deprive the state of its legitimacy. As established by the Noahic covenant, the legitimate human use of the sword in defense of justice ends not with Jesus' first coming, but at his second coming, when the earth in present form no longer "endures" (cf. Gen. 8:22).

I appreciate the powerful simplicity of the case for consistent nonviolence and thus for Christians' refusal to participate in the state's use of the sword. For that matter, I also understand the powerful simplicity of the case for "Christendom" and the identification of the kingdom of God with geopolitical success in the name of Christ. The case for a Christian's dual citizenship in

---

13. E.g., Craig A. Carter affirms that a sinful world will always need somebody to maintain order by the sword, but denies that Christians should ever be the ones to take up this responsibility. See *Rethinking Christ and Culture: A Post-Christendom Perspective* (Grand Rapids: Brazos, 2006).

14. Hauerwas, *The Peaceable Kingdom*, p. 61; see pp. 60-64 for his larger critique of natural law.

two covenants, with ethics that are organically related but in crucial respects distinct, may not have the same simplicity as these other options but, as I have argued especially in Chapter 9, it allows us to affirm both strands of biblical teaching that ought to shape the Christian's present life: new covenant *and* Noahic covenant, eschatological new creation *and* protological present creation, redemption *and* preservation, saving grace *and* common grace, the church *and* natural institutions — the Sermon on the Mount *and* the natural law. Jesus and the apostles surely intended their converts in the Roman military to embrace the eschatological ethic just as their other converts did, but they never commanded them to leave their posts (Matt. 8:5-13; Luke 7:1-10; Acts 10:24-48).[15] In Chapter 9 I suggested that the eschatological ethic was to be specially embodied in the corporate life of the church, but that Christians are evidently to seek opportunities to testify to their unique identity in all sorts of times and places, yet without undermining the legitimacy of the state or other natural institutions. I did not offer a neat formula specifying how exactly to do so, nor do I here. I suspect there is no such formula, but God leaves much to believers' Christ-sanctified wisdom. This may be, I suggested, *the* challenge of a robustly biblical Christian ethics.

Natural institutions are legitimate, but *limited* in their authority. This point has special significance with respect to civil government, the natural institution most prone to usurp authority and to exercise raw power. As I claimed earlier, civil government is a basic natural institution precisely because its work is to carry out the minimalist natural law requirement of enforcing retributive justice. The promotion of justice, in other words, is the very basis for civil government's legitimacy. Thus its authority is inherently limited by the obligation to do what is just. Any injustice is usurpation. Civil authority is also limited by the important fact that there are other natural institutions. The presence of legitimate authority in other natural institutions means that civil government does not have unlimited authority. All of this is true even on terms internal to the Noahic covenant and its natural law, and thus relevant for all human beings.

But Christians have an additional, and ultimately more important, reason to recognize the limited character of civil authority. As argued in Chapter 9, the humiliation and exaltation of Christ and the consequent dawning of new creation have not de-legitimized natural institutions for Christians, but they

---

15. See Nigel Biggar's response to Richard Hays's (nonviolent) interpretation of these texts: "Specify and Distinguish! Interpreting the New Testament on 'Non-Violence,'" *Studies in Christian Ethics* 22, no. 2 (2009): 169-70.

have penultimized them. While Christians recognize that the state and other natural institutions are important, they also profess that they are not the *most* important, because they are temporary, rooted in and thus dependent upon the soon-to-expire Noahic covenant. In comparison to the future full revelation of the eschatological kingdom — and even in comparison to the suffering and sinful church of Jesus Christ as it presently manifests that kingdom inchoately — the wealth and power of the state look small indeed. A Christian's deep appreciation for and industrious service to her own particular civil community — a humble patriotism, we might say — seems an appropriate response to God's blessings through the Noahic covenant. But a Christian's militaristic or imperialistic pride in one's nation — a hubristic patriotism — displays a flagrant disregard not only of the internal limitations on each state's authority but also of the ultimate loyalty due to Christ's eschatological kingdom.

Justice: Retribution with Restoration

The second issue for reflection is justice, a topic crucial for political and legal theory and an ideal almost universally honored, though so inconsistently practiced. Justice has also been a pervasive subject of this book, something I have associated with the minimalist natural law ethic. Though my biblical theology of natural law does not inherently provide a comprehensive theory of justice, the brief statement in Genesis 9:5-6 suggests a number of significant things about justice relevant for a more detailed exploration of political and legal theory. Specifically, justice grounded in the natural law should be proportionate, retributive, restorative, and forbearing (and therefore flexible in application).

Genesis 9:5-6 conveys at least three general ideas about justice. First, Genesis 9:5 indicates that God himself is concerned about justice in the social order and is its ultimate enforcer: "For your lifeblood I will require a reckoning." Second, in Genesis 9:6 God commissions human beings to enforce justice in their interrelationships: "Whoever sheds the blood of man, *by man* shall his blood be shed." God is the ultimate enforcer of justice, but he uses human beings as instruments. Finally, Genesis 9:6 also communicates the principle that should guide the human pursuit of justice: "Whoever *sheds the blood of man,* by *man shall his blood be shed.*" This is the *lex talionis,* or law of retribution, mentioned so often in previous chapters of this book. All three things Genesis 9:5-6 says about justice are important, but I focus upon the third: since human beings should pursue intrahuman justice as instruments of God's justice, what insight might the natural law principle in Genesis 9:6 provide for the development of a political or legal theory?

First, the *lex talionis* expresses the important legal principle of proportionate justice, that is, that the response to a wrong should match the harm done. As William Ian Miller puts it in his wonderful study of the *lex talionis*, "the eye/tooth statement perfectly captures the rule of equivalence, balance, and precision in a stunning way. It holds before us the possibility of getting the measure of value right."[16] While people may widely agree that justice requires some sort of punishment and/or compensation when one person harms another, measuring the harm done is no simple matter. How to determine the value of the harm if I lose my eye due to your violent act? What is an eye worth? It is difficult to think of anything more nearly equivalent than another eye. The natural law principle of *lex talionis,* therefore, suggests a conception of justice as equivalence and proportionality.

Second, the *lex talionis* expresses the idea of retributive justice. The formula in Genesis 9:6 identifies three people: the wrongdoer, the victim, and the one who metes out punishment. In contemplating the just outcome following the crime, however, Genesis 9:6 focuses not upon the victim but only upon the wrongdoer and the one who punishes. The latter should shed the blood of the wrongdoer to give him his just deserts. The appeal to the image of God at the end of 9:6 actually reinforces this focus. As argued in Chapter 2, the appeal to the image likely serves primarily to explain why human beings (and not God alone) have authority to administer just punishment (i.e., human beings can justly punish one another because they image a God who brings just punishment). In short, the *lex talionis* seeks to ensure that wrongdoers receive a proportionate harm as recompense for their deeds, by someone properly authorized to deal it out. I take it that this expression of "rectifying justice" presumes the reality of "primary justice" — in this case, the obligation of each person not to inflict harm on others and a corresponding right not to be harmed[17] — though the focus of Genesis 9:6 is the former.

Retribution receives bad press from many quarters, for various reasons

---

16. William Ian Miller, *Eye for an Eye* (Cambridge: Cambridge University Press, 2006), p. 30.

17. I borrow the language here of Nicholas Wolterstorff, *Justice: Rights and Wrongs* (Princeton: Princeton University Press, 2008), and concur with his basic claim that rectifying justice requires primary justice. Primary justice refers to the positive obligations and corresponding rights that people have with respect to each other, while rectifying justice refers to the equitable response to violations of primary justice, which entails inflicting a proportionate harm on wrongdoers and/or seeking to restore victims to their original position.

that often have initial plausibility. I discuss below why I do not believe retribution is the only purpose of criminal punishment — or even the only principle embedded in the *lex talionis* — but first a brief word in defense of retributive justice. In terms of the present study, the frequent biblical depictions of God's retributive justice against human beings throughout history, culminating at the final judgment,[18] calls into question any principled objection to the idea of retribution on allegedly biblical or other Christian grounds. And one of the chief points of Genesis 9:5-6 is that God commissions human beings, precisely as his image-bearers, to carry out retributive justice on his behalf. Intrahuman retributive justice, I suggest, is an expression of human dignity, both for the victim and the wrongdoer. In terms of wrongdoers, retributive justice deals with them as image-bearers of God who have a grand calling from God, unique among created beings, to exercise just and benevolent dominion in this world, but who instead have failed in this calling and inflicted unjust harm upon fellow image-bearers. This is not simply misguided or inefficient, but *wrong* and *sinful*. Therefore they *deserve* a just recompense. Created beings of lesser dignity can in some cases be deterred from future undesirable behavior through punishment, but only a divine image-bearer can receive retributive justice. In terms of the victim, retributive justice provides an appropriate expression of a righteous desire for vengeance, and hence is attentive to the violation of dignity victims suffer. Most people desire vengeance when wronged, and a number of scholars from various philosophical perspectives have defended the righteousness of vengeance under proper bounds.[19] The anthropology presumed in Genesis 9:6 offers perhaps the best defense: I am a human being created in the image of God, and to harm me is objectively wrong, not just subjectively inconvenient to me. To desire disproportionate vengeance against a wrongdoer is selfish and unrighteous, but historically the *lex talionis* served precisely to prevent disproportionate vengeance. By providing a lawful and measured outlet for the desire for vengeance, the *lex talionis* is actually more sensitive to the victim's harm and what it will take to

---

18. Regarding the destruction of "Babylon" on the last day, Revelation 18:6-7a states: "Pay her back as she herself has paid back others, and repay her double for her deeds; mix a double portion for her in the cup she mixed. As she glorified herself and lived in luxury, so give her a like measure of torment and mourning." See also 2 Peter 2:13; Revelation 11:18; 16:6.

19. Among significant studies, see Miller, *Eye for an Eye;* Jeffrie G. Murphy, *Getting Even: Forgiveness and Its Limits* (Oxford: Oxford University Press, 2003); Peter A. French, *The Virtues of Vengeance* (Lawrence: University Press of Kansas, 2001); and Susan Jacoby, *Wild Justice: The Evolution of Revenge* (New York: Harper & Row, 1983).

restore her and to break down lingering ill-will than are visions of justice that treat vengeance as too depraved to be honored.

Third, the natural law principle of *lex talionis* also points toward the restoration of victims. Advocates of the restorative justice movement have often contrasted restoration and retribution as opposite goals in the context of criminal justice, but others have embraced a more helpfully balanced view that attention to the latter need not, and should not, eliminate the former.[20] The claim that the *lex talionis* can account for the restoration of victims, and even the healing of fractured relationships, is perhaps surprising. Certainly the *lex talionis* cannot provide the holistic restoration that the eschatological ethic can provide through its embrace of forgiveness, rooted in Christ's atonement (see Chapter 9). But a few considerations justify the claim that the *lex talionis* can promote a meaningful restoration among victims, wrongdoers, and their communities. For one thing, as just discussed, by providing an outlet for properly bounded vengeance the *lex talionis* accounts for and deals with this aspect of the harm victims experience, rather than suppressing it, and thus ought to hasten victims' healing. Second, the *lex talionis* shows concern for the restoration of victims through its ability to provide for material compensation. Concern for victims requires not simply providing an outlet for vengeance but also compensating them for pain, medical bills, lost wages, or the like. Whatever satisfaction there may be for one who has lost his arm because of another's cruelty to see that person lose her arm, he may no longer be able to practice his profession and thus be unable to feed his family. Historical evidence indicates that societies in which the *lex talionis* was judicially prominent regularly enforced it through monetary compensation rather than hacking off body parts. In such cases the threat of literal enforcement hanging in the background could effectively help to establish the monetary value of a particular harm. How many dollars is an eye worth? If we know how many dollars an assailant is willing to pay to keep her eye, and how many dollars a victim is willing to accept to forgo the right to take his assailant's eye, we can probably determine a pretty good answer to that question.[21] Finally, it is worth noting that the Mosaic law at times utilizes the *lex talionis* formula precisely in order to regulate compensation for victims. For example, Leviticus 24:18 states: "Whoever takes an animal's life shall make it good, life for life." Jon-

20. E.g., see Christopher D. Marshall, *Beyond Retribution: A New Testament Vision for Justice, Crime, and Punishment* (Grand Rapids: Eerdmans, 2001); and Jonathan Burnside, "Retribution and Restoration in Biblical Texts," in *Handbook of Restorative Justice*, ed. Gerry Johnstone and Daniel W. Van Ness (Cullompton, UK: Willan, 2007), pp. 132-48.

21. See Miller, *Eye for an Eye*, chap. 4.

athan Burnside notes that the word "for" (תחת) can mean "in the place of," suggesting that this regulation requires the wrongdoer (the animal slayer) to compensate the victim (the owner of the slain animal) by replacing the dead beast with a living one.[22]

Finally, the natural law principle of *lex talionis,* when considered *in the context of the Noahic covenant* (which I have argued it should be!), ought to be tempered by forbearance in human legal systems. There is no place for true forgiveness to mitigate the strict principle of talionic justice, because legal systems exist under the auspices of the Noahic covenant, and this covenant makes no provision for the atonement of sins.[23] But the Noahic covenant exhibits God's common grace, whereby he temporarily postpones the final judgment. While God withholds the full manifestation of strict and merciless retributive justice, so also must his human image-bearers. Not every single wrong in this world can be justly punished, and not every wrong should be. Forbearance is a noble virtue in the administration of justice in the present world. This is further evidence that civil law must be, to an important extent, imprecise, prudential, flexible, and approximate. There is no calculus for determining when and how forbearance ought to stay the hand of justice. Legislators and judges must exercise wise judgment to define and interpret the law in ways that respect the ever-shifting peculiarities of societies and the people within them. The natural law ideal of justice that is proportionate, retributive, restorative, and forbearing can only be implemented imperfectly. People must leave room for the law, as the saying goes, to work itself pure. In the present world we must usually be content with incremental improvements and finding ever better approximations of the ideal. The state of justice perfectly satisfied is found only in the full manifestation of the eschatological kingdom.

Religious Freedom (with Modest Appreciation for the Liberal and the Secular)

The final matter for reflection is religious liberty. Often regarded as one of the great, though hard-won, achievements of Western civilization, which Western nations have in turn sought to import throughout the world, it remains a

---

22. Burnside, "Retribution and Restoration," p. 139.

23. See Chapter 9 for discussion of how Christ's redemptive work provides such atonement and thus provides forgiveness without neglecting the claims of justice, a benefit enjoyed through the covenants of grace. For a different account of mercy in human legal systems, see Oliver O'Donovan, *The Ways of Judgment* (Grand Rapids: Eerdmans, 2005), chap. 6.

fragile and controversial ideal. What exactly religious freedom really is, and whether it is desirable or even possible, are not settled questions, either in Western nations or elsewhere in the world. In several places in this book I have suggested that my biblical theology of natural law implies the propriety of recognizing a right to religious freedom. In this final section I return to this subject and argue more thoroughly (though still briefly) why I believe there is a natural law right to religious freedom, yet only a penultimate right to such. This in turn encourages a modest appreciation for the "liberal" and the "secular," even while opposing much that liberal*ism* and secular*ism* often represent.

Before defending a penultimate right to religious liberty under the natural law, I think it important to note that there is no *ultimate* natural law right to religious liberty. This is evident in Paul's discussion of natural revelation in Romans 1:21-23, immediately after his claim that God holds all people inexcusable before him: "For although they knew God, they did not honor him as God or give thanks to him, but they became futile in their thinking, and their foolish hearts were darkened. Claiming to be wise, they became fools, and exchanged the glory of the immortal God for images resembling mortal man and birds and animals and creeping things." These verses indicate that human beings have *no ultimate* natural law right to religious freedom *before God*. No human being can stand before God and claim the right to be religious or commune with the divine in whatever way she chooses. Rather, natural law requires each person to worship *the one true God* — the creator of heaven and earth — and to worship him properly. While natural law may not provide a great deal of information on what that proper worship consists of, natural law at least communicates the foolishness of idolatry. What is more, Paul's larger point, both in Romans 1:18-32 and especially as he brings this larger section of Romans to a conclusion in 3:9-20, is that natural law (as well as the law of Moses) exposes the dire sinfulness of every person, such that no one by his own efforts can meet the standard of God's judgment. According to Paul, only through the redemptive work of Jesus Christ and faith in him can anybody be justified before God (3:21–5:21), and such faith comes through the hearing of God's word preached (10:9-17). As an ultimate matter, natural law does not leave people claiming rights of religious freedom before God, but brings them face-to-face with their responsibilities to serve the one true God aright and with their failure in this regard (apart from Christ).

These considerations encourage critical evaluation of the way natural law is sometimes invoked in defense of religious freedom. For example, though Robert George advocates certain notions of human dignity that I also affirm, Romans 1 calls other aspects of his natural law conception of religious freedom into question. After making a case for religious freedom in terms of "practical reason," George, now speaking specifically as a Roman Catholic, appeals to the idea "that there is much that is good and worthy . . . in non-Christian faiths" and that religion generally "enriches, ennobles, and fulfils the human person in the spiritual dimension of his being." This leads to "a rational affirmation of the value of religion as embodied and made available to people in and through many traditions of faith." Similarly, he states later that the right to religious freedom permits people of many faiths to "engage in the sincere religious quest and live lives of authenticity reflecting their best judgments as to the truth of spiritual matters."[24]

George's conclusions are consistent with the documents of the Second Vatican Council he cites in support, as these reflect the evolving teaching of Rome on matters of religious freedom and the spiritual status of non-Christians.[25] But these conclusions sit awkwardly next to Paul's discussion of natural law and the human condition in Romans 1 and the rest of that epistle. According to Paul, all people's natural condition is not one of seeking religious and spiritual truth with sincerity, honesty, and integrity, but of suppressing the truth about God manifest in natural revelation. Rather than non-Christian religion enriching and ennobling people, Paul describes it as degrading people made to know and serve the one true God. Natural law, in Romans, does not lead humanity down the road to spiritual enlightenment and nobility, but makes its condemnation before God more plain. The only solution to the human plight Paul offers is one not known through the light of nature: the death and resurrection of Jesus and faith in him through the preaching of the gospel. There may well be a certain earthly profit that people gain through participation in other religions, due to God's common grace, but according to Scripture they do not bring true spiritual enlightenment before God.

In light of this I conclude that human beings do not have an *ultimate* natural law right to religious freedom *before God*. God holds all people accountable for serving him properly, and by the light of nature alone all people know who God is but respond to him sinfully, a condition rectified only through Christian faith. This conclusion makes problematic natural law arguments

24. Robert P. George, "Religious Liberty and the Human Good," *International Journal of Religious Freedom* 5, no. 1 (2012): 35-44.

25. The Vatican II documents he cites are *Dignitatis Humanae* and *Nostra Aetate*. For the background of these documents, see John O'Malley, *What Happened at Vatican II* (Cambridge, MA: Belknap, 2010). For my own interpretation of how Roman Catholic doctrine on the spiritual status of non-Christians has changed over the centuries, see David VanDrunen, "Inclusive Salvation in Contemporary Roman Catholicism," *New Horizons* (October 2011): 6-8.

for religious freedom (such as George's) based upon the spiritual profit that humanity generally gains through sincerely seeking God by the light of nature in a host of different religions.

Nevertheless, Romans 1 also makes evident that one of the chief sins of people under natural law is a failure to treat their fellow human beings with proper respect. Paul mentions murder, for example, as evidence of how people violate God's natural law (Rom. 1:29). In other words, one of the things required by natural law is treating fellow human beings with the dignity they deserve. This raises the question whether this mutual respect human beings owe to one another includes respect for freedom of religion. I believe the answer is yes, and this points the way to a different, but better, argument for a natural law right to religious liberty. My conclusion, derived from the Noahic covenant, is that there is a *penultimate* natural law right to religious freedom *before fellow human beings,* and this right is granted by God.

As argued in Chapter 2, the postdiluvian Noahic covenant is universal, established with the human race as a whole. No religious qualification is necessary for participation. Through it God requires all human beings to pursue their natural obligations, regardless of religious profession or membership in a particular community of faith. The Noahic covenant thereby creates common space for the cultural interaction of all people, though this cultural space is nevertheless not morally neutral space.[26]

The implication for the question of religious freedom is simple, but deeply significant. The simple implication is this: if God has called the entire human race (regardless of religious identification) to participate in the cultural life of society while he preserves this present world, then no human being has the authority to exclude other human beings from full participation because of their religious profession or practice. The covenant with Noah is a common grace *blessing of God* (Gen. 9:1). Therefore the minimalist natural law ethic concerning procreation, eating, and justice (9:1-7) does not merely involve obligations but also a privilege that God grants to all people to be active members of civil society — and this despite the ongoing blight of human sin (8:21) and the specter of a final judgment in the distant future. Since God blesses people with these privileges without respect to religious profession, if a human being

26. I believe, therefore, that the Noahic covenant provides an excellent foundation for explaining the possibility of having "neither a naked nor a sacred public square, but a civil public square open to the full range of convictions" (Evangelicals and Catholic Together, "In Defense of Religious Freedom," in *First Things* [March 2012]: 32), and for avoiding "the extremes of imperialism on the one hand and obsequiousness on the other" (David Novak, *In Defense of Religious Liberty* [Wilmington, DE: ISI Books, 2009], p. x; cf. p. 106).

strips another human being of these privileges because of religious profession, he defies the post-fall natural order established by God. (Whether one can strip another of these privileges because of some other reason is a different question, addressed below.)

Here, then, is one reason from Genesis 9 to recognize a natural law right to religious freedom. As part of the natural order sustained in the covenant with Noah, God has granted to each human being in the present age the common blessing of participating in the life of human society, without religious qualification, and thus each person may claim, against any fellow human beings who would seek to add such a qualification, the unhindered right to this participation.

A reader might lodge the following objection to my argument in the previous paragraphs: Yes, the Noahic covenant indicates that all human beings, whatever their religion, have the right not to be obstructed in their participation in activities such as procreation, eating, and administration of justice, but this does not necessarily mean that no one may obstruct them from performing certain acts of religious devotion. In other words, even if the Noahic covenant grants universal natural rights to engage in general human endeavors whatever one's religious profession, does it leave open the possibility that society might justly suppress the worship and teaching of certain religions? I believe the answer is negative. In the Noahic covenant God grants one kind of religious freedom as well as the other.

To defend this claim I turn again to Genesis 9:6: "Whoever sheds the blood of man, by man shall his blood be shed, for God made man in his image." Of the many significant things about this verse, perhaps most profound is the fact that God, the supreme governor and judge of the world, has delegated aspects of the administration of justice to human beings. In the previous verse (9:5), God states that *he himself* will "require a reckoning for the life of man," but then in 9:6 states that he who sheds the blood of a man will receive retribution "by man." As also argued in Chapter 2, this delegation is really not surprising, since the very nature of image-bearing entails the commission to rule the world under God's supreme authority. Though dispensing retributive justice against fellow humans would have been unnecessary in an unfallen world, in a fallen world imposing just punishment upon wrongdoers becomes a necessary aspect of human rule. To rule a sinful world means, in part, ensuring that those who injure another human person receive appropriate and proportionate retribution.

What God delegates to human beings here is the administration of *intrahuman* justice. To put it another way, God ordains that human beings should impose punishments for injuries inflicted *upon each other*. God does not delegate authority to impose just punishment upon wrongs that a human being commits *against God himself*. From one perspective, of course, any injury inflicted upon a human being is a wrong against the God whose image that person bears, so I will modify my claim in this way: God delegates to human beings the authority to impose punishments for wrongs insofar as they are injuries inflicted upon each other, but not for wrongs insofar as they are inflicted upon God.

Thus to return to the question at hand: Does the Noahic covenant shed any light on whether human society might prohibit or penalize the worship or instruction of a particular religion? Yes, and it indicates that human beings do not have such authority. According to the Noahic covenant, human beings have the authority to use force against one another in order to impose proportionate penalties for intrahuman wrongs. For intrahuman crimes such as murder or theft, there are concrete and definable injuries, and just legislators and judges can design penalties that match their severity. But acts of improper religious worship are offenses against God. In such cases human beings are inherently incapable of imposing a proportionate penalty. What sort of human punishment is proportionate to a wrong done against an infinite and eternal God? Even if one were to claim that a teacher of a false religion is corrupting the religious sensibilities of the youth, for example, and thus is guilty of an intrahuman injury, it is difficult to perceive how any human court could objectively determine the character and extent of this injury so as to impose a proportionate penalty.

This distinction between an ultimate and penultimate natural law right to religious freedom has the additional benefit of helping to explain why there was no protected right to religious freedom *in Old Testament Israel under the Mosaic law*. If there is no ultimate right to religious freedom, then God was free, for his own purposes at a particular point in history, to call accounts for idolatry early, as it were, requiring human law to punish this natural law violation during this historical time and place rather than merely waiting for the final judgment. If the right to religious freedom is in some way absolute, then God's requirements under the Mosaic law — let alone the final judgment — become deeply problematic.

These conclusions about religious liberty concur with the broad argument in previous chapters about natural law under the Noahic covenant. The natural law does communicate that the worship of false gods is wrong, but the minimalist natural law ethic, made explicit in Genesis 9:1-7, concerns intrahuman relations that represent basic requirements for the preservation of human society. Procreation, eating, and the administration of civil justice are necessary for human society to survive in this world; worshiping the true God in the right way is not. Thus, given his purposes in the Noahic covenant, God's temporal judgments against particular communities in the course of history transpire because of flagrant disregard for the minimalist natural law ethic, not for sins of religious profession or worship. Even so, in his inscrutable providence God does hand over idolaters to a variety of other sins (Rom. 1:24, 26, 28) — but without requiring human beings to bring civil penalties against each other for sins of religious creed or practice.

Because of these conclusions about religious freedom, I suggested in the Introduction that my biblical theology of natural law, though essentially a premodern natural law theory in most respects, also has modern features that are sympathetic to some of the broad goals of the Enlightenment. These conclusions also suggest a modest appreciation for the "liberal" and the "secular," understood in a certain way, even while the biblical theology of natural law defended in these pages is sharply at odds with much that passes for liberal*ism* and secular*ism*.

The notion that my biblical theology of natural law suggests a positive view of "liberalism" requires clarification of how I use the term. I use it here not in the colloquial sense denoting leftist political views but, generally, in the classical sense. More specifically, I reflect here not upon certain ideas often associated with classical liberalism, such as a free-market economy or representative democracy, but upon the basic liberal idea that the multitudes should be brought together in a common social life despite their not sharing a common religious or metaphysical commitment. Is this an attractive or even a viable idea? My biblical theology of natural law suggests that this liberal idea is both attractive and viable, but only so long as it is a *pragmatic* liberalism rather than an *ideological* liberalism; or, a *penultimate* liberalism rather than an *ultimate* liberalism.[27]

One of the great dangers of the liberal tradition is its tendency to wed its embrace of a social order not united by a common religious or metaphysical creed to the idea that moral and political issues ought to be religiously and metaphysically neutral or even that there is no real religious or metaphysical truth at all. Accordingly, religious convictions may be tolerated as a private matter but political discourse can and ought to be conducted independently of such convictions. There is a basic (and ironic) problem with such a perspec-

---

27. For a similar suggestion, see Glenn A. Moots, *Politics Reformed: The Anglo-American Legacy of Covenant Theology* (Columbia: University of Missouri Press, 2010), chap. 12.

tive: the belief that religious conviction should be only a private matter that does not encumber one's social life is itself a kind of religious or metaphysical conviction that entails the rejection of key aspects of the teaching of so many of the world's major religions. Such a "liberalism" is thus illiberal at its core. This is what I mean by an ideological or ultimate liberalism. It expands the practical desire for people to get along in civil society despite religious differences into a metaphysical conviction that religion ought to be politically and legally irrelevant. Such a liberalism is contradictory to the biblical theology of natural law developed in this book, because the latter holds that the social order owes its very existence to a divine covenant with the human race and that God is its ongoing governor. Such a liberalism is not even viable because in the name of religious neutrality it is fundamentally biased against Christianity and many other religions.

Yet my biblical theology of natural law is harmonious with what I called a pragmatic or penultimate liberalism. From the perspective of the Noahic covenant the alternative to the failures of ideological liberalism need not be pining for the bygone days of Christendom. A theology of natural law grounded in the Noahic covenant must reject a religiously skeptical metaphysic but upholds the *practical* goal of a social order in which people of many religious convictions participate in a common cultural life. Such a social order should be attractive because God has ordained it, though it must not become attractive as an end in itself, given the temporary and provisional character of the Noahic covenant. Such a social order is also possible — as fragile and tenuous as the fabric of a religiously diverse society inevitably is — because God himself has promised to maintain order and regularity (to *some* degree) in the world.

Distinguishing between ultimate and penultimate perspectives on liberalism provides reason both to appreciate and finally to dissent from some popular theological responses to liberalism. A number of prominent contemporary theologians, including Stanley Hauerwas, John Milbank, and Oliver O'Donovan, have prosecuted serious critiques of modern liberal society, calling attention variously to its moral fragmentation, internalization of morality, exaltation of autonomous reason, and loss of ability to resolve disputes through the pursuit of truth and persuasion.[28] All of them, in distinctive ways, promote

28. See generally Hauerwas, *The Peaceable Kingdom*; and John Milbank, *Theology and Social Theory: Beyond Secular Reason* (Oxford: Blackwell, 1990). O'Donovan's critique of liberalism is more tempered than that of Hauerwas and Milbank. See e.g. Oliver O'Donovan, *The Desire of the Nations: Rediscovering the Roots of Political Theology* (Cambridge: Cambridge University Press, 1996), pp. 8-9, 221-22, 227-31, 252-71. Around the time I was writing this, Patrick J. Deneen issued a similar sort of grand critique of liberalism; see "Unsustainable

an alternative kind of social order that manifests the eschatological kingdom of Christ here and now and that recovers or reinvents some form of Christendom.[29] Their identification of the problems of modern liberal society, and of the dangers to virtuous Christian life in such a context, are in many respects accurate and penetrating. Each of these theologians, however, critiques liberalism as a worldview or all-encompassing vision, analyzing it from an *ultimate* perspective, from the standpoint of the eschatological reign of God in Christ. From this perspective a liberal society indeed falls far short. But so inevitably must *any* social system of this present age, since God upholds the social order through the Noahic covenant, not for its perfection but for its preservation. If, alternatively, a person evaluates liberal society from a *penultimate* perspective, as a social system for a fallen world, whose goal can be no more than preserving human society and providing a context for limited human flourishing, one's conclusions might look rather different. A Christian may concur about the serious flaws inherent to any liberal society and oppose any pretentious attempt to turn liberalism into a worldview, while still judging that a liberal society is better than any other option yet attempted or possible to achieve at present. This is a matter of prudential judgment, but I am inclined to agree with the opinion, for example, that modern capitalism (the economic system generally associated with classical liberalism), while by no means bringing utopia, is "pretty good," and definitely worth keeping in light of the other options heretofore attempted or proposed in human history.[30] In any area of

---

Liberalism," *First Things* (Aug./Sept. 2012): 25-31. In response to Deneen, Daniel J. Mahoney defends a more modest — i.e., penultimate — kind of liberalism that seems similar to what I defend here; see "The Art of Liberty," *First Things* (Aug./Sept. 2012): 33-35.

29. The Christendom theme is clear in Milbank, nuanced yet explicit in O'Donovan, and surprisingly present even in Hauerwas, a severe critic of the Christendom that actually existed for more than a millennium of Western history. For O'Donovan, Christendom, "the idea of a confessionally Christian government," is not a project of, but a response to, the church's mission. It is not a seizing of power by the church but the alien power becoming attentive to the church. He argues that the Christian state need not be coercive and should not try to protect itself against constitutional reform; rather, the Christian state may be disclosed from time to time, in anticipation of the eschatological age, but Christians may not expect that it will have the permanence of Byzantium here and now. See *Desire of the Nations,* pp. 195, 224. Hauerwas explains that his critiques of Christendom have specifically targeted its Constantinian version, and that he does uphold a vision of Christendom in seeking a society fully integrated under Christ's lordship. See Stanley Hauerwas, *A Better Hope: Resources for a Church Confronting Capitalism, Democracy, and Postmodernity* (Grand Rapids: Brazos, 2000), p. 44.

30. See Deidre N. McCloskey, *Bourgeois Dignity: Why Economics Can't Explain the Modern World* (Chicago: University of Chicago Press, 2010), p. xii. McCloskey appeals here to John Mueller, *Capitalism, Democracy, and Ralph's Pretty Good Grocery* (Princeton: Princeton

social life under the Noahic covenant, "pretty good" is, in the words of golf analyst Gary Koch, "better than most."[31]

Similar conclusions are appropriate with respect to secularity. The term "secular" has nefarious connotations among many Christians, and some Christian intellectuals have warned us about dividing life into "sacred" and the "secular" spheres.[32] Such a mindset is understandable and emerges out of legitimate theological concerns. Nevertheless, I believe this mindset is also problematic and strips Christianity of a profoundly important concept for understanding the world. My biblical theology of natural law unequivocally re-

---

University Press, 1999). McCloskey says of capitalism (or her preferred term, "innovation"): "Not perfect, not a utopia, but probably worth keeping in view of the worse alternatives so easily fallen into. Innovation backed by liberal economic ideas has made billions of poor people pretty well off, without hurting other people." I recognize that some of my interlocutors would disagree strongly with the last four words of this quotation (e.g., see Hauerwas, *A Better Hope*, pp. 50-51), but those who are truly concerned about the poor must surely be impressed by an economic system able to lift *billions* out of poverty.

31. I also suggest another way to look at this issue if we consider (classical) liberalism generally, and not simply in terms of religious liberty. We may ask how the human race has done, in the liberal age, with the minimalist natural law ethic identified in this book. With respect to being fruitful and filling the earth, it has done very well in the liberal age, with human population booming over the past couple of centuries. This has not been because of increasing fertility in liberal societies — indeed, fertility rates have tended to decrease in such societies — but because of the unprecedented improvements in agriculture and medical technology that have drastically lowered child-mortality rates and drastically increased life-expectancy, thanks to the innovations fueling the free-market economic system of classical liberalism. These comments already touch upon the second element of the minimalist natural law ethic: eating well. That the human race under liberalism has done a stellar job here hardly needs argument. Unlike for so many people in previous ages of human history (and still today where liberalism has not reached), no one has to starve in liberal societies. In fact, a humble grocery store in any contemporary liberal society would have utterly astounded even the rich in preliberal ages. The third aspect of the minimalist natural law ethic is retributive justice. The rule of law has been a hallmark (or at least a professed ideal) of liberal societies, so liberalism seems to be on the right track here as well. It is not as though preliberal Western societies did not practice retributive justice, but modern forensics techniques (again, an indirect product of the technological innovations of the free market) increase the likelihood of determining guilt and innocence with accuracy. What is more, liberal societies have also tended to enhance the social standing of women and various minority groups (religious, ethnic, racial), and all of them are generally more likely to receive just treatment in courts now than they were in preliberal ages. That liberal societies seem to have done better with the minimalist natural law ethic — the ethic of the Noahic covenant — than preliberal Christendom societies did, in these important ways, is surely a point in their favor.

32. For one example, see Albert M. Wolters, *Creation Regained: Biblical Basics for a Reformational Worldview* (Grand Rapids: Eerdmans, 1985), pp. 10-11, 53-58, 65, 74.

jects any *ideological* secularity (or "secularism") but may support a *penultimate* secularity, or what David Novak calls "finite secularity."[33] By an ideological secularism I mean the conviction that there is nothing sacred; all of reality must be viewed apart from the existence of God and theological truth (or at least *public* reality, since people may still be permitted to believe in God privately). Alternatively, penultimate or pragmatic secularity refers to the existence of social space that is not holy or religiously particularistic, but does not deny that holy things exist or that God himself rules this secular social space.[34] Why should "secular" not be able to refer to the *saeculum,* that is, to this present age — in Christian terms, to this age preceding the second coming of Christ? "Secular" need not mean "godless," but may simply refer to the common social space that is distinct from the holy social space that Christ has formed in his church; it may refer to the life of this present age that is distinct from the life of the age to come in the new creation.[35]

That my biblical theology of natural law must reject ideological secularism needs no explanation. But it also suggests that a penultimate or finite secularity is an eminently useful and even necessary idea. What has the Noahic covenant done if not create common social space in which God commissions the human race at large to procreation, eating, enforcing justice, and other responsibilities under the natural moral order? This covenant governs an age that is temporary and passing, in force only so long as "the earth remains" (Gen. 8:22). It must be distinguished from the eschatological heavenly kingdom, which is a "holy city" (Rev. 21:2) and is inchoately manifest today in the church as a "holy nation" (1 Pet. 2:9). The idea of a penultimate or finite secularity should be of great value to Christians. A holy (nonsecular) social order could only be attractive to Christians if they themselves are in charge. But since the NT calls Christians "sojourners and exiles" in the world (1 Pet. 2:11), rather

33. David Novak, *The Jewish Social Contract* (Princeton: Princeton University Press, 2005), p. 5; see also pp. 121-22, 203. See also the similar idea in Zimmerman, *Humanism and Religion,* pp. 20-22.

34. I am speaking here of two kinds of *theories* of what a desirable "secularity" might be. This is clearly a different issue from identifying what concretely characterizes the "secular age" in which nearly everyone agrees Western people now live. Charles Taylor considers the latter issue, identifying two plausible candidates and then choosing a third, which is closely related to the other two: "The change I want to define and trace is one which takes us from a society in which it was virtually impossible not to believe in God, to one in which faith, even for the staunchest believer, is one human possibility among others." See *A Secular Age,* pp. 1-3.

35. For a thoughtful consideration of such questions, with many concerns similar to mine, see Robert A. Markus, *Christianity and the Secular* (Notre Dame: University of Notre Dame Press, 2006).

than its rulers, they do not have the privilege of defining what the holiness of society would look like. A nonideological secularity, therefore, serves for Christians' protection. Holiness is an all-encompassing concept. Much better for Christians to live in a social order marked by a penultimate secularity, in which space is reserved for them to exist as the church and to profess their ultimate convictions, than to live in a social order that claims all-encompassing authority over its participants, as many Christians in the Middle East would probably attest when faced with "Islamist" or "secularist" alternatives.

Natural Law in Contemporary Literature

In the Introduction I interacted with several Protestant and Roman Catholic scholars — and one Jewish scholar — who have developed constructive theories of natural law in recent years and whose work constitutes an important part of the contemporary context for my own work. In this appendix I provide additional background concerning the perspectives and arguments of these projects, though I do not engage them critically here. The four Roman Catholic works are Robert George's *In Defense of Natural Law*, Russell Hittinger's *The First Grace: Rediscovering the Natural Law in a Post-Christian World*, Matthew Levering's *Biblical Natural Law*, and Jean Porter's *Nature as Reason: A Thomistic Theory of Natural Law*. The three Protestant works are Craig A. Boyd's *A Shared Morality: A Narrative Defense of Natural Law*, J. Daryl Charles's *Retrieving the Natural Law: A Return to Moral First Things*, and Alister McGrath's *The Open Secret: A New Vision for Natural Theology*.[1] The Jewish natural law proposal is the one set forth in David Novak's *Natural Law in Judaism*.

I begin with the Roman Catholic works. Many Protestants are not familiar with contemporary Roman Catholic natural law literature and instinctively impute to Roman Catholic natural law theory the assumptions of human autonomy characterizing other natural law theories (often imprecisely associated with the Enlightenment), for some understandable historical reasons. They may be surprised, therefore, at the degree to which many recent Roman Catholic writers reject such assumptions and seek to develop

---

1. Two other Protestant volumes worth mentioning, though difficult to summarize since they are multi-author works, are *Natural Law: A Lutheran Reappraisal*, ed. Robert C. Baker and Roland Cap Ehlke (St. Louis: Concordia, 2011); and *Natural Law and Evangelical Political Theory*, ed. Jesse Covington, Bryan McGraw, and Micah Watson (Lanham, MD: Lexington, 2012).

theological, tradition-dependent, and even biblical accounts of natural law. Hittinger, Levering, and Porter all fall into this category. The natural law theory that George has rigorously defended is a useful place to begin, however, since he pursues a theoretical course clearly distinct from these other three and which they reject.

In his *Defense of Natural Law,*[2] George defends the so-called "new natural law theory" pioneered by Germain Grisez and John Finnis.[3] This theory roots natural law in the practical reason and not in any anthropological, theological, or metaphysical account of reality. As George explains, the human person apprehends the first principles of practical reason as self-evident and underived from other premises. Sensitive to the charge often made against neo-scholastic Roman Catholic natural law theories that one cannot validly derive what ought to be done from what is (the naturalistic fallacy), George asserts that the human intellect grasps these first principles of morality without deducing them from a theology or philosophy of nature. The practical intellect understands that certain goods are intrinsically valuable. In distinction from instrumental goods that require justification in order to be rationally comprehensible, intrinsically valuable goods are rationally comprehensible on their own terms and for their own sake. As an illustration, George speaks of money as an instrumental good that makes sense as a good worthy of pursuit only insofar as it is a means to something else, such as prestige or financial security. On the other hand, he asserts that health is an intrinsically valuable good that needs no further justification to be appreciated as a good worthy of pursuit. In his well-known account of the new natural law theory, Finnis identifies seven intrinsically valuable goods: life, knowledge, play, aesthetic experience, sociability (friendship), practical reasonableness, and religion.[4] These goods are incommensurable. That is, they cannot be placed in a hierarchical relationship to one another but are equally pursued for their own sakes.

This account of the first practical principles of natural law becomes a full-fledged moral theory through the idea that all people ought to pursue these goods in a way that is compatible with attaining integral human fulfillment. This does not mean that any moral choice can seek all the intrinsically valuable goods simultaneously or realize integral human fulfillment, for this

2. Robert P. George, *In Defense of Natural Law* (Oxford: Clarendon, 1999). On the material summarized in the following two paragraphs, see especially chapter 2 of this work.

3. E.g., see John Finnis, *Natural Law and Natural Rights* (Oxford: Clarendon, 1980); and Germain Grisez, *The Way of the Lord Jesus 1: Christian Moral Principles* (Chicago: Franciscan Herald Press, 1983).

4. Finnis, *Natural Law and Natural Rights,* chap. 4.

is impossible. But no moral act should choose against the fulfillment of any of the basic goods, and any act that does is inherently immoral.

A distinctive feature of this theory, as mentioned above, is its attempt to ground natural law purely in practical reason without recourse to a philosophy of nature from which it is derived. Another significant feature, at least as expounded by George, is the legitimacy and defensibility of the theory independent of the existence of God. Though practitioners of the new natural law theory have generally employed it in defense of traditional Roman Catholic moral teaching, George explains that the speculative judgment about whether God exists will affect how one pursues the good of religion, but "nothing in these judgments need alter one's grasp of foundational practical and moral principles, nor one's basic understanding of how to employ these principles in one's practical thinking."[5] This description of natural law suggests that the new natural law theory, despite claims of its Thomistic provenance,[6] is better categorized as an example of a post-Enlightenment theory that attempts to ground natural law in autonomous practical reason.[7]

Many of George's fellow Roman Catholic natural lawyers evaluate his work similarly.[8] In contrast to the new natural law theory, writers such as

---

5. George, *In Defense of Natural Law,* p. 72.

6. E.g., see George, *In Defense of Natural Law,* pp. 36-42; and especially John Finnis, *Aquinas: Moral, Political, and Legal Theory* (Oxford: Oxford University Press, 1998).

7. George's discussion in chapter 3 of *In Defense of Natural Law* prompts the need to nuance some of these claims about the new natural law theory and its relation to other recent Roman Catholic theories described below. In this chapter George continues to assert that ethics is not to be derived from metaphysics, which commits the naturalistic fallacy of inferring moral norms from facts about human nature. But he affirms strongly that basic moral norms are in some sense grounded in human nature. Knowledge of the self-evident basic moral principles, though underived, is itself knowledge of human well-being and fulfillment. Thus human nature understood as a moral matter, but not understood as a metaphysical matter, is closely connected to the practical reason's self-evident knowledge of the basic goods. As evident below, the difference between George and a critic such as Porter lies in Porter's conviction that a proper understanding of human flourishing entails an interconnected knowledge of biology and morality, human nature being both pre-rational and rational.

8. Russell Hittinger offered an early and penetrating critique of the Grisez-Finnis view in his *A Critique of the New Natural Law Theory* (Notre Dame: University of Notre Dame Press, 1987). George presents a detailed response to this book in *In Defense of Natural Law,* pp. 59-75. Another Roman Catholic critique of the new natural law theory appears in Jean Porter, *Nature as Reason: A Thomistic Theory of the Natural Law* (Grand Rapids: Eerdmans, 2005), pp. 37-40, 127-31. Porter sees the new natural law theory as an example of a modern (as opposed to medieval scholastic) version of natural law that tries to appeal to all people of good will and works with natural law in terms of rationality but not in terms of pre-rational nature. The new

Porter, Hittinger, and Levering expound accounts of natural law that seek to be theological, biblical, and grounded in the Roman Catholic tradition. Porter's book is the most theoretically ambitious. She sets out to develop a contemporary version of the Thomistic and medieval scholastic view of natural law, which she identifies as rooted in Scripture and grounded in a theological context that makes it meaningful.[9] Her theory affirms not only the centrality of reason for moral reflection but also the moral significance of pre-rational human nature. Thus she begins by developing an account of pre-rational human nature through a detailed study of evolutionary biology, turns to the virtues to specify what it means for such a human being to flourish and thus what the moral content of human flourishing is, and then discusses the importance of reason and a proper understanding of the precepts of natural law. In the big picture, Porter emphasizes that her theory not only incorporates various sorts of philosophical arguments (concerning both metaphysics and biology) but also is thoroughly theological in character. In contrast to George, therefore, she seeks to ground her natural law theory in a sophisticated philosophy of nature and a theology of creation and providence. For her, natural law is both a universal human phenomenon as well as a crucial resource for a distinctively Christian account of ethics. Whereas George presents the naturalistic fallacy as a major obstacle to be avoided, Porter rejects the strict distinction between factual and normative claims that the naturalistic fallacy, as classically articulated, presupposes. As she puts it, with reference to the work of Philippa Foot, "evaluative terms have an inextricable descriptive content, which cannot be

natural law theory, she concludes, is very modern in its attempt to specify a comprehensive system of rules from first principles. See also Matthew Levering, *Biblical Natural Law: A Theocentric and Teleological Approach* (Oxford: Oxford University Press, 2008), pp. 217-19, which critiques the new natural law theory for failing to affirm the necessity of grounding natural law in a conception of the eternal law, that is, in God's providential and teleological ordering of all things. Another recent work on natural law by a Roman Catholic philosopher offers a critique of the new natural law theory, though within the context of a reconstructed Thomistic natural law theory distinct from that of Porter, Hittinger, or Levering; see Douglas Kries, *The Problem of Natural Law* (Lanham, MD: Lexington, 2007), chap. 6.

9. Though the description of Porter's work in this paragraph is drawn from her *Nature as Reason*, important background for this work appears in a prior study of medieval scholastic natural law; see Jean Porter, *Natural and Divine Law: Reclaiming the Tradition for Christian Ethics* (Grand Rapids: Eerdmans, 1999). More recently she has reiterated and extrapolated some of her arguments in *Nature as Reason* in an important essay responding to Alasdair MacIntyre; see Jean Porter, "Does the Natural Law Provide a Universally Valid Morality?" in *Intractable Disputes about the Natural Law: Alasdair MacIntyre and Critics,* ed. Lawrence S. Cunningham (Notre Dame: University of Notre Dame Press, 2009), pp. 53-95.

separated from the attitudes they express without intolerable distortions of meaning."[10]

The recent presentations of natural law by Hittinger and Levering are not identical, but share some characteristic features that differentiate them from Porter's approach. While Porter, Hittinger, and Levering all seek to be Thomistic in their accounts, the latter two emphasize Aquinas's conception of eternal law in a way that Porter does not. For Aquinas, eternal law is associated with God's providential governing of all things and natural law is human reason's participation in the eternal law.[11] Chiefly by means of this idea Hittinger argues for a thoroughly theological account of natural law. Beginning with the Enlightenment, he claims, people began to think of the natural law in terms of the autonomous human mind, apart from the constraints of law and authority. Hittinger asserts that the proliferation of nontheological treatments of natural law among Roman Catholics is a modern aberration and that modern secular constructions of natural law are contrary to the gospel. In response to the Enlightenment's conception of natural law in terms of human autonomy, Hittinger appeals to the idea of natural law as truly *law*. Natural law puts human beings under the authority of a divine lawgiver who providentially governs all things and leaves no sphere of ethics immune from his authority.[12] Levering's account places a similar emphasis upon the grounding of natural law in eternal law and thus in God's wise teleological ordering of creation. He repudiates the anthropocentric turn in modern, post-Enlightenment natural law theories and argues instead for an "explicitly theocentric" approach to natural law.[13] One particular contribution that Levering seeks to make is developing an account of natural law through the integration of biblical teaching with Christian theological claims and the philosophical analysis of human nature. This includes a lengthy exploration, through the concept of *ecstasis,* of the relationship of natural law to humanity's return to God by grace, and thus of law to love.

These last three writers, therefore, illustrate the contemporary Roman Catholic interest in developing a theologically rich and biblically attuned concept of natural law that does not associate natural law with human autonomy. Other Roman Catholic scholars could provide further examples, such

---

10. Porter, *Nature as Reason,* p. 123; cf. 232.

11. See Thomas Aquinas, *Summa Theologiae,* 1a2ae 91, 93-94.

12. See Russell Hittinger, *The First Grace: Rediscovering the Natural Law in a Post-Christian World* (Wilmington, DE: ISI Books, 2003), especially the Introduction and chapters 1-2.

13. This quotation appears in Levering, *Biblical Natural Law,* p. 19. The rest of the description of Levering's thought in this paragraph is a summary of the book as a whole.

as J. Budziszewski and (more ambiguously) Alasdair MacIntyre.[14] Recent attempts by Protestants to develop a positive account of natural law show the same interest.

One interesting Protestant example is Boyd's account of natural law, which bears certain resemblances to Porter's. His approach is largely Thomistic, seeking to combine an understanding of human nature with the fulfillment of the natural law through the theological virtues and pursuit of goods that transcend earthly goods. One significant feature of his book, however, is his substitution of Aquinas's Aristotelian metaphysical view of human nature with a conception of human nature drawn from sociobiology and evolutionary psychology. Boyd interacts with a number of influential schools of thought that have presented challenges to natural law ethics, including postmodernism, divine command ethics, and analytic philosophy. He embraces aspects of truth that he finds in each of these but responds to their objections to natural law. Though Boyd does not develop any detailed biblical account of natural law, he too firmly rejects the association of natural law with human autonomy: "Accepting an account of morality based upon natural law does not result in committing one to the autonomy thesis; rather, a true understanding of natural law morality reveals that God is the *sine qua non* of the natural law."[15] The work of Daryl Charles is helpful to mention at this point. Charles's primary concern is to reinvigorate appreciation for the natural law in order to combat moral relativism and to provide Christians with a means for engaging in meaningful moral discourse in a pluralistic society, particularly with regard to questions of bioethics. His approach to defending natural law is rather eclectic. He does

14. In a recent volume J. Budziszewski argues, among other things, that a full-orbed theory of natural law requires acknowledging God and the insights of theology, and he skewers Enlightenment liberalism's pretensions of neutrality; see *The Line Through the Heart: Natural Law as Fact, Theory, and Sign of Contradiction* (Wilmington, DE: ISI Books, 2009), pp. xviii-xix and chapters 2, 3, and 10. In two recent essays Alasdair MacIntyre has undertaken a strong defense of reason's ability to perceive the precepts of the (Thomistic) natural law, but only in conjunction with his longstanding critique of the Enlightenment, and especially its utilitarian manifestation; see "Intractable Moral Disagreements" and "From Answers to Questions: A Response to the Responses," in *Intractable Disputes about the Natural Law*, pp. 1-52, 313-51. Among special points of interest for present purposes are his calls to engage other moral traditions at the level of basic premises and presuppositions (pp. 24, 52, 347-50) and, at least as I read him, a simultaneous resistance and openness to the necessity of theology for an understanding of natural law (pp. 315, 349-50).

15. Craig A. Boyd, *A Shared Morality: A Narrative Defense of Natural Law Ethics* (Grand Rapids: Brazos, 2007), p. 159. The rest of the description of Boyd's theory of natural law is a general summary of this book.

a little biblical exposition and appeals to a number of theological concepts, often with special concern to combat the "prejudice" against natural law that he sees afflicting many of his fellow evangelicals. But he does not build a rigorous theoretical account of natural law or ground it in an explicit theological system. Interestingly, his two trustiest theological guides on the question of natural law seem to be Thomas Aquinas and John Paul II.[16] Thus, as with fellow Protestant Boyd and the four Roman Catholic writers surveyed earlier, Aquinas is luminary *par excellence* in the natural law pantheon.

The same cannot be said for McGrath's treatment of natural law in his recent development of a Christian natural theology. In distinction from Thomistic theories of natural law that, in one way or another, ground natural law in God's work of creation and providence and see it brought to higher fulfillment through redemptive grace, McGrath treats natural law as an aspect of a natural theology that is Christological and redemptive from the outset. Truths about God cannot simply be read from nature by observing it objectively, contrary to many approaches to natural theology generated by the "Age of Reason" that assumed a human capacity to prove God's existence without recourse to religious presuppositions. Instead, truth about God can only be learned from nature if it is "seen" in certain ways, that is, with "discernment." The Christian way of seeing is anchored in Christ and his incarnation, and when seen in this light nature discloses the kingdom of God. For McGrath, nature and supernature are simply two aspects of the same reality. Thus when McGrath addresses natural law specifically toward the end of his work he argues that a concept of natural law must be founded in an understanding of the "economy of salvation" associated with a Christian natural theology.[17] Though McGrath does not explicitly say so, his general approach resembles that of the later Karl Barth, who reincorporated a Christological natural theology into his thought years after rejecting any notion of natural theology in his famous exchange with Emil Brunner.[18]

I conclude this appendix by calling attention to the Jewish theory of

16. The work of J. Daryl Charles described in this paragraph is *Retrieving the Natural Law: A Return to Moral First Things* (Grand Rapids: Eerdmans, 2008).

17. Alister McGrath, *The Open Secret: A New Vision for Natural Theology* (Malden, MA: Blackwell, 2008). His discussion of natural law appears in chapter 12. See also Alister McGrath, *A Fine-Tuned Universe* (Louisville: Westminster John Knox, 2009).

18. In *The Open Secret*, pp. 158-64, McGrath expresses appreciation for and criticism of both their perspectives. For my analysis of Barth's views, see David VanDrunen, *Natural Law and the Two Kingdoms: A Study in the Development of Reformed Social Thought* (Grand Rapids: Eerdmans, 2010), chap. 8.

natural law developed in recent years by David Novak, with whose work I interact at various points in this book. Novak's approach is certainly not shared by all Jewish thinkers, but in my judgment it is one of the most stimulating contemporary approaches to natural law. Here I note two brief points. First, Novak develops an account of natural law from complementary philosophical and theological angles, both of which entail radical rejection of Enlightenment social contract theory, which rests on the idea of an autonomously constructed human society. Second, Novak explicitly builds his theory of natural law from within the context of his own Jewish tradition, both biblical and rabbinic.[19] Thus several of the trends that I identified as characterizing recent Roman Catholic and Protestant natural law theories — such as the rejection of assumptions about human autonomy and the interest in a theologically rich and biblically based natural law — also find expression in this Jewish natural law theory.

19. See especially David Novak, *Natural Law in Judaism* (Cambridge: Cambridge University Press, 1998), though he has developed key ideas here in subsequent works, such as *The Jewish Social Contract* (Princeton: Princeton University Press, 2005) and *Covenantal Rights: A Study in Jewish Political Theory* (Princeton: Princeton University Press, 2000).

APPENDIX 2

Neo-Calvinism and Natural Law

In the Introduction I set my biblical theology of natural law in historical context with particular reference to Thomism and neo-Calvinism. Given my attempt to develop a *Reformed* theology of natural law in this book, as well as the tremendous influence of neo-Calvinism upon Reformed thought over the past century — at least in the North American circles with which I am most familiar — a few more comments on this movement seem appropriate. These comments may also shed a little more light on the hostility to natural law among many Reformed people in recent years.

The story of neo-Calvinism begins with the prodigious efforts of Abraham Kuyper and Herman Bavinck to reform and revitalize the Dutch Reformed Church in the late nineteenth and early twentieth centuries. It continues through their scores of disciples who have embraced their legacy and sought to advance and develop it through intellectual work in many academic fields and through the establishment of numerous institutions to support this work. To speak at a personal level, this movement has had profound influence upon the schools in which I was trained in my youth, the church I serve as a minister of the gospel, and the seminary where I am now a professor. What accounts for later neo-Calvinists' tendency to be indifferent or even hostile toward natural law theory, despite their persistent affirmation of the reality of natural revelation and the deep sympathy of both Kuyper and Bavinck toward much of the Reformed natural law tradition?[1]

1. On Kuyper and the Reformed natural law tradition, see David VanDrunen, *Natural Law and the Two Kingdoms: A Study in the Development of Reformed Social Thought* (Grand Rapids: Eerdmans, 2010), chap. 7. On Bavinck and the Reformed natural law tradition, see Theodore G. Van Raalte, "Unleavened Morality? Herman Bavinck on Natural Law," in *Five Studies in the Thought of Herman Bavinck, a Creator of Modern Dutch Theology*, ed. John Bolt

The explanation, unfortunately, is complicated, and I am still not sure I understand the full answer, even after many years of pondering the question. I think the answer goes something like this. The movement instigated especially by the indefatigable labors of Kuyper (and to a lesser and quieter degree by Bavinck) was motivated to a large extent by the harmful legacy of the Enlightenment, through the many philosophies and theories it spun off (often in directions overtly hostile to orthodox Christianity) and the fruit it bore in the liberalization of the Dutch Reformed state church. A significant part of the response, therefore (and here again I think primarily of Kuyper), was to reassert the sovereignty and authority of God over all things, in response to all human-centered worldviews that glorified human reason and failed to account for the depths of human depravity. To the extent that natural law theory had become associated with Enlightenment philosophies, it could understandably come under suspicion by those who followed Kuyper's line of thought.

Reinforcing this negative cast hanging over natural law theory in the perception of many neo-Calvinists is their association of natural law theory not only with Enlightenment philosophies but also with medieval thought. As discussed in the Introduction, neo-Calvinism has taken a very critical posture toward medieval views on nature and grace. This part of the story is complicated by what seems to be a somewhat caricatured view of the medieval nature-grace doctrine(s) among many neo-Calvinists (though the view they critique may well be represented among some Roman Catholic thinkers subsequent to the Reformation).[2] A common neo-Calvinist critique is that medieval thought was infected by a nature-grace dualism, in which grace was an ontological superstructure built upon an inferior realm of nature. This dualism constituted too low a view of nature as God's good creation, since it required, even before the fall, supernatural perfection through grace. It also held too rosy a view of post-fall nature and natural human faculties such as reason. According to a typical neo-Calvinist critique, grace should be seen as restoring nature rather than perfecting it. Thus, insofar as natural law theory is associated with the nature-grace dualism imputed to medieval thought, the critical posture of many neo-Calvinists toward natural law theory is all the more understandable.

(Lewiston, NY: Edwin Mellen, 2011), pp. 57-99; and David VanDrunen, "'The Kingship of Christ is Twofold': Natural Law and the Two Kingdoms in the Thought of Herman Bavinck," *CTJ* 45 (April 2010): 147-64.

2. See Paul Helm, *Calvin at the Centre* (Oxford: Oxford University Press, 2010), chap. 10, which focuses especially on Bavinck.

An additional, but related, part of the explanation of the neo-Calvinist attitude toward natural law theory that seems necessary to mention is its frequently caricatured notions about its own Reformed heritage. Much twentieth-century Reformed thought suffered under considerable ignorance about sixteenth- and seventeenth-century post-Reformation Reformed orthodoxy, frequently associating it with a "scholasticism" that was by definition inferior to and a degeneration from the supposedly more biblical theology of John Calvin.[3] The problems with this view of Reformed orthodoxy are numerous, and have been persuasively critiqued in recent years,[4] but it has had considerable effect upon perceptions of natural law theory. Insofar as natural law theory in the early Reformed tradition is associated with an unfortunate revival of a medieval, rationalistic, and nonbiblical scholasticism, it is bound to look suspicious to neo-Calvinists.

In spite of these considerations, it may be the case that some of the neo-Calvinist negativity toward natural law is deeper rhetorically than it is substantively. As Jonathan Chaplin notes regarding Herman Dooyeweerd (perhaps the most influential neo-Calvinist thinker in the generation after Kuyper and Bavinck), his "attack on legal positivism is certainly more damning than that on Thomistic natural law theory. Indeed he pays tribute to the latter's 'imperishable' contribution to legal theory in having demonstrated its need for recognition of material principles of law standing above the arbitrary will of legislators. When viewed against the background of the variety of historical schools of legal philosophy, there is no doubt that the affinities between his theory of law and natural law theory are far more significant than the differences between them."[5] Yet given Dooyeweerd's penchant for critiquing other writers down to the core of their thought, a trait he shared with other

---

3. As one of the most influential neo-Calvinist thinkers put it, Protestant scholasticism "even today opposes the truly biblical approach in scientific thought with the unbending resistance of an age-old tradition. . . . The inherent dialectic of the unscriptural nature-grace ground motive also infiltrated the protestant mind." See Herman Dooyeweerd, *Roots of Western Culture: Pagan, Secular, and Christian Options,* trans. John Kraay (Toronto: Wedge, 1979), pp. 142-43.

4. See especially the work of Richard A. Muller; for an overview of his conclusions regarding Reformed orthodoxy, see his *Post-Reformation Reformed Dogmatics: The Rise and Development of Reformed Orthodoxy, c. 1520 to c. 1725,* vol. 1, *Prolegomena to Theology,* 2nd ed. (Grand Rapids: Baker Academic, 2003), chap. 1.

5. Jonathan Chaplin, *Herman Dooyeweerd: Christian Philosopher of State and Civil Society* (Notre Dame: University of Notre Dame Press, 2011), p. 320. I offer reflection on Dooyeweerd's relation to the earlier Reformed natural law tradition in *Natural Law and the Two Kingdoms,* pp. 359-68.

neo-Calvinists, as noted below, his interaction with natural law proponents tended to be quite negative.[6]

Where does my biblical theology of natural law relate to this neo-Calvinism that has so significantly shaped my own theological and ecclesiastical environment? In my short writing career I have already offered critiques of neo-Calvinism, but it is worth acknowledging several areas in which I am indebted to neo-Calvinist emphases and wish to embrace their substantive burdens, even while rejecting the exaggerations and historical caricatures often accompanying them. First, I appreciate and hope I have sufficiently absorbed neo-Calvinism's heightened sense of the goodness of physical creation and the identity of the new creation as the consummation of the original creation. I say "heightened" sense because I believe historic Christian theology has ultimately maintained a positive view of the goodness of physical creation, thanks especially to key doctrines such as creation, incarnation, and resurrection, yet has also too often succumbed to the temptation to elevate soul over body and to conceive of the beatific vision in ways that make the resurrection seem rather unimportant. My appropriation of this neo-Calvinist emphasis — though in a way no neo-Calvinist has pursued, as far as I am aware — is perhaps especially evident in my conception of the integrity of the original creation and the image of God, such that human beings were able, by the gifts of their original nature and without need of any superadded gift, to complete their commission made known in natural law and to attain the goal of new creation. The doctrine that the original goal has been achieved through the redemptive work of Jesus Christ as the Last Adam subsequently shapes my treatment of the relationship of natural law and the new covenant.

A second emphasis of neo-Calvinism that I believe has shaped my own theology of natural law is the non-neutrality and non-autonomy of human reason, and even of nature generally. Again, this affirmation is not unique to neo-Calvinism, but an implication of Christian orthodoxy in a broad sense. If God is creator and judge of all things, then human reason is what it is because God made it such, and people are ultimately answerable to him for how they use it. Nevertheless, neo-Calvinism seems to have emphasized this theme and made it explicit in heightened ways in comparison to other Christian traditions or even the earlier Reformed tradition. In my biblical theology of natural law I

---

6. Chaplin notes that Dooyeweerd "adopts a markedly 'antithetical' stance toward his interlocutors. . . . While his strategic goal . . . is ultimately to promote dialogue across perspectival divides, his method is to penetrate to and expose the deepest differences between his own thought and that of his opponents rather than to search out existing or potential points of convergence with a view to maximizing consensus." See *Herman Dooyeweerd*, p. 2.

have appropriated this theme especially through the central place I give to the divine covenants. Insofar as God promulgates natural law and human beings respond to it in covenant relationships, natural law can never be associated with illusions of human autonomy or the neutrality of reason.

With respect to what I take to be the main line of neo-Calvinist thought in North America, I wish to highlight one major point of substantive disagreement that has had major implications for the theology of natural law developed in this book.[7] This neo-Calvinism tends to view Christians' cultural endeavors as the taking up again of Adam's original mandate (Gen. 1:28), seeking to bring the claims of Christ's kingdom to bear upon every sphere of human activity, and (through faithful service in these spheres) producing the material that will adorn the new heavens and new earth.[8] Neo-Calvinism's quest for the redemptive transformation of all activities and institutions according to the ways of the eschatological kingdom, I believe, leaves little space for a genuine *natural law* theory.

In contrast to these neo-Calvinist motifs, I have argued that the original creation mandate, broken in Adam, continues to be promulgated to the whole world by natural revelation, but only as refracted through God's universal covenant of preservation with Noah. Furthermore, the message of salvation in Christ proclaims not that Christians take up Adam's task once again but that Jesus Christ is the Last Adam, who was perfectly faithful to God's law (both natural and Mosaic) and thus has already attained Adam's original goal, the new creation. Justified and made citizens of this eschatological kingdom through him, Christians should not seek to be new Adams but to rest by faith in the Last Adam. Christians' ongoing responsibilities in this world include both fidelity under the protological Noahic natural law, with its structures and institutions, and anticipation of the new creation through pursuit of the eschatological ethic, which is grounded in the finished work of Christ and comes to special expression in the life and ministry of the church. This is in

---

7. I take this main line of North American neo-Calvinism to be represented by popular books such as Albert M. Wolters, *Creation Regained: Biblical Basics for a Reformational Worldview*, 2nd ed. (Grand Rapids: Eerdmans, 2005); and Cornelius Plantinga Jr., *Engaging God's World: A Christian Vision of Faith, Learning, and Living* (Grand Rapids: Eerdmans, 2002). I have offered some analysis of this school of thought in *Natural Law and the Two Kingdoms*, pp. 368-85; and *Living in God's Two Kingdoms: A Biblical Vision for Christianity and Culture* (Wheaton, IL: Crossway, 2010), chap. 1.

8. As Anthony A. Hoekema puts it, "Through our kingdom service the building materials for that new earth are now being gathered." See *The Bible and the Future* (Grand Rapids: Eerdmans, 1979), p. 287.

many respects a different conception of the main storyline of Scripture, and it provides, I believe, significant room for a genuine natural law theory — room that neo-Calvinism does not provide.

A few comments are also in order about the stream of the Kuyper-Bavinck legacy pioneered by Cornelius Van Til. This is the stream of particular influence in my own ecclesiastical home (the Orthodox Presbyterian Church) and academic institution (Westminster Seminary California), for Van Til was a minister of the Orthodox Presbyterian Church and professor at Westminster Theological Seminary in Philadelphia, out of which my own institution emerged several decades ago. Van Til wrote nothing explicitly about the Reformed or broader Christian natural law traditions, though he did strongly affirm the reality of natural revelation. Many of his devoted disciples, however, tend to have a decidedly negative reaction to the idea of natural law. Van Til and these disciples seem to have interacted little with the Reformed tradition of natural law, and also seem to have a somewhat caricatured view of Thomas Aquinas and medieval conceptions of nature and grace. Given my close association with the Van Tilian school of thought and its typical unease with natural law, I wish to say a few words about where I see my biblical theology of natural law in relation to it.

One of Van Til's goals was to take many of the chief insights of Kuyper and Bavinck — such as the sovereignty and authority of God over all things — and apply them consistently to the field of apologetics, the intellectual defense of the Christian faith. He did not think Kuyper and Bavinck themselves had done so sufficiently. Van Til emphasized that natural revelation confronts every person at every moment, such that each human thought and action is a response to the claims of God himself. Human beings never run across a "brute fact" in the universe, that is, some fact that God has not already interpreted. Thus human beings are obligated to interpret everything according to God's interpretation, and at every moment are either obedient or disobedient to him. Human reason is therefore never neutral or autonomous, but stands in constant obligation to think God's thoughts after him, in ways appropriate for finite creatures. If unbelievers were perfectly consistent in their rebellion against God ("epistemologically self-conscious," in Van Til's terms), they would explicitly reject all truth and have nothing in common with believers, insofar as believers are consistent in their obedience. But God's common grace keeps unbelievers now from being perfectly consistent, and they do acknowledge many truths, even if they cannot place them accurately in their ultimate context. This permits "relative" or "penultimate" agreement among believers and unbelievers.

With these basic points I am in hearty agreement, and acknowledging them creates no barrier to developing a natural law theory.[9] In fact, in placing all natural law in the context of God's covenanting with the natural order and the entire human race, I have embraced the idea that all human beings at every moment are confronted by God and called to obey him (making ideas of human rational autonomy an illusion), and that God's preservative grace under the Noahic covenant enables a common life among all people without bringing them all to true faith. What, then, accounts for the negative attitude toward natural law amongst most enthusiastic Van Tilians, beyond the issue of historical blind spots? I offer a few thoughts.[10]

First, while Van Til wrote very strongly about the reality of natural revelation and decried any "biblicism" that failed to take it seriously,[11] he also wrote at times as though he were just this kind of biblicist, claiming, for example, that all moral questions must be answered in the light of Scripture only.[12] While I would take the latter kind of statement as a rhetorical exaggeration that could not be consistently followed even if one believed it to be literally true, I fear that many Van Tilians emphasize such exaggerations, rather than his critique of biblicism, and this has deleterious implications for a robust view of natural law.[13] Similarly, when Van Til says that natural and special revelation "are mutually meaningless without one another and mutually fruitful when taken together," I believe he is partially correct.[14] Surely natural revelation and special revelation are mutually fruitful when taken together, and imagining someone reading Scripture without natural revelation is conceptually impossible, since what Scripture says constantly presumes knowledge of the

9. For another argument (similar to my analysis) that Van Til's overall thought is compatible with a sound natural law theory, see Thomas K. Johnson, *Natural Law Ethics: An Evangelical Proposal* (Bonn: Verlag für Kultur und Wissenschaft, 2005), pp. 108-15.

10. See also my analysis in *Natural Law and the Two Kingdoms,* chap. 10.

11. See e.g. Cornelius Van Til, *The Defense of the Faith* (Philadelphia: Presbyterian and Reformed, 1955), p. 203.

12. See Cornelius Van Til, *Christian Theistic Ethics* (Phillipsburg, NJ: Presbyterian and Reformed, 1980), pp. 22-23.

13. A recent example of this is perhaps found in K. Scott Oliphint, "The Prolegomena Principle: Frame and Bavinck," in *Speaking the Truth in Love: The Theology of John M. Frame,* ed. John J. Hughes (Phillipsburg, NJ: Presbyterian and Reformed, 2009), pp. 201-32. Though Oliphint expresses many convictions I share, he seems to alternate between insisting generally upon divine revelation/Logos (in nature and Scripture) as the only basis for a sound epistemology and insisting specifically on Scripture alone as this basis.

14. Cornelius Van Til, "Nature and Scripture," in *The Infallible Word,* ed. N. B. Stonehouse and Paul Woolley (Grand Rapids: Eerdmans, 1946), p. 261.

world. But to say that natural revelation alone is meaningless seems to obscure Scripture's own teaching: natural revelation is certainly not meaningless for people without access to Scripture who are held accountable to God through nature (Rom. 1:18-32).

Second, Van Til wrote extensively, on the one hand, about the antithesis between believing and unbelieving thought (rooted in each person's fundamental posture toward God as obedient or disobedient) and, on the other hand, the common grace that permits relative agreement among them and the maintenance of peaceful coexistence in society. I think it is accurate to say, however, that his primary mode of analysis was in terms of the antithesis, which again led to certain exaggerations in rhetoric.[15] Again, I fear that some especially devoted Van Tilians often take the rhetorical exaggerations to lie at the heart of what Van Til's thought was all about, such that the antithesis idea swallows up everything else. The manifold genuine achievements of unbelievers, gained through natural abilities they have developed through response to the natural order, are thus greatly downplayed.[16]

Finally, I observe that Van Til himself offered very little discussion of *how* Christians are supposed to fulfill their various callings in the world, which they so often pursue in peaceful collaboration with their unbelieving neighbors. I do not necessarily mean this as a point of criticism of Van Til; few theologians address every issue of theological interest (though one might argue that what Van Til does address urgently invites this *how* question). In any case, in my experience this question seems to be practically a forbidden topic among some devoted Van Tilians. Yet it is surely necessary that at least some of us wrestle with this question and seek to provide guidance for Christians, for few topics are of more constant practical relevance to the ordinary believer. Whether I have done so helpfully or not, my attempt to think through the Noahic cov-

15. As one of Van Til's students and proponents puts it, Van Til was an "apostle of antithesis"; see John M. Frame, *Cornelius Van Til: An Analysis of His Thought* (Phillipsburg, NJ: Presbyterian and Reformed, 1995), pp. 187-88, 210-11. As an example of his exaggeration in rhetoric driven by concern for the antithesis, I think of some of his statements about why arithmetic must be taught in Christian schools and cannot be taught anywhere else; see Cornelius Van Til, "Antithesis in Education," in *Foundations of Christian Education: Addresses to Christian Teachers*, ed. Dennis E. Johnson (Phillipsburg, NJ: Presbyterian and Reformed, 1990), pp. 7, 18.

16. I think for example of a letter to the editor in *New Horizons* (January 2012), pp. 21-22, by William D. Dennison, in criticism of an article by my colleague Michael Horton. Dennison, describing how a "true Van Tilian" should read Horton's article, contrasts "Van Til's militantly antithetical stance against Roman Catholic thought" with Horton's allegedly "compromising position that gives way to a nature-grace dualism," the latter of which is revealed in Horton's utilization of concepts of common grace, the two kingdoms, and natural law.

enant and the natural law has sought to offer some way forward on this issue that Van Til himself did little to address, and has done so from the perspective of one sympathetic to most of Van Til's concerns, even if also wary of some of his rhetorical exaggerations, one-sided emphases, and historical caricatures.

David Kelsey's Anthropology and the Image of God

In Chapter 1, I developed a theology of natural law in the original creation in significant measure through investigating the meaning of humanity's creation in the image of God. From the perspective of historic Christian theological anthropology, there is nothing unusual about according a central place to the image of God as first described in Genesis 1:26-27. David Kelsey, however, has recently raised serious questions about this approach.[1] The importance of Kelsey's work, and its relevance for a number of issues with which I wrestle in the present book, suggests that I should interact with his claims. It is a long, rich, and thorough work, and I admit with regret that this short appendix can hardly do justice to it.

Eccentric Existence derives its memorable title from Kelsey's basic conviction that human beings are centered outside of themselves — specifically, in the distinctive ways in which God relates to them. Kelsey develops his proposal with a sense of leisure, and the book progresses by repeatedly circling around its subjects and often retracing ground before building a new point. This approach beneficially draws patient readers into Kelsey's orbit and reinforces important claims that he has made and defended earlier. But it does require patience. One unusual feature of *Eccentric Existence* is that many chapters are divided into A and B sections. The B sections consist of more detailed and technical arguments in support of conclusions Kelsey draws in the A sections. He intends that people can read only the A sections should they not wish to wrestle with the more technical material. But readers will miss many rich discussions if they pursue this route.

---

1. David H. Kelsey, *Eccentric Existence: A Theological Anthropology,* 2 vols. (Louisville: Westminster John Knox, 2009).

The book is organized into three parts, preceded by several substantive introductory chapters and followed by three "Codas" that integrate the various claims made throughout the work. The three parts correspond to three claims about human beings that Kelsey believes are nonnegotiable for the Christian faith. They concern how God relates to human beings: to create them, to draw them to eschatological consummation, and to reconcile them when alienated from God. These, he says, are "three inseparable, but irreducibly different ways" in which God relates to us. In each part he reflects upon what is implied about human beings by the claim that God relates to them in these three ways. According to Kelsey, God's relating to create does not presuppose that God relates to draw to eschatological consummation or to reconcile, while God's relating to draw to eschatological consummation presupposes God's relating to create but not his relating to reconcile, and God's relating to reconcile presupposes both of the other ways of relating. The basic human responses appropriate to God's three ways of relating are, respectively, faith, hope, and love.

Kelsey also gives structure to *Eccentric Existence* by continually exploring three perennial questions of anthropology: *What* is a human being, *who* am I/*who* are we, and *how* ought we "to be existentially 'set' into, and oriented toward, our ultimate and proximate contexts"?

One especially noteworthy feature of Kelsey's development of a *Christian* anthropology is that he does not deal with the idea of the image of God until his three Codas, nearly 900 pages into the book. This is a calculated move rather than an oversight. As he warns readers early in the work, and defends at considerable length in one of the codas, he does not see the classic text, Genesis 1:26, as providing much help for Christian anthropology. He does, however, regard the New Testament's identification of Jesus as the image of God as highly significant for tying together the three parts of *Eccentric Existence* into a coherent "triple helix." Jesus, as described in the canonical Gospels, is the paradigmatic human being who shows how God relates to human beings in the three ways and how human beings are to respond to such a God in their ultimate and proximate contexts. According to Kelsey, it is not so much that we image God but that we image the image of God.

Evaluating a book requires attention to its stated purposes. Kelsey has aimed to offer proposals for how Christians might view important theological questions rather than to offer dogmatic pronouncements about what Christians must assert about them. Judged by this intention, Kelsey has succeeded, giving the theological world a wealth of material upon which to reflect. His work lacks dependence upon or commitment to a particular theological tradition, and this will likely prohibit it from becoming a standard text for training ministers and theologians in confessional churches. This freedom from confessional constraints, however, probably has enhanced Kelsey's ability to think outside of traditional boxes and to make this a very stimulating piece of academic theology.

Most stimulating, in my judgment, is his building an anthropology upon a threefold relation of God toward the human race. Over against temptations — seemingly perennial in Western theology — of centering anthropology in a static conception of the image of God, Kelsey opens lines of thought for conceiving anthropology more dynamically, according to the various plots that Scripture unfolds. I must wonder, however, at a fundamental level, whether Kelsey has identified the proper three categories. His first category, concerning God as creator, does not distinguish how God relates to human beings in an originally sinless creation from how he relates to them after the fall into sin. Scripture makes this crucial distinction, and does so with reference to the image of God at climactic points (compare Genesis 1:26 and 9:6 in their contexts). This suggests the need to identify two very different ways of God's relating to human beings where Kelsey has identified only one. With respect to Kelsey's second category I again express appreciation for his extensive attention to God's drawing human beings to eschatological consummation, a central biblical theme too infrequently recognized as such in Christian anthropology. What is ultimately unpersuasive about Kelsey's development of this category, however, is his decision to treat it as a theme distinct (albeit inseparable) from God's work of creation and reconciliation. As argued in the present volume, Scripture presents God's eschatological drawing of humanity as a *constitutive* aspect of both his creative work and his reconciling work. God creates and reconciles precisely to draw human beings into eschatological life. This purpose, however, does not characterize his relation with fallen human beings. Thus I suggest that a better threefold categorization would be God relating (a) to create so as to draw human beings into eschatological consummation, (b) to preserve human beings after they have fallen, until the final judgment, and (c) to reconcile human beings so as to bring human beings into eschatological consummation.[2]

These three ways of God's relating to human beings correspond with

2. My suggested alternative presumes an important conviction that Kelsey does not embrace: the historicity of the fall through the sin of the first man Adam. Kelsey asks early in the book whether such a conviction is logically necessary given Christian beliefs about salvation. I believe that it is — though I would add that this "logical" necessity concerns the logic of the biblical narrative itself rather than an abstract logic. Kelsey does well to conclude

the three contexts in which Scripture describes human beings as bearing his image: a) in an original state of integrity (Gen. 1:26-27); b) in a fallen but preserved state (Gen. 9:6); and c) in a state of salvation through Christ (Rom. 8:29; 2 Cor. 3:18; Eph. 4:24; Col. 3:10). If the theology of the image of God developed in the present book (see especially Chapters 1, 2, and 9) is sound, then I believe it corresponds to and supports many of Kelsey's chief concerns. In my judgment, a biblical doctrine of the image of God should enrich any Christian anthropology, such as Kelsey's, that wishes to capture the dynamic and layered character of the divine-human relationships.

---

his anthropology by pointing readers to the New Testament Jesus, but in the New Testament he is only *the* image of God insofar as he is the *second* Adam.

The Heavenly Court View of Genesis 1:26

In Chapter 1, I stated that the heavenly court view of Genesis 1:26 adds further depth to the portrayal of God as a just king in the opening chapter of Scripture. According to this view, Genesis 1:26 anthropomorphically reveals God as a king seated in splendor on his royal throne, attended by his angelic host, and issuing judicial decrees. I did not defend this view in Chapter 1, but here I offer a few considerations that lend credence to it.

First, the idea of God as a king enthroned among the angelic host is a common biblical image. Among the striking OT examples are Micaiah's vision of God "sitting on his throne and all the host of heaven standing beside him on his right hand and on his left" (1 Kgs. 22:19-22), the heavenly scenes in Job 1-2, the commission of Isaiah by "the Lord sitting upon a throne" while "above him stood the seraphim" (Isaiah 6), and Daniel's vision of the "Ancient of days" taking his seat upon a throne while "a thousand thousands served him, and ten thousand times ten thousand stood before him" and "the court sat in judgment and the books were opened" (Dan. 7:9-10). This imagery appears in the Psalms (89:5-14; 99:1; 103:19-21; and perhaps 82:1-8). Other Old Testament references to God's "council" may also be allusions to the same reality (e.g., Job 15:8; Jer. 23:18). In the New Testament, a "multitude of the heavenly host" appears to the shepherds (though God himself does not appear in this scene) (Luke 2:8-14) and, most prominently, Revelation 4 describes God as "seated on the throne" in heaven, surrounded by the twenty-four elders and the four living creatures, and he repeatedly puts angels to his service in subsequent chapters. The king enthroned in heaven is, as the Old Testament proclaims hundreds of times, "the Lord of hosts."

An initial consideration suggesting that this is the portrait of God communicated in Genesis 1:26 is an interconnected web of biblical imagery that closely associates three realities with one another: the "Spirit of God . . . hovering over the face of the waters" (Genesis 1:2), the theophanic pillar of cloud and fire leading the Israelites through the wilderness, and the angelic court. The heavenly court and the theophanic cloud share a number of characteristic features, such as lightning, thunder, smoke, and fire (e.g., Exod. 19:16-19; Ps. 97:2-4; Isa. 6:4; Rev. 4:5). Psalm 99 explicitly connects the court and cloud, first describing God as he who "sits enthroned upon the cherubim" and then stating that "in the pillar of the cloud he spoke to them" (99:1, 7). Haggai 2:4-5 further associates both of these realities with the visible revelation of the Holy Spirit. Here God identifies himself as "the Lord of hosts" who made a covenant with Israel when they "came out of Egypt. My Spirit remains in your midst." Isaiah 63:10-14 three times refers to the "Holy Spirit" or "Spirit of the Lord" as the one who was "in the midst of" Israel as he "brought them up out of the sea," "divided the waters before them," "led them through the depths," and "gave them rest" (see similarly Neh. 9:19-20). In Revelation 4:2, furthermore, John when "in the Spirit" sees the throne in heaven and the one seated upon it surrounded by his court of glory.

In addition to these general associations of the Spirit, angelic court, and the theophanic cloud is the specific description of the theophanic cloud in Deuteronomy 32:10-11 in terms clearly evocative of the Spirit of God in Genesis 1:2. As the earth was "without form [תהו] and void" and "the Spirit of God was hovering [מרחפת] over the face of the waters" (Gen. 1:2) so, according to the Song of Moses, the one caring for and guiding Israel through the wilderness found him "in the howling waste [ובתהו] of the wilderness" and encircled him like an eagle "that flutters [ירחף] over its young" (Deut. 32:10-11). The Hebrew word רחף appears in only these two places in the Pentateuch. The Spirit of God who superintended the original creation also visibly manifested God as he led his people through the wilderness in the cloud. The reference a few verses earlier to the "sons of God" who have authority over the human race in their national divisions (Deut. 32:8) may also bring the angelic court into view in the immediate context.

In short, the reference to the Spirit of God in Genesis 1:2 ought to bring readers' minds to the theophanic cloud and thus also to the heavenly court, and therefore, 24 verses before the first person plural occurs in 1:26, the God who created the heavens and earth reveals himself as the one who sits enthroned amidst the angels. Furthermore, the language of the divine first person plural is the language of the heavenly court. In other words, those rare occasions in which the Old Testament records God speaking of "we" or "us" are ordinarily in the context of his angelic council (and not in the context of a plurality of divine Persons).

This is most explicit in Isaiah 6, where God reveals himself as highly exalted and sitting on a throne surrounded by his angelic servants (6:1-7) and then asks: "Whom shall I send, and who will go for us" (6:8)? The other two divine first person plurals in the Old Testament, in Genesis 3:22 and 11:7, are also significant. Various linguistic markers connect these two texts with Genesis 1:26, suggesting that a similar reality is in view in all three.[1] In 3:22-24 the presence of God's angelic servants is again overt, for when the Lord God states that "the man has become like one of us" he proceeds to place the cherubim at the east of the Garden to prohibit reentrance. Genesis 11:7, where the tower of Babel provokes God to say "come, let us go down," does not explicitly identify an angelic presence. But its context — God's coming in judgment — is similar to that of Genesis 3:22, where the angels were instruments of enforcing justice. The rest of Scripture frequently describes God coming in judgment accompanied by the angelic host (e.g., Zech. 14:5; 1 Thess. 3:13; 4:16; Rev. 18:1; 19:14-17).

Seeing the heavenly court in Genesis 1:26 is also confirmed by later biblical interpretation of God's work of creation. The Scriptures frequently praise the creator God as the Lord of hosts whose angels were present as he made the world, and especially as he made human beings. This is true of God's own reflections on creation recorded in Job 38. God asks Job where he was "when I laid the foundation of the earth" (38:4), "when the morning stars sang together and all the sons of God shouted for joy" (38:7). A similar dynamic is present in several of the Psalms that look back to creation. Psalm 24, for example, which begins by acclaiming the Lord who "has founded it [the earth] upon the seas and established it upon the rivers" (24:2) ends with praise to the "King of glory," the "Lord of hosts" (24:7-10) who arrives at the top of his holy hill (perhaps evocative of the seventh day of Genesis 2:1-3). Likewise, the creation imagery in Psalm 29 is bracketed by a call to the sons of God to ascribe glory and strength to the Lord (29:1) and by the pronouncement that "the Lord sits enthroned over the flood; the Lord sits enthroned as king forever" (29:10). Most significant is Psalm 8. After a general statement about God's work of creation (8:3), the psalmist asks: "what is man that you are mindful of him, and the son of man that you care for him" (8:4)? This human creature is "made a little lower than the heavenly beings" and "crowned with glory and honor," given "dominion over the work" of God's hands (8:5-6). The human beings created by God and entrusted with dominion in Genesis 1:26, therefore, are defined in relation to the heavenly host.

1. For extensive discussion of this, see W. Randall Garr, *In His Own Image and Likeness: Humanity, Divinity, and Monotheism* (Leiden: Brill, 2003), chaps. 2-5.

Those who reject the heavenly court view of Genesis 1:26 often seem to be driven more by objections to this view than by weighty positive arguments for other interpretations. Though I will not address objections related to the worldview of the Priestly writer, allegedly the author of Genesis 1:1–2:3,[2] I offer brief response to a couple of general theological objections. First, the heavenly court view does not, in my judgment, commit its proponents to the heterodox idea that angels are co-creators with God. Genesis 1:27 attributes creation solely to God, and analogy with Isaiah 6:8 suggests that joint divine-angelic creation is not intended in 1:26. When Isaiah 6:8 asks "who will go for us?," a going that is primarily for the purpose of speaking (see 6:9), there is no suggestion that the prophet will speak on behalf of God and angels together — for Isaiah and the other prophets it is "thus says the Lord." The first person plural exalts God as a majestic king through anthropomorphic language without necessarily implying cooperation.

Second, and for similar reasons, the heavenly court view of Genesis 1:26 does not necessarily mean that human beings were created in the image of angels as well as in the image of God. If the use of the first person plural in "let us make" does not necessarily mean co-creation, then "in our image, after our likeness" does not necessarily mean that both God and angels bestow their image upon the human being. At the same time, there are plausible theological reasons to suppose that human beings may, in a lesser and indirect sense, bear the image of angels. If image-bearing was indeed a royal-judicial task in the original creation, which is a key claim of Chapter 1, then human beings as image-bearers resembled both God and angels. In Scripture angels often exercise judicial authority over earthly affairs as God's underlings (as is likely evident in Gen. 18:1-2; 19:1; Deut. 32:8; and Ps. 82:1).[3] When human beings execute justice properly, Scripture sometimes likens them to angels. In addition to Psalm 8:5-6, in which the exercise of dominion places humans "a little lower" than the angels, 2 Samuel 14:17 expresses this idea in the words of the wise woman who says to king David after he judges her case, "my lord the king is like the angel of God to discern good and evil." To similar effect, and of special interest to the context of Genesis 1–3, is God's condemnation of the king of Tyre in Ezekiel 28. God speaks of the king of Tyre as being "in Eden, the garden of God" (28:13) and "blameless in your ways from the day you

---

2. For discussion of this issue with regard to P, see the discussion throughout Garr, *In His Own Image and Likeness,* especially chaps. 8-9.

3. For defense of this reading of Deuteronomy 32:8 and Psalm 82, see Michael S. Heiser, "Deuteronomy 32:8 and the Sons of God," *Bibliotheca Sacra* 158 (January-March 2001): 52-74.

were created" (28:15) until he was cast down from the holy mountain because of pride and unrighteousness (28:2, 15-18). In his original state, however, he was "an anointed guardian cherub" (28:14). In this pregnant Edenic imagery, therefore, the originally blameless king is likened to the angels.

Noahic Natural Law and the Noahide Laws in Jewish Ethics

My appeal to the Noahic covenant as the foundation for present-day natural law has certain similarities and important dissimilarities to aspects of traditional Jewish theological ethics. Judaism has taught, since at least the Tannaitic period after the destruction of the Second Temple, that while Jews alone are bound by the law of Moses, Gentiles are bound by seven universal precepts commonly called the "Noahide" commandments or laws. These seven laws include six prohibitions — of idol worship, taking God's name in vain, murder, adultery, theft, and eating the torn limb of an animal — and one requirement, administering a legal system.[1] Certain similarities with my proposal are evident. One is the strong recognition within Judaism that the demands of later biblical covenants (particularly the Sinaitic) are binding not universally but only upon those with whom the covenants are made. Second is the Jewish conviction that all people are morally accountable to God, despite the non-universality of later biblical covenants. Hence there is no ultimate human moral autonomy.[2] Third is the appeal to the "Noahide" in the attempt to specify where Gentile moral accountability to God lies. Though this is perhaps little more than a surface similarity, in that only two of the seven Noahide laws are

1. For a thorough description of the Noahide commandments in Judaism, see David Novak, *The Image of the Non-Jew in Judaism: An Historical and Constructive Study of the Noahide Laws* (Lewiston, NY: Edwin Mellen, 1983).

2. As one Jewish writer explains, "Noahides are always obligated to obey the law and culpability is thus always present. Thus, it is well established that gentiles benefit from being taught the Noahide laws." See Michael J. Broyde, "The Obligation of Jews to Seek Observance of Noahide Laws by Gentiles: A Theoretical Review," in *Tikkun Olam: Social Responsibility in Jewish Thought and Law,* ed. David Shatz, Chaim I. Waxman, and Nathan J. Diament (Northvale, NJ: Jason Aronson, 1997), pp. 108-9.

prescribed in Genesis 9 and Jewish writers do not ordinarily attempt to root the Noahide laws in this revelation to Noah,[3] the instinct that Noah represents a universal relationship between God and humanity resembles the perspective of my proposal at a basic level.

Nevertheless, the dissimilarities between Judaism's idea of the Noahide laws and my own conception of natural law as grounded in the Noahic covenant are substantial. First, as I understand it, Judaism's idea of the Noahide laws does not express the notion of *commonality* in precisely the same way that I am suggesting it here.[4] I see the Noahic covenant as a universal covenant that not only obligated all people at that time but also obligates all people today, and this means that it *directly* obligates Christians *in their participation in earthly cultural activities.* Judaism does not see Jews as directly bound by the Noahide laws. Though these laws obligated the line of Abraham before Sinai, the Sinai covenant ended that relationship with God and initiated a new one. Thus Jews avoid idolatry, blasphemy, murder, adultery, theft, and eating torn limbs because of the Mosaic law, not the Noahide laws. The fact that the things prohibited in the Noahide laws are also prohibited in the Mosaic law, however, does provide ground for a measure of common life among Jews and non-Jews. The positive Noahide command to administer a legal system also provides some sense of commonality among Jews and Gentiles, though this is rather limited in nature. Jews have few obligations with respect to Gentile legal systems other than recognizing and respecting them.[5]

Second, Judaism teaches that Gentiles who keep the Noahide commandments are the "righteous" and hence will share in eternal bliss.[6] Thus, in contrast to my conception of the Noahic covenant as promising preservation and not redemption (no matter how assiduously its precepts are followed), the Noahide laws in Judaism can serve a salvific function.

A final difference concerns how people know the universally binding commandments. It seems that Jewish writers have been long divided about this

3. For some reflection on these issues, see Novak, *The Image of the Non-Jew,* p. 10; and David Novak, *Natural Law in Judaism* (Cambridge: Cambridge University Press, 1998), p. 151.

4. I am grateful to David Novak for his critical comments on the way I explained this point in an earlier draft. I hope that what I now say captures the view of Judaism accurately, if not comprehensively.

5. On the Noahide commandment to establish a legal system and Jews' relationship to it, see Broyde, "The Obligation of Jews," pp. 103-43; and Naḥum Raḳover, *Law and the Noahides: Law as a Universal Value* (Jerusalem: Library of Jewish Law, 1998).

6. E.g., see Elliot N. Dorff, *To Do the Right and the Good: A Jewish Approach to Modern Social Ethics* (Philadelphia: Jewish Publication Society, 2002), pp. 70-71, 83.

issue. They generally acknowledge that at least most of the Noahide commandments can be perceived by reason, but many also insist that these commandments are ultimately *revealed* in character and ought to be obeyed as such.[7]
A few writers have tried to use the Noahide laws as a means for developing a
Jewish theory of natural law, in recent years most notably David Novak. But
even Novak does not clearly ground this natural law in the Noahic *covenant*,
and he tends to treat natural law as something distinct from revelation and history.[8] In comparison, this book grounds humanity's universal moral obligation
in natural law and grounds natural law in the Noahic covenant, which means
that even natural law is *revelation* and intimately tied to the movement of
history rather than hovering somewhere above history and abstracted from it.

7. For discussion of this issue within Judaism, see e.g. Rakover, *Law and the Noahides*,
pp. 12-13; Nahum M. Sarna, *Genesis* (Philadelphia: Jewish Publication Society, 1989), p. 377;
Louis E. Newman, *An Introduction to Jewish Ethics* (Upper Saddle River, NJ: Prentice Hall,
2005), pp. 117-18, 122; Aharon Lichtenstein, "Does Jewish Tradition Recognize an Ethic Independent of Halakha?" in *Modern Jewish Ethics: Theory and Practice*, ed. Marvin Fox (Columbus: Ohio State University Press, 1975), pp. 62-64; and J. David Bleich, "*Tikkun Olam:* Jewish
Obligations to Non-Jewish Society," in *Tikkun Olam*, pp. 76-77.

8. Novak's most sustained effort to build a Jewish theory of natural law is *Natural Law
in Judaism*. He acknowledges, however, that this endeavor has been a debated issue within
Judaism for a very long time; see *Natural Law in Judaism*, pp. 27, 191-92. Though I have great
appreciation for Novak's work on natural law, I find a certain bifurcation of the natural from
revelation, history, community, and covenant in his work — at least if I am reading him accurately in, e.g., *Natural Law in Judaism*, pp. 13-18, 145. In subsequent works Novak seems to
have increasing appreciation for the Noahic *covenant* and its significance for natural law and
universal moral obligation, though this line of thought still seems to me to be underdeveloped.
See David Novak, *Covenantal Rights: A Study in Jewish Political Theory* (Princeton: Princeton
University Press, 2000), pp. 84-85; and *The Jewish Social Contract: An Essay in Political Theology*
(Princeton: Princeton University Press, 2005), chap. 2.

Bibliography

Alexander, T. Desmond. "Lot's Hospitality: A Clue to His Righteousness," *Journal of Biblical Literature* 104, no. 2 (1985): 289-91.

Alter, Robert. *Genesis: Translation and Commentary.* New York: W. W. Norton, 1996.

―――. "Sodom as Nexus: The Web of Design in Biblical Narrative," *Tikkun* 1 (1986): 30-38.

Andersen, Francis I., and David Noel Freedman. *Amos: A New Translation with Introduction and Commentary.* New York: Doubleday, 1989.

Aquinas, Thomas. *Summa Theologica.* Translated by the Fathers of the English Dominican Province. New York: Benzinger, 1948.

Arkes, Hadley. *Constitutional Illusions and Anchoring Truths: The Touchstone of the Natural Law.* Cambridge: Cambridge University Press, 2010.

Arnold, Bill T. "The Use of Aramaic in the Hebrew Bible: Another Look at Bilingualism in Ezra and Daniel," *Journal of Northwest Semitic Languages* 22, no. 2 (1996): 1-16.

Arnold, Clinton E. *The Colossian Syncretism: The Interface between Christianity and Folk Belief at Colossae.* Grand Rapids: Baker, 1996.

―――. "Returning to the Domain of the Powers: STOICHEIA as Evil Spirits in Galatians 4:3, 9," *Novum Testamentum* 38 (January 1996): 55-76.

Augustine. *City of God.* Translated by Marcus Dods. New York: Random House, 1950.

Auld, Graeme. "*Imago Dei* in Genesis: Speaking in the Image of God," *Expository Times* 116 (2005): 259-62.

Bahnsen, Greg L. *Theonomy in Christian Ethics.* Nutley, NJ: Craig, 1979.

Baker, Robert C., and Roland Cap Ehlke, eds. *Natural Law: A Lutheran Reappraisal.* St. Louis: Concordia, 2011.

Balogh, Csaba. *The Stele of YHWH in Egypt: The Prophecies of Isaiah 18–20 Concerning Egypt and Kush.* Leiden: Brill, 2011.

Balthasar, Hans Urs von. *The Theology of Karl Barth.* Translated by John Drury. New York: Holt, Rinehart & Winston, 1971.

Bar-Efrat, Shimon. *Narrative Art in the Bible.* Sheffield: Almond, 1989.

Barclay, John M. G. *Obeying the Truth: Paul's Ethics in Galatians.* Minneapolis: Fortress, 1988.

Barr, James. *Biblical Faith and Natural Theology.* Oxford: Clarendon, 1993.

———. "Reflections on the Covenant with Noah." In *Covenant as Context: Essays in Honour of E. W. Nicholson,* edited by A. D. H. Mayes and Robert B. Salters, pp. 11-22. Oxford: Oxford University Press, 2003.

———. *The Semantics of Biblical Language.* Oxford: Clarendon, 1961.

Barré, Michael L. "The Meaning of *l' 'sybnw* in Amos 1:3–2:6," *Journal of Biblical Literature* 105, no. 4 (1986): 611-31.

Barth, Karl. *Church Dogmatics III/1.* London: T. & T. Clark, 2004.

Bartholomew, Craig G. "A Time for War, and a Time for Peace: Old Testament Wisdom, Creation and O'Donovan's Theological Ethics." In *A Royal Priesthood? The Use of the Bible Ethically and Politically: A Dialogue with Oliver O'Donovan,* edited by Craig G. Bartholomew, Jonathan Chaplin, Robert Song, and Al Wolters, pp. 91-112. Grand Rapids: Zondervan, 2002.

Barton, John. *Understanding Old Testament Ethics: Approaches and Explorations.* Louisville: Westminster John Knox, 2003.

Bartor, Assnat. *Reading Law as Narrative: A Study in the Casuistic Laws of the Pentateuch.* Atlanta: Society of Biblical Literature, 2010.

Bash, Anthony. "Forgiveness: A Re-appraisal," *Studies in Christian Ethics* 24, no. 2 (2011): 133-46.

Bauckham, Richard. *Living with Other Creatures: Green Exegesis and Theology.* Waco, TX: Baylor University Press, 2011.

Baugh, S. M. "Galatians 5:1-6 and Personal Obligation: Reflections on Paul and the Law." In *The Law Is Not of Faith: Essays on Works and Grace in the Mosaic Covenant,* edited by Bryan D. Estelle, J. V. Fesko, and David VanDrunen, pp. 259-80. Phillipsburg, NJ: Presbyterian and Reformed, 2009.

Bavinck, Herman. "Calvin and Common Grace." In *Calvin and the Reformation,* edited by William Park Armstrong, pp. 99-130. New York: Fleming H. Revell, 1909.

———. *God and Creation.* Vol. 2 of *Reformed Dogmatics.* Translated by John Vriend. Edited by John Bolt. Grand Rapids: Baker Academic, 2004.

———. *Prolegomena.* Vol. 1 of *Reformed Dogmatics.* Translated by John Vriend. Edited by John Bolt. Grand Rapids: Baker Academic, 2003.

————. *Sin and Salvation in Christ.* Vol. 3 of *Reformed Dogmatics.* Translated by John Vriend. Edited by John Bolt. Grand Rapids: Baker Academic, 2006.

Bayes, Jonathan F. *The Weakness of the Law: God's Law and the Christian in New Testament Perspective.* Carlisle: Paternoster, 2000.

Beale, G. K. "The Eschatological Conception of New Testament Theology." In *"The Reader Must Understand": Eschatology in Bible and Theology,* edited by K. E. Brower and M. W. Elliot, pp. 11-52. Leicester: InterVarsity, 1997.

————. *The Temple and the Church's Mission: A Biblical Theology of the Dwelling Place of God.* Downers Grove, IL: InterVarsity, 2004.

Bechtel, Lyn M. "What if Dinah Is Not Raped? (Genesis 34)," *Journal for the Study of the Old Testament* 19 (1994): 19-36.

Bell, Richard H. *No One Seeks for God: An Exegetical and Theological Study of Romans 1.18–3.20.* Tübingen: Mohr Siebeck, 1998.

Belleville, Linda J. "'Under Law': Structural Analysis and the Pauline Concept of Law in Galatians 3:21–4:11," *Journal for the Study of the New Testament* 26 (1986): 53-78.

Berkhof, Louis. *Systematic Theology.* 4th ed. Grand Rapids: Eerdmans, 1993.

Berlin, Adele. *Lamentations: A Commentary.* Louisville: Westminster John Knox, 2002.

Betz, Hans Dieter. *Galatians: A Commentary on Paul's Letter to the Churches in Galatia.* Philadelphia: Fortress, 1979.

Biggar, Nigel. "Specify and Distinguish! Interpreting the New Testament on 'Non-Violence'," *Studies in Christian Ethics* 22, no. 2 (2009): 164-84.

Bird, Phyllis A. "'Male and Female He Created Them': Gen 1:27b in the Context of the Priestly Account of Creation," *Harvard Theological Review* 74, no. 2 (1981): 129-60.

Bleich, J. David. "*Tikkun Olam:* Jewish Obligations to Non-Jewish Society." In *Tikkun Olam: Social Responsibility in Jewish Thought and Law,* edited by David Shatz, Chaim Isaac Waxman, and Nathan J. Diament, pp. 61-102. Northvale, NJ: Jason Aronson, 1997.

Blenkinsopp, Joseph. *Isaiah 1–39: A New Translation with Introduction and Commentary.* New York: Doubleday, 2000.

————. *Wisdom and Law in the Old Testament: The Ordering of Life in Israel and Early Judaism.* Oxford: Oxford University Press, 1983.

Blocher, Henri. *In the Beginning: The Opening Chapters of Genesis.* Downers Grove, IL: InterVarsity, 1984.

Blount, Brian K. "Reading and Understanding the New Testament on Homosexuality." In *Homosexuality and Christian Community,* edited by C. L. Seow, pp. 28-38. Louisville: Westminster John Knox, 1996.

Bockmuehl, Markus. *Jewish Law in Gentile Churches: Halakhah and the Beginning of Christian Public Ethics.* Grand Rapids: Baker Academic, 2000.

Boecker, Hans Jochen. *Law and the Administration of Justice in the Old Testament and Ancient East.* Translated by Jeremy Moiser. Minneapolis: Augsburg, 1980.

Bolin, Thomas M. "The Role of Exchange in Ancient Mediterranean Religion and Its Implications for Reading Genesis 18–19," *Journal for the Study of the Old Testament* 29, no. 1 (2004): 37-56.

Bolt, John. "Bavinck's Use of Wisdom Literature in Systematic Theology," *Scottish Bulletin of Evangelical Theology* 29 (Spring 2011): 4-23.

Boswell, John. *Christianity, Social Tolerance, and Homosexuality: Gay People in Western Europe from the Beginning of the Christian Era to the Fourteenth Century.* 8th ed. Chicago: University of Chicago Press, 2005.

Botterweck, G. Johannes, and Helmer Ringgren, eds. *Theological Dictionary of the Old Testament.* 2 vols. Grand Rapids: Eerdmans, 1975.

Boyd, Craig A. *A Shared Morality: A Narrative Defense of Natural Law Ethics.* Grand Rapids: Brazos, 2007.

Brague, Rémi. *The Law of God: The Philosophical History of an Idea.* Translated by Lydia G. Cochrane. Chicago: University of Chicago Press, 2007.

Brakel, Wilhelmus à. *The Christian's Reasonable Service.* 4 vols. Translated by Bartel Elshout. Ligonier, PA: Soli Deo Gloria, 1992-95.

Braulik, Georg. *The Theology of Deuteronomy.* Richland Hills, TX: BIBAL, 1994.

Bray, Gerald, ed. *Romans.* Ancient Christian Commentary on Scripture. Downers Grove, IL: InterVarsity, 1998.

Brooten, Bernadette J. *Love between Women: Early Christian Responses to Female Homoeroticism.* Chicago: University of Chicago Press, 1996.

Brown, William P. *Character in Crisis: A Fresh Approach to the Wisdom Literature of the Old Testament.* Grand Rapids: Eerdmans, 1996.

————. *The Ethos of the Cosmos: The Genesis of Moral Imagination in the Bible.* Grand Rapids: Eerdmans, 1999.

————. "The Law and the Sages: A Reexamination of Tora in Proverbs." In *Constituting the Community: Studies on the Polity of Ancient Israel in Honor of S. Dean McBride, Jr.,* edited by John T. Strong and Steven Shawn Tuell, pp. 251-80. Winona Lake, IN: Eisenbrauns, 2005.

————. *The Seven Pillars of Creation: The Bible, Science, and the Ecology of Wonder.* Oxford: Oxford University Press, 2010.

Broyde, Michael J. "The Obligation of Jews to Seek Observance of Noahide Laws by Gentiles: A Theoretical Review." In *Tikkun Olam: Social Responsibility in Jewish Thought and Law,* edited by David Shatz, Chaim Isaac Waxman, and Nathan J. Diament, pp. 103-43. Northvale, NJ: Jason Aronson, 1997.

Bruckner, James K. *Implied Law in the Abraham Narrative: A Literary and Theological Analysis.* Sheffield: Sheffield Academic Press, 2001.

Brueggemann, Walter. *Genesis.* Atlanta: John Knox, 1982.

————. *In Man We Trust: The Neglected Side of Biblical Faith.* Atlanta: John Knox, 1972.

Brunner, Emil, and Karl Barth. *Natural Theology: Comprising "Nature and Grace" by Professor Dr. Emil Brunner and the Reply "No!" by Dr. Karl Barth.* Eugene, OR: Wipf & Stock, 2002.

Buchanan, James. *The Doctrine of Justification. An Outline of Its History in the Church and of Its Exposition from Scripture.* Edinburgh: 1867.

Budziszewski, J. *The Line Through the Heart: Natural Law as Fact, Theory, and Sign of Contradiction.* Wilmington, DE: ISI Books, 2009.

Burns Jr., J. Patout, ed. and trans. *Romans: Interpreted by Early Christian Commentators.* Grand Rapids: Eerdmans, 2012.

Burnside, Jonathan P. *God, Justice, and Society: Aspects of Law and Legality in the Bible.* Oxford: Oxford University Press, 2011.

————. "Retribution and Restoration in Biblical Texts." In *Handbook of Restorative Justice,* edited by Gerry Johnstone and Daniel W. Van Ness, pp. 132-48. Cullompton, UK: Willan, 2007.

Calvin, John. *Commentaries on the Book of the Prophet Daniel.* Vol. 1. Translated by Thomas Myers. Grand Rapids: Eerdmans, 1948.

————. *Commentaries on the First Book of Moses Called Genesis.* Vol. 1. Translated by John King. Grand Rapids: Eerdmans, 1963.

————. *Commentaries on the Twelve Minor Prophets.* Vol. 2. Translated by John Owen. Grand Rapids: Eerdmans, n.d.

————. *Commentary on a Harmony of the Evangelists, Matthew, Mark, and Luke.* Vol. 2. Translated by William Pringle. Grand Rapids: Baker, 2003.

————. *Commentary on the Book of the Prophet Isaiah.* 2 vols. Translated by William Pringle. Grand Rapids: Eerdmans, 1948.

————. *Commentary on the Epistles of Paul the Apostle to the Corinthians.* 2 vols. Translated by John Pringle. Grand Rapids: Eerdmans, 1948.

————. *Institutes of the Christian Religion.* Translated by Henry Beveridge. Grand Rapids: Eerdmans, 1953.

————. *The Second Epistle of Paul the Apostle to the Corinthians and the Epistles to Timothy, Titus, and Philemon.* Translated by T. A. Smail. Grand Rapids: Eerdmans, 1964.

Bibliography

Camp, Claudia V. *Wisdom and the Feminine in the Book of Proverbs.* Sheffield: Almond, 1985.

Campbell, Douglas A. *The Deliverance of God: An Apocalyptic Rereading of Justification in Paul.* Grand Rapids: Eerdmans, 2009.

―――. "Natural Theology in Paul? Reading Romans 1.19-20," *International Journal of Systematic Theology* 1 (November 1999): 231-52.

Carmichael, Calum M. *Law, Legend, and Incest in the Bible: Leviticus 18–20.* Ithaca, NY: Cornell University Press, 1997.

Carson, D. A. "The Vindication of Imputation: On Fields of Discourse and Semantic Fields." In *Justification: What's at Stake in the Current Debates,* edited by Mark Husbands and Daniel J. Treier, pp. 46-77. Downers Grove, IL: InterVarsity, 2004.

Carter, Craig A. *Rethinking Christ and Culture: A Post-Christendom Perspective.* Grand Rapids: Brazos, 2006.

Carter, T. L. *Paul and the Power of Sin: Redefining 'Beyond the Pale.'* Cambridge: Cambridge University Press, 2002.

Carter, Warren. "Jesus' 'I Have Come' Statements in Matthew's Gospel," *Catholic Biblical Quarterly* 60 (2001): 44-62.

Cassuto, Umberto, and Israel Abrahams. *A Commentary on the Book of Genesis: Part 1, From Adam to Noah.* Jerusalem: Magnes, 1972.

Chalmers, Aaron. "The Importance of the Noahic Covenant to Biblical Theology," *Tyndale Bulletin* 60, no. 2 (2009): 207-16.

Chan, Michael. "Rhetorical Reversal and Usurpation: Isaiah 10:5-34 and the Use of Neo-Assyrian Royal Idiom in the Construction of an Anti-Assyrian Theology," *Journal of Biblical Literature* 128, no. 4 (2009): 717-33.

Chaplin, Jonathan. *Herman Dooyeweerd: Christian Philosopher of State and Civil Society.* Notre Dame: University of Notre Dame Press, 2011.

Charles, J. Daryl. *Retrieving the Natural Law: A Return to Moral First Things.* Grand Rapids: Eerdmans, 2008.

Childs, Brevard S. *Isaiah.* Louisville: Westminster John Knox, 2001.

Chisholm, Robert B. "The 'Everlasting Covenant' and the 'City of Chaos': Intentional Ambiguity and Irony in Isaiah 24," *Criswell Theological Review* 6, no. 2 (1993): 237-53.

Christensen, Duane L. *Deuteronomy 21:10–34:12.* Nashville: Thomas Nelson, 2001.

Clark, R. Scott. "Christ and Covenant: Federal Theology in Orthodoxy." In *Companion to Reformed Orthodoxy,* edited by Herman Selderhuis, pp. 403-28. Leiden: Brill, 2013.

Clark, W. Malcolm. "A Legal Background to the Yahwist's Use of Good and Evil in Genesis 2–3," *Journal of Biblical Literature* 88 (September 1969): 266-78.

Clements, R. E. *Isaiah 1–39*. Grand Rapids: Eerdmans, 1980.

———. "Solomon and the Origins of Wisdom in Israel," *Perspectives in Religious Studies* 15 (1988): 23-26.

———. *Wisdom in Theology*. Grand Rapids: Eerdmans, 1992.

Clifford, Richard J. *Proverbs: A Commentary*. Louisville: Westminster John Knox, 1999.

Clines, D. J. A. "Humanity as the Image of God." In *On the Way to the Postmodern: Old Testament Essays, 1967-1998*, vol. 2, edited by D. J. A. Clines, pp. 447-97. Sheffield: Sheffield Academic Press, 1998.

Collins, C. John. "Echoes of Aristotle in Romans 2:14-15: Or, Maybe Abimelech Was Not So Bad After All," *Journal of Markets and Morality* 13 (Spring 2010): 123-73.

Collins, John J. *Daniel, First Maccabees, Second Maccabees*. Wilmington, DE: Michael Glazier, 1981.

Cotter, David W. *Genesis*. Collegeville, MN: Liturgical, 2003.

Countryman, L. William. *Dirt, Greed, and Sex: Sexual Ethics in the New Testament and Their Implications for Today*. Philadelphia: Fortress, 1988.

Covington, Jesse, Bryan McGraw, and Micah Watson, eds. *Natural Law and Evangelical Political Theory*. Lanham, MD: Lexington, 2013.

Craigie, Peter C. *The Book of Deuteronomy*. Grand Rapids: Eerdmans, 1976.

Cranfield, C. E. B. *The Epistle to the Romans,* vol. 1. Edinburgh: T. & T. Clark, 1975.

Crenshaw, James L. *Old Testament Wisdom: An Introduction*. Louisville: Westminster John Knox, 1998.

———. *Urgent Advice and Probing Questions: Collected Writings on Old Testament Wisdom*. Macon, GA: Mercer University Press, 1995.

Curtis, Byron G. "Hosea 6:7 and Covenant-Breaking like/at Adam." In *The Law Is Not of Faith: Essays on Works and Grace in the Mosaic Covenant,* edited by Bryan D. Estelle, J. V. Fesko, and David VanDrunen, pp. 170-209. Phillipsburg, NJ: Presbyterian and Reformed, 2009.

Das, A. Andrew. "Galatians 3:10: A 'Newer Perspective' on an Omitted Premise." In *Unity and Diversity in the Gospels and Paul: Essays in Honor of Frank J. Matera,* edited by Christopher W. Skinner and Kelly R. Iverson, pp. 203-23. Atlanta: Society of Biblical Literature, 2012.

———. "Paul and Works of Obedience in Second Temple Judaism: Romans 4:4-5 as a 'New Perspective' Case Study," *Catholic Biblical Quarterly* 71 (October 2009): 795-812.

———. *Paul, the Law, and the Covenant.* Peabody, MA: Hendrickson, 2001.

———. *Solving the Romans Debate.* Minneapolis: Fortress, 2007.

Davies, John A. "'Discerning between Good and Evil': Solomon as a New Adam in 1 Kings," *Westminster Theological Journal* 73 (Spring 2011): 39-57.

Davies, Margaret. "New Testament Ethics and Ours: Homosexuality and Sexuality in Romans 1:26-27," *Biblical Interpretation* 3 (October 1995): 315-31.

Davies, W. D., and Dale C. Allison. *A Critical and Exegetical Commentary on the Gospel According to Saint Matthew.* 2 vols. Edinburgh: T. & T. Clark, 1988.

Davis, James F. *Lex Talionis in Early Judaism and the Exhortation of Jesus in Matthew 5:38-42.* New York: T. & T. Clark, 2005.

Day, John. "Foreign Semitic Influence on the Wisdom of Israel and Its Appropriation in the Book of Proverbs." In *Wisdom in Ancient Israel: Essays in Honour of J. A. Emerton,* edited by John Day, R. P. Gordon, and H. G. M. Williamson, pp. 55-70. Cambridge: Cambridge University Press, 1995.

———. "Why Does God 'Establish' Rather Than 'Cut' Covenants in the Priestly Source?" In *Covenant as Context: Essays in Honour of E. W. Nicholson,* edited by A. D. H. Mayes and Robert B. Salters, pp. 91-109. Oxford: Oxford University Press, 2003.

De Boer, Martinus C. *Galatians: A Commentary.* Louisville: Westminster John Knox, 2011.

De Vaux, Roland. *Ancient Israel: Its Life and Institutions.* Translated by John McHugh. New York: McGraw-Hill, 1961.

Dell, Katharine J. *The Book of Proverbs in Social and Theological Context.* Cambridge: Cambridge University Press, 2006.

———. "Covenant and Creation in Relationship." In *Covenant as Context: Essays in Honour of E. W. Nicholson,* edited by A. D. H. Mayes and Robert B. Salters, pp. 111-33. Oxford: Oxford University Press, 2003.

Dempster, Stephen G. *Dominion and Dynasty: A Theology of the Hebrew Bible.* Downers Grove, IL: InterVarsity, 2003.

Deneen, Patrick J. "Unsustainable Liberalism," *First Things* (Aug.-Sept. 2012): 25-31.

Dequeker, L. "Noah and Israel: The Everlasting Divine Covenant with Mankind." In *Questions disputées d'Ancien Testament: Méthode et théologie,* edited by C. Brekelmans, pp. 115-29. Leuven: Leuven University Press, 1972.

Dooyeweerd, Herman. *Roots of Western Culture: Pagan, Secular, and Christian Options.* Translated by John Kraay. Toronto: Wedge, 1979.

Dorff, Elliot N. *To Do the Right and the Good: A Jewish Approach to Modern Social Ethics.* Philadelphia: Jewish Publication Society, 2002.

Doyle, Brian. "'Knock, Knock, Knockin' on Sodom's Door': The Function of

פתח/דלת in Genesis 18–19," *Journal for the Study of the Old Testament* 28, no. 4 (2004): 431-48.

Driver, G. R., and John Charles Miles, eds. *The Babylonian Laws.* Vol. 2 of *Ancient Codes and Laws of the Near East.* Oxford: Clarendon, 1955.

Driver, S. R. *A Critical and Exegetical Commentary on Deuteronomy.* Edinburgh: T. & T. Clark, 1895.

Dumbrell, W. J. *Covenant & Creation: A Theology of the Old Testament Covenants.* Carlisle: Paternoster, 1984.

———. *Romans: A New Covenant Commentary.* Eugene, OR: Wipf & Stock, 2005.

Dunn, James D. G. *The Epistle to the Galatians.* Peabody, MA: Hendrickson, 1993.

———. "In Search of Common Ground." In *Paul and the Mosaic Law,* edited by James D. G. Dunn. Grand Rapids: Eerdmans, 2001.

———. *Romans 1–8.* Dallas: Word, 1988.

———. *The Theology of Paul the Apostle.* Grand Rapids: Eerdmans, 1998.

Durham, John I. *Exodus.* Waco, TX: Word, 1987.

Edwards, Mark J., ed. *Galatians, Ephesians, Philippians.* Ancient Christian Commentary on Scripture. Downers Grove, IL: InterVarsity, 1999.

Eisen, Robert. "The Education of Abraham: The Encounter between Abraham and God over the Fate of Sodom and Gomorrah," *The Jewish Bible Quarterly* 28 (April-June 2000): 80-86.

Elazar, Daniel. *Covenant & Polity in Biblical Israel: Biblical Foundations & Jewish Expressions.* New Brunswick, NJ: Transaction, 1995.

Erlandsson, Seth. *The Burden of Babylon: A Study of Isaiah 13:2–14:23.* Lund, Sweden: CWK Gleerup, 1970.

Estelle, Bryan D. "The Covenant of Works in Moses and Paul." In *Covenant, Justification, and Pastoral Ministry: Essays by the Faculty of Westminster Seminary California,* edited by R. Scott Clark, pp. 89-135. Phillipsburg, NJ: Presbyterian and Reformed, 2007.

———. "Proverbs and Ahiqar: Revisited," *The Biblical Historian* 1 (2004): 1-9.

———, J. V. Fesko, and David VanDrunen, eds. *The Law Is Not of Faith: Essays on Works and Grace in the Mosaic Covenant.* Phillipsburg, NJ: Presbyterian and Reformed, 2009.

Evangelicals and Catholics Together. "In Defense of Religious Freedom," *First Things* (March 2012): 29-34.

Fesko, J. V. *Justification: Understanding the Classic Reformed Doctrine.* Phillipsburg, NJ: Presbyterian and Reformed, 2008.

———. *Last Things First: Unlocking Genesis 1–3 with the Christ of Eschatology.* Fearn, Ross-shire: Mentor, 2007.

Fewell, Danna Nolan, and David M. Gunn. "Tipping the Balance: Sternberg's

Reader and the Rape of Dinah," *Journal of Biblical Literature* 110, no. 2 (1991): 193-211.

Fields, Weston W. *Sodom and Gomorrah: History and Motif in Biblical Narrative.* Sheffield: Sheffield Academic Press, 1997.

Finkelstein, J. J. *The Ox That Gored.* Philadelphia: American Philosophical Society, 1981.

Finnis, John. *Aquinas: Moral, Political, and Legal Theory.* Oxford: Oxford University Press, 1998.

———. *Natural Law and Natural Rights.* Oxford: Clarendon, 1980.

Fishbane, Michael. "The Treaty Background of Amos 1:11 and Related Matters," *Journal of Biblical Literature* 89 (September 1970): 313-18.

Fitzmyer, Joseph A. *First Corinthians: A New Translation with Introduction and Commentary.* New Haven: Yale University Press, 2008.

———. *Romans: A New Translation with Introduction and Commentary.* New York: Doubleday, 1993.

Fox, Michael V. *Proverbs 1–9.* The Anchor Bible. New York: Doubleday, 2000.

———. *Proverbs 10–31.* The Anchor Bible. New Haven: Yale University Press, 2009.

Frame, John M. *Cornelius Van Til: An Analysis of His Thought.* Phillipsburg, NJ: Presbyterian and Reformed, 1995.

Freedman, David Noel. "Dinah and Shechem: Tamar and Amnon," *Austin Seminary Bulletin* 105 (Spring 1990): 51-63.

French, Peter A. *The Virtues of Vengeance.* Lawrence: University Press of Kansas, 2001.

Fretheim, Terrence E. *The Book of Genesis.* The New Interpreter's Bible. Nashville: Abingdon, 1994.

Friedman, Richard E. "The Hiding of the Face: An Essay on the Literary Unity of Biblical Narrative." In *Judaic Perspectives on Ancient Israel,* edited by Jacob Neusner et al., pp. 207-22. Philadelphia: Fortress, 1987.

Frydrych, Tomáš. *Living Under the Sun: Examination of Proverbs and Qoheleth.* Leiden: Brill, 2002.

Gaffin, Richard B., Jr. *By Faith, Not by Sight: Paul and the Order of Salvation.* Waynesboro, GA: Paternoster, 2006.

Gage, Warren Austin. *The Gospel of Genesis: Studies in Protology and Eschatology.* Winona Lake, IN: Carpenter, 1984.

Gagnon, Robert A. J. *The Bible and Homosexual Practice: Texts and Hermeneutics.* Nashville: Abingdon, 2001.

Gammie, John G. "The Theology of Retribution in the Book of Deuteronomy," *Catholic Biblical Quarterly* 32 (1970): 1-12.

Garlington, Don. *An Exposition of Galatians: A New Perspective/Reformational Reading.* 2nd ed. Eugene, OR: Wipf & Stock, 2004.

Garr, W. Randall. *In His Own Image and Likeness: Humanity, Divinity, and Monotheism.* Leiden: Brill, 2003.

Gathercole, Simon J. "The Cross and Substitutionary Atonement," *The Southern Baptist Journal of Theology* 11 (Summer 2007): 64-73.

———. "Justified by Faith, Justified by His Blood: The Evidence of Romans 3:21–4:25." In *Justification and Variegated Nomism: The Paradoxes of Paul,* vol. 2, edited by D. A. Carson, Peter Thomas O'Brien, and Mark A. Seifrid, pp. 147-84. Grand Rapids: Baker Academic, 2004.

———. *The Pre-Existent Son: Recovering the Christologies of Matthew, Mark, and Luke.* Grand Rapids: Eerdmans, 2006.

———. *Where Is Boasting? Early Jewish Soteriology and Paul's Response in Romans 1–5.* Grand Rapids: Eerdmans, 2002.

Gemser, B. "The Importance of the Motive Clause in Old Testament Law." In *Supplements to Vetus Testamentum,* vol. 1, pp. 50-66. Leiden: Brill, 1953.

George, Robert P. *In Defense of Natural Law.* Oxford: Clarendon, 1999.

———. "Religious Liberty and the Human Good," *International Journal of Religious Freedom* 5, no. 1 (2012): 35-44.

Geyer, John B. "Mythology and Culture in the Oracles Against the Nations," *Vetus Testamentum* 36, no. 2 (1986): 129-45.

Gieschen, Charles A. "Original Sin in the New Testament," *Concordia Journal* 31 (2005): 366-70.

Goldingay, John. *Daniel.* Dallas: Word, 1989.

———. *Isaiah.* Peabody, MA: Hendrickson, 2001.

Gowan, Donald E. *The Book of Amos: Introduction, Commentary, and Reflections.* The New Interpreter's Bible. Nashville: Abingdon, 1996.

Grabill, Stephen John. *Rediscovering the Natural Law in Reformed Theological Ethics.* Grand Rapids: Eerdmans, 2006.

Gregory, Eric. *Politics and the Order of Love: An Augustinian Ethic of Democratic Citizenship.* Chicago: University of Chicago Press, 2008.

Grenz, Stanley J. *The Social God and the Relational Self: A Trinitarian Theology of the Imago Dei.* Louisville: Westminster John Knox, 2001.

Grisez, Germain. *The Way of the Lord Jesus 1: Christian Moral Principles.* Chicago: Franciscan Herald, 1983.

Griswold, Charles L. *Forgiveness: A Philosophical Exploration.* Cambridge: Cambridge University Press, 2007.

Grundke, Christopher L. K. "A Tempest in a Teapot? Genesis III 8 Again," *Vetus Testamentum* 51, no. 4 (2001): 548-51.

Gundry, Robert H. "The Nonimputation of Christ's Righteousness." In *Justifica-tion: What's at Stake in the Current Debates,* edited by Mark Husbands and Daniel J. Treier, pp. 17-45. Downers Grove, IL: InterVarsity, 2004.

Hahn, Scott. *Kinship by Covenant: A Canonical Approach to the Fulfillment of God's Saving Promises.* New Haven: Yale University Press, 2009.

Hamborg, G. R. "Reasons for Judgement in the Oracles against the Nations of the Prophet Isaiah," *Vetus Testamentum* 31, no. 2 (1981): 145-59.

Hamilton, Victor P. *The Book of Genesis Chapters 1–17.* Grand Rapids: Eerdmans, 1990.

———. *The Book of Genesis: Chapters 18–50.* Grand Rapids: Eerdmans, 1995.

Hart, H. L. A. *The Concept of Law.* 2nd ed. Oxford: Oxford University Press, 1997.

Hartley, John E. *Leviticus.* Dallas: Word, 1992.

Hartman, Louis Francis, and Alexander A. di Lella. *The Book of Daniel.* Garden City, NY: Doubleday, 1978.

Hauerwas, Stanley. *A Better Hope: Resources for a Church Confronting Capital-ism, Democracy, and Postmodernity.* Grand Rapids: Brazos, 2000.

———. *The Peaceable Kingdom: A Primer in Christian Ethics.* Notre Dame: University of Notre Dame Press, 1983.

Hawthorne, Gerald F. *Philippians.* Waco, TX: Word, 1983.

Hayes, John H. "Amos's Oracles against the Nations," *Review and Expositor* 92 (1995): 153-67.

Hays, Richard B. "Christology and Ethics in Galatians: The Law of Christ," *Cath-olic Biblical Quarterly* 49 (1987): 268-90.

———. *The Letter to the Galatians: Introduction, Commentary, and Reflections.* New Interpreter's Bible. Nashville: Abingdon, 2000.

———. *The Moral Vision of the New Testament: Community, Cross, New Cre-ation: A Contemporary Introduction to New Testament Ethics.* New York: HarperSanFrancisco, 1996.

Heaton, E. W. *Solomon's New Men: The Emergence of Ancient Israel as a National State.* New York: Pica, 1974.

Heiser, Michael S. "Deuteronomy 32:8 and the Sons of God," *Bibliotheca Sacra* 158 (January-March 2001): 52-74.

Helm, Paul. *Calvin at the Centre.* Oxford: Oxford University Press, 2010.

———. "Image of the Spirit and Image of God." In *Creator, Redeemer, Consum-mator: A Festschrift for Meredith G. Kline,* edited by Howard Griffith and John R. Muether, pp. 203-14. Greenville, SC: Reformed Academic Press, 2000.

Hepner, Gershon. "Abraham's Incestuous Marriage with Sarah: A Violation of the Holiness Code," *Vetus Testamentum* 53 (2003): 143-55.

Hittinger, Russell. *A Critique of the New Natural Law Theory.* Notre Dame: University of Notre Dame Press, 1987.

——. *The First Grace: Rediscovering the Natural Law in a Post-Christian World.* Wilmington, DE: ISI Books, 2003.

Hoekema, Anthony A. *The Bible and the Future.* Grand Rapids: Eerdmans, 1979.

Hoffmeier, James K. "The Wives' Tales of Genesis 12, 20 & 26 and the Covenants at Beer-Sheba," *Tyndale Bulletin* 43, no. 1 (1992): 81-100.

Hogue, Arthur R. *Origins of the Common Law.* Bloomington: Indiana University Press, 1966.

Hollander, H. W. "The Meaning of the Term 'Law' in 1 Corinthians," *Novum Testamentum* 40 (1998): 117-35.

——, and J. Hollemna. "The Relationship of Death, Sin, and Law in 1 Cor 15:56," *Novum Testamentum* 35 (1993): 270-91.

Hong, In-Gyu. *The Law in Galatians.* Sheffield: Sheffield Academic Press, 1993.

Hooker, M. D. "Adam in Romans 1," *New Testament Studies* 6 (1959-60): 297-306.

——. "A Further Note on Romans 1," *New Testament Studies* 13 (1966-67): 181-83.

Horton, Michael S. *The Christian Faith: A Systematic Theology for Pilgrims on the Way.* Grand Rapids: Zondervan, 2000.

——. *God of Promise: Introducing Covenant Theology.* Grand Rapids: Baker, 2006.

——. *Lord and Servant: A Covenant Christology.* Louisville: Westminster John Knox, 2005.

——. *People and Place: A Covenant Ecclesiology.* Louisville: Westminster John Knox, 2008.

Hubbard, David Allen. *Joel and Amos: An Introduction and Commentary.* Downers Grove, IL: InterVarsity, 1989.

Hubbard, Moyer V. *New Creation in Paul's Letters and Thought.* Cambridge: Cambridge University Press, 2002.

Hübner, Hans. *Law in Paul's Thought.* Translated by James C. G. Greig. Edinburgh: T. & T. Clark, 1984.

Hultgren, Arland J. *Paul's Letter to the Romans: A Commentary.* Grand Rapids: Eerdmans, 2011.

Hütter, Reinhard. "Attending to the Wisdom of God — from Effect to Cause, from Creation to God: A *relecture* of the Analogy of Being according to Thomas Aquinas." In *The Analogy of Being: Invention of the Antichrist or the Wisdom of God?* edited by Thomas Joseph White, pp. 209-45. Grand Rapids: Eerdmans, 2011.

Hyldahl, Niels. "A Reminiscence of the Old Testament at Romans i.23," *New Testament Studies* 2 (1955-56): 285-88.

Hyman, Ronald T. "Final Judgment: The Ambiguous Moral Question That Culminates Genesis 34," *Jewish Bible Quarterly* 28 (April-June 2000): 93-101.

Irenaeus. "Against Heresies." In *Ante-Nicene Fathers,* vol. 1, edited by Alexander Roberts and James Donaldson, pp. 315-567. Peabody, MA: Hendrickson, 1994.

Jackson, Bernard S. *Wisdom-Laws: A Study of the Mishpatim of Exodus 21:1–22:16.* Oxford: Oxford University Press, 2006.

Jackson, Timothy P. *The Priority of Love: Christian Charity and Social Justice.* Princeton: Princeton University Press, 2003.

Jacob, B. *The First Book of the Bible: Genesis.* Translated by Ernst Jacob and Walter Jacob. New York: Ktav, 1974.

Jacoby, Susan. *Wild Justice: The Evolution of Revenge.* New York: Harper & Row, 1983.

Jeremias, Joachim. *The Sermon on the Mount.* Translated by Norman Perrin. Philadelphia: Fortress, 1963.

Jeremias, Jörg. *The Book of Amos: A Commentary.* Translated by Douglas W. Stott. Louisville: Westminster John Knox, 1998.

Jervis, L. Ann. "'Commandment Which Is for Life' (Romans 7.10): Sins' Use of the Obedience of Faith," *Journal for the Study of the New Testament* 27 (2004): 193-216.

Jewett, Robert. *Romans: A Commentary.* Minneapolis: Fortress, 2007.

John of Damascus. "The Orthodox Faith." In *The Fathers of the Church,* vol. 37, translated by Frederic C. Chase Jr., pp. 165-406. New York: Fathers of the Church, 1958.

Johnson, Dan G. *From Chaos to Restoration: An Integrative Reading of Isaiah 24–27.* Sheffield: Sheffield Academic Press, 1988.

Johnson, Dennis. "The Function of Romans 7:13-25 in Paul's Argument for the Law's Impotence and the Spirit's Power, and Its Bearing on the Identity of the Schizophrenic 'I.'" In *Resurrection and Eschatology: Theology in Service of the Church: Essays in Honor of Richard B. Gaffin, Jr.,* edited by Lane G. Tipton and Jeffrey C. Waddington, pp. 3-59. Phillipsburg, NJ: Presbyterian and Reformed, 2008.

Johnson, Luke Timothy. *Reading Romans: A Literary and Theological Commentary.* New York: Crossroad, 1997.

Johnson, Thomas K. *Natural Law Ethics: An Evangelical Proposal.* Bonn: Verlag für Kultur und Wissenschaft, 2005.

Jones, Brian C. *Howling over Moab: Irony and Rhetoric in Isaiah 15–16.* Atlanta: Scholars, 1996.

Jones, L. Gregory. *Embodying Forgiveness: A Theological Analysis.* Grand Rapids: Eerdmans, 1995.

Jónsson, Gunnlaugur A. *The Image of God: Genesis 1:26-28 in a Century of Old Testament Research.* Lund, Sweden: Almqvist & Wiksell, 1988.

Joüon, Paul, S.J. *A Grammar of Biblical Hebrew.* Translated and revised by T. Muraoka. Rome: Editrice Pontificio Instituto Biblico, 1991.

Käsemann, Ernst. *Commentary on Romans.* Translated and edited by Geoffrey William Bromiley. Grand Rapids: Eerdmans, 1980.

Kass, Leon. *The Beginning of Wisdom: Reading Genesis.* Chicago: University of Chicago Press, 2003.

Kaufman, Steven A. "The Second Table of the Decalogue and the Implicit Categories of Ancient Near Eastern Law." In *Love & Death in the Ancient Near East: Essays in Honor of Marvin H. Pope,* edited by John H. Marks and Robert M. Good, pp. 11-16. Guilford, CT: Four Quarters, 1987.

Kelsey, David H. *Eccentric Existence: A Theological Anthropology.* 2 vols. Louisville: Westminster John Knox, 2009.

Kim, Seyoon. *Paul and the New Perspective: Second Thoughts on the Origin of Paul's Gospel.* Grand Rapids: Eerdmans, 2001.

Kline, Meredith G. "Death, Leviathan, and Martyrs: Isaiah 24:1–27:1." In *A Tribute to Gleason Archer,* edited by Walter C. Kaiser and Ronald F. Youngblood, pp. 229-49. Chicago: Moody, 1986.

———. "Double Trouble," *Journal of the Evangelical Theological Society* 32 (June 1989): 171-79.

———. *God, Heaven and Har Magedon: A Covenantal Tale of Cosmos and Telos.* Eugene, OR: Wipf & Stock, 2006.

———. *Images of the Spirit.* Grand Rapids: Baker, 1980.

———. *Kingdom Prologue: Genesis Foundations for a Covenantal Worldview.* Overland Park, KS: Two Age, 2000.

———. "Lex Talionis and the Human Fetus," *Journal of the Evangelical Society* 20 (1977): 193-201.

———. *Treaty of the Great King: The Covenant Structure of Deuteronomy.* Grand Rapids: Eerdmans, 1963.

Kloosterman, Nelson D. "Review Article: *A Biblical Case for Natural Law,*" *Ordained Servant* 16 (2007): 101-7.

Knierim, Rolf P. *The Task of Old Testament Theology: Method and Cases.* Grand Rapids: Eerdmans, 1995.

Koch, Klaus. "Is There a Doctrine of Retribution in the Old Testament?" In

Theodicy in the Old Testament, edited by James L Crenshaw, pp. 57-87. Philadelphia: Fortress, 1983.

Krašovec, J. "Punishment and Mercy in the Primeval History," *Ephemerides Theologicae Lovanienses* 70 (April 1994): 5-33.

Kries, Douglas. *The Problem of Natural Law.* Lanham, MD: Lexington, 2007.

Kuhn, Karl A. "Natural and Unnatural Relations between Text and Context: A Canonical Reading of Romans 1:26-27," *Currents in Theology and Mission* 33 (August 2006): 313-29.

Kuula, Kari. *The Law, the Covenant and God's Plan.* 2 vols. Göttingen: Vandenhoeck & Ruprecht, 1999.

Kuyper, A. *De Gemeene Gratie.* Kampen: J. H. Kok, 1945.

Lemaire, André. "Wisdom in Solomonic Historiography." In *Wisdom in Ancient Israel: Essays in Honour of J. A. Emerton,* edited by John Day, R. P. Gordon and H. G. M. Williamson, pp. 106-18. Cambridge: Cambridge University Press, 1995.

Lessing, R. Reed. *Interpreting Discontinuity: Isaiah's Tyre Oracle.* Winona Lake, IN: Eisenbrauns, 2004.

———. "Satire in Isaiah's Tyre Oracle," *Journal for the Study of the Old Testament* 28, no. 1 (2003): 89-112.

Letellier, Robert Ignatius. *Day in Mamre, Night in Sodom: Abraham and Lot in Genesis 18 and 19.* Leiden: Brill, 1995.

Levenson, Jon. *Creation and the Persistence of Evil: The Jewish Drama of Divine Omnipotence.* San Francisco: Harper & Row, 1988.

———. *Sinai and Zion: An Entry into the Jewish Bible.* San Francisco: HarperSanFranciso, 1985.

Levering, Matthew. *Biblical Natural Law: A Theocentric and Teleological Approach.* Oxford: Oxford University Press, 2008.

Levine, Nachman. "Sarah/Sodom: Birth, Destruction, and Synchronic Transaction," *Journal for the Study of the Old Testament* 31, no. 2 (2006): 131-46.

Lichtenstein, Aharon. "Does Jewish Tradition Recognize an Ethic Independent of Halakha?" In *Modern Jewish Ethics: Theory and Practice,* edited by Marvin Fox, pp. 62-88. Columbus: Ohio State University Press, 1975.

Lincoln, Andrew T. *The Letter to the Colossians.* The New Interpreter's Bible. Nashville: Abingdon, 2000.

Linville, James R. *Amos and the Cosmic Imagination.* Aldershot: Ashgate, 2008.

Loader, J. A. *A Tale of Two Cities: Sodom and Gomorrah in the Old Testament, Early Jewish and Early Christian Traditions.* Kampen: Kok, 1990.

Lohfink, Norbert, S.J. "Poverty in the Laws of the Ancient Near East and of the Bible," *Theological Studies* 52 (1991): 36-42.

Long, Steven A. *Natura Pura: On the Recovery of Nature in the Doctrine of Grace.* New York: Fordham University Press, 2010.

Longenecker, Richard. *Biblical Exegesis in the Apostolic Period.* Grand Rapids: Eerdmans, 1975.

―――. *Galatians.* Dallas: Word, 1990.

Longman, Tremper, III. *How to Read Exodus.* Downers Grove, IL: IVP Academic, 2009.

―――. *Proverbs.* Grand Rapids: Baker Academic, 2006.

Lossky, Vladimir. *Orthodox Theology: An Introduction.* Crestwood, NY: St. Vladimir's Seminary Press, 1978.

Louth, Andrew, ed. *Genesis 1–11.* Ancient Christian Commentary on Scripture. Downers Grove, IL: InterVarsity, 2001.

Lubac, Henri de. *The Mystery of the Supernatural.* Translated by Rosemary Sheed. New York: Herder & Herder, 1967.

Lucas, Ernest. *Daniel.* Downers Grove, IL: InterVarsity, 2002.

Lust, Johan. "'For Man Shall His Blood Be Shed' Gen 9:6 in Hebrew and in Greek." In *Tradition of the Text: Studies Offered to Dominique Barthelemy in Celebration of His 70th Birthday,* edited by Gerard J. Norton and Stephen Pisano, pp. 91-102. Fribourg: Biblical Institute of the University, 1991.

Luther, Martin. "The Freedom of a Christian." In *Luther's Works,* vol. 31, edited by Harold J. Grimm, pp. 327-77. Philadelphia: Fortress, 1957.

―――. "How Christians Should Regard Moses." In *Luther's Works,* vol. 35, edited by E. Theodore Bachmann, pp. 155-74. Philadelphia: Fortress, 1960.

―――. "Lectures on Romans." In *Luther's Works,* vol. 25, edited by Hilton C. Oswald. St. Louis: Concordia, 1972.

―――. "Temporal Authority: To What Extent It Should be Obeyed." In *Luther's Works,* vol. 45, edited by Walther I. Brandt, pp. 81-139. Philadelphia: Muhlenberg, 1962.

Lyons, William John. *Canon and Exegesis: Canonical Praxis and the Sodom Narrative.* Sheffield: Sheffield Academic Press, 2002.

MacIntyre, Alasdair C. *After Virtue: A Study in Moral Theory.* 2nd ed. Notre Dame: University of Notre Dame Press, 1984.

―――. "From Answers to Questions: A Response to the Responses." In *Intractable Disputes about the Natural Law: Alasdair MacIntyre and Critics,* edited by Lawrence Cunningham, pp. 313-51. Notre Dame: University of Notre Dame Press, 2009.

―――. "Intractable Moral Disagreements." In *Intractable Disputes about the Natural Law: Alasdair MacIntyre and Critics,* edited by Lawrence Cunningham, pp. 1-52. Notre Dame: University of Notre Dame Press, 2009.

Mahoney, Daniel J. "The Art of Liberty," *First Things* (Aug.-Sept. 2012): 33-35.

Marcus, Joel. "The Gates of Hades and the Keys of the Kingdom (Matt 16:18–19)," *Catholic Biblical Quarterly* 50 (1988): 443-55.

Markus, Robert A. *Christianity and the Secular.* Notre Dame: University of Notre Dame Press, 2006.

Marlow, Hilary. "The Lament over the River Nile — Isaiah xix 5-10 in Its Wider Context," *Vetus Testamentum* 57 (2007): 229-42.

Marshall, Christopher. *Beyond Retribution: A New Testament Vision for Justice, Crime, and Punishment.* Grand Rapids: Eerdmans, 2001.

Martens, John W. "Romans 2.14-16: A Stoic Reading," *New Testament Studies* 40 (1994): 55-67.

Martin, Dale B. "Heterosexism and the Interpretation of Romans 1:18-32," *Biblical Interpretation* 3 (October 1995): 332-55.

Martyn, J. Louis. *Galatians: A New Translation with Introduction and Commentary.* New York: Doubleday, 1997.

———. *Theological Issues in the Letters of Paul.* Nashville: Abingdon, 1997.

Mason, Stephen D. "Another Flood? Genesis 9 and Isaiah's Broken Eternal Covenant," *Journal for the Study of the Old Testament* 32, no. 2 (2007): 177-98.

———. *"Eternal Covenant" in the Pentateuch: The Contours of an Elusive Phrase.* New York: T. & T. Clark International, 2008.

Matlock, R. Barry. "Zeal for Paul but Not According to Knowledge: Douglas Campbell's War on 'Justification Theory,'" *Journal for the Study of the New Testament* 34 (December 2011): 115-49.

Mayr, Ernst. *What Evolution Is.* New York: Basic, 2001.

Mays, James Luther. *Amos: A Commentary.* Philadelphia: Fortress, 1969.

McBride, S. Dean. "Divine Protocol: Genesis 1:1–2:3 as Prologue to the Pentateuch." In *God Who Creates: Essays in Honor of W. Sibley Towner,* edited by William P. Brown and S. Dean McBride. Grand Rapids: Eerdmans, 2000.

———. "Polity of the Covenant People: The Book of Deuteronomy." In *Constituting the Community: Studies on the Polity of Ancient Israel in Honor of S. Dean McBride, Jr.,* edited by John T. Strong and Steven Shawn Tuell, pp. 17-33. Winona Lake, IN: Eisenbrauns, 2005.

McCarthy, Dennis J. *Treaty and Covenant: A Study in Form in the Ancient Oriental Documents and in the Old Testament.* Rome: Biblical Institute, 1963.

McCartney, Dan, and Charles Clayton. *Let the Reader Understand: A Guide to Interpreting and Applying the Bible.* 2nd ed. Phillipsburg, NJ: Presbyterian and Reformed, 2002.

McCloskey, Deirdre N. *Bourgeois Dignity: Why Economics Can't Explain the Modern World.* Chicago: University of Chicago Press, 2010.

McGrath, Alister E. *A Fine-Tuned Universe*. Louisville: Westminster John Knox, 2009.

———. *The Open Secret: A New Vision for Natural Theology*. Malden, MA: Blackwell, 2008.

McIver, Robert K. "The Parable of the Weeds among the Wheat (Matthew 13:24-30, 36-43) and the Relationship between the Kingdom and the Church as Portrayed in the Gospel of Matthew," *Journal of Biblical Literature* 114 (1995): 643-59.

McKinion, Steven A., ed. *Isaiah 1–39*. Ancient Christian Commentary on Scripture. Downers Grove, IL: InterVarsity, 2004.

Mendenhall, George E. *Law and Covenant in Israel and the Ancient Near East*. Pittsburgh: Biblical Colloquium, 1955.

Meyer, Jason C. *The End of the Law: Mosaic Covenant in Pauline Theology*. Nashville: Broadman & Holman, 2009.

Meyer, Paul W. "The Worm at the Core of the Apple: Exegetical Reflections on Romans 7." In *The Conversation Continues: Studies in Paul & John in Honor of J. Louis Martyn*, edited by Robert Tomson Fortna and Beverly Roberts Gaventa, pp. 62-84. Nashville: Abingdon, 1990.

Middleton, J. Richard. *The Liberating Image: The* Imago Dei *in Genesis 1*. Grand Rapids: Brazos, 2005.

Milbank, John. *Theology and Social Theory: Beyond Secular Reason*. Oxford: Blackwell, 1990.

Milgrom, Jacob. *Leviticus 1–16: A New Translation with Introduction and Commentary*. New York: Doubleday, 1991.

———. *Leviticus 23–27: A New Translation with Introduction and Commentary*. New York: Doubleday, 2001.

Miller, Patrick D. "Constitution or Instruction? The Purpose of Deuteronomy." In *Constituting the Community: Studies on the Polity of Ancient Israel in Honor of S. Dean McBride, Jr.*, edited by John T. Strong and Steven Shawn Tuell, pp. 125-41. Winona Lake, IN: Eisenbrauns, 2005.

———. *Deuteronomy*. Louisville: Westminster John Knox, 1990.

Miller, William Ian. *Eye for an Eye*. Cambridge: Cambridge University Press, 2006.

Mohrmann, Douglas C. "Making Sense of Sex: A Study of Leviticus 18," *Journal for the Study of the Old Testament* 29 (2004): 57-79.

Möller, Karl. *A Prophet in Debate: The Rhetoric of Persuasion in the Book of Amos*. Sheffield: Sheffield Academic Press, 2003.

Moo, Douglas J. *The Epistle to the Romans*. Grand Rapids: Eerdmans, 1996.

———. "Nature in the New Creation: New Testament Eschatology and the Environment," *Journal of the Evangelical Theological Society* 49 (September 2006): 449-88.

Moots, Glenn A. *Politics Reformed: The Anglo-American Legacy of Covenant Theology.* Columbia: University of Missouri Press, 2010.

Morschauser, Scott. "'Hospitality', Hostiles and Hostages: On the Legal Background to Genesis 19.1-9," *Journal for the Study of the Old Testament* 4 (2003): 461-85.

Mueller, John E. *Capitalism, Democracy, and Ralph's Pretty Good Grocery.* Princeton: Princeton University Press, 1999.

Muller, Richard A. "Divine Covenants, Absolute and Conditional: John Cameron and the Early Orthodox Development of Reformed Covenant Theology," *Mid-America Journal of Theology* 17 (2006): 11-56.

———. *Post-Reformation Reformed Dogmatics: The Rise and Development of Reformed Orthodoxy, ca. 1520 to ca. 1725.* Vol. 1 of *Prolegomena to Theology.* 2nd ed. Grand Rapids: Baker Academic, 2003.

Murphy, Jeffrie G. *Getting Even: Forgiveness and Its Limits.* Oxford: Oxford University Press, 2003.

Murphy, Roland E. *Proverbs.* Word Biblical Commentary. Nashville: Thomas Nelson, 1998.

———. *The Tree of Life: An Exploration of Biblical Wisdom Literature.* 3rd ed. Grand Rapids: Eerdmans, 2002.

Murray, John. *The Covenant of Grace. A Biblico-Theological Study.* Phillipsburg, NJ: Presbyterian and Reformed, 1953.

———. *The Epistle to the Romans.* Grand Rapids: Eerdmans, 1959.

———. *The Imputation of Adam's Sin.* Grand Rapids: Eerdmans, 1959.

Murray, Robert. *The Cosmic Covenant: Biblical Themes of Justice, Peace and the Integrity of Creation.* London: Sheed & Ward, 1992.

Newman, Louis. *An Introduction to Jewish Ethics.* Upper Saddle River, NJ: Prentice Hall, 2005.

Niehaus, Jeffrey. "In the Wind of the Storm: Another Look at Genesis 3:8," *Vetus Testamentum* 44, no. 2 (1994): 263-67.

Nissinen, Martti. *Homoeroticism in the Biblical World: A Historical Perspective.* Minneapolis: Fortress, 1998.

Noble, Paul. "Israel Among the Nations," *Horizons in Biblical Theology* 15 (June 1993): 56-62.

Novak, David. *Covenantal Rights: A Study in Jewish Political Theory.* Princeton: Princeton University Press, 2000.

———. *The Image of the Non-Jew in Judaism: An Historical and Constructive Study of the Noahide Laws.* Lewiston, NY: Edward Mellen, 1983.

———. *In Defense of Religious Liberty.* Wilmington, DE: ISI Books, 2009.

———. *The Jewish Social Contract: An Essay in Political Theology.* Princeton: Princeton University Press, 2005.

———. *Natural Law in Judaism.* Cambridge: Cambridge University Press, 1998.

Novick, Tzvi. "'Almost, at Times, the Fool': Abimelekh and Genesis 20," *Prooftexts* 24 (2004): 277-90.

Nygren, Anders. *Agape and Eros.* Translated by Philip S. Watson. London: SPCK, 1953.

O'Brien, Peter T. *Colossians, Philemon.* Waco, TX: Word, 1982.

O'Connell, Robert H. "Isaiah XIV 4B-23: Ironic Reversal Through Concentric Structure and Mythic Allusions," *Vetus Testamentum* 38, no. 4 (1988): 407-18.

O'Donovan, Oliver. *The Desire of the Nations: Rediscovering the Roots of Political Theology.* Cambridge: Cambridge University Press, 1996.

———. *Resurrection and Moral Order: An Outline for Evangelical Ethics.* 2nd ed. Grand Rapids: Eerdmans, 1994.

———. *The Ways of Judgment.* Grand Rapids: Eerdmans, 2005.

Oliphint, Scott K. "The Prolegomena Principle: Frame and Bavinck." In *Speaking the Truth in Love: The Theology of John M. Frame,* edited by John J. Hughes, pp. 201-32. Phillipsburg, NJ: Presbyterian and Reformed, 2009.

O'Malley, John W. *What Happened at Vatican II.* Cambridge, MA: Belknap, 2010.

Overstreet, R. Larry. "Man in the Image of God: A Reappraisal," *Criswell Theological Review* 3 (2005): 43-70.

Owen, John. "A Dissertation on Divine Justice." In *The Works of John Owen,* vol. 10, edited by William H. Goold, pp. 483-624. Edinburgh: Banner of Truth, 1967.

———. *An Exposition of the Epistle to the Hebrews.* Vol. 11 of *The Works of John Owen.* Edited by William H. Goold. London/Edinburgh, 1850; Philadelphia: Leighton, 1869.

Pannenberg, Wolfhart. *Systematic Theology.* Vol. 2. Translated by Geoffrey W. Bromiley. Grand Rapids: Eerdmans, 1994.

Pate, C. Marvin. *The Reverse of the Curse: Paul, Wisdom, and the Law.* Tübingen: Mohr Siebeck, 2000.

Paul, Shalom M. *A Commentary on the Book of Amos.* Minneapolis: Fortress, 1991.

———. *Studies in the Book of the Covenant in the Light of Cuneiform and Biblical Law.* Leiden: Brill, 1970.

Pennington, Jonathan T. *Heaven and Earth in the Gospel of Matthew.* Leiden: Brill, 2007.

Perdue, Leo G. "Cosmology and the Social Order in the Wisdom Tradition." In *The Sage in Israel and the Ancient Near East,* edited by John G. Gammie and Leo G. Perdue, pp. 457-78. Winona Lake, IN: Eisenbrauns, 1990.

———. *Proverbs.* Louisville: Westminster John Knox, 2000.

———. *The Sword and the Stylus: An Introduction to Wisdom in the Age of Empires.* Grand Rapids: Eerdmans, 2008.

———. *Wisdom & Creation: The Theology of Wisdom Literature.* Nashville: Abingdon, 1994.

Phillips, Anthony. "NEBALAH," *Vetus Testamentum* 25, no. 2 (1975): 237-41.

Plantinga, Cornelius. *Engaging God's World: A Christian Vision of Faith, Learning, and Living.* Grand Rapids: Eerdmans, 2002.

Plucknett, Theodore Frank Thomas. *A Concise History of the Common Law.* 5th ed. Boston: Little, Brown and Co., 1956.

Poirier, J. C. "Romans 5:13-14 and the Universality of Law," *Novum Testamentum* 38 (1996): 344-58.

Polaski, Donald C. "Reflections on a Mosaic Covenant: The Eternal Covenant (Isaiah 24.5) and Intertextuality," *Journal for the Study of the Old Testament* 77 (1998): 55-73.

Porter, Jean. "Does the Natural Law Provide a Universally Valid Morality?" In *Intractable Disputes About the Natural Law: Alasdair MacIntyre and Critics,* edited by Lawrence Cunningham, pp. 53-95. Notre Dame: University of Notre Dame Press, 2009.

———. *Natural and Divine Law: Reclaiming the Tradition for Christian Ethics.* Grand Rapids: Eerdmans, 1999.

———. "The Natural Law and Innovative Forms of Marriage: A Reconsideration," *Journal of the Society of Christian Ethics* 30 (Fall-Winter 2010): 79-97.

———. *Nature as Reason: A Thomistic Theory of the Natural Law.* Grand Rapids: Eerdmans, 2005.

Priest, John. "The Covenant of Brothers," *Journal of Biblical Literature* 84 (1965): 400-406.

Pryor, C. Scott. "Looking for Bedrock: Accounting for Human Rights in Classical Liberalism, Modern Secularism, and the Christian Tradition," *Campbell Law Review* 33, no. 3 (2011): 609-40.

Rahner, Karl. "Concerning the Relationship between Nature and Grace." In *Theological Investigations,* vol. 1, pp. 297-317. Baltimore: Helicon, 1969.

Räisänen, Heikki. *Paul and the Law.* Philadelphia: Fortress, 1983.

Rakover, Naḥum. *Law and the Noahides: Law as a Universal Value.* Jerusalem, Israel: Library of Jewish Law, 1998.

Reichenbach, Bruce. "Genesis 1 as a Theological-Political Narrative of Kingdom Establishment," *Bulletin for Biblical Research* 13, no. 1 (2003): 47-69.

Reumann, John. *Philippians: A New Translation with Introduction and Commentary.* New Haven: Yale University Press, 2008.

Ridderbos, Herman N. *The Coming of the Kingdom.* Translated by H. De Jongste. Edited by Raymond O. Zorn. Phillipsburg, NJ: Presbyterian and Reformed, 1962.

———. *Paul: An Outline of His Theology.* Translated by John R. De Witt. Grand Rapids: Eerdmans, 1975.

Ridderbos, J. *Deuteronomy.* Translated by Ed M. van der Maas. Grand Rapids: Regency Reference Library, 1984.

Robertson, O. Palmer. *The Christ of the Prophets.* Phillipsburg, NJ: Presbyterian and Reformed, 1980.

Sanders, E. P. *Paul and Palestinian Judaism: A Comparison of Patterns of Religion.* Philadelphia: Fortress, 1977.

Sarna, Nahum. *Genesis.* Philadelphia: Jewish Publication Society, 1989.

Scarry, Elaine. *On Beauty and Being Just.* Princeton: Princeton University Press, 1999.

Schenker, Adrian. "What Connects the Incest Prohibitions with the Other Prohibitions Listed in Leviticus 18 and 20?" In *The Book of Leviticus: Composition and Reception,* edited by Rolf Rendtorff and Robert A. Kugler, pp. 162-85. Leiden: Brill, 2003.

Schnabel, Eckhard J. *Law and Wisdom from Ben Sira to Paul: A Tradition Historical Enquiry into the Relation of Law, Wisdom, and Ethics.* Tübingen: Mohr Siebeck, 1985.

Schnelle, Udo. *Apostle Paul: His Life and Theology.* Translated by M. Eugene Boring. Grand Rapids: Baker Academic, 2005.

Schoors, A. "The Particle כי." In *Remembering All the Way . . . : A Collection of Old Testament Studies Published on the Occasion of the Fortieth Anniversary of the Oudtestamentisch Werkgezelschap in Nederland,* edited by B. Albrektson, pp. 240-76. Leiden: Brill, 1981.

Schreiner, Thomas R. *The Law and Its Fulfillment: A Pauline Theology of Law.* Grand Rapids: Baker, 1993.

———. *Romans.* Grand Rapids: Baker, 1998.

Schubeck, Thomas. *Love That Does Justice.* Maryknoll, NY: Orbis, 2007.

Schüle, Andreas. "Made in the 'Image of God': The Concepts of Divine Images in Genesis 1–3," *Zeitschrift für die Alttestamentliche Wissenschaft* 117, no. 1 (2005): 1-20.

Scobie, Charles H. H. *The Ways of Our God: An Approach to Biblical Theology.* Grand Rapids: Eerdmans, 2003.

Scroggs, Robin. *The Last Adam: A Study in Pauline Anthropology.* Philadelphia: Fortress, 1966.

———. *The New Testament and Homosexuality: Contextual Background for Contemporary Debate.* Philadelphia: Fortress, 1983.

Seifrid, Mark A. "Natural Revelation and the Purpose of the Law in Romans," *Tyndale Bulletin* 49, no. 1 (1998): 115-29.

———. "Unrighteous by Faith: Apostolic Proclamation in Romans 1:18–3:20." In *Justification and Variegated Nomism: The Paradoxes of Paul,* vol. 2, edited by D. A. Carson, Peter Thomas O'Brien, and Mark A. Seifrid, pp. 105-45. Grand Rapids: Baker Academic, 2004.

Seitz, Christopher R. *The Character of Christian Scripture: The Significance of a Two-Testament Bible.* Grand Rapids: Baker Academic, 2011.

———. *Isaiah 1–39.* Louisville: Westminster John Knox, 1993.

Shemesh, Yael. "Rape Is Rape Is Rape: The Story of Dinah and Shechem (Genesis 34)," *Zeitschrift für die Alttestamentliche Wissenschaft* 119, no. 1 (2007): 2-21.

Sheridan, Mark, ed. *Genesis 12–50.* Ancient Christian Commentary on Scripture. Downers Grove, IL: Intervarsity, 2002.

Shipp, R. Mark. *Of Dead Kings and Dirges: Myth and Meaning in Isaiah 14:4b-21.* Atlanta: Society of Biblical Literature, 2002.

Simonetti, Manlio. *Matthew 1–13.* Ancient Christian Commentary on Scripture. Downers Grove, IL: InterVarsity, 2001.

Skeel, David, and Tremper Longman III. "The Mosaic Law in Christian Perspective." In *The Bible and the Law,* edited by Robert F. Cochran Jr. and David VanDrunen, pp. 80-100. Downers Grove, IL: IVP Academic, 2013.

Smail, Thomas A. "The Image of the Triune God," *International Journal of Systematic Theology* 5 (March 2003): 22-32.

Smith, Mark D. "Ancient Bisexuality and the Interpretation of Romans 1:26-27," *Journal of the American Academy of Religion* 64 (Summer 1996): 223-56.

Smith, Mark S. *The Priestly Vision of Genesis 1.* Minneapolis: Fortress, 2010.

Smith, Steven D. *The Disenchantment of Secular Discourse.* Cambridge, MA: Harvard University Press, 2010.

Smith-Christopher, Daniel L. "Engendered Warfare and the Ammonites in Amos 1.13." In *Aspects of Amos: Exegesis and Interpretation,* edited by Anselm C. Hagedorn and Andrew Mein, pp. 15-40. New York: T. & T. Clark, 2011.

Sonsino, R. *Motive Clauses in Hebrew Law: Biblical Forms and Near Eastern Parallels.* Chico, CA: Scholars, 1980.

Sprinkle, Joe M. *The Book of the Covenant: A Literary Approach.* Sheffield: Sheffield Academic Press, 1994.

Stanton, Graham. "The Law of Moses and the Law of Christ: Galatians 3:1–6:2." In *Paul and the Mosaic Law,* edited by James D. G. Dunn, pp. 99-116. Grand Rapids: Eerdmans, 2001.

Steinmann, Andrew E. "The Order of Amos's Oracles against the Nations: 1:3–2:16," *Journal of Biblical Literature* 111, no. 4 (1992): 683-89.

Steinmetz, Devora. "Vineyard, Farm, and Garden: The Drunkenness of Noah in the Context of Primeval History," *Journal of Biblical Literature* 113, no. 2 (1994): 193-207.

Sternberg, Meir. *The Poetics of Biblical Narrative: Ideological Literature and the Drama of Reading.* Bloomington: Indiana University Press, 1985.

Stevenson, Kenneth, and Michael Glerup, eds. *Ezekiel, Daniel.* Ancient Christian Commentary on Scripture. Downers Grove, IL: InterVarsity, 2008.

Stowers, Stanley Kent. *A Rereading of Romans: Justice, Jews, and Gentiles.* New Haven: Yale University Press, 1994.

Streett, Daniel R. "As It Was in the Days of Noah: The Prophets' Typological Interpretation of Noah's Flood," *Criswell Theological Review* 5 (Fall 2007): 33-51.

Stuart, Douglas K. *Hosea-Jonah.* Waco, TX: Word, 1987.

Stump, Eleonore. *Aquinas.* London: Routledge, 2003.

Talbert, Charles H. *Romans.* Macon, GA: Smyth & Helwys, 2002.

Taylor, Charles. *A Secular Age.* Cambridge, MA: Belknap, 2007.

Terrien, Samuel. "Amos and Wisdom." In *Israel's Prophetic Heritage: Essay in Honor of James Muilenburg,* edited by Berhard W. Anderson and Walter Harrelson, pp. 108-15. New York: Harper & Brothers, 1962.

Thielman, Frank. *Paul & the Law: A Contextual Approach.* Downers Grove, IL: InterVarsity, 1994.

Thompson, John L., ed. *Genesis 1–11.* Reformation Commentary on Scripture. Downers Grove, IL: IVP Academic, 2012.

Turner, Laurence A. *Genesis.* Sheffield: Sheffield Academic Press, 2000.

Turretin, Francis. *Institutes of Elenctic Theology.* 3 vols. Translated by George Musgrave Giger. Edited by James T. Dennison Jr. Phillipsburg, NJ: Presbyterian and Reformed, 1992-97.

Ursinus, Zacharias. "Larger Catechism." In *An Introduction to the Heidelberg Catechism: Sources, History, and Theology,* edited by Lyle D. Bierma, Charles D. Gunnoe Jr., Karin Y. Maag, and Paul W. Fields, pp. 163-223. Grand Rapids: Baker Academic, 2005.

Vander Hart, Mark D. "Creation and Covenant: Part One," *Mid-America Journal of Theology* 6, no. 1 (1990): 3-18.

VanDrunen, David. "Inclusive Salvation in Contemporary Roman Catholicism," *New Horizons* (October 2011): 6-8.

———. " 'The Kingship of Christ Is Twofold': Natural Law and the Two Kingdoms in the Thought of Herman Bavinck," *Calvin Theological Journal* 45 (April 2010): 147-64.

———. *Law & Custom: The Thought of Thomas Aquinas and the Future of the Common Law.* New York: Peter Lang, 2003.

———. *Living in God's Two Kingdoms: A Biblical Vision for Christianity and Culture.* Wheaton, IL: Crossway, 2010.

———. *Natural Law and the Two Kingdoms: A Study in the Development of Reformed Social Thought.* Grand Rapids: Eerdmans, 2010.

———. "Natural Law and the Works Principle under Adam and Moses." In *The Law Is Not of Faith: Essays on Works and Grace in the Mosaic Covenant,* edited by Bryan D. Estelle, J. V. Fesko, and David VanDrunen, pp. 283-314. Phillipsburg, NJ: Presbyterian and Reformed, 2009.

———. "The Reformed Two Kingdoms Doctrine: An Explanation and Defense," *The Confessional Presbyterian* 8 (2012): 177-90.

———. "To Obey Is Better Than Sacrifice: A Defense of the Active Obedience of Christ in the Light of Recent Criticism." In *By Faith Alone: Answering the Challenges to the Doctrine of Justification,* edited by Gary L. W. Johnson and Guy Prentiss Waters, pp. 127-46. Wheaton, IL: Crossway, 2006.

———. "VanDrunen in the Hands of an Anxious Kloosterman: A Response to a Review of *A Biblical Case for Natural Law,*" *Ordained Servant* 16 (2007): 107-13.

———, and R. Scott Clark. "The Covenant before the Covenants." In *Covenant, Justification, and Pastoral Ministry: Essays by the Faculty of Westminster Seminary California,* edited by R. Scott Clark, pp. 167-96. Phillipsburg, NJ: Presbyterian and Reformed, 2007.

Van Ee, Joshua. "Adam and Other Carnivores: Questions Regarding Primitive Vegetarianism in Genesis 1:28-30." Paper presented at the International Society of Biblical Literature annual conference, London, 2011.

Van Huyssteen, J. Wentzel. *Alone in the World?: Human Uniqueness in Science and Theology.* Grand Rapids: Eerdmans, 2006.

Van Leeuwen, Raymond C. *Proverbs.* The New Interpreter's Bible. Nashville: Abingdon, 1997.

Van Raalte, G. "Unleavened Morality? Herman Bavinck on Natural Law." In *Five Studies in the Thought of Herman Bavinck, a Creator of Modern Dutch Theology,* edited by John Bolt, pp. 57-99. Lewiston, NY: Edwin Mellen, 2011.

Van Til, Cornelius. "Antithesis in Education." In *Foundations of Christian Edu-*

cation: Addresses to Christian Teachers, edited by Dennis E. Johnson, pp. 3-24. Phillipsburg, NJ: Presbyterian and Reformed, 1990.

———. *Christian Apologetics.* Phillipsburg, NJ: Presbyterian and Reformed, 1976.

———. *Christian Theistic Ethics.* Phillipsburg, NJ: Presbyterian and Reformed, 1980.

———. *The Defense of the Faith.* Philadelphia: Presbyterian and Reformed, 1955.

———. "Nature and Scripture." In *The Infallible Word: A Symposium,* edited by Ned B. Stonehouse and Paul Woolley, pp. 255-93. Grand Rapids: Eerdmans, 1946.

Van Wolde, Ellen. "Does 'INNÂ Denote Rape? A Semantic Analysis of a Controversial Word," *Vetus Testamentum* 52, no. 4 (2002): 528-44.

Venema, Cornelis P. *The Gospel of Free Acceptance in Christ: An Assessment of the Reformation and New Perspectives on Paul.* Edinburgh: Banner of Truth, 2006.

———. "The Mosaic Covenant: A 'Republication' of the Covenant of Works? A Review Article: *The Law Is Not of Faith: Essays on Works and Grace in the Mosaic Covenant,*" *Mid-America Journal of Theology* 21 (2010): 35-101.

Vlachos, Chris A. *The Law and the Knowledge of Good & Evil: The Edenic Background of the Catalytic Operation of the Law in Paul.* Eugene, OR: Pickwick Publications, 2009.

Volf, Miroslav. *Free of Charge: Giving and Forgiving in a Culture Stripped of Grace.* Grand Rapids: Zondervan, 2005.

Von Rad, Gerhard. *Genesis: A Commentary.* Rev. ed. Philadelphia: Westminster, 1972.

———. *Old Testament Theology.* 2 vols. New York: Harper & Row, 1962-65.

Vos, Geerhardus. *Biblical Theology: Old and New Testaments.* Grand Rapids: Eerdmans, 1949.

———. "The Doctrine of the Covenant in Reformed Theology." In *Redemptive History and Biblical Interpretation: The Shorter Writings of Geerhardus Vos,* edited by Richard B. Gaffin Jr., pp. 234-67. Phillipsburg, NJ: Presbyterian and Reformed, 1980.

———. *Redemptive History and Biblical Interpretation: The Shorter Writings of Geerhardus Vos.* Edited by Richard B. Gaffin. Phillipsburg, NJ: Presbyterian and Reformed, 1980.

———. *The Teaching of Jesus Concerning the Kingdom of God and the Church.* Grand Rapids: Eerdmans, 1958.

Waltke, Bruce K. *Genesis: A Commentary.* Grand Rapids: Zondervan, 2001.

———, and M. O'Connor. *An Introduction to Biblical Hebrew Syntax.* Winona Lake, IN: Eisenbrauns, 1990.

Walton, John H. *Ancient Israelite Literature in Its Cultural Context: A Survey of Parallels between Biblical and Ancient Near Eastern Texts.* Grand Rapids: Zondervan, 1989.

Washington, Harold C. *Wealth and Poverty in the Instruction of Amenemope and the Hebrew Proverbs.* Atlanta: Scholars, 1994.

Waters, Guy Prentiss. *The Federal Vision and Covenant Theology: A Comparative Analysis.* Phillipsburg, NJ: Presbyterian and Reformed, 2006.

————. *Justification and the New Perspectives on Paul: A Review and Response.* Phillipsburg, NJ: Presbyterian and Reformed, 2004.

————. "Romans 10:5 and the Covenant of Works." In *The Law Is Not of Faith: Essays on Works and Grace in the Mosaic Covenant,* edited by Bryan D. Estelle, J. V. Fesko, and David VanDrunen, pp. 210-39. Phillipsburg, NJ: Presbyterian and Reformed, 2009.

Watson, Francis. *Text and Truth: Redefining Biblical Theology.* Grand Rapids: Eerdmans, 1997.

Watts, John D. W. *Isaiah 1–33.* Waco, TX: Word, 1985.

Weeks, Stuart. *Early Israelite Wisdom.* Oxford: Oxford University Press, 1994.

————. *Instruction and Imagery in Proverbs 1–9.* Oxford: Oxford University Press, 2007.

Weinfeld, Moshe. *Deuteronomy 1–11: A New Translation with Introduction and Commentary.* New York: Doubleday, 1991.

————. *Deuteronomy and the Deuteronomic School.* Oxford: Clarendon, 1972.

Weir, David A. *Early New England: A Covenanted Society.* Grand Rapids: Eerdmans, 2005.

Wells, Bruce. "The Covenant Code and Near Eastern Legal Traditions: A Response to David P. Wright," *Maarav* 13, no. 1 (2006): 85-118.

Wenham, Gordon J. *The Book of Leviticus.* Grand Rapids: Eerdmans, 1979.

————. *Genesis 1–15.* Word Biblical Commentary. Waco, TX: Word, 1987.

————. "Sanctuary Symbolism in the Garden of Eden Story." In *I Studied Inscriptions from Before the Flood: Ancient Near Eastern, Literary, and Linguistic Approaches to Genesis 1–11,* edited by Richard S. Hess and David Toshio Tsumura. Winona Lake, IN: Eisenbrauns, 1994.

Westbrook, Raymond. "The Laws of Biblical Israel." In *The Hebrew Bible: New Insights and Scholarship,* edited by Frederick E Greenspahn. New York: New York University Press, 2008.

————. *Studies in Biblical and Cuneiform Law.* Paris: J. Gabalda, 1988.

Westerholm, Stephen. "The Law in the Sermon on the Mount: Matt 5:17-48," *Criswell Theological Review* 6, no. 1 (1992): 43-56.

————. *Perspectives Old and New on Paul: The "Lutheran" Paul and His Critics.* Grand Rapids: Eerdmans, 2004.

Westermann, Claus. *Genesis 1–11: A Commentary.* Translated by John J. Scullion. Minneapolis: Augsburg, 1984.

————. *Genesis 12–36: A Commentary.* Translated by John J. Scullion. Minneapolis: Augsburg, 1985.

White, Thomas Joseph, O.P. *Wisdom in the Face of Modernity: A Study in Thomistic Natural Theology.* Ave Maria, FL: Sapientia, 2009.

Whitelam, Keith W. *The Just King: Monarchical Judicial Authority in Ancient Israel.* Sheffield: JSOT, 1979.

Whybray, R. N. *Proverbs.* New Century Bible Commentary. Grand Rapids: Eerdmans, 1994.

————. "'Shall Not the Judge of All the Earth Do What Is Just?' God's Oppression of the Innocent in the Old Testament." In *Shall Not the Judge of All the Earth Do What Is Right? Studies on the Nature of God in Tribute to James L. Crenshaw,* edited by David Penchansky and Paul L. Redditt, pp. 1-19. Winona Lake, IN: Eisenbrauns, 2000.

————. *Wealth and Poverty in the Book of Proverbs.* Sheffield: Sheffield Academic Press, 1990.

Wildberger, Hans. "Das Abbild Gottes: Gen. 1,26-30," *Theologische Zeitschrift* 21 (1965): 245-49, 481-501.

————. *Isaiah: A Continental Commentary.* Translated by Thomas H. Trapp. Minneapolis: Fortress, 1997.

Wilder, William N. "Illumination and Investiture: The Royal Significance of the Tree of Wisdom in Genesis 3," *Westminster Theological Journal* 68 (Spring 2006): 51-69.

Williamson, Paul R. *Sealed with an Oath: Covenant in God's Unfolding Purpose.* Downers Grove, IL: InterVarsity, 2007.

Winger, Michael. "Hard Sayings," *Expository Times* 115 (2004): 266-73.

Witherington, Ben, III. *Grace in Galatia: A Commentary on St Paul's Letter to the Galatians.* Grand Rapids: Eerdmans, 1998.

————. *Paul's Letter to the Romans: A Socio-Rhetorical Commentary.* Grand Rapids: Eerdmans, 2004.

Witsius, Herman. *The Economy of the Covenants between God and Man: Comprehending a Complete Body of Divinity.* 2 vols. Translated by William Crookshank. Phillipsburg, NJ: Presbyterian and Reformed, 1990.

Witte, John. *The Reformation of Rights: Law, Religion, and Human Rights in Early Modern Calvinism.* Cambridge: Cambridge University Press, 2007.

Wold, Donald J. *Out of Order: Homosexuality in the Bible and the Ancient Near East.* Grand Rapids: Baker, 1998.

Wolff, Hans W. *Joel and Amos: A Commentary on the Books of the Prophets Joel and Amos.* Translated by Waldemar Janzen, S. Dean McBride, and Charles A. Muenchow. Philadelphia: Fortress, 1977.

Wolters, Albert M. *Creation Regained: Biblical Basics for a Reformational World-view.* Grand Rapids: Eerdmans, 1985.

Wolterstorff, Nicholas. *Justice in Love.* Grand Rapids: Eerdmans, 2011.

———. *Justice: Rights and Wrongs.* Princeton: Princeton University Press, 2008.

Wright, David P. *Inventing God's Law: How the Covenant Code of the Bible Used and Revised the Laws of Hammurabi.* Oxford: Oxford University Press, 2009.

Wright, N. T. *The Climax of the Covenant: Christ and the Law in Pauline Theology.* Minneapolis: Fortress, 1992.

———. *The Letter to the Romans.* New Interpreter's Bible. Nashville: Abingdon, 2002.

———. *Paul: In Fresh Perspective.* Minneapolis: Fortress, 2005.

———. *What Saint Paul Really Said: Was Paul of Tarsus the Real Founder of Christianity?* Grand Rapids: Eerdmans, 1997.

Yee, Gale A. "The Anatomy of Biblical Parody: The Dirge Form in 2 Samuel 1 and Isaiah 14," *Catholic Biblical Quarterly* 50 (1988): 565-86.

Yinger, Kent L. *Paul, Judaism, and Judgment According to Deeds.* Cambridge: Cambridge University Press, 1999.

Yoder, Christine Elizabeth. *Wisdom as a Woman of Substance: A Socioeconomic Reading of Proverbs 1–9 and 31:10-31.* Berlin: Walter de Gruyter, 2001.

Yoder, John Howard. *The Politics of Jesus.* Grand Rapids: Eerdmans, 1972.

Young, Edward J. *The Book of Isaiah.* 2 vols. Grand Rapids: Eerdmans, 1965.

Zehnder, Markus. "Cause or Value? Problems in the Understanding of Gen 9,6a," *Zeitschrift für die Alttestamentliche Wissenschaft* 122, no. 1 (2010): 81-89.

Zimmermann, Jens. *Humanism and Religion: A Call for the Renewal of Western Culture.* Oxford: Oxford University Press, 2012.

Index of Names and Subjects

Selective Index of Biblical Texts Discussed